Hans-Jürgen Feulner (Hg./Ed.)

Liturgies in East and West
Ecumenical Relevance of Early Liturgical Development

Österreichische Studien zur Liturgiewissenschaft
und Sakramententheologie
(früher *Liturgica Oenipontana*)

Austrian Studies
of Liturgy and Sacramental Theology
(previously *Liturgica Oenipontana*)

herausgegeben von
edited by

Hans-Jürgen Feulner (Wien)
und
Reinhard Meßner (Innsbruck)

zusammen mit
together with

Basilius J. Groen (Graz), *N. N.* (Salzburg)
und P. Ewald Volgger OT (Linz)

ÖSLS

Band / Volume 6

LIT

Liturgies in East and West
Ecumenical Relevance of Early Liturgical Development

Acts of the International Symposium Vindobonense I,
Vienna, November 17 – 20, 2007

herausgegeben von
edited by

Hans-Jürgen Feulner

LIT

Dieses Buch ist Margareta Feulner
(27. 9. 1928; † 10. 4. 2009)*
gewidmet

Umschlagbild: Gabriele Hübel/Wien (www.hellschwarz.at)

Bibliographic information published by the Deutsche Nationalbibliothek
The Deutsche Nationalbibliothek lists this publication in the Deutsche Nationalbibliografie; detailed bibliographic data are available in the Internet at http://dnb.d-nb.de.

ISBN 978-3-643-90412-6

A catalogue record for this book is available from the British Library

Klosbachstr. 107
CH-8032 Zürich
Tel. +41 (0) 44-251 75 05
Fax +41 (0) 44-251 75 06
E-Mail: zuerich@lit-verlag.ch
http://www.lit-verlag.ch

LIT VERLAG Dr. W. Hopf
Berlin 2013
Fresnostr. 2
D-48159 Münster
Tel. +49 (0) 2 51-62 03 20
Fax +49 (0) 2 51-23 19 72
E-Mail: lit@lit-verlag.de
http://www.lit-verlag.de

Distribution:
In Germany: LIT Verlag Fresnostr. 2, D-48159 Münster
Tel. +49 (0) 2 51-620 32 22, Fax +49 (0) 2 51-922 60 99, E-mail: vertrieb@lit-verlag.de

In Austria: Medienlogistik Pichler-ÖBZ, e-mail: mlo@medien-logistik.at
In the UK: Global Book Marketing, e-mail: mo@centralbooks.com
In North America: International Specialized Book Services, e-mail: orders@isbs.com
e-books are available at www.litwebshop.de

Inhaltsverzeichnis

Einleitung zur neuen Reihe ÖSLS

Mit dieser Publikation beginnt zugleich auch die neue liturgiewissenschaftliche Reihe „Österreichische Studien zur Liturgiewissenschaft und Sakramententheologie / Austrian Studies of Liturgy and Sacramental Theology" [ÖSLS] als Band 6, in die die bisherige Reihe „Liturgica Oenipontana" (Münster 2000ff.) mit ihren fünf Bänden aufgehen wird.

In Österreich sind an den staatlichen bzw. kirchlichen Theologischen Fakultäten die Lehrstühle/Institute für Liturgiewissenschaft in der Regel auch mit der Sakramententheologie verbunden. An einigen Instituten liegt außerdem ein Forschungsschwerpunkt auch auf den orientalischen Liturgien bzw. gibt es interreligiöse/interkulturelle liturgiewissenschaftliche Forschungsprojekte. Damit unterscheidet sich innerhalb des deutschsprachigen Raums das Bild in Österreich grundsätzlich von dem in Deutschland oder in der Schweiz.

Seit 2002 kam es in Österreich fast überall zu Neubesetzungen der Lehrstühle und damit auch zu einem Anwachsen der an österreichischen Fakultäten betreuten (internationalen) Dissertationsprojekte, teilweise auf sehr hohem und daher publikationswürdigem Niveau. Keine der vorhandenen einschlägigen Reihen im deutschsprachigen Raum deckt jedoch die Spezifika der österreichischen Situation umfassend ab. Da bereits einige sehr gute Dissertationen in Österreich abgeschlossen wurden oder vor dem Abschluss stehen, stellte sich seit einiger Zeit sehr dringend die Frage nach angemessenen Publikationsmöglichkeiten in einer Reihe, die den besonderen Anforderungen weitgehendst entspricht.

Um der österreichischen Situation und den vielfältigen, hier entstandenen Dissertationen, auch aus dem Bereich der Sakramententheologie, der Ostkirchen, dem Islam und dem Judentum, gerecht zu werden, wurde der Vorschlag eingebracht, nicht eine weitere ortsgebundene Reihe zu gründen, sondern eine gesamtösterreichische Reihe unter Einbezug der staatlichen und kirchlichen Institute, um primär für solche Dissertationsprojekte ein finanziell tragbares Publikationsorgan auf hohem wissenschaftlichen Niveau zu schaffen. Dies soll ausdrücklich nicht in Konkurrenz zu den bestehenden liturgiewissenschaftlichen bzw. pastoralliturgischen Reihen geschehen, sondern als sinnvolle und notwendige Ergänzung dazu. Nicht zuletzt soll eine gesamtösterreichische Reihe auch der Zusammenarbeit der liturgiewissenschaftlichen Institutionen untereinander dienen.

Die neue Reihe soll primär der Veröffentlichung von hervorragenden, an österreichischen Fakultäten entstandenen Dissertationen (und Habilitationen) aus dem Bereich Liturgiewissenschaft und Sakramententheologie, unter Einbeziehung der ost- und westkirchlichen sowie der interreligiösen liturgischen Traditionen, dienen. Aber auch andere hervorragende liturgiewissenschaftliche (oder sakramententheologische) Forschungsleistungen aus dem In- und Ausland sollen Aufnahme finden.

Als Publikationssprachen sind deutsch, englisch und französisch erwünscht. In Ausnahmefällen (z.B. in Tagungs- oder Sammelbänden oder Festschriften) können auch andere westeuropäische Sprachen zugelassen werden.

Die Reihe ÖSLS wird in Zusammenarbeit mit dem LIT-Verlag in Wien herausgegeben. Es ist angestrebt, die Reihe im internationalen Ranking als mindestens „B-wertig" zu etablieren, mittelfristig und auf Dauer sogar als „A-wertig", was eine qualifizierte Begutachtung der für eine Publikation eingereichten Studien (als reproduktionsfähige Druckvorlagen) voraussetzt.

Zum Herausgeber-Gremium der Reihe gehören die jeweiligen Ordinarien für Liturgiewissenschaft (und Sakramententheologie) der staatlichen und kirchlichen Theologischen Fakultäten in Wien, Innsbruck, Graz, Salzburg und Linz.

Nähere Informationen (Zitierrichtlinien, Layoutvorlagen, Einreichungs- und Begutachtungskriterien, Statuten usw.) finden sich unter:

http://ktf.univie.ac.at/lit

Für das Herausgeber-Kollegium

gez. *Hans-Jürgen Feulner* gez. *Reinhard Meßner*
Wien Innsbruck

Vorwort

Bereits 2004 hatte das damalige *Institut für Liturgiewissenschaft* der Katholisch-Theologischen Fakultät an der Universität Wien erstmals überlegt, ob, wann und unter welchem Thema ein internationales Liturgie-Symposium in Wien organisiert werden könnte. Nach umfänglichen Planungen, unzähligen Gesuchen um finanzielle Unterstützung, terminlichen Verschiebungen und vielen Vorarbeiten ist es dann schließlich gelungen, vom 17. – 20. November 2007 ein kleines mehrtägiges Symposium in der österreichischen Hauptstadt durchzuführen, dessen Vorträge in diesem Sammelband (fast vollständig) publiziert sind.

Die Liturgiekonstitution „Sacrosanctum Concilium" (4. Dezember 1963) des II. Vatikanischen Konzils billigt dem Gottesdienst in Artikel 10 einen hohen Stellenwert zu – was auch über den römisch-katholischen Bereich hinaus Gültigkeit besitzt –, wenn es dort gleich eingangs heißt:

> „[D]ie Liturgie [ist] der Höhepunkt, dem das Tun der Kirche zustrebt, und zugleich die Quelle, aus der all ihre Kraft strömt …"

Die Feier der Liturgie ist also zentral für das Glaubensleben (*lex credendi – lex orandi*) und auch für das Selbstverständnis der verschiedenen Kirchen in Ost und West. Im Bereich der Liturgie sowie der Liturgiewissenschaft hat sich seit dem II. Vatikanischen Konzil – nicht zuletzt auch aufgrund wegweisender liturgiehistorischer Untersuchungen der letzten Jahrzehnte – eine erstaunliche Annäherung der christlichen Konfessionen vollzogen, bis in die liturgische Feierpraxis hinein.

Schon jede Form menschlichen Tuns ist ein äußerst komplexes Gebilde, zu dessen Erklärung oft verschiedene Wissenschaften herangezogen werden müssen. Noch mehr gilt das für das liturgische Tun der Kirche. Hier müssen auch die verschiedensten theologischen Disziplinen herangezogen werden, um die je verschiedenen Seiten des liturgischen Geschehens zu erfassen.

Die Versuche, die Komplexität des liturgischen Geschehens durch die eine oder andere der klassischen theologischen Disziplinen *allein* in den Griff zu bekommen, müssen als gescheitert angesehen werden. Nur das Zusammenspiel aller theologischen Disziplinen und die Anwendung der verschiedenen Methoden kann es ermöglichen, zu einer gewissen Gesamtschau zu gelangen.

Vielenorts ist in diesem Zusammenhang oft der Vorwurf zu vernehmen, dass eine *historische* Beschäftigung mit der Liturgie und deren geschichtlicher Entwicklung für die heutige Feierpraxis irrelevant sei oder zumindest kaum Nutzen brächte. Dass dies nicht unbedingt so sein muss, lässt sich bei genauerer Betrachtung durchaus erschließen, zumal die Liturgie in den verschiedenen Kirchen im Laufe der Jahrhunderte mehr oder weniger organisch gewachsen ist.

Mit Hilfe einer historischen Methode gelang auch der Aufbau einer eigenen *Liturgiegeschichte*, die Unterscheidung der wichtigsten Epochen und der in ihnen wirkenden Kräfte. Nur so wird es möglich, die *heutige* Liturgie in ihrem geschichtlichen Werden zu erkennen, den Bedeutungsgehalt der einzelnen Akte auszumachen und das Wichtige vom Unwichtigen zu unterscheiden (SC 21). Natürlich genügt es dabei nicht, *allein* auf die Geschichte der liturgischen Handlungen zu sehen. Es muss das gesamte christliche Leben der verschiedenen Jahrhunderte im Hinblick auf seinen Einfluss auf die Liturgie untersucht werden. Auch die Liturgiereform, die durch das II. Vatikanum eingeleitet wurde, ist ohne die liturgie-geschichtliche Forschung nicht denkbar. Die historische Forschung hat die Grundstrukturen der Liturgie erarbeitet, an denen die liturgietheologischen Überlegungen der Reform dann anknüpfen konnten.
Die Liturgiegeschichte lehrt außerdem, den rechten Zusammenhang zur Tradition des kirchlichen Lebens zu wahren, die Erfahrung über den Erfolg oder auch Misserfolg bestimmter liturgischer Maßnahmen auszuwerten. Damit kann auch die Richtung erkannt werden, in die das liturgische Leben der Kirche treibt. Die Liturgiegeschichte kann also positive Impulse geben für eine ständig sich erneuernde Liturgie. Sie ebnet die Wege, wieder aufzuzeigen oder wieder stärker zu betonen, was einmal bewährter Bestandteil der Liturgie in den verschiedenen Riten war, später dann leider in den Hintergrund trat oder sogar vergessen und aufgegeben wurde. Eine historisch-philologische Methode darf aber natürlich nicht dazu verleiten, nur wohlgeordnete Archive anzulegen, sondern sie muss zugleich die Möglichkeit schaffen, diese Ergebnisse für die lebendige Liturgie der Gegenwart fruchtbar zu machen, und zwar im ökumenischen Kontext.

Deshalb hatten wir uns entschlossen, ein Symposium unter das Leitthema *Liturgies in East and West: Ecumenical Relevance of Early Liturgical Development* zu stellen. Der ökumenische Beitrag und die jüdischen Wurzeln der christlichen Liturgie sollten in diesem Symposium durch international anerkannte WissenschaftlerInnen aus verschiedenen christlichen Konfessionen aufgezeigt und auf die Praxis hin fruchtbar gemacht werden.

Die sich oft schwierig gestaltende Bearbeitung der eingegangenen Beiträge hat sich bis zur Drucklegung leider immer wieder um viele Jahre verzögert, nicht zuletzt aufgrund eines schweren Autounfalls des Herausgebers, der sich verschlechternden Krankheit und schließlich des Todes seiner Mutter in Deutschland sowie anderer widriger Umstände, die nicht vorhersehbar waren.

In diesem Sammelband sind fast alle während des Symposiums gehaltenen Vorträge publiziert (bis auf drei), sowie zwei zusätzliche Beiträge aufgenommen, darunter der Artikel von Heinzgerd BRAKMANN, der damals als Vortragender vorgesehen war, aber kurzfristig aus gesundheitlichen Gründen nicht kommen konnte.

Im Dokumentationsteil ist neben dem damaligen Symposiums-Poster und Grußwort auch der Abschlussbericht abgedruckt (der im Wesentlichen auf Frau Mag. Manuela ULRICH zurückgeht).

Dank gilt zunächst den verschiedenen Sponsoren, die durch ihre finanzielle Unterstützung die Durchführung erst ermöglicht hatten: neben der Stiftung *Pro Oriente* sind dies die *Erzdiözese Wien*, das *Bundesministerium für Wissenschaft und Forschung*, die *Universität Wien* mit ihrem damaligen Rektor Univ.-Prof. Dr. Georg WINCKLER, die *Superiorenkonferenz der männlichen Ordensgemeinschaften Österreichs* und auch die *Stadt Wien*. Ein besonderer Dank sei an alle Vortragenden gerichtet, die u.a. auch aus den USA angereist waren.

Außerdem gilt ein ganz herzlicher Dank den damaligen Mitarbeiterinnen unseres Instituts, die ganz besonders erwähnt werden sollen. Ohne die Mithilfe aller Mitarbeiterinnen wäre das Symposium nicht zustande gekommen: an erster Stelle die damalige Sekretärin, Frau Renate KOS, sowie die damalige Assistentin, Frau Mag. Manuela ULRICH; daneben auch Frau Dr. Monika SCALA, Frau Mag. Petra SCHILLER und Frau Ing. Justyna OKOLOWICZ. Dank auch an Herrn Florian MAYR von der damaligen Studentenvertretung unserer Fakultät, der die Homepagegestaltung für das Symposium mitübernommen hatte.

Schließlich möchte ich mich ganz besonders bei meinen gegenwärtigen MitarbeiterInnen am Institut bedanken, die beim Korrekturlesen, bei der Layoutbearbeitung, Korrespondenz u.v.m. eine unschätzbare und unverzichtbare Hilfe waren: Herr Dr. Johannes SPORER (Assistent bis 2013), Frau Mag. Karin SULZ (Organisationsassistentin seit 2010), Herr Dr. Daniel GALADZA (Assistent seit 2013) und Frau Mag. Pia HECHT (Studienassistentin). Dr. GALADZA hat außerdem das Abkürzungs- und Autorenverzeichnis erstellt und die Harmonisierung der Beiträge vorgenommen.

Auch bei Herrn Richard KISLING vom LIT-Verlag (Wien) möchte ich mich für die Betreuung bedanken sowie bei Frau Gabriele HÜBEL für die Gestaltung des Buchcovers.

Wien, im Sommer 2013

Hans-Jürgen Feulner

Univ.-Prof. Dr. Hans-Jürgen Feulner
Institut für Historische Theologie
Liturgiewissenschaft und Sakramententheologie
Universität Wien

Already in 2004 we first considered when, where, and how to best organize a liturgy symposium in Vienna. After an extensive period of planning, writing various grant applications, managing time conflicts and immersing ourselves in preparatory work, we succeeded in organizing the small but constructive Symposium Vindobonense in the capital city of Austria, November 17–20, 2007.

Article 10 of the Constitution on Sacred Liturgy, "Sacrosanctum Concilium" (December 4, 1963), of the Second Vatican Council awards the liturgy a high significance – even beyond the Roman-Catholic sphere – when one reads at the very beginning:

> "[T]he liturgy is the summit toward which the activity of the Church is directed; at the same time it is the font from which all her power flows …"

Celebrating liturgy is the central element of a living faith (*lex credendi – lex orandi*) and the mission of different churches in the East and West. Ever since Vatican II and due to seminal work in the field of historico-liturgical studies, various Christian denominations have been striving to approach each other, reaching out to each other also in terms of how to celebrate the liturgy.
Any aspect of human action is an extremely complex structure and can often only be explained by employing various methodologies. This applies even more to the liturgical activity of the Church. One has to employ various theological disciplines in order to understand the manifold aspects of the liturgical events.
It has been shown that all attempts to explain the complexity of liturgical actions by relying upon one or another theological discipline *alone* have failed. Only the cooperation of all theological disciplines and the application of the various methods can help to achieve a certain kind of overall view.
In this respect, in many places one can hear complaints that it is irrelevant or at least of no use for the current way of celebrating the liturgy to look at liturgy from a *historical* point of view as well as observing its historical development. However, this does not necessarily need to be the case as one can see when taking a closer look at things and particularly when accepting the fact that the liturgy has, more or less, been growing organically over the last centuries. It was possible to establish a *Liturgical History* with the aid of a historical method. Liturgical History in this sense means a differentiation of the most important eras and their most influencing powers. With that in hand, this is the only way possible to recognize our *current* liturgy in its historical development, to understand the significant content of single passages and articles, and to distinguish between important and unimportant aspects (*Sacrosanctum Concilium* 21). Of course, it is not enough to *only* focus on the history of liturgical acts. In order to fully understand liturgical developments, it is necessary to research Christian life as a whole, looking at various centuries and examining how far Christian life as such has influenced the celebration of the liturgy. The liturgical reform, initiated by Vatican II, cannot be imagined without liturgico-historical research. It is the seminal work of historical research that developed a basic structure for

liturgy, and which was then followed by liturgico-theological thoughts and research.

This is why we decided and chose "*Liturgies in East and West: Ecumenical Relevance of Early Liturgical Development*" as a guiding theme for our Symposium. In their talks and presentations, different internationally renowned scholars belonging to various Christian denominations tried to indicate the ecumenical aspect and the Jewish roots of Christian liturgy. Hereby our aim was to gain fruitful aspects for the practical experience of the different liturgies.

The final publication of the submitted articles, which were sometimes difficult to edit, was delayed for many years, partially due to a severe car accident of the editor, the serious illness and subsequent death of the editor's mother and other adverse conditions, which were unforeseeable.

This anthology contains almost all lectures given during the symposium, except for three. Two more articles were added to this volume, among them the article of Heinzgerd BRAKMANN, who was scheduled to be one of the lecturers at the Symposium but, for health reasons, could not attend.

The documentation of the Symposium shows the Symposium poster, the word of welcome, and the final report, primarily compiled by Manuela ULRICH.

Let me express my thanks to our various sponsors. Their generous financial support enabled us to organize and realize this Symposium. Along with the *Pro Oriente* Foundation, we would like to thank the *Archdiocese of Vienna*, the *Federal Ministry of Science and Research*, the *University of Vienna*, its former rector, Georg WINCKLER, and also the *Conference of the Major Superiors of Austria*, as well as the *City of Vienna*.

Moreover, I sincerely thank my entire staff at our Department at the time of the Symposium. Without their help, this Symposium would not have taken place: my former secretary Renate KOS, my former assistant Manuela ULRICH, Monika SCALA, Petra SCHILLER, and Justyna OKOLOWICZ. Thanks also to Florian MAYR, one of the faculty's student representatives, for helping design our symposium-webpage.

Last but not least I would like to thank my present staff members at the Department who helped with the proofreading, the layout, the correspondence, and much more, for their invaluable and essential help: Johannes SPORER (assistant until 2013), Karin SULZ (organizational assistant since 2010), Daniel GALADZA (assistant since 2013), who created the list of abbreviations and the list of authors, and coordinated the various articles, and Pia Maria HECHT (assisting student).

Thank you very much to Richard KISLING from the publishing house LIT-Verlag Wien for his support and to Gabriele HÜBEL for creating the book cover.

Vienna, Summer 2013

Hans-Jürgen Feulner

Univ.-Prof. Dr. Hans-Jürgen Feulner
Department of Historical Theology
Liturgical Studies and Sacramental Theology
University of Vienna

ABKÜRZUNGSVERZEICHNIS

ALW	Archiv für Liturgiewissenschaft
Aug.	Augustinianum. Roma
BEL.S	Bibliotheca ephemerides liturgicae – Subsidia
BFPUL	Bibliothèque de la faculté de philosophie et lettres de l'université de Liège
CChr.SL	Corpus Christianorum – Serie Latina
CPG	Clavis Patrum Graecorum
CRAI	Comptes rendus des séances de l'académie des inscriptions et belles lettres
CSCO	Corpus scriptorum Christianorum orientalium
CSCO.A	Corpus scriptorum Christianorum orientalium – Scriptores Arabici
CSCO.C	Corpus scriptorum Christianorum orientalium – Scriptores Coptici
CSCO.I	Corpus scriptorum Christianorum orientalium – Scriptores Iberici
CSCO.S	Corpus scriptorum Christianorum orientalium – Scriptores Syri
CSEL	Corpus scriptorum ecclesiasticorum Latinorum
DH	Denzinger/Hünermann (Hg.), Kompendium der Glaubensbekenntnisse und kirchlichen Lehrentscheidungen. 43. Auflage. Freiburg im Breisgau u. a. 2010
EL	Ephemerides liturgicae
EOr	Échos d'Orient
FCCO	Fonti. Sacra congregazione per la chiesa orientale. Codificazione canonica orientale
GCS	Die griechischen christlichen Schriftsteller der ersten drei Jahrhunderte
GLS	Grove Liturgical Study
GdK	Gottesdienst der Kirche
HBS	Henry Bradshaw Society
HDG	Handbuch der Dogmengeschichte
IThS	Innsbrucker theologische Studien
JAC	Jahrbuch für Antike und Christentum
JEH	Journal of Ecclesiastical History
JLH	Jahrbuch für Liturgik und Hymnologie
JThS	Journal of Theological Studies
KStT	Kanonistische Studien und Texte
LCPM	Letture cristiane del primo millennio
LF	Liturgiegeschichtliche Forschungen
LJ	Liturgisches Jahrbuch
LO	Lex orandi
LQF	Liturgiegeschichtliche Quellen und Forschungen
LThK	Lexikon für Theologie und Kirche
LWQF	Liturgiewissenschaftliche Quellen und Forschungen

Mansi	Sacrorum conciliorum nova et amplissa collectio
MD	Maison-Dieu
OCA	Orientalia Christiana Analecta
OCP	Orientalia Christiana Periodica
OrChr	Oriens Christianus
OrSyr	Orient syrien
OLA	Orientalia Lovaniensia Analecta
PG	Patrologiae cursus completus. Accurante Jacques-Paul Migne. Series Graeca
PL	Patrologiae cursus completus. Accurante Jacques-Paul Migne. Series Latina
PO	Patrologia orientalis
Quat.	Quatember [Kassel]
RCatT	Revista Catalana de Teologia
REArm	Revue des études arméniennes
RED	Rerum ecclesiasticarum documenta
RevSR	Revue des sciences religieuses
RM	Religionen der Menschheit
RSR	Recherches de science religieuse
RThAM	Recherches de théologie ancienne et mediévale
SC	Sources chrétiennes
SE	Sacris erudiri
SJ	Studia Judaica
SPAW.PH	Sitzungsberichte der preußischen Akademie der Wissenschaften – Philosophisch-historische Klasse
STAC	Studien und Texte zu Antike und Christentum
StAns	Studia Anselmiana
StLi	Studia liturgica
StPatr	Studia patristica
StT	Studi e testi
StTh	Studia theologica
SVTQ	St. Vladimir's Theological Quarterly
TRE	Theologische Realenzyklopädie
TS	Theological Studies [Woodstock/MD, u. a.]
TU	Texte und Untersuchungen zur Geschichte der altchristlichen Literatur
UTB	Uni-Taschenbücher
ZKG	Zeitschrift für Kirchengeschichte
ZKTh	Zeitschrift für katholische Theologie

Accepting Converts in the Orthodox Church: Theory and Practice *

Stefanos Alexopoulos

1. Introduction

There is no doubt that the number of converts in the Orthodox Church is rising, both in the Diaspora and in traditionally Orthodox countries. In the first case, the Orthodox communities have been assimilated into the local culture enough to open up to people of different ethnic and cultural backgrounds. In the second case, most Orthodox countries coming out of communism have to deal with a large number of unbaptized people, while in countries like Greece the rising number of immigrants[1] has increased the number of adult baptisms.[2]
The questions that arise are the following: How are these people accepted in the Orthodox Church? What is the process of catechesis? Is there something equivalent to the Roman Catholic Rites of Christian Initiation for Adults? In trying to answer these questions, I will examine the Byzantine liturgical tradition as regards: (1) the catechetical process, (2) the baptismal and post-baptismal rites for unbaptized converts, and (3) the rites of admission for baptized converts, comparing all these with today's practices. I will then (4) evaluate the current practice and, finally, (5) offer suggestions pointing to areas where the current practice needs reform. I have to note that it is not my purpose to give a detailed description of the whole catechetical process, baptismal and post-baptismal rites either in Byzantium[3] or in the current practice.[4] Rather, I will only highlight what I believe is important for our purposes.

* An earlier version of this article appeared in: Stefanos Alexopoulos, Initiation of Adults in Greece Today: Challenges and Suggestions, in: Šimon Marinčák (Ed.), Sväté Tajomstvá na Krestanskom Vychode (Orientalia et Occidentalia 3), Košice 2008, 145–158 with a particular emphasis on current catechetical process and procedures.

1 According to the Mediterranean Migration Observatory of Panteion University, the number of immigrants in Greece (with a conservative estimate of illegal immigrants) amounted to about 950.000 in 2004. That is about 8.5% of the total population. See http://www.mmo.gr/pdf/general/IMEPO_Final_Report_English.pdf (accessed 15/12/2010).

2 For example, in the parish of St. George in Halandri (Athens), where I serve as a parish priest, over 50 baptisms of adults were celebrated since 1999, a number that is much higher than the total number of baptisms of adults from the beginning of the parish in the 50s until 1999. See also Alexopoulos, Initiation of Adults, 145–156.

3 For an overview of the evidence, see Stefanos Alexopoulos, Gestalt und Deutung der christlichen Initiation im mittelalterlichen Byzanz, in: Christian Lange – Clemens Leonhard – Ralph Olbrich (Eds.), Die Taufe. Einführung in Geschichte und Praxis, Darmstadt 2008, 49–66.

4 Alexopoulos, Initiation of Adults.

2. CATECHETICAL PROCESS

Important documents that reflect the practice of the Great Church of Constantinople in the tenth century allow us to reconstruct the catechumenate in the cathedral liturgical practice of the City.[5] According to these documents, the admission of a candidate to the catechumenate was marked by the prayer for the Making of a Catechumen. During the period of his or her catechesis exorcisms were read over that person. The collective catechumenate was an ecclesial and not a private event, as the petitions and prayer for the Catechumens in the Divine Liturgy (and the Liturgy of the Hours) demonstrate.[6]

In the final phase of the catechumenate, a select group among the catechumens deemed ready was prepared for Baptism. Hence their various names in the Christian tradition: *electi*, *competentes*, or *illuminandi* in the Western Liturgical tradition, *photizomenoi* in the Byzantine liturgical tradition. This final phase was initiated on the third Sunday of Lent, the Sunday of the Exaltation of the Cross, a liturgical high point in Lent. On that Sunday the following announcement was read after the *trisagion*:

> I appeal to your love, Christ-loving brothers, those of you that have some people that ought to be brought to holy Baptism, knowing that Christ's resurrection is at hand, bring these to our most holy church from tomorrow, so that from tomorrow they may receive the seal in Christ and that they may be kept and catechized. However, if some would like to join after this week, knowing that they have not thought about it, these we will not accept unless it is necessary.[7]

After that Sunday,[8] petitions and a prayer relative to the *photizomenoi* appear within the Liturgy of the Presanctified Gifts, following the petitions and

5 Stefano PARENTI – Elena VELKOVSKA (Eds.), L'Eucologio Barberini gr. 336 (BEL.S 80), Rome ²2000; Miguel ARRANZ, L'eucologio costantinopolitano agli inizi del secolo XI, Rome 1996; Juan MATEOS, Le Typicon de la Grande Église (OCA 165–166), Rome 1962–1963; Heinzgerd BRAKMANN, Der griechische Text des Konstantinopler prosphonetikon ton katechoumenon, in: OCP 52 (1986) 211–213; Gudrun ENGBERG – Carsten HÖEG – Günter ZUNTZ (Eds.), Prophetologium. (Monumenta Musicae Byzantinae, Lectionaria), Copenhagen 1939–1981.

6 PARENTI – VELKOVSKA, L'Eucologio Barberini, 119–122, n. 114–117; ARRANZ, L'Eucologio Constantinopolitano, 172–173; Miguel ARRANZ, Les Sacraments de l'ancien Euchologe constantinopolitain 1:1–10, in: OCP 48 (1982) 284–335; 49 (1983) 42–90, 284–302; 50 (1984) 43–64, 372–397; 51 (1985) 60–86; 52 (1986) 145–178; 53 (1987) 59–106; 55 (1989) 33–62, 317–338, here (1984) 52–60; Stefano PARENTI, Christian Initiation in the East, in: Anscar CHUPUNGCO (Ed.), Handbook for Liturgical Studies IV: Sacraments and Sacramentals, Collegeville 2000, 29–48, here 35.

7 Juan MATEOS, Le Typikon 2:38. ARRANZ, Les Sacraments (1984), 47–49. Apparently this text was also read on the previous Sunday, as a rubric in the provisions for the Second Sunday of Lent in the Typikon of the Great Church indicates. See MATEOS, Le Typicon 2:30. For a French translation of the Greek text from Dresden A 104, see MATEOS, Le Typicon 2:31 note 2. For the Greek text, see BRAKMANN, Der griechische Text, 212.

8 On the three–week distance between the enrollment of the *photizomenoi* and Lazarus Saturday, see Thomas TALLEY, The Origins of the Liturgical Year, Collegeville ²1986, 189–214; Maxwell JOHNSON, Preparation for Pascha? Lent in Christian Antiquity, in: Paul BRADSHAW – Lawrence HOFFMAN (Eds.), Passover and Easter. The Symbolic Structuring of Sacred Seasons (Two Liturgical Traditions 6), Notre Dame 1999, 36–54;

dismissal of the catechumens (originally, also within the Divine Liturgy on Saturdays and Sundays[9]).

Following the three exorcisms one finds in the manuscript tradition a prayer that is titled "Prayer after one is made a catechumen, [said over] him who is about to be baptized,"[10] followed by the renunciation and profession of faith, and a prayer of invitation to Baptism.[11]

This final stage of the catechumenate in the collective catechesis is reflected in the renunciation and acceptance rites of Holy Friday in the Cathedral Rite of Constantinople. According to these rites, as reflected in the Euchologion *Barberini gr. 336*, the Patriarch would arrive at the Church of *Hagia Eirene* in Constantinople around noon on Holy Friday. There all the catechumens would be gathered, and the patriarch would ascend the ambo. After a diaconal command to be attentive, the bishop would command them to stand with awe, cross themselves, strip, and take off their shoes.[12] Then the "catechesis", a long exhortation pointing out and explaining to them their renunciation of the devil and their acceptance of Christ, would start.[13] After that, he would guide them to turn towards the West, raise their hands, renounce Satan three times and blow upon him. After that, he would guide them to turn towards the East, accept Christ, recite the Nicene/Constantinopolitan Creed, and accept Christ again. Then the bishop would exclaim: "Blessed is God who desires that every human being be saved and come to the knowledge of truth, now and ever and unto the ages of ages."[14] After that the bishop would continue his catechetical exhortation.[15]

At the conclusion of his catechetical exhortation the bishop would call them to raise their hands again, and three petitions were said: for the well-being of the Church, the Emperor and the people, protection from the devil and for peace in the City. After giving peace, he would order them to dress and wear their shoes. Then he would descend from the ambo, enter the sanctuary, and pray the usual

IDEM, From Three Weeks to Forty Days. Baptismal Preparation and the Origins of Lent, in: IDEM, Living Water, Sealing Spirit, Collegeville 1995, 118–136.

9 Stefanos ALEXOPOULOS, The Presanctified Liturgy in the Byzantine Rite. A Comparative Analysis of its Origins, Evolution, and Structural Components (Liturgia Condenda 21), Leuven 2009, 196–217. Since in the cathedral practice of Constantinople the PRES was celebrated up to Holy Friday, the petitions of the *photizomenoi* were also said up to that point, but after the PRES ceased to be celebrated on Holy Friday, the petitions of the *photizomenoi* were said up to Holy Wednesday, the last day the Presanctified would be celebrated.

10 PARENTI – VELKOVSKA, L'Eucologio Barberini, 122–123, n. 118; ARRANZ, L'eucologio costantinopolitano, 178; ARRANZ, Les Sacraments (1984), 60–61.

11 PARENTI – VELKOVSKA, L'Eucologio Barberini, 124, n. 119; ARRANZ, L'eucologio costantinopolitano, 181.

12 PARENTI – VELKOVSKA, L'Eucologio Barberini, 146, n. 143.1–3; ARRANZ, Les Sacraments (1984), 377.

13 PARENTI – VELKOVSKA, L'Eucologio Barberini, 146, n. 143.4–5.

14 IBID. 148, n. 143.23.

15 IBID. 148–149, n. 143.24–25.

prayers for the *photizomenoi,* and recite the prayer of invitation to Baptism[16] Then the *photizomenoi* were invited to proceed and receive the laying-on of hands, after which a final prayer was read.[17]

Turning to current practice, we observe that most of the ritual elements are present, but the ritual structure and process is absent. The whole process is initiated by the person interested to be baptized. He comes to a parish and approaches the priest, either alone or usually with a member of the parish. After the priest talks to him or her and sees that his or her motives are genuine, the priest initiates the paperwork. The candidate fills in an application to the local bishop, stating his will to become Orthodox. That application is accompanied by a letter of the parish priest to the local bishop, asking that the bishop accept the candidate's application. The bishop then replies, usually accepting the application, assigns a catechist for the candidate, and notes that the candidate should be baptized after the catechism is completed. The catechist is usually the priest who sent the letter accompanying the candidate's application. Now, if there is a language barrier, then the priest is responsible for finding a translator and books in the language of the candidate.

The catechesis then starts. It varies in length, depending on the background of the candidate, his discipline and willingness to study and learn, and the frequency of meetings. The whole process of catechesis is a series of classes, devoid of any ritual signpost of its beginning, its process, and its nearing completion. Usually the catechesis takes place within private study meetings, once or twice a week. What material and what method is used depends entirely upon the priest/catechist. The minimum duration for a catechesis is, in theory, six months. There is no ritual associated either with the beginning or the process of catechesis. The liturgical elements of the process of catechesis that we saw earlier are now all piled one on top of the other right before Baptism proper, as is done in cases of infant Baptism:

Enarxis: In the name of the Father …

1 Prayer for the Making of a Catechumen[18]

2 Three Exorcisms[19]

16 IBID., 149–150, n. 144.1–10.

17 We find details of this whole process, but especially of the laying-on of hands, in a manuscript of the Prophetologion, the liturgical book that contained the readings of the Old Testament. In that manuscript, at the service of Trithekte (Terce-Sext) of Holy Friday, after the reading, the rubrics that follow give these directions: "And then the Patriarch ascends to the ambo, he makes three prostrations, the archdeacon lifts the omophoron, and the patriarch does the catechesis. And after he finishes, he descends and stands in front of the holy table. The deacon then says the petitions for the *photizomenoi.* And when he says "Catechumens depart" the catechumens are brought up (lit. offered) by one of the deacons to the left barrier of the bema. And leaning there, the patriarch blesses the catechumens on the forehead, the mouth, the chest, and then washes his hands and says: "For you are our illumination" and the deacon says: "Let us depart in peace." [Prophetologion 1960 (see fn 5), 401].

18 PARENTI – VELKOVSKA, L'Eucologio Barberini, 119, n. 114.

19 IBID. 120–122, n. 115–117.

3 Prayer for the One about to be Baptized[20]

4 Renunciation of Satan and Acceptance of Christ[21]

5 Prayer for Invitation to Baptism[22]

Dismissal

These ritual elements, stacked one on top of the other, and completed today within ten or fifteen minutes, once marked the whole process of the catechumenate.

3. BAPTISMAL AND POST-BAPTISMAL RITES

We described the Byzantine catechetical and initiation process up to and including Holy Friday. Now we will continue with the baptism itself. The *Typikon of the Great Church* provides us with a brief description of Baptism on Holy Saturday vigil:

> And the Patriarch goes to the large Baptistery and puts on his white *sticharion*, and enters where the baptismal font is, and in the usual manner censes three times around the baptismal font, followed by the deacons, and performs the baptisms there according to the ordo. In the meantime, the rest of the readings are read in the church.[23]

The deacons in the baptistery would proclaim "the diaconal petitions of Holy Saturday at baptism"[24] while the celebrant silently read a private prayer, a kind of apologia, asking God's forgiveness for his sins as he is to perform the Baptism.[25]

After the completion of the petitions and the silent recitation of the above prayer, the blessing of the baptismal waters followed.[26] Upon the completion of the prayer, the celebrant gave the peace, and the deacons called everyone to bow their head. The celebrant then breathed on the container of the oil three times, signed it, and read a prayer of the blessing of the oil for the prebaptismal anointing.[27] The priest poured some of the oil in the baptismal waters and the

20 IBID. 122–123, n. 118.
21 IBID. 124, n. 119.1–10.
22 IBID. 124, n. 119.11.
23 MATEOS, Le Typicon 2:84.
24 PARENTI – VELKOVSKA, L'Eucologio Barberini, n. 120, 125; ARRANZ, L'eucologio costantinopolitano, 182; ARRANZ, Les Sacraments (1985), 75.
25 PARENTI – VELKOVSKA, L'Eucologio Barberini, n. 121, 125–126; ARRANZ, L'eucologio costantinopolitano, 183–184; ARRANZ, Les Sacraments (1985), 77. This prayer is of the same genre as the prayers "No one is worthy..." of the Divine Liturgy; see PARENTI – VELKOVSKA, L'Eucologio Barberini, n. 12, 62. and "Lord Jesus Christ, the only begotten son..." of the office of the sanctification of the waters on Epiphany. IBID. n. 128, 133–134.
26 PARENTI – VELKOVSKA, L'Eucologio Barberini, n. 122, 126–128; ARRANZ, L'eucologio costantinopolitano, 184–187; ARRANZ, Les Sacraments (1985), 78–79.
27 PARENTI – VELKOVSKA, L'Eucologio Barberini, n. 123, 129; ARRANZ, L'eucologio costantinopolitano, 187–188; ARRANZ, Les Sacraments (1985), 81.

candidate for Baptism was brought forth. The priest anointed the candidate's forehead, chest, and back and then the deacon anointed the candidate's body with the oil.[28] Male and female candidates were brought forth separately. Male candidates were accompanied, undressed, anointed, and dressed (after the Baptism) by the deacons. Then, female candidates would be brought forth by deaconesses, who would bring forth, undress, anoint, and dress them (after the Baptism).[29] The current practice, where the candidate for Baptism is anointed by the godparent, is first reflected in the manuscript tradition in the fifteenth century.[30]

Each candidate would be baptized by the celebrant with the well-known formula: "N is baptized in the name [of the Father and the Son and the Holy Spirit]." After the triple immersion, the newly baptized would come out of the water, and Psalm 31:1 would be chanted.[31]

The celebrant then would read the prayer of Chrismation. After the prayer was read, Galatians 3:27 was chanted and during the chant the celebrant would anoint the baptized with Chrism using the formula: "The seal of the Gift of the Holy Spirit" tracing the sign of the Cross on the forehead, the nostrils, the mouth, and the ears. The celebrant then would start to chant Psalm 31:1 and enter with the neophytes into the church, and the Divine Liturgy would take place.[32]

We saw that the candidates for Baptism would be totally naked as they entered the baptismal font. The older manuscripts imply that the vesting with white garments took place after the triple immersion and before Chrismation, but it becomes explicit in some manuscripts of the twelfth/thirteenth century, where we read:

> After baptizing everyone, (the patriarch) washes (his hands), takes off the *lention* [white piece of cloth protecting his white *sticharion*] and the cuffs and takes off his baptismal vestments [the white *sticharion*] and wears the vestments of the Divine Liturgy, and comes out of the sacristy of the Baptistery, and chrismates the ones baptized with holy chrism.[33]

The neophytes, then, would not wait in the nude for the bishop to change. Rather, they would be dressed in their white garments after their Baptism and before their Chrismation. A rite associated with the vesting of the white baptismal

28 PARENTI – VELKOVSKA, L'Eucologio Barberini, n. 124.4, 130.

29 On the history and the role of the deaconesses in the Orthodox liturgical tradition see the article "Deaconess" in the Oxford Dictionary of Byzantium 1: 592–593. For detailed information and bibliography, see Euaggelos THEODOROU, Ho Thesmos ton Diakonisson eis ten Orthodoxon Ekklesian kai he Dynatotis Anabioseos autou, in: Gennadios LIMOURIS (Ed.), He Thesis tes Gynaikos en te Orthodoxo Ekklesia kai ta peri Cheirotonias ton Gynaikon, Katerini 1994, 309–357.

30 Panagiotis TREMPELAS, Mikron Euchologion vol. 1, Athens 1950, 233, see critical apparatus on 359.

31 PARENTI – VELKOVSKA, L'Eucologio Barberini, n. 124.6–7, 130.

32 IBID., n. 125.1–5, 130–131. There is a variety in later codices as to which and how many parts of the body the celebrant anoints, and in some cases different formulae are used for different parts of the body. In some codices there are even up to three prayers of Chrismation. TREMPELAS, Mikron Euchologion, 303–305.

33 TREMPELAS, Mikron Euchologion, 297.

garments is first attested to in manuscripts dating from the twelfth century on.[34] In a few codices, the earliest being of the thirteenth century, there is also a rite associated with giving a lit candle to the neophyte.[35]

Lections from the Old Testament were read in church for the duration of the Baptisms. The amount of readings depended upon the number of the candidates for Baptism, as the *Typikon of the Great Church* informs us. Psalm 31:1 was read during their entry into the church, and then Galatians 3:27 in the place of the Trisagion.[36] The neophytes would then attend the Divine Liturgy and commune of the Body and Blood of Christ. We should also note that no Epistle and Gospel readings are provided in the outlined rites of Baptism, as Baptism and Chrismation were celebrated in the context of the Divine Liturgy.[37]

Two post-baptismal rites appear in the Byzantine liturgical tradition; that of ablution, and that of tonsure. The ablution would take place on the eighth day, following a week of daily communion and mystagogy,[38] a remnant of the mystagogical catecheses of the fourth and fifth centuries, and the tonsure, a rite for children originally independent from Baptism, would take place when the baptized would have his or her hair cut.[39]

The above description of Baptism has Easter and its vigil as its context. Easter, however, was not the only time for baptisms. Of course, the evidence that we have seen up to now, for example the enrollment of the *photizomenoi* on the Third Sunday of Lent, and especially the Holy Friday renunciations and profession of faith, point to Easter Baptism. A rubric in manuscript *Athens National Library 662* of the twelfth/thirteenth century introducing the baptismal liturgy characteristically notes: "Prayers of the Holy Baptisms, which the Patriarch makes after the litany of peace, especially on Holy Saturday evening."[40] This rubric highlights the Easter vigil as the time for Baptisms, but implies that Baptisms could take place at other times as well. The *Typikon of the Great Church* of the tenth century foresees baptisms on Easter, on Lazarus Saturday, on Pentecost, and on Epiphany.[41]

But already we have indications in the *Typikon of the Great Church* that as infant Baptism dominated, Baptism became privatized. In a rubric, it examines the

[34] IBID., 298–300.

[35] IBID., 299.

[36] MATEOS, Le Typicon 2:86–90. See also Gabriel BERTONIÈRE, The Historical Development of the Easter Vigil and Related Services in the Greek Church (OCA 193), Rome 1972, 127–139.

[37] The readings on the Easter vigil are Romans 6:3–11 and Matthew 28:1–20. MATEOS, Le Typicon 2:90.

[38] See, for example, Canon 66 of the Council of Trullo. TREMPELAS, Mikron Euchologion 310, 371–377, critical apparatus; L'Eucologio Barberini, 131–132, n. 126; ARRANZ, L'eucologio costantinopolitano, 194–195; ARRANZ, Les Sacraments (1989) 39–42.

[39] PARENTI – VELKOVSKA, L'Eucologio Barberini, 198, 200, §§ 208, 209, 212; TREMPELAS, Mikron Euchologion 378–382. See also ARRANZ, L'eucologio costantinopolitano, 196–197; ARRANZ, Les Sacraments (1989), 48–54.

[40] TREMPELAS, Mikron Euchologion, 348, manuscript H.

[41] MATEOS, Le Typicon 2, 84–90 (Easter); 2, 62–64 (Lazarus Saturday); 2, 136–138 (Pentecost); 2, 184–186 (Epiphany).

possibility that no Baptisms might take place on the Easter vigil.[42] There is no doubt that by the 15th century, Baptism was totally privatized, even in the case of an adult. St. Symeon of Thessalonike (†1429) characteristically writes:

> The work achieved in the holy Baptism is the greatest. That is why *in the past* the Church had the bishops celebrate the Baptisms of those that came forth [to be baptized] at the cathedral churches, when on the feasts in the liturgy the "As many as have been baptized" was sung, and especially on Holy Saturday, before the divine liturgy, during the many readings from the holy prophets.[43]

Not only is the connection to Easter lost and Baptism privatized, but after the fifteenth century even the connection with the Eucharistic celebration is severed. The neophyte would not attend the liturgy right after his or her Baptism and commune there, but would commune after his or her Baptism from the reserved Eucharist.[44]

In current liturgical practice we observe this privatization of Baptism, not only in the case of infants, but also when adults are baptized. The Baptism proper today has maintained its structural unity, although it is now not celebrated within the context of a Divine Liturgy. The elements of the service are:

Enarxis

1 Litany of Peace [Private Prayer of Celebrant read during the litany]
2 Blessing of the Baptismal Waters
3 Blessing of the Oil of Gladness
4 Anointing of the Font
5 Anointing of the Candidate
6 Triple Immersion with passive formula
7 Psalm 31:1
8 Prayer of Chrism and anointing with Chrism
9 Clothing with White Garment
10 Galatians 3:27
11 Romans 6:3-11
12 Matthew 28:16-20
13 Prayers of Ablution
14 Prayer of Tonsure

Dismissal

Items (1) to (9), the Baptismal proper, reflect both the current and the Byzantine practice. The only difference is that in the Byzantine practice, as we have seen, these would take place in the Baptistery, while the community, gathered for the Eucharist, would listen to a series of readings, waiting for the baptisms to be completed. Today the Baptism is celebrated privately and not in the context of a Eucharistic liturgy.

42 MATEOS, Le Typicon 2, 90.
43 De Sacramentis (PG 155, 221C); emphasis added.
44 PARENTI, Christian Initiation in the East, 45.

Item (10) acts as a transition. In current practice the newly baptized processes around the font three times, standing opposite the priest who censes in the meantime. He or she is not led to the Eucharistic Assembly, as Baptism is no longer within a Eucharistic context, but have to wait until the first Divine Liturgy to be celebrated after his or her Baptism to receive communion!
Items (11) and (12), the readings, are remnants of the Divine Liturgy, while items (13) and (14) are part of the rites that would take place after Baptism. Today they are also compressed, attached to the end of the Baptismal proper concluding Baptism, and the rite of tonsure is administered to adults too. Finally, administering the Eucharist to the neophyte is in some cases deferred to the closest Eucharist celebrated, or in other cases the neophyte is communed by the reserved sacrament.

4. ACCEPTANCE OF BAPTIZED CONVERTS

The admission and initiation of baptized converts[45] would naturally become an issue in Byzantium. Canon 95 of the Quinisext Council stipulated with much

[45] On the issue of the acceptance of converts into the Orthodox Church in Byzantine and current practice, see the following studies: Miguel ARRANZ, Les Sacraments de l'ancien Euchologe Constantinopolitan. 1: Étude préliminaire des sources, in: OCP 48 (1982) 284–335; IDEM, Les Sacraments de l'ancien Euchologe constantinopolitan. 2: Ière partie – admission dans l'Église des convertis des hérésies ou d'autres religions non-chrétiennes, in: OCP 49 (1983) 42–90; CHRYSOSTOMOS, Metropolitan of Myra, Response to Thomas Hopko. 'Tasks Facing the Orthodox', in: Gennadios LIMOURIS – Michael VAPORIS (Eds.), Orthodox Perspectives on Baptism, Eucharist, and Ministry (Faith and Order Paper 128), Brookline 1985, 149–158. John ERICKSON, The Reception of Non–Orthodox into the Orthodox Church, in: Diakonia 19 (1984–1985) 68–86; IDEM, Divergences in Pastoral Praxis in the Reception of Converts, in: Theodore STYLIANOPOULOS (Ed.), Orthodox Perspectives on Pastoral Praxis, Brookline 1988, 150–177; IDEM, The Reception of Non–Orthodox into the Orthodox Church. Contemporary Practice, in: SVTQ 41 (1997) 1–17; Thomas HOPKO, Tasks Facing the Orthodox in the 'Reception' Process of BEM, in: Gennadios LIMOURIS – Michael VAPORIS (Eds.), Orthodox Perspectives on Baptism, Eucharist, and Ministry (Faith and Order Paper 128), Brookline 1985, 135–147; Bishop Peter L' HUILLIER, The Reception of Roman Catholics into Orthodoxy. Historical Variations and Norms, in: SVTQ 24 (1980) 75–82; John KLENTOS, Rebaptizing Converts in the Orthodox Church. Old Perspectives on a New Problem, in: StLi 29 (1999) 216–234; George METALLINOS, I Confess One Baptism: Interpretation and Application of Canon VII of the Second Ecumenical Council by the Kollyvades and Constantine Oikonomos (translated by Priestmonk Seraphim), Mount Athos 1994; Orthodox–Roman Catholic Consultation in North America. "Statement on Baptism and Sacramental Economy" June, 1999. Archimandrite Ambrose POGODIN, On the Question of the Order of Reception of Persons into the Orthodox Church Coming to Her from Other Christian Churches, in: Vestnik Russkogo Khristianskogo Dvizheniya [Messenger of the Russian Christian Movement] 173 (1–1996) 174 (2–1996/1–1997), English translation available at: http://www.holy–trinity.org/ecclesiology/pogodin–reception; Robert STEPHANOPOULOS (Ed.), Guidelines for Orthodox Christians in Ecumenical Relations, New York ²1973, 18–19; Francis THOMSON, Economy. An Examination of the Various Theories of Economy Held Within the Orthodox Church, in: JThS 16 (1965) 368–420; Max THURIAN (Ed.), Churches Respond to BEM vols. 1–5, Geneva 1986–1988, vol. 1, 122–129; vol. 2, 5–29; vol. 3, 1–25; vol. 4, 1–6; vol. 5, 1–3.

detail this process of initiation[46] which is also reflected in the liturgical practice, and witnessed in the manuscript tradition of the Church of Constantinople. The witness of these manuscripts is very important because "canons dictate abstract principles while liturgical texts testify to actual practices."[47] In examining Constantinopolitan liturgical sources representing the practice of the Great Church,[48] John Klentos observes that there are three distinct ways of receiving converts. Some were treated as pagans, and had to go through the whole process of catechesis, exorcisms, Baptism, and Chrismation before being allowed to share in the Eucharist. Others were required to submit a *libellus* (petition or certificate) and renounce any pertinent heresies before being admitted to a brief two-week period of fasting and catechesis. This culminated in a public renunciation of heresy and submission to the Orthodox faith, anointing with Chrism, and Communion. After eight days the convert returned for a ritual ablution. Finally, others were required simply to submit a *libellus* before receiving Communion. Observing the above, Prof. John Klentos notes:

> If we were to compare this well-established and durable liturgical tradition with the requirements of canon law, we would find that these three routes to conversion are exactly those prescribed in Canon 95 of the Pethekte Council. The only alteration is that the list of heresies in each group has expanded over time."[49]

In general the following criteria seem to hold true: Heretics who had a *divergent christological confession* were received by means of a *libellus* and Eucharist

[46] "Those who from the heretics come over to orthodoxy, and to the number of those who should be saved, we receive according to the following order and custom. Arians, Macedonians, Novatians, who call themselves Cathari, Aristeri, and Testareskaidecatitae, or Tetraditae, and Apollinarians, we receive on their presentation of certificates and on their anathematizing every heresy which does not hold as does the holy Apostolic Church of God: then first of all we anoint them with the holy chrism on their foreheads, eyes, nostrils, mouth and ears; and as we seal them we say – 'The seal of the gift of the Holy Ghost.' But concerning the Paulianists it has been determined by the Catholic Church that they shall by all means be rebaptized. The Eunomeans also, who baptize with one immersion; and the Montanists, who here are called Phrygians; and the Sabellians, who consider the Son to be the same as the Father, and are guilty in certain other grave matters, and all the other heresies – for there are many heretics here, especially those who come from the region of the Galatians – all of their number who are desirous of coming to the Orthodox faith, we receive as Gentiles. And on the first day we make them Christians, on the second Catechumens, then on the third day we exorcise them, at the same time also breathing thrice upon their faces and ears; and thus we initiate them, and we make them spend time in church and hear the Scriptures; and then we baptize them. And the Manichaeans, and Valentinians and Marcionites and all of similar heresies must give certificates and anathematize each his own heresy, and also Nestorius, Eutyches, Dioscorus, Severus, and the other chiefs of such heresies, and those who think with them, and all the aforesaid heresies; and so they become partakers of the Holy Communion." For the Greek text see Georgios RALLES – Michael POTLES, Syntagma ton Theion kai Ieron Kanonon, vols. 1–6, Athens 1852–1859, 2:531. The English translation is from Philip SCHAFF – Henry WACE (Eds.), Nicene and Post Nicene Fathers, Second Series, vol. 14: The Seven Ecumenical Councils, Peabody ^{2}1995, 405.

[47] KLENTOS, Rebaptizing Converts, 223.

[48] *Barberini gr. 336* of the end of the eighth century, the eleventh–century *Coislin 213*, the eleventh–century *Grottaferrata Γ.β. I*, and the twelfth/thirteenth–century *Athens 662.*

[49] KLENTOS, Rebaptizing Converts, 224.

(e.g. Nestorians, Eutychians, Apollinarians, Jacobites). Those who *differed in their theology of the Trinity* were required to submit a *libellus*, fast, pray, learn the Creed (which implies a more serious dogmatic deviation), publicly renounce their heresy, and be anointed with *Myron* before receiving Communion (e.g. Arians, Macedonians, Dioscoriens, Sabbatians, Nabatians, Quartodecimans). Finally, converts who came from communities with *a radically deficient understanding of God* had to go through the entire initiation process for pagans or non-believers (e.g. Eunomians, Montanists, Manichaeans, Sabellians).[50] In other words, canon 95 of Trullo became the guiding principle in Byzantium regarding the way converts would be accepted in the Orthodox Church.

In current liturgical practice accepting baptized converts has also become an issue, as most of the people approaching the Orthodox Church are already baptized Christians. But this guiding principle is totally ignored. Either there is a distinction made between mainstream, Trinitarian Christians, and others, where the former are accepted by Chrismation while the latter are baptized, or in a number of cases all converts, no matter where they come from, are baptized, as any prior Baptism is considered invalid and non-existent. One may observe these two divergent practices not only within the same Church, but even within the same diocese. There are even cases where people are accepted into the Orthodox Church by Chrismation, partake of the Sacraments, and then after a while are rebaptized because either they feel something is lacking, or they are told to do so.

[50] There is also supporting evidence of the above practice. When John Scholasticus, Patriarch of Constantinople from 565–577, forced re–ordination upon some Monophysite bishops, he met with considerable opposition; see THOMPSON, Economy, 415. In 1195, Balsamon, the famous canonist and Byzantine commentator of canons, officially responding in the name of the Synod of Constantinople to questions put by Patriarch Mark of Alexandria, wrote that "since the Church of the West has been separated for a long time from spiritual communion with the other four patriarchates, no Latin ought to be admitted to communion before first presenting a declaration rejecting the doctrines and customs and being instructed according to the canons;" see RALLES – POTLES, Syntagma, 4:460. Demetrios Chomatianos, Archbishop of Ochrid (1216/17–c. 1234) noted that many were criticizing Balsamon's answer as too rigorous; see PG 119, 956–960. Niphon, Archbishop of Novgorod (1130–1156) stipulated that as far as he was concerned, Westerners were to be received into Orthodoxy by Chrismation; see L' HUILLIER, The Reception, 77. In addition, the Synod of Constantinople of 1260, after the expulsion of the Crusaders, rejected the theory that the Latins should be re–baptized; see THOMSON, Economy, 415. Finally, Mark of Ephesus, the well–known anti–unionist who refused to sign the Ferarra–Florence union, notes that in the event some want to return to Orthodoxy, they are to be catechized and anointed with chrism. It is extremely important to note that in the period of St. Mark and the controversy regarding the union, and the language used, that St. Mark speaks of catechism and anointing, not re–baptizing. This would later be the foundation for the official post–fall policy of the Great Church; see L' HUILLIER, The Reception, 78.

5. EVALUATION OF CURRENT PRACTICE

From this summary, I believe it is obvious that the difference between theory and practice regarding the manner of acceptance of converts in the Orthodox Church is great. In brief, we can observe the following: The ritual elements of the whole period of catechesis are compressed to a ten to fifteen minute service before Baptism proper, Baptism itself has lost its connection with the Eucharistic celebration, turning Baptism into a private enterprise, and the rites of the eighth day have lost their meaning by being attached to the end of the baptismal service. Finally, there is confusion as to how to accept baptized Christians in the Orthodox community.

Although the Byzantine liturgical tradition has maintained the structural framework within which the Initiation of the adult could be restored, nothing is done to that measure. In other words:

1. The local bishop does not have any active role in the whole process of initiation.
2. Although Great Lent offers the structure for the catechetical process, such as the petitions for the catechumens and *photizomenoi* (after the fourth week of Lent) in the Presanctified, with the Old Testament Readings, and with the Vesperal Liturgy of Basil on Holy Saturday, it is not employed at all. In general, although Great Lent, Holy Week, and Easter are the natural *loci* for the final preparation of the catechumens, they are not employed as such.
3. Traditional baptismal days in the Byzantine liturgical tradition such as Holy Saturday, Christmas Eve, Epiphany Eve, Saturday of Lazarus, and Pentecost are not employed.
4. Oftentimes fonts for adults are not available!
5. Baptisms almost never take place within the context of the Divine Liturgy.
6. There is no Mystagogy during the period of Easter Week.
7. Baptism has become a private endeavor; the community is not part of it.
8. The criteria as to how one accepts a baptized convert vary from diocese to diocese, even sometimes from parish to parish.

6. TOWARDS A REFORM OF CURRENT PRACTICE

Great Lent provides us with an already existing structure within and around which an active catechumenate can be re-established, thus also restoring meaning to elements of Lent that now make no sense to the non-specialists (e.g. petitions of the *photizomenoi* from the fourth week of Lent on, the series of readings at Vesperal Basil on Holy Saturday). More concretely, I would suggest that the bishop should have an active role in the whole process of the catechumenate. In other words, (1) set days during the year should be established when new

catechumens are enrolled in the presence of the local bishop, who meets with them, and reads over them the prayer of the making of catechumen. (2) The bishop should have an active role in the catechesis by meeting with the catechumens and reading the exorcisms over them. (3) On the Third Sunday of Lent (Sunday of the Adoration of the Cross) a formal announcement is made regarding those who enter the final stage of the catechumenate and become *photizomenoi*. The petitions for the *photizomenoi* are reintroduced on Sundays. (4) On Holy Friday the bishop gathers all the *photizomenoi*, the renunciation of Satan and acceptance of Christ takes place, and the bishop reads over them the Prayer of invitation to Baptism. (5) Baptism takes place during the readings of Vesperal Liturgy of Basil on Holy Saturday, and is celebrated by the bishop. (6) Mystagogy during Bright Week is also restored. It is also obvious that each diocese should make sure it has a font designed for adults. On the parish level, the existing structure (petitions for catechumens and *photizomenoi*) will regain their meaning and thus the community will become part of the process.
This restoration is relevant to Great Lent and Easter. I would also suggest that a second such structure is formed around Christmas and the Christmas Lent, thus providing us with two major baptismal days in current liturgical practice, Easter and Christmas:

Event	Easter	Christmas
Enrollment of *Photizomenoi*	3rd Sunday of Lent	3rd Sunday before Christmas
Petitions for *Photizomenoi*	4th week of Lent	3rd week before Christmas
Final Renunciation and Acceptance	On Holy Friday	On December 23
Baptism	During Readings at Vesperal Basil on Holy Saturday	During Readings at Vesperal Basil on December 24
Mystagogy	Bright Week	Between Christmas and Epiphany

Thus Christmas and Christmas Lent imitate the catechetical process organized around Great Lent and Easter. In such a case, the enrollment of the *photizomenoi* would take place on the third Sunday before Christmas, after which the petitions for the *photizomenoi* would be incorporated in liturgical use. The final renunciation would take place on December 23, and Baptism itself would take place during the readings of Vesperal Liturgy of Basil on December 24. Finally, the mystagogical catechesis would take place between Christmas and Epiphany. The other baptismal days (Epiphany, Lazarus Saturday, and Pentecost) could be restored as days when group Baptisms of infants in the local communities can take place.
What I suggest is not an exercise in creative ritual planning but an ecclesiological statement. Liturgical reform is not a movement to "modernize" liturgy. Rather, it is a movement to restore to liturgy its original vitality and meaning,

making liturgy again the center of Christian life and spirituality. It is towards this goal that I have suggested the restoration of adult initiation to its proper ritual framework and context, to bring again practice in line with theory.

Die Typika des Schenute-Klosters: Die Vorstellung eines Projektes[1]

Diliana Atanassova

1. Einleitung

Auf der Grundlage erstmalig oder verbessert zu edierender liturgischer Quellen, besonders der koptischen (sahidischen = sa) Typikon-Fragmente, steht der Gottesdienst des auf Schenute (um 361/62 – 465) zurückgehenden Weißen Klosters[2] (Ägypten) im Mittelpunkt der Forschungen des vorliegenden Projektes. Die Typika – genannt auch Perikopen- und Hymnen-Direktorien (oder „directory" und „index")[3] – sind gottesdienstliche „Verzeichnisse, die angeben, an

[1] Das am 01.03.2007 beim Österreichischen Wissenschaftsfonds (FWF) eingereichte Projekt „Der Gottesdienst des Schenute-Klosters anhand der koptischen (sahidischen) Typika. Edition. Kommentar. Untersuchung" wurde in der FWF-Sitzung vom 25. Juni 2007 für drei Jahre bewilligt und ist am 1. September 2007 in Kraft getreten. Das Projekt wird am Fachbereich Bibelwissenschaft und Kirchengeschichte der Paris-Lodron Universität Salzburg unter der Leitung von Univ.-Prof. Dr. Dietmar Winkler von Dr. Diliana Atanassova durchgeführt. Der vorliegende Aufsatz entspricht dem Projektzustand aus dem Jahr 2007. Die danach folgenden Jahre haben Veränderungen mit sich gebracht, die allerdings nicht die Substanz des Vorhabens betreffen, sondern sich eher auf Details beziehen. Z.B. hat sich die Zahl der Blätter mit ihren Signaturangaben aus der Beilage erhöht. Die Änderungen werden hier absichtlich nicht mehr berücksichtigt, um besser den Entwicklungsprozess, dem sich die Typika-Untersuchung unterzogen hat, darzustellen. Die endgültigen Ergebnisse werden in einer Monographie publiziert werden.

[2] Obwohl der Name „Weißes Kloster" urspr. nur die erhaltene Kirche meint und nicht den gesamten Komplex, hat es sich nunmehr eingebürgert, dass man die Bezeichnung „so genannt" weglassen kann, vgl. Heinzgerd Brakmann, Fragmenta Graeco-Copto-Thebaica. Zu Jutta Henners Veröffentlichung alter und neuer Dokumente südägyptischer Liturgie, in: OrChr 88 (2004) 117–172, hier 120, Fußn. 8.

[3] Untersuchungen zu den Typika finden sich teilweise bei: Heinzgerd Brakmann, Zu den Liturgien des Christlichen Ostens, in: ALW 24 (1982) 377–410; Heinzgerd Brakmann, Συναξις καθολικη in Alexandreia. Zur Verbreitung des christlichen Stationsgottesdienstes, in: JAC 30 (1987) 74–89; Heinzgerd Brakmann, Neue Funde und Forschungen zur Liturgie der Kopten 1984-1988, in: ICCoptS 4 (1988) 419–435; Heinzgerd Brakmann, Neue Funde und Forschungen zur Liturgie der Kopten 1988-1992, in: ICCoptS 5 (1992) 9–32; Heinzgerd Brakmann, Die Kopten – Kirche Jesu Christi in Ägypten. Ihre Geschichte und Liturgie, in: Albert Gerhards– Heinzgerd Brakmann (Hg.), Die koptische Kirche. Einführung in das ägyptische Christentum, Stuttgart [u.a.] 1994, hier 9–27, mit Anm. auf 196–221; Heinzgerd Brakmann, Neue Funde und Forschungen zur Liturgie der Kopten 1992-1996, in: ICCoptS 6 (1996) 451–464; Heinzgerd Brakmann, Der christlichen Bibel erster Teil in den gottesdienstlichen Traditionen des Ostens und Westens. Liturgiehistorische Anmerkungen zum sog. Stellenwert des Alten/Ersten Testaments im Christentum, in: Ansgar Franz (Hg.), Streit am Tisch des Wortes? Zur Deutung und Bedeutung des Alten Testaments und seiner Verwendung in der Liturgie, St. Ottilien 1997, 565–604; Heinzgerd Brakmann, Neue Funde und Forschungen zur Liturgie der Kopten 1996-2000, in: ICCoptS 7 (2000) 575–606; Heinzgerd Brakmann, Zwischen Pharos und Wüste. Die Erforschung alexandrinisch-ägyptischer Liturgie durch und nach Anton Baumstark, in: Gabriele Winkler – Robert Taft (Ed.), Comparative Liturgy Fifty

welchen Tagen welche Texte zu verwenden waren"[4]. Sie bieten demnach in der Regel keine vollständigen Gebete oder sonstige liturgischen Formulare[5], sondern nur ihre Initien, manchmal auch Endverse. Man kann die Typika somit als liturgische Quellen mit sehr knappem Umfang, allerdings sehr großer Informationsdichte charakterisieren. Die Termini Typikon (pl. Typika) und Direktorium werden in der koptologischen und liturgiehistorischen Forschung synonym verwendet. In unserem Projekt verwenden wir Typikon als allgemeinen Begriff und für die konkreten Blätter die Bezeichnungen „Perikopen-Direktorium" und „Hymnen-Direktorium".[6]

2. PROJEKTZIELE

Ziel des Forschungsvorhabens ist es, alle sa Typika (Perikopen- und Hymnendirektorien[7]) des Weißen Klosters bei Sohag (Oberägypten) zu identifizieren, zu edieren und zu untersuchen. Diese Typikon-Handschriften (= Hss) sind die

Years after Anton Baumstark (1872-1948). International Congress at the Pontificio Istituto Orientale/Centro di Studi Ezio Aletti, Rome 15-29 September 1998 (OCA 265), Roma 2001, 323–376; Heinzgerd BRAKMANN, Neue Funde und Forschungen zur Liturgie der Kopten 2000-2004, in: ICCoptS 8 (2006) 127–149; James DRESCHER, A Coptic Lectionary Fragment, in: Annales du Service des Antiquités d'Égypte 51 (1951) 247–256, Pl. 1–4; Hans QUECKE, Untersuchungen zum koptischen Stundengebet (Publications de l'Institut Orientaliste de Louvain 3), Louvain 1970; Hans QUECKE, Zukunftschancen bei der Erforschung der koptischen Liturgie, in: Coptic Studies 1 (1978) 164-196; Hans QUECKE, Koptische "Hermeniai"-Fragmente in Florenz, in: Orientalia 47 (1978) 215–219; Hans QUECKE, Zwei Blätter aus koptischen Hermeneia-Typika in der Papyrussammlung der Österreichischen Nationalbibliothek (P.Vindob. K 9725 und 9734), in: Festschrift Papyrussammlung der ÖNB. Papyrus Erzherzog Rainer (P. Rainer cent.), Wien 1983, 194–206, Tf. 13-16; Hans QUECKE, Ein koptischer Psalmenindex, in: Orientalia 56 (1987) 263–291; Hans QUECKE, Psalmverse als »Hymnen« in der koptischen Liturgie?, in: Christianisme d'Égypte. Hommages à René-Georges Coquin (Cahiers de la Bibliothèque Copte 9), Paris/Louvain 1995, 101–114; Ugo ZANETTI, Premières recherches sur les lectionnaires coptes, in: EL 98 (1984) 1–34; Ugo ZANETTI, Les lectionnaires coptes annuels Basse-Égypte (Publications de l'Institut Orientaliste de Louvain 33), Louvain-la-Neuve 1985; Ugo ZANETTI, La distribution des psaumes dans l'horologion copte, in: OCP 56/1 (1990) 323–369; Ugo ZANETTI, Abû-l-Barakât et les lectionnaires de Haute-Égypte, in: ICCoptS 4 (1988) 450–462; Ugo ZANETTI, Un index liturgique du Monastère blanc, in: Christianisme d'Égypte. Hommages à René-Georges Coquin (Cahiers de la Bibliothèque Copte 9), Paris – Louvain 1995, 55–75, Tf. 1–2; Ugo ZANETTI, Les lectionnaires coptes, in: La lecture liturgique des Épitres catholiques dans l'Église ancienne (Histoire du texte biblique 1), Lausanne 1996, 141–190; Ugo ZANETTI, Liturgy in the White Monastery, in: Gawdat GABRA – Hany N. TAKLA (Ed.), Christianity and Monasticism in Upper Egypt. Vol. 1: Akhmim and Sohag, Cairo – New York 2007, 201–210; Ugo ZANETTI, Leçons liturgiques au Monastère Blanc. Six Typika, in: Bulletin de la Société d'Archéologie Copte 46 (2007) 231–304.

4 BRAKMANN, Die Kopten (s. Anm. 3), 215, Anm. 157.

5 QUECKE, Zwei Blätter (s. Anm. 3), 195.

6 Vgl. BRAKMANN, Neue Funde 1996-2000 (s. Anm. 3), 589, 591; QUECKE, Stundengebet (s. Anm. 3), 76, Fußn. 123; ZANETTI, Index (s. Anm. 3), 55.

7 Die Bezeichnung erfolgt nach BRAKMANN, Neue Funde 1996-2000 (s. Anm. 3), 591, Fußn. 48.

Hauptquellen des Projektes. Mit ihrer Hilfe werden die jeweiligen Perikopen (Bibelabschnitte), Hymnen und Homilien für jeden bezeugten Sonn- und Festtag der im Schenute-Kloster gefeierten Liturgie ermittelt. Demnach wird das Projekt

- einerseits die weltweit verstreuten Blätter bzw. Fragmente von Typika des Weißen Klosters aufspüren, ihre Zusammengehörigkeit zu bestimmten Manuskripten untersuchen und danach die wiedergewonnenen liturgischen Bücher edieren
- andererseits die im Weißen Kloster begangenen Feiern und Feste mit ihren genauen heortologischen Angaben (d.h. Datum und Namen) feststellen sowie die Bestandteile der jeweiligen Liturgie – Perikopen, Hymnen und Homilien – erfassen und untersuchen.

Wie im Weiteren zu erläutern ist, werden die wiedergewonnenen Blätter einer Typikon-Hs diplomatisch ediert und kommentiert. Diese Edition wird künftig beim Auffinden einer neuen sa liturgischen Hs oder beim Entziffern eines bisher unidentifizierten liturgischen Fragmentes ein grundlegendes Arbeitsinstrumentarium bilden.

Um dies zu erreichen, sind Schwierigkeiten verschiedenster Art zu bewältigen. Die größte davon ist, dass die Begrenztheit der Hauptquellen es bisher nicht erlaubte, die Liturgie des Weißen Klosters in ihrer Vollständigkeit zu ermitteln. Das wird dazu führen, dass einige Feste und ihre Bestandteile a) vorerst fehlen werden[8], b) nur durch eine einzelne Hs zu belegen sind oder c) in mehreren Typika ihre Bestätigung finden und diese damit eventuell eine Entwicklung oder Vielfalt der Perikopen- oder Hymnenauswahl zu ein und demselben Fest aufzeigen werden.

Ein Spezifikum der liturgischen Hss, das auch zu berücksichtigen sein wird, ist deren „Sitz im Leben" in einem lebendigen Gottesdienst. Im vorliegenden Fall gilt es, sich mit den konkreten liturgischen Consuetudines des Weißen Klosters – also einem monastischen Gottesdienst – zu beschäftigen. Allerdings liefern die Typika auch Hinweise dafür, dass Laien, darunter hochgestellte Beamte[9], der Liturgie des Schenute-Klosters beiwohnten. Auch die Bevölkerung der Umgebung des Klosters war eingeladen[10].

[8] Dies kann Feste betreffen, die aus anderen christlichen Traditionen bekannt sind, im Kirchenkalender des Schenute-Klosters an sich zu erwarten wären, jedoch in den Hss nicht zu belegen sind.

[9] Vgl. die liturgischen Rubriken von Leiden, RMO, Ins. 34.

[10] Jutta HENNER, Fragmenta liturgica coptica. Editionen und Kommentar liturgischer Texte der Koptischen Kirche des ersten Jahrtausends (STAC 5), Tübingen 2000, 87–88.

3. STRUKTUR UND METHODIK DES FORSCHUNGSVORHABENS

Einleitend wird auf das Weiße Kloster allgemein und konkret auf seine in der ganzen Welt verstreuten Bibliotheksbestände eingegangen sowie der Stand der Forschung[11] referiert. Sodann beinhaltet das Forschungsvorhaben:

- die vollständige Zusammenstellung der Typikon-Blätter bzw. –Fragmente des Weißen Klosters nach den Bibliothekskatalogen und –beständen weltweit
- die Untersuchung noch unidentifizierter Fragmente, die möglicherweise früher einer Typikon-Hs angehört haben[12]
- die Identifizierung zusammengehöriger Blätter und Fragmente
- die Edition der dadurch wieder gewonnenen Typikon-Hss und ihre umfassende Untersuchung.

Die Schwerpunkte der geplanten Untersuchung sind Erarbeitung der unbeweglichen und beweglichen Feste des liturgischen Jahres anhand der Typika des Weißen Klosters, die Feststellung des Typus der liturgischen Feier sowie des Typus des Vortragenden und dessen „Rolle“[13], wie sie in der jeweiligen Typikon-Hs niedergeschrieben und festgelegt wird.

a. Art der Feste
Die beiden Festarten – die unbeweglichen und die beweglichen – findet man gleichzeitig auf ein und demselben Typikon-Blatt verzeichnet, wobei sie chronologisch miteinander abgestimmt sind.

- Zu den unbeweglichen Festen zählen u.a. die Hochfeste im Jahreskreis mit ihrer Vor- und Nachfeier, wie z.B. die Christus- und Marien-Feste, und andere Feste mit Abend- und Morgengottesdienst sowie Heiligenfeste.
- Unter den beweglichen Festen sind v.a. die 40-tägige Fastenzeit (ⲡⲉϩⲙⲉ), die 4 Sabbat-Sonntag-Feiern vor Christi Geburt sowie die Sabbat-Sonntag-Feiern, die an einen Monat oder einen unbeweglichen Festtag gebunden sind. Für die Pascha-Woche (Karwoche und Osterfest) sind Hermeneiai-Gesänge für die Ostersonntag-Nacht-Feier[14] erhalten.

b. Art des Gottesdienstes
Bezüglich der Art der liturgischen Feier ist das Forschungsvorhaben an zwei Typen interessiert:

[11] Zum Stand der Forschung sei auf meinen Vortrag „Zu den Perikopen- und Hymnendirektorien des Schenute-Klosters“ beim „9th International Congress of Coptic Studies“ in Kairo (14.–20. September 2008) verwiesen.
[12] Vgl. z.B. die Bestände der Pariser Bibliothèque Nationale de France mit den vielen Handschriften-Schnipsel in den Kartonagen 133 (1–2).
[13] Für den Begriff „Rollenbücher“ vgl. BRAKMANN, Neue Funde (s. Anm. 3), 589.
[14] Leiden, RMO, Ins. 32.

- Der erste Typus präsentiert Hss mit den Bibellesungen und Gesängen für die Messfeier des Schenute-Klosters. Heinzgerd Brakmann spricht von zwei Ordnungen anhand der Perikopenreihenfolge und –zusammensetzung: *ordo minor* und *ordo major*[15]. Der *ordo minor* weist nur je eine Perikope aus den Paulus-Briefen, aus dem Psalter und aus einem der vier Evangelien auf. Der *ordo major* bietet eine viel reichere Zusammensetzung von biblischen Abschnitten, und zwar in folgender Reihenfolge: Prokeimenon, Perikopen der Paulinischen Briefe, Katholischen Briefe, Acta, Psalter und Evangelien. Diese zwei Typen von Perikopenordnungen – *ordo minor* und *ordo major* – sind an den meisten Tagen des Kirchenjahres anzutreffen. Die Ausnahmen davon bilden die Wochen der Großen Fastenzeit und die Pascha-Woche, an denen auch alttestamentliche Perikopen vorkommen. Solche Perikopeninitien sind z.B. aus dem Wiener Typikon K 9741[16] bekannt. Für die Abgrenzung beider Ordnungen spielt die Bedeutsamkeit eines Festes eine große Rolle. So war der *ordo major* für die Festtage „höheren Ranges[17]" vorgesehen und dementsprechend spiegelt sich das auch in der beträchtlichen Hymnenanzahl bei solchen Festen wieder.
- Der zweite Typus ist die Tagzeitenliturgie mit ihren Perikopen. Der eucharistischen Liturgie geht die abendliche und morgendliche Weihrauchdarbringung voraus.[18] Die Ps- und Ev-Perikopen waren auch hier die Hauptlesungen, jedoch von den Bibelabschnitten der Messe verschieden. Über die konkrete Auswahl und Ordnung der Lesungen und Hymnen[19] im nichteucharistischen Gottesdienst des Weißen Klosters wird dieses Forschungsvorhaben Näheres erbringen.

c. Der Vortragende

Wie Heinzgerd Brakmann[20] betont, werden „die Mitspieler des liturgischen Geschehens" in der koptischen Liturgie mit den sog. „Rollenbüchern" ausgestattet, wo jeder von ihnen – die Sänger, die Vorleser, die Diakone (auch Archidiakone), die Priester, die Bischöfe – seine Rolle ablesen kann. Die Typika des Schenute-Klosters haben Hinweise für den Sänger[21] sowie für den Priester[22] aufbewahrt. Allerdings wird der Sänger mit unterschiedlichsten Aufgaben be-

[15] BRAKMANN, Neue Funde 1996–2000 (s. Anm. 3), 591.

[16] Stephen L. EMMEL, Shenoute's Literary Corpus, 1–2 (CSCO 599-600/111-112), Louvain 2004, hier 77, typ. frg. C; QUECKE, Stundengebet (s. Anm. 3), 77.

[17] QUECKE, Zwei Blätter (s. Anm. 3), 195.

[18] QUECKE, Stundengebet (s. Anm. 3), 2–13.

[19] Z.B. Hermeneiai: QUECKE, Stundengebet (s. Anm. 3), 98–101.

[20] BRAKMANN, Neue Funde (s. Anm. 3), 589 u.a.

[21] Vgl. ⲡⲥⲁϩ: Leiden, RMO, Ins. 34, pag. 56, 58; Ins. 38a, f; London, BL, Or. 3580 A.1; Wien, ÖNB, K 9741.

[22] Vgl. Leiden, RMO, Ins. 34, pag. 58 (ⲡⲉⲡⲣⲉⲥⲃⲩⲧⲉⲣⲟⲥ).

traut.[23] Meistens ist jedoch der Vortragende nicht spezifiziert, sondern nur durch die zweite Person Sg. gekennzeichnet. Zu identifizieren, ob sich dahinter der erwähnte Sänger oder ein Vorleser verbirgt, wird eine der Aufgaben des vorliegenden Projekts sein. Dabei ist genauso mit zusätzlichen Erkenntnissen[24] bei der Differenzierung der Rolle des Sängers und über eventuelle andere „Mitspieler" zu rechnen.

3.1. Hauptquellen des Forschungsvorhabens

Die in der Beilage zusammengestellte Liste[25] präsentiert die uns bekannten und für das Projekt als Hauptquellen herangezogenen Typikon-Blätter bzw. Fragmente des Schenute-Klosters. Sie soll keineswegs als abgeschlossen und vollständig betrachtet werden, sondern nur eine erste Vorstellung über das Ausmaß an Hss-Blättern bzw. Fragmenten bieten, mit welchen das Projekt zu tun haben wird. Diese Hss-Blätter bzw. Fragmente, die einst zum Hss-Inventar des Weißen Klosters gehörten und heute die in der Liste aufgezählten Bibliothekssammlungen schmücken, sind in zwei Hauptgruppen geteilt und nach ihren Signaturen alphabetisch geordnet. Diese Tabelle (siehe Beilage) stellt den Kern der Quellen des Projektes dar. Es ist unsere Überzeugung, dass sie sich in Laufe der Untersuchung ergänzen lässt und zwar sowohl durch eine präzisere Erforschung des publizierten Materials (Bibliothekskataloge und andere koptologische Werke) als auch durch die direkte Arbeit vor Ort in den in Beilage aufgelisteten Hss-Abteilungen sowie durch die Bearbeitung der bekannten Nachlässe berühmter Koptologen der Vergangenheit. Der gegenwärtige Stand der Forschung erlaubt keine genauere Zuordnung jedes Blattes bzw. Fragmentes zu seiner ursprünglichen Hs. In diese Richtung sind schon Versuche unternommen worden,

[23] Er muss ebenso Hermeneiai (Leiden, RMO, Ins. 34, pag. 56; 38a, pag. 33–34; 38f, pag. 108; Wien, ÖNB, K 9725.9741), wie Homilien (Leiden, RMO, Ins. 34, pag. 58; Paris, BnF, Copte 129(20) f. 168) vorlesen.

[24] Aufschlussreich sind Queckes Ausführungen über die unterschiedlichen Akteure des koptischen Gottesdienstes, vgl. QUECKE, Stundengebet (s. Anm. 3), 72–78.

[25] Diese Liste ist anhand der bis 2007 publizierten koptologischen Untersuchungen entstanden, vgl. hier in der Anm. 3 die Werke von BRAKMANN, QUECKE, ZANETTI sowie EMMEL, Shenoute's Literary Corpus (s. Anm. 16); Walter E. CRUM, Catalogue of the Coptic Manuscripts in the British Museum, London 1905; Walter E. CRUM, Catalogue of the Coptic Manuscripts in the Collection of the John Rylands Library – Manchester, Manchester 1909; Catherine LOUIS, Catalogue raisonné des manuscrits littéraires coptes conservés à l'IFAO du Caire. Contribution à la reconstitution de la Biblliothèque du monastère Blanc, im Druck; Henri MUNIER, Catalogue général des antiquités égyptiennes du Musée du Caire, N^OS 9201–9304, Manuscrits coptes, Le Caire 1916; Willem PLEYTE – Pieter A. A. BOESER, Manuscrits coptes du Musée d'Antiquités des Pays-Bas à Leide, Leide 1897; Carl WESSELY, Griechische und Koptische Texte theologischen Inhalts 1, 2, 3, 4, 5 (Studien zur Palaeographie und Papyruskunde 9, 1, 12, 13, 15, 18), Leipzig 1909, 1911, 1912, 1913, 1914, 1917 (Nachdr. Amsterdam 1966, 1967); Georg ZOËGA, Catalogus codicum copticorum manu scriptorum qui in museo Borgiano velitris adservantur. Avec une introduction historique et des notes bibliographiques par Joseph-Marie Sauget, Hildesheim – New York 1973. (Nachdruck Rom 1810) u.a.

zumeist von Hans Quecke und Ugo Zanetti. Allerdings kann nur eine gleichzeitige und komplexe Erforschung des gesamten Materials zu richtigen Feststellungen führen. Die beiden Gruppen – Perikopen- und Hymnendirektorien – sind keinesfalls homogen und werden in weitere Untergruppen, die wichtiger Teil der Untersuchung sind, untergliedert[26].

3.2. Sekundäre Quellen für das Forschungsvorhaben

Typika können als liturgische Quellen mit sehr geringem Umfang, jedoch mit großer Informationsdichte charakterisiert werden. Zur Entschlüsselung benötigt man mehrere Quellen verschiedenster Art. Folgende Quellen spielen eine unterstützende Rolle; sie werden lediglich bei der Klärung schwieriger Fälle herangezogen werden. Sie seien hier nur unkommentiert aufgelistet:

3.2.1. Aus dem koptischen Ritus: a) sa liturgische Hss sowohl des Weißen Klosters, als auch anderer;[27] b) die Liturgie des faijumischen Deir El-Naqlun[28]; c) die Liturgie aus Oxyrhynchos (POxy XI 1357)[29]; d) liturgische Lesungshinweise in sa Bibelhandschriften[30]; e) Werke der Kirchenväter, insbesondere des

[26] Für eine ausführlichere Darstellung der Untergruppen sei erneut auf meinen Vortrag „Zu den Perikopen- und Hymnendirektorien des Schenute-Klosters“ beim „9th International Congress of Coptic Studies“ in Kairo (14.–20. September 2008) verwiesen.

[27] Darunter sind Lektionare und weitere sa liturgische Hss. Aus dem Weissen Kloster et al.: Karlheinz SCHÜSSLER, Biblia Coptica. Die koptischen Bibeltexte. Das sahidische Alte und Neue Testament. Bde.: 1/1: sa 1–20; 1/2: sa 21–48; 1/3: sa 49–92; 1/4: sa 93–120; 3/1: sa 500–520; 3/2: sa 521–540; 3/3: sa 541–560; 3/4: sa 561–585; 4/1: sa 586–620. Wiesbaden 1995, 1996, 1998, 2000, 2001, 2003, 2004, 2006, 2008: sa 16^{lit}, sa 40^{lit}, sa 54^{lit}, sa 65^{L}, sa 74^{L}, sa 105^{L}, sa 108^{L}, sa 112^{lit}, sa 570^{L}, sa 589^{L}, sa 590^{L}, sa 591^{lit}, sa 609^{L}, sa 613^{lit}, sa 620^{L}; vgl. auch Franz-Jürgen SCHMITZ – Gerd MINK, Liste der Koptischen Handschriften des Neuen Testaments. 1. Die sahidischen Handschriften der Evangelien, Teil 1; Teil 2, 1–2. (Arbeiten zur Neutestamentlichen Textforschung 8, 13, 15), Berlin – New York 1986, 1989, 1991: sa 14^{L}–sa 16^{L}; sa 291^{L}–sa 349^{L}; aus dem Michael-Kloster: New York, PML, M 573 (Leo Depuydt, Catalogue of Coptic Manuscripts in the Pierpont Morgan Library. Album of Photographic Plates (Corpus of Illuminated Manuscripts 4-5, Or. Ser. 1-2), Leuven 1993, Nr. 51; SCHÜSSLER, Biblia Coptica, sa 530^{L}); M 574 (Depuydt, Catalogue, Nr. 59); M 575 (Depuydt, Catalogue, Nr. 58); Ann Arbor, UML, Ms 4942+Freiburg i. Br., UB, Hs. 615+New York, PML, M 615 (Depuydt, Catalogue, Nr. 54); aus dem Merkurios-Kloster von Tbo/Edfu: Signatur: London, BL, Or. 6801 f. 22a–31a.

[28] Katarzyna URBANIAK-WALCZAK, “Hermeneiai”-Fragmente oder den “Hermeneiai” verwandte Texte aus Deir El-Naqlun (Faijum), in: ICCoptS 7 (2000) 647–663, Abb. I–III u.a.

[29] Hippolyte DELEHAYE, Le calendrier d’Oxyrhynque pour l’année 535–6, in: Analecta Bollandiana 42 (1924) 83–99; Herbert J. M. MILNE, Early Psalms and Lections for Lent, in: Journal of Egyptian Archaeology 10 (1924) 278–282; Arietta PAPACONSTANTINOU, La liturgie stationnale à Oxyrhynchos dans la première moitié du 6e siècle. Réédition et commentaire du POxy XI 1357, in: Revue des études byzantines 54 (1996) 135–159.

[30] Vgl. z.B. SCHÜSSLER, Biblia Coptica (s. Anm. 27), sa 523, sa 525, sa 532, sa 538, sa 569, sa 615.

Schenutes[31]; f) der Kalender des Ibn Kabar Abu l-Barakat[32]; g) aus dem bohairischen (= bo) Ritus[33] u.a.: Alexandrinisches Synaxarium[34]; Koptisch-Arabisches Menologium[35]; Jakobitisches Synaxarium (arabisch)[36]; das heutige Lektionar[37].

3.2.2. Aus dem Ritus anderer orthodoxer und orientalischer Kirchen: a) aus dem byzantinischen Ritus u.a.: Konstantinopolitanisches Synaxarium[38] und das Typikon der Großen Kirche von Konstantinopel[39] sowie andere griechische und slawische Hss[40]; b) aus der Jerusalemer Liturgie[41] u.a.: armenisches Lektionar[42] und georgisches Lektionar[43]; c) aus dem Äthiopischen Ritus[44]; d) aus dem westlichen und östlichen Syrischen Ritus[45].

[31] Vgl. EMMEL, Shenoute's Literary Corpus (s. Anm. 16) und dort aufgelistete Bibliographie.

[32] Louis VILLECOURT – Eugène TISSERANT – Gaston WIET, Le livre de la Lampe des Ténèbres et de l'exposition (lumineuse) du servise (de l'Église), par Abu 'l-Barakât connu sous le nom d'Ibn Kabar, in: PO 20 (1929) 575–734; ZANETTI, Lectionnaires (s. Anm. 3), 221–248; ZANETTI, Abû-l-Barakât (s. Anm. 3), 450–462.

[33] ZANETTI, Lectionnaires (s. Anm. 3).

[34] Jacques FORGET, Synaxarium Alexandrinum (CSCO.A 47–49, 67, 78, 90/3–5, 11–13), Louvain 1953–1954.

[35] François NAU, Les ménologes des évangéliaires coptes-arabes (PO 10/2), Paris 1913 (Repr. 1993).

[36] René BASSET, Le synaxaire arabe jacobite (rédaction copte) 1.–5. Texte arabe publié, traduit et annoté. 6. Additions et corrections. – Tables. Tables des matières des tomes XI a XX rédigées par F. Nau. (PO 1/3, 3/3, 11/5, 16/2, 17/3, 20/5), Paris 1904–1929 (Réimpression Turnhout 1993, 2003).

[37] Maurice DE FENOYL, Le Sanctoral Copte (Recherches publiées sous la direction de l'institut de Lettres orientales de Beyrouth 15), Beyrouth 1960.

[38] Hippolyte DELEHAYE, Synaxarium Ecclesiae Constantinopolitanae e codice Sirmondiano nunc Berolinensi adiectis synaxariis selectis. Opera et studio, Bruxellis 1902.

[39] Juan MATEOS, Le Typicon de la Grande Église. Ms. Saint-Croix n° 40, Xe siècle. Introduction, texte critique, traduction et notes. Tome 1. Le Cycle des douze mois. Tome 2. Le Cycle des fêtes mobiles. (OCA 165-166), Roma 1962–1963.

[40] Aleksej DMITRIEVSKIJ, Opisanie liturgitseskich rukopisej, 1–3, Hildesheim 1965; arch. Sergij, Polnyj mesjaceslov Vostoka, 1–2, Vladimir 1901.

[41] Anton BAUMSTARK, Die sonntägliche Evangelienlesung im vorbyzantinischen Jerusalem, in: Byzantinische Zeitschrift 30 (1930) 350–359; Charles RENOUX, La lecture biblique dans la liturgie de Jérusalem, in: Claude MONDÉSERT (Ed.), Le monde grec ancien et la Bible, Paris 1984, 399–420.

[42] Athanase RENOUX, Un manuscrit du lectionnaire arménien de Jérusalem (cod. Jérus. arm. 121), in: Le Muséon 74 (1961) 361–385; Athanase RENOUX, Addenda et corrigenda, in: Le Muséon 75 (1962) 385–398 u.a.

[43] Gerard GARITTE, Le calendrier palestino-géorgien du Sinaiticus 34, in: Subsidia hagiographica 30 (1958) 23–27.

[44] Gérard COLIN, Le synaxaire éthiopien. État actuel de la question, in: Analecta Bollandiana 106 (1988) 280–283; Ugo ZANETTI, Is the ethiopian Holy Week Service translated from sahidic? Towards a study of the Gebra Hemamat, in: Bahru ZEWDE – Richard PANKHURST – Taddesse BEYENE (Eds.), Proceedings of the Eleventh International Conference of Ethiopian Studies. Addis Ababa, April 1–6 1991, Addis Ababa 1994, 765–783 u.a.

[45] Anton BAUMSTARK, Festbrevier und Kirchenjahr der syrischen Jakobiten (Studien zur Geschichte und Kultur des Altertums 3,3/5), Paderborn 1910; Anton BAUMSTARK, Nichtevangelische syrische Perikopenordnungen des ersten Jahrtausends. Im Sinne vergleichender Liturgiegeschichte (LWQF 15), Münster 1921.

3.3. Edition, Kommentar und Untersuchung der Hauptquellen

Die Typika des Weißen Klosters werden wie folgt dargestellt:

- die einzelnen Fragmente werden daraufhin untersucht, welcher Hs sie ursprünglich angehörten;
- sodann werden die wiedergewonnenen Typikon-Hss ein Abkürzungssigel, wie z.B. von MONB.WA bis MONB.WT, von der Datenbank Tito Orlandis[46] *Corpus dei Manoscritti Copti Letterari* (Rom)[47] erhalten;
- es werden Signatur, kodikologischer Zustand und Paläographie beschrieben, sowie eine Bibliographie zu jeder Hs zusammengestellt.
- Jede wiedergewonnene Hs wird transkribiert und ihr Inhalt identifiziert. Die Identifizierung jeder Hs-Zeile wird auf der linken Seite der zukünftigen Monographie gegenüber der jeweiligen Transkription erfolgen. In der Edition wird der genaue Text-Wortlaut der jeweiligen Hs mit ihren orthographischen und diakritischen Besonderheiten wiedergegeben. Allerdings wird die Edition das Gesamtbild der jeweiligen Typikon-Hs aus technischen Gründen nicht exakt widerspiegeln. Das könnte man bei den farbigen Fotos, die die Arbeit begleiten werden, nachvollziehen. Bei der Worttrennung des koptischen Textes orientiert sich das Forschungsvorhaben an den gängigen Schenute-Editionen – von Ariel Shisha-Halevy[48], Stephen Emmel[49], Heike Behlmer[50] u.a. – und folgt dem Prinzip „Zusammengehörige Wortgruppen werden zusammengeschrieben“ [51]. Wegen der vielfach schlecht erhaltenen oder problematischen Stellen einer Hs wird es erforderlich sein, die Edition mit einem umfangreichen Kommentar zu versehen.
- Die genannten Hauptquellen werden einander ergänzen und korrigieren. Bei den problematischen Fällen werden an erster Stelle die edierten sa Quellen aus den anderen südägyptischen Klöstern und bo Publikationen herangezogen. Sollten diese sich als nicht hilfreich erweisen, werden andere ostkirchliche Riten (vgl. hier 3.2.2.) zu Hilfe genommen.
- Die detaillierte Untersuchung wird sich mit der unter den Pkt. 3 a, b, c schon erwähnten Problematik befassen.

[46] Mein Dank gilt an dieser Stelle Professor Orlandi, der mir für meine Arbeit an den Typika Abkürzungssigel in seiner Datenbank zur Verfügung gestellt hat.

[47] Corpus dei Manoscritti Copti Letterari (CMCL), Direttore: Tito Orlandi, http://rmcisadu.|let.uniroma1.it/cmcl/ammini/entrata.html

[48] Vgl. Ariel SHISHA-HALEVY, Unpublished Shenoutiana in the British Library, in: Enchoria 5 (1975) 53–108.

[49] Vgl. Stephen L. EMMEL, Theophilus's Festal Letter of 401 as Quoted by Shenute, in: Cäcilia FLUCK u.a. (Hgg.), DIVITIAE AEGYPTI. Koptologische und verwandte Studien zu Ehren von Martin Krause, Wiesbaden 1995, 93–98 u.a.

[50] Vgl. Heike BEHLMER, Schenute von Atripe. De iudicio (Torino, Museo Egizio, Cat. 63000, Cod. IV) (Catalogo del Museo Egizio di Torino. Serie 1, Vol. 8), Torino 1996 u.a.

[51] Vgl. BEHLMER, Schenute von Atripe (s. Anm. 50), CVII.

3.4. Register und Bibliographie

Ein angefügtes Register wird das Auffinden der Heiligen, Feste, Perikopen, Bibelstellen, Hss, Signaturen, Orte etc. erleichtern. Eine Bibliographie wird die Publikation abschließen.

4. SCHLUSS

Einerseits wird sich die vorliegende Erforschung der liturgischen Ordnungen und Gewohnheiten des Weißen Klosters als erhellend und hilfreich erweisen, sowohl für andere ägyptische Klosterliturgien – z.B. die des Michael-Klosters oder des Merkurios-Klosters von Tbo/Edfu – als auch für den Gottesdienst der Kathedraltradition in Alexandrien und Ägypten. Andererseits ist das Projekt implizit fächerübergreifend, da es nicht allein die Koptologie betrifft, sondern auch den konkreten liturgischen Vollzug und dessen Theologie (Liturgiewissenschaft), wie auch die Geschichte des koptischen Christentums im Gesamtkontext der orientalischen Kirchen.

BEILAGE

Perikopendirektorien	Bl.		Hymnendirektorien	Bl.
Ann Arbor, UML, Ms. 110	1		Ann Arbor, UML, Ms. 158 (12)	1
Berlin, SBB, Ms. or. oct. 409 f. 42	1		Ann Arbor, UML, Ms. 4559a	3
Kairo, IFAO, Copte 225A	1		Ann Arbor, UML, Ms. 6037	6
Kairo, IFAO, Copte 279 A-B	2		Berlin, SBB, Ms. or. oct. 409 f. 39-41	3
Kairo, IFAO, Copte 291-294	4		Berlin, SBB, Ms. or. oct. 409 f. 43	1
Leiden, RMO, Ms. Copte 77 (Ins. 34)	5		Berlin, SBB, Ms. or. oct. fol. 1609 Bl. 3-6	4
Leiden, RMO, Ms. Copte 81 (Ins. 38a)	2		Kairo, IFAO, Copte 161	1
Leiden, RMO, Ms. Copte 82A (Ins. 38b)	1		Kairo, IFAO, Copte 162	1
Leiden, RMO, Ms. Copte 83 (Ins. 38f)	1		Kairo, IFAO, Copte 224	1
London, BL, Or. 3580 A.1	1		Kairo, IFAO, Copte 225B	1
London, BL, Or. 3580 A.2	1		Leiden, RMO, Ms. Copte 75 (Ins. 32)	3
London, BL, Or. 3580 A.4-5 (= A.3 β, γ)	2		Leiden, RMO, Ms. Copte 76 (Ins. 33)	1
London, BL, Or. 6954 (25)-(29)	5		Leiden, RMO, Ms. Copte 78 (Ins. 35)	1
Paris, BnF, Copte 129(6) f. 43	1		Leiden, RMO, Ms. Copte 79 (Ins. 36)	1
Paris, BnF, Copte 129(20) f. 161	1		Leiden, RMO, Ms. Copte 80 (Ins. 37)	1
Paris, BnF, Copte 129(20) f. 162	1		Leiden, RMO, Ms. Copte 82B, C, D (Ins. 38c-e)	3
Paris, BnF, Copte 129(20) f. 164	1		Leiden, RMO, Ms. Copte 84 (Ins. 39)	4
Paris, BnF, Copte 129(20) f. 165	1		Leiden, RMO, Ms. Copte 85 (Ins. 40)	4
Paris, BnF, Copte 129(20) f. 166	1		Leiden, RMO, Ms. Copte 86 (Ins. 41)	1
Paris, BnF, Copte 129(20) f. 168	1		Leiden, RMO, Ms. Copte 87 (Ins. 42)	2
Paris, BnF, Copte 129(20) f. 169	1		Leiden, RMO, Ms. Copte 92 (Ins. 47)	1
Paris, BnF, Copte 129(20) f. 174	1		Leiden, RMO, Ms. Copte 93 (Ins. 48)	1
Paris, BnF, Copte 132(2) f. 30	1		London, BL, Or. 3580 A.3 (= A.3 α)	1
Paris, BnF, Copte 161(44)	1		London, BL, Or. 3580 A.6 (= A.4)	1
Paris, Louvre, n° 9972 (R 164)	1		London, BL, Or. 3580 A.7 (= A.5)	1
Rom, BAV,Borgia copto 109, cass. XXIV, fasc. 108, f. 2	1		London, BL, Or. 3580 A.8 (= A.6)	1
St. Petersburg, Eremitage, 55	1		London, BL, Or. 3580 A.19 (= A.14)	1
Venezia, Biblioteca Naniana copt. frg., Mingarelli-Fragm. XIX	1		London, BL, Or. 3580 A.20 (= A.15)	1
Wien, ÖNB, P.Vindob. K 211	1		London, BL, Or. 3580 A.22 (= A.17)	1
Wien, ÖNB, P.Vindob. K 9718	1		London, BL, Or. 3580 A.23-25 (= A.18)	3
Wien, ÖNB, P.Vindob. K 9728	1		Manchester, JRL, n° 53 [20a]	3
Wien, ÖNB, P.Vindob. K 9729	1		Oxford, BL, Clarendon Press b.3, Frg. 18	1
Wien, ÖNB, P.Vindob. K 9731	1		Oxford, BL, Clarendon Press b.3, Frg. 19	5

Wien, ÖNB, P.Vindob. K 9732	1		Paris, BnF, Copte 129(20) f. 159	1
Wien, ÖNB, P.Vindob. K 9733	1		Paris, BnF, Copte 129(20) f. 160	1
Wien, ÖNB, P.Vindob. K 9738	1		Paris, BnF, Copte 129(20) f. 163	1
Wien, ÖNB, P.Vindob. K 9741	1		Paris, BnF, Copte 129(20) f. 167	1
			Paris, BnF, Copte 129(20) f. 170+173	1
			Paris, BnF, Copte 129(20) f. 171	1
			Paris, BnF, Copte 129(20) f. 172	1
			Paris, BnF, Copte 129(20) f. 177	1
			Paris, BnF, Copte 133(2) f. 24b	1
			Paris, BnF, Copte 161(10) f. 153	1
			Rom, BAV, Borgia copto 109, cass. XXIV, fasc. 103, f. 4	1
			Wien, ÖNB, P.Vindob. G 39789 (= K 9740)	1
			Wien, ÖNB, P.Vindob. K 9725	1
			Wien, ÖNB, P.Vindob. K 9726	2
			Wien, ÖNB, P.Vindob. K 9734	1
			Wien, ÖNB, P.Vindob. K 9735	1
			Wien, ÖNB, P.Vindob. K 9736	1
			Wien, ÖNB, P.Vindob. K 9737	1
			Wien, ÖNB, P.Vindob. K 9739	1
Gesamt	51		Gesamt	84

ABKÜRZUNGEN

Für die internationalen Koptologenkongresse der IACS wird die übliche Abkürzung ICCoptS und die Zahl des Kongresses verwendet.

ICCoptS 4 Actes du IVe congrès copte: Louvain-la-Neuve, 5–10 septembre 1988, ed. par Marguerite RASSART-DEBERGH. 1: Art et archéologie, 2: De la linguistique au gnosticisme (Publications de l'Institut Orientaliste de Louvain 40–41), Louvain-la-Neuve 1992.

ICCoptS 5 Acts of the Fifth International Congress of Coptic Studies, Washington, 12–15 August 1992, eds. by Tito ORLANDI and David W. JOHNSON, 2 vols, Rome 1993.

ICCoptS 6 Ägypten und Nubien in spätantiker und christlicher Zeit: Akten des 6. Internationalen Koptologenkongresses, Münster, 20.–26. Juli 1996, hrsg. von Stephen EMMEL (Sprachen und Kulturen des christlichen Orients 6,1–2), Wiesbaden 1999.

ICCoptS 7 Coptic studies on the threshold of a new millennium. I-II. Proceedings of the Seventh International Congress of Coptic Studies Leiden, 27 August–2 September 2000 edited on behalf of the International Association for Coptic Studies (IACS), ed. by Mat IMMERZEEL and Jacques VAN DER VLIET with the assistance of Maarten KERSTEN und Carolien VAN ZOEST (OLA 133), Leuven – Paris – Dudley/MA 2004.

ICCoptS 8 Huitième congrès international d'études coptes (Paris 2004). Vol. 1: Bilans et perspectives 2000–2004, éd. par Anne BOUD'HORS et Denyse VAILLANCOURT (CBCo 15) Paris 2006; Vol. 2: Actes du huitième congrès international d'études coptes. Paris, 28 juin–3 juillet 2004, éd. par Nathalie BOSSON et Anne BOUD'HORS, 2 vols. (OLA 163), Leuven – Paris – Dudley/MA 2007.

JEWISH INFLUENCE ON EARLY CHRISTIAN LITURGY
A REAPPRAISAL

PAUL F. BRADSHAW

Although right from the beginning of the scientific study of early Christian worship there were some who examined its Jewish background to look for possible antecedents, yet this line of enquiry was relatively slow in becoming widely established. For a very long time many scholars did not look in that direction at all, seemingly out of a dogmatic conviction that the Christian faith would necessarily have involved a radical transformation or even rejection of the former religion.[1] Gerhard Delling, for example, writing in 1952 asserted that 'the Worship which belongs to the kingdom which has come in Jesus is fundamentally and completely detached from that of Israel',[2] and Ferdinand Hahn, writing around 1970, believed that the early Christians were originally free from Jewish ritual practices, but then gradually returned to such customs as fasting and Sabbath observance.[3] More recently, however, it has become almost axiomatic for liturgical historians to look for a possible link between Jewish and Christian forms – so much so that there appears to be a tendency sometimes to overstate the case, to claim to find such links where in reality there do not seem to have been any, or at least none as close as is alleged. This lecture, therefore, is an attempt to re-examine some of the claims that have been made in the hope of arriving at a more realistic evaluation and avoiding many of the false conclusions that have been reached.

Part of the problem stems from a propensity among some Christian scholars to continue to utilize outdated Jewish scholarship in order to demonstrate a connection between practices. Thus, it has been natural for Christians to suppose that the weekly Sabbath service might have left marks on the early Christian Sunday liturgy. Indeed, so hard did Louis Bouyer try to establish a link between the two that he came up with an ingenious theory to explain the difference in the two orders of the service – the Christian having readings first and then prayers, and the Jewish having the prayers before the readings. He claimed that it was the Jews who had subsequently reversed the order in their service in order to differentiate themselves from the Christians.[4] As we shall see later, while there

1 See, for example, the critical comments on such scholars made by Louis BOUYER, Eucharist, Notre Dame 1968, 15–19.

2 Gerhard DELLING, Der Gottesdienst im Neuen Testament, Göttingen 1952; English translation, Worship in the New Testament, London/Philadephia 1962, 6.

3 Ferdinand HAHN, Der urchristliche Gottesdienst, Stuttgart 1970; English translation, The Worship of the Early Church, Philadelphia 1973, 32–39, 50–52.

4 BOUYER, Eucharist, 60.

is no evidence whatsoever for this particular action having taken place, he was not so wide of the mark in imagining that some liturgical changes might have been made by Jews rather than always by Christians in order to establish their own identity.

Although many of the Jewish texts with which parallels were sought were known only from sources dating from much later times than the first century, in the past this was not viewed as a problem: older generations of Jewish scholars believed that the Jewish liturgical tradition had exhibited remarkable stability through the ages, and thus a reference to some custom in the Talmud could safely be taken as evidence for its existence many centuries earlier, especially if what was said about it were attributed to some figure from antiquity. This, however, is no longer the case in mainstream Jewish scholarship. It is now recognized that, like Christian liturgy, Jewish practices underwent significant changes and development in the course of their history, and especially after the destruction of the Temple, which brought about such a fundamental transformation to Judaism. The majority now believe that a Sabbath synagogue liturgy as such was entirely a product of the post-Temple period,[5] when many practices formerly carried out exclusively in the Temple were transferred to the synagogue and other elements were newly created there as substitutes for Temple rituals that could no longer be performed.[6]

This is not to say that there would not have been any synagogue gatherings on the Sabbath prior to this time, but that these assemblies were not liturgies in the sense in which that word is usually understood. They were instead primarily for the purpose of studying the Law (and if Luke 4:16-20 and Acts 13:15 are reliable testimony for Jewish practices of the period, for the reading of the Prophets too). Far from being a liturgical service of a fixed and limited duration, Philo reports that in Alexandria this time of study did not end until the late afternoon (*Apol.* 7.12-13), although things were no doubt quite different in places that were not major centres of intellectual life. Consequently, it seems highly improbable that there would have been any fixed lectionaries in use at these gatherings in the first century, except possibly in relation to the greater feasts of the

5 See for example the studies by Lee LEVINE, The Ancient Synagogue, New Haven – London 2000, 134–159; Heather A. MCKAY, Sabbath and Synagogue. The Question of Sabbath Worship in Ancient Judaism, Leiden 1994; and the briefer survey by Daniel FALK, Jewish Prayer Literature and the Jerusalem Church in Acts, in: Richard BAUCKHAM (Ed.), The Book of Acts in its Palestinian Setting, Carlisle – Grand Rapids 1995, 267–301, here at 277–285. McKay has been rightly criticized by Pieter W.VAN DER HORST, Was the synagogue a place of Sabbath worship before 70 C.E.?, in: Steve FINE (Ed.), Jews, Christians and Polytheists in the Ancient Synagogue, London – New York 1999, 18–43, for defining 'worship' too narrowly and ignoring the probability that study included some prayer.

6 See further Richard S. SARASON, Religion and Worship. The Case of Judaism, in: Jacob NEUSNER (Ed.), Take Judaism, For Example: Studies toward the Comparison of Religions, Chicago 1983, 49–65; Ruth LANGER, To Worship God Properly. Tensions between Liturgical Custom and Halakhah in Judaism, Cincinnati 1998.

year, still less a uniform lectionary observed throughout a whole region. Thus, the many attempts made by a whole range of Christian scholars to find points of contact between such putative Jewish lections and the books of the New Testament, or even later Christian lectionaries, must largely fall to the ground, as also must the claim often made that Jesus would have sung the psalms in the synagogue service week by week and that is why Christians should continue to do the same.[7] All that can now be said is that Jews studied their scriptures each week, and so did Christians in one way or another.

Even the annual Jewish festivals that we know were being celebrated during Jesus' lifetime almost certainly did not have the form that is described in later rabbinic literature. In particular, there is almost complete consensus among Jewish scholars today that the later Passover *seder* did not exist during the Second Temple period, and although some have attempted to reconstruct the ritual pattern of the feast prior to the destruction of the Temple, those efforts have also been questioned.[8] Thus, cautious scholars would now hesitate to draw any direct parallels between the Last Supper and the rabbinic *seder*.

Equally doomed are the frequent attempts that have been made to find close verbal similarities between later Jewish prayer texts and those of the early Christians. For instance, generations of scholars have searched for parallels between Christian texts and what became the standard form of Jewish daily prayer, the *'Amidah* or *Shemoneh 'Esreh*, 'The Eighteen Benedictions'. Similarly, what appear to be the earliest extant Christian meal prayers in the church order known as the *Didache* have also been a particular focus of attention in efforts to find parallels. Bouyer, for example, made the astonishing claim that here no more than a few words and phrases had been changed from the alleged Jewish original, the *Birkat ha-mazon* or grace after meals.[9] This assertion is patently untrue, but other scholars have come up with alternative theories in order to try to demonstrate some connection between the two prayers. The conclusion reached by the Jewish scholar Louis Finkelstein nearly eighty years ago, that the first and second of the three units of the Jewish prayer had been inverted in the Christian version,[10] has been repeated by many Christian scholars in the years in between, although Louis Ligier preferred to speak of the first unit being integrated into the second and absorbed by it,[11] and Enrico Mazza argued that the

[7] See the critical observations of James MCKINNON, On the Question of Psalmody in the Ancient Synagogue, in: Early Music History 6 (1986) 159–191, here at 170–180 = IDEM, The Temple, the Church Fathers and Early Western Chant, Aldershot 1998, VIII.

[8] See Joshua KULP, The Origins of the Seder and the Haggadah, in: Currents in Biblical Research 4 (2005–2006) 109–134, especially 114–116.

[9] BOUYER, Eucharist, 115.

[10] Louis FINKELSTEIN, The Birkat Ha–Mazon, in: Jewish Quarterly Review 19 (1928/9) 211–262.

[11] Louis LIGIER, The Origins of the Eucharistic Prayer. From the Last Supper to the Eucharist, in: StLi 9 (1973) 161–185, here at 177.

Didache had instead eliminated the first unit altogether and substituted a quite different beginning.[12]

The earliest text of the *Birkat ha-mazon* known to us, however, dates only from the ninth century of the Common Era, and so we have no way of knowing what form it might have taken many centuries earlier. It is true that in the *Book of Jubilees*, usually thought to have been written in the middle of the second century BCE, there is a form of grace put into the mouth of Abraham that displays a somewhat similar tripartite structure to the *Birkat ha-mazon*: a blessing of God for creation and the gift of food; a thanksgiving for the long life granted to Abraham; and a supplication for God's mercy and peace.[13] The Mishnah too speaks of a grace after meals composed of three blessings (*Ber*. 6.8), but does not indicate their contents, presumably because they were expected already to be familiar to its readers. Nevertheless, we should beware of drawing too straight a line from these sources to the text first known hundreds of years later. What they do show is the existence of a tripartite prayer after meals with a defined pattern. But they do not suggest that the detailed contents were already fixed or that it was the only form in use at the time. Similarly, most extant early forms of Christian intercession are quite different in style from the later texts used in the *'Amidah*, the Jewish daily prayer. Hence those desperate to find parallels between the two have generally been reduced to pointing out similarities merely in their general themes, and not in their particular linguistic style or vocabulary nor even in their order, resemblances that are simply too vague to support a theory of direct dependency.[14]

In any case, once again most recent Jewish scholars have grave doubts that any Jewish prayers existed in a standardized form in the first century. Thus Joseph Heinemann, one of the pioneers of the revolution in Jewish scholarship in this area in the 1960s, wrote:

> The Jewish prayers were originally the creations of the common people. The characteristic idioms and forms of prayer, and indeed the statutory prayers of the synagogue themselves, were not in the first place products of the deliberation of the Rabbis in their academies, but were rather the spontaneous, on-the-spot improvisations of the people who gathered on various occasions to pray in the synagogue. Since the occasions and places of worship were numerous, it was only natural that they should give rise to an abundance of prayers, displaying a wide variety of forms, styles, and patterns. Thus, the first stage in the development of the liturgy was characterized by diversity and variety, and the task of the Rabbis was to systematize and to impose order on this multiplicity of forms, patterns, and structures. This task they undertook after the fact; only after the numerous prayers had come into being and were familiar to the masses did the Sages decide that the time had come to estab-

12 Enrico MAZZA, The Origins of the Eucharistic Prayer, Collegeville 1995, 18–20. See also Huub VAN DE SANDT – David FLUSSER, The Didache. Its Jewish sources and its place in early Judaism and Christianity, Assen – Minneapolis 2002, 310–329.

13 Jubilees 22.6–9; for an English translation, see James H. CHARLESWORTH (Ed.), Old Testament Pseudepigrapha 2, Garden City/NY 1985 / London 1986, 97.

14 For examples, see BOUYER, Eucharist, 197–199, 213–214, 233–234, 303; Stéphane VERHELST, La 'kéryxie catholique' de la liturgie de Jérusalem et le Shemoneh 'Esreh, in: Questions Liturgiques 81 (2000) 5–47.

> lish some measure of uniformity and standardization. Only then did they proceed carefully to inspect the existing forms and patterns, to disqualify some while accepting others, to decide which prayers were to be statutory on which occasions, and by which prayers a man 'fulfilled his obligation.[15]

Heinemann argued that the process of standardization took place only gradually. By the second century CE 'only the number of the benedictions, their order of recitation, and their general content had been fixed, as well as the occasions of their recitation and the rules which governed them, but not their exact wording'.[16] While some of his conclusions have been challenged by more recent Jewish scholars – for instance, that a direct evolutionary line could be traced from what he called 'the creations of the common people' to the later rabbinic prayer texts[17] – yet much of what he wrote has become generally accepted, and especially the view that there was never a single original standard text of Jewish prayers, but rather a wide range of variants in existence among different Jewish groups. Some of these earlier variants can in fact be detected in the later prescriptions. Thus, for example, the same passage of the Mishnah that prescribes a grace composed of three blessings also allows a single blessing composed of the substance of the three to be said instead. Similarly, while the prayer composed of eighteen blessings came to be required to be said three times every weekday, a variant form composed of only seven blessings was to be used on Sabbaths and festivals. In both these cases and others, it seems probable that there had been a rival tradition that was simply too well established in some circles for it to be entirely suppressed by the one favoured by the legislators and so a compromise was reached of retaining both in some way.

Indeed, even the conservative Jewish scholar Ezra Fleischer lent his support to the view that the three times of daily prayer only became obligatory for all Jews after the destruction of the Temple. Where he seemed to be mistaken, however, was in supposing that once the Rabbis came to prescribe the practice, the people would immediately have adopted it, and that not only the specific times for praying but also the content of the prayers would have sprung fully formed *ex nihilo* at the time.[18] As Ruth Langer remarked in a critique of his work, he assumed that 'Rabban Gamliel could decree that everyone must pray a new complex set of prayers three times a day, and people simply rearranged their lives to

[15] Joseph HEINEMANN, Prayer in the Period of the Tanna'im and the Amora'im. Its Nature and its Patterns (in Hebrew), Jerusalem 1964; ^{2}1966; English translation, Prayer in the Talmud. Forms and Patterns, Berlin 1977, 37.

[16] Ibid. 26.

[17] See Richard S. SARASON, On the Use of Method in the Modern Study of Jewish Liturgy, in: William Scott GREEN (Ed.), Approaches to Ancient Judaism. Theory and Practice, Missoula 1978, 97–172, here at 146 = Jacob NEUSNER (Ed.), The Study of Ancient Judaism 1, New York 1981, 107–179, here at 161.

[18] Ezra FLEISCHER, On the Beginnings of Obligatory Jewish Prayer, in: Tarbiz 59 (1990) 397–441 (in Hebrew; English summary, iii–v); IDEM, The Shemone Esre – Its Character, Internal Order, Contents and Goals, in: Tarbiz 62 (1993) 179–223 (in Hebrew; English summary, vi–vii).

accommodate this'.[19] And he ignored the strong probability that the specific times chosen for prayer and at least the outlines of what was then to be prayed would have had existing antecedents among some groups of pious Jews prior to this time, rather than the much less likely possibility that they were invented on the spot as a complete innovation.[20]

This raises another aspect of the question – the tendency of many Christian scholars, like many earlier Jewish scholars, to restrict their investigation of Jewish antecedents exclusively to rabbinic Jewish traditions found in the Mishnah, Talmud, and other writings. While it was these traditions that subsequently formed later Jewish orthodoxy and consequently created the impression that they had also formed the dominant mainstream of Jewish practice earlier in the first century, we should beware of taking that impression at face value. Indeed, a recent, though controversial, school of Jewish scholarship has argued that the rabbinic movement remained peripheral in Jewish society until at least the third or fourth centuries of the Common Era, and that even then it gained influence very gradually and only became socially and religiously dominant in the sixth century or even later.[21] We can form a similar misleading impression of primitive Christianity if we assume that the Gentile, and especially Pauline, version of the faith which fills so much of the New Testament and eventually formed the mainstream of later orthodoxy was already in this position in the first generation or two of the movement. This would make us relegate Jewish Christianity to the sidelines in looking at the earliest roots, whereas in reality it appears to have been Paul and his Gentile movement that constituted the breakaway from what had been the heart of the nascent religious tradition. We have no reason to suppose that the first Christian converts were drawn from the Pharisaic party, and every reason to expect the opposite to have been the case from the controversies documented in the New Testament, and hence we need to look at what we know about other forms of Jewish belief and practice in the first century for possible influences on the earliest traditions of Christian worship.

One simple example will illustrate this point. We know that a custom emerged in early Christianity of facing in the direction of the east in order to pray, whether a believer was alone or in a group. Earlier generations of scholars assumed that the Christians chose to do this in order to differentiate themselves from Jews, who would have faced towards Jerusalem. In other words, they saw

[19] Ruth LANGER, Revisiting Early Rabbinic Liturgy. The Recent Contributions of Ezra Fleischer, in: Prooftexts 19 (1999) 179–194, here at 190; see also their subsequent correspondence, Controversy, in: Prooftexts 20 (2000) 380–387.

[20] See the comments by Stefan REIF, On the Earliest Development of Jewish Prayer, in: Tarbiz 60 (1991) 677–681 (in Hebrew; English summary, viii), and Fleischer's response, Rejoinder to Dr. Reif's Remarks, ibid. 683–688 (in Hebrew; English summary, viii–ix). For evidence of the existence of regular daily prayer within the Qumran community, see the works cited in n. 26 below.

[21] See for example Seth SCHWARTZ, Imperialism and Jewish Society 200 B.C.E. to 640 C.E., Princeton 2001.

it as the result of Jewish influence, but an influence that led the early Christians to do the opposite of the prevailing tradition, and this naturally appealed to those who wanted to see Christianity as a rejection of Judaism. More recent scholarship, however, suggests that the Christian practice may in truth be the continuation of an earlier custom of facing east to pray that was observed by some groups of Jews, and especially the Essenes.[22]

Something similar may also be the case with regard to the Christian choice of Wednesday and Friday as regular days of fasting. The *Didache*, which mentions these days, has often been understood to mean that they too were a Christian innovation intended to distinguish Jewish Christians from other Jews who fasted on Mondays and Thursdays. But other scholars have raised the question, why were these particular days selected? Moving a Monday fast to Tuesday and a Thursday fast to Friday might make some sense, but why *Wednesday* and Friday? As the French biblical scholar Annie Jaubert pointed out, religious movements do not usually make simply random choices in such matters.[23] This has led to the hypothesis that it may have been the prominence of these days in the solar calendar used by the Essenes (and perhaps other Jews) that accounts for their adoption by Christians.[24]

Thus, far from being innovations to mark out their identity from that of other Jews, a number of Christian customs may well be the perpetuation of older traditions practised in certain Jewish sects that did not survive in Judaism after its transformation following the destruction of the Temple. It is thus important that, when looking for antecedents and parallels, what we know about all the practices of all the varieties of Jewish groups that were in existence in the first century should be taken into account. Although such material may not be in as great an abundance as we might wish, quite a number of texts do exist,[25] not least those from Qumran that are eventually being published and analysed for the light they can shed on early Jewish liturgy in general as well as upon the practices of that particular sect. The recent literature in this field will well repay careful attention, especially with regard to possible antecedents of patterns of Christian daily prayer.[26] We can also discern references to variant worship practices in other

[22] See Paul F. BRADSHAW, Daily Prayer in the Early Church, London 1981/New York 1982, 10–11, 58–59.

[23] Annie JAUBERT, Jésus et le calendrier de Qumrân, in: New Testament Studies 7 (1960) 1–30, here at 27: 'Ces vues superficielles ne tiennent aucum compte de la profondeur d'enracinement des usages liturgiques'.

[24] See Annie JAUBERT, The Date of the Last Supper, Staten Island, New York 1965; Thomas J. TALLEY, The Eucharistic Prayer of the Ancient Church According to Recent Research. Results and Reflections, in: StLi 11 (1976) 138–158, here at 149.

[25] See James H. CHARLESWORTH, Jewish Hymns, Odes, and Prayers (ca. 167 B.C.E – 135 C.E.), in: Robert A. KRAFT – George W. E. NICKELSBURG (Eds.), Early Judaism and its Modern Interpreters, Atlanta – Philadelphia 1986, 411–436; David FLUSSER, Psalms, Hymns and Prayers, in: Michael E. STONE (Ed.), Jewish Writings of the Second Temple Period, Assen – Philadelphia 1984, 551–577.

[26] See James R. DAVILA, Liturgical Works, Grand Rapids, Michigan 2000; Daniel FALK, Daily, Sabbath, and Festival Prayers in the Dead Sea Scrolls, Leiden 1998; IDEM, The

sources, including rabbinic literature itself, which occasionally mentions disparagingly the ritual activities of the common people.

At this point in our survey, however, we need to ask the fundamentally important question as to whether Jewish influence on Christian liturgy was restricted to the first century or whether it continued in later times. It is obvious that the primary influence must have been exerted at the historical roots of the Christian movement while it was still very much part of the broader Jewish culture. But were there also influences that were felt after that period? Here there is a division within both Jewish and Christian scholarship. The traditional position has been to see a sharp separation between church and synagogue as having taken place at a quite early date, as a result of which all communication between the two then ceased and so influence came to an end. The point at which the ways parted has been variously fixed, between a date in the middle of the first century all the way up to 135 CE, but not usually beyond.[27] However, this has been challenged in recent years by some scholars, who have argued instead for a slower process of separation and a continuing, if diminishing, influence of the two on each other for at least several centuries longer.[28] It is well known that at least in Antioch and probably elsewhere some Christians attended both synagogue and church in the late fourth century, as they were severely criticized by John Chrysostom in his sermons for doing so,[29] but it is perhaps less well-known that canons from several fourth-century councils prohibit clergy and laity from keeping fasts or festivals with Jews or accepting gifts of food sent from their festivals – regulations that would hardly have been necessary had there not been a real risk of them doing so.[30] And recently Daniel Stökl Ben

Contribution of the Qumran Scrolls to the Study of Ancient Jewish Liturgy, in: Timothy H. LIM – John J. COLLINS (Eds.), The Oxford Handbook of the Dead Sea Scrolls, Oxford 2010, 616–651; Bilhah NITZAN, Qumran Prayer and Religious Poetry, Leiden 1994; EADEM, The Dead Sea Scrolls and the Jewish Liturgy, in: James R. DAVILA (Ed.), The Dead Sea Scrolls as Background to Postbiblical Judaism and Early Christianity, Leiden 2003, 195–219; Stefan C. REIF, The Second Temple Period, Qumran Research, and Rabbinic Liturgy. Some Contextual and Linguistic Comparisons, in: Esther G. CHAZON (Ed.), Liturgical Perspectives. Prayer and Poetry in Light of the Dead Sea Scrolls, Leiden 2003, 133–149; and especially the cautions expressed by Richard S. SARASON, Communal Prayer at Qumran and Among the Rabbis. Certainties and Uncertainties, in: ibid. 151–172.

27 See for example, James D. G. DUNN (Ed.), Jews and Christians. The Parting of the Ways, A.D. 70 to 135, Tübingen 1992.

28 See for example Adam H. BECKER – Annette Yoshiko REED (Eds.), The Ways that Never Parted. Jews and Christians in Late Antiquity and the Early Middle Ages, Tübingen 2003.

29 English translation in JOHN CHRYSOSTOM, Discourses against Judaizing Christians, translated by Paul W. HARKINS (The Fathers of the Church 68), Washington/DC 1979. See also Marcel SIMON, Verus Israel. A Study of the Relations between Christians and Jews in the Roman Empire (135–425), Oxford 1985.

30 Council of Elvira (c. 306), canons 49 and 50; Council of Laodicea (c. 363), canons 29, 37, and 38; canon 70 of The Ecclesiastical Canons of the Holy Apostles in Apostolic Constitutions 8.47.

Ezra has argued for the continuation of a tradition of some Christians keeping Jewish autumn festivals, and specifically Yom Kippur, for several centuries.[31] Moreover, the notion of some continuing cross-fertilization helps explain the emergence in the fourth century of two Christian liturgical texts with a strongly Jewish appearance that do not seem to have been part of the tradition from its earliest inception. The first of these is a collection of prayers in Book 7 of the late-fourth-century church order known as *Apostolic Constitutions* that really do have some striking resemblances to the Jewish *'Amidah*, especially in its shorter Sabbath form. This particular liturgical material is quite exceptional in character among Christian texts both earlier and later, and so it seems likely that it was introduced at a fairly late date, perhaps the third century, from a deviant Jewish group.[32] While this text appears not to have had any wide influence on Christian liturgy but merely within a limited group, it was otherwise with the emergence of the Sanctus in some fourth-century eucharistic prayers. As the question of how the Sanctus came to find a place in Christian usage has been extensively examined by others, I do not intend to pursue that subject in any further detail here, except to say that it is more likely to have been a late borrowing from Judaism than something that had enjoyed a continuous existence in Christian worship from early times while simultaneously remaining completely invisible in the extant sources.[33]

Obviously influences such as these would have directly affected only certain Christian groups and not all, even if in the case of the Sanctus the practice was later copied more widely. In most places church authorities were anxious to distance themselves and their practices from those of Jews. Such phenomena as

[31] See Daniel STÖKL BEN EZRA, "Christians" observing "Jewish" festivals of Autumn, in: Peter J. THOMSON – Doris LAMBERS-PETRY (Eds.), The Image of the Judaeo-Christians in Ancient Jewish and Christian Literature, Tübingen 2003, 53–73; IDEM, Whose Fast Is It? The Ember Day of September and Yom Kippur, in: The Ways that Never Parted, 259–281.

[32] See David A. FIENSY, Prayers Alleged to be Jewish. An Examination of the Constitutiones Apostolorum (Brown Judaic Studies 65), Chico 1985; Pieter W. VAN DER HORST, The Greek Synagogue Prayers in the Apostolic Constitutions, Book 7, in: Joseph TABORY (Ed.), From Qumran to Cairo: Studies in the History of Prayer, Jerusalem 1999, 32–36; Esther G. CHAZON, A 'Prayer Alleged to be Jewish' in the Apostolic Constitutions, in: Esther G. CHAZON et al. (Eds), Things Revealed: Studies in Early Jewish and Christian Literature in Honor of Michael E. Stone, Leiden 2004, 261–277.

[33] See Bryan SPINKS, The Sanctus in the Eucharistic Prayer, Cambridge 1991, 1–121; Robert F. TAFT, The Interpolation of the Sanctus into the Anaphora. When and Where? A Review of the Dossier, in: OCP 57 (1991) 281–308; 58 (1992) 83–121; Gabriele WINKLER, Nochmals zu den Anfängen der Epiklese und des Sanctus im Eucharistischen Hochgebet, in: Theologische Quartalschrift 74 (1994) 214–231, especially 216–219; EADEM, Weitere Beobachtungen zur frühen Epiklese (den Doxologien und dem Sanctus). Über die Bedeutung der Apokryphen für die Erforschung der Entwicklung der Riten, in: OrChr 80 (1996) 177–200; EADEM, Das Sanctus. Über den Ursprung und die Anfänge des Sanctus und sein Fortwirken, Rome 2002; Maxwell E. JOHNSON, The Origins of the Anaphoral Sanctus and Epiclesis Revisited. The Contribution of Gabriele Winkler, in: Hans–Jürgen FEULNER et al. (Eds.), Crossroad of Culture. Studies in Liturgy and Patristics in Honor of Gabriele Winkler (OCA 260), Rome 2000, 405–42.

the efforts to abolish the Quartodeciman observance of Easter and the need felt by some Christians to compile their own tables to predict the date of Easter each year, rather than face the embarrassment of having to go down the road to the neighbouring synagogue to ask when Passover would fall, that are found even in the third century are signs of the struggle that was going on in the new religious movement to establish its own independent identity and abolish as far as possible the more obvious signs of any connection to Jewish customs.[34]

However, a similar diversity in the degree of Jewish influence on different Christian communities should also be recognised for the first century too. In the past we liturgical historians have tended to expect to find roughly the same effect, or lack of effect, of Judaism everywhere in primitive Christianity, and credit should be given in particular to Gerard Rouwhorst for attempting to persuade us to look differently at Christian liturgical traditions on the basis of their particular point of origin, and thus correct our misapprehensions. Those searching for Jewish antecedents to Christian liturgical practices need to recognize that there will probably be significant differences between churches that emerged out of a predominantly Gentile background and those that have stronger roots in Jewish Christianity. Indeed, Rouwhorst has rightly argued that even making a distinction between churches with Jewish roots and those with Gentile origin is too simplistic a categorization: there are likely to have been intermediate forms, as for example, churches that were Gentile in origin but having hardly any affinity to Pauline theology and for one reason or another still being open to Jewish influences.[35]

Rouwhorst has shown how such an approach helps to explain a number of divergent phenomena in early Christian liturgical practice. It explains why there is so much polemic in early Christian writings over some Christians following Jewish observances, and in particular the keeping of the Sabbath. While their opponents may have characterized this as 'Judaizing' – falling back into unreformed ways – for those groups it was nothing of the kind but simply the continuation of their traditional practices. It also explains the honour accorded to Saturdays in some churches in fourth-century sources, so that it was not a day on which the Christians fasted but was a day on which they regularly celebrated the eucharist, alongside the opposite treatment in other churches. It explains why in some churches the eucharistic ministry of the word regularly included an

[34] See Timothy C. G. THORNTON, Problematical Passovers. Difficulties for Diaspora Jews and Early Christians in Determining Passover Dates during the First Three Centuries A.D., in: Studia Patristica 20 (1989) 402–408; Anscar CHUPUNGCO, Shaping the Easter Feast, Washington/DC 1992, 43–50, 61–73.

[35] See Gerard ROUWHORST, Liturgical Time and Space in early Christianity in Light of their Jewish Background, in: Alberdina HOUTMAN – Marcel POORTHUIS – Joshua SCHWARTZ (Eds.), Sanctity of Time and Space in Tradition and Modernity, Leiden 1998, 265–284, here at 267. On the difficulties in classifying 'Jewish Christians', see Matt A. JACKSON–MACCABE, (Ed.), Jewish Christianity Reconsidered. Rethinking ancient groups and texts, Minneapolis 2007.

Old Testament reading, or even two – from the Law and from the Prophets – while in others it did not. It explains why in some churches the celebration of Easter is known to us at an early date as a Christianized Passover held on 14 Nisan, while in other churches the feast is not observed at all until it is adopted at a later date as a Saturday night–Sunday celebration with a thoroughly Christianized meaning. And it explains why the eucharistic prayers of some churches have a strong Semitic flavour in their vocabulary and style, while in others it is hard to show any connection with a Jewish grace after meals, as the prayers seem to belong to an entirely different cultural milieu. We may contrast, on the one hand, the anaphora of Addai and Mari with, on the other, the eucharistic canon of the Roman church.[36]

Although all the examples cited so far are of instances where Christians have derived liturgical customs from Jews, we should not automatically assume that the traffic was all one-way. Israel Yuval has opened up an interesting line of possible research by suggesting that sometimes it may have been Jews who changed their customs in order to differentiate themselves from Christians, rather than always the other way round. He claimed:

> The Jewish view that sees Judaism as always influencing Christianity, but never the other way around, is theologically grounded, based on the assumption that Judaism is the mother-religion of Christianity. But early Christianity and tannaitic Judaism are two sister religions that took shape during the same period and under the same conditions of oppression and destruction. There is no reason not to assume a parallel and mutual development of both religions, during which sometimes Judaism internalized ideas of its rival rather than the other way around. During the second and third centuries there were all kinds of Jews and all kinds of Christians, all struggling against pagan Rome and all sharing the centrality of the messianic idea and the ritual of Passover.[37]

He then went on to expand on this idea in detail in relation to the development of the Passover. Seth Schwartz has suggested that something similar may be true with regard to the emergence of elaborate synagogue buildings in the fourth century, as being a direct response to the Christian church-building programme that was taking place at the time.[38] To this we may add the rabbinic demand that every prayer text should be conformed to the *berakah* pattern, incorporating the phrase, 'Blessed are you, Lord God,' etc. that we see being imposed even on traditional prayer material in the codification of Judaism after the destruction of the Temple. Any prayers that did not already begin in this way were modified

[36] On all these, see further ROUWHORST as in the above note, and also his Continuity and Discontinuity between Jewish and Christian Liturgy, in: Bijdragen 54 (1993) 72–83; Jewish Liturgical Traditions in Early Syriac Christianity, in: Vigiliae Christianae 51 (1997) 72–93; The reception of the Jewish Sabbath in early Christianity, in: Paul POST et al. (Eds.), Christian Feast and Festival, Leuven 2001, 223–266; The Reading of Scripture in Early Christian Liturgy, in: Leonard V. RUTGERS (Ed.), What Athens has to do with Jerusalem, Leuven 2002, 305–331.

[37] Israel J. YUVAL, Easter and Passover as Early Jewish–Christian Dialogue, in: Paul F. BRADSHAW – Lawrence A. HOFFMAN (Eds.), Passover and Easter. Origin and History to Modern Times, Notre Dame 1999, 98–124, here at 103–104.

[38] SCHWARTZ, Imperialism and Jewish Society, chapters 8–9.

by appending this formula to the end of the prayer as a seal or *chatimah* rather than by re-writing the entire text from the beginning. Why did the authorities choose this *berakah* pattern as normative and discard all other possible constructions? Could it have been because the early Christians were already showing a preference for using prayers cast in the *eucharistia* form, 'We give thanks to you, O Lord', etc. which previously had been a quite acceptable variant of the *berakah* form in Jewish praying? Rather than this being a Christian deviation from an already established norm, could it be that the imposition of the *berakah* on Jewish liturgy was a reaction to the Christian trend as a further marker of orthodox Jewish identity over against it?

On the other hand, we cannot completely discount the possibility that all these may simply be cases of quite independent parallel developments rather than the reaction of one to the other.[39] Whatever may be the truth of that, there are certainly instances where scholars have too rashly jumped to the conclusion of a direct literary dependency when they have encountered similarities in phrases and expressions in later Jewish and Christian prayers. Frequently, on closer examination, these turn out to not to be due to direct borrowing by one from the other – whether by Jews from Christians, or by Christians from Jews – but to be the result of the use of a common source, their shared scriptures, which the Christians came to call the Old Testament. It is now also being recognized that some of the commonalities that exist between certain practices from Qumran and those in later rabbinic liturgy may also be explained in the same way.[40]

The Christian use of Temple imagery presents a particular case in point. It is tempting to imagine that Christian references to Temple practices are based upon authentic historical recollections of what went on in the Jerusalem Temple, handed down from the earliest converts through succeeding generations of believers; and quite a number of Christian scholars have all too easily fallen into that very temptation.[41] But even in the case of later Jewish traditions about Temple customs, some Jewish scholars suspect that what may sometimes be happening is a projecting back of what later generations thought *should* have happened rather than what actually *was* the case. For example, the material in the Mishnah tractate *Middot* seems at times to be more closely related to biblical projections of the Temple than to what is now known through archaeological research to have been true of the actual Temple site. Similarly, the liturgical descriptions in the tractate *Tamid* do not yield a single consistent picture such as one might expect if its purpose had really been to record accurately the daily ritual. So much more so, then, in the case of Christian traditions concerning

39 See KULP, The Origins of the Seder and the Haggadah, 118–125.

40 See for example REIF, The Second Temple Period, Qumran Research, and Rabbinic Liturgy, 139; SARASON, Communal Prayer at Qumran and Among the Rabbis, 171.

41 A recent example is Margaret BARKER, The Great High Priest. The Temple Roots of Christian Liturgy, London 2003; EADEM, Temple Themes in Christian Worship, London 2007.

Jewish cultic practices, which seem to be based on Old Testament descriptions and prescriptions rather than any independent source. This is as applicable at the earliest point in the two traditions – anti-Jewish polemic among the Apostolic Fathers – as it is in the appropriation of cultic language and imagery in reference to Christian worship practices in the fourth century.

In conclusion, therefore, what can we say about Jewish influence on early Christian liturgy? Evidence of it certainly exists, but not to the extent that former generations of scholars imagined. We cannot expect to find precise parallels in the wording of texts or the details of ceremonial. Nor can we expect to see the same degree of influence in every part of the ancient Christian world. And sometimes the influence was not in Christians adopting the same customs as Jews, but doing the opposite in order to distinguish themselves from Jews, while at other times it may have been Jews who needed to differentiate their practices from those of Christians. More often than not the influences seem to have come out of the traditions of first-century Jewish movements that disappeared from view in the shake-up in the culture after the destruction of the Temple rather than from the rabbinic traditions that became codified as orthodox Judaism in later centuries. And it is possible that further discoveries are yet to be made in research in this area.

No, Christianity was not a new religion that owed little or nothing to the Jewish roots from which it emerged, but its relationship with those roots and with the orthodox Judaism that was gradually being formed alongside it is rather more complex than a simple parent-child association. The connection is rather that of two estranged siblings, siblings who are today finally beginning to discover their common ancestors, and for that we should give thanks.[42]

[42] This article was also published in a German translation in July 2008 by the Austrian „Koordinierungsausschuss für christlich-jüdische Zusammenarbeit / Coordination Committee for Christian-Jewish Cooperation“: Paul F. BRADSHAW, Der jüdische Einfluss auf die frühe christliche Liturgie: Eine Neubewertung, in: Dialog – DuSiach. Christlich-jüdische Informationen 72 (Juli 2008) 14–31.

Pseudoapostolische Ordinationsgebete in Apostolischen Kirchen
Beobachtungen zur gottesdienstlichen Rezeption der Traditio Apostolica und ihrer Deszendenten

Heinzgerd Brakmann

»Geliebtes Kind trägt viele Namen« (Sprichwort). Die nicht allein bei Liturgikern hochgeschätzte Schrift CPG 1737, vormals bekannt als »Ägyptische Kirchenordnung« (»Constitutiones [ecclesiae] aegyptiacae«, »Egyptian Church Ordinances«, »Ordinance ecclésiastique égyptienne«), reist gegenwärtig auch unter Namen wie »Dokument x« oder διατάξεις τῶν ἁγίων ἀποστόλων, nachdem der zwischenzeitlich gemeinhin angenommene Werktitel ἀποστολικὴ παράδοσις (»Traditio apostolica«) unter den Verdacht der Täuschung geriet, weil die solche *nomendatio* begründende Autorschaft des Hippolytos von Rom († 235) Ende des 20. Jahrhunderts nicht mehr so sicher galt, wie dies zu seinem Anfang durch gleich mehrere Autoren nachgewiesen schien[1]. Unbeschadet dessen sei CPG 1737 hier, weil bequem und eindeutig, weiterhin beim vertrauten ›Künstlernamen‹ Traditio apostolica genannt. Im Übrigen geht es mir nicht um Literatur–, sondern nur um Liturgiegeschichte, und dies zudem in engsten Grenzen, nämlich um die Frage post-spätantiker gottesdienstlicher Nutzung der in der Traditio apostolica und ihren Nachfolgeschriften versammelten Gebetsliteratur zur Bestellung kirchlicher Amtsträger[2].

In dieser Hinsicht scheint eine aktuelle Bestandaufnahme bekannter Fakten, jüngerer Erkenntnisse und offener Fragen aus doppeltem Grunde nicht überflüssig. Zum Einen, weil über die Wirkungsgeschichte der Traditio apostolica allgemein und ihrer Ordinationsgebete im Besonderen übertriebene Einschätzungen im Umlauf sind. So hielt etwa Harry Boone Porter (1923–1999) das Werk für »most widely read in Eastern Christendom« mit daraus folgendem »immense influence on ancient and modern usages«[3]. Zum Zweiten erfuhr in unserer Generation das Bischofsweihegebet der Traditio apostolica: Ὁ θεὸς καὶ πατὴρ τοῦ κυρίου ἡμῶν ..., eine Revitalisierung vornehmster Art, indem es 1968,

1 Zur neueren Debatte vgl. Andrea Nicolotti, Che cos'è la Traditio apostolica di Ippolito? In margine ad una recente pubblicazione, in: Rivista di Storia del Cristianesimo 2, 1 (2005) 219–237 mit Lit.

2 Mit Wien ist vorliegende Studie insofern verbunden, weil dort die erste moderne Monographie zur Entwicklung der abendländischen Bischofsweiheliturgie entstand: Adalbert Flittner, Der Ritus der Bischofsweihe in der abendländischen Kirche in geschichtlicher Entwicklung bis zum 11. Jahrhundert, Diss. Wien (1926); leider ungedruckt und wissenschaftlich einflusslos.

3 Harry Boone Porter, The Ordination Prayers of the Ancient Western Churches (Alcuin Club Collections 49), London 1967, XI.

leicht überarbeitet, in das Pontificale Romanum aufgenommen wurde[4], ab 1969 unter Verdrängung der bisherigen, weit über tausendjährigen Weihepräfation des Römischen Ritus: »Deus honorum omnium ...«[5], die seither nur noch in mittelalterlicher Übersetzung bei den orthodoxen wie katholischen Armeniern in regelmässigem Gebrauch ist[6].

Neben redaktionellen und amtstheologischen ›Schwächen‹[7] des in den Ruhestand verabschiedeten alt-lateinischen Formulars[8], darunter seinem heute nachgerade peinlichem Schweigen vom »munus apostolicum Episcoporum«, wurde zugunsten des Rückgriffs auf Ὁ θεὸς καὶ πατὴρ τοῦ κυρίου ἡμῶν vom Leiter (*relator*) der zuständigen Arbeitsgruppe, Bernard Botte OSB (1883–1980) — selbst Urheber einer wissenschaftlichen Rekonstitution der Traditio apostolica[9] — ein »argument œcuménique« vorgetragen. In seinen Memoiren (1973) begründet er dies knapp: »en étudiant les rites orientaux, j'avais constaté que la formule [scil. der Traditio apostolica] était toujours vivante sous les formes plus évoluées«[10]. Im Detail abgebildet finden sich Argumente und Argumentationsgang in den Arbeitspapieren, die schließlich zur Editio typica des römischen

4 Pontificale Romanum ex decreto Sancrosancti Oecumenici Concilii Vaticani II instauratum auctoritate Pauli PP. VI promulgatum: De Ordinatione Diaconi, Presbyteri et Episcopi. Editio Typica, Urbs Vaticana 1968, 62–79. 105–114; die Oratio consecrationis des Bischofs ebd. 70–75. 110f; zu dieser vgl. Giuseppe FERRARO, Le preghiere di ordinazione al diaconato, al presbiterato, all'episcopato, Napoli 1977, 149–260 mit Lit.; Ovidio VEZZOLI, « Et nunc effunde super hunc electum spiritum principalem ». Per una lettura della preghiera di ordinazione del vescovo, in: Il vescovo e la sua Chiesa (Quaderni teologici del Seminario di Brescia 6), Brescia 1996, 171–202; Giuseppe FERRARO, La liturgia dei sacramenti, Roma 2008, 282–324.

5 Zum Formular »Deus honorum omnium ...« vgl. Antonio SANTANTONI, L'ordinazione episcopale. Storia e teologia dei riti dell'ordinazione nelle antiche liturgie dell'occidente (Studia Anselmiana 69), Roma 1976, 53–62; Klemens RICHTER, Die Ordination des Bischofs von Rom (LWQF 60), Münster i. W. 1976, 23–26. 40f. 64. 98; Bruno KLEINHEYER, Geschicke eines Textes. Zu Struktur und Geschichte des altrömischen Gebetes zur Bischofsweihe, in: Weisheit Gottes – Weisheit der Welt [FS Joseph Ratzinger], St. Ottilien 1987, 713–728.

6 Italienische Übersetzung des armenisch–orthodoxen Ordos der Bischofsweihe bei Claudio GUGEROTTI, La liturgia armena delle ordinazioni e l'epoca ciciliana. Esiti rituali di una teologia di comunione tra Chiese (OCA 264), Roma 2001, 362–386, die gemeinte Oration ebd. 381 Nr. 647.

7 Bernard BOTTE, Le mouvement liturgique. Témoignage et souvenirs, Tournai 1973, 166f; SANTANTONI, L'ordinazione episcopale (wie Anm. 5) 61f: »Una preghiera che presenta molti difetti, ...«. Die amtstheologischen ›Schwächen‹ beinhalten in Wahrheit eine ausgeprägt gloriose Theorie des Bischofsamtes, die in der Gegenwart nicht länger präsentabel scheint, mag auch die von »Deus honorum omnium ...« implizierte Kleiderpracht des Episkopos noch heute ihre Amateure finden.

8 Die Ordinationen zu den Ordines maiores gehören nicht zu dem 2007 von Benedikt XVI. Ratzinger qua »Chef du rite romain« (Achille M. Triacca) begründeten Sonderbrauch (usus extraordinarius) der Römischen Liturgie. Das durch Paul VI. Montini ersetzte vorherige Pontifikale wurde einstweilen nur noch ein Mal bei einer erlaubten abendländischen Bischofsweihe benutzt, nämlich am 18. August 2002 durch Castrillón Card. Hoyos für die »Indult-Ordination« des Fernando Arêas Rifan, jetzt Ordinarius der mit Rom unierten altritualistischen Apostolica Administratio personalis Sancti Ioannis Mariae Vianney, Campos dos Goytacazes (Brasilien).

9 Siehe unten Anm. 26.

10 BOTTE, Le mouvement liturgique (wie Anm. 7) 165–178, hier 167.

Ordinales von 1968 führten[11]: Als Modell eines befriedigenden Textes wird gleich anfangs (im Schema 102, datiert 11.09.1965), die »oratio consecratoris Traditionis Apostolicae S. Hippolyti Romani saec. III ineunte scripta« eingeführt. Neben der Romanitas[12] spreche zu ihren Gunsten die Ökumenizität: »usque hodie in ordinatione episcopi Coptorum [...] et in forma evoluta qualem induit in Testamentum Domini [...] in liturgia ordinationis Syrorum occidentalium in honore habetur«[13]. Die zwei Belege aus der Liturgienvergleichung dienen auch in der Folgezeit als wesentliche Stütze der Kandidatur des ›Hippolytschen Gebets‹. Bezogen auf den ersten, die Verwendung der »oratio consecratoris Traditionis Apostolicae« bei der koptischen Bischofsweihe, unterbleibt beständig jede Reserve. Ab Schema 180 (datiert 29.08.1966) wird sogar die anfangs eingeführte Sondergruppe »Kopten« durch vorzugsweise die breite Berufung auf Patriarchat und Ritus Alexandriens ersetzt[14]. Beim zweiten Argument, aus dem antiochenischen Bereich, tritt neben das schon anfängliche Eingeständnis dortiger Benutzung nicht des Traditio–Gebetes selbst, sondern einer jüngeren Überarbeitung (Testamentum Domini; 5. Jh.), wenigstens sporadisch die Anerkennung faktischer Beschränkung des Gebrauchs als »oratio consecrationis patriarchae«, also nicht jeglichen Bischofs[15]. Gleichzeitig wird mit wachsender Wucht zugunsten römischer Übernahme von Ὁ θεὸς καὶ πατὴρ τοῦ κυρίου ἡμῶν das »argument œcuménique« der Ost–West–Einheit vorgebracht: »Sic affirmatur unitas trium antiquiorum patriarchatuum, Romae, Antiochiae et Alexandrinae«[16]. Der Hinweis auf das ursprüngliche Terzett der Patriarchate[17] – vor der kirchlichen Rangerhöhung Konstantinopels – suggeriert allerhöchstes Alter der beobachteten Tradition und entsorgt zugleich den Ausfall der Bezeugung des Gebetes ausgerechnet im byzantinisch–konstantinopolitanischen Ritus, neben dem Romanus der einzige von Weltgeltung. Bottes »ökumenisches Argu-

11 Jan Michael JONCAS, The work of the Consilium in the reform of Roman Rite episcopal ordination: 1965–1968, in: EL 108 (1994) 81–127. 183–204 mit Abdruck der Dokumente im lateinischen Original und Übersetzung in das Englische.

12 Dass Hippolyt von Rom die Traditio apostolica verfasst habe, war in den 1960er Jahren so gut wie allgemeine Überzeugung, begründet von Eduard VON DER GOLTZ, Unbekannte Fragmente altchristlicher Gemeindeordnungen, in: Sitzungsberichte der Preußischen Akademie der Wissenschaften 56 (1906) 141–157; Eduard SCHWARTZ, Über die pseudapostolischen Kirchenordnungen (Schriften der Wissenschaftlichen Gesellschaft in Straßburg 6), Straßburg 1910, und Richard Hugh CONNOLLY, The so-called Egyptian church order and derived documents (Texts and Studies 8, 4), Cambridge 1916. Einzelne Gegenstimmen (Hieronymus Engberding 1948; Jean Magne 1965) blieben Außenseitermeinungen bis zu der mit dem Namen Marcel METZGER zu verbindenden Neuorientierung: Nouvelles perspectives pour la prétendue Tradition Apostolique, in: Ecclesia Orans 5 (1988) 241–259; DERS., Enquêtes autour de la prétendue »Tradition Apostolique«, in: ebd. 9 (1992) 7–36 u. a.

13 JONCAS, Work (wie Anm. 11) $86f_{16}$; in italienischer Sprache wiederholt in Schema 220 (31.03.1967): ebd. 187_{7}.

14 Ebd. 123_{124}. 126. 127_{128}. 196_{41}.

15 Ebd. 123_{124}; die auf die Patriarchenbestellung beschränkte Nutzung des Formulars wird in Schema 220 nicht wiederholt: ebd. $195f_{37.\,41}$.

16 Ebd. 124_{126}.

17 Ebd. 200_{62}.

ment« fand Gefallen, wurde daher abschließend im Schema 220 (31.03.1967) wiederholt[18] und im Frühjahr 1968, auf Nachfrage Pauls VI. († 1978), dem römischen Papst in folgender Weise übermittelt: »haec formula unitatem cum Ecclesia orientali testaretur, cum in tribus antiquioribus patriarchatibus eadem doctrina de Episcopo in ipso ordinationis actu enuntiaretur«[19]. In Übereinstimmung damit versteht die päpstliche Konstitution »Pontificalis Romani« vom 18. Juni 1968 die für den Westen wiederbelebte Prex consecratoria der Traditio apostolica als Testimonium der Concordia östlicher und westlicher Tradition hinsichtlich der apostolischen Bischofstheorie[20]. Über das östliche Pendant heißt es im päpstlichen Schreiben knapp, aber korrekt: »... quaeque, magna ex parte, in liturgia Ordinationis Coptorum et Syrorum occidentalium adhuc servatur«. Das »magna ex parte« leugnet die textlichen Unterschiede zwischen den überlieferten Gebetsformularen nicht[21], das »in liturgia Ordinationis« vermeidet geschickt die genauere Beschreibung der verschiedenen Gelegenheiten ostkirchlicher Nutzung des mit der römischen Neuerwerbung korrespondierenden Gebetes. Über geschichtliche Details hat in der Tat nicht eine päpstliche Konstitution zu informieren, sondern die Liturgiewissenschaft in Schrift und Wort, eine Aufgabe, die leider das deutschsprachige Groß-Handbuch »Gottesdienst der Kirche« wenig vorbildlich erledigt[22].

[18] Ebd. $196_{39.41}$.

[19] Ebd. 196_{39}.

[20] In: Pontificale Romanum ... (wie Anm. 4) 8 = Reiner KACZYNSKI (Hg.), Enchiridion documentorum instaurationis liturgicae. Bd. 1, Torino 1976, 392 Nr. 1081; deutsche Übersetzung bei Heinrich RENNINGS – Martin KLÖCKENER, Dokumente zur Erneuerung der Liturgie, Bd. 1, Kevelaer 1983, 553 Rz. 1081.

[21] Gegenüber Kritikern Pauls VI. ist festzuhalten, dass dieser in »Pontificalis Romani« nicht behauptet, das in sein Pontificale Romanum aufgenommene Ordinationsgebet der Traditio apostolica sei als solches bis in die Gegenwart bei Kopten und Syrern in Gebrauch.

[22] Korrekt informiert BOTTE, Le mouvement liturgique (wie Anm. 2) 167f: »dans le rite syrien, la prière pour l'ordination du patriarche n'était autre que celle du Testament de Notre Seigneur, remaniement de la Tradition apostolique. ... dans le rite copte, la prière pour l'ordination de l'évêque est proche de celle des Constitutions apostoliques, autre remaniement du texte d'Hippolyte. On retrouvait partout les idées essentielles de la Tradition apostolique«. Vgl. damit die seltsam verrätselten Auskünfte bei Bruno KLEINHEYER, Ordinationen und Beauftragungen, in: DERS. – Emmanuel v. SEVERUS – Reiner KACZYNSKI, Sakramentliche Feiern 2 (GdK 8), Regensburg 1984, 53: »... das Hippolytsche Gebet zur Bischofsweihe [...] bestimmt bis heute in ununterbrochener Tradition in Teilen des Patriarchats Alexandrien (äthiopische Bischofsweihe) und des Patriarchats Antiochien (Weihe des Patriarchen im maronitischen Ritus) die Weihepraxis«. Zutreffend ist mit diesem Text ausschließlich jener Benutzer informiert, der (a) das »bestimmt« so versteht, dass in den angeführten Patriarchaten »das Hippolytsche Gebet«, d. h. das Bischofsweihegebet der Traditio, nicht etwa selbst, sondern nur in abgeleiteten Formen benutzt wird. Er muss ferner (b) begreifen, dass die in Klammern angeführten Gelegenheiten der Anwendung der Gebete nicht identisch sind mit den im selben Satz genannten »Teilen« der Patriarchate, sondern nur Teile, und zwar keineswegs die wichtigsten, jener »Teile« darstellen. Eine nach Ort und Sprache »äthiopische Bischofsweihe« ist ohnehin erst ein Produkt des 20. Jh. Besser unterrichtete Kleinheyers Erstinformation (DERS., Weiheliturgie in neuer Gestalt, in: LJ 18 [1968] 210-229, hier 215): »sowohl im koptischen als auch im westsyrisch–maronitischen Ritus der Bischofsweihe ist der Text des Hippolyt die Grundlage des (freilich da und dort erheblich erweiterten) Weihegebetes«. Der irreführende nachträgliche Austausch des »koptisch« gegen »äthiopisch« wird

Im Gefolge der Übernahme einer bearbeiteten Version von Ὁ θεὸς καὶ πατὴρ τοῦ κυρίου ἡμῶν in das heutige Pontificale Romanum sind am Rande der Catholica Zweifel an der Wirksamkeit dieses Gebetes für die Bestellung katholischer Bischöfe laut geworden[23]. Ich halte sie für unbegründet. Der vorliegende Aufsatz soll mithin solche Schatten weder werfen noch vertreiben, sondern will allein weitere liturgiehistorische Untersuchungen anregen, die dringend nötiges Licht in die noch unzureichend ausgeleuchtete Geschichte der Ordinationseuchologie bringen.

Im ersten Teil meines Beitrags werden der Bestand an Ordinationsgebeten in den einzelnen altchristlichen Kirchenordnungen[24] registriert sowie erste Nachrichten zu jener Nutzung in Kirchen der verschiedenen Regionen und Konfessionen eingesammelt[25]. Der zweite Teil befragt die einzelnen Liturgien der Ostkirchen nach Gegebenheit, Umfang und Umständen einer Verwendung pseudapostolischer Orationen, insbesondere des Bischofsweihegebetes aus der Traditio apostolica und ihren literarischen Derivaten.

RICHTER, Die Ordination (wie Anm. 5) 121_{36} oder seinen namenlosen Gewährsleuten verdankt.

23 Zum Sprecher der Bedenkenträger macht sich ein »Comité international de recherches scientifiques sur les origines et la validité de *Pontificalis Romani*«, das im Netz die Seite http://www.rore-sanctifica.org betreibt, für die Paul Schoonbroodt († 2012) verantwortlich zeichnete. Einer der Hauptmitwirkenden, der deutsche Dipl.-Ing. Thilo STOPKA, veröffentlichte im Netz die umfängliche Abhandlung »Die Frage der Gültigkeit der Priester- und Bischofsweihen nach dem Ritus von „Papst" Paul VI« (http://www.rore-sanctifica.org/bibliotheque_rore_sanctifica/04-rite_de_paul_6-invalidite_du_rite_episco|pal/2009-02-28_Etude_de_STOPKA-Thilo_Das-Pontifikale-Pauls-VI/RORE_2009-02-26-DE_Das-Pontifikale-Pauls-VI_-_ePaper(f).pdf; auch im Buchhandel: ISBN 2- 84519-880-9). Darin benutzt er unabgesprochen und mit eigener Zielsetzung ausgewählte Inhalte aus einem mit mir geführten Telefonat. Gegen die von genannter Gruppe verbreiteten Thesen wendet sich aus dem Kreis der von Marcel Lefebvre begründeten Bewegung Frère PIERRE-MARIE [DE KERGORLAY] O.P., Sont-ils évêques? Le nouveau rituel de consécration épiscopale est-il valide?, Avrillé 2006. Darin veröffentlicht sind Aktenstücke aus dem Nachlass Kleinheyer im Deutschen Liturgischen Institut, Trier.

24 Die benutzten Editionen sind an Ort und Stelle bibliographiert. Hinsichtlich der Einleitungsfragen der einzelnen Kirchenordnungen stütze ich mich in der Regel auf Bruno STEIMER, Vertex Traditionis. Die Gattungen der altchristlichen Kirchenordnungen (Beihefte zur Zeitschrift für die neutestamentliche Wissenschaft und die Kunde der älteren Kirche 63) Berlin 1992, der auch die Forschungsgeschichte ausführlich referiert. Außerdem beigezogen: Eduard SCHWARTZ, Über die pseudapostolischen Kirchenordnungen [1910], in: DERS., Gesammelte Schriften 5. Zum Neuen Testament und zum frühen Christentum, Berlin 1963, 192–273; Walter SELB, Orientalisches Kirchenrecht, Bd. 2 (Österr. Akademie der Wiss., Phil.-hist. Kl., Sitzungsberichte 543), Wien 1989; Hubert KAUFHOLD, La littérature pseudo-canonique syriaque, in: Muriel DEBIÉ [u. a.] (Hgg.), Les apocryphes syriaques (Études syriaques 2), Paris 2005, 147–167; David Ferguson WAGSCHAL, The Nature of Law and Legality in the Byzantine Canonical Collections 381–883, Diss. Durham (2010); Wilfried HARTMANN – Kenneth PENNINGTON (Hgg.), The History of Byzantine and Eastern Canon Law to 1500, Washington 2012; Hubert KAUFHOLD, Sources of Canon Law in the Eastern Churches, ebd. 215–342.

25 In dieser Hinsicht noch immer hilfreich: Jean Michel HANSSENS, Les oraisons sacramentelles des ordinations orientales, in: OCP 18 (1952) 297-318; überarbeitete Fassung: DERS., La liturgie d'Hippolyte. Documents et études, Roma 1970 [Nachdruck: Cadillac: Éd. Saint–Remi 2008] 263–285, danach hier zitiert.

1. TEIL

Die *Traditio apostolica*[26] (CPG 1737), Ausgangspunkt unserer Untersuchung, überliefert die folgenden drei Ordinationsgebete[27]:

Amt	Gebet	Textüberlieferung	Rezeption
Bischof	Ὁ θεὸς καὶ πατὴρ τοῦ κυρίου ἡμῶν Ἰησοῦ Χριστοῦ, ὁ πατὴρ τῶν οἰκτιρμῶν ...[28]	griechisch (Epit. Const. apost. VIII); lateinisch; aethiopisch	Can. Hipp.; Const. apost.; Epit. Const. apost. VIII; Test. Dom.; ➤ romEpisc (seit 1968)
Presbyter	Deus [...] respice super servum tuum ...[29]	lateinisch; aethiopisch	Const. apost.; Test. Dom.
Diakon	Deus, qui omnia creasti et verbo perordinasti ...[30]	lateinisch; aethiopisch	Can. Hipp.; Test. Dom.

Ein Lektor wird gemäß Trad. apost. 11 (30 BOTTE) ohne Handauflegung und ohne besonderes Gebet für seinen Dienst bestellt, ebenso ein Subdiakon (13 [32]).

Die 38 *Canones Hippolyti* (CPG 1742)[31] bilden eine eigenständige Überarbeitung (›Neuauflage‹) der Traditio apostolica, hier erstmals mit dem Namen des Hippolyt von Rom in Verbindung gebracht. Die Schrift, ursprünglich wohl in Griechisch abgefasst, wurde, möglicherweise über eine koptische Zwischenstufe, in das Arabische übersetzt und ist nur in dieser Sprache erhalten. Als Abfassungszeit gilt die Mitte des vierten Jahrhunderts. Als Heimat wird mehrheitlich das Nilland, Alexandrien oder die Provinz, angesehen, vereinzelt Kleinasien[32]. Enthalten sind folgende Ordinationsgebete:

26 Benutzte Ausgabe: Bernard BOTTE, La Tradition apostolique de Saint Hippolyte. Essai de reconstitution. 5. verb. Aufl. (LQF 39), Münster i. W. 1989; vgl. Paul F. BRADSHAW – Maxwell E. JOHNSON – L. Edward PHILLIPS, The Apostolic Tradition. A commentary (Hermenaia), Minneapolis 2002.

27 Der älteste Wortlaut der in unterschiedlichen Zuständen überlieferten Gebetsformulare ist nicht einfach zu rekonstruieren, einen bedenkenswerten Versuch bietet Eric SEGELBERG, The Ordinations Prayers in Hippolytus, in: StPatr 13 (TU 116), Berlin 1975, 397–408.

28 Trad. apost. 3 (6–10 BOTTE).

29 Ebd. 7 (20–22).

30 Ebd. 8 (26).

31 Benutzte Ausgabe: René Georges COQUIN, Les Canons d'Hippolyte (PO 31, 2), Paris 1966; deutsche Übersetzung: Wilhelm RIEDEL, Die Kirchenrechtsquellen des Patriarchats Alexandrien, Leipzig 1900, 200–230, hier 201f (für den Bischof: »O Gott, Vater unseres Herrn Jesu Christi, Vater der Barmherzigkeit und Gott alles Trostes ...«). 203 (für den Presbyter: »ganz wie beim Bischof geschehen ist; mit Ausnahme des Wortes ›Bischof‹«). 203 (für den Diakon: »O, Gott, Vater unseres Herrn Jesu Christi, wir flehen dich an, dass du deinen Heiligen Geist ausgießest über deinen Knecht ...«).

32 STEIMER, Vertex (wie Anm. 24) 72–79.

Amt	Gebete	Quellen	Rezeption
Bischof	Ô Dieu, Père de notre Seigneur Jésus–Christ, père des miséricordes et dieu de toute consolation ...	Trad. apost. 3 (vermindert um die alttestamentliche Typologie)	unbelegt
Presbyter	Ô Dieu, Père de notre Seigneur Jésus–Christ, père des miséricordes et dieu de toute consolation ...	Bischofsweihegebet der Can. Hipp. unter Anpassung der Amtsbezeichnung	unbelegt
Diakon	O Dieu, Père de notre Seigneur Jésus–Christ ... répands ton Esprit–Saint sur N., compte le parmi ceux qui te servent ... comme Étienne ...		unbelegt

Die *Apostolischen Konstitutionen* (CPG 1740) mit ergänzenden *Canones Apostolorum* sind die erste in der Neuzeit wiederentdeckte altchristliche Kirchenordnung[33]. Ihre Szenerie ist »die einer apostolischen Vollversammlung in Jerusalem«[34]. Als Sekretär der versammelten Apostel tritt Clemens von Rom auf. Das Werk setzt sich ausdrücklich gegenüber den Pseudepigrapha ab und beansprucht kanonische Geltung[35]. Die zu Beginn der Moderne von dieser Schrift ausgehende Faszination durch das vermeintlich Apostolische, nicht zuletzt im gottesdienstlichen Bereich, wich erst nach längerer Frist nüchterner historischer Einordnung: Das in griechischer Sprache abgefasste und vollständig in der Originalsprache, offenbar nicht ohne gewisse Bearbeitungen, erhaltene kirchenrechtliche Sammelwerk entstand etwa in den Jahren 375–400, wahrscheinlich im Gebiet des spätantiken Syrien, anscheinend in oder bei Antiochien[36]. Die als Oktateuch organisierte Schrift überarbeitet in Buch I–VI die Didascalia apostolorum (»Syrische Didaskalie«[37]; CPG 1738) und verwertet in Buch VII, nebst

[33] Ausgaben: Frank Xaver FUNK, Didascalia et Constitutiones Apostolorum, Bd. 1–2, Paderborn 1905; Marcel METZGER, Les Constitutions apostoliques, Bd. 1–3 (SC 320. 329. 336), Paris 1985/87.

[34] STEIMER, Vertex (wie Anm. 24) 132.

[35] Can. apost. 85 (Const. apost. 8, 47 can. 85).

[36] STEIMER, Vertex (wie Anm. 24) 114–133. Reserven äussern SCHWARTZ, Kirchenordnungen (wie Anm. 24) 244f und Michael KOHLBACHER, Zum liturgischen Gebrauch der Apostolischen Konstitutionen, in: James M. S. COWEY – Bärbel KRAMER (Hgg.), Paramone. Editionen und Aufsätze von Mitgliedern des Heidelberger Instituts für Papyrologie zwischen 1982 und 2004 (Archiv für Papyrusforschung und verwandte Gebiete. Beiheft 16), München 2004, 296–312, hier 296f.

[37] Trotz dieser Benennung eine griechische Schöpfung, die Übersetzung in das Syrische erfolgte nach STEIMER, Vertex (wie Anm. 24) 51 noch im 4. Jh., nach KAUFHOLD, La littérature pseudo-canonique syriaque (wie Anm. 24) 157 mit Anm. 33: um 700, Handschriften ab 7./8. Jh.

anderen Quellen, die Doctrina apostolorum (»Didache«; CPG 1735). Buch VIII schöpft erkennbar aus der Traditio apostolica und ist liturgiehistorisch wie gebetsgeschichtlich besonders wertvoll, weil es eine Art Euchologion einschliesst[38], u. a. mit der sog. Klementinischen Liturgie (8, 5,11–15, 11), einer Ordnung der Eucharistiefeier in antiochenischer Form[39], sowie einem Ordinale (8, 3, 1–5, 9. 16, 1–26, 3) mit dem folgenden Orationenbestand:

Amt	Gebet	Quellen	Liturg. Rezeption
Bischof	Ὁ ὤν, δέσποτα Κύριε ὁ θεὸς ὁ παντοκράτωρ, ὁ μόνος ἀγέννητος καὶ ἀβασίλευτος ...[40]	Trad. apost. (mit erweiterter alttestamentlicher Typologie)	➤ coptEpisc (*nicht* bei Patriarch oder Metropolit); ➤ maronEpisc (Nebengebet)
Presbyter	Κύριε παντοκράτορ, ὁ βασιλεὺς ἡμῶν ...[41]		➤ coptPresb; ➤ byzPresb (vereinzelt)
Diakon	Ὁ θεὸς ὁ παντοκράτωρ, ὁ ἀληθινὸς καὶ ἀψευδής ...[42]		➤ coptDiac; ➤ byzDiac (vereinzelt)
Diakonin	Ὁ θεὸς ... ὁ ἀνδρὸς καὶ γυναικὸς δημιουργός ...[43]		unbekannt
Subdiakon	Δέσποτα ὁ θεὸς ... ὁ καὶ ἐν τῇ σκηνῇ τοῦ μαρτυρίου τοὺς νεωκόρους ἀναδείξας ...[44]		➤ coptSubd ➤ byzDiac (vereinzelt)
Lektor	Ὁ θεὸς ὁ αἰώνιος, ὁ πολὺς ἐν ἐλέει ...[45]		➤ coptLect[46]

38 Nicht abschließend beantwortet ist die Frage, ob und in welcher Weise der Constitutor ein in gottesdienstlichem Gebrauch befindliches Buch verwendete und dessen Gebete in seinem Sinne überarbeitete; vgl. METZGER, Les Constitutions (wie Anm. 33) 1, 21f. 24; 2, 67–74: »L'euchologe des *CA*«. Zu den Weihegebeten ebd. 67: »l'origine [...] des ordinations [...] ne nous est pas connue. Pourtant [...] le compilateur semble bien avoir puisé dans des recueils antérieurs«. An der Möglichkeit der Existenz eines Euchologions zur Wirkungszeit des Constitutors besteht kein Zweifel.

39 Vgl. Paul DREWS, Untersuchungen über die sogen. clementinische Liturgie im VIII. Buch der apostolischen Konstitutionen. Bd. 1. Die clementinische Liturgie in Rom (Studien zur Geschichte des Gottesdienstes und des gottesdienstlichen Lebens 2 u. 3), Tübingen 1906; Jan A. A. A. STOOP, Die Klementynse Liturgie, Pretoria 1992.

40 Const. apost. 8, 5, 1–7 (SC 336, 144–148).

41 Const. apost. 8, 16, 3–5 (SC 336, 216–218). Erwägungen zu den Quellen bei Jean MAGNE, Tradition apostolique sur les charismes et Diataxeis des saints Apôtres, Paris 1975, 139–145. 157–179.

42 Const. apost. 8, 18, 1–3 (218–220).

43 Ebd. 8, 20, 1–2 (220–222).

44 Ebd. 8, 21, 3–4 (222).

45 Ebd. 8, 22, 3–4 (224).

Die Rechtgläubigkeit des Werkes wirkte aus der Warte des Nicaeno-Constantinopolitanums verdächtig. Insofern überrascht nicht, dass es — im Unterschied zu den Apostolischen Kanones — vom 691/92 in Konstantinopel zusammengetretenen Concilium Quinisextum (Trullanum II) wegen vermeintlicher Verfälschungen durch Häretiker verworfen wurde[47]. Die erfolgte Verurteilung konnte die weitere Wirkung des in den Apostolischen Konstitutionen enthaltenen Gebetsgutes im byzantinischen Bereich eingrenzen, brachte sie aber nicht vollends zum Erliegen[48]. Zum literarischen Fortleben der inkorporierten Ordinationsgebete tragen in Sonderheit bei:
(a) ein griechischer Paralleltext von Const. apost. VIII, die sog. Epitome (CPG 1741), sowie
(b) der syrische Octateuchus Clementinus[49] (CPG 1733)[50], der in seinen Büchern 4 bis 7 Const. apost. VIII breit übernahm, so in seinem das Ordinale umfassenden 5. Buch Const. apost. 8, 3–5. 16–26[51]. Damit schuf oder erleichterte er die Möglichkeit der Übernahme der Gebete in den Gottesdienst syrischer Zunge.

Die bekannte koptisch-sahidische Version hingegen hat die Gebete ausgelassen[52], vielleicht gerade deshalb, weil sie zur Zeit der Abschriften bereits Eingang in gottesdienstliche Bücher gefunden hatten[53].

Die *Epitome libri VIII Constitutionum Apostolorum* (CPG 1741; *alias* »Canones per Hippolytum«, »Règlements Apostoliques«), ein fünfteiliger Neben– oder Paralleltext zum Buch VIII der Apostolischen Konstitutionen[54], gehört nicht, wie gelegentlich vermutet, einer Vorform an, sondern war offensichtlich zur Ablösung der Apostolischen Konstitutionen bestimmt[55]. Die Schrift entstand wahrscheinlich um oder bald nach 400 ebenfalls in Syria. Die Überlieferung des griechischen Textes ist verbunden mit jener der *Canones Apostolorum*[56] und erfolgte vor allem im Kontext der *Synagoge L titulorum* des Johannes Scholas-

[46] Vgl. unten Anm. 167.
[47] Can. 2 (Mansi 11, 940f.).
[48] Siehe unten nach Anm. 79.
[49] In französischer Übertragung veröffentlicht: François NAU, La version syriaque de l'Octateuque de Clément (Ancienne Littérature Canonique Syriaque 4), Paris 1913, Nachdruck mit neuer Einführung durch Pio CIPRIOTTI (ebd. 1967), hier benutzt. Ebd. 13–22: »Tableaux des correspondances«. Eine erste Gesamtausgabe des syrischen Octateuchus Clementinus bereitet Hubert Kaufhold, München, vor.
[50] STEIMER, Vertex (wie Anm. 24) 141–148.
[51] Pio CIPRIOTTI, in: NAU, La version (wie Anm. 49) 17f.
[52] Johannes LEIPOLDT, Saïdische Auszüge aus dem 8. Buche der Apostolischen Konstitutionen (TU 26, 1b), Leipzig 1904, 3.
[53] Emmanuel LANNE, Les ordinations dans le rite copte. Leurs relations avec les Constitutions Apostoliques et la Tradition de saint Hippolyte, in: OrSyr 5 (1960) 81–106, hier 90.
[54] Ausgabe: FUNK, Didascalia et Constitutiones (wie Anm. 33) 2, 72–96, vgl. die Einleitung ebd. XI–XIX und STEIMER, Vertex (wie Anm. 24) 80–86; WAGSCHAL (wie Anm. 24) 88f.
[55] Bedenken gegenüber der herrschenden Meinung äußert KAUFHOLD, La littérature pseudo-canonique syriaque (wie Anm. 24) 151. 160.
[56] Dazu STEIMER, Vertex (wie Anm. 24) 87–94.

tikos aus Antiochien (565–577 Konstantinopler Patriarch) sowie des *Syntagma XIV titulorum* (629–640).
Für das im 2. Teil der griechischen Schrift enthaltene Ordinale findet sich die Überschrift Διατάξεις τῶν ἁγίων ἀποστόλων περὶ χειροτονιῶν διὰ Ἱππολύτου (par. Const. apost. 8, 4, 5. 16–28. 30, 31). Angeführt sind folgende Formulare:

Amt	**Gebete**	**Quellen**	**Liturg. Rezeption**
Bischof	Ὁ θεὸς καὶ πατὴρ τοῦ κυρίου ἡμῶν Ἰησοῦ Χριστοῦ, ὁ πατὴρ τῶν οἰκτιρμῶν ...[57]	Trad. apost. 3 Botte (*nicht* Const. apost. 8, 5, 1-7)	Barb. gr. 390 (16. Jh.) parr.
Presbyter	Κύριε παντοκράτορ, ὁ βασιλεὺς ἡμῶν, ὁ διὰ Χριστοῦ τὰ πάντα δημιουγήσας ...[58]	Const. apost. 8, 16, 3–5 (leicht gekürzt[59])	
Diakon	Ὁ θεὸς, ὁ παντοκράτωρ, ὁ ἀληθινός, ὁ ἀψευδής ...[60]	Const. apost. 8, 18, 1–3	
Diakonin	Ὁ θεός, ὁ αἰώνιος, ὁ πατὴρ τοῦ κυρίου ἡμῶν Ἰησοῦ Χριστοῦ, ὁ ἀνδρὸς καὶ γυναικὸς δημιουργός ...[61]	Const. apost. 8, 20, 1–2	
Subdiakon	Δέσποτα θεέ, δημιουργὲ ... ὁ καὶ ἐν τῇ σκηνῇ τοῦ μαρτυρίου τοὺς νεωκόρους ἀναδείξας ...[62]	Const. apost. 8, 21, 3–4	
Lektor	deest[63]	*Getilgt:* Const. apost. 8, 22, 3–4	

Hinsichtlich der Ordinationsliturgie verließ der Epitomator, wie sich zeigt, seine Vorlage (Const. apost. 8, 4f. 16–28. 30f) in der Hauptsache zwei Mal: (1) Für das Weihegebet des Bischofs übernimmt er nicht den von den Apostolischen Konstitutionen gebotenen Text, sondern greift auf eine ihm vorliegende griechische Version des Formulars der Traditio apostolica zurück. Ferner untersagt er

57 Epit. Const. apost. VIII B 4 (5), 1–4 (2, 78f FUNK).
58 Ebd. B 6, 1–2 (2, 79f).
59 SCHWARTZ, Kirchenordnungen (wie Anm. 24) 254 mit Anm. 1.
60 Epit. Const. apost. VIII B 8 (18), 1–3 (2, 80 FUNK).
61 Ebd. B 10, 1–2 (20), 1–2 (2, 81).
62 Ebd. B 12, 1–2 (2, 81f).
63 Ebd. B 13 (22) (2, 82); vgl. SCHWARTZ, Kirchenordnungen (wie Anm. 24) 256–258.

(2) beim Lektor — nach dem Muster von Trad. apost. 11 — den sakramentlichen Ritus der Handauflegung und tilgt im Zuge dessen das zugehörige Ordinationsgebet.

Das *Testamentum Domini nostri Jesu Christi*[64] (CPG 1743) gilt gemeinhin als »die späteste Kirchenordnung überhaupt«[65]. Die Schrift, ein weiterer fleissiger Verwerter der Traditio apostolica, entstand im griechischen Original wohl im frühen oder fortgeschrittenen fünften Jahrhundert, nach Einschätzung mancher noch im späten vierten Jahrhundert.[66] Hinsichtlich ihrer Heimat gibt man heute gewöhnlich Syria den Vorzug gegenüber Ägypten oder Kleinasien. Michael Kohlbacher sucht sie in Palaestina[67]. In Griechisch haben sich vom Testamentum Domini nur Fragmente erhalten. In das Syrische wurde die Kirchenordnung im Jahre 686/87 durch Jakob von Edessa (ca. 633–708) übersetzt und dem syrischen Octateuchus Clementinus eingefügt[68]. Erhalten sind ferner eine äthiopische sowie mehrere arabische Übersetzungen. Zumindest in Teilen erfolgte eine Übertragung des Werkes auch in das Koptische und in das Georgische, in beiden Fällen ab dem 10. Jahrhundert greifbar[69]. Die Ordinationsgebete:

Amt	**Gebete**	**Quellen**	**Liturg. Rezeption**
Bischof	Deus, qui omnia in vitute fecisti et fermasti ...[70]	Trad. apost. 3; vgl. Const. apost. 8, 5	➢ jacobPatriarch ➢ maronPatriarch

[64] Benutzte Ausgabe: Ignatius Ephraem II. RAHMANI, Testamentum Domini Nostri Jesu Christi, Mainz 1899, = Rezension S² (Teil des Octateuchus Clementinus) bei René-Georges COQUIN, Le Testamentum Domini. Problèmes de tradition textuelle, in: Parole de l'Orient 5 (1974) 165–188. Zur Überlieferung des Werkes und zu seinen Ausgaben vgl. Tinatin CHRONZ – Heinzgerd BRAKMANN, Fragmente des *Testamentum Domini* in georgischer Übersetzung, in: Zeitschrift für Antikes Christentum 13 (2009) 395–402, bes. 395–397; KAUFHOLD, Sources of Canon Law (wie Anm. 24) 242 u. ö.

[65] STEIMER, Vertex (wie Anm. 24) 100. Zu den jüngeren »Canones des Basileios« vgl. unten Anm. 77.

[66] Ältester handschriftlicher Belege ist das jüngst identifizierte Fragment in Cambridge, das für das letzte Viertel des 5. Jahrhundert bespruch wird: Simon CORCORAN – Benet SALWAY, The Newly Identified Greek Fragment of the *Testamentum Domini*, in: JThS NS 62 (2011) 118–135.

[67] Michael KOHLBACHER, Wessen Kirche ordnete das Testamentum Domini Nostri Jesu Christi? Anmerkungen zum historischen Kontext von CPG 1743, in: Martin TAMCKE – Andreas HEINZ (Hgg.), Zu Geschichte, Theologie, Liturgie und Gegenwartslage der syrischen Kirchen (Studien zur Orientalischen Kirchengeschichte 9), Münster i. W. 2000, 55–137.

[68] Herman G. B. TEULE, Jacob of Edessa and Canon Law, in: Bas TER HAAR ROMENEY (Hg.), Jacob of Edessa and the Syriac Culture of His Day (Monographs of the Peshịtta Institute 18), Leiden – Boston 2008, 83–100, bes. 84–86.

[69] Georgisch: CHRONZ – BRAKMANN (wie Anm. 64) 399: Cod. Sinait. iber. 12/O, 10. Jh.; zur Überlieferung in koptischer Sprache ebd. 396: ab 926/27 nC.; das ebd. erwähnte sahidische Euchologion »Z 100« (= MONB.VE im Corpus dei Manoscritti Copti Letterari) wird jetzt um das Jahr 990 datiert; vgl. Alin SUCIU, À propos de la datation du manuscrit contenant le Grand Euchologe du Monastère Blanc, in: Vigiliae Christianae 65 (2011) 189–198.

[70] Test. Dom. 1, 21 (29–31 RAHMANI), engl. Übers. James COOPER – A. J. MACLEAN, The Testament of Our Lord, Edinburgh 1902, 65–67.

			➤ iberCatholic–1 ➤ coptPatriarch/Metrop
Presbyter	Deus Pater Domini nostri Jesu Christi, qui es ineffabilis ...[71]		➤ iberPresb–2
Diakon	Deus, qui omnia creasti, et per verbum ornasti ...[72]		➤ iberDiac–2
Diakonin[73]	vacat	o	o
Vidua	Deus sancte excelse, qui humilia respicis ...[74]		

Der vorstehende Überblick gestattet eine erste Feststellung: Die Traditio apostolica wird in der etablierten Ordinationsliturgie der östlichen Kirchen nirgendwo direkt genutzt, wohl aber zwei ihrer Derivate, die Apostolischen Konstitutionen und das Testamentum Domini. Dabei wurden die Ordinationsgebete der Konstitutionen, wie sich unten zeigen wird, im alexandrinischen Patriarchat der Kopten in einer besonderen Form rezipiert, in byzantinische Euchologien in nur begrenztem Umfang aufgenommen. Aus dem Testamentum Domini schöpfen das antiochenisch–syrische und das koptische Patriarchat. Beide erheben jedoch nur die Texte zur Bischofsweihe und wenden sie allein bei der Ordination zu höchsten Kirchenämter an. In breiterem Umfang, für alle Ordines maiores, greift allein das chalcedonensische Katholikat von Mzcheta in Georgien auf das Ordinale des Testamentum zurück[75].

In unserem Zusammenhang nicht übersehen werden sollte der Umstand, dass die Ordinationsgebete der frühchristlichen Kirchenordnungen — bis in die Neuzeit wahrgenommen als neben–kanonische apostolische Texte — nicht die einzigen aus der Spätantike erhaltenen christlichen Gebete zur Bestellung kirchlicher Amtsträger bilden. Literarisch überliefert sind eine Gebetsserie, die das — mit eigenen Problemen behaftetete — Serapion–Euchologion (4. Jh.) enthält[76], und ein einzelnes Formular für die Bischofsweihe in den »Canones des Basi-

71 1, 30 (69–71 R.); vgl. COOPER – MACLEAN (wie Anm. 70) 91f.

72 1, 38 (93 R.); vgl. COOPER – MACLEAN (wie Anm. 70) 104f.

73 Das Amt der Diakonin ist dem Testamentum Domini bekannt, doch über ihre Ordination »nullum fit verbum«: RAHMANI, Testamentum (wie Anm. 64) 165; vgl. Aimé-Georges MARTIMORT, Les diaconesses. Essai historique (BEL.S 24), Roma 1982, 45f.

74 Test. Dom. 1, 41 (98f R.).

75 Im »Alt-Georgischen Archieratikon« bilden innerhalb der in diesem versammelten Ordinationsgebete die Übernahmen aus dem Testamentum Domini eine geschlossene Schicht; vgl. Heinzgerd BRAKMANN, Die altkirchlichen Ordinationsgebete Jerusalems. Mit liturgiegeschichtlichen Beobachtungen zur christlichen Euchologie in Palaestina, Syria, Iberia und im Sasanidenreich, in: JAC 47 (2004 [2006]) 108–127.

76 Maxwell E. JOHNSON, The Prayers of Sarapion of Thmuis (OCA 249), Roma 1995, 58. 60.

leios«[77] (5. Jh.?). Bei solchen Texten ist nicht gesichert, dass sie in der Spätantike, in engen Grenzen oder in größerem Umfang, Teil lebendiger Liturgie gewesen sind. Unmittelbar spätantikem Gottesdienst, somit der Periode der Kirchenordnungen, entstammen hingegen nicht wenige jener anonymen Orationen zur Bestellung kirchlicher Amtsträger, die innerhalb der Hauptkirchen der Christenheit, u. a. Rom und Konstantinopel, bis zur Gegenwart praktische Verwendung finden[78]. Folglich ist stets die Möglichkeit zu berücksichtigen, dass in lebendiger Liturgie späterer Zeit begegnende Orationen aus pseudapostolischer Literatur ihren Platz auch als Konkurrenten, Partner und sogar Nachfolger der vor Ort traditionell gepflegten Gebetsformulare erlangt haben können.

2. TEIL

2.1 PATRIARCHAT KONSTANTINOPEL – AUTOKEPHALE KIRCHE VON ZYPERN

In Euchologien der byzantinischen Kirchen ist die Übernahme von Orationen aus frühchristlichen Kirchenordnungen einerseits nicht wirklich »tutt'altro que sporadica«[79], doch andererseits in der Tat nicht zur Gänze unbekannt. Soweit bisher zu sehen, begegnen Übernahmen vor allem in Euchologion–Exemplaren aus dem griechischen Süditalien (mit möglichem nahöstlichen Hintergrund). Gleich mehrfach nachgewiesen, auch im palästinischen Sinait. gr. 959 (11. Jh.), ist das Vorkommen des Gebets zur Darbringung der Erstlingsfrüchte aus Trad. apost. 31 (76 BOTTE) parr. Const. apost 8, 40, 2–4 (SC 336, 254) und Test.

[77] RIEDEL, Die Kirchenrechtsquellen (wie Anm. 31) 260f. Zu den koptisch-arabischen Pseudo–Basileios–Kanones vgl. KAUFHOLD, Sources of Canon Law (wie Anm. 24) 275f. (Lit.); hiesige Datierung nach John WORDSWORTH, The 106 Canons of Basil, an Egyptian Church Order, probably of the fifth century, in: DERS., The Ministry of Grace. London ²1903, 445-461. Eine bisher unbekannte koptische Handschrift (Papyrus, 7./8. Jh.) der »Canones des Basileios« wurde 2005 in al-Qurna (am Nil gegenüber von Luxor) aufgefunden: Tomasz GÓRECKI, Sheikh Abd el-Gurna (Hermitage in Tomb 1152). Preliminary report, 2005, in: Polish Archaeology in the Mediterranean 17 (2007) 263–274, hier 266–271 mit Fig. 5. 7; Daria KORDOWSKA, Conservation Work on Three Coptic Manuscripts from Sheikh Abd el-Gurna, ebd. 18 (2008) 311–315, hier 314 mit Fig. 4.

[78] Übersichten: Jean Michel HANSSENS, Les oraisons sacramentelles des ordinations orientales [1952], in: DERS., La Liturgie d'Hippolyte. Documents et études, Roma 1970, 263–285; Pierre–Marie GY, La théologie des prières anciennes pour l'ordination des évêques et des prêtres, in: Revue des Sciences Philosophiques et Théologiques 58 (1974) 599–617; resümiert und weitergeführt durch DERS., Les anciennes prières d'ordination, in: MD 138 (1979) 93–122 = DERS., Ancient ordination prayers, in: StLi 13 (1979) 70–93 ≈ D. BAKAROS, Οἱ εὐχές τῆς Χειροτονίας, in: Gregorios ho Palamas 71 (1988) 463–479 und BRADSHAW (wie Anm. 96).

[79] Stefano PARENTI – Elena VELKOVSKA, L'Eucologio Barberini gr. 336. Seconda edizione riveduta (BEL.S 80), Roma 2000, 31.

Dom. 2, 16 (138 RAHMANI)[80]. Ferner begegnen in italo-griechischen Euchologien Const. apost. 8, 29, 3 (232) als »Gebet des Apostels Matthaios« zur Segnung von Öl und Honig[81], Const. apost. 8, 41, 4f (256–258) als ein Gebet für Verstorbene[82] sowie ein Exorzismusgebet aus Test. Dom. 2, 7 (120 R.) im Euchologion Barb. gr. 329 (12. Jh., Kalabrien[83]) und in der Sammel-Handschrift Sinait. gr. 531 (15. Jh.)[84]. Die anzutreffenden Formulare — keines von ihnen, wie man sieht, hochrangigen Zwecken zugedacht — wirken insgesamt wie einzelne in gottesdienstliche Praxis umgesetzte Lesefrüchte und nicht wie Zeugen einer breiten, systematischen Auswertung der in Kirchenordnungen gefundenen Gebetsliteratur oder gar wie inselförmig aufragende Reste einer ansonsten versunkenen kompletten Pflege dieserart Euchologie in frühchristlicher Zeit.
Das Corpus der byzantinisch–konstantinopolitanischen Ordinationsgebete[85] kommt für gewöhnlich ohne jegliche Anleihe bei der pseudapostolischen Literatur aus. Zudem ist in Konstantinopel, im Unterschied zu anderen östlichen Patriarchaten und Katholikaten, ein Sondergebet für die Bestellung des Ersthierarchen nicht ausgebildet worden[86]. Vereinzelt freilich führen gewisse griechische Euchologien auch Ordinationsgebete aus frühchristlichen Kirchenordnungen an. Gleich im ältesten erhaltenen byzantinischen Euchologion, dem Cod. Barb. gr. 336 (olim III, 55), einer süditalienischen Kopie (8. Jh.?) des mit nahöstlichem Material erweiterten Konstantinopler Patriarchaleuchologions, findet sich am heutigen Ende der Handschrift (fol. 266r–279r), ursprünglich aber wohl an ihrem Anfang, ein Exzerpt aus den Apostolischen Konstitutionen[87] mit den Apostolischen Kanones (65-70. 74-80, hier gezählt als 62-67. 70-80) sowie — unter dem Titel Διατάξεις ἁγίων ἀποστόλῶν μυστικῆς λατρίας — aus den Bestimmungen und Gebeten für die Bestellung der Amtsträger, absteigend vom Bischof bis zum Exorzisten (Const. apost. 8, 4–8, 27; lückenhaft). Der eine wie

80 Richard Hugh CONNOLLY, An ancient prayer in the medieval euchologia, in: JThS 19 (1917/18) 132–137; COOPER – MACLEAN (wie Anm. 70) 231.
81 Giovanni MERCATI, Una benedizione delle Costituzioni Apostoliche in Eucologi medievali, in: DERS., Opere minori 4 (Studi e Testi 79), Città del Vaticano 1939, 143–148.
82 PARENTI – VELKOVSKA (wie Anm. 79) 31f.
83 Zur Handschrift André JACOB, Les euchologes du fonds Barberini grec de la Bibliothèque Vaticane, in: Didaskalia 4 (1974) 150–154, hier 152.
84 Pierre de PUNIET, Art. Baptême, in: DACL 2, 1 (1907) 277; Benoît GAIN, Fragments grecs inédits du Testamentum Domini attribués à Saint Basile, in: Augustinianum 32 (1992) 261–277.
85 Panagiotes N. TREMPELAS, Μικρὸν Εὐχολόγιον. Bd. 1, Ἀθῆναι 1950, 192–256; vgl. Heinzgerd BRAKMANN, Metrophanes von Nyssa und die Ordnungen der byzantinisch-griechischen Bischofsweihe, in: Hairesis [FS Karl Hoheisel] (JAC Erg.-Bd. 34), Münster i. W. 2002, 303–326.
86 Zum Sonderzeremoniell *vor* der Ordination eines Konstantinopler Patriarchen mit Überreichung des Patriarchenstabes durch den Kaiser s. Vitalien LAURENT, Le rituel de l'investiture du patriarche byzantin au début du 15e siècle, in: Académie Roumaine. Bulletin de la section historique 28, 2 (1947) 218–232.
87 Marcel METZGER, in: SC 320, Paris 1985, 68, Handschrift »f«; PARENTI – VELKOVSKA (wie Anm. 79) 25f. 31f.; die von ihnen vorgelegte Edition verzichtet auf fol. 266r–279r des Barb. gr. 336.

der andere Auszug führt an dieser Stelle apostolische Autorität ins Feld, bietet hingegen keine Vorlagen zum unmittelbaren Gebrauch im Gottesdienst. Die genannten Pseudapostolica sind nämlich nicht dem eigentlichen Gebetbuch zugerechnet, weil von dessen originaler Nummerierung ausgeschlossen, und besitzen im Barb. gr. 336 ihr gebrauchsfertiges Gegenstück unter den Nummern 123–134 (§§ 157–168 P./V.)[88], einem byzantinischen Ordinale mit den üblichen konstantinopolitanischen Gebetsformularen. Doch lassen sich einzelne Fälle nicht ausschließen, in denen pseudapostolisches Gebetsgut zur tatsächlichen Verwendung bei Ordinationen aufgegriffen wurde. Ein solches Zeugnis fand Joannes Morinus († 1659) in einem griechischen Kodex der Theatiner–Bibliothek bei S. Andrea della Valle, Rom[89], den jüngst Stefano Parenti als den heutigen Cod. II C 21 der Biblioteca Nazionale di Napoli »Vittorio Emanuele III« identifizieren konnte[90]. In dieser süditalienischen Handschrift des 13. Jahrhundert ist das Ordinale insgesamt ausdrücklich auf »die Tradition der göttlichen Apostel« (κατὰ τὴν θείων ἀποστόλων παράδοσιν) zurückgeführt und sind in dieses die Orationen der Apostolischen Konstitutionen zur Subdiakonen–, Diakonen– u. Presbyterweihe, nicht aber zur Bestellung eines Bischofs, als Zusätze in eine gewöhnliche Konstantinopler Ordinations– und Gebetsordnung eingearbeitet.

Eine wiederum andere Situation läßt sich beobachten mit dem sog. Euchologium Allatianum (Barb. gr. 390; kopiert 1575/80)[91], um hier nur den bekanntesten Vertreter einer insgesamt bemerkenswerten Gruppe von Euchologien aus der autokephalen Kirche von Zypern zu nennen. Hier ist das Ordinale einerseits erkennbar beeinflusst von der Epitome Const. apost. VIII, »da es die Handauflegung nur dem Lektor [...] vorenthält und die Verordnungen über die einzelnen Ordines von dem Subdiakon an aufwärts [...] einzelnen Aposteln in den Mund legt«[92], anderseits umfasst es einer Reihe ungewöhnlicher Orationen zur Bestellung kirchlicher Funktionsträgern, so für Kantor, Lektor[93], Protopresbyter, Oi-

[88] Schematische Übersicht über den Inhalt des Euchologions Barb. gr. 336 mit Angabe der Originalnummerierung seiner einzelnen liturgischen Bestandteile bei PARENTI – VELKOVSKA (wie Anm. 79) 28–31.

[89] Joannes MORINUS, Commentarius de Sacris Ecclesiae Ordinationibus. Ed. nova, Antverpiae 1695, 74–78 mit 103 Anm. d, g und h (»in Constitutionibus Clementis«); Nachdruck: Joseph Aloysius ASSEMANUS, Codex Liturgicus Ecclesiae Universae. Bd. 11 (8 [De ordine], 4), Romæ 1763,166–178 mit Anm. d, g und h ebd. 249; in beiden Fällen ohne Abdruck der pseudapostolischen Gebetstexte.

[90] Stefano PARENTI, Preghiere delle « Costituzioni Apostoliche » in alcuni eucologi italo–greci del medioevo, in: EL 113 (1990) 47–52, Zweitauflage in: DERS., A oriente e occidente di Costantinopoli (Monumenta Studia Instrumenta Liturgica 54), Città del Vaticano 2010, 149–154, mit Textauszügen.

[91] Zur Handschrift JACOB, Les euchologes (wie Anm. 83) 169–173; weitere Literatur bei Gregorios A. IOANNIDES, La Constitutio o Bulla Cypria Alexandri Papae IV del Barberinianus graecus 390, in: OCP 66 (2000) 349_{71}.

[92] Franz Xaver FUNK, Das Testament unseres Herrn und die verwandten Schriften (Forschungen zur Christlichen Litteratur– und Dogmengeschichte 2, 1–2), Mainz 1901, 39.

[93] Die für die Bestellung eines Anagnosten verwendete Oration Εὐλογητὸς εἶ Κύριε [...] ὁ ἀποστείλας τὸν Ἀβραὰμ ... (TREMPELAS, Μικρὸν Εὐχολόγιον [wie Anm. 85] 244) rezi-

konomos und Archidiakon. Keines dieser extravaganten Gebete entstammt, soweit zu sehen, dem euchologischen Reservoir der altchristlichen Kirchenordnungen[94].

2.2 ORIENTALISCHE KIRCHEN

2.2.1 Westsyrische Liturgien

Das westsyrisch–antiochenische Ordinale[95] der ›Jakobiten‹ und der Maroniten tritt in drei zeremoniell wie euchologisch miteinander verwandten Hauptformen auf:
(1) Die durch Patriarch Michael I. d. Gr. († 1199) gestaltete Rezension des syrisch-orthodoxen Patriarchats für die Ordinationen im immediaten Jurisdiktionsbereich[96], vertreten u. a. durch die Handschriften Paris. syr. 113 (1166/70 ?; Autograph Michaels ?), Vat. syr. 51 (1188/89; olim Ecchellensis 4[97]) sowie

piert die apokryphe *Historia de Melchisedech*; nachzutragen bei Görge K. HASSELHOFF, Art. Melchisedech, in: Reallexikon für Antike und Christentum 24 (2011) 624f.

94 Texte: MORINUS, Commentarius (wie Anm. 89) 85–102; TREMPELAS, Μικρὸν Εὐχολόγιον (wie Anm. 85) 243f. 254–256 (mit falscher Datierung des Allatianon auf AD 1260: ebd. 243); Gregorios A. IOANNIDES, « Τάξις ἐπὶ προχειρίσεως πρωτοπρεσβυτέρου, μεγάλου οἰκονόμου καὶ ἀρχιδιάκονου » στὸ κυπριακὸ εὐχολόγιο *Barberini greco 390*, in: Ὑψίστου κλῆσις. Ἀναμνηστικὸς τόμος ἐπὶ τῇ συμπληρώσει πεντήκοντα ἐτῶν ἀπὸ τῆς ἱδρύσεως τῆς Ἱερατικῆς Σχολῆς « Ἀπόστολος Βαρνάβας », Λευκωσία 2003, 53–72.

95 Das vor-byzantinische Ordinale der Chalcedonenser des Patriarchats Antiochien ist noch unerforscht. Für jüngere Ausgestaltungen vgl. Hanna GHONEIM, Ein Bischofsweiheritus in der melkitischen Kirche nach einem Dokument aus dem 15. Jahrhundert, in: Parole de l'Orient 34 (2009) 361–411.

96 Zu den Handschriften der Pontifikale–Rezension Michaels d. Gr. siehe Hermann ZOTENBERG, Catalogue des manuscrits syriaques et sabéens (mandaïtes) de la Bibliothèque Nationale, Paris 1874) 72–76 und besonders Hubert KAUFHOLD, Über Datum und Schreiber der Handschrift Vaticanus Syriacus 51, in: Aram Periodical 5 (1993 [1996]) 267–275. Zugängliche Texte: (1) Paris. syr. 112 (Lektor bis Bischof) in Eusèbe Renaudots Latein bei Henricus DENZINGER, Ritus Orientalium Coptorum Syrorum et Armenorum in administrandis sacramentis 2, Wiceburgi 1864, 78–108, bes. 82–100; (2) Vat. syr. 51 in J. A. ASSEMANIS ungedruckt gebliebener Übersetzung (Borg. lat. 166) des Borg. syr. 57, einer Kopie des Vat. syr. 51, bei [I.- M. VOSTÉ], Pontificale iuxta ritum Ecclesiae Syrorum Occidentalium id est Antiochiae. Versio Latina. Bd. 2: Continens chirotonias sacerdotales usque ad patriarchatum inclusive, Typis polyglott. Vat. 1941 (nicht im Buchhandel), 167–241, danach in Auswahl bei Paul F. BRADSHAW, Ordination Rites of the Ancient Churches of East and West, New York 1990,174–187; (3) französische Übersetzung aus dem (nicht veränderungsfreien) gottesdienstlichen Pontifikale–Druck für syrisch–*katholische* Bischöfe (Ktaba d-ṭekse kumraye) von 1950/52 bei Bernard DE SMET, Le rituel du sacre des évêques et des patriarches dans l'église syrienne d'Antioche. in: OrSyr 8 (1963) 165–212 mit nützlicher Einführung durch Gabriel KHOURI–SARKIS ebd. 137–164. Angesichts der Bedeutung des Pontifikales Michaels d. Gr. überrascht das Fehlen einer wissenschaftlichen Ausgabe.

97 Giuseppe Simone ASSEMANI, Bibliotheca Orientalis Clementino-Vaticana 1. De Scriptoribus Syris Orthodoxis, Romae 1719, 573f.

Paris. syr. 112 (1238/39; Renaudots »Codex Florentinus [Jacobiticus]«, illuminiert)[98].
(2) die Rezension des den Ostteil der syrisch–orthodoxen Kirche umfassenden Maphrianats[99] (»Ritus von Tagrit«, »Eastern Rite«[100]), vertreten u. a. durch Paris. syr. 110 u. 114, beide 15. Jh.[101], Oxon. Bodl. Hunt. 444 v.J. 1493[102], alle drei ohne Bischofsweihe, sowie die verlorenen handschriftlichen Vorlagen syrischer Texte im »Commentarius de sacris Ecclesiae Ordinationibus« (1655) des Joannes Morinus († 1659)[103].
(3) das Pontifikale der Kirche der Maroniten[104], ihrem Patriarchen Stephan ad–Duwaihī (1670–1704) zufolge ehedem organisiert in zwei Teilen, einem ersten für die Hand des Bischofs und einem zweiten für die Zwecke der Diakone. Ein derartiges Diakonale liegt der syrisch–lateinischen Ausgabe des Joannes Morinus zugrunde[105]. Den episkopalen Teil vertritt u. a. der 1505 kopierte Paris. syr.

[98] Näheres zum Ordinale des Paris. syr. 112 bei R. GRAFFIN, Ordination du prêtre dans le rite jacobite, in: Revue de l'Orient Chrétien 1, 2 (1896) 1–36.
[99] Monographisch behandelt diese Rezension René MOURET, Le rituel syrien d'ordination de Jean Morin (1655), Diss. (masch.) Paris-Sorbonne (1990). Näheres zu den in Europa verwahrten Handschriften beider Rezensionen des syrisch–orthodoxen Pontifikale ebd. 79–93. Der für die »Patrologia Orientalis« angekündigte Druck der Monographie Mourets (BRADSHAW [wie Anm. 96] 255_{41}) ist bis heute nicht erschienen, wohl aber eine Art Resümee: René MOURET, Un rituel d'ordination de Tagrit, in: Rituels [FS Pierre–Marie Gy], Paris 1990, 417–422. Dem verstorbenen französischen Kollegen danke ich ergebenst für freundliche Überlassung eines Exemplars seiner Dissertation.
[100] Ignatius Aphram I. BARSOUM, The Scattered Pearls. A History of Syriac Literature and Sciences. 2nd rev. ed. (Piscataway 2003) 73–75. 88f; ein Pontificale »according to the Eastern Rite« ebd. 111: Jerusalem, St. Mark's Convent, Ms. 109 v.J. 1300.
[101] Zu den Pariser Kodizes ZOTENBERG, Catalogue (wie Anm. 96) 67–69. 76f.
[102] Zur Handschrift Robert PAYNE SMITH, Codices Syriacos, Carshunicos, Mendaeos (Catalogi codicum manuscriptorum Bibliothecae Boleianae 6), Oxonii 1864, 240–248.
[103] MORINUS, Commentarius (wie Anm. 89) 406–416, Nachdruck: DENZINGER, Ritus Orientalium (wie Anm. 96) 2, 67–76, mit Einschüben.
[104] Zu Pontifikale und Ordinale der Maroniten vgl. Pierre CHÉBLI, Le livre maronite de la chirotonie ou de l'imposition des mains du Patriarche Douayhi [1899], in: Youakim MOUBARAC (Hg.), Pentalogie antiochienne / domaine maronite. Bd. 4, Beyrouth 1984, 321–330; Pierre DIB, Étude sur la liturgie maronite, Paris 1919, 169–224. Weitere Arbeiten sind ungedruckt: Maschinenschriftlich liegen bei der vatikanischen Ostkirchenkongregation (AZ: 916/1948) eine Studie (Du Pontifical Maronite, 1947, LXVIII, 205 S.) und eine lateinische Übersetzung (Pontifical Maronite, 1948) des maronitischen Liturgikers Michel AR-RAJJI, beides Aktenstücke eines gescheiterten Reformprojektes. Ebenso unveröffentlicht ist Joseph MERHEJ, Jalons pour l'histoire du Pontifical maronite, Diss. Paris: Institut Catholique (1975). Aus den genannten Studien sowie dem Manuskript »Étude de la Chirotonie Maronite« von Ibrahim Harfouche (»dans la bibliothèque des Missionnaires Libanais«) schöpft die e-Publikation Nasser GEMAYEL, Patriarche Estephan Douaïhy: vie et œuvres. 2ème Edition, Beyrouth 2004, Abschnitt: »Le Livre de la Chirotonie« (unpaginiert).
[105] MORINUS, Commentarius (wie Anm. 89) 314–363 (Bischofsweihe 349–352, Patriarchenweihe 352–363) nach einem Codex des Maroniten Abraham Ecchellensis (Ibrahim al-aqilani, 1640–1653 in Paris, † 1663 in Rom). Zur Gattung der Quelle vgl. DENZINGER, Ritus Orientalium (wie Anm. 96) 2, 108: kein Pontifikale, »sed librum ministerii diaconici episcopi ordinantis«.

120 (»Codex Seguerianus Maroniticus«)[106]. Das reformierte Maroniten–Pontifikale des Stephan ad-Duwaihī (1683) publizierte Joseph Aloysius Assemani († 1782) in seinem »Codex Liturgicus Ecclesiae Universae« indirekt aus der für den — unterbliebenen — Erstdruck vorgesehenen Vorlage Vat. syr. 311 (ab 1685/95 in Rom) *via* dessen Kopie Rom, Bibliothek des Ordo Maronita BMV, Cod. 75 (I) v.J. 1728 mit eigener lateinischer Übersetzung[107].
Der jetzige Stand der Edition von Zeugen der westsyrischen Pontifikalien gestattet keine textgeschichtlichen Feinuntersuchungen, reicht aber für die hier nötige Erhebung des von jenen verbreiteten Bestandes an Orationsformularen. Entlehnungen von Ordinationsgebeten aus altchristlichen Kirchenordnungen sind im Raum der westsyrischen Liturgien bislang, von einer Ausnahme abgesehen, allein bei der Bestellung der höchsten Kirchenoberhäupter, der Patriarchen, nachgewiesen. Michael Kohlbacher hat ihr jüngst neuerliche Aufmerksamkeit zugewandt[108]. Doch bleibt einiges zu verdeutlichen. Zu betrachten sind die folgenden drei liturgischen Texte, die sowohl bei den Syrisch–Orthodoxen[109] wie bei den Maroniten[110] auftreten (von B und C sind auch die unten genannten koptischen Parallelen bekannt[111]):

	Rubrizierung	**Gebet**	**Quelle**
A	*precatio invocationis Spiritus Sancti*:	Deus, qui virtute tua omnia coelestia fecisti et orbem fundasti voluntate Unigeniti tui ...	Anfangsabschnitt vielleicht aus dem syrischen Testamentum Domini[112]
B	*alia oratio invocationis Spiritus Sancti, quae est Clementis* ...:	Imponimus manus nostras ...	Oct. Clem. syr.: Test. Dom. 1, 21 (28f RAHMANI)[113]
C	*invocatio ordinationis*	Deus, qui omnia in virtute	Oct. Clem. syr.: Test. Dom.

[106] ZOTENBERG, Catalogue (wie Anm. 96) 79f: Vorlage der Übersetzung Eusèbe Renaudots (Psaltes bis Periodeutes), veröffentlicht bei DENZINGER, Ritus Orientalium (wie Anm. 96) 2, 108–186.
[107] Joseph Aloysius ASSEMANUS, Codex liturgicus ecclesiae universae in XV libros distributus; in quo continentur libri rituales, missales, pontificales, officia, dypticha &c. Ecclesiarum Occidentis, & Orientis. Bd. 9 u. 10 (*alias* 8 [De ordine], 2 u. 3, so hier gezählt), Romæ 1756/58.
[108] Michael KOHLBACHER, Georgische Paralleltexte zum Testament unseres Herrn Jesus Christus (CPG 1743), in: Rainer VOGT (Hg.), Akten des 5. Symposiums zur Sprache, Geschichte, Theologie und Gegenwartslage der syrischen Kirchen (V. Deutsche Syrologentagung), Berlin 14.–15. Juli 2006 (Semitica and Semitohamitica Berolinensia 9), Aachen 2010, 97–126, bes. 119–126.
[109] VOSTÉ, Pontificale (wie Anm. 96) 2, 231–234, »Imponimus ...« in margine; DE SMET, Le rituel (wie Anm. 96) 202.
[110] ASSEMANUS, Codex liturgicus (wie Anm. 107) 8, 3, 102–104 (mit syrischem Text); DENZINGER, Ritus Orientalium (wie Anm. 96) 2, 219–221.
[111] Vgl. unten zu Anm. 175, 181 und 181.
[112] KOHLBACHER, Georg. Paralleltexte (wie Anm. 108) 122 mit Synopse ebd. 126.
[113] COOPER – MACLEAN (wie Anm. 70) 156: »The declaration seems to be the work of the Test. Compiler himself«.

	sanctissimae:	fecisti et firmasti ac fundasti conceptu mentis orbem habitabilem ...	1, 21 (28–31 RAHMANI)

Text A, Kohlbachers »Gebet zur Geist–Anrufung«, ist das traditionelle Ordinationsgebet der syrisch-orthodoxen Kirche für die Weihe aller bischöflichen Amtsträger, auch, aber nicht allein des Patriarchen[114]. Nähere Verwandschaft mit bekannten Orationen nichtsyrischer Kirchen und Traditionen bestehen offensichtlich nicht[115]. Doch findet sich eine abweichende Rezension des Textes unter den nicht wenigen Ordinationsgebeten, die der maronitische Ritus — »surabondant comme a son ordinaire« — für seinen Ordo der Bischofsweihe eingesammelt hat: »Potestate verbi tui, Domine deus, qui omnia clementia tua fecisti, et fundasti orbem voluntate Unigeniti tui ...« [116]. Wenn unter diesen Umständen das Gebet in seiner Rezension A ausgerechnet bei der Bestellung des maronitischen Patriarchen, und nur bei dieser, auftritt[117], wird dies liturgiegeschichtlich besagen, dass sich die Maroniten bei diesem Anlass — wie auch sonst nicht selten — am Vorbild der syrisch–orthodoxen Schwesterkirche auszurichten suchten.

Text B, von Kohlbacher »Gebet zur Handauflegung« genannt, und Gebet C (»das eigentliche Bischofsweihe-Gebet«) sind *en bloc* aus dem syrischen Oktateuch herübergenommen, genauer aus dem Testamentum Domini, wo sie in gleicher Zusammenstellung und Abfolge zu lesen sind[118]. Text B bildet freilich kein Gebet im eigentlichen Sinn, sondern die Begleitformel (»declaration«) zur Handauflegung der ordinierenden Bischöfe. Der Trabant »Imponimus ...« (B) der Oration C fehlt im modernen syrisch-katholischen Pontifikale[119], vielleicht, um bei einer Patriarchenbestellung heutiger Art den Anschein erneuter Weihe eines bereits ordinierten Bischofs zu vermeiden.

Text C, das Bischofsweihegebet des Testamentum Domini »avec quelques amplifications«[120], gehört zum euchologischen Proprium bei der Amtsein-

[114] DENZINGER, Ritus Orientalium (wie Anm. 96) 2, 97 (nach Paris. syr. 113); BRADSHAW (wie Anm. 96) 183f (nach Vat. syr. 51); DENZINGER, Ritus Orientalium 2, 219; DE SMET, Le rituel (wie Anm. 96) 202; vgl. HANSSENS, Les oraisons (wie Anm. 78) 265. Das Pontifikale Michaels d. Gr. enthält jeweils einen gemeinsamen Ordo für (a) die »Chirotonia patriarchae et metropolitae et episcopi« (VOSTÉ, Pontificale [wie Anm. 96] 2, 209–241) und (b) ihre Inthronisierung (ebd. 245-250).

[115] BRADSHAW (wie Anm. 96) 243.

[116] HANSSENS, Les oraisons (wie Anm. 78) 280f. Vgl. DENZINGER, Ritus Orientalium (wie Anm. 96) 2, 198 mit ebd. 219. DIB, Étude (wie Anm. 104) 210 nennt diese Oration »la grande formule consécratoire«, das bei der Patriarchenordination verwendete Gebet A entspricht jener »avec quelques modifications«.

[117] ASSEMANUS, Codex liturgicus (wie Anm. 107) 8, 3, 105–109 (mit syr. Text).

[118] Testamentum Domini 1, 21, 2. 4 (28–33 RAHMANI) = DENZINGER, Ritus Orientalium (wie Anm. 96) 2, 220. Es ist somit nicht so, wie DREWS, Rez. Rahmani (wie Anm. 175) 155 meinte, dass das Testamentum Domini »in Syrien [...] keinerlei liturgische Spuren hinterlassen« hätte.

[119] DE SMET, Le rituel (wie Anm. 96) 202.

[120] LANNE, Les ordinations (wie Anm. 53) 86.

setzung eines syrisch-orthodoxen Patriarchen (und seines maronitischen Kollegen)[121]. Bei der hochrangigen gottesdienstlichen Gelegenheit der Bestellung eines Kirchenoberhauptes finden demnach zwei ihrem Ursprung nach veritable Bischofsweihegebete Verwendung.

Doch unterscheiden sich beide, zumindest in der uns bekannten Endgestalt des Ordos, sowohl im Gebrauch wie in der Bedeutung. Oration C bildet hier einen Zusatztext zu A, dem eigentlichen Bischofsweihegebet auch für einen erwählten Patriarchen. Die unterschiedliche Bewertung beider Gebete ist dem Umstand zu entnehmen, dass nach einheimischem Kirchen– und Liturgierecht die Oration A bei der Bestellung eines Patriarchen nur dann Verwendung findet, wenn der Electus den Weihegrad eines Presbyters innehat, hingegen entfällt, falls ein ordinierter Bischof auf den Patriarchenstuhl erhoben wird[122]. Anderseits werden bei der Patriarchenordination B und C immer benutzt. Das Bischofsweihegebet des Testamentum Domini (C) ist nunmehr also zum euchologischen Distinctivum des antiochenischen Patriarchen geworden, und zwar nicht im Sinne einer amtsbezogenen Alternative zum Ordinationsgebet sonstiger Bischöfe (= A), sondern als Hinzufügung zu diesem, falls eine bischöfliche Ordination des Erwählten ansteht, bzw. ohne das Gebet A, falls sich eine Bischofsweihe erübrigt bzw. verbietet, weil der neue Patriarch aus den Reihen der bereits ordinierten Bischöfe erwählt wurde. C ist gleichwohl kein Text nebensächlicher Bedeutung. Er »macht« keinen Bischof, aber einen solchen zum Patriarchen. Mit diesem Gebet promoviert die Kirche den Erwählten zu ihrem irdischen Oberhaupt, indem sie durch das Kollegium der Bischöfe mit allem nötigen Ernst Gott um seinen Beistand für den neuen Patriarchen und seine Amtsführung bittet. Wenn die Liturgiker des Patriarchats ausgerechnet für diesen Zweck auf ein, wie man damals meinte, apostolisches Gebetsformular zurückgriffen, darf dahinter Absicht vermutet werden, nämlich die Einbindung der Verfasser jenes ehrwürdigen Textes in das Bitten der gegenwärtigen Kirche.

Die Übertragung von Ordinationstexten aus dem 686/87 erstmals in das Syrische übersetzten Testamentum Domini in den syrisch–orthodoxen Patriarchalgottesdienst lässt sich bislang nicht genau datieren. Ihre Benutzung steht jedenfalls nicht, wie Kleinheyer meinte[123], »in ununterbrochener Tradition«, sondern

[121] Syrisch-orthodox: VOSTÉ, Pontificale (wie Anm. 96) 2, 233; syrisch-katholisch: DE SMET, Le rituel (wie Anm. 96) 202–205; maronitisch: ASSEMANUS, Codex liturgicus (wie Anm. 107) 8, 3, 105; DENZINGER, Ritus Orientalium (wie Anm. 96) 2, 220f.

[122] Ecclesiae Antiochenae Syrorum Nomocanon a Gregorio Abulpharagio Bar-Hebraeo syriace compositus et a Iosepho Aloysio Assemano in latinam linguam conversus, in: Angelo MAI (Hg.), Scriptorum veterum nova collectio e Vaticanis codicibus edita 10, 2 (Romae 1838) 44f. Translationen ordinierter Bischöfe auf den Patriarchenstuhl begegnen in der Geschichte der syrisch–orthodoxen Kirche früh und wiederholt; vgl. Wolfgang HAGE, Die syrisch–jakobitische Kirche in frühislamischer Zeit, Wiesbaden 1966, 13; Peter KAWERAU, Die jakobitische Kirche im Zeitalter der syrischen Renaissance. Zweite erg. Aufl. (Berliner Byzantinistische Arbeiten 3), Berlin 1960, 16; SELB, Kirchenrecht (wie Anm. 24) 216.

[123] Vgl. oben Anm. 22.

bildet eine Neuerung unter Rückgriff auf ›archivierte‹ Gebetsliteratur, wobei schon die Einführung einer gegenüber dem Ritus der gewöhnlichen Bischofsweihe abgesetzten Gestalt der Patriarchenbestellung selbst eine Innovation darstellt. Zwar wurden in patristischer Zeit an den Sitzen der Oberbischöfe eigene Ordnungen für deren Weihe ausgebildet, die man mehr oder minder unverändert auch für die Ordination von Suffraganen benutzte, doch scheint man generell nicht vor dem 8./9. Jahrhundert auf einem unverkennbaren Sonderritual für die Bestellung des regionalen Ersthierarchen bestanden zu haben[124]. Bekannt ist, dass um 800 n. Chr. im antiochenisch–syrischen Raum das Problem diskutiert wurde, warum eine Kirche, die das Testamentum Domini als authentische Aufzeichnung des Willens Jesu Christi ansehe, dessen Gebete in ihrer eigenen Liturgie nicht verwende. Der damalige syrisch-orthodoxe Patriarch Kyriakos aus Tagrit (793–817) bestreitet dieses Faktum gar nicht, sondern verteidigt es mit dem Argument der wenngleich nicht wörtlichen, so doch inhaltlichen Übereinstimmung der, wie er ausdrücklich bekennt, vom Herrn selbst hinterlassenen Texte mit jenen Gebeten, die man im Gottesdienst vorzutragen pflege[125]. Angesichts dessen wird es vermutlich erst unter einem seiner nächsten oder späteren Nachfolger, jedenfalls nach Ende der Spätantike, zur liturgischen Verwendung der Testamentum–Texte bei der antiochenischen Patriarchenweihe gekommen sein.

Die zu jener Zeit bei den Syrern erfolgte Aufnahme vermeintlich apostolischer Gebetsliteratur in die Patriarchenordination stellt einerseits kaum nur ein verspätetes und teilweises Nachgeben gegenüber den Bedenken oder Wünschen jener dar, denen Patriarch Kyriakos entgegengetreten war, und ist wohl anderseits mehr als absichtslose oder nur dekorative Beigabe zum Textrepertoire einer liturgisch hochwertigen Feier. Im Zeremoniell der Patriarchenweihe ist nämlich zu beobachten, dass der rituelle Vollzug der beiden Textkomplexe A und B+C bemerkenswerte Unterschiede aufweist. Das Ordinationsgebet eines Bischofs (A) wird vom Hauptzelebranten solo und leise gesprochen[126]. Den Begleittext »Imponimus ...« (B) zur gemeinsamen Handauflegung hingegen rezitieren alle mitwirkenden Bischöfe gemeinsam und laut[127]. Die ebenfalls »klementinische« Oration C spricht sodann entweder einer der Bischöfe im

[124] Vgl. Charles RENOUX, L'ordination du catholicos arménien, in: Achille M. TRIACCA – Alessandro PISTOIA (Hgg.), Ordination et ministères. Conférences Saint-Serge. 42e Semaine d'études liturgiques, Paris, 27–30 juin 1995 (BEL.S 85), Roma 1996, 247-274, hier 247f.

[125] Adolf RÜCKER, Das dritte Buch der Mêmrê des Kyriakos von Antiochien und seine Väterzitate, in: OrChr 31 (1934) 114f. Kyriakos verfasste selbst gottesdienstliche Gebete, vgl. K. KAISER, Die syrische »Liturgie« des Kyriakos von Antiochien, ebd. 5 (1905) 174–197.

[126] DENZINGER, Ritus Orientalium (wie Anm. 96) 2, 97: »Patriarcha dicit hanc orationem invocationis Spiritus Sancti secreto«.

[127] Ebd. 2, 97. 219: »omnes episcopi praesentes manus imponunt ei dicentes: ›Imponimus ....‹«.

Auftrag aller Kollegen[128], so dass sie gemeinsam als dessen Beter zu gelten haben, oder alle Bischöfe tun dies gemeinsam[129]. Auf die sinnfällig wahrnehmbare Einheit der ordinierenden Bischöfe kommt es offensichtlich an. Damit werden alle an der Wahl des Patriarchen Beteiligten, Minderheit wie Mehrheit, in das unter Anrufung Gottes gefeierte Geschehen eingebunden, ein Sicherungsmittel, das angesichts des für jede kirchliche Gemeinschaft nicht ungefährlichen Moments der Erlangung eines neuen irdischen Oberhauptes als durchaus plausibel gelten darf[130].

M. Kohlbacher merkt an, dass im hiesigen Kontext »anscheinend noch ein anderes Gebet ›des Clemens‹« auftritt[131]. Von dessen Gebrauch liest man im Nomokanon des Bar Hebraeus[132] (cap. VII. sect. III. directio): »Super patriarcham praecipue dum atollitur evangelium supra caput eius, oratio illa, quae in libro quinto Clementis est, dicitur: qui ostendisti Abraham, et illos reliquos patriarchas, fideles tui placatores, Moysen, et Aaron, et Eleazarum et Phinees«[133]. Die Quelle, der diese Oration entstammt, ist somit ausdrücklich genannt: das 5. Buch des syrischen Octateuchus Clementinus (CPG 1733)[134]. Dessen Benutzung wird durch das in die Anweisung eingewobene Zitat aus dem Gebetstext

[128] DENZINGER, Ritus Orientalium (wie Anm. 96) 2, 220.

[129] Das Pontifikale Michaels d. Gr., z. B. der Vat. syr. 51 (olim Ecchellensis 4), zählt die drei Eigentümlichkeiten der Bestellung eines syrisch–orthodoxen Patriarchen auf, darunter als der zweiten: »invocatio sancti Spiritus, quae tribuitur Clementi [...] et quae super patriarcham tantummodo ab episcopis consecrantibus recitatur«: DENZINGER, Ritus Orientalium (wie Anm. 96) 2, 76; VOSTÉ, Pontificale (wie Anm. 96) 2, 210; maronitische Parallele: ASSEMANUS, Codex liturgicus (wie Anm. 107) 8, 3, 65 (syr.-lat.). Die zwei anderen Propriäteten sind die Wahl durch sämtliche Bischöfe und die gemeinsame Überreichung des Patriarchenstabes, bei der die Hand des Patriarchen über die Hände der Bischöfe gelegt wurde (ebd.; VOSTÉ, Pontificale [wie Anm. 96] 2, 210; SELB, Kirchenrecht [wie Anm. 24] 216; vgl. u. Anm. 182). Vgl. ASSEMANUS, Codex liturgicus (wie Anm. 107) 8, 3, IX: »Tum omnes Episcopi unacum Præside manus capiti Electi impositas, dicunt *Imponimus manus nostras super hunc servum Dei Electum in Spiritu* &c. Et Praeses Synodi & reliqui Episcopi prosequuntur Invocationem Spiritus Sancti, suas adhuc manus super caput Electi impositas tenenetes: *Deus, qui omni in virtute fecisti* &c.«.

[130] Der Bestellung eines syrisch-orthodoxen Patriarchen gingen nicht selten langwierige Meinungsverschiedenheiten der Bischöfe voraus oder es folgten ihr schmerzliche Patriarchalschismen; vgl. HAGE, Die syrisch-jakobitische Kirche (wie Anm. 122) 12; Ilse NABE–VON SCHÖNBERG, Die westsyrische Kirche im Mittelalter (800–1150), Diss. Heidelberg (1976) 6–8; SELB, Kirchenrecht (wie Anm. 24) 214; Dorothea WELTECKE, The Syriac Orthodox in the Principality of Antioch during the Crusader Period, in: Krijnie N. CIGGAAR – Michael METCALF (Hgg.), East and West in the Medieval Eastern Mediterranean. Bd. 1 (OLA 147), Leuven [u.a.] 2006. 103f.

[131] KOHLBACHER, Georg. Paralleltexte (wie Anm. 108) 122.

[132] Gregorius Bar-Hebraeus wurde am 20. Januar 1264 Katholikos (syrisch: Maphrian) des autonom verwalteten Ostteiles des syrisch-orthodoxen Patriarchats Antiochien. In Anwesenheit von Hethum I., dem König von Armenien, wurde er in der Kirche H. Theotokos in Sis (heute: Kozan, Prov. Adana, Türkei) geweiht, konnte aber wegen der politischen Unruhen erst 1266 sein Amt in Tagrit (heute: Tikrit) bzw. Barelli (Bartella) antreten. Vgl. Jean Marie FIEY, Esquisse d'une bibliographie de Bar Hebraeus, in: Parole de l'Orient 13 (1986) 279–312 (Editionen, Literatur); Sebastian BROCK, Art. Gregor ibn al-ʿIbri, in: LThK³ 4 (1995) 1001f.

[133] Ecclesiae Antiochenae Syrorum Nomocanon (wie Anm. 122) 44f.

[134] NAU, La version (wie Anm. 49) 80f.

bestätigt. Mit Kohlbacher darf man somit davon ausgehen, dass hier »das ausführliche Gebet der Apostolischen Konstitutionen«[135]: Ὁ ὤν, δέσποτα Κύριε ὁ Θεός ὁ παντοκράτωρ ... (Const. apost. 8, 5, 1–7), in seiner syrischen Version gemeint ist.

Für den Gebrauch des Formulars Ὁ ὤν, δέσποτα Κύριε ὁ Θεός ὁ παντοκράτωρ als ein Hauptgebet der syrisch-orthodoxen Patriarchenweihe finde ich in den veröffentlichten syrischen Pontifikalien keine unterstützende Bestätigung. Es muss jedoch nicht notwendigerweise ein Versehen des Bar Hebraeus, ab 1264/66 Maphrian des Ostens und in dieser Eigenschaft legitimer Konsekrator des Patriarchen[136], vorliegen. Vielmehr kann seine Nachricht auch eine Bestimmung wiedergeben, die sich in einem konkurrierende Entwurf des Ordos der Patriarchenweihe befand und keine dauerhafte Geltung behielt[137]. In diesem Zusammenhang muss man sich vergegenwärtigen, dass die heute greifbaren Exemplare des Pontifikales nach dem »Ritus von Tagrit«, also des Maphrianats, die Bischofsweihen nicht behandeln[138]. Ausgenommen ist das allenfalls verlorene »breue compendium ... olim ad Congregationem de propaganda fide ex oriente missum«, das allerdings kein bischöfliches Gebetbuch war, sondern eine Art Zeremoniell. Der daraus von Joannes Morinus mit lateinischer Übersetzung veröffentlichte syrische »Ordo chirotoniae episcoporum, metropolitarum et pat-

[135] KOHLBACHER, Georg. Paralleltexte (wie Anm. 104) 122.

[136] Vgl. KAWERAU, Die jakobitische Kirche (wie Anm. 122) 31 mit Anm. 201; SELB, Kirchenrecht (wie Anm. 24) 214–216.

[137] Differenzen im Orationenbestand zwischen der Redaktion Michaels d. Gr. und dem »Ritus von Tagrit« vermeldet MOURET, Le rituel syrien (wie Anm. 99) 35. 37f. Gleich dem Patriarchen besaß der Maphrian das Recht, Bischöfe und Metropoliten zu weihen; KAWERAU, Die jakobitische Kirche (wie Anm. 122) 30. Im Jahr 1189, also zu Lebzeiten Michaels d. Gr., ordinierten die Orientalen selbst einen Maphrian, gegen die Gewohnheit ohne Mitwirkung des Patriarchen; ebd. 28.

[138] Enthalten war der Ordo der Bischofsweihe in Morins »Goensis antiquior«, einem heute verschollenen syrischen Codex, der aus Goa über Lissabon Morin zugänglich geworden war (kurz vor 1655, Erscheinungsjahr des Commentarius de Sacris Ecclesiae Ordinationibus, »jam sub prelo«), den er jedoch, weil »obscurus & deturpatus«, nicht verwerten konnte; MORINUS, Commentarius (wie Anm. 89) 404; MOURET, Le rituel syrien (wie Anm. 99) 11. Erstaunlich ist, dass Morin aus dem südindischen Goa ein Pontifikale des *westsyrischen* Ritus bekam, weil im zeitlichen Umfeld des »Coonan Cross Oath« 1653 noch sämtliche indischen Thomaschristen, auch die Rebellen gegen die Lateiner, den *ostsyrischen* (»chaldäischen«) Ritus pflegten und generell Pontifikalien eher rare Bücher sind. Unter diesen Umständen nehme ich an, dass die zwei von Morin benutzten Pontifikalien aus dem Buchbesitz des früheren syrisch-orthodoxen Bischofs Gregor ʿAtallah (ʿAhatallah) von Damaskus stammten, der 1652 in Malabar Fuß zu fassen suchte; im Spätsommer 1653 ist er in Lissabon nachgewiesen und soll bald danach in Paris gestorben sein (vgl. Edouard R. HAMBYE, An Eastern Prelate in India. Mar Aithalaha, 1652-53, in: Indian Church History Review 2 [1968] 1-5, hier 5 unter Berufung auf ein Schreiben des Erzbischofs Garcia an die Propaganda-Kongregation [m.W. unveröffentlicht]; Joseph THEKEDATHU, The troubled days of Francis Garcia S.J., Archbishop of Cranganore [Analecta Gregoriana 187], Roma 1972, 73–127; anders noch Karl WERTH, Das Schisma der Thomaschristen unter Erzbischof Franciscus Garzia, Limburg a. d. Lahn 1937, 49: 1654 in Goa zum Feuertod verurteilt und hingerichtet). Die betreffenden syrischen Handschriften gelangten an ihren Vorbesitzer, Honoré de Bonfils, zur Zeit Morins Kanonikus an Saint–Sauveur d'Aix, freilich nicht aus Paris, sondern, so MORINUS, Commentarius (wie Anm. 89) 404, aus Lissabon.

riarchae« zitiert zwar einige Formeln wörtlich, erwähnt auch das Gebet zur Handauflegung, gibt aber die eigentlichen Ordinationsorationen nicht wieder[139]. Ein weiterer Hinweis findet sich mit Marcel Metzgers Anmerkung zu Const. apost. 8, 5, das Bischofsweihegebet der Apostolischen Konstitutionen sei »encore en usage dans les rites copte et maronite«[140]. Der Hinweis führt über Franz Xaver Funk[141] zurück auf Denzingers »Ritus orientalium« und somit auf das Gebet »Tu es, Domine deus, qui omnia contines, qui solus es sine principio ...«[142]. Dieses findet sich in der Tat »à peu près littéralement«[143] im maronitischen Pontifikale des Stephan ad–Duwaihī, dort aber nicht als eine der eigentlichen Weiheorationen, sondern als eines des Nebengebete, hier zur Übergabe des Evangeliars und der von Duwaihī selbst als Neuerung eingeführten Salbung des Ordinandus.

2.2.2 Georgien

Aus der »vor–athonitischen Periode« der georgischen Liturgiegeschichte[144], also jener langen Phase vor dem Landeskonzil von Ruis-Urbnisi 1105, in der die Kirche der Georgier ihre jerusalemisch geprägten liturgischen Gebräuche noch nicht für die byzantinischen Konstantinopels eingetauscht hatte, ist bisher nur ein einziges Ordinale bekannt: Codex Tbilisi, Nationales Zentrum für Handschriften, A–86 (10./11. Jh.)[145]. Dieses ›Alt-Georgische Archieratikon‹ ließ ein Katholikos von Kartli (Iberien, Ost–Georgien) namens Symeon, wahrscheinlich Symeon III. (im Amt 1001/2-1012), zu seinem und seiner Nachfolger Nutzen anfertigen. Im Ordinale–Teil des Pontifikales sind für die Weihe eines Bischofs, eines Presbyters und eines Diakons neben anderen Orationen die entsprechen-

139 Ebd. 413–416, bes. 415; DENZINGER, Ritus Orientalium (wie Anm. 96) 74–76; vgl. MOURET, Le rituel syrien (wie Anm. 99) 24.

140 SC 336, 144_5; vgl. auch LANNE, Les ordinations (wie Anm. 53) 86 und KOHLBACHER, Georg. Paralleltexte (wie Anm. 108) 122.

141 FUNK, Didascalia et Constitutiones (wie Anm. 33) 1, 475 Anm. zu Zeile 1–7.

142 DENZINGER, Ritus Orientalium (wie Anm. 96) 2, 200; vgl. ebd. 23f.

143 LANNE, Les ordinations (wie Anm. 53) 86 mit Anm. 16; 97; Text: ASSEMANUS, Codex liturgicus (wie Anm. 107) 8, 3, 41–45.

144 Beste verfügbare liturgiehistorische Übersicht in westlicher Sprache: Bernadette MARTIN–HISARD, Liturgie eucharistique et pratiques eucharistiques dans le monde géorgien (IVe–XIe siècle), in: Nicole BÉRIOU – Béatrice CASEAU – Dominique RIGAUX (Hgg.), Pratiques de l'eucharistie dans les Églises d'Orient et d'Occident (Antiquité et Moyen Âge). Bd. 2: Les réceptions (Coll. de l'Institut d'Études augustiniennes, Série Moyen Âge et Temps Modernes 46), Paris 2009, 671-698. Die von MARTIMORT, Les diaconesses (wie Anm. 73) 181 unterstellte weitgehende Abhängigkeit der georgischen von der armenischen Liturgie entspricht nicht liturgiegeschichtlicher Realität.

145 Zur Handschrift vgl. Lili KHEVSURIANI, in: Liturgia Ibero–Graeca Sancti Iacobi (Jerusalemer Theologisches Forum 17), Münster i. W. 2011, 19f mit Farb–Abb. 3f. Edition des georgischen Textes: Korneli KEKELIDZE, Древнегрузинскій архіератиконъ, Tiflis 1912; englische Übersetzung: Frederick C. CONYBEARE – J. Oliver WARDROP, The Georgian Version of the Liturgy of St. James, in: Revue de l'Orient Chrétien 18 (1913) 395–410; 19 (1914) 155–173.

den Gebete aus dem Testamentum Domini in georgischer Übersetzung verzeichnet:

Amt	Gebete	Quelle
Bischof	O God, who madest all things by Thy might ...	Test. Dom. 1, 21 (29/31 RAHMANI)
Presbyter	Lord and Father of our Lord Jesus Christ, Light ineffable ...	Test. Dom. 1, 30 (69 RAHMANI)
Diakon	O God, who didst create and adorn by the word all things ...	Test. Dom. 1, 38 (93 RAHMANI)
Diakonin	O Lord God of Hosts who before all women didst command Mariam the sister of Moses ...	unbekannt, vgl. Const. apost 8, 20, 1f (SC 336, 220–2)[146]

Diese Orationenreihe aus dem Testamentum Domini[147] bildet eine der im altgeorgischen Ordinale bei den Ordines maiores deutlich erkennbaren drei Schichten von Ordinationstexten unterschiedlicher Herkunft, wobei die zwei anderen Schichten einerseits palästinisch–jerusalemischer Euchologie und anderseits der ostsyrischen Liturgie des vormaligen Sasanidenreiches entstammen[148]. Warum der ohnehin nicht arme Bestand an Orationen des Archieratikons durch eine pseudapostolische Schicht noch erweitert wurde, liegt nicht offen zutage. »An der Bildung von Ternaren (= Dreiergruppen) kann es nicht gelegen haben«[149]. Stellt man jedoch die bewährte Kriminalistenfrage *Cui bono?* fällt der Blick unweigerlich auf den einen Begünstigten: Für die Weihe des georgischen Katholikos, so besagt die beigegebene Rubrik, soll, anders als für einfache Diözesanbischöfe, speziell das — an erster Stelle des einschlägigen Ternars — genannte Gebet aus dem Testamentum Domini verwendet werden. Die offensichtlich angestrebte Alleinstellung des iberischen Kirchenoberhauptes durch Verwendung eines vermeintlich apostolischen Weihegebetes findet eine Parallele und wohl auch ihr Vorbild in der oben erwähnten Regelung für die Ordination der in der Nachbarschaft wirkenden syrisch–antiochenischen Patriarchen und eine zeitnahe Analogie in der Ausbildung einer von der gewöhnlichen Bischofsweihe abgehobenen Sonderordnung für die Bestellung des Katho-

[146] Im Testamentum Domini fehlt, soweit zu sehen, ein Gebet zur Bestellung einer Diakonin. Die Entstehungsumstände der georgischen Oration sind unbekannt; auf dem Internationalen Symposium »Georgian Manuscripts«, Tbilisi 2009, hielt Paul Crego einen Vortrag: The »Ordination« of St. Nino, with Reference to the Prayers for Women Deacons in the Archieratikon of MS. 86 of the Former Church–Archeological Museum of Tbilisi«, dessen voller Text mir leider nicht zugänglich wurde (Buba Kudava [Hrsg.]. 1st International Symposium »Georgian Manuscripts«. Abstracts of Papers, Tbilisi 2009, 39f.).

[147] Über die Umstände georgischer Übertragungen aus dem Testamentum Domini besteht noch keine Klarheit; vgl. CHRONZ – BRAKMANN, Fragmente (wie Anm. 64) 395–402.

[148] BRAKMANN, Die altkirchlichen Ordinationsgebete (wie Anm. 75) 118–121.

[149] KOHLBACHER, Georg. Paralleltexte (wie Anm. 108) 108.

likos der Armenier in Dvin[150]. In Prestigefragen bilden konfessionellen Gegensätze, erst recht, wenn wie hier im Kern nicht betroffen, keine unüberwindlichen Schranken, und da die Authentizität des Testamentum Domini seinerzeit nicht in Frage stand, ist eine georgische Imitation der syrisch–antiochenischen Übung, auch ohne dogmatisch engere kirchliche Verbindung, durchaus vorstellbar. Möglicherweise erfolgte der Rückgriff der mit dem Tblisi A–86 greifbaren Redaktion des georgischen Ordinales auf das pseudapostolische Testamentum Domini insgesamt aus dem Motiv, dem Kirchenoberhaupt der Georgier ein euchologisches Distinctivum nämlicher Art wie seinen benachbarten nichtchalcedonensischen Kollegen zuzuordnen. Scheuten die Betreiber davor zurück, den Katholikos innerhalb des euchologischen Repertoires gänzlich zu isolieren, war es unzweifelhaft ein kluger Schachzug, die komplette Folge der Weihegebete für die Ordines maiores aus dem Testamentum herüber zu nehmen.

2.2.3 Patriarchat Alexandrien

In Alexandrien und Ägypten bilden nach der Spaltung des dortigen Patriarchats über das Reichskonzil von 451 die beiden sich im 6. Jahrhundert als getrennte Kirchen organisierenden Hauptkonfessionen — die chalcedonensischen Melkiten (»Kaiserlinge«) und die sich auf Severos von Antiochien († 538 in Ägypten) berufenden griechisch–koptischen »Theodosianer« — zwei unterschiedliche Ordnungen pontifikaler Gottesdienste aus, die man als alexandrinisch–melkitische und neo–alexandrinisch–koptische Ordines unterscheiden kann, wobei auch letztere (a) auf Griechischem basieren und es nie ganz verlieren sowie (b) der Namenszusatz »neo« die offensichtliche Nichtkontinuität gegenüber den gottesdienstlichen Gepflogenheiten früherer alexandrinischer Patriarchen, etwa Dioskoros (444–451, † 454) und Proterios (451–† 457), anzeigen soll.

Die beiden konkurrierenden, wenngleich nicht total geschiedenen Corpora der Gebete für die Bestellung von Amtsträgern überschneiden sich auffälligerweise in einer pseudapostolischen Oration: Δέσποτα παντοκράτωρ καὶ Κύριε τῶν ὅλων, Πατὴρ τῶν οἰκτιρμῶν, καὶ Θεὸς πάσης παρακλήσεως ... || ⲫⲛⲏⲃ ⲡⲓⲡⲁⲛⲧⲟⲕⲣⲁⲧⲱⲣ ⲟⲩⲟϩ ⲡϭ̅ⲥ̅ ⲙⲓⲡⲓⲉⲡⲧⲏⲣϥ ⲫⲓⲱⲧ ⲛⲧⲉ ⲛⲓⲙⲉⲧϣⲉⲛϩⲏⲧ... (»Dominator omnipotens, et Dominator universi, Pater misericordiarum et Deus totius consolationis ...«)[151]. Bei den Melkiten Alexandriens findet sich dieses Gebet (a) inner-

[150] Vgl. RENOUX, L'ordination du catholicos (wie Anm. 124) 250f. Französische Übersetzung des gesamten Ordos ebd. 260–274: »Canon de l'ordination du Catholicos«.

[151] Näheres bei Heinzgerd BRAKMANN, Pseudo–Clemens Romanus, homilia 3, 72 als petrinisches Konsekrationsgebet der Kopten und der ägyptischen Melchiten, in: Zeitschrift für Antikes Christentum 10 (2007) 233–251. Gemeinsam ist ferner Melkiten und Kopten das allerdings auch mit den Syrisch–Orthodoxen (einschließlich des »Ritus von Tagrit«) und den Maroniten geteilte, im Nahen Osten offenbar allgemeine Vorbereitungsgebet des Or-

halb der Ordnung für die Inthronisation eines (Suffragan–) Bischofs sowie (b) — in leicht erweiterter Gestalt — in der Taxis für die Ordination des Patriarchen[152]. Bei den Kopten begegnet sie (a) bei der Bestellung von Bischöfen (diversen Ranges)[153] und, sicher davon abgeleitet, (b) bei der Konsekration von Kirchengebäuden[154]. Die genannte Oration entstammt der Schrift Κλήμεντος τοῦ Πέτρου ἐπιδημιῶν κηρυγμάτων ἐπιτομή (CANT 209 [4] = BHG 322/41). In diesen sog. pseudoklementinischen Homilien des 3./4. Jahrhunderts wird der Text vom Apostel Petrus bei der Einsetzung des Zakchaios zum Bischof von Kaisareia in Palaestina als Weihegebet gesprochen (PsClem. Rom. hom. 3, 72). Die in Alexandrien und Ägypten verwendete liturgische Redaktion trägt in das in den Gottesdienst herübergenommene Formular kaum mehr als zusätzliche Gottesprädikationen ein und gleicht die Schlußdoxologie aktuellem Gebrauch an. Offensichtlich ist ferner die Übereinstimmung von Melkiten und Kopten in allen charakteristischen Veränderungen gegenüber der literarischen Vorlage. Somit spricht einiges dafür, dass das Weihegebet aus PsClem. Rom. hom. 3, 72 bereits vor dem Chalcedonense zum euchologischen Repertoire alexandrinischer Ordinationen gehörte[155].

dinators Κύριε ὁ θεὸς τῶν δυνάμεων, ὁ θέμενος ἡμᾶς εἰς τὸν κλῆρον τῆς διακονίας ...; dazu vgl. BRAKMANN, Die altkirchlichen Ordinationsgebete (wie Anm. 75) 114–115.

152 Alexius A. DMITRIEVSKIJ, Описаніе литургическихъ рукописей, хранящихся въ библіотекахъ православнаго востока. Bd. 2, Кіевъ 1901, 694f. 699.

153 Koptische Texte: Oswald H. E. KHS–BURMESTER, The Rite of Consecration of the Patriarch of Alexandria (Text according to MS. 253 Lit., Coptic Museum) (Publ. de la Soc. d'Arch. Copte, Textes et documents 8) Le Caire 1960; DERS., Ordination Rites of the Coptic Church (according to MS. 253 Lit., Coptic Museum) (Publ. de la Soc. d'Arch. Copte, Textes et documents 16), Le Caire 1985, jeweils nach einem koptischen Patriarchaleuchologion des Jahres 1364. Auf Handschriften in europäischen Bibliotheken bzw. dem katholischen Druck des 18. Jahrhunderts beruhen die älteren Übersetzungen bei DENZINGER, Ritus Orientalium (wie Anm. 96) 2, 1–64 und Eusèbe RENAUDOT, Liturgiarum Orientalium Collectio. Bd. 1, Francofurti ad Moenum ²1847, 441–463: koptische Patriarchenweihe nach Cod. Petropol. Dorn 627 (Elanskaja Nr. 15), 13./14. Jh. Zu Renaudots und Denzingers Vorlagen vgl. Heinzgerd BRAKMANN, Renaudots »Pontificale Seguierianum«, die »Fourmont«–Manuskripte in Leningrad und andere Coptica Coisliniana, in: Tesserae [FS Josef Engemann] (JAC Erg.–Bd. 18), Münster i. W. 1991, 406–415.

154 George William HORNER, The service for the consecration of church and altar according to the Coptic rite, London 1902, 4f. 350-352, nach Birmingham, Mingana Chr. Arab. 6 v.J. 1307. Vgl. René–Georges COQUIN, La Consécration des Églises dans le rite copte; ses relation avec les rites syrien et byzantin, in: OrSyr 9 (1964) 149–188.

155 BRAKMANN, Pseudo–Clemens (wie Anm. 151) 247; zur Bedeutung vgl. Alberto CAMPLANI, La funzione religiosa del vescovo di Alessandria. A proposito di alcune recenti prospettive di ricerca, in: S. PERNIGOTTI – M. ZECCHI (Hgg.), Sacerdozio e società civile nell'Egitto antico. Atti del terzo Colloquio Bologna – 30/31 maggio 2007 (Archeologia e Storia della Civiltà Egiziana e del Vicino Oriente Antico 14), Imola 2008, 149–165, bes.153–156; Ewa WIPSZYCKA, Les élections épiscopales en Égypte au VIe–VIIe siècles, in: Johann LEEMANS [u. a.] (Hgg.), Episcopal Elections in Late Antiquity (Arbeiten zur Kirchengeschichte 119), Berlin 2011, 258–291, hier 263.

2.2.3.1 Chalcedonenser

Die Ordinationsliturgie der alexandrinischen Chalcedonenser (»Melkiten«)[156], bislang kaum mehr denn ansatzweise erforscht, lässt neben der gerade erwähnten Oration aus dem pseudoklementinischen Roman auch ein Echo aus dem Bischofsweihegebet der Apostolischen Konstitutionen bzw. seines textgeschichtlichem Umfelds, d. h. Traditio apostolica (CPG 1737) und Epitome (CPG 1741), vernehmen. Es verlautet in dem vom Euchologion Sinait. gr. 974 (v.J. 1510) tradierten Nebengebet Ὁ Θεὸς καὶ Πατὴρ τοῦ Κυρίου ἡμῶν Ἰησοῦ Χριστοῦ δεδώρηται τοῖς ἁγίοις αὐτοῦ ἀποστόλοις κτλ. der Patriarchenordination[157], hier gesprochen vom 2. Konzelebranten der Weihe und, dem ersten Eindruck nach, ein redigierter Auszug aus dem Bischofsweihegebet der Epitome oder ihrer Vorlage:

Const. apost. 8, 5, 6	**Trad. apost. par. Epit. Const. apost. VIII**	**Alex.–melkitische Patriarchenweihe**
...	Ὁ θεὸς καὶ πατὴρ τοῦ κυρίου ἡμῶν Ἰησοῦ Χριστοῦ ...	Ὁ θεὸς καὶ πατὴρ τοῦ κυρίου ἡμῶν Ἰησοῦ Χριστοῦ ...
Δὸς ἐν τῷ ὀνόματί σου, καρδιογνῶστα Θεέ,	δὸς	καὶ δὸς
ἐπὶ τόν δοῦλόν σου τόνδε, ὃν ἐξελέξω εἰς ἐπισκοπὴν,	ἐπὶ τόν δοῦλόν σου τοῦτον ὃν ἐξελέξω εἰς ἐπισκοπὴν,	τῷ δούλῳ σου δεῖνα
ποιμαίνειν ποίμνην	⟨ποιμαίνειν τὴν ποίμνην⟩ σου τὴν ἁγίαν,	ποιμαίνειν ποίμην σου ἁγίαν,
καὶ ἀρχιερατεύειν σοι, ἀμέμπτως λειτουργοῦντα νυκτὸς καὶ ἡμέρας καί ἐξιλασκόμενόν σου τό πρόσωπον,	καὶ ἀρχιερατεύειν σοι, ἀμέμπτως λειτουργοῦντα νυκτὸς καὶ ἡμέρας, ἀδιαλείπτως, τε ἱλάσκεσθαι τῷ προσώπῳ σου, καὶ	λειτουργεῖν σοι ἡμέρας καὶ νυκτὸς ἀδιαλείπτως,
ἐπισυναγαγεῖν τὸν ἀριθμὸν τῶν σῳζομένῳν καὶ		
προσφέρειν σοι τὰ δῶρα τῆς ἁγίας σου Ἐκκλησίας.	προσφέρειν σοι τὰ δῶρα τῆς ἁγίας σου ἐκκλησίας.	προσφέρειν τὰ δῶρα τῆς ἁγίας σου ἐκκλησίας,
Δὸς αὐτῷ, δέσποτα παντοκράτορ, δὶα τοῦ Χριστοῦ σου τὴν μετουσίαν τοῦ ἁγίου Πνεύματος, ὥστε	καὶ τῷ πνεύματι τῷ ἀρχιερατικῷ	
ἔχειν ἐξουσίαν	ἔχειν ἐξουσίαν	
ἀφιέναι ἁμαρτίας κατὰ τὴν ἐντολήν σου,	ἀφιέναι ἁμαρτίας κατὰ τὴν ἐντολήν σου,	ἀφιέναι ἁμαρτίας κατὰ τὴν ἐντολήν σου,
διδόναι κλήρους κατά τὸ πρόσταγμά σου, λύειν δὲ πάντα σύνδεσμον	διδόναι κλήρους κατά τὸ πρόσταγμά σου, λύειν δὲ πάντα σύνδεσμον	

[156] Zu den Quellen vgl. BRAKMANN, Pseudo–Clemens (wie Anm. 151) 236f.
[157] DMITRIEVSKIJ, Описание (wie Anm. 152) 696; zur Handschrift ebd. 668–705; Viktor GARDTHAUSEN, Catalogus codicum Graecorum Sinaiticorum, Oxonii 1886, 209f; Murad KAMIL, Catalogue of all manuscripts in the Monastery of St. Catharine on Mount Sinai, Wiesbaden 1970, Nr. 1303.

κατά τὴν ἐξουσίαν, ἣν ἔδωκας τοῖς ἀποστόλοις, εὐαρεστεῖν δέ σοι ἐν πραότητι καὶ καθαρᾷ καρδίᾳ, ἀτρέπτῶς, ἀμέμπτως, ἀνεγκλήτως προσφέροντά σοι καθαρὰν καὶ ἀναίμακτον θυσίαν,	κατά τὴν ἐξουσίαν, ἣν ἔδωκας τοῖς ἀποστόλοις, εὐαρεστεῖν τέ σοι ἐν πραότητι καὶ καθαρᾷ καρδίᾳ, προσφέροντά σοι ὀσμὴν εὐωδίας καθαρὰν καὶ ἀναίμακτον θυσίαν, διὰ τοῦ παιδός σου	 εὐχαριστεῖν καὶ εὐαρεστεῖν σοι ἐν πραότητι καὶ καθαρᾷ καρδίᾳ.

2.2.3.2 Kopten

Hinsichtlich der Ordinationseuchologie des in der heutigen Kirche der Kopten fortlebenden Patriarchats der »Theodosianer«, ist seit Längerem die »erhebliche Bedeutung« pseudapostolischer Gebetsliteratur bekannt, besonders aus den Apostolischen Konstitutionen oder ihrer Nachbarschaft[158]. Gleichwohl lassen sich die Forschungslücken nicht übersehen; denn noch immer ist die Frage nicht befriedigend beantwortet, unter welchen Umständen jene pseudapostolischen Texte ihre notorisch herausragende Bedeutung bei den Kopten erlangten. Die Formulare:

Amt	Gebet	Quelle	Parallelen
Patriarch	Dominator Domine Deus omnipotens ... qui creasti omnia per potentiam et sapientiam suam ...[159]	Testamentum Domini 1, 21	jacobPatr; maronPatr; iberCathol
Metropolit	Dominator Domine Deus omnipotens ... qui creasti omnia per potentiam et sapientiam suam ...[160]	coptPatr	
Bischof	Dominator Domine Deus omnipotens Pater Domini nostri et Dei nostri et Salvatoris nostri Jesu Christi,	Const. apost. 8, 5, 1-7 + »van de Paverd–Oration«[162]	

[158] Jüngst KOHLBACHER, Zum liturgischen Gebrauch (wie Anm. 36) 304f.; zuvor schon u. a. P. ANTOINE, L'Ordination sacerdotale chez les coptes unis, in: Revue de l'Orient Chrétien 28 (1931/32) 362–374; HANSSENS, Les oraisons sacramentelles (wie Anm. 78); LANNE, Les ordinations (wie Anm. 53).

[159] RENAUDOT, Liturgiarum Orientalium Collectio^2 (wie Anm. 153) 1, 448f; DENZINGER, Ritus Orientalium (wie Anm. 96) 2, 48f; BURMESTER, The Rite of Consecration (wie Anm. 153) 22–24.

[160] DENZINGER, Ritus Orientalium (wie Anm. 96) 2, 33f; BURMESTER, Ordination Rites (wie Anm. 153) 68–70.

	une sole ingenite, sine principio nullum regem habens super te, ...[161]		
Presbyter	Dominator Domine qui creasti omnia per verbum tuum coaeternum ...[163]	Const. apost. 8, 16, 3–5	
Diakon	Dominator Domine Deus omnipotens verus, verax in repromissionibus tuis. ...[164]	Const. apost. 8, 18, 1–3	
Subdiakon	Dominator Domine Deus omnipotens, qui manifestati in tabernaculo testimonii ...[165]	Const. apost. 8, 21,3	
Lektor	Dominator Domine Deus, qui praescis numerum electorum tuorum ... qui elegisti Esdram servum tuum ...[166]	Const. apost. 8, 22,3f.[167]	

Handschriften koptischer Pontifikalien mit Ordinale–Teil — gewöhnlich bohairisch–arabische Bilinguen — sind erst aus einer Zeit erhalten, die weit diesseits der Anfänge und der maßgeblichen Entwicklungsstufen der verzeichneten Ordinationsordines liegt. Ältestes datiertes Exemplar ist Brit. Libr. Or. 8774 v.J. 1302[168], bestimmt für einen Suffraganbischof, daher ohne die Aufzeichnung von Bischofsweihen, weil in Ägypten die Ordination von Diözesanbischöfen seit dem Konzil von Nikaia i.J. 325 (can. 6) dem alexandrinischen Patriarchen reserviert ist. Die Bischofsweihen tradierende Patriarchalpontifikalien stehen ab Vat. copt. 44 (olim 13) aus der Zeit 1305–1320[169] und der Kairener Handschrift

162 Mit dem Namen »van de Paverd–Oration« bezeichne ich das Formular eines Bischofsweihegebets, das in verschiedener Textgestalt in der byzantinischen, der ostsyrischen, der alt-georgischen und der koptischen Liturgie begegnet, seinen deprekativen Abschnitt aber überall gemeinsam hat; Frans VAN DE PAVERD, Ein Gebet zur Bischofsweihe aus dem vorbyzantinischen Jerusalem, in: Εὐλόγημα [FS Robert F. Taft] (Studia Anselmiana 110), Roma 1993, 511–523, bes. 523. Die Jerusalemer Herkunft der Oration bzw. ihrer Vorlage ist nicht gesichert; vgl. BRAKMANN, Die altkirchlichen Ordinationsgebete (wie Anm. 75) 122.

161 DENZINGER, Ritus Orientalium (wie Anm. 96) 2, 23f; BURMESTER, Ordination Rites (wie Anm. 153) 61f.

163 DENZINGER, Ritus Orientalium (wie Anm. 96) 2, 12; BURMESTER, Ordination Rites (wie Anm. 153) 40.

164 DENZINGER, Ritus Orientalium 2, 8; BURMESTER, Ordination Rites 33f.

165 DENZINGER, Ritus Orientalium 2, 5; BURMESTER, Ordination Rites 28.

166 DENZINGER, Ritus Orientalium 2, 3; BURMESTER, Ordination Rites 27.

167 Zum Verhältnis des koptischen Lektorenweihegebets zum Formular der Apostolischen Konstitutionen vgl. HANSSENS, Les oraisons (wie Anm. 78) 268 (»étroitement apparentée«); LANNE, Les ordinations (wie Anm. 53) 85. 100. 104; eher reserviert KOHLBACHER, Gebrauch (wie Anm. 36) 304_{55}.

168 Bentley LAYTON, Catalogue of Coptic literary manuscripts in the British Library acquired since the year 1906, London 1987, 364–366 Nr. 233.

169 Microfiche–Veröffentlichung: Pontificale Copticum (Corpus des Liturgies Chrétiennes du Centre Intern. de Publ. Œcum. des Liturgies A0007), Paris 1973. Zur Handschrift vgl.

Copt. Museum 142/Lit. 253 v.J. 1364[170] zur Verfügung. Etwas älter ist vielleicht die Abschrift allein der Patriarchenweihe im Codex Dorn 627 (13./14. Jh.), vormals in Paris, heute in Sankt-Petersburg[171].

Die der handschriftlichen Bezeugung voraufgehenden Stationen mehrhundertjähriger Entwicklung sind demnach nur mit den Methoden der historischen und vergleichenden Liturgiewissenschaft zu ermitteln. Die grundlegenden Einsichten verdanken wir Emmanuel Lanne († 2010): Die Ordinationsliturgie der Kopten bezieht in ihrer Endgestalt den ganzen Rahmen sowie die Formulare der meisten ›Nebengebete‹ aus der Kirche Syriens[172]. Die zentralen Ordinationsgebete jedoch sind aus dem euchologischen Vorrat frühchristlicher Kirchenordnungen herübergenommen, in aller Regel, vom Lektor aufwärts bis zum Bischof, aus dem Umkreis von Buch VIII der Apostolischen Konstitutionen, bei den höchsten Ämtern aus dem Testamentum Domini. Für die Bestellung der Bischöfe findet sich als gewöhnliches Weihegebet nicht, wie 1965/68 in Europa suggeriert[173], das Formular der Traditio apostolica (3 BOTTE), sondern ein Paralleltext zur Oration Const. apost. 8, 5, 1–7: Ὁ ὤν, δέσποτα Κύριε ὁ Θεός ὁ παντοκράτωρ, ὁ μόνος ἀγέννητος καὶ ἀβασίλευτος κτλ.[174].

Freilich gehören die Kopten zu jenen orientalischen Kirchen, die (a) für die Bestellung ihrer höchsten kirchlichen Leiter spezielle Ordinationsgebete vorsehen und sich dabei (b) für den Gebrauch des Modells aus dem Ordinale des Testamentum Domini entschieden haben[175]. In diesem Fall findet das Formular nicht allein bei der Ordination der Patriarchen Verwendung, sondern, jedenfalls seit gehöriger Zeit, auch bei der eines Metropoliten. Noch für Ibn Sabbāʿ (13./14. Jh.) jedoch unterschied sich die Bestellung eines Metropoliten nicht von der

Adolphe HEBBELYNCK – Arnold VAN LANTSCHOOT, Codices Coptici Vaticani Barberiani Borgiani Rossiani. Bd. 1, Città del Vaticano 1937, 226–248.

170 Ausgabe: BURMESTER, The Rite of Consecration (wie Anm. 153); DERS., Ordination Rites (wie Anm. 153). Zur Kairener Handschrift s. Georg GRAF, Catalogue de manuscrits arabes chrétiens conservés au Caire (StT 63), Città del Vaticano 1934, 251–253; Marcus SIMAIKA – Yassa ʿABD AL-MASIḤ, Catalogue of the Coptic and Arabic Manuscripts in the Coptic Museum, the Patriarchate, the Principal Churches of Cairo and Alexandria and the Monasteries of Egypt. Bd. 1 (Publications of the Coptic Museum), Cairo 1939, 72; vgl. Maria CRAMER, Koptische Paläographie, Wiesbaden 1964, Nr. 47 Taf. 84.

171 RENAUDOT, Liturgiarum Orientalium Collectio (wie Anm. 153) 1, 441–463; deutsche Übersetzung bei Alexis VON MALTZEW, Die Sacramente der Orthodox–Katholischen Kirche des Morgenlandes, Berlin 1898, Anhang 16–32. Zur Handschrift vgl. A. I. ELANSKAJA, Description des manuscrits coptes de la Bibliothèque Nationale publique « Saltykoff-Chtchédrine » de Saint-Pétersbourg, in: Études coptes IV (Cahiers de la Bibliothèque Copte 8) Paris – Louvain 1995, 18 Nr. 15.

172 Emmanuel LANNE, Les ordinations dans le rite copte. Leurs relations avec les Constitutions Apostoliques et la Tradition de saint Hippolyte, in: OrSyr 5 (1960) 81–106; DERS., Dans la tradition alexandrine. L'ordination du patriarche, in: Ordination et ministères (wie Anm. 124) 139–155.

173 Vgl. oben zu Anm. 13.

174 Text: BURMESTER, Ordination Rites (wie Anm. 153) 61f.

175 Beobachtet schon von Paul DREWS, Rez. zu Rahmani, Testamentum Domini, in: Theologische Studien und Kritiken 74 (1901) 141–170, hier 147–149. Liturgischer Text: BURMESTER, The Rite of Consecration (wie Anm. 153) 22–24.

üblichen Weihe eines koptischen Bischofs[176]. Die handschriftliche Überlieferung verbindet den gesonderten koptische Ordo für die Ordination eines Metropoliten mit der Bestellung des Metropoliten Michael von Äthiopien (amtierte bis 1449/50) unter dem 89. Koptenpatriarchen Johannes XI. (im Amt 1427–1452)[177]. Eine Metropolitenweihe enthält allerdings schon das frühere Patriarchaleuchologion Kairo, Coptic Museum, 142/Lit. 253 v.J. 1364[178]. Nach seinen Angaben tritt die Oration aus dem Testamentum Domini bei der Feier nicht an die Stelle des gewöhnlichen Bischofsweihegebetes, sondern wird am Ende der Ordinationsriten als Zusatz angefügt[179]. Bei der Umwidmung des koptischen Formulars auf diesen Sekundärzweck hat man den vorgegebenen Text durch Streichung einiger Wendungen, die anscheinend als spezifisch patriarchal gewertet wurden, leicht adaptiert.

Die aus dem Testamentum Domini und den syrischen Liturgien bekannte Begleitformel »Imponimus ...«[180] findet auch bei den Kopten Verwendung, und zwar gleich den Syrisch–Orthodoxen und Maroniten allein bei der Patriarchenbestellung, jedoch in Ägypten nicht unmittelbar vor dem Konsekrationsgebet, sondern erst später, bei einer erneuten Handauflegung vor der Investitur und Inthronisation, und zwar der Reihe nach von jedem einzelnen der konzelebrierenden Bischöfe gesprochen[181]. Nach struktureller Stellung und Bedeutung entspricht dieses Ritual der Kopten der syrischen Sitte, jeden der konzelebrierenden Bischöfe an der Überreichung des Patriarchenstabes an den Neoordinatus mitwirken zu lassen[182], und dürfte darin sein Vorbild besitzen.

[176] Vicentius MISTRÎḤ, Jûḥnnâ ibn abi Zakariâ ibn Siba', Pretiosa margarita de scientiis ecclesiasticis (Studia Orientalia Christiana Aegyptiaca), Cairo 1966, 510–513: »Caput LXXIX: De consecratione episcopi et metropolitae: ambo eodem modo consecratur«.

[177] DENZINGER, Ritus Orientalium (wie Anm. 96) 2, 33 Anm. * unter Berufung auf den von Renaudot benutzten »codex Seguerianus«, der sich als der heutige Paris. copt. 71 (Delaporte Nr. 112) identifizieren lässt; vgl. BRAKMANN, Renaudots »Pontificale Seguierianum« (wie Anm. 153) 412. Zum genannten Metropoliten Äthiopiens Michael vgl. Salvatore TEDESCHI, Art. Ethiopian prelates, in: Coptic Encyclopedia 4 (1991) 1013–1015 mit Lit. Wem unbekannt ist, dass bis in das 20. Jh. die Metropoliten Äthiopiens stets in Ägypten ordinierte Kopten waren, kann es leicht unterlaufen, die mit der Bestellung Michaels *für* Äthiopien verbundene Ordnung *in* Äthiopien anzusiedeln; vgl. oben Anm. 22.

[178] BURMESTER, Ordination rites (wie Anm. 153) 67–70 bzw. 117–119.

[179] Ebd. 117; DENZINGER, Ritus Orientalium (wie Anm. 96) 2, 33. Ein Stück aus Test. Dom. 1, 20 (27 RAHMANI) ist als rechtliche Regelung auch dem koptischen Bischofsweihe-Ordo vorangestellt: DENZINGER, Ritus Orientalium (wie Anm. 96) 2, 18; vgl. DREWS, Rez. Rahmani (wie Anm. 175) 146f.

[180] Vgl. oben zu Anm. 112.

[181] BURMESTER, The Rite of Consecration (wie Anm. 153) 36f; RENAUDOT, Liturgiarum Orientalium Collectio² (wie Anm. 153) 1, 452, dem »Imponimus ...« vorangestellt ist die griechische Aufforderung des Archidiakons Συνεύξασθε πάροντες οἱ ὅσιοι ἐπίσκοποι, die auf eine verständig vorgenommene Redaktionstätigkeit schließen lässt. Synopse von Test. Dom. 21 und koptischem »Imponimus ...« (nach anderer Quelle) bei DREWS, Rez. Rahmani (wie Anm. 175) 147. Eine Überreichung des Patriarchenstabes ist im koptischen Ordo nicht vorgesehen.

[182] Ecclesiae Antiochenae Syrorum Nomocanon (wie Anm. 122) 45; ASSEMANUS, Codex liturgicus (wie Anm. 107) 8, 3, VII. X. 65f mit der Begründung: »hoc demonstratur, quod

Die Vor– und Redaktionsgeschichte der im Koptenpatriarchat gepflegten Ordinationseuchologie pseudapostolischer Herkunft liegt noch weitestgehend im Dunkeln. Von den oben vorgetragenen Fällen der Syrer und der Georgier unterscheidet sich der koptische Befund wesentlich dadurch, dass die von den Kopten liturgisch benutzten Fassungen sich merklich bis erheblich unterscheiden von den Gebetstexten, wie sie heute in den leihgebenden Kirchenordnungen zu lesen sind. So sind die den Apostolischen Konstitutionen eindeutig verwandten Ordinationsorationen der Kopten nicht direkt aus einer der uns bekannten Fassungen jener Kirchenordnung entnommen oder übersetzt worden. Lanne zufolge gehen die Weihegebete auf einen älteren griechischen Paralleltext von Const. apost. VIII zurück, der allerdings nicht identisch sei mit der uns bekannten Epitome, sondern älter als diese und sogar älter als die von ihr epitomierte Fassung der Apostolischen Konstitutionen. Deren Redaktor habe sich der euchologischen Quelle bedient wie ansonsten der Didache und Didascalia apostolorum[183].

Die aus den pseudoklementinischen Apostolischen Konstitutionen bekannten bischöflichen Gebetstexte begegnen bei den Kopten in bohairischer Sprache und textlich »erheblich bearbeitet«[184]. Das zu Const. apost. 8, 5, 1–7 parallele Bischofsweihegebet zum Beispiel ist in der koptischen Liturgie durch eine diakonale Admonitio Τοῦ κυρίου δεηθῶμεν zweigeteilt[185]: Nur der 1. Teil entspricht, mit einigen Varianten und Interpolationen, dem Formular der Apostolischen Konstitutionen. Der 2. Teil ist zugesetzt und enthält u. a. einen Abschnitt aus der verbreiteten, ursprünglich zweifellos griechischen »van de Paverd–Oration«[186]. Die schließlich in das Pontifikale der koptischen Kirche eingegangene Überarbeitung der pseudoklementinischen Vorlagetexte erfolgte nach Lanne auf der Ebene des Griechischen und unter dem Einfluß von in Syria beheimateten Vorstellungen und Formulierungen[187]. Dabei ist freilich nicht von vornherein auszuschließen, dass die von Lanne beobachtete »influence syrienne postérieure«[188] bei der liturgischen Redaktion der pseudoklementinischen Weihegebete nicht in Syria, sondern in Ägypten erfolgte; denn wir wissen, dass manche Texte der syrisch-orthodoxen Liturgie von ihren Verfassern im ägyptischen Exil und ursprünglich in griechischer Sprache komponiert wurden[189].

ex voluntate, & consensu totius Ecclesiae [...] tradita illi sit potestas unica, super omnes Ordines Ecclesiae Sanctae Dei«.

183 LANNE, Les ordinations (wie Anm. 53) 103f.

184 KOHLBACHER, Zum liturgischen Gebrauch (wie Anm. 36) 304f.

185 LANNE, Les ordinations (wie Anm. 53) 92.

186 Vgl. oben Anm. 162.

187 LANNE, Les ordinations (wie Anm. 53) 92f.

188 Ebd. 101.

189 Übersicht der sicher oder wahrscheinlich aus griechischem Originaltext in das Syrische übertragenen Anaphoren des 6./7. Jh. bei Hermann FUCHS, Die Anaphora des monophysitischen Patriarchen Jôḥannàn I. (Liturgiegeschichtliche Quellen 9), Münster i. W. 1926, XXXII-LII.

Dazu gehört, neben den Anaphoren eines Johannes von Bostra[190] und des antiochenischen Patriarchen Severos[191], das unter dem Namen des Alexandriners Timotheos III. (518–535) umlaufende Eucharistieformular[192]. In letzteres eingearbeitet begegnen, wie von Kennern längst erkannt, zwei eucharistische Texte aus dem Testamentum Domini[193].
Von der Redaktion der mit Lanne vorausgesetzten ursprünglich griechischen Fassungen für die alexandrinisch–ägyptische Liturgie aufbereiteter Weihegebete der Apostolischen Konstitutionen bis zu den uns erhaltenen Formularen der mittelalterlichen bohairischen Handschriften war somit notwendigerweise die Sprachgrenze zu überwinden, bei Unterstellung einer sahidischen Zwischenstufe[194] gleich zwei Mal. Weder der Zeitpunkt der liturgischen Redaktion noch jener der Koptisierung sind bisher bestimmt.
Die Datierung der Erstfassung des ›neo-alexandrinischen‹ Ordinales nach der Organisation einer neuen Hierarchie und eigenen liturgischen Ordnung des von Anhängern des Severos von Antiochien (518–†538 in Ägypten), den »Theodosianern«, begründeten nichtchalcedonensischen Patriarchats Alexandrien ist weiterhin unklar[195]. Bei der Suche nach einer dies alles ordnenden Hand denkt man an Severos selbst[196], an Jakob Baradai[197] († 578), an den aus Syria stammenden Patriarchen Damian[198] († 605) oder an Benjamin I.[199] († 665).

190 Humphrey William CODRINGTON, Anaphora Ioannis Bostrensis, in: Anaphorae Syriacae 3, 1, Roma 1981, 36f.
191 DERS., Anaphora Severi Antiocheni, ebd. 1, 1, Roma 1939, 80f.
192 Adolf RÜCKER, Anaphora Timothei Alexandrini, ebd. 10–47.
193 Ebd. 41,11–43,11 und 45, 18–25 (nach Cod. Brit. Libr. Add. 14.520; 8./9. Jh.). Zu notieren ist, dass sich eben diese zwei Texte auch in sahidischer Sprache in Euchologien aus dem sog. Weißen Kloster finden (Borg. copt. 109^{100} und 109^{110}). Die beiden Gebete müssen demnach nicht für eine sahidische Testamentum–Übersetzung stehen, sondern könnten auch auf griechische liturgische Vorlagen zurückgehen; vgl. CHRONZ – BRAKMANN, Fragmente (wie Anm. 64) 396f.
194 LANNE, Les ordinations (wie Anm. 53) 93. 98. 100.
195 Heinzgerd BRAKMANN, Neue Funde und Forschungen zur Liturgie der Kopten [1984–1988], in: Actes du IVe Congrès Copte, Louvain–la–Neuve, 5–10 sept. 1988. Bd. 2 (Publ. de l'Inst. Orientaliste de Louvain 41), Louvain–la–Neuve 1992, 419–435, hier 426.
196 Severos von Antiochien ist zweifelsohne die Fundamentalautorität für jene Antichalcedonenser, die ein dauerhaftes alexandrinisches Patriarchat ausbilden konnten, veranschaulicht in der einzigartigen Stellung, die er als einziger Nichtalexandriner innerhalb der koptischen Diptychen einnimmt, deren hohes Alter das Diptychon des 7. Jh. in Boston belegt; Heinzgerd BRAKMANN, Severos unter den Alexandrinern, in: JAC 25 (1983) 54–58. Severos wird auch ein eucharistisches Liturgieformular zugeschrieben, von dem sich Teile noch im Gottesdienst der Kopten erhalten haben; vgl. Anton BAUMSTARK, Die syrische Anaphora des Severus von Antiocheia, in: Jahrbuch für Liturgiewissenschaft 2 (1922) 92–98. Wenn anderseits Severos jedoch die Apostolischen Konstitutionen generell nicht benutzte (KAUFHOLD, La littérature pseudo-canonique syriaque [wie Anm. 24] 155), dürfte er persönlich kaum ein sich gerade auf diese stützendes Ordinale organisiert haben.
197 LANNE, Les ordinations (wie Anm. 53) 105. Jakob Baradai weihte Bischöfe »in einer Notzeit und im Untergrund« (SELB, Kirchenrecht [wie Anm. 24] 213), kaum besonders geeignete Umstände für die Durchführung einer umfassenden liturgischen Reorganisation.
198 KOHLBACHER, Zum liturgischen Gebrauch (wie Anm. 36) 303_{53}.
199 Irenée-Henri DALMAIS, Art. Egitto I. Liturgia, in: Dizionario Patristico e di Antichità Cristiane 1 (Casale 1983) 1112f.

Jedenfalls lässt sich der von Lanne beschriebene »cadre syriaque« (= Zeremoniell + euchologische Anteile) nicht nur bei den Weihen, sondern als grundlegendes liturgiehistorisches Faktum der sakramentlichen Feiern der koptischen Liturgie beobachten[200]. Daraus ergibt sich hier die Frage, in welcher Weise bei den Ordinationen der nach Ägypten eingemeindete »cadre syriaque« vereinigt wurde mit (a) der pseudapostolischen Gebetsliteratur sowie (b) mit ägyptisch–alexandrinischem »Heimatgut«[201]: Gehören die Pseudapostolica, sämtlich oder zu einem Teil, bereits zur Erstredaktion des ›neo–alexandrinischen‹ Ordinales? Falls ja, als gleichfalls importierte Beifracht des »cadre syriaque« oder als in Ägypten dem neuen Ordinale allein oder zusätzlich beigegebene Stammtexte? Oder wurde das aus der pseudapostolischen Literatur entwickelte Gebetsgut einem etablierten alexandrinisch–koptischen Ordinale erst im weiteren Verlauf seiner Geschichte eingefügt?

Letztere Möglichkeit kann heute nicht mehr schlechthin ausgeschlossen werden, nachdem René Mouret aufdeckte, dass die Handschrift Brit. Libr. Or. 434 (Lond. copt. 850; 13. Jh.?[202]), ein vergleichsweise frühes koptisches Pontifikale für die Hand eines Suffraganbischofs (daher ohne Bischofsweihe), neben den üblichen Weiheorationen in pseudoklementinischer Tradition zusätzlich eine koptische Übersetzung von Ordinationsgebeten antiochenisch–syrischer Herkunft enthält[203]. Diese Orationen treten im Londoner Kodex allerdings ohne hinzugesetzte arabische Übertragung auf[204], waren demnach entweder inzwischen aus dem lebendigen Gebrauch ganz ausgebürgert oder wurden allenfalls noch eingeschränkt benutzt.

Angesichts dessen kommt dem Nachweis einiges Gewicht zu, dass das paarweise Auftreten von Ordinationsgebeten antiochenisch–syrischer Provenienz und solchen pseudapostolischer Herkunft nicht auf den Brit. Libr. Or. 434 beschränkt war, sondern einst weiter verbreitet gewesen sein muss, und zwar auch in jenem Bereich, der maßgeblich für die Entwicklung des koptischen Ordinale Sorge trug, also im Gottesdienst des Patriarchen. Dafür spricht das in der Endgestalt des Pontificale copticum anzutreffende Rituale der Bestellung eines Lektors.

Im genannten Ordo zeigen sich der »cadre syriaque« und das ägyptische Sondergut in folgender Weise:

[200] BRAKMANN, Neue Funde (wie Anm. 195) 425.

[201] Vgl. BRAKMANN, Pseudo–Clemens (wie Anm. 151) 233–251.

[202] Walter E. CRUM, Catalogue of the Coptic manuscripts in the British Museum. London 1905, 358. Eine genauere liturgiewissenschaftliche Untersuchung des Brit. Libr. Or. 434 ist erwünscht.

[203] René MOURET, L'ordination d'un diacre copte, (masch.) Mémoire de Diplômé de l'É.P.H.É. V[e] sect., Paris (1976) 3.19–28. 30. 74–77.

[204] MOURET, L'ordination (wie Anm. 203) 128f Anm. 16; näherhin bezogen auf den Ordo der Diakonenweihe: »Pour les prières le texte arabe semble avoir été ajouté plus tard, en particulier pour la prière d'ordination [...] Les deux prières propre à ce rituel sont en copte sans traduction arabe«; vgl. ebd. 143.

	Koptischer Ordo[205]	Syrisch–orth. Ordo[206]	Parallelen
1	Suppliciter rogamus et obsecramus te ... suscipe tibi servum tuum N. in anagnosten ...	Rogamus et precamur te Domine Deus, suscipe servum tuum istum in lectorem ...	➤ maronLect
2	Deus magne, dives in donis tuis, qui donasti Ecclesiae tuae ordines et constituisti eos in ea per grados ...	Deus magne, et donorum dives, qui ordines Ecclesiae tuae concessisti, et gradus ministerii in ea constituisti ...	➤ maronLect
3	Deus magne et amator hominum, tenens universa manu tua et effundens spiritum tuum super omnes ... ad annuntianda eloquia tua sancta veteris et novi Testamenti ...	Deus magne et amator hominum, in cujus manibus omnia comprehenduntur ... aspice huc servum tuum ... ut sit praedicator sermonum tuorum sanctorum, Testamenti Veteris et Novi ...	Barb. gr. 336[207]; Sinait. gr. 973[208]; palLect–2[209]; iberLect–2
4	Dominator Domine Deus, qui praescis numerum electorum tuorum ... qui elegiste Esdram servum tuum ...	Const. apost. 8, 22, 3[210]	

Die vorstehende Übersicht lässt bei der Bestellung eines koptischen Lektors dieselbe Vorgehensweise beobachten, wie sie in dem von Mouret angeführten Londoner Kodex als historische Praxis erkennbar wurde: Ein pseudapostolisches Gebet (hier Nr. 4) ist eingefügt in den vorgegebenen »cadre syriaque«, d. h. in Struktur und Euchologie eines Ordos, der aus der Kirche Syrias nach Ägypten übernommen wurde (mit Nr. 1–3). Nr. 4 erscheint als pseudapostolischer Zusatz zu einem gegebenen Bestand von Ordinationsorationen nichtägyptischer Provenienz, die im gegebenen Fall jedoch — im Gegensatz zu antiochenisch–syrischen Weihegebeten der Ordines maiores — nicht mit der Zeit zugunsten der Pseudapostolica aus dem aktuellen liturgischen Brauch ausgeschieden wurden.

Michael Kohlbacher zufolge wär die Verwendung des Bischofsweihegebetes des Testamentum Domini zur Ordination des Patriarchen der syrisch-orthodoxen und der maronitischen Kirche »sichtlich unter koptischem Einfluss«

[205] BURMESTER, Ordination Rites (wie Anm. 153) 23–25 bzw. 73–77; DENZINGER, Ritus Orientalium (wie Anm. 96) 2, 2–4.

[206] DENZINGER, Ritus Orientalium (wie Anm. 96) 2, 78f nach dem »Codex Florentinus«, dem heutigen Paris. syr. 112 (vgl. oben zu Anm. 96).

[207] Κύριε ὁ ϑεὸς ὁ παντοκράτωρ, ἔκλεξαι τὸν δοῦλόν σου κτλ.: PARENTI – VELKOVSKA (wie Anm. 79) 175 Nr. 166, 3.

[208] DMTRIEVSKIJ, Описаніе (wie Anm. 30) 2, 115.

[209] Matthew BLACK, Rituale Melchitarum. A Christian Palestinian Euchologion (Bonner Orientalistische Studien 22), Stuttgart 1938, 83.

[210] Zum Verhältnis von Text Nr. 4 und Const. apost. 8, 22, 3 vgl. HANSSENS, Les oraisons (wie Anm. 78) 268 (Synopse) sowie oben Anm. 167.

erfolgt[211]. Das gegenläufige Gefälle von Vorbild und Nachahmung wurde von uns erwogen[212]. Tatsächlich ist bisher nicht bekannt, wann eine Fassung von Test. Dom. 21 zum Spezialgebet der Bestellung eines Koptenpatriarchen geworden ist: Gleich bei der Redaktion des ›neo-alexandrinischen‹ Ordinales oder erst in einer späteren Entwicklungsphase? In jedem Fall nicht ohne Kenntnis und Mitwirkung der Liturgiker in unmittelbarer Umgebung des Patriarchen, die aufgrund dessen Weiheprivilegs für die Ordinationsordines aller drei bischöflichen Ämter, Bischof, Metropolit und Patriarch, zu sorgen hatten. Das Einfallstor für die Einführung neuer Gebete ist daher denkbar schmal und muss in Alexandrien gestanden haben, solange der Koptenpatriarch dort residierte und zelebrierte. Geht man, um einen Ansatz zu haben, von der ältesten überlieferten Ordnung der Weihe eines Patriarchen der Kopten aus, gefeiert, wie im liturgischen Ordo ausdrücklich festgehalten, in der Angelion–Kathedrale zu Alexandrien[213], dann sollte das von Test. Dom. 21 abhängige Gebet in bohairischer Übersetzung vor Ende des 10. Jahrhunderts in Übung gewesen sein, weil etwa in dieser Zeit die Angelion–Kirche ihre Bedeutung verlor. Anderseits setzt der vorliegende Ordo bereits den vollendeten Bau des alexandrinisch-koptischen Patriarcheions voraus, der unter Johannes IV. (755-799) errichtet wurde[214].
Einen mit dem Testamentum Domini verbundenen reichen Bestand an Liturgica (Bischofsweihe, »Mystagogia«, Eucharistiefeier, Ordination von Presbyter, Diakon und Witwe, Initiatio Christiana) umfasste die verschollene koptische, möglicherweise bohairische[215] Handschrift aus dem Besitz des Patriarchen Kosmas III. v.J. 926/27[216]. Das Material überlebte in Rechtshandschriften mit Coquins Rezension B des arabischen Testamentums[217], so Borg. arab. 22 (olim K IV 24 bzw. Borg. syr. 60) v.J. 1348. Die in dieser Sammlung überlieferten Mess– und Taufliturgien erwiesen sich als Ergebnis ägyptischer Bearbeitungen[218], Theodor Schermann zufolge »nicht vor das 8. bis 9. Jh.« zu setzen[219].

211 KOHLBACHER, Gebrauch (wie Anm. 36) 310_{100}; wiederholt, jetzt in Frageform, DERS., Georg. Paralleltexte (wie Anm. 108) 123f.
212 CHRONZ – BRAKMANN (wie Anm. 64) 397; vgl. auch LANNE, Les ordinations (wie Anm. 53) 85.
213 BURMESTER, The Rite of Consecration (wie Anm. 153) 9f. 46. 55. 83; RENAUDOT, Liturgiarum Orientalium Collectio² (wie Anm. 153) 1, 441; zur Angelion–Kirche vgl. Heinzgerd BRAKMANN, Σύναξις καθολική in Alexandreia, in: JAC 30 (1987) 74–89, bes. 83f.
214 Ebd. 88 mit Anm. 107.
215 Das Bohairische als Sprache der verlorenen Handschrift des Kosmas nimmt Jean–Michel HANSSENS, La Liturgie d'Hippolyte. Ses documents – son titulaire – ses origines et son caractère (OCA 155), Roma 1959,71 an, für den sahidischen Dialekt spricht sich KAUFHOLD, Sources of Canon Law (wie Anm. 24) 270 aus.
216 Vgl. den Kolophon des Cod. Borg. arab. 22: Jean PÉRIER – Augustin PÉRIER, Les »127 Canons des Apôtres« (PO 8, 4), Paris 1912, 565–567.
217 COQUIN, Le Testamentum (wie Anm. 64) 169f.
218 Anton BAUMSTARK, Eine aegyptische Mess– und Taufliturgie vermutlich des 6. Jh., in: OrChr 1 (1901) 1–45; Ignace Ehrem II. RAHMANI, Les Liturgies Orientales & Occidentales. Beyrouth 1929, 446–470.

Die mitgeteilten Ordinationsgebete hingegen sind im Wesentlichen unveränderte Übertragungen aus der Kirchenordnung[220]. Dies erlaubt die Frage, ob auf ein Exemplar wie das des Patriarchen Kosmas vielleicht sämtliche Auszüge aus dem Testamentum Domini zurückzuführen sind, die Eingang in die koptisch–bohairische Liturgie gefunden haben, die »Mystagogie« wie auch das Bischofsweihegebet für die Ordination von Patriarchen und Metropoliten.

RESÜMEE

Pflege oder Übernahme pseudapostolischer Ordinationsgebete in die gottesdienstliche Praxis vorreformatorischer Kirchen begegnen vor der Neuzeit, soweit zu sehen, nicht im Westen, nicht in Konstantinopel, nicht in Armenien, nicht im Katholikat Seleukia–Ktesiphon, vielmehr nur in der syrisch-orthodoxen (»jakobitischen«), der maronitischen und der koptischen Liturgie, die Hieronymus Engberding unter der Bezeichnung »westsyrisch–ägyptischer Gürtel« zusammenschließt[221], sowie in Georgien, das über Jerusalem sowie palästinische und syrische Mönchskolonien ebenso mit dem Nahen Osten zu verbinden ist wie die als gelegentliche Verwerter pseudapostolischer Orationen in Erscheinung tretenden süditalienischen und zypriotischen Euchologien. In all diesen Fällen handelt es sich offensichtlich um ein jüngeres Zurückgreifen auf unter apostolische Autorität gestellte Kirchenrechtsliteratur, nicht um kontinuierlich im lebendigen Gottesdienst bewahrtes Gut. Das Bischofsweihegebet der Traditio apostolica findet sich als Feiertext allein im Pontificale Romanum seit 1968. Im Osten werden nur zwei seiner Derivate aus den Apostolischen Konstitutionen und dem Testamentum Domini gebraucht, letzteres nur bei besonderen Gelegenheiten, nämlich der Bestellung zu den vor Ort höchsten bischöflichen Ämtern. Gleichwohl stellt das aus der Traditio apostolica hervorgegangene Bischofsweihegebet das einzige unter Seinesgleichen dar, das Grenzen überwindet und Traditionen verbindet, den Westen und den Osten einerseits sowie Chalcedonenser und Nichtchalcedonenser anderseits. In diesem Sinn ist es wahrhaft ein »ökumenisches Gebet«. Seine Paul VI. Montini zu verdankende Präsenz an prominenter Stelle im gegenwärtigen Pontificale Romanum erscheint wie ein euchologisches Denkmal jener großen Hoffnung, die Johannes XXIII. Roncalli

[219] Theodor SCHERMANN, Ägyptische Abendmahlsliturgien des ersten Jahrtausends in ihrer Überlieferung dargestellt (Studien zur Geschichte und Kultur des Altertums 6, 1-2), Paderborn 1912, 190.

[220] Dem Testamentum Domini entnommen sind auch die Kap. 35–39 der Didascalia Arabica (2, 226–236 FUNKE); darin enthalten sind die »Imponimus«–Formel und das Bischofsweihegebet.

[221] Hieronymus ENGBERDING, Eine neuerschlossene, bedeutsame Urkunde zur Geschichte der östlichen Weiheriten, in: OrChr 36 (1941) 38–49, hier 43.

On the Early History of Quadragesima A New Look at an Old Problem and Some Proposed Solutions[*]

Harald Buchinger

Quadragesima has long been famous as a highly problematic field of liturgical history: while the sources are abundant enough to indicate a multifaceted development, even the earliest evidence already is so complex as to raise the question of a possible prehistory, which is not documented by the extant testimonies. It is not merely matters of detail that have to remain open; the origins and early development of the Quadragesima as such are so obscure that substantially different scenarios have recently been proposed.

The classical view has been summarized in such publications as Hansjörg Auf der Maur's authoritative manual on the Liturgical Year and assumes a gradual growth of the pre-paschal time of preparation:[1] In the third century the Paschal Fast was occasionally extended to the whole week before Easter.[2] At a some-

* Earlier versions of this paper were presented in July 2005 as a Short Communication at the Societas Liturgica Congress in Dresden and discussed at the 2007 meeting of the Problems in Early Liturgical History Seminar of the North American Academy of Liturgy in Toronto. I am grateful to the members of this uniquely stimulating group and especially to Nicholas Russo, who in the meantime has finished a doctoral dissertation on the early history of Lent at the University of Notre Dame under the direction of Maxwell E. Johnson: Nicholas V. Russo, The Origins of Lent, PhD Diss., University of Notre Dame, Indiana, 2009; cf. also Id., A Note on the Role of Secret Mark in the Search for the Origins of Lent, in: StLi 37 (2007) 181–197. I am preparing a more elaborate German version of the present article (aiming to incorporate an exhaustive bibliography and a more comprehensive range of source-references) probably to be published in Archiv für Liturgiewissenschaft. I am grateful to John Nicholson, Vienna, for the revision of the English version.

Abbreviations in bibliographical references follow Siegfried Schwertner, Internationales Abkürzungsverzeichnis für Theologie und Grenzgebiete. International glossary of abbreviations for theology and related subjects, Berlin ^{2}1992 [cf. ^{1}1976]; for the titles of patristic works, cf. the abbreviations used by G. W. H. Lampe, A Patristic Greek Lexicon, Oxford 1961, and Albert Blaise, Dictionnaire latin-français des auteurs chrétiens, Turnhout 1954.

1 Hansjörg Auf der Maur, Feiern im Rhythmus der Zeit. 1: Herrenfeste in Woche und Jahr (GdK 5), Regensburg 1983, 144f.; 146f.; 2nd totally revised and augmented edition in preparation by Harald Buchinger and Reinhard Meßner. A similar view is held by other standard works such as Pierre Jounel, L'année, in: Aimé Georges Martimort (ed.), La liturgie et le temps (EeP 4), Paris 1983, 43–166, here 80, or Adrien Nocent, Panoramica storica dell'evoluzione dell'anno liturgico, in: L'anno liturgico. Storia, teologia e celebrazione (Anàmnesis 6), Genova ^{2}1989 [^{1}1988], 35–55, here 44f.; id., La Quaresima, in: ibid., 139–173, here 152f.

2 Cf. Dionysius of Alexandria, ep. 14 (ad Basiliden) (101, 9–102, 3; Charles Lett Feltoe): ἐπεὶ μηδὴ τὰς ἓξ ἡμέρας ἴσως μηδὲ ὁμοίως πάντες διαμένουσιν· ἀλλ᾿ οἱ μὲν καὶ πάσας ὑπερτιθέασιν ἄσιτοι διατελοῦντες, οἱ δὲ δύο, οἱ δὲ τρεῖς, οἱ δὲ τέσσαρας, οἱ δὲ οὐδεμίαν; Didasc. syr. 21 (CSCO 407 = CSCO.S 179, 208, 9–11; 214, 5–10 [syr.] / CSCO 408 = CSCO.S 180, 191, 16f.; 198, 19–199, 2 [engl.]; Arthur Vööbus). In the

what later stage, Socrates Scholasticus is quoted as recording a three-week-period;[3] and in the fourth century a period of basically forty days gained universal acceptance, the only substantial variations being related to the exact calculation of its duration, beginning, and end.

Only in one sceptical footnote[4] did Auf der Maur make reference to a more recent departure in modern scholarship that was triggered off by a paper read by Thomas J. Talley at the Oxford Patristics Conference 1979,[5] developed in more detail in his epochal book "The Origins of the Liturgical Year",[6] and described as a "standard answer to this question"[7] by Maxwell E. Johnson, whose study "Baptismal Preparation and the Origins of Lent" can also be called a classic contribution to the debate.[8] Taking up earlier essays by René-Georges Coquin,[9] this model does not present the pre-paschal Quadragesima as a result of gradual growth of the preparatory period before Easter, but rather as a period of forty days first occurring in Egypt independently of Easter and following Epiphany, the celebration of the Lord's baptism, in imitation of his fast as narrated by Mark 1:12/Matthew 4:1. This Quadragesima would thus originally have been connected with the motif of Christ's temptation in the desert and would furthermore have served as preparation for baptism as celebrated in mid-February. Only later, Talley suggests, after the council of Nicaea, was it transferred to before Easter, which only then took pride of place as the preferred date for baptism.[10]

preceding century, Irenaeus of Lyons, as quoted by EUSEBIUS OF CAESAREA, h. e. 5, 24, 12 (GCS 2/1, 494, 16–19; Eduard SCHWARTZ), mentions only "one, two or more" days or 40 hours of continuous fasting.

3 Socrates begins his account on the differences regarding duration and observance of Quadragesimal fasting with a reference to Roman use: οἱ μὲν γὰρ ἐν Ῥώμῃ τρεῖς πρὸ τοῦ πάσχα ἑβδομάδας πλὴν σαββάτου καὶ κυριακῆς συνημμένας νηστεύουσιν. (h.e. 5, 22, 32 [GCS 300, 11f.; Günther Christian HANSEN]) On the problems of this account, see section 3 below.

4 AUF DER MAUR, Feiern (see fn. 1), 145, n. 64.

5 Thomas J. TALLEY, The Origin of Lent at Alexandria, in: StPatr 17/2 (1982) 594–612.

6 Thomas J. TALLEY, The Origins of the Liturgical Year, Collegeville [2]1991 [[1]1986], 163–230.

7 Maxwell E. JOHNSON, Preparation for Pascha? Lent in Christian Antiquity, in: Paul F. BRADSHAW – Lawrence A. HOFFMAN (eds.), Passover and Easter. The Symbolic Structuring of Sacred Seasons (Two Liturgical Traditions 6), Notre Dame/IN 1999, 36–68, here 44 [repr. in: Maxwell E. JOHNSON (ed.), Between Memory and Hope. Readings on the Liturgical Year, Collegeville/MN 2000, 207–222]. In Paul BRADSHAW (ed.), The New SCM Dictionary of Liturgy and Worship, London 2002, 278f. s.v. Lent, Johnson distinguishes the two models as "traditional" and "modern scholarship".

8 Maxwell E. JOHNSON, From Three Weeks to Forty Days. Baptismal Preparation and the Origins of Lent, in: StLi 20 (1990) 185–200 [repr. in: ID. (ed.), Living Water, Sealing Spirit. Readings on Christian Initiation (A Pueblo Book), Collegeville/MN 1995, 118–136 (Quotations here taken from this reprint); ID., Worship: Rites, Feasts, and Reflections, Portland/OR 2004, 199–213].

9 René-Georges COQUIN, Les origines de l'Épiphanie en Égypte, in: Noël – Épiphanie – Retour du Christ. Semaine liturgique de l'Institut Saint-Serge (LO 40), Paris 1967; ID., Une réforme liturgique du Concile de Nicée (325)?, in: CRAI 1967, 178–192.

10 Cf. Paul F. BRADSHAW, "Diem baptismo sollemniorem": Initiation and Easter in Christian Antiquity, in: E. CARR – S. PARENTI – A.-A. THIERMEYER – E. VELKOVSKA (eds.),

In view of the substantially revised and augmented new edition of Auf der Maur's handbook, both theories have to be reviewed; the purpose of the following pages is to present the main evidence on which they are based and to assess their import for a balanced presentation of the earliest history of the Quadragesima and its inherent problems. As the Quadragesima is quasi-universally attested by the end of the fourth century, this investigation will limit itself to those traditions in which there is evidence before the second half of that century, namely, in the putative historical sequence of the earliest testimonies, Palestine, Alexandria, and Rome.[11]

1. ON THE EARLY HISTORY OF QUADRAGESIMA IN JERUSALEM

1.1. The sources

In Palestine, *Eusebius of Caesarea* in his work "On the Paschal Feast", which can be dated between 325 and 337, records that the Christians of his time and region "undertake the exercise of forty days in preparation for the feast, according to the zeal of the saints Moses and Elijah."[12] A little further on he gives the concrete indication that this "exercise of forty days" lasted six weeks.[13] Although Eusebius does not yet use the word τεσσαρακοστή, his testimony – perhaps the earliest of all those available – brings out three constitutive features of the Quadragesima: firstly, it was an exercise in preparation for Easter; secondly, it lasted for forty days, which in concrete practice amounted to six weeks; and thirdly, this number was determined by biblical symbolism. Strikingly, Eusebius draws only on Old Testament types, not on the example of Jesus.

A little later, most likely still in the first half of the fourth century, *Cyril of Jerusalem* speaks to the catechumens about a "conversion of forty days",[14] using the technical term ἁγία τεσσαρακοστή.[15]

Still in Cyril's era, in the early 380s, *Egeria* gives a detailed account of a fast that now appears for the first time with a proper liturgical order and takes eight

ΕΥΛΟΓΗΜΑ. [FS Robert TAFT] (StAns 110 = Analecta Liturgica 17), Roma 1993, 41–51 [repr. in: Living Water (see fn. 8), 137–147].

[11] Other allegedly early testimonies cannot be dated securely; cf., for example, the Syrian Doctrina Apostolorum as translated and commented by Reinhard MESSNER, Die "Lehre der Apostel" – eine syrische Kirchenordnung. Übersetzung und Anmerkungen, in: Konrad BREITSCHING – Wilhelm REES (eds.), Recht – Bürge der Freiheit. [FS Johannes MÜHLSTEIGER] (KStT 51), Berlin 2006, 305–335, here 316.

[12] Pasch. 4 (PG 24, 697 C): … προέορτα μὲν προπαρασκευῆς ἕνεκα τὴν τεσσαρακονθήμερος ἄσκησιν παραλαμβάνοντες κατὰ τὸν τῶν ἁγίων ζῆλον Μωϋσέως καὶ Ἠλίου …

[13] Pasch. 5 (PG 24, 700 B–C).

[14] Procatech. 4 (6; Wilhelm Karl REISCHL): τεσσαράκοντα ἡμερῶν μετάνοιαν ἔχεις.

[15] Catech. 4, 3 (92; REISCHL).

weeks in all[16] (seven weeks plus *septimana paschale, quam hic appellant septimana maior*[17]), this duration being the result of the concern to count forty days of actual fasting.[18] By virtue of making this calculation, Egeria is by far the earliest witness to a tendency that was later to lead to a general prolongation of the pre-paschal fast in many parts of the Christian East; in the context of other evidence of her time, however, her account remains isolated, erratic, and ultimately inexplicable.[19]

The *Armenian Lectionary*, the lost Greek prototype of which goes back to Hagiopolite practice of the period between 417 and 439, offers a Quadragesima of only six weeks plus Holy Week, the latter being clearly distinguished as the week of the "Paschal Fast".[20] *Peter*, patriarch of Jerusalem in the second quarter of the sixth century (524–552), still unequivocally refers to this status of seven weeks in all in a Festal letter;[21] it is only somewhat later in the same century that *Dorotheus of Gaza* († between 560 and 580) recalls the transition to a fasting period of eight weeks in all.[22] This fully developed status is also reflected by the *Georgian Lectionary* (the date of which is difficult to determine exactly and to prove separately for every detail attested, though it is in any case significantly later than the Armenian Lectionary), which provides for an additional week of "cheese-fasting" (ყველიერისასა < τῆς Τυροφάγου/Τυρινῆς) before Quadragesima proper.[23]

Setting aside the difficulties related to the concrete calculation of forty days increasingly counted as days of actual fasting, it seems clear that Quadragesima was introduced in Palestine by the second quarter of the fourth century as a

16 Pereg. 27–29 (SC 296, 256–270; Pierre MARAVAL).

17 Pereg. 30, 1 (SC 296, 270; MARAVAL).

18 Pereg. 27 (SC 296, 256–258; MARAVAL).

19 The various theories presented by the commentaries on Egeria have only one feature in common: they cannot offer a satisfactory explanation. A more detailed assessment of the various scholarly opinions will be given in the expanded German version of this paper (cf. n. *).

20 The end of Quadragesima proper – Armenian Lectionary § XIX–XXXII (PO 168 = 36/2, 238 [100]–254 [116]; Athanase RENOUX) – with the stational service on Friday of the 6th week is marked by a rubric in § XXXII: "Finished is the canon of the sixth week of the Holy Quadragesima." (ibid. 254 [116]); Monday of Holy Week, in turn, is introduced as "Monday of the Paschal Fast" in § XXXV (ibid. 258 [120]). For ample discussion of further evidence, see Sebastià JANERAS, Le vendredi avant le Dimanche des Palmes dans la tradition liturgique hagiopolite, in: Studi sull'Oriente Cristiano 4 (2000) 59–86.

21 As quoted by the florilegium – most likely spuriously – attributed to John of Damascus (cf. n. 24): … θεοῦ χάριτι, τῆς νενομισμένης ἀπαρξώμεθα νηστείας, τῶν ἑπτὰ ἑβδομάδων, ἀπὸ τῆς ἑβδόμης τοῦ Φεβρουαρίου μηνὸς, τὴν τοῦ σωτηρίου Πάθους, καὶ τῆς Χριστοῦ Ἀναστάσεως ἐπιτελοῦντες πανήγυριν, τῇ εἰκάδι ἑβδόμῃ τοῦ λεγομένου Μαρτίου μηνός. (PG 95, 76 B)

22 DOROTHEUS, Doct. 15, 159 (SC 92, 446–448; Lucien REGNAULT – Jacques de PRÉVILLE), distinguishes the "seven weeks of fasting", which he derives from the apostles, from the additional week which he suggests was introduced as a convention of the Fathers with the aim of "honouring the fast by the number of the holy Quadragesima which our Lord fasted."

23 Georgian Lectionary § 290 (CSCO 188 = CSCO.I 9, 47 [georg.] / CSCO 189 = CSCO.I 10, 43 [lat.]; Michael TARCHNISCHVILI).

symbolical period at first spanning six weeks (Eusebius). In addition, Holy Week was developed, most likely in the third quarter of the same century (being attested from Egeria onwards), thus permitting the mimetic celebration of the events of Christ's Passion; this addition obviously shifted Quadragesima back one week (Armenian Lectionary), resulting in seven weeks of fasting in all. Another week of fasting was added – most likely in the later sixth century – to comply with the desire for forty days of actual fasting, but in most sources it is clearly distinguished from Quadragesima as such.[24] Egeria's account of an eight-week fast as early as the late fourth century remains erratic against the background of these developments.

1.2. Theories regarding a prehistory

Although Quadragesima in Palestine is quite well attested from the earliest available testimonies onwards as having been a period of basically forty days, research over the years has repeatedly postulated shorter predecessors. On the one hand, the independence of Holy Week has been interpreted as evidence for it being a remnant of an early fast of one week;[25] on the other hand, a three-week period has been sought in reconstructions of the prehistory of the liturgical orderings transmitted from the fifth century on.[26]
While the Paschal Fast may possibly have been extended to a whole week in Jerusalem in early times, as is attested elsewhere,[27] this ascetic practice was motivated by factors not essentially linked with liturgy and should not be seen as the root of the liturgical development of Holy Week, the shape of which was determined not by the extension of the fast (though it coincides with the latter, as reflected, for example, in the nomenclature applied by the Armenian Lectionary) but by the desire for mimetic celebration of the Passion. Thus, the furnishing of the Holy Week Lectionary is more a secondary phenomenon than a relic of earliest times.[28] Whether Holy Week developed at the same time as

[24] The question continued to be discussed as late as the 8th century, as is documented by the Letter of JOHN DAMASCENE, De sacris jejuniis and the attached florilegium (PG 95, 64–77); cf. Vassa CONTICELLO, Un florilège sur le Grand Carême attribué à Jean Damascène. Authenticité, sources, nouveaux fragments de Sévère d'Antioche, in: Bart JANSSENS – Bram ROOSEN – Peter VAN DEUN (eds.), Philomathestatos. Studies in Greek and Byzantine Texts. [FS Jacques NORET] (OLA 137), Leuven 2004, 77–104; EAD., La Quarantaine hiérosolymitaine dans le De sacris jejuniis de Jean Damascène, in: Job GETCHA – André LOSSKY (eds.), Θυσία αἰνέσεως. Mélanges liturgiques. [GS Georges Wagner] (Analecta Sergiana 2), Paris 2005, 77–94.

[25] Stéphane VERHELST, Histoire ancienne de la durée du carême à Jérusalem, in: QuLi 84 (2003) 23–50, esp. 24–26.

[26] Mário FERREIRA LAGES, Étapes de l'évolution du Carême à Jérusalem avant le Ve siècle. Essai d'analyse structurale, in: REArm 6 (1969) 67–102, taken up by VERHELST, Histoire (see fn. 25), 26–30.

[27] Cf. n. 2.

[28] FERREIRA LAGES, Étapes (see fn. 26), 91, takes this possibility into consideration, though he himself tends towards the priority of Holy Week.

Quadragesima or, as would appear to me more plausible, a little later (their earliest attestations being separated by half a century), they are independent phenomena that cannot be derived from one another. This is also clear from the fact of the one immediately following the other in the liturgical sources, beginning with the Armenian Lectionary: had Holy Week been the nucleus of an organic development, the two periods would not be so clearly distinguished. Their liturgical outline follows different principles; and the celebrations of Holy Week are not the nucleus of Quadragesimal liturgy.

The theory that the Hagiopolite Quadragesima might at an earlier stage have lasted three weeks rests on the one hand on traces of a series of Psalms sung in their biblical order at the stational services during the last three weeks of Quadragesima in the Armenian Lectionary,[29] though the evidence seems to require too much interpretational effort for it to be able to carry the burden of proof; and on the other hand on the number and distribution of the eighteen or nineteen lections that show remarkable continuity from their first occurrence as the basis of Cyril's Catecheses until the Georgian Lectionary,[30] though their liturgical sequence and concrete distribution remain obscure because of tensions and contradictions between various details in the different sources, especially as the development of baptismal practice and preparation is an area where one has to be particularly aware of significant changes in the centuries under discussion. Although here is not the place to enter this complex debate,[31] it may be noted that the liturgical distribution as provided by the Georgian Lectionary comes only from the latest source available and thus may be the product of a secondary systematization;[32] but even if it did conserve the original disposition of

[29] FERREIRA LAGES, Étapes (see fn. 26), 81–85; 97.

[30] FERREIRA LAGES, Étapes (see fn. 26), 98f.

[31] See, among others, Anthony A. STEPHENSON, The Lenten Catechetical Syllabus in Fourth-Century Jerusalem, in: TS 15 (1954) 103–116; Maxwell E. JOHNSON, Reconciling Cyril and Egeria on the Catechetical Process in Fourth-Century Jerusalem, in: Paul F. BRADSHAW (ed.), Essays in Early Eastern Initiation (Alcuin GROW Liturgical Study 8 = GLS 56), Bramcote 1988, 18–30; John F. BALDOVIN, A Lenten Sunday Lectionary in Fourth Century Jerusalem, in: J. Neil ALEXANDER (ed.), Time and Community. [FS Thomas Julian TALLEY], Washington/D.C. 1990, 115–122, esp. 119f.; Juliette DAY, Lent and the Catechetical Program in Mid-Fourth-Century Jerusalem, in: StLi 35 (2005) 129–147; Sebastià JANERAS, À propos de la Catéchèse XIVe de Cyrille de Jérusalem, in: EO 3 (1986) 307–318; ID., Novament sobre la Catequesi XIV de Ciril de Jerusalem, in: RCatT 21 (1996) 333–341; ID., En quels jours furent prononcées les Catéchèses 14–18 de Cyrille de Jérusalem, in: OCP 74 (2008) 195–207.

[32] Rolf ZERFASS, Die Schriftlesung im Kathedraloffizium Jerusalems (LQF 48), Münster 1968, 68–70. There are two indications of the secondary character of the distribution provided by the Georgian Lectionary: Firstly, the catechetical lections are incorporated in a liturgical framework not attested in earlier sources, indicating a general development. Secondly, the later Armenian tradition, which generally preserves the ordering of the Hagiopolite Quadragesimal readings extremely faithfully, assigns the catechetical lections to other days than the Georgian Lectionary, namely, to the days that in the early Hagiopolite order documented by the earlier witnesses of the Armenian Lectionary did not have proper readings: Mondays, Tuesdays and Thursdays of the 1st, 3rd, 4th, 5th and 6th week; cf. Charles RENOUX, Le lectionnaire de Jérusalem en Arménie. Le Čašocʿ. 2. Édition synoptique des plus anciens témoins, in: PO 214 = 48/2 (1999) 119 [33].

catechetical lections (and thus services), this would not necessarily tell us too much about the duration of Quadragesima as such, which is already described by Cyril as a period of forty days, though the liturgical circumstances of his catecheses remain disputed.

Finally, mention should be made of another suggestion about the prehistory of Quadragesima in Jerusalem: Charles Renoux, without doubt the most prominent expert on the Jerusalem liturgy, noted correspondences between pericopes provided by Hagiopolite lectionaries for Quadragesima and the lections on which Origen had preached in Jerusalem in the first half of the 3rd century.[33] Invited by Bishop Alexander of Jerusalem, Origen had preached what was perhaps a whole series of homilies on 1 Samuel; however, all that has survived of his exposition is two homilies transmitted in different contexts and some catena fragments that might, but need not necessarily, stem from homilies.[34] The Armenian Lectionary provides not only lections for the stational services on every Wednesday and Friday of the Quadragesima already known to Egeria, but in the second week also for the rest of the feriae, i. e., Monday, Tuesday, and Thursday, the first lesson of these additional services being taken from the beginning of 1 Samuel. The first pericope (to be read on Monday) is the very beginning of the book, on which Origen did demonstrably deliver a sermon in Jerusalem;[35] furthermore, there is a catena fragment attributed to Origen from the range of the second pericope (assigned to Tuesday by the Lectionary).[36] Further correspondences can be traced between what has been reconstructed as Origen's series of sermons and the order of readings provided by the Georgian Lectionary for the rest of Quadragesima, which generally fills up both the formerly vacant days with additional services and also the reading programme of prior stational dates, but leaves the old material mostly intact. From this evidence, Renoux draws the conclusion that an antecedent of the system of readings documented by the Georgian Lectionary would have been known to Origen; by the time of Egeria, who does not mention services beyond Wednesday and Friday, this ordering would have fallen into disuse and would have come to the surface only later, the Georgian Lectionary being a more faithful witness of the original disposition than the Armenian.

33 Charles RENOUX, La Quarantaine pré-pascale au 3e siècle à Jérusalem, in: MD 196 (1993) 111–129; ID., Origène dans la liturgie de l'Église de Jérusalem, in: Adamantius 5 (1999) 37–52. For a reassessment of both the circumstances of Origen's exposition of 1 Sam and the history of the Hagiapolite lectionary for the weekdays of the Quadragesima, see Harald BUCHINGER, Origenes und die Quadragesima in Jerusalem: Ein Diskussionsbeitrag, in: Adamantius 13 (2007) 174–217.

34 Pierre & Marie-Thérèse NAUTIN (eds.), Origène, Homélies sur Samuel (SC 328), Paris 1986.

35 Hom. 1, 1 in Sam. alludes to Bishop Alexander (SC 328, 96, 23; NAUTIN); the summary of the preceding lection (§ 2, ibid. p. 100–102) ranges from 1 Sam 1:1 to 2:11.

36 For detailed references and a critical discussion of the evidence, see BUCHINGER, Origenes (see fn. 33).

A close view, however, shows that the only exact correspondence is to be found in the very first lection, 1 Samuel 1:1–2:11 according to the Georgian Lectionary[37] (but only 1 Samuel 1:1–23 according to the Armenian Lectionary,[38] generally documenting an earlier stage). The beginning of the book is probably not a parallel strong enough to carry the weight of complex historical hypotheses, especially as the evidence can be explained more easily in a simpler way: rather than assuming an underground tradition running from the third to the fifth century, temporarily dormant in the late fourth century, it would seem more plausible to propose a continuous growth and development of the liturgical order of Quadragesima in Jerusalem. Egeria describes a stage at which Quadragesima contained only the stational days also observed in the rest of the year; only later on were the other weekdays to be furnished with services – a process the beginning of which can be observed in the Armenian Lectionary and the completion of which is documented by the Georgian Lectionary.

2. ON THE EARLY HISTORY OF QUADRAGESIMA IN ALEXANDRIA

2.1. Sources on the institution of Quadragesima

Roughly at the same time as Eusebius, *Athanasius*, in his sixth Festal letter of 334, gives us evidence of the introduction of pre-paschal Quadragesima in Alexandria.[39] Like Eusebius, he takes the number forty as a symbol. In Athanasius, however, the only biblical point of reference is the forty years' migration in the desert, by which the Israelites were purified for going up to Jerusalem, which would correspond to the Christians' going up to the upper room (cf. Mark 14:15/Luke 22:12) to hold the paschal meal with the Lord.[40] Like Eusebius, Athanasius testifies to a duration of six weeks but at the same time distinguishes Quadragesima from the ensuing (!) "holy days of the Pascha", even though these six days overlap with the last of the (in all) six weeks of fasting.[41]

[37] § 367 TARCHNISCHVILI.
[38] § XX RENOUX.
[39] Ep. fest. 6 (of 334) 12f. = 28f.; (the numbering of paragraphs follows the Italian translation of Alberto CAMPLANI [tr., intr., comm.], Atanasio di Alessandria, Lettere Festali. Anonimo: Indice delle Lettere Festali [LCPM 34], Milano 2003, 295f.; syr. text: William CURETON [ed.], The Festal Letters of Athanasius Discovered in an Ancient Syriac Version, London 1848, ܘ [6]). Having discussed the question of the Quadragesima already in his dissertation, Le lettere festali di Atanasio di Alessandria. Studio storico-critico (Unione Accademica Nazionale. Corpus dei Manoscritti Copti Letterari), Roma 1989, esp. 159–189, Alberto Camplani turns to the question in the comprehensive introduction to his translation of the Festal letters, esp. 178–181.
[40] This motif was introduced into Christian paschal theology by Origen; cf. Harald BUCHINGER, Pascha bei Origenes (IThS 64), Innsbruck 2005, 2, 644f.
[41] Sever J. VOICU, Settimana santa, digiuno e Quaresima nelle sottoscrizioni delle Lettere festali di Atanasio, in: Aug. 47 (2007) 283–297.

The fact that the previous Festal letters had not announced a Quadragesima, but only the "holy fast" of "the six great and holy days",[42] constitutes clear evidence from the writings of Athanasius for the official introduction of Quadragesima in Egypt, superseding but not replacing the old Paschal Fast. Where had the inspiration come from? The reassessment of the chronology of the Festal letters rules out Roman influence, which leaves us with two possibilities: either Athanasius transformed a period that already existed but was independent from Easter into a pre-paschal preparation, or this use was newly instituted by him.

In any case it seems clear that the idea as well as the practice of a forty-day fast must have been older than the Festal letter of 334. *Athanasius* himself, when appealing in his first Festal letter of 329 for the fast to be observed – nota bene the Paschal Fast of six days – mentions the idea of a forty-day fast and recalls the examples of Moses, Elijah, and Daniel.[43] A real period of forty days is known to Athanasius' immediate predecessor, *Peter I of Alexandria*, as early as the first decade of the fourth century; from certain of those who had lapsed under the persecution he demands "a further forty days" after a repentance of three years, "for which our Lord and Saviour Jesus Christ also fasted after having been baptized."[44] Whether, and if so when, this period of forty days was attached to a certain season of the year, and if or in what manner it had a liturgical shape,[45] is not clear.

In the Middle Ages, several sources claim to know that Quadragesima was originally held – in accordance with the example of Jesus – subsequent to Epiphany, the commemoration of his baptism, and only later, at the council of Nicaea, became associated with the Passion;[46] some later sources even ascribe

42 Ep. fest. 1 (of 329) 10 = 20 (syr. text Cureton 19; it. tr. LCPM 34, 235f.; Camplani). A fast of only six days is also announced in ep. fest. 14 (of 331) 6 = 26 (syr. text Cureton ܠܙ [37]; it. tr. LCPM 34, 257; Camplani); ep. fest. 4 (of 332) 5 = 7 (syr. text Cureton 35; it. tr. LCPM 34, 266; Camplani); ep. fest. 5 (of 333) 13 (syr. text Cureton 40; it. tr. LCPM 34, 280; Camplani). The chronology of the Festal letters remains a matter of debate; cf. Camplani, LCPM 34, 616–620. Furthermore, the announcement of the Quadragesima in ep. fest. 24 (of 330) 21 (copt. text CSCO 150 = CSCO.C 19, 41, 25f.; Louis Théophile Lefort; it. tr. LCPM 34, 246; Camplani) must be considered an interpolation; cf. Camplani, ibid. n. 24.

43 Ep. fest. 1, 6 = 13 (copt. text CSCO 150 = CSCO.C 19, 5f.; Lefort; syr. text Cureton 16f.; it. tr. LCPM 34, 231f.; Camplani). One notes that OT types of Christian fasting were indeed familiar to Athanasius, as they were to Eusebius and have remained quasi-canonical in later Quadragesimal theology.

44 Ep. can. 1 (FCCO 9/2; Périclès-Pierre Joannou / PG 18, 468 B): … ἄλλας τεσσαράκοντα ἡμέρας, ἃς καίπερ νηστεύσας ὁ κύριος καὶ σωτὴρ ἡμῶν Ἰησοῦς Χριστὸς μετὰ τὸ βαπτισθῆναι, ἐπειράσθη ὑπὸ τοῦ διαβόλου.

45 Peter says that the penitents should "watch in order to pray" (FCCO 9/2, 19f.; Joannou; cf. PG 18, 468 B): γρηγορήσουσιν εἰς προσευχάς.

46 Expositio Officiorum Ecclesiae 1, 13 (CSCO.S 3/91, 61, 12f. 22–25 [syr.] / 2/91, 51, 16f. 24–27 [lat.]; Richard H. Connolly); the attribution to the tenth-century Bishop George of Arbela is spurious.
The History of the Patriarchs of the Coptic Church of Alexandria, compiled by Severus of Ashmunein (10th century), ch. 7 & 8, mentions no more than that "the days of the fast and the day of the feast of Easter were fixed" by the council of Nicaea presided over by patriarch Alexander (PO 1/4, 402 [138]; 407 [143]; Basil Thomas Alfred Evetts); it does

the shift to Patriarch Demetrius (in office 189–232?).[47] Although the latter attribution is clearly anachronistic,[48] a core of historical truth has been claimed for the theory of a shift since Coquin, who held Athanasius responsible for it.[49] In some currents of recent scholarship, the institution of pre-paschal Quadragesima has also been connected with the spread of Easter as the time for baptisms in the church of Alexandria in the course of the 4th century. This conviction seems to be confirmed by an episode that ascribes the institution of Paschal baptism in Alexandria to Patriarch Theophilus (in office 385–412) and Horsiesi, leader of the Pachomian monasticism († 380/390?);[50] the account makes a clearly etiological point: "and thus it has been practised until today."[51] The case seems to be strengthened further by the Canones Hippolyti (mid-fourth century?), which in different contexts mention "Wednesday, Friday and the Forty" as "the appointed days of the fast", associating them with "God, who fasted for

not use the term "Quadragesima", but speaks only of "the fast" (الصوم), as does the East-Syrian ("Nestorian") Chronicle of Seert (after the 9th century), ch. 18 (PO 4, 281 [71]; Addai SCHER; the translation ibid. 280 [70] "le Carême" is misleading).
Attention was drawn to a western parallel – an Irish homily transmitted by a fifteenth-century manuscript containing homilies dated to the eleventh century – by Marc SCHNEIDERS, The Pre-paschal "Quadragesima": An Innovation of the First Nicaean Council? A Piece of "Evidence" from Ireland, in: ALW 33 (1991) 285–289.

47 The most detailed account is given by the latest source, Abu 'l-Barakat (14th century): L. VILLECOURT, Les observances liturgiques et la discipline du jeûne dans l'Église copte, in: Le Muséon 36 (1923) 249–292; 37 (1924) 201–280; 38 (1925) 261–320, here p. 314f. (French translation; Arabic original of Ms. Paris ar. 203 unpublished).
The account of Patriarch Eutychius (10th century; arab. text CSCO.A 3/6, 104f.; Louis CHEIKHO / lat. tr. PG 111, 989 C) remains obscure in some of its details. Later on, he refers to the Nicene decision about the calculation of the date of Easter and the Fast; he describes it as a confirmation of the computation made by Demetrius and the other bishops and patriarchs of his time (CSCO.A 3/6, 127; CHEIKHO / PG 111, 1007 D). The latter idea might ultimately go back to the account given by Eusebius of the Paschal controversy of the later 2nd century, though that text does not of course prove such an historical reconstruction: although the concurrence of Roman and Alexandrian practice is indirectly supposed, Victor and Demetrius are only mentioned together in the preceding chronological notice of h. e. 5, 22 (GCS 2/1, 486, 20–23; SCHWARTZ).
The Synaxarium Alexandrinum in one place seems to suggest an – obviously impossible – immediate succession of the feast of Christ's baptism, the Quadragesima, and Pascha (lat. tr. CSCO 3/18, 65; Jacobus FORGET / PO 1/3, 334f. [119f.]; René BASSET); elsewhere, however, it gives clearer and more detailed information, fictitiously speaking even of a council in Rome, involving Pope Victor and Patriarch Demetrius (CSCO 3/18, 111; FORGET / PO 3/3, 274f. [198f.]; the other sources only speak of an agreement).

48 Even Dionysius, successor to Demetrius, testifies only to the Paschal Fast of variable duration; see n. 2.

49 COQUIN, origines (see fn. 9), 148f.

50 Historia Horsiesi: Walter Ewing CRUM (ed., tr.), Der Papyruscodex saec. VI-VII der Phillipsbibliothek in Cheltenham. Koptische theologische Schriften (Schriften der wissenschaftlichen Gesellschaft in Straßburg 18), Straßburg 1915, papyrus p. 38–49 (copt. text p. 12–15; germ. tr. p. 65–69). It is not easy to determine the date of the text in the extant form, as the evidence allows any date during the 5th and the 6th centuries. A much shorter version is included in the History of the Patriarchs of the Coptic Church of Alexandria 11 (PO 1, 427; EVETTS; tenth century); it confuses Horsiesi with the Deacon Arsenius and does not stress the aspect of date.

51 Papyrus ed. Crum p. 49 (copt. p. 15; germ. tr. p. 69).

us" and referring to the catechumens,[52] and the Paschal Fast of the "Week of the Pascha of the Jews",[53] thus indicating a certain independence between Quadragesima and the Paschal Fast. However, it should be noted that the earliest dating proposed for the redaction of the Canones Hippolyti is mid-4th century,[54] at which time the pre-paschal Quadragesima had already been introduced in Alexandria, if not yet in its Egyptian hinterland.[55] This is even more true of the anecdote about Theophilus, which furthermore is not concerned with Quadragesima at all.

2.2. Scholarly debate on the interpretation

The thesis, developed above all by Thomas Talley, that Quadragesima was transferred from its original place after Epiphany to its later pre-paschal position by Athanasius, has been criticized by Alberto Camplani,[56] among others, on the following grounds. Firstly, Athanasius does not seem to have been unfamiliar with Paschal baptism: he himself is reported to have baptized before being exiled, possibly in the Paschal vigil of 339,[57] and Easter clearly was a baptismal date in the Pachomian monasteries,[58] with which he had close relations. The argumentum e silentio from the Festal letters' failure to mention Paschal baptism is not a strong one, as Theophilus and Cyril of Alexandria, in whose times Paschal baptism can safely be assumed, do not talk of it very much in their Festal letters either.

Secondly, the accounts of the institution of Paschal baptism by Theophilus need not necessarily be understood historically; Camplani in his turn proposes interpreting the etiological story as an argument against the diffusion of non-paschal

52 Can. Hipp. 20 (PO 149 = 31/2, 386f. [118f.]; René-Georges COQUIN).
53 Can. Hipp. 22 (PO 149 = 31/2, 388f. [120f.]; COQUIN).
54 Paul F. BRADSHAW – Maxwell E. JOHNSON – L. Edward PHILLIPS, The Apostolic Tradition. A Commentary (Hermeneia), Minneapolis 2002, 10.
55 Cf. n. 65.
56 In addition to the works quoted in n. 39, see Alberto CAMPLANI, Sull'origine della Quaresima in Egitto, in: David W. JOHNSON (ed.), Acts of the Fifth International Congress of Coptic Studies, Washington, 12–15 August 1992, Roma 1993, 2, 105–121.
57 CAMPLANI, LCPM 34, 345f. and 569 (it. tr.), with reference to Annick MARTIN, Introduction to SC 317, 82f. ("Ceci fait manifestement allusion à la fête de Pâques"), which, however, does not seem exempt from the suspicion of circular reasoning; the meaning of text may simply be that the baptism took place in the night before the twenty-second of Phamenoth (March 18), which would have been the second Sunday of the Quadragesima in that year: "... Athanasius, having been pursued on the night of the twenty-second of the month Phamenoth, escaped the next morning from the church of Theonas, after having baptized many." (English trans. CURETON xlviii).
58 Paul F. BRADSHAW, Baptismal Practice in the Alexandrian Tradition: Eastern or Western?, in: ID. (ed.), Essays (see fn. 31), 5–17 [repr. in Living Water [see fn. 8], 82–100], especially 8; Emmanuel LANNE, Catéchèse et initiation chrétienne dans la tradition pachômienne, in: Achille M TRIACCA – Alessandro PISTOIA (eds.), Mystagogie: Pensée liturgique d'aujourd'hui et liturgie ancienne. Conférences Saint-Serge. XXXIXe Semaine d'Études liturgiques, Paris, 30 juin–3 juillet 1992 (BEL.S 70), Roma 1993, 145–162.

baptism at the time when the *Historia Horsiesi* was composed towards the end of late antiquity: "The text's particular ideological orientation and its author's ignorance of fourth-century Pachomian baptismal practices invalidate its testimony with regard to the history of Egyptian Quadragesima."[59]
Thirdly, the medieval testimonies are late and inconsistent, and can all be explained otherwise as well:[60] their repeated account of a Quadragesima originally being attached to Epiphany displays traits of a reconstruction (possibly even of an ideological legitimization of contemporary practice),[61] the hypothetical character of which is clear not only from anachronistic elements but also from the inconsistency of the concrete data.[62] Furthermore, one could argue that the assertion made in various sources to the effect that the council of Nicaea reordered Quadragesima suffers under the same misunderstanding of the Nicene statement on the τεσσαρακοστή that caused pre-twentieth century scholars to confuse the fortieth day after Easter with a pre-paschal period of forty days.[63]

If this critique is valid, what can be said about the motivation and circumstances of the introduction of Quadragesima by Athanasius? It is clear that at the beginning of the fourth century there existed a fast of forty days in the context of the reconciliation of fallen members of the community, which Peter I associated with Jesus's fast after his baptism. It cannot be proved that this fast was held after Epiphany (the origins and original contents of which remain debated[64]),

59 CAMPLANI, origine (see fn. 56), 118: "Sia l'orientamento ideologico specifico del testo, sia l'ignoranza del suo autore circa le usanze battesimali pacomiane del IV secolo, rendono la sua testimonianza inutilizzabile per la storia della Quaresima egiziana."

60 CAMPLANI, origine (see fn. 56), 118f.

61 Clemens LEONHARD, The Jewish Pesach and the Origins of the Christian Easter. Open Questions in Current Research (SJ 35), Berlin 2006, 209f., summarizes his detailed analysis of what is probably the earliest source for the claim of a Nicene shift of the Quadragesima: "The author of the Expositio [cf. n. 46; H. B.] tries to reconstruct ante-Nicene customs on his own. His foregoing discussion of Biblical precedents for the Christian fast before Easter Sunday did not yield unequivocal parallels in the Gospel on which he could build a system of mimetic representation in the liturgy. Thus, he changes his strategy and explains the existing liturgy as the result of ecclesiastical legislation." Cf. also n. 86.

62 Apart from the abstruse projection of the putative Nicene decision into the time of Demetrius in several sources, one notes the contradictions regarding the date of baptism of the apostles by Christ: The letter of Macarius of Memphis (tenth century), which does not mention a fast other than the pre-paschal one, speaks of Friday of the sixth week of the fast (French translation: Louis VILLECOURT, La Lettre de Macaire, évêque de Memphis, sur la liturgie antique du Chrême et du Baptême à Alexandrie, in: Le Muséon 36 [1923] 33–46, here 39; Arabic original of Paris ar. 100 unpublished), Abu 'l-Barakat (VILLECOURT see fn. 47, p. 269) of the preceding Sunday. Neither a fixed Friday nor a Sunday can have been the end of a fast which would have begun on January 6, a changing day of the week.

63 The historical question seems to be have been settled by S. SALAVILLE, La ΤΕΣΣΑΡΑΚΟΣΤΗ du Ve Canon de Nicée (325), in: EOr 13 (1910) 65–72; ID., Tessaracoste: Carême ou Ascension, in: EOr 14 (1911) 355–357; ID., Τεσσαρακοστή, Ascension et Pentecôte au IVe siècle, in: EOr 32 (1929) 257–271.

64 The notion that Epiphany was dedicated to the baptism of Christ before the account of JOHN CASSIAN, Coll. 10, 2, 1 (CSEL 13, 286f.; Michael PETSCHENIG), which reflects the

nor can a link with Easter be established on the basis of the Pascha being mentioned in the Epistula canonica.[65] Is it not possible that Athanasius was inspired from outside? It cannot be precluded that he drew on the example of Palestine when he introduced the institution of fasting 40 days before Easter, especially since the theology of his Festal letters also draws heavily upon Palestinian sources (Eusebius and Origen).[66] However, unlike the lines of theological tradition, the historical development cannot be clearly traced.

3. ON THE EARLY HISTORY OF QUADRAGESIMA IN ROME

3.1. The earliest testimonies

It is possible that the church of Rome was also acquainted with the Quadragesima as early as the first half of the fourth century: in a letter to Serapion of Thmuis, *Athanasius* urges his colleague in office "to proclaim Quadragesima to the brethren and to persuade them to fast, lest only we from Egypt become the object of derision, because we do not fast but rejoice, while the whole world is fasting."[67] If the letter was composed in the year 340 in Rome, it attests to the existence of a Quadragesima in Rome more than forty years before the first indisputable testimony: in 384, *Jerome* writes that "we on the whole earth fast a Quadragesima according to a tradition of the apostles."[68] One year later, *Pope Siricius* in his letter to Himerius of Tarragona speaks of "forty or more days" of immediate preparation for baptism, which is to be conferred "at *Pascha* and its *Pentecost*".[69]

These are not the only statements that clearly contradict the church historian *Socrates*, who at a date as late as somewhat after 439 claims to know that in Rome a Quadragesima was held that only lasted three weeks.[70] *Leo I* in his roughly contemporaneous sermons not only makes frequent mention of a Quadragesima of forty days, but also unequivocally reveals that it lasted six weeks.[71]

situation of the later fourth century, has recently been questioned; Hans FÖRSTER, Die Anfänge von Weihnachten und Epiphanias. Eine Anfrage an die Entstehungshypothesen (STAC 46), Tübingen 2007, 57–120, esp. 82f., has argued that originally – according to his view not much earlier than somewhat before 374/377 – only the birth of Christ was commemorated in Egypt.

65 Ep. can. 1 (FCCO 9/2, 33, 12; JOANNOU / PG 18, 468 A).

66 CAMPLANI, Lettere (see fn. 39), 167–178. Palestinian influence on Athanasius has also been assumed by VOICU, Settimana (see fn. 41).

67 Ep. ad Serapionem 3 (syr. text CURETON ܟܗ–ܟܘ [25f.]; it. tr. LCPM 34, 376; CAMPLANI).

68 Ep. 41, 3, 2 ad Marcellam (CSEL 54^2, 313, 11–13; Isidor HILBERG): Nos unam quadragesimam secundum traditionem apostolorum toto nobis orbe ieiunamus.

69 Ep. 1, 2. 3 (PL 13, 1134 B–1135 A).

70 See n. 3.

71 For detailed references, see Winfried BÖHNE, Beginn und Dauer der römischen Fastenzeit im sechsten Jahrhundert, in: ZKG 77 (1966) 224–237, here 226–228.

3.2. Traces of even earlier prehistory and/or more recent developments?

Nevertheless, from the middle of the last century onwards Antoine Chavasse tried to collect indications of the history of Quadragesima in Rome, and above all arguments in favour of an early stage of three weeks.[72] Attention has repeatedly been drawn to the fragility of some of the data adduced to corroborate the case: the distance of three weeks between the earliest possible Easter date on March 22 and the beginning of the civil year on the first of the same month may be a mere coincidence of no further significance, and the distribution of Sanctoral celebrations is not a very safe starting point for historical conclusions. Apart from several other substantial problems,[73] both observations can only provide explanations for specific years, and they lose their validity in view of the changing date of Easter. The sheer variety of the hypotheses that have sprung up around the *Dominica in mediana* makes it clear that no reliable conclusions may be drawn from this anomaly.[74]

What remains to be explained, however, are two features of the Roman Quadragesimal liturgy as documented in the medieval sources. On the one hand there is firstly a series of readings from the gospel of John running from Friday of the third week until Tuesday of the sixth week of Quadragesima (which makes something more than two or something less than three weeks) and secondly a series of Sunday lections from the same gospel that can be reconstructed on the basis of irregularities in the ferial series mentioned above and in the light of non-Roman Italic liturgies; on the other hand, the number of originally three scrutinies can be inferred from this reconstruction of evidently catechetical dominical gospel readings, as it can from the Old Gelasian sacramentary. Furthermore, it is clearly attested by Johannes Diaconus, later (523–526) Pope John I.[75]

[72] Antoine CHAVASSE, Le Carême romain et les scrutins prébaptismaux avant le IXe siècle, in: RSR 35 (1948) 325–381; ID., Les messes quadragésimales du sacramentaire gélasien (Vat. Reg. 136), in: EL 63 (1949) 257–275; ID., La préparation de la Pâque, à Rome, avant le Ve siècle. Jeûne et organisation liturgique, in: Memorial J. Chaine (Bibliothèque de la Faculté Catholique de Théologie de Lyon 5), Lyon 1950, 61–80; ID., Temps de préparation à la Pâque d'après quelques livres liturgiques romains, in: RSR 37 (1950) 125–145; ID., La structure de Carême et les lectures des messes quadragésimales dans la liturgie romaine, in: MD 31 (1952) 76–119; ID., Les féries de Carême célébrées au temps de Saint Léon le Grand (440–461), in: Miscellanea Liturgica. [FS Giacomo LERCARO], Roma 1966, 1, 551–557; ID., L'organisation stationale du Carême romain avant le VIIIe siècle. Une organisation "pastorale", in: RevSR 56 (1982) 17–32 [repr. in: ID., La liturgie de la ville de Rome du Ve au VIIIe siècle. Une liturgie conditionnée par l'organisation de la vie in urbe et extra muros (StAns 112 = ALit 18), Roma 1993, 231–246].
For a useful review of the relevant theses and some critical remarks see Josef Andreas JUNGMANN, Die Quadragesima in den Forschungen von Antoine Chavasse, in: ALW 5/1 (1957) 84–95, and JOHNSON, Three Weeks (see fn. 8).

[73] JUNGMANN, Quadragesima (see fn. 72), 92f.

[74] JUNGMANN, Quadragesima (see fn. 72), 90f.; AUF DER MAUR, Feiern (see fn. 1), 146f.

[75] Ep. ad Senarium 2 (StT 59, 171, 6f. André WILMART = PL 59, 401 C): … tertio ante Pascha scrutinentur infantes.

Standing on its own, this line of reasoning can be relativized at every point: the number of three scrutinies is but one stage in a complex development the chronology of which remains highly hypothetical both in relative and in absolute terms,[76] the more so as the Gelasianum Vetus concerns itself with scrutinies in four contexts.[77] Although the (reconstructed) dominical series of readings from the gospel of John clearly includes four rather than three pericopes,[78] the ferial series of somewhat less than three weeks remains a remarkable phenomenon. However, since Chavasse himself assumes that this part of the lectionary is later than the development of Holy Week that in Rome can be substantiated from the fifth century on, the Lenten weekday readings transmitted in lectionaries from the seventh century on may be a secondary development within an existing Quadragesima rather than the remnant of an earlier stage that would have to reach back at least to the first half of the fourth century, i. e., to the time before the emergence of Quadragesima as a distinct entity.[79]

[76] It seems safe to assume a number of three scrutinies in the earlier sixth century on the basis of Johannes Diaconus, but generally the catechumenal rites are undoubtedly among the elements of baptismal liturgy that changed most between late antiquity and early Middle Ages.

[77] In addition to the formularies pro scrutinio at the third, fourth, and fifth Sundays, there is the Denuntiatio pro scrutinio inserted between Saturday of the fifth week and Palm Sunday (N° XXVIIII / § 283f. RED.F 4; Leo Cunibert MOHLBERG). On the problems of this order, see Dominic E. SERRA, New Observations About the Scrutinies of the Elect in Early Roman Practice, in: Worship 80 (2006) 511–527.

[78] For a convenient overview of the non-Roman evidence cf. Kl(aus) GAMBER, Die kampanische Lektionsordnung, in: SE 13 (1962) 326–352, here 346–349 (the problems of Gamber's interpretation of the material need not concern in the present context). In addition to the renowned pericopes of John 4, 9, and 11 one has to take into account John 8:12–59 attested on the third Sunday of the Quadragesima in the non-Roman traditions.

[79] Cf. JUNGMANN, Quadragesima (see fn. 72), 92: "Wenn wir diese Sonntagslesungen um eine Woche verschieben, so daß die Reihe lautet: Jo 4; 6; 8; 9; 10; 11 (Passion); 12; 13, so ergäbe sich zwar eine ungebrochene Reihe; aber da sonst nichts dafür spricht, begingen wir doch eine petitio principii. Und dürften wir, selbst wenn diese Operation zugelassen wird, eine festgelegte Perikopenreihe auch schon für die Wochentage ins 3./4. Jahrhundert (‚vor 384') zurückprojizieren? Zur Erklärung des Sachverhaltes genügt es durchaus, anzunehmen, daß in der Zeit, da die Quadragesima schon eine feste Einrichtung war, innerhalb dieser von der von jeher bevorzugten mediana-Woche an Johanneslesungen angesetzt wurden, die zugleich eine Vorstufe waren für die nachösterlichen Johanneslesungen." [If we shift these Sunday readings by one week so that the series runs: John 4; 6; 8; 9; 10; 11 (Passion); 12; 13, the result would admittedly be an uninterrupted sequence; but as there is no other evidence to this effect, we would be committing a petitio principii. And even if this procedure were to be allowed, would we really be justified in also projecting back to the third/fourth century ('before 384') a fixed sequence of pericopes allotted to weekdays? In order to explain the matter it is quite sufficient to assume that in the period in which Quadragesima was already established, within it readings from John were laid down for the period from the long since-favoured mediana week onwards that were at the same time antecedents of the post-paschal readings from John.]

4. CONCLUSION: OBSERVATIONS AND THESES

This trial and review of facts and interpretations has a bearing both on the "traditional" convictions and also on the "modern" alternative: the origin and character of Quadragesima cannot be explained satisfactorily either in terms of a gradual growth of the Paschal Fast into a preparatory time of forty days, or by the theory of its originating independently of Easter.

(1) There is no proof for *a successive growth from a one-week preparation* before Easter to a period of six or seven weeks (the position taken by "traditional scholarship"). The week before Easter is of course clearly discernible, but one has to distinguish two phenomena that are different in origin as well as in character.

On the one hand, the casual extension of the *Paschal Fast* from one, two, or three days to a whole week can occasionally be observed from the third century onwards. At its beginning, it is an individual ascetic exercise; its institutionalization at a later stage does not as such lead to a liturgical arrangement. The Paschal Fast exists long before the occurrence of a Quadragesima; and later documents show that it maintained its identity after the latter had become established. The final coexistence of the two institutions (as testified, for example, by Athanasius and the liturgical sources of Hagiopolite origin[80]) demonstrates that there is no genetic connection between them.

Holy Week as a liturgical institution, on the other hand, is a totally different phenomenon. It can only be observed much later, beginning with the later fourth century; it follows other – namely, liturgical – rules and is not primarily concerned with fasting. The special liturgical organization of the week before Easter either supersedes an already existing Quadragesima or shifts the latter a week back, thus demonstrating the genetic independence of the two phenomena. There is no proof that the Holy Week lectionary preserves a stratum older than Quadragesima; it may just as well be a special development of a more recent period of liturgical creativity.

(2) The theory that *a Quadragesima originally independent from Easter* was only secondarily moved to its later pre-paschal position (the explanation given by "modern scholarship"[81]) is able to maintain the original integrity of the forty-day period (which seems crucial in view of its symbolic value, the latter not being otherwise explicable: Quadragesima per definitionem means basically forty days, however they be counted, and not a shorter period). In other respects, however, it rests on somewhat shaky foundations: the few documents relating to the transposition come too late and are too heterogeneous to provide reliable information on the early fourth century, especially since from that time

[80] Further early evidence (around 375) is provided by the Palestinian-born EPIPHANIUS OF SALAMIS, fid. 22, 9f. (GCS 3^2, 523, 16–20; Karl HOLL – Jürgen DUMMER).

[81] The terminology is Johnson's (see fn. 7).

and for centuries thereafter there is no hint of the existence of a Quadragesima after Epiphany. A causal nexus between the universal spread of the pre-paschal Quadragesima and the rise of Paschal baptism in Alexandria cannot be proven, even though from the middle of the fourth century onwards Quadragesima increasingly coincides with the intensive phase of baptismal instruction in many places.

(3) Thus, the *appearance of a pre-paschal Quadragesima in the 330s* – between 325 and 337 in Palestine, from 334 on in Alexandria, and perhaps distinctly before 340 in Rome – remains the only firm date in its early history; every reconstruction trying to lead further back must remain hypothetical. Hansjörg Auf der Maur was definitively right in one respect at least: "The real origins of Quadragesima are shrouded in darkness."[82] Nevertheless, it may be asked, what objection is there to understanding the Quadragesima as a pre-paschal period of forty days, introduced as such in the first half of the fourth century, most likely in Palestine or perhaps in Alexandria? It is neither necessary to assume a shorter antecedent, nor must its origin be sought independently of Easter. Quadragesima appears as a phenomenon sui generis. As its first witnesses (Eusebius and Athanasius) testify, its fundamental duration of forty days with their biblical symbolism, is constitutive for Quadragesima to a degree that renders superfluous the search for any other explanation. Uncertainties in and differences between various practices only result from the concrete enactment of this principle.

The original reason for the introduction of Quadragesima remains obscure. To me, the most plausible theory would seem to be that the Paschal Fast may simply have been the hook on which to hang a period of fasting inspired by biblical prototypes and here or there practised previously for other reasons (e. g., public penance)[83] – to quote Eusebius, the first testimony available: "A period of forty days of preparation before the feast …, according to the example of the saints Moses and Elijah."[84] Speculation in medieval sources about a Quadragesima subsequent to the celebration of Christ's baptism and the practice of a liturgical period of this kind in some traditions[85] may well be late parallel

[82] AUF DER MAUR, Feiern (see fn. 1), 145: "Die eigentliche Herkunft der Quadragesima liegt im Dunkeln."

[83] On an heuristic level, this might appear as a prolongation of the Paschal Fast; nevertheless, the Quadragesima is a phenomenon sui generis and not an extension of the Paschal Fast as such.

[84] See n. 12.

[85] The Irish Martyrology of Oengus the Culdee (before 804) mentions "the beginning of Jesu's (sic) Lent" (HBS 29, 34; Whitley STOKES) on January 7, the day after Epiphany, the latter conceived as "the great baptism of Mary's son" (ibid.). The other fast known to this source is "Moses' Lent", held before Christmas, beginning on November 13 (ibid. 234).

Beginning the pre-paschal fast on the day after Epiphany obviously was quite common in certain monastic traditions; the Rule of the Master (first half of sixth century?) 45, 9–11 (SC 106, 18–23; Adalbert DE VOGÜÉ) prohibits the Alleluia as from (the day after)

phenomena rather than linear antecedents of the pre-paschal period of fasting, especially since such post-Epiphany fasts always occur in sources that already know several periods of fasting throughout the year.[86]

(4) What, then, remains of Socrates' presentation of a *three-week practice*, which is obviously wrong when taken in its actual wording, i. e., referring to the Roman practice of his time? One has to take into account the possibility that Socrates may here be just as ill-informed as he is in the second part of the same sentence,[87] and in instances where he gives historical details of liturgical practice (for example when referring to Alexandrian liturgy of Origen's time[88]); it is also possible that pieces of information containing a reliable core were handed down by him in a mistaken context and/or interpretation. However, the phenomenon of three-week periods as such is attested in several places in the context of pre-baptismal preparation,[89] and it may well be the case that practices of this kind formed the historical core of Socrates' account. Yet it does not seem necessary to regard them as anachronistic and relegate them to the, liturgically speaking, somewhat dark times before the later fourth century. The examples of both Rome and Jerusalem demonstrate that three-week periods need not necessarily be archaic institutions, but may also be the result of later systematizing tendencies (in Jerusalem, only the latest source – the Georgian Lectionary – gives a concrete liturgical arrangement for the catechetical lections, assigning them to the feriae of the last three weeks before Easter and integrating them in a liturgical framework previously unknown). Furthermore, one has to recognize, as has been underlined by Maxwell E. Johnson, that this three-week period of pre-baptismal preparation is a phenomenon not only ideally but also historically independent from the pre-paschal Quadragesima as such;[90] although it mostly

Epiphany, quia centesima Paschae ab eo die ieiunantibus incoatur et abstinentibus inputatur.

86 It is probably significant that the earliest source to raise the theory of the alleged shift of a post-Epiphany Quadragesima to its pre-paschal position, the Expositio Officiorum Ecclesiae of Ps-George of Arbela (see n. 46 and 61), is also the first known witness to the existence of three forty-day-periods of fasting in the East; on Expositio 1, 13 (CSCO.S 3/91, 61, 25–27; 62, 25–27 [syr.] / CSCO.S 2/91, 51, 27–30; 52, 19–21 [lat.]; CONNOLLY) cf. Karl HOLL, Die Entstehung der vier Fastenzeiten in der griechischen Kirche, in: ID., Gesammelte Aufsätze zur Kirchengeschichte. Band 2. Der Osten, Tübingen 1928, 155–203 [Repr. Darmstadt 1964; originally in SPAW.PH 1923/5, Berlin 1924], 177. Might Ps-George's historicizing idea of an allegedly original post-Epiphany Quadragesima have been influenced by his contemporary practice of a post-Pentecost Quadragesima (the "Fast of the Apostles")? On the similar three periods of fasting in the old British church, see ibid. 192, and Josef Andreas JUNGMANN, Advent und Voradvent. Überreste des gallischen Advents in der römischen Liturgie, in: ID., Gewordene Liturgie. Studien und Durchblicke, Innsbruck 1941, 232–294 [originally in: ZKTh 61 (1937) 341–390], esp. 253f. (on Oengus; cf. above n. 85); 257f.

87 The opinion that Saturdays in Rome were exempt from fasting is in any case misguided.

88 On h. e. 5, 22, 45–49 (GCS 301, 13–25; HANSEN), see BUCHINGER, Pascha (see fn. 40), 1, 147–152.

89 JOHNSON, Three Weeks (see fn. 8).

90 JOHNSON, Three Weeks (see fn. 8), 133 (emphasis original): "However, granted that the indications of this three-week period in the various sources do occur during the final

coincides with the latter in terms of liturgical time, it may not be taken as a genetic root in terms of historical explanation. (As a result, at least for Rome, it seems that there is a need to review the complex stratigraphy of the liturgical sources codified only in the Middle Ages and to think about alternative models to the ever more complex hypotheses about the prehistory of the Roman Quadragesima that have been developed since Antoine Chavasse.)
(5) Finally, I would like to propose that the phenomena with a distinguishable history and character should also be differentiated terminologically, and that the term *Quadragesima* should thus be reserved for a period of basically forty days, for which the symbolism of the biblical number is absolutely constitutive. And one has to make a clear distinction between a "Quadragesima" and two other phenomena: firstly, pre-paschal *one-week* periods of different origins and character – the ascetic practice of the Paschal Fast, which certainly is earlier than Quadragesima and which only in some cases was extended to a whole week, and the liturgical arrangement of Holy Week, which is probably a more recent invention but in any case follows different rules and interests; and, secondly, the *three-week* periods that occur in the course of baptismal preparation. The coexistence of these different phenomena, which accounts for the complexity of the liturgical orders as finally codified, is, rather, a secondary development involving various distinctive features; although interferences can be observed, I suggest avoiding the assumption of genetic dependence between institutions when their respective origins can be explained independently.

portion of Lent, this period devoted to baptismal preparation need not be understood only in relationship to Easter." Cf. ID., Preparation (see fn. 7), 42: "... when we first see whatever evidence there is for this three-week 'Lent' (with the exception of Socrates' general reference to fasting), it is 1. already closely associated with the final preparation of catechumens for baptism, and 2. not always clearly associated with Easter baptism." Cf. already JUNGMANN, Advent (see fn. 86), 246f., n. 49.

Ordination of Deaconesses or Widows in the Syrian Tradition

Anthony F. Carr

1. Introduction

The earliest Christian sources originating in Syria make no mention of deaconesses. Women who have a particular position in the Church are named widows and/or virgins (e.g. Ignatius, *To the Smyrnians* 13, 1: "to the virgins called widows"; and in some of the Pseudo Ignatian and Pseudo Clementine literature).[1] In the New Testament itself, the "women" who are set in strict parallel to the deacons are given no specific title (see 1 Timothy 3:11 [8–12]: "[Deacons like the bishop must be serious, not double-tongued, not addicted to much wine, not greedy for gain…] The women likewise must be serious, no slanderers, but temperate, faithful in all things. [Let deacons…]"). Are they spouses or deaconesses? More likely they were deaconesses like Phoebe "διάκονος of the Church at Cenchrae" (Romans 16:1).[2] The renowned preacher John Chrysostom, in his *Homilies on 1 Timothy* delivered at Antioch in Syria, calls the women in question deacons (διακόνοι) and affirms without hesitation that in the verse of 1 Timothy: "He (Paul) spoke about those who had the dignity of the diaconate (τὸ ἀξίωμα τῆς διακονίας)".[3] He offers no other alternative. It would seem a long-standing and unquestioned tradition of the Antiochene Church.

2. Didascalia of the Apostles

The first certain evidence is found in the Syriac *Didascalia of the Apostles* (ca. 230). The two groups, widows, and deaconesses are distinct and are treated as

1 Ignatius, To the Smyrnians 13, 1 (110; Karl Bihlmeyer – Wilhelm Schneemelcher); See also Pseudo Ignatius, To the Philippians 15, 1: "I salute the company of virgins and the order of widows", (PG 5, 940); Pseudo Clement, Recognitions 6, 15: "He also instituted the order of widows"; and Idem, Homily 11, 36, 2: "he regulated matters relating to widows", (PG 2, 301); The translations throughout the paper are mine.

2 See Luke Timothy Johnson, The First and Second Letters to Timothy (The Anchor Bible 35A), New York [etc.] 2001, 228–229; George T. Montague, First and Second Timothy, Titus (Catholic Commentary on Sacred Scripture), Grand Rapids/MI 2008, 82–83. Cf. the studies of Barry L Blackburn, The Identity of 'The Women' in 1 Tim 3:11, in: Carroll D. Osburn (ed.), Essays on Women in Early Christianity 1, Joplin/MO 1995, 303–319 and Jennifer H. Stiefel, Women Deacons in 1 Timothy: A Linguistic and Literary Look at 'Women likewise…' (1 Tim 3,11), in: New Testament Studies 41 (1995) 442–457.

3 John Chrysostom, Homily 11 in 1 Timothy 1 (PG 62, 553; Bernard de Montfaucon).

such. Following the admonition of 1 Timothy 5:9, widows are "appointed" (*qom*, aphel or *som*, ethpe'el)[4] to the office (*duko/duktho*) of widow.[5] Their qualities, conduct and ministry (*tešmešto* – especially prayer and alms) occupies a lengthy section.[6] They should, however, not presume to teach! A model recommended for their imitation is the poor widow who offered her two small coins in the Temple (Mark 12:41–44).

The deaconesses are treated together with the deacons in a short chapter (16).[7] The office of deaconess is presented as parallel to that of the deacon, but it is limited to the ministry (*tešmešto*) of women. For the baptism of women, for visiting women who are ill and "for many other matters, the office (*duktho*) of deaconess is required". The chapter is entitled: "On the Institution (the Syriac text uses the Greek word κατάστασις transliterated) of Deacons and Deaconesses". The phrase implies some sort of formal rite of "institution", but no liturgical ritual is supplied. The section begins with the admonition to the bishop:

> O bishop, constitute (*maqim*, aphel) righteous workers for yourself, helpers who may cooperate with you for the salvation [of all]. Those who are suitable according to you from among all the people you shall choose (*tegbe*) and shall constitute (*taqim*) as deacons, a man for the administration of many necessary things [and] a woman for the ministry of women.

The double duty of the bishop, on the one hand to "select, choose, elect" (*gbo*)[8], and on the other to "appoint, erect, constitute, establish" (*aqim*), could well reflect the effort of a Syriac translator to render adequately the two senses of the Greek verb χειροτονέω, namely "to choose, elect (by raising hands)" and "to appoint, install (by some gesture of the hand)".[9]

The verb χειροτονέω is already the expression for selection of one for a definite office found in the Syrian *Didache*: "Choose (χειροτονήσατε) then for yourself bishops and deacons worthy of the Lord".[10] An influence of the *Didache* cannot be excluded. A ritual gesture of raising or imposing hands could thus be implied in the Greek, although less evident in the Syriac. The instituting of deacons and deaconesses supposes some external sign(s), an "ordination" in the broad sense

4 See Jessie Payne SMITH (Margoliouth) (comp.), A Compendious Syriac Dictionary, Oxford 1903, 495.366.

5 Didascalia apostolorum syriace 14 (Didascalia apostolorum syriace, ed. Paul de LAGARDE, Leipzig 1854, 61, 62); cf. The Didascalia Apostolorum in Syriac 2, 1 (Text) (CSCO.S 179, 155–156; Arthur VÖÖBUS). For an English translation see Didascalia apostolorum, trans. Richard Hugh CONNOLLY, Oxford 1929 and The Didascalia Apostolorum in Syriac 2, 2 (Version) (CSCO.S 180), trans. Arthur VÖÖBUS, Louvain 1979. The Syriac word *duko/dukhto* means literally "post" or "position", see Payne SMITH (Margoliouth), Compendious Syriac Dictionary, 85.

6 Didascalia, 15 (ed. LAGARDE, 63–70; ed. VÖÖBUS, 157–172).

7 Didascalia, 16 (ed. LAGARDE, 70–72; ed. VÖÖBUS, 172–174).

8 See Payne SMITH (Margoliouth), Compendious Syriac Dictionary, 58.

9 See William F. ARNDT – Felix W. GINGRICH, A Greek-English Lexicon of the New Testament, Chicago–London ²1979, 881. The Apostolic Constitutions 3, 16, 1, however, use the related verb προχειρίζω.

10 Didache 15 (Karl BIHLMEYER – Wilhelm SCHNEEMELCHER).

even if it is not clear how the ministry was conferred. The only model cited for the deaconess in the *Didascalia* is the ministry to Jesus of the holy women – Mary Magdalene, Mary the mother of James and Joseph, and the mother of the sons of Zebedee (Matthew 27:56).

3. COUNCIL OF NICAEA

The next testimony comes from the Ecumenical Council gathered at Nicaea in 325. The council fathers were confronted by the question of the followers of the heretic Paul of Samosata (Syria) who returned to the Catholic Church. The Council decided they should be baptized *de novo* since their former baptism was void. If they were among the clergy and were without reproach, those (re)baptized were to be ordained by the Catholic bishop. If unfit, they were to be deposed. Among those coming back to the Church were some deaconesses and the fathers of Nicaea concluded: "As regards the deaconesses, and in short, any who have been enrolled among the clergy, the same convention shall be observed. Moreover, we considered those deaconesses who are counted in that status although they do not have any imposition of hands (χειροθεσία); they are by all means to be ranked among the laity".[11] For the Council, membership in the clergy clearly comes by ordination through a bishop's imposition of hands. That deaconesses are enrolled among the clergy is not brought into question. There seem, however, to have been two groups of Paulinianist deaconesses – one which had rightly received ordination at the hands of a bishop and another which had not. Prayer to accompany the χειροθεσία is not mentioned in the canon.

4. APOSTOLIC CONSTITUTIONS

The first complete description of the ordination of deaconesses comes in the Apostolic Constitutions (ca. 380). This church order comes from the ranks of one of the three rival Christian communities at Antioch that resulted from the Arian controversy. Its theology is neither radically Arian nor wholly Nicene, but rather a moderate Origenism – Biblical and archaic.[12]

[11] Council of Nicaea, canon 19 (Conciliorum oecumenicorum decreta, Bologna ³1973, 15; Josephus ALBERIGO et alii); The last part of the canon is not entirely clear in its expression.

[12] See the remarks of Marcel METZGER in the introduction to his edition and translation of Apostolic Constitutions, Books 3–6 (SC 329), Paris 1986, 10–39: "La théologie des *CA*".

Book three parallels, in a slightly different version in Greek, the information mentioned above in the Syriac Didascalia of the Apostles.[13] The rite of ordination proper in Book eight follows that of deacons, although it lacks the specific term χειροτονία – "ordination" – found for the rite of ordaining a presbyter and a deacon.[14] On the other hand the principal gesture in the ritual is the laying on of hands[15] as in the ordination of the presbyter and the deacon, as well as in those of a subdeacon or a lector.[16] The Apostolic Constitutions distinguish between "ordain" (χειροτονεῖ) and "impose hands" (χειροθετεῖ): the bishop ordains and he imposes hands; the presbyter imposes hands but he does not ordain.[17] This imposition of hands is contrary to the regulations of the so-called Apostolic Tradition on which Book eight is based. At the installation of women (widows and virgins), of lectors, and of subdeacons according to the earlier church order, "hands shall not be laid on her/him".[18] The presence of the presbytery, the deacons and the deaconesses is explicitly mentioned by the Apostolic Constitutions.[19]

The structure of the prayer for a deaconess, which has no counterpart in the Apostolic Tradition, is parallel to that for a deacon: address to God, commemoration of some relevant mirabilia Dei, a petition to look upon the one selected for the diaconate (εἰς διακονίαν), an epiclesis over the person so that she may fulfill worthily the office entrusted to her, and a doxology.[20]

The introduction of the prayer appeals to "O God, the eternal". The features of God's mighty works cited are:

> "Father of our Lord Jesus Christ" (2 Corinthians 1:3);
>
> "Creator of man and woman" (Genesis 1:27);
>
> "Who filled with the Spirit Miriam (Exodus 15, 20), Deborah (Judges 4:4), Hannah (Luke 2:36), and Huldah (4 Kings 22:14)";
>
> "Who did not consider it unworthy that your only-begotten Son be born of a woman" (Luke 1:26-38);
>
> "Who chose/installed (προχειρισάμενος) in the tent of witness and the temple women keepers of your holy gates" (see Exodus 3:88 and 1 Kings 2:2).

After a reference to the sonship of Jesus, the text turns to God's choice of woman from the beginning on various occasions for service in the history of salvation. The first instance was the creation of woman as partner of man. Like those

[13] Apostolic Constitutions 3 (SC 329, 120–164; Marcel METZGER).
[14] Apostolic Constitutions 8, 19, 1 (SC 336, 220; Marcel METZGER), in contrast to 8, 16, 1 and 8, 17, 1 (216–217; Marcel METZGER). Hereafter abbreviated AC.
[15] Επιθήσεις αὐτῇ τὰς χειρας, AC 8, 19, 2 (220; Marcel METZGER).
[16] AC 8, 16, 2; 17, 2; 21, 2; 22, 2 (216.218.222.224; Marcel METZGER).
[17] AC 8, 28, 2–3 (228.230; Marcel METZGER).
[18] Apostolic Tradition, chapters 10, 11 (οὐδὲ γὰρ χειροθετεῖται), 12, 13 (LWQF 39, 30.32; Bernard BOTTE).
[19] AC 8, 19, 2 (220; Marcel METZGER).
[20] AC 8, 20 (220.222; Marcel METZGER).

elected and established witnesses of old, the deaconess being ordained is to receive the Holy Spirit. The fundamental role of a woman (Mary) in the incarnation is highlighted. The only ministry as such hinted at in the list of women favored by God is that of porter at the doors of the church. It is confirmed by a notice in Book two: "Let the porters stand near the entrances of the men to guard them and the deaconesses near those of the women like a ship's steward, for the same pattern (τύπος) was traced in the tent of witness".[21] There is a mixture of Old Testament and New Testament allusions. The model of the holy women who ministered to Jesus according to the *Didascalia* is absent.

The text then turns from the past actions of God to the present: "And so you yourself now look down upon (imperative!) your servant, N., who is being installed (προχειριζομένην) in the diaconate". The list of God's mighty works gives confidence in his activity here and now in favor of the woman presented for admission to the order of deaconesses. The rite uses an historical anamnesis as basis for a demand (imperative) for the present and ongoing operation of God in the actual ordination. The person presented for the order of deaconess is called by name (τήνδε). The term used for her diaconal work is the same as for the male deacon (εἰς διακονίαν).[22] No detail is supplied, however, about what that service might involve concretely outside of the reference to serving as porters in common with male deacons. Elsewhere a supervisory role over widows is attributed to deaconesses alongside the deacons and higher clergy.[23]

The prayer then calls upon the purifying presence of the Holy Spirit in order to bring to a fitting end the work put into her hands for the glory and praise of Christ: "Give (imperative) her the Holy Spirit and 'cleanse (imperative!) her from all defilement of flesh or spirit' (2 Corinthians 7:1) in order to accomplish (ἐπιτελεῖν) worthily the work (ἔργον) entrusted (ἐγχειρισθὲν) to her for the glory and approval of your Christ". The Spirit epiclesis is to realize the physical and spiritual purification of the deaconess for the purpose of fulfilling and completing her years of diaconal service not for her own sake but for the glorification of God's Anointed One whom their life and work is to please. The Pauline text inserted in the prayer originally came between a commemoration (anamnesis) of the promises of God (2 Corinthians 6:16-18) and the invitation to "complete (ἐπιτελοῦντες) a life of holiness in fear of God" (2 Corinthians 7:1). The influence of these Pauline verses is notable in the expression of the "fruit" of the Spirit's presence. The frequency of words derived from the root χεῖρ, "hand" is suggestive in regard to the "gesture" associated with the rite.

21 AC 2, 57, 10 (SC 320, 314; Marcel METZGER). See also AC 8, 28, 6 (230; Marcel METZGER). There is an interesting parallel in part of the closing greeting of the fourth century PSEUDO IGNATIUS, To the Antiochians 12: "I salute the keepers of the holy gates, the deaconesses in Christ", (PG 5, 908).

22 AC 8, 20, 2 (222; Marcel METZGER), cf. AC 8, 18 (220; Marcel METZGER).

23 AC 3, 8, 1 (140; Marcel METZGER): "Widows should be obedient to bishops, presbyters, deacons as well as to deaconesses".

The oration ends with a doxology simpler than that of the other ordination prayers in the series: “through whom to you (be) glory and adoration in the Holy Spirit to the ages”, and the “Amen”.
The ordination of a deaconess in this document includes her in the ranks of the clergy, but the significance of the laying on of hands is unclear because it is also used for subdeacons and lectors as mentioned above. The rank of deaconess is fluid: in the rites of ordination it follows that of deacons and the deaconess is said to be representative of the Holy Spirit as the deacon is of Christ in an earlier section evolved from the *Didascalia*.[24] This implies a close connection of the two. In other texts, however, the reference to deaconesses follows after the orders of subdeacons, readers, cantors, porters, and even ascetics, but ahead of widows and virgins.[25] Their liturgical functions are limited to keepers of the entrances to church, examination of foreign women entering the church,[26] and the baptism of women.[27] The information on hand about the import of the ordination of deaconesses is, unfortunately, not consistent.

5. TESTAMENTUM DOMINI NOSTRI JESU CHRISTI

In the *Testament of our Lord Jesus Christ* (late fourth–fifth century), a Syrian church order derived from the so-called *Apostolic Tradition*, there is no ordination rite for deaconesses. Where one would expect to find the same, after the ordination of deacons, there is a special blessing for widows instead! They have the rank and duties that in other sources appertain to deaconesses. This may to some extent depend on the earlier document, the *Apostolic Tradition*, which does not mention deaconesses. In it widows are appointed (καθίστασθαι)[28] by word, or named, not ordained. Thus hands are not to be laid on her – ordination (χειροτονία) is for the clergy on account of the liturgy and she has no liturgical role.[29] No prayer is provided there.
In contrast to the ritual for a bishop, a presbyter, or a deacon, which is called “χειροτονία” – the Greek word is transliterated into Syriac[30] –, the ritual for a widow is designated as an “institution” (*m^{e}qimonutho*)[31] of widows who sit in

24 AC 2, 26, 5–6 (238; Marcel METZGER).
25 AC 2, 26, 3 (236; Marcel METZGER); cf. 8, 13, 14 (208–210; Marcel METZGER); 8, 28, 7 (230; Marcel METZGER) and 8, 31, 2 (234; Marcel METZGER).
26 AC 2, 58, 6 (322; Marcel METZGER).
27 AC 8, 28, 6 (230; Marcel METZGER); see especially 3, 16, 1–4 (154–158; Marcel METZGER).
28 The word appears four times in the short paragraph of Apostolic Tradition 10.
29 Apostolic Tradition 10 (30; Bernard BOTTE). The Greek terminology comes from the Coptic version.
30 Testamentum domini nostri Jesu Christi, ed. tr. Ignatius Ephraem RAHMANI, Mainz 1899, 28, 68, 92.
31 The word corresponds to the Greek καθίστασθαι.

the first places. The introductory rubric has her praying with face bowed at the entrance to the altar. The bishop prays quietly so that the priests alone can hear. The humble attitude of the candidate is matched by the quiet atmosphere of the prayer itself.[32]

The structure of the oration is more complicated than the *Apostolic Constitutions*: the titles with which God is addressed are not all in one place; in place of an historical anamnesis of God's mighty works, the prayer names God's dealings with the humble, the weak, the scorned, the poor ones; there is no epiclesis calling down the Holy Spirit as such, but a series of petitions to grant a spirit of power, of humility, of patience; the gifts requested are to strengthen and sanctify her in her works; finally there is a lengthy doxology and "Amen".[33]

The appellatives of God are simple: "O holy and most high God", "O venerable One", "O Lord" (three times), "O Lord God", "O God the Father". The prayer is clearly addressed to God the Father. God's relationship to humankind is kenotic and salvific: "You look upon lowly women, you have chosen the weak as well as the strong, O honored One, you have created also those things which are contemptible [of no account],… You know our weakness". The titles are distributed throughout the prayer – a phenomenon that creates a certain lack of integration and unity. On the other hand the frequent interjections give the prayer a more intimate tone. There is decided contrast built between the divine holiness and power on one hand and the weakness and lowliness of human beings, the widows being one, on the other.

The most extensive part of the prayer consists in the "epiclesis" and accompanying petitions. The epicletic passages are, in order:

> Confer (*hab*) the spirit of power upon this your servant and make her strong in your truth.
>
> Confer (*hab*) on her the power to carry out joyfully those teachings of yours, which you have laid down as a rule [of life, κανών] for your servant.
>
> Give her, Lord, a spirit of humility, and of power, and of patience, and of kindness.
>
> Perfect your servant for the praise of your house, make her strong in instruction and good example, sanctify [her], give her wisdom, encourage [her], O God.

God is enjoined, in imperatives, to give the spirit or power (thrice), to strengthen (twice), to perfect, to sanctify, to give wisdom, and to encourage the widow, his "servant" (twice). The specific gifts requested are vigor, truth, right conduct, humility, long-suffering, benevolence, knowledge, holiness, wisdom and courage. It is an impressive list to mark the life of attentive care and observance of a widow at the service of the Church. Some duties of the widows are alluded to in sections of the petitions, namely, prayer in church ("praise of your house"), instruction of female catechumens and believers ("strong in your truth"; "strong in instruction and example"; "give her wisdom"); observing a set rule of life

[32] Testamentum domini nostri Jesu Christi, 41 (98; Ignatius Ephraem RAHMANI).
[33] Testamentum domini nostri Jesu Christi, 41 (98; Ignatius Ephraem RAHMANI).

("observe your teachings"; "good example"; "make her holy"; "give her courage").

The hoped-for results of the abundant gifts granted to the widow by God are expressed in the following terms:

> … so that, observing your commandment and laboring in your holy house, she may be for you a precious vessel and sing praise on the day on which you are prepared to glorify your lowly ones.
>
> … so that, bearing your burden with inexpressible joy, she may sustain her toils.

The text accentuates her conduct in a prescribed rule of life and her service in God's house. The consequence is to become a vessel sacred to the Lord in the church (holy house) and to join the heavenly choirs. This is reminiscent of the role of the "daughters of the covenant" in Syriac Christianity. The second passage alludes to the words of Jesus in Matthew (11:28, 30): "Come to me, all who labor and are heavily laden, and I will give you rest… For my yoke is easy and my burden is light". The reference to a life according to Christ's teaching in the preceding section may also suggest the influence of 1 John (5:3): "For this is the love of God, that we keep his commandments. And his commandments are not burdensome".

The doxology begins with a transitional phrase. "Because blessed and praiseworthy is your kingdom, O God the Father". It brings to mind the "Our Father". The text of the doxology itself is lengthy and involved, especially in its reference to the Holy Spirit: "And to you be glory and to your only-begotten Son, our Lord Jesus Christ, and to the Holy Spirit, good and worthy of worship and life-giving, and equal to you in essence (= consubstantial), now, before all ages, and forever and ever". The extended section on the Spirit indicates a time after 381 (Council of Constantinople) when the discussion on the divinity of the Holy Spirit was still a burning issue. *Homoousios* was not immediately applied to the Spirit at the Council.

The prayer for the installation of a widow is an anomaly. The duties assigned to her in the *Testament* are those normally assigned to deaconesses elsewhere. Widows and deaconesses are, however, distinct groups in the document. In the community of the *Testament of our Lord*, the widows were members of the clergy with special seating in the sanctuary, etc. Although there is no laying on of hands, they are said to be chosen (*m^ethgabayo*) and ordained (*tetasrah̲*).[34] That is true of deaconesses in other documents of the era. The reversal of roles, widow = deaconess, is singular for the period (fourth–fifth century). It may depend on the particular tradition of the local church or it may represent the great

[34] Testamentum domini nostri Jesu Christi, 40 (94; Ignatius Ephraem RAHMANI). The noun, *mettasr^eh̲onutho*, "ordination", from the aphel of the same root *srh̲*, is used for priests and deacons as well as for widows in the document! See Testamentum domini nostri Jesu Christi, ed. Ignatius Ephraem RAHMANI, 68. 90. 98. The significance of the "ordination" of a widow is at best ambiguous.

respect on the part of the compiler for the mother document, the *Apostolic Tradition*.

The inconsistencies and unclear organization of the prayer said over the widow hint at a prayer composed of elements from other orations that may or may not have been specifically intended for the "order" of widows. It also has all the marks of a translation into Syriac from another tongue whose structure has determined that of the actual text, in word order, etc. The Greek original is not extant.

In the patristic sources considered, the deaconesses have a liturgical and pastoral ministry towards women. They assist at the baptism of women, especially with the anointing for the sake of propriety. They welcome (ὑποδέχεσθαι) the newly baptized women, probably helping them get out of the water and get dressed. They teach and instruct these women so that the seal of baptism might be solid. They have custody of the doors through which women enter the church. The paradigms for the service of women (deaconesses or widows) in the Church are varied: the poor woman with her two pennies; the holy women who ministered to Jesus; the Spirit-filled women Miriam, Deborah, Hannah, and Huldah; Mary, the mother of the Savior; the women door-keepers at the tent and the temple; lowly women (allusion to Luke 1:48?), but never the "deaconess" Phoebe of the Letter to the Romans (16:1). They are all Biblical models, but they have little in common. That may indicate confusion about the interpretation of their ministry.

6. THE ECLIPSE OF DEACONESSES IN THE SYRIAN TRADITION

In the following period there are increasingly restrictive canonical regulations about the ministry of deaconesses gathered by John bar Qursos, bishop of Tella († 538) and Jacob of Edessa († 708). Typical is the canonical reply of Jacob that finds its way into a later ordination rite for deaconesses in the West Syrian tradition:

> From Jacob of Edessa: She has no power at all at the altar, because even though she is ordained she is not ordained <in the sanctuary> but in the church only. She has the power only to sweep the sanctuary and to light the lamps in the sanctuary, but <she does> these things when there is no presbyter or deacon present. If she is in a monastery of nuns, she may take the mysteries from the repository where there is no presbyter or deacon and she may give them to women or younger children. She may not take them (the mysteries) from the altar nor may she place them on it nor may she touch it at all. When adult women are baptized, she may anoint them. She may visit women who are ill and minister to them. The above alone constitutes her power in the church.[35]

[35] In a manuscript of Paris, Bibliothèque nationale de France, ms. Syr 113, fol. 111r (page 223) of the fourteenth century, which I have in microfilm.

Deaconesses continued to be ordained for a time, but they are increasingly excluded from the sanctuary and from any significant service if priests or deacons are present. Adult women to be baptized and anointed were certainly few. The deaconess may visit and minister to women who are sick. Otherwise, little is left for her to do.

Gebet und Fasten nach der orientalischen orthodoxen Tradition

Biji Markose Chirathilattu

„Und dann wird es geschehen, dass der Anbetende alle Gebete empfängt. Nun ist er nicht mehr der, der anbetet; er ist nicht mehr der, der fragt, sondern der, der alle Fragen beantwortet, weil ihm sein reicher Vater Macht gegeben hat über seinen Reichtum. Und der Anbetende ist derselbe geworden wie derjenige, der in ihm wohnt."[1] Diese Worte aus dem „Buch der Taube" und dem „Ethikon", den beiden Spätwerken von Gregor Bar-Hebraeus, bringen sehr deutlich den Höhepunkt des Gebets, welche ein Gläubiger/eine Gläubige der Syrisch-Orthodoxen Kirche durch Gebete erreichen kann, zum Ausdruck. Die wesentlichen Elemente auf dem Weg dorthin sind Gebet und Fasten. Bar-Hebraeus, der syrische Maphrian des 13. Jahrhunderts, „einer der leuchtenden Sterne unter den syrischen Schriftstellern"[2], wie ihn Anton Baumstark genannt hat, ist uns allen bekannt. Seine Äußerungen zu Gebet und Fasten sind bis jetzt allerdings noch nicht zusammenhängend untersucht worden. Mein Vortrag versucht, dazu einen systematisierenden Überblick zu geben.

Die Hauptquellen seiner asketischen und spirituellen Lehre sind das Ethikon[3], der Nomokanon[4] und das Buch der Taube[5]. Als wohl wichtigster syrisch-orthodoxer Sammler von Kanones verwendet Bar-Hebraeus viel Mühe darauf, für seine Kirche die Regelungen für die Gebete und das Fasten zusammenzustellen. Besonders bemerkenswert daran sind seine eigenen Erklärungen für einzelne Vorschriften. Es gibt unterschiedliche Anweisungen für die Laien, die Asketen und die Priester, aber auch gemeinsame Bestimmungen, die alle Gläubigen betreffen[6].

Für alle Gläubigen gelten dieselben Grundlagen des Betens. Konzentration zählt zu den wichtigsten Voraussetzungen. Bevor man betet, muss die Seele von allen leidenschaftlichen Gedanken befreit werden. Nur mit ständiger Anstrengung ist es möglich, die richtige Achtsamkeit zu erreichen. Reine Gedanken, das Verständnis der im Gebet gesprochenen Wörter, das Lob des Herrn in der Seele, die

[1] Paul Bedjan (ed), Ethicon seu Moralia Gregorii Bar-Hebraei, Paris – Leipzig 1898, 492–493; Arent J. Wensinck (transl.), Bar Hebraeus' Book of the Dove together with Some Chapters from his Ethicon, Leyden 1919, 104.

[2] Anton Baumstark, Geschichte der syrischen Literatur mit Ausschluß der christlich-palästinensischen Texte, Bonn 1922 [Nachdruck: Berlin 1968], 312–313.

[3] Bedjan, Ethicon (siehe Anm. 1).

[4] Paul Bedjan (ed), Nomocanon Gregorii Barhebraei, Paris – Leipzig 1898.

[5] Wensinck, Book of the Dove (siehe Anm. 1).

[6] Biji Markose Chirathilattu, Prayers and Fasts according to Bar Ebroyo, Münster 2004, 40–87.

Ehrfurcht vor dem allmächtigen Gott, das Beschämt-Werden über eigene Sünden und die Hoffnung auf Gottes Gnade führen zur Vollkommenheit im Gebet[7]. Auf den Kanones der Apostel basierend erklärt Bar-Hebraeus ausführlich, warum es die sechs täglichen Stundengebete gibt[8]. Zum Beispiel muss man am Morgen beten, weil der Herr am Morgen das Licht erschaffen hat. Zur dritten Stunde (der Zeit zwischen Sonnenaufgang und Mittag) wird gebetet, weil Jesus zu dieser Zeit verurteilt wurde. Zu den kanonischen Gebeten kommen weitere Gebete zu Situationen des Alltags und in verschiedenen Lebenslagen[9]. Eine ausführliche Beschreibung der Regelungen für die Gebete bei den Mahlzeiten findet sich im Ethikon, sowie die Verpflichtungen für Gebete in Freundschaft und Ehe[10]. Gebete vor dem Betreten einer Kirche wie auch Gebete für die Reisenden finden ihren Platz im Werk des Bar-Hebraeus. Das ganze Leben der Gläubigen soll von Gebeten geprägt sein. So gibt es selbst für diejenigen Gebete, die sich waschen oder ein Bad nehmen. Am Morgen, nach dem Aufstehen, soll der Gläubige beten, während er sich wäscht. Wenn möglich, soll er dabei den ganzen Psalm 51 beten. Hier ist natürlich Vers 9 im Blick: „Entsündige mich mit Ysop, dann werde ich rein. Wasche mich, dann werde ich weißer als Schnee.“ Zur Not kann der Gläubige auch nur diesen Vers sprechen. In öffentlichen Badeanstalten soll man allerdings nicht laut sprechen und auch keine Psalmen singen[11].

Interessant ist es, wie der Maphrian mit den traditionellen Reinheitsregelungen seiner Kirche umgeht. Er rät dazu, diese Vorschriften zu vernachlässigen, wenn sie der Verrichtung von Gebeten hinderlich sind. So erlaubt er den Frauen, die ihre Menstruation haben, in die Kirche zu kommen und zu beten, obwohl dies traditionell für sieben Tage verboten ist. Als Begründung für diese Abweichung von der überlieferten kirchlichen Norm nennt Bar-Hebraeus den Gedanken, dass der Heilige Geist, den wir durch die Taufe empfangen haben, trotz Menstruation in uns bleibt. Analoges gilt für Männer nach Samenerguss[12].

Das Fasten zielt auf die Erhöhung der Menschen zu den Stufen der Engel[13]. Die geistlichen Sinne des Menschen werden von allen „Essensgerüchen“ gereinigt, die die Seele blind machen[14]. Bar-Hebraeus vergleicht die verschiedenen Arten von Fasten miteinander und erteilt für jede einzelne von ihnen detaillierte Regelungen. Dies trifft etwa zu für seine Beschreibung über die Speisen, die am Mittwoch und Freitag erlaubt bzw. verboten sind, sowie für die Einzelheiten der

7 Herman G. B. TEULE (ed.), Gregory Barhebraeus Ethicon Memra 1 (CSCO.S 219), Louvain 1993, 14–16.
8 TEULE, Ethicon, 21; BEDJAN, Nomocanon, 63–64.
9 CHIRATHILATTU, Prayers and Fasts, 50–51.
10 BEDJAN, Ethicon, 121–128.
11 CHIRATHILATTU, Prayers and Fasts, 60–64.
12 BEDJAN, Ethicon, 165–167.
13 Antoine TORBEY (ed. and transl.), Le Candélabre du Sanctuaire de Grégoire Abou'l Faradj dit Barhebraeus, Cinquième base: Des Anges (PO 30), Paris 1963, 694.
14 TEULE, Ethicon, 85; WENSINCK, Book of the Dove, 27; Paul BEDJAN (ed.), Liber Columbae Seu Directorium Monachorum Gregorii Barhebraei, Paris – Leipzig 1898, 545.

fünf Fastenzeiten der syrisch-orthodoxen Kirche. Hierzu ein Beispiel, wie Bar-Hebraeus eine kirchenrechtliche Quelle zitiert und anschließend präzisiert. Im Nomokanon Kapitel 5[15] zitiert er aus den Kanones der Apostel, dass am Samstag und Sonntag das Fasten verboten ist. In seiner anschließenden Auslegung (syrisch: *hudoyo*) fügt Bar-Hebraeus hinzu: An diesen Tagen ist dennoch das Essen in den Morgenstunden untersagt. Denn die Gläubigen sollen zur dritten Stunde nüchtern die eucharistische Liturgie besuchen und erst danach essen.
Bar-Hebraeus ist sehr verständnisvoll, was die begrenzten Möglichkeiten der Laien angeht, die Fastenzeiten zu halten und die vorgeschriebenen Gebete zu verrichten. Er reduziert die Zahl der Stundengebete für die Laien auf drei. Als einziges Pflichtgebet schreibt er den Laien das sogenannte „allgemeine Gebet" vor (syrisch: *sluto gawwonoyo* oder *qawmo*). Dies sind die Eröffnungsgebete, mit denen alle Gottesdienste der syrisch-orthodoxen Kirche eingeleitet werden: unter anderem das Trishagion und das Vaterunser. Bar-Hebraeus kann also davon ausgehen, daß jeder Gläubige zumindest diese Gebete auswendig beherrscht. Entsprechende Erleichterungen gibt es auch bei den Fastengeboten für Laien[16].
Andererseits ist Bar-Hebraeus sehr streng in seinen Vorschriften für die Asketen[17]. Quelle hierfür ist hauptsächlich das Buch der Taube, eine Art „Directorium Spirituale" für Mönche. Gebete und Fasten werden darin als äußerst wichtige Bestandteile der asketischen Praxis behandelt. Im Gegensatz zu den Laien müssen Asketen auch auf den Verzehr von Öl während der Fastenzeiten verzichten. Im Gebet muss der Asket einen so hohen Grad an Konzentration erreichen, dass er während der gemeinsamen Gebetszeiten nicht mehr weiß, wer an seiner linken oder an seiner rechten Seite steht. Ein Asket hat pro Tag acht Mal zu beten. Nach Bar-Hebraeus' Meinung soll jeder Moment im Leben eines Asketen so gestaltet sein, dass er ihn näher zu Gott bringt. Deshalb soll er die Zeit zwischen den acht Fixgebetszeiten mit verschiedenen spirituellen Tätigkeiten ausfüllen wie Fürbitten, Lesungen, der Psalmoldie und anderem mehr. Ferner werden einige Gebete angegeben, die eigens für den Gebrauch der Asketen bestimmt sind. Ein Beispiel: Wenn der Mönch von jemandem beleidigt wird, soll er ihm vergeben und sich dann nach Osten wenden, seine Hände erheben und demütig zur Erde sehen. Dabei soll er sprechen: „O Gott, sei gnädig mit mir, einem Sünder. Herr, sei mir gnädig. Herr, gewähre mir, was nützlich ist für mich."[18] Zusammengefasst werden alle Regeln für Asketen in dem Kanon, dass die Seele auf keinen Fall mit irgendeinem bösen Gedanken beschmutzt werden soll.

[15] BEDJAN, Nomocanon, 52.
[16] CHIRATHILATTU, Prayers and Fasts, 65–72.
[17] Ibid. 75–85.
[18] WENSINCK, Book of the Dove, 22; BEDJAN, Liber Columbae, 540.

Für die Priester und Laien gelten zu einem großen Teil dieselben Regeln. Sonderegelungen für die Priester bestehen hauptsächlich in Anweisungen für Strafverfahren, wenn Priester nicht ordnungsgemäß fasten oder beten[19].

Die eben genannten Regelungen für die Gebets- und Fastenspraxis sind vom theologischen Gottesbild des Bar-Hebraeus geprägt. Es lassen sich zwei Aspekte in seinem Gottesbild unterscheiden: ein theoretischer und ein praktischer Aspekt[20]. Sein theoretisches Gottesbild ist vergleichbar mit dem traditionellen philosophischen Gottesbild. Peter Kawerau charakterisierte die Theologie des Bar-Hebraeus mit folgenden Worten: „Es bietet sich uns also bei Bar-Hebraeus das eigentümliche Bild, dass die vom Platonismus geprägte alexandrinisch-monophysitische Theologie im formalen Gewande der aristotelischen Philosophie auftritt und deshalb so auffällig der scholastischen Theologie des abendländisch-lateinischen Mittelalters ähnelt."[21] Bar-Hebraeus sieht Gott als das notwendige Sein, als den ewigen und fortwährenden Schöpfer. Wir verehren ihn im Gebet. Gott ist der Absolute, er unterliegt keiner Veränderung und er ist nicht zeitlich begrenzt. Er ist körperlos, aber er sieht und hört doch alles[22].

Über diese eher philosophisch-theoretische Grundlage der Gotteslehre hinaus versteht Bar-Hebraeus Gott aber auch als einen mitfühlenden Gott. Er ist der Gütige, der unsere Herzen mit Frieden und Liebe füllt. Er wohnt in allen und will alle zu dem Hafen des Lebens führen, wenn wir ihm alle unsere Sorgen, Krankheiten, Ruhelosigkeiten, Versehen und Fehler übergeben. Gott ist uns nahe und will uns erhören. Er weiß, was für den Betenden nützlich ist und gewährt ihm Gnadengaben noch über sein Bitten hinaus[23].

Nach Bar-Hebraeus besteht das höchste Ziel des Gebetes in der Anbetung Gottes. Durch das Gebet nähert sich der Mensch Gott; im Gebet löst die Nähe Gottes unbeschreibliche Freude im Menschen aus. Das Gebet selbst ist Einigung mit Gott. Alle Gebete erreichen ihre Höhepunkt im sogenannten „reinen Gebet", in dem man die „Theologia" erfährt, das heißt: in dem man der Vision der Dreieinigkeit gewürdigt wird. Dort kann es auch zu dem Zustand der Vereinigung kommen, auf den ich am Anfang dieses Vortrages hingewiesen habe.

Doch findet sich bei Bar-Hebraeus neben diesem höchsten Ziel des Gebetes (der Vereinigung mit Gott) auch das Verständnis des Gebetes als Bittgebet. Wichtiger als die Bitten um materielle Vorteile sind freilich die spirituellen Güter, um die der Gläubige bitten soll: um den Frieden im Herzen und um die Erleuchtung der Seele. Die ewigen Güter sollen beim Bittgebet im Vordergrund stehen. Obwohl es an sich nicht empfehlenswert ist, macht Bar-Hebraeus das Zugeständnis, dass man Gott daneben auch um irdische Dinge bitten kann. Als Beispiel

19 CHIRATHILATTU, Prayers and Fasts, 85–87.
20 TEULE, Ethicon, 7.
21 Peter KAWERAU, Das Christentum des Ostens (RM 30), Stuttgart 1972, 63.
22 Herman F. JANSSENS (ed and transl.), L'entretien de la sagesse. Introduction aux œuvres Philosophiques de Bar Hebraeus (BFPUL 75), Liège – Paris 1937, 91–92.
23 CHIRATHILATTU, Prayers and Fasts, 30–31.

nennt er das Gebet um Hilfe bei einem Unfall. Das Fasten unterstützt das Gebet. Dazu erzählt Bar-Hebraeus in seinem „Chronicon Ecclesiasticum“ folgende Geschichte, die in der Zeit des Katholikos Henanischo spielt, der sein Amt im Jahre 686 angetreten hatte. Die Ereignisse finden statt in der Zeit nach dem Epiphaniefest: „Als Abdul Malik, der Sohn des Marwan, von der Schönheit der Frauen in Hirto hörte, befahl er dem dortigen Gouverneur, alle Jungfrauen zu ihm zu bringen. Der Gouverneur begann, alle Jungfrauen zusammenzutreiben. Daraufhin versammelten sich die Christen in der Kirche und beteten und fasteten. Sie warfen sich nieder vor dem Herrn und flehten ihn an, daß sie vor dieser Strafe verschont würden. Am dritten Tag empfing Bischof Johannes eine Vision, als er das Evangelium verlas: nämlich den Tod von Abdul Malik. Er verkündete dies dem Volk. Nach einigen Tagen traf die Nachricht vom Tode des Herrschers ein. Man sagt – so Bar Hebraeus – dass die Gläubigen seither diese Fastenzeit einhalten.“[24] So erklärt der Maphrian den Brauch der syrischen Kirche, drei Tage nach Epiphanie zu fasten.

In seiner Lehre über Gebet und Fasten bemüht sich Bar-Hebraeus darum, die gesamte christliche Tradition bis zu seiner Zeit zu verarbeiten. Er ist Enzyklopädist, der von den Schriften der früheren christlichen Väter ausgiebig Gebrauch macht. Seine Anleihen beschränken sich nicht auf die Väter der eigenen – miaphysitischen – Tradition. Er zitiert auch griechische und ostsyrische Autoren und entlehnt selbst islamischen Philosophen einige Argumente. In der Regel dienen die Zitate allerdings dazu, die Normen der westsyrischen rechtlichen Literatur zu untermauern. Evagrius Ponticus ist der Autor, der wohl den größten Einfluß auf Bar-Hebraeus ausgeübt hat. Evagrius ist der einzige Autor, den Bar Hebraeus im „Buch der Taube“ namentlich erwähnt[25]. Er übernimmt das gestufte spirituelle System des Evagrius: Die gefallenen Intellekte (syrisch: *hawne*) erlangen die Vereinigung mit Gott durch die Praktike mit dem Ziel der Leidenschaftslosigkeit (Apátheia), die Theoria Physike und die Theoria Theologike[26]. Auffällig ist die redaktionelle Bearbeitung, wenn Bar-Hebraeus Evagrius zitiert. Denn Bar-Hebraeus achtet darauf, mögliche origenistische Aussagen in den Zitaten aus Evagrius wegzulassen. Ein Beispiel: Im Ethikon zitiert Bar-Hebraeus das 49. Kapitel des Praktikos nur unvollständig. In diesem Kapitel betont Evagrius zunächst, dass das Gebet wichtiger ist als alle anderen asketischen Leistungen. Dann gibt er eine Erklärung dafür, warum das so ist. Um die anderen asketischen Leistungen ausführen zu können, braucht man einen Körper. Dieser ist von Natur aus schwach. Dagegen braucht das Gebet nicht notwendig einen Körper, um verrichtet zu werden. Das Gebet bekämpft die Dämonen allein dadurch, daß es den Intellekt stärkt und reinigt. Eben diesen Teil des

[24] Jean Baptiste ABBELOOS – Thomas Josephus LAMY (ed. and transl.), Gregorii Bar-Hebraei Chronicon Ecclesiasticum, 1 – 3, Paris – Louvain 1872 – 1877, Col. 139–141.

[25] CHIRATHILATTU, Prayers and Fasts, 88–89.

[26] Karl PINGGÉRA, Wort- und Schweigegebet in der Tradition des Christlichen Ostens, in: Quat. 64 (2000) 83–87.

Textes gibt Bar-Hebraeus nur stark verkürzt wieder: Er beschränkt sich auf die Aussage, dass das Gebet den Intellekt stärke im Kampf gegen den Feind. Wie mir scheint, hat Bar-Hebraeus den Satz, wonach das Gebet ohne Leib verrichtet werden könne, nicht ohne Grund ausgelassen. Denn Evagrius folgt in seinen Schriften der origenistischen Ansicht, dass der Körper ein Resultat des Sündenfalles sei. Damit steht der Körper unter dem Intellekt. Der Körper wird keinen Anteil haben an der Auferstehung. In diesem Zusammenhang ist die Äußerung zu sehen, dass der Körper auch für das Gebet entbehrlich ist. Bar-Hebraeus versucht mit seiner Auslassung zu verhindern, dass der Leser sich an dieses theologische Konzept erinnert.

Bar-Hebraeus war in seinen Spätwerken zu der Einsicht gekommen, dass der Streit der Kirchen um das richtige christologische Bekenntnis nur ein Streit über Wörter, nicht über Tatsachen war. Wenn ostsyrische Autoren zitiert werden, fällt dennoch auf, dass nur solche Aussagen übernommen werden, die für den Miaphysiten Bar-Hebraeus nicht anstößig sind. Inhaltlich gering ist der Einfluss von Al-Ghazali. Dessen Einfluss macht sich hauptsächlich daran bemerkbar, wie Bar-Hebraeus den Stoff in seinen Büchern anordnet.

Nach Wolfgang Hage hat Bar-Hebraeus in seinem Werk nahezu das gesamte syrische Erbe zusammengefasst und ist in der syrischen-orthodoxen Kirche die maßgebliche Autorität in allen Bereichen des kirchlichen Lebens[27]. Deshalb ist es wichtig danach zu fragen, welche Bedeutung seine Lehre in der Gegenwart besitzt. Ich nenne drei Punkte:

(1) Das spirituelle Leben der Gläubigen in der syrisch-orthodoxen Kirche ist heute einem rasanten Wandel ausgesetzt. Die starke Betonung der Fastens und der Gebete geht heute verloren. Viele Menschen empfinden die Gebete als zu lang und als bedeutungslos. Andere beten nur noch um materielle Vorteile. Ich meine: Bar-Hebraeus kann uns heute zeigen, dass das Gebet mehr ist. Die vorgeschriebenen täglichen Gebete sind nicht der Endpunkt des geistlichen Lebens, sondern sind ein Mittel für den Aufstieg zu Gott und zur Erfahrung seiner Gegenwart. Außerdem ist seine Betonung wichtig, sich auf das Gebet zu konzentrieren und die Bedeutung der Gebetsworte zu verstehen. Die Kirche sollte akzeptieren, dass es sinnvoller ist, wenige Worte bewusst und konzentriert zu beten, als die täglichen kanonischen Stundengebete monoton zu sprechen, ohne bei der Sache zu sein.

(2) Bar-Hebraeus, ein Theologe des 13. Jahrhunderts, war bereit, die Reinheitsvorschriften für Frauen an bestimmten Punkten zu relativieren. Leider ist ihm die kirchliche Gesetzgebung darin bis heute nicht gefolgt. Die Methode des Bar-

[27] Wolfgang HAGE, Gregory Bar-Hebraya the Syrian Orthodox Scholar and Maphrian of the East, Syriac Christianity in the East, Moran 'Etho 1, Kottayam 1988 [reprint 1997], 96.

Hebraeus sollte die Kirche ermutigen, die traditionellen Reinheitsvorschriften den Einsichten und Anforderungen der Gegenwart behutsam anzupassen.

(3) Schließlich ist Bar-Hebraeus ein bleibendes Vorbild dafür, die verschiedenen christlichen Konfessionen zu respektieren und voneinander zu lernen. Das gilt auch für die ostsyrische Kirche. Bar-Hebraeus könnte ein Prototyp sein für die ökumenischen Beziehungen der syrisch-orthodoxen Kirche der Gegenwart.

„Ut omnes unum sint“
Zur ökumenischen Bedeutung einer *Vergleichenden Liturgiewissenschaft*

Hans-Jürgen Feulner

Fünf Jahrzehnte nach dem II. Vatikanischen Konzil mit seiner wegweisenden ökumenischen Ausrichtung und der nachfolgenden ökumenischen Aufbruchstimmung sowie 18 Jahre nach der vielbeachteten Ökumene-Enzyklika „Ut unum sint“[1] von Papst Johannes Paul II. († 2005) scheint es durchaus angemessen, auch von *liturgiewissenschaftlicher* Seite her einige Dimensionen und Möglichkeiten im gegenwärtig teilweise stockenden ökumenischen Dialog zumindest kurz anzuskizzieren.[2]

1. Zur Bedeutung der Ökumene für die Kirche(n)

Ut unum sint! Mit diesen Worten beginnt die Ökumene-Enzyklika Papst Johannes Pauls II. vom 25. Mai 1995, und zwar in Anlehnung an die Worte Jesu in der Stunde seines Leidens, als er seinen Vater selbst für seine Jünger und alle, die an ihn glauben, bittet, „dass alle eins seien“ – „ut omnes unum sint“ (Joh 17,21). Christus ruft also alle seine Jünger und an ihn Glaubenden zur Einheit. Mit dem II. Vatikanischen Konzil hat sich die Katholische Kirche mit dem Ökumenismus-Dekret *Unitatis redintegratio* (*UR*)[3] vom 21. November 1964 unumkehrbar dazu verpflichtet, den Weg der Suche nach der Einheit aller Christen umfassend einzuschlagen.[4] Das Konzil bringt nämlich die Entschlos-

1 Acta Apostolicae Sedis [= AAS] 57 (1995) 921–982 [lat. Text]; Sekretariat der Deutschen Bischofskonferenz, Enzyklika *Ut unum sint* von Papst Johannes Paul II. über den Einsatz für die Ökumene (25. Mai 1995)(Verlautbarungen des Apostolischen Stuhls [= VAS] 121), Bonn 1995 [dt. Übers.].

2 Auch in liturgischer Hinsicht [vgl. z.B. Paul-Werner Scheele, Ökumenische Impulse der Liturgiekonstitution, in: Martin Stuflesser (Hg.), Sacrosanctum Concilium. Eine Relecture der Liturgiekonstitution des II. Vatikanischen Konzils, (Theologie der Liturgie 1), Regensburg 2011, 57–65; Ulrich Kühn, Ökumenische Aspekte der Liturgiekonstitution des Zweiten Vatikanums, in: ebd., 67–73].

3 AAS 57 (1965) 90–107. – Vgl. auch Peter Neuner, Das Dekret über die Ökumene *Unitatis redintegratio*, in: Franz Xaver Bischof – Stephan Leimgruber (Hgg.), Vierzig Jahre II. Vatikanum. Zur Wirkungsgeschichte der Konzilstexte, Würzburg 2004, 117–140; Wolfgang Thönissen (Hg.), „Unitatis redintegratio“. 40 Jahre Ökumenismusdekret – Erbe und Auftrag, Paderborn – Frankfurt/M. 2005.

4 Vgl. Johannes Paul II., Ut unum sint, Nr. 3 [VAS 121, 6f.]. – Siehe auch Hermann Josef Pottmeyer, Die Öffnung der römisch-katholischen Kirche für die Ökumenische Bewegung und die ekklesiologische Reform des 2. Vatikanums. Ein wechselseitiger Einfluss, in: Paolo VI e l'Ecumenismo. Colloquio Internationale di Studio Brescia 1998, Brescia – Roma 2001, 98–117; Bernd-Jochen Hilberath, Theologischer Kommentar zum Dekret über den Ökumenismus *Unitatis redintegratio*, in: Herders Theologischer Kommentar zum Zweiten Vatikanischen Konzil, Bd. III, Freiburg u.a. 2005, 67–223.

senheit der Kirche zum Ausdruck, die ökumenische Aufgabe zugunsten der Einheit der Christen anzunehmen und sie mit Überzeugung und Entschiedenheit voranzutreiben.
In seiner Enzyklika *Ut unum sint* beschreibt JOHANNES PAUL II. im zweiten Kapitel die Früchte des ökumenischen Dialogs, darunter auch die bereits erreichten Übereinstimmungen im *Wort Gottes* und in der *Liturgie*.[5] Da die Liturgie die „erste und unentbehrliche Quelle ist, aus der die Gläubigen wahrhaft christlichen Geist schöpfen sollen" (*SC* 14),[6] leistet sie einen bedeutenden Beitrag zur Einheit aller, die an Christus glauben.
Der von der katholischen Kirche vollzogenen liturgischen Erneuerung entsprach nämlich vor allem in mehreren reformatorischen Kirchen und kirchlichen Gemeinschaften die Initiative, ihren Gottesdienst ebenfalls zu erneuern. Einige von ihnen haben auf Grund eines auf ökumenischer Ebene geäußerten Wunsches beispielsweise die Gewohnheit aufgegeben, ihren Abendmahlsgottesdienst nur bei sehr seltenen Gelegenheiten zu feiern, und sich für eine sonntägliche Abendmahlsfeier entschieden. Des Weiteren stellt man bei einem Vergleich der Zyklen der liturgischen Lesungen verschiedener christlicher Gemeinschaften im Westen fest, dass sie im Wesentlichen übereinstimmen. Ebenso werden auf ökumenischer Ebene ganz besonders die Liturgie und die liturgischen Zeichen (also Bilder, Ikonen, Paramente, Licht, Weihrauch, Gebärden usw.) hervorgehoben. Darüber hinaus beginnt man in den theologischen Instituten, in denen die künftigen Geistlichen ausgebildet werden, dem Studium der Geschichte und der Bedeutung der Liturgie einen festen Platz in den Studienprogrammen einzuräumen.[7]
Neben gewissen Stagnationen[8] ist aber auch auf anderen Gebieten natürlich ein fortschreitendes Wachsen des ökumenischen Dialogs und der kirchlichen Beziehungen festzustellen.[9] Aber welchen Beitrag kann die Liturgiewissenschaft beitragen, die mit der Liturgiekonstitution *Sacrosanctum Concilium* nach dem II. Vatikanum als eigenständiges „Hauptfach"[10] aufgewertet wurde (*SC* 16)?

Der Ökumene kommt für die Kirche und die Theologie sowie für das gottesdienstliche Leben der Kirche zweifellos eine große Bedeutung zu. Daher ge-

5 JOHANNES PAUL II., Ut unum sint, Nr. 44–46 [VAS 121, 34–36].
6 AAS 56 (1964) 104. – Der gesamte latein. Text der am 4. Dezember 1963 promulgierten Liturgiekonstitution *Sacrosanctum Concilium* findet sich in: AAS 56 (1964) 97–134.
7 JOHANNES PAUL II., Ut unum sint, Nr. 45 [VAS 121, 35].
8 Vgl. Hans HALTER (Hg.), Neue ökumenische Eiszeit?, Zürich 1989; Heinrich DÖRING, Ist die Ökumene am Ende?, Regensburg 1994; Michael WEINRICH, Ökumene am Ende? Plädoyer für einen neuen Realismus, Neukirchen 1995; Kurt KOCH, Gelähmte Ökumene. Was jetzt noch zu tun ist, Freiburg u.a. 1991; DERS., Dass alle eins seien. Ökumenische Perspektiven, Augsburg 2006, bes. 57–68; Manfred KOCK, Wider die ökumenische Eiszeit. Die Vision von der Einheit der Kirchen, Neukirchen 2006 u.a.
9 Vgl. z.B. Kurt KOCH, Ökumene im Wandel. Zum Zukunftspotential des Ökumenismusdekrets *Unitatis redintegratio*, in: Jan-Heiner TÜCK (Hg.), Erinnerung an die Zukunft. Das Zweite Vatikanische Konzil, Freiburg [2]2013, 403–436.
10 AAS 56 (1964) 104f.

winnt eine *ökumenisch* ausgerichtete Liturgiewissenschaft,[11] die sich mit dem vergleichenden Studium der verschiedenen östlichen und *westlichen* Liturgien und ihren Quellen sowie ihrer Theologie beschäftigt, zunehmend an Gewicht.[12] Ein wichtiges Arbeitsinstrument hierfür ist unter anderem – aber nicht nur – eine *liturgievergleichende* Methodik. Eine Liturgiewissenschaft, die sich nicht ganz selbstverständlich als eine *ökumenische* versteht, würde von vornherein eigentlich ihr Thema verfehlen. Über die Grenzen des Christentums hinaus wird auch die sog. „große Ökumene“ der Weltreligionen durch die engen Kontakte vieler Bekenntnisse in der heutigen Gesellschaft immer wichtiger und dringlicher. Dies betrifft in ganz besonderer Weise das Judentum, zunehmend auch den Islam.

Die liturgievergleichende Methodik sei zunächst in der gebotenen Kürze vorgestellt, ohne dabei jedoch eine umfassende liturgiewissenschaftliche Methodendiskussion aufgreifen zu wollen.[13]

2. DIE KLASSISCHE „VERGLEICHENDE LITURGIEWISSENSCHAFT“

Eine *vergleichende Methodik* haben sich bereits andere Geisteswissenschaften mit großem Erfolg zunutze machen können, wie z.B. eine *vergleichende Sprachwissenschaft* oder eine *vergleichende Religionswissenschaft*. Auch innerhalb der Liturgiewissenschaft hat sich für das wissenschaftliche Studium von liturgischen Texten und Strukturen eine vergleichende Methodik bewährt, wobei jedoch ausdrücklich betont sei, dass eine solche Methodik nicht der einzige Weg ist, auf dem man sich dem wissenschaftlichen Umgang mit der Liturgie nähern kann oder sollte. Es gibt hier viele Möglichkeiten, die im Zusammenspiel untereinander zu fruchtbaren Ergebnissen führen können: eine systematisch-theologische, eine pastoralliturgische oder eine liturgierechtliche Arbeitsweise, um nur einige zu nennen.[14]

[11] Karl-Heinrich BIERITZ, Chancen einer ökumenischen Liturgik, in: Zeitschrift für Katholische Theologie 100 (1978) 470–483; Angelus HÄUSSLING, Was heißt: Liturgiewissenschaft ist ökumenisch?, in: Karl SCHLEMMER (Hg.), Gottesdienst – Weg zur Einheit. Impulse für die Ökumene (Quaestiones Disputatae 122), Freiburg u.a. 1989, 62–88; Friedrich LURZ, Die Feier des Abendmahls nach der Kurpfälzischen Kirchenordnung von 1563. Ein Beitrag zu einer ökumenischen Liturgiewissenschaft (Praktische Theologie heute 38), Stuttgart 1998, 17–47; DERS., Für eine ökumenische Liturgiewissenschaft, in: Trierer Theologische Zeitschrift 108 (1999) 273–290.

[12] Vgl. auch Hans-Jürgen FEULNER, Die Armenische Athanasius-Anaphora. Kritische Edition, Übersetzung und liturgievergleichender Kommentar (Anaphorae Orientales 1 – Anaphorae Armeniacae 1), Roma 2001, 63–73; DERS., „Ex oriente lux“ – Die Ostkirchen und ihre Liturgien. Ein liturgiewissenschaftlicher Beitrag zum ökumenischen Dialog, in: Ostkirchliche Studien 61 (2012) 10–42, hier 25–31; DERS., Liturgiewissenschaft in Wien. Selbstverständnis einer „Konzilswissenschaft“ zwischen Gestern, Heute und Morgen, in: Johann REIKERSTORFER – Martin JÄGGLE (Hgg.), Vorwärtserinnerungen. 625 Jahre Katholisch-Theologische Fakultät der Universität Wien, Wien 2009, 221–253, bes. 224–240, 248–250.

[13] Siehe dazu FEULNER, Liturgiewissenschaft in Wien, 224–240.

[14] Vgl. ebd. 231–240.

a) Allgemeine Bemerkungen zu einer „liturgievergleichenden" Methodik[15]

Der Orientalist Anton BAUMSTARK (1872–1948)[16] befasste sich in seinen liturgiegeschichtlichen Studien neben den gesamten orientalischen Riten auch mit den westlichen Liturgietraditionen. Er war es wohl auch, der den Begriff „Liturgie*wissenschaft*" erstmals in gedruckter Form vorgelegt hat.[17] BAUMSTARK entwickelte den Ansatz einer *Vergleichenden Liturgiewissenschaft*, den er in seinem in französischer Sprache erschienenen Werk *Liturgie Comparée* schließlich umfassender ausführte.[18] Sein Interesse galt der Liturgiegeschichte, die dem Wissenschaftler als etwas Gewachsenes entgegentrete, das gleichzeitig Gegebenes und Bestehendes sei. Der Entfaltung der Liturgie entspreche die *Vergleichende Liturgiewissenschaft*, die durch Vergleich und Zusammenschau zwischen den verschiedenen östlichen und westlichen Liturgiefamilien die Hauptentwicklungslinien der Liturgie und ihre Gesetzmäßigkeiten erheben und untersuchen solle. Eine *Vergleichende Liturgiewissenschaft* will den größeren religionsgeschichtlichen Kontext, die jüdische Liturgie und in ganzer Breite die Liturgien der verschiedenen christlichen Kirchen berücksichtigen.[19] Diesem Denkansatz kommt auch heute im Hinblick auf die Ökumene ein besonderes Gewicht zu. In der klassischen Sicht einer *Vergleichenden Liturgiewissenschaft* kristallisierte sich die Idee heraus, dass die einzelnen Riten in ihren jeweiligen Originalsprachen zu erfassen sind, dass die einzelnen *liturgischen Einheiten*

[15] Vgl. hierzu auch die in Notre Dame/IN entstandene Dissertation von Fritz (Frederic S.) WEST, Anton Baumstark's Comparative Liturgy in Its Intellectual Context, Ann Arbor University Microfilms International 1988; sowie DERS., The Comparative Liturgy of Anton Baumstark (Joint Liturgical Studies 31), Bramcote 1995.

[16] Vgl. Hans-Jürgen FEULNER, Anton Baumstark (1872–1948), in: Benedikt KRANEMANN – Klaus RASCHZOK (Hgg.), Gottesdienst als Feld Theologischer Wissenschaft im 20. Jahrhundert. Deutschsprachige Liturgiewissenschaft in Einzelporträts I (LQF 98/1), Münster 2011, 158–170.

[17] Anton BAUMSTARK, Ein liturgiewissenschaftliches Unternehmen deutscher Benediktinerabteien, in: Deutsche Literaturzeitung 40 (1919) 897–905, 921–927. – Er hat den Begriff „Liturgiewissenschaft" wohl von Kunibert MOHLBERG übernommen, mit dem er in ständigem Briefkontakt stand [s. hierzu ausführlich Stefan K. LANGEBAHN, Fürs Archiv des „Archivs". Die Vorgeschichte des *Jahrbuch für Liturgiewissenschaft*, in: Archiv für Liturgiewissenschaft 50 (2008) 31–61, hier bes. 50f., 52–54].

[18] Anton BAUMSTARK, Liturgie Comparée. Principes et méthodes pour l'étude historique des liturgies chrétiennes, Chevetogne 1939 (^{3}1953); Comparative Liturgy. Revised by Bernard BOTTE. English edition translated by Frank L. CROSS, Westminster/MD 1958. – In seiner Rezension von Gustav DIETTRICH, Die nestorianische Taufliturgie, skizzierte BAUMSTARK zum ersten Mal das Konzept einer „Vergleichenden Liturgiewissenschaft" als eine „allseitige Orientierung über das Ganze" betreibende „Wissenschaft, die noch zu begründen wäre" [Anton BAUMSTARK, Rez. „G. Diettrich, Die nestorianische Taufliturgie", in: Oriens Christianus 3 (1903) 219–226, hier 220f.]. – Vgl. dazu auch Anton BAUMSTARK, Ein liturgiewissenschaftliches Unternehmen deutscher Benediktinerabteien (s. Anm. 17), 901–905, 921–924; DERS., Arbeiten zur Literaturgeschichte, Kirchengeschichte und Liturgie des christlichen Orients, in: Literarische Rundschau für das katholische Deutschland 37 (1911) 225–230, 386–388, hier 388.

[19] Benedikt KRANEMANN, Liturgiewissenschaft angesichts der „Zeitenwende". Die Entwicklung der theologischen Disziplin zwischen den beiden Vatikanischen Konzilien, in: Hubert WOLF (Hg.), Die katholisch-theologischen Disziplinen in Deutschland 1870–1962. Ihre Geschichte, ihr Zeitbezug (Programm und Wirkungsgeschichte des II. Vatikanums 3), Paderborn u.a. 1999, 351–375, hier 367.

(*„liturgical units"*)[20] und *Strukturen* miteinander verglichen werden müssen und schließlich auch noch der historische Wandel vergleichend gegenüberzustellen ist.
Einschlägige Untersuchungen haben nämlich gezeigt, dass sich weder liturgische Texte noch Strukturen – zumindest nicht immer und notwendigerweise – gleichförmig als umfassende Liturgieformulare weiterentwickeln. Große liturgische Texteinheiten, wie z.B. das Eucharistische Hochgebet, bestehen aus mehreren Unter-Einheiten, die wiederum je eine eigenständige Form- und Redaktionsgeschichte aufweisen, und zwar unabhängig von den übrigen liturgischen Einheiten. So hat etwa das *Sanctus–Benedictus* eine andere liturgiegeschichtliche Entwicklung als die *Epiklese*, und beide Elemente sind zudem noch zu unterschiedlichen Zeiten in das Eucharistische Hochgebet eingefügt worden. Es ist also deshalb häufig notwendig, liturgische Formulare in sinnvolle liturgische Einheiten und Unter-Einheiten zu gliedern, einzeln zu analysieren und innerhalb sowie außerhalb der eigenen liturgischen Tradition zu vergleichen, gegebenenfalls auch unter Heranziehung von außerliturgischen Quellen:

Feier der:		Eröffnungsdialog	
	Eröffnung	Präfation	
Initiation	Wortgottesdienst	Sanctus–Benedictus	
Eucharistie	Gabenbereitung	Postsanctus	**Einleitung z. Brotwort**
Krankensalbung	***Euchar. Hochgebet***	Epiklese I	**Herrenwort über Brot**
Ordination	Kommunionkreis	***Einsetzungsworte***	**Einleitung z. Kelchwort**
...	Abschluss	Anamnese	**Herrenwort über Kelch**
		Epiklese II	**(Akklamation)**
		Interzessionen	
		Doxologie	

Mit und nach BAUMSTARK suchte man nach grundlegenden Prinzipien, mit denen die Evolution der Liturgie erfasst werden konnte, und zwar aufgrund (1) einer vergleichenden *strukturellen* Analyse der liturgischen Texte, (2) einer vergleichenden *textlichen* Untersuchung auf *philologischer* Grundlage und (3) einer vergleichenden *historischen* Studie.[21] Anton BAUMSTARK und besonders

[20] Robert F. TAFT, The Structural Analysis of Liturgical Units. An Essay in Methodology, in: Worship 52 (1978) 314–329 [= DERS., Beyond East and West. Problems in Liturgical Understanding, Roma ^{2}1997, 187–202].

[21] Zu diesen grundlegenden Ansätzen der „Vergleichenden Liturgiewissenschaft" siehe z.B. BAUMSTARK, Liturgie Comparée: «La première tâche de l'étude comparée des textes liturgiques est de nature purement *philologique* [...] On voit immédiatement que la connaissance des langues est de toute nécessité pour ce genre d'études et l'on doit ajouter que l'on ne peut aborder la liturgie comparée sans une science étendue des langues orientales» (ebd. 59); «Nous commencerons par étudier *la structure* de ces unités liturgiques [...] *Ces structures*, soit en leur état définitif, soit à un moment déterminé de leur évolution, sont

seine beiden Schüler Fritz HAMM (1901–1970) und Hieronymus (Karl) ENGBERDING OSB (1899–1969) fanden durch den Vergleich und die Zusammenschau der verschiedenen Liturgiefamilien wichtige Entwicklungsstränge heraus und formulierten einige grundlegende „*Gesetzmäßigkeiten*“ (nicht „Gesetze“),[22] die zur Erklärung der Entwicklung der Liturgie dienen. Diese „Gesetzmäßigkeiten“, die in den frühen Formen der Liturgie bis etwa zur ausgehenden Antike auftreten, sind auch für das Verständnis der späteren liturgischen Traditionen von großer Tragweite.[23]

b) Gesetzmäßigkeiten der „Vergleichenden Liturgiewissenschaft“

Bezüglich der genauen Anzahl der „Gesetzmäßigkeiten“ der *Vergleichenden Liturgiewissenschaft* herrscht unter den Fachleuten eine gewisse Uneinigkeit. Das liegt zum einen daran, dass nicht alle „Gesetzmäßigkeiten“ von BAUMSTARK selbst explizit formuliert wurden, sondern auch auf seine beiden Schüler Fritz HAMM und Hieronymus ENGBERDING zurückgehen; zum anderen sind einige „Gesetzmäßigkeiten“ nur indirekt aus den verstreuten Schriften BAUMSTARKS rekonstruierbar. Sie lassen sich im Anschluss an den amerikanischen Liturgiewissenschaftler und anerkannten Vertreter einer *Vergleichenden Liturgiewissenschaft*, Robert F. TAFT SJ, im Wesentlichen wie folgt umrisshaft zusammenfassen:[24]

très souvent le résultat d'un développement fort compliqué» (ebd. 35); «Par ce rapprochement, on entend délimiter nettement la place occupée par *l'histoire de la liturgie* dans l'ensemble des sciences» [ebd. 3; *eigene Hervorhebungen*]. – Siehe auch Gabriele WINKLER – Reinhard MESSNER, Überlegungen zu den methodischen und wissenschaftstheoretischen Grundlagen der Liturgiewissenschaft, in: Theologische Quartalschrift 178 (1998) 229–243, hier 240f.

22 Anton BAUMSTARK spricht an einigen Stellen von „Gesetzen“ („lois“ bzw. „laws“), was wohl in manchen Zusammenhängen einer gewissen Modifizierung bedarf (siehe auch die Stellungnahme von Bernard BOTTE im Vorwort zur 3. Auflage: Liturgie Comparée [s. Anm. 18], VI–VII; Comparative Liturgy [s. Anm. 18], viii–ix). – Man sollte hier also bewusst nicht von „Gesetzen“ sprechen, wie dies leider oft missverständlich getan wird. Es handelt sich eben nicht um feste „Gesetze“ im naturwissenschaftlichen Sinne, sondern um auf induktivem Wege gewonnene Prinzipien, die dazu dienen, die durch die liturgischen Quellen aufgezeigten Fakten besser zu erklären.

23 Vgl. auch Ernst HAMMERSCHMIDT, Probleme der orientalischen Liturgiewissenschaft, in: Ostkirchliche Studien 10 (1961) 28–47, bes. 28–32. – Siehe zudem die Ausführungen von Gabriele WINKLER und Robert F. TAFT in ihrer „Introduction“ zum Tagungsband: Acts of the International Congress „Comparative Liturgy Fifty Years after Anton Baumstark (1872–1948)“ […] (OCA 265), ed. by Robert F. TAFT – Gabriele WINKLER, Roma 2001, 9–29, bes.14–27.

24 Robert F. TAFT, Anton Baumstark's Comparative Liturgy Revisited, in: Acts of the International Congress, 191–232. – Siehe aber auch: Paul DE CLERCK, Les lois de Baumstark, l'évolution de la liturgie et ses réformes, in: ebd., 233–249; FEULNER, Die armenische Athanasius-Anaphora (s. Anm. 12), 63–75; DERS., Anton Baumstark (s. Anm. 16), 166f.; DERS. The Anglican Use within the Western Liturgical Tradition. Importance and Ecumenical Relevance from the Perspective of Comparative Liturgy, in: Stephen CAVANAUGH (ed.), Anglicans and the Roman Catholic Church. Reflections on Recent Developments, San Francisco 2011, 184–224, hier 191–196; DERS., „Ex oriente lux“ (s. Anm. 12), 28–31.

ALLGEMEINE PRINZIPIEN

1. *Die Entwicklung von der Mannigfaltigkeit zur Einheitlichkeit:*[25] Die divergierenden örtlichen liturgischen Feiern wurden auf Dauer in überörtliche Liturgiefamilien gefasst, die sich um die damaligen bedeutenden kulturellen und theologischen Zentren wie Alexandrien, Antiochien, Rom und Konstantinopel bildeten. Rom und Konstantinopel übten dabei den nachhaltigsten Einfluss aus.

   BAUMSTARK formulierte diese allgemein anerkannte „Gesetzmäßigkeit“ als Antwort auf die vom Tübinger Liturgiker Ferdinand PROBST (1816–1899) vertretene These, dass am Anfang aller liturgischen Entwicklung *eine* apostolische Urliturgie stand, aus der sich alle heute existierenden Riten herausgebildet hätten.[26] Es ist in der Forschung mittlerweile natürlich unstrittig, dass die gegenwärtigen liturgischen Riten am Ende eines komplizierten Prozesses der Verschmelzung, Vereinheitlichung und Überformung stehen.

2. *Die zunehmende Anreicherung der liturgischen Riten und Texte:*[27] Ein ursprünglich einfacher, schlichter Ritus oder liturgischer Text wurde oft auf Kosten der Durchschaubarkeit durch Hinzufügungen erweitert. Bei einer einsetzenden Gegenbewegung kam es manchmal wieder zu Kürzungen, jedoch nicht der sekundären Anreicherungen, sondern oftmals sogar der substantiellen Elemente.

   Erfolgreich bewährte sich diese „Gesetzmäßigkeit“ z.B. bei der Erhellung der Entwicklungsgeschichte der *Basilius-Anaphora*, die in mehreren orientalischen Redaktionen vorliegt.[28]

3. *Die Entwicklung von freien und improvisierten Gebeten zu Formulargebeten:*[29] Ein fest fixiertes Formulargebet steht oftmals am Ende einer längeren mündlichen Überlieferung.

[25] Vgl. Anton BAUMSTARK, Vom geschichtlichen Werden der Liturgie (Ecclesia Orans 10), Freiburg [1/5]1923, 29–31, 32–35, 37–47; DERS., Liturgie Comparée (s. Anm. 18), 17–20, 21f.; DERS., Comparative Liturgy (s. Anm. 18), 15–17, 18f.

[26] Vgl. Ferdinand PROBST, Liturgie der ersten drei christlichen Jahrhunderte, Tübingen 1870; DERS., Sakramente und Sakramentalien in den ersten drei christlichen Jahrhunderten, Tübingen 1872; DERS., Liturgie des vierten Jahrhunderts und deren Reform, Münster 1893.

[27] Vgl. BAUMSTARK, Liturgie Comparée (s. Anm. 18), 22–25; DERS., Comparative Liturgy (s. Anm. 18), 19–22.

[28] Vgl. vor allem Gabriele WINKLER, Die Basilius-Anaphora. Edition der beiden armenischen Redaktionen und der relevanten Fragmente, Übersetzung und Zusammenschau aller Versionen im Licht der orientalischen Überlieferungen (Anaphorae Orientales 2 – Anaphorae Armeniacae 2), Roma 2005. – Siehe auch Achim BUDDE, Die ägyptische Basilios-Anaphora. Text – Kommentar – Geschichte (Jerusalemer Theologisches Forum 7), Münster 2004.

[29] Vgl. BAUMSTARK, Vom geschichtlichen Werden (s. Anm. 25), 31f.; DERS., Liturgie Comparée, 20f.; DERS., Comparative Liturgy, 17f. – Siehe auch Allan BOULEY, From Freedom to Formula. The Evolution of the Eucharistic Prayer from Oral Improvisation to Written Texts (Studies in Christian Antiquity 21), Washington/DC 1981.

Klassisches Beispiel sind die überlieferten liturgischen Texte in der dem HIPPOLYT von Rom zugeschriebenen so genannten *Traditio Apostolica* aus dem dritten Jahrhundert.[30]

4. *Die liturgischen Verwandtschaftsverhältnisse*:[31] Aufgrund des Vergleiches einzelner Riten miteinander können bedeutsame liturgische Beziehungen bzw. Verwandtschaftsverhältnisse ausgemacht werden, und zwar:

   - zwischen dem stadtrömischen Ritus und der lateinischen Liturgie Nordafrikas, sowie dem (stadt-)römischen Ritus und der alexandrinischen Liturgiefamilie,
   - zwischen altgallischem, altspanischem (und keltischem) Ritus einerseits und dem westsyrischen Liturgiebereich andererseits,
   - zwischen maronitischem Ritus und syro-mesopotamischem („nestorianischem") Ritus ostsyrischen Typus',
   - zwischen armenischem Ritus und Jerusalem, sowie den liturgischen Gebräuchen Persarmeniens und Syriens,
   - zwischen der west-syrischen Liturgiefamilie und dem alexandrinischen Liturgiebereich.

SPEZIELLE „GESETZMÄSSIGKEITEN"

A. Texte

5. *Die Einfügung biblischer Zitate in liturgische Texte*:[32] Liturgische Texte, in denen Bibelzitate unsystematisch bzw. in paraphrasierter Form eingefügt sind, sind oft älter als Texte, in denen Bibelzitate wörtlich und zu doktrinellen Zwecken thematisch gezielt eingesetzt wurden.

Klassisches Beispiel sind die Einsetzungsworte, die schon in den ältesten Anaphoren nie wörtlich von einer der neutestamentlichen Redaktionen übernommen wurden, wie Fritz HAMM sehr ausführlich gezeigt hat.[33] Hier haben wir übrigens eine

[30] Zur sog. „Traditio Apostolica" siehe z.B. Bruno STEIMER, Vertex Traditionis. Die Gattung der altchristlichen Kirchenordnungen (Beihefte zur Zeitschrift für die neutestamentliche Wissenschaft 63), Berlin – New York 1992, 28–48, 211–222; Christoph MARKSCHIES, Wer schrieb die sogenannte *Traditio Apostolica*? Neue Beobachtungen und Hypothesen zu einer kaum lösbaren Frage aus der altkirchlichen Literaturgeschichte, in: Wolfram KINZING – Christoph MARKSCHIES – Markus VINZENT (Hgg.), Tauffragen und Bekenntnis (Arbeiten zur Kirchengeschichte 74), Berlin – New York 1999, 1–74; DERS., Neue Forschungen zur sogenannten „Traditio Apostolica", in: TAFT – WINKER, Acts of the International Congress (s. Anm. 23), 583–598.

[31] Vgl. BAUMSTARK, Vom geschichtlichen Werden (s. Anm. 25), 38f.; DERS., Liturgie Comparée (s. Anm. 18), 5f.; DERS., Comparative Liturgy (s. Anm. 18), 5f.; DERS., Orientalisches in altspanischer Liturgie, in: Oriens Christianus III/10 (1935) 1–37 u.a.

[32] Vgl. BAUMSTARK, Liturgie Comparée, 67; DERS., Comparative Liturgy, 59.

[33] Fritz HAMM, Die liturgischen Einsetzungsberichte im Sinne vergleichender Liturgieforschung untersucht (LQF 23), Münster 1928. – Siehe künftig die ausführliche Studie von Predrag BUKOVEC, Der Einsetzungsbericht in der Eucharistiefeier. Genese, Geschichte und Stellenwert der Narratio institutionis aus liturgievergleichender Sicht (Dissertation der Universität Wien; in Vorbereitung).

Fehleinschätzung der Reformatoren vor uns, die oft meinten, dass die ältesten liturgischen Texte auch die bibeltreuesten seien.

6. *Das Prinzip der Symmetrie:*[34] Bei manchen liturgischen Texten (wie z.B. bei den Einsetzungsworten) ist die jüngere Textgestalt symmetrischer strukturiert als die ältere.

7. *Die Anreicherung liturgischer Texte mit doktrinellen Elementen:*[35] Ab dem vierten Jahrhundert wurden die liturgischen Texte mit doktrinellen Elementen durchsetzt, die die theologischen Kontroversen der frühen Konzilien widerspiegeln.

8. *Die zunehmende rhetorische Prägung der liturgischen Sprache.*[36]

B. Strukturen, Handlungen und ihre Symbolisierung

9. *Die Verdrängung älterer Elemente durch neue:*[37] Im zweifachen, entgegengerichteten Prozess der Anreicherung und Kürzung (vgl. oben Gesetzmäßigkeit Nr. 2) konnten zwar eine Zeit lang jüngere Elemente mit älteren zusammen bestehen, bevor letztere schließlich verdrängt wurden. Gewöhnlich machten aber die ältesten Elemente Platz, bevor die neuen übernommen wurden.

   Diese von BAUMSTARK als „Gesetz der organischen Entwicklung“[38] bezeichnete „Gesetzmäßigkeit“ hat mit den besonderen liturgischen Einheiten (Antiphonen, Litaneien *etc.*) innerhalb von Ritualen wie Taufe, Eucharistie *etc.* zu tun.

10. *Die Bewahrung des Alten in „liturgisch hochwertiger Zeit“:*[39] Vor allem an liturgischen Hochfesten und in geprägten Zeiten während des Kirchenjahres haben sich ansonsten verschwundene liturgische Bräuche und Texte noch

[34] Vgl. BAUMSTARK, Liturgie Comparée (s. Anm. 18), 67; DERS., Comparative Liturgy (s. Anm. 18), 59.

[35] Vgl. BAUMSTARK, Liturgie Comparée, 68f.; DERS., Comparative Liturgy, 59f.

[36] Vgl. BAUMSTARK, Liturgie Comparée, 69–79; DERS., Comparative Liturgy, 61–70. – Dieses stilistische Gesetz ist z.B. hinsichtlich einiger griech. Texte bestätigt worden, denn die Chrysostomus-Anaphora wäre ein anschauliches Beispiel für die Regeln der klassischen Rhetorik [vgl. Daniel J. SHEERIN, The Anaphora of the Liturgy of St. John Chrysostom. Stylistic Notes, in: David JASPER – Ronald C.D. JASPER (ed.s), Language and the Worship of the Church, New York 1990, 44–81; Robert F. TAFT, John Chrysostom and the Byzantine Anaphora that Bears his Name, in: Paul F. BRADSHAW (ed.), Essays on Early Eastern Eucharistic Prayers, Collegeville 1997, 195–226, hier 224–226].

[37] Vgl. BAUMSTARK, Liturgie Comparée, 26–30; DERS., Comparative Liturgy, 23–26.

[38] Vgl. BAUMSTARK, Liturgie Comparée, 26; DERS., Comparative Liturgy, 23. – Siehe auch den Ansatz von Alcuin REID, The Organic Development of the Liturgy, San Francisco ²2005; DERS., Eine Präzisierung von “The Organic Development of Liturgy”. Das grundlegende Prinzip zur Beurteilung der Reform, in: Stephan WAHLE u.a. (Hgg.), Römische Messe und Liturgie in der Moderne, Freiburg u.a. 2013, 73–102.

[39] Vgl. Anton BAUMSTARK, Das Gesetz der Erhaltung des Alten in liturgisch hochwertiger Zeit, in: Jahrbuch für Liturgiewissenschaft 7 (1927) 1–23; DERS., Liturgie Comparée, 30–34; DERS., Comparative Liturgy, 27–30. – Diese „Gesetzmäßigkeit“ wurde 1912 erstmals von Adrian FORTESCUE formuliert (The Mass: A Study of the Roman Liturgy, New York 1912, 270).

erhalten können. Diese „Gesetzmäßigkeit“ umschreibt also die Entwicklung vom regelmäßigen liturgischen Brauch hin zur späteren Ausnahmeerscheinung an liturgischen Festen oder Intensivzeiten im Kirchenjahr.

Für den Westen hat Martin KLÖCKENER in einem interessanten Aufsatz einige repräsentative Beispiele für das *Triduum Paschale* aufzeigen können:[40] so erhielten sich z.B. in der Karfreitagsliturgie die bis zur Mitte des 5. Jahrhunderts allgemein übliche, sehr schlichte Eröffnung eines Gottesdienstes (mit [Prostratio und] Stillgebet des Zelebranten); in der Abendmahlsmesse am Gründonnerstag findet sich im *Canon Missae* beim Einsetzungsbericht eine auffällige Erweiterung, die einst in mehreren westlichen nicht-römischen Hochgebetstexten auch über den Gründonnerstag hinaus anzutreffen war. Auch das Abdecken des Altares nach der Abendmahlsmesse am Gründonnerstag [= bis ins 7./8. Jahrhundert allgemeine Praxis] und die Übertragung der Eucharistie in eine Seitenkapelle sind weitere anschauliche Beispiele.[41]

11. *Die Symbolisierung liturgischer Handlungen*:[42] Rein utilitaristische liturgische Handlungen bekamen eine symbolische Bedeutung, was dann später in eine *allegorische Liturgieerklärung* einmündete.

Durch diese und noch andere „Gesetzmäßigkeiten“,[43] die bereits größtenteils von der klassischen *Vergleichenden Liturgiewissenschaft* aufgezeigt wurden, konnte man auf Entwicklungen in der Liturgiegeschichte rückschließen. Die

[40] Vgl. Martin KLÖCKENER, Die Auswirkungen des „Baumstarkschen Gesetzes“ auf die Reform des II. Vaticanums, dargestellt anhand des Triduum Paschale, in: Ecclesia Lacencis. Beiträge aus Anlaß der Wiederbesiedlung der Abtei Maria Laach durch Benediktiner aus Beuron vor 100 Jahren [...](Beiträge zur Geschichte des alten Mönchtums und des Benediktinerordens. Supplement 6), hg. v. Emmanuel VON SEVERUS, Münster 1993, 371–402.

[41] In diesem Zusammenhang sei noch auf eine sonderbare Rubrik in der Feier der Osternacht hingewiesen: „Zum Evangelium werden *keine* Leuchter getragen, sondern nur Weihrauch“ (Die Feier der Heiligen Messe. Messbuch für die Bistümer des deutschen Sprachgebietes, Regensburg u.a. ²1988, [93] Nr. 35; *eigene Hervorhebung*); „35. [...] Ad Evangelium non portantur luminaria, sed tantum incensum.“ (Missale Romanum ex decreto Sacrosancti Oecumenici Concilii Vaticani II [...], Città del Vaticano ³2002, 360). Diese Rubrik wird nur verständlich, wenn man bedenkt, dass sie noch den alten Zustand widerspiegelt, als Kerzen rein funktional und weniger zum Ausdruck der Festlichkeit verwendet wurden, weshalb beim Lesen in der Osternacht wegen des erhellten Raumes auf sie verzichtet werden konnte.

[42] Vgl. BAUMSTARK, Liturgie Comparée, 144; DERS., Comparative Liturgy, 130.

[43] Ernst HAMMERSCHMIDT macht auf ein mögliches weiteres Prinzip der Methode der *Vergleichenden Liturgiewissenschaft* aufmerksam, das er „liturgisches Formkriterium“ nennt und das er auch zu belegen versucht: „Wenn die Gleichheit zwischen liturgischen Texten (Wort- oder Satzgruppen) durch die gleichen *Quellen*, das gleiche *Anliegen*, den gleichen *Zweck* (Bestimmung) oder den gleichen geistigen *Hintergrund* bedingt ist, kann nicht ohne weiteres eine Verwandtschaft bzw. eine Abhängigkeit zwischen ihnen angenommen werden“ (DERS., Das liturgische Formkriterium. Ein Prinzip in der Erforschung der orientalischen Liturgien, in: Frank L. CROSS, (ed.), Studia Patristica V/3 (TU 80), Berlin 1962, 50–68, hier 52; vgl. auch Hieronymus ENGBERDING, in: Oriens Christianus 42 (1958) 136: „Die grundsätzlich zurückhaltende Beurteilung der Fragen der gegenseitigen Abhängigkeit von Texten, bei denen ‚das generelle Anliegen das gleiche und von den gleichen Faktoren bestimmt ist‘ ... verdient uneingeschränkte Anerkennung“].

klassische *Vergleichende Liturgiewissenschaft* hat im deutschen Sprachgebiet mit einer Reihe beachtlicher Untersuchungen nur eine relativ kurze Zeit der Blüte erlebt, besonders mit dem Benediktiner Hieronymus ENGBERDING, der mit seiner 1931 veröffentlichten Dissertation über alle orientalischen Rezensionen der sogenannten *Basilius-Anaphora*[44] die Methodik der *Vergleichenden Liturgiewissenschaft* verfeinern konnte. Anton BAUMSTARKS methodische Grundlegung der klassischen *Vergleichenden Liturgiewissenschaft* ist in den sechziger Jahren in Rom am *Päpstlichen Orientalischen Institut* durch die von Juan MATEOS SJ (1917–2003) begründete „School of Comparative Liturgiology“ rezipiert und weiterentwickelt worden.[45] Aus dieser Schule mit internationaler Besetzung sind mehrere namhafte Vertreter des Faches hervorgegangen (z.B. Robert F. TAFT SJ, Miguel ARRANZ, Sebastià JANERAS und Gabriele WINKLER).

Es gab oder gibt natürlich nicht *die* (eine) „Vergleichende Liturgiewissenschaft“, sondern wir haben auch hier eine gewisse differenzierte Methodenvielfalt innerhalb des skizzierten Ansatzes vor uns.

3. KRITISCHE WEITERFÜHRUNG EINER „LITURGIEVERGLEICHENDEN“ METHODIK

Die von BAUMSTARK ausgeprägte Methodik ist jedoch nicht unumstritten gewesen. Bernard BOTTE OSB (1893–1980) hat im Vorwort zur dritten Auflage von *Liturgie Comparée* – bei aller betonter Zustimmung im Grundsätzlichen – auf das Problem hingewiesen, dass durch die von BAUMSTARK aufgestellten „Gesetze“ die Gefahr der Verwechslung von logischer Konstruktion und historischer Realität drohe.[46] Auch die Schüler von BAUMSTARK haben bereits nur von einer *relativen* Gültigkeit solcher „Gesetzmäßigkeiten“ sprechen wollen.[47] In der neueren englischsprachigen Literatur wird diese Seite der *Vergleichenden Liturgiewissenschaft* einer deutlichen Kritik unterzogen,[48] die allerdings in vielen Punkten nicht haltbar ist.

44 Hieronymus ENGBERDING, Das Eucharistische Hochgebet der Basileiosliturgie. Textgeschichtliche Untersuchungen und kritische Ausgabe (Theologie des Christlichen Ostens 1), Münster 1931. – Vgl. jetzt aber abgelöst durch die wegweisende Studie von WINKLER, Basilius-Anaphora (s. Anm. 28).

45 Vgl. Gabriele WINKLER, The Achievements of the Pontifical Oriental Institute in the Study of Oriental Liturgiology, in: Robert F. TAFT – James L. DUGAN (ed.s.), Il 75° anniversario del Pontificio Istituto Orientale. Atti delle celebrazioni giubilari, 15–17 ottobre 1992 (OCA 244), Roma 1994, 115–141.

46 Vgl. BAUMSTARK, Liturgie Comparée, VII; DERS., Comparative Liturgy, ix.

47 So z.B. HAMM, Die liturgischen Einsetzungsberichte (s. Anm. 33), 97.

48 So z.B. von Fritz WEST, The Comparative Liturgy of Anton Baumstark (GROW Joint Liturgical Studies 31), Bramcote 1995, 25; Martin STRINGER, Liturgy and Anthropology. The History of a Relationship, in: Worship 63 (1989) 503–521 [s. dazu Robert F. TAFT, Comparative Liturgy Fifty Years after Anton Baumstark (d. 1948). A Reply to Recent Critics, in: Worship 73 (1999) 521–540, hier 528–531]; John R.K. FENWICK, The Anaphoras of St. Basil and St. James. An Investigation into their Common Origin (OCA 240), Roma 1992, 61-69 (“Methodology”)[s. dazu die ausführliche Rezension von Gabriele WINKLER, in: Oriens Christianus 78 (1994) 269–277]; Paul F. BRADSHAW, The Search for

Weitere ernstzunehmende Einwände sind von Benedikt KRANEMANN und besonders von Friedrich LURZ vorgebracht worden.[49] Das bisherige Materialobjekt einer *Vergleichenden Liturgiewissenschaft* waren nämlich fast ausschließlich die orientalischen Liturgien, da diese Liturgien aufgrund ihrer starken Beharrungskraft in die Zeit der antiken Liturgien zurückblicken lassen. In der ersten Hälfte des 20. Jahrhunderts kam es in der klassischen *Vergleichenden Liturgiewissenschaft* zu einer auffallenden Ausklammerung der reformatorischen Liturgien. Der tiefere Grund für die *bisherige* Ignorierung der reformatorischen Tradition in der klassischen *Vergleichenden Liturgiewissenschaft* liegt nicht in einer konfessionellen Voreingenommenheit, sondern in der Anwendung einer Methodik und der Übertragung des dahinterstehenden Entwicklungsparadigmas auf die Liturgie.[50] Die Liturgie wird nach BAUMSTARK nämlich als etwas Gewachsenes und Organisches gesehen, und nicht als Produkt menschlicher Willkür oder bewusster Planung.[51] Das Spezifische dieser Sicht ist, dass ihr zufolge die Liturgie wie die Natur in ihrer Entwicklung bestimmten liturgischen „Gesetzmäßigkeiten" folge,[52] von denen oben einige kurz skizziert wurden. Ein radikaler Umbruch aber, wie ihn die reformatorischen Liturgien tatsächlich beinhalten und der oftmals die innere Gesetzlichkeit aufhebt, lässt sich in diese klassische Methodik nur schwer einbinden, wie auch kulturelle Veränderungen in ihr weitgehend unberücksichtigt bleiben.[53]

Eine auch die reformatorischen Traditionen integrierende *Vergleichende Liturgiewissenschaft* vermag jedoch über bloße „Gesetzmäßigkeiten" hinaus – und das darf bei aller berechtigter Kritik *nicht* übersehen werden – sowohl für das Mittelalter als auch für die Neuzeit bedeutsame Ergebnisse zu liefern.[54] Im Hinblick auf die reformatorischen Liturgien können nämlich ebenso wesentliche Abhängigkeitsverhältnisse bzw. wechselseitige Einflüsse herausgearbeitet werden, obgleich die *klassischen* „Gesetzmäßigkeiten" hier natürlich nicht mehr zur Anwendung kommen. Aber in einer solch einseitigen und ausschließlichen Beobachtung von bloßen „Gesetzmäßigkeiten" erschöpft sich eine *Vergleichende Liturgiewissenschaft* ja durchaus nicht.

the Origins of Christian Worship. Sources and Methods for the Study of Early Liturgy, London – Cambridge 1992, 56–79 ("Ten Principles for Interpreting Early Christian Liturgical Evidence") u.a. – Siehe schon die Bezweiflung der Allgemeingültigkeit durch Theodor KLAUSER, Kleine Abendländische Liturgiegeschichte, Bonn 1965, 176.

49 KRANEMANN, Liturgiewissenschaft angesichts der „Zeitenwende" (s. Anm. 19), 368f.; LURZ, Die Feier des Abendmahls (s. Anm. 11), 24–27; DERS., Für eine ökumenische Liturgiewissenschaft (s. Anm. 11), 276f.

50 Vgl. LURZ, Feier des Abendmahls, 25.

51 Vgl. BAUMSTARK, Vom geschichtlichen Werden (s. Anm. 25), 2.

52 Vgl. WEST, Comparative Liturgy (s. Anm. 48), 16–19.

53 Von BAUMSTARK wird die Reformation als „riesenhafte[r] Abfall von der alten Kirche" verstanden (DERS., Vom geschichtlichen Werden, 126), da die Substanz für ihn immer gleich bleiben muss (DERS., Comparative Liturgy, 1).

54 Vgl. Bryan D. SPINKS, Evaluating Liturgies of the Reformation: The Limitations of the Comparative Methods of Baumstark, in: TAFT – WINKLER, Acts of the International Congress (s. Anm. 23), 283–303.

Auch die westlichen Liturgieformulare des Römischen, des Altspanischen, des Ambrosianischen oder Mailändischen Ritus, und natürlich auch die der reformatorischen Liturgietraditionen lassen sich in ihre liturgischen Einheiten bzw. Bestandteile gliedern, philologisch analysieren, historisch-kritisch sowie theologisch untersuchen und vergleichend gegenüberstellen, wobei oftmals interessante Entwicklungen und gegenseitige Einflüsse auszumachen sind.[55]
Bei der historisch-kritischen Arbeitsweise einer *Vergleichenden Liturgiewissenschaft* geht es ja nicht nur um Vergangenes, sondern letztlich auch um das Verstehen der Gegenwart.[56] Einer historisch-kritisch arbeitenden Liturgiewissenschaft wird es zudem wesentlich leichter fallen, konvergente wie divergente Entwicklungen in den verschiedenen Liturgien und ihre Ursachen wahrzunehmen. Aber auch die gegenseitige Beeinflussung liturgischer Traditionen wird so deutlicher (auch im interreligiösen Bereich, zumindest bezüglich des Judentums). Das Verstehen der anderen Liturgien und der Motivation für ihre Änderungen bringen ein besseres Verständnis der eigenen liturgischen Tradition mit sich.[57]

Anhand der nachfolgenden, aus einer großen Fülle ausgewählten Beispiele soll dies nun näher illustriert werden, was aber im Rahmen dieses kurzen Beitrags unmöglich mit der gebotenen Gründlichkeit und im nötigen Umfang geschehen kann.

4. BEISPIELE DER „VERGLEICHENDEN“ METHODIK IN ÖKUMENISCHER HINSICHT[58]

(1) Das erste Beispiel ist aus dem Bereich der Ordinationen genommen, da die Erforschung der Ordinationsliturgie innerhalb der Liturgiewissenschaft lange Zeit eine vergleichsweise untergeordnete Rolle eingenommen hat:

• Besonders symbolträchtig erscheint eine Entscheidung von Papst PIUS XII., der am 30. November 1947 in seiner Apostolischen Konstitution *Sacramentum Ordinis*[59] mit einem Rückgriff auf die liturgische Überlieferung als Norm des sakramentalen Vollzugs der Ordination gegen die *materia-forma*–Umschreibung der Ordinationhandlungen im *Decretum pro Armenis* (1439)[60] des Konzils von Florenz argumentierte. Diese Sichtweise wurde erst u.a. durch intensive vorausgegangene *liturgievergleichende* Forschungen ermöglicht.[61]

[55] Vgl. beispielsweise Hans-Jürgen FEULNER, Das „Anglikanische Ordinale“. Eine liturgiegeschichtliche und liturgietheologische Studie, Bd. I: Von den altenglischen Pontifikalien zum Ordinale von 1550/52, Neuried 1997, *passim.*
[56] Vgl. TAFT, Beyond East and West (s. Anm. 20), 153–154.
[57] Vgl. LURZ, Ökumenische Liturgiewissenschaft (s. Anm. 11), 283.
[58] Die folgenden Beispiele sind nur kurz anskizziert und sollen teilweise in künftigen Einzelstudien liturgiewissenschaftlich weiter vertieft werden. – Siehe dazu auch FEULNER, „Ex oriente lux“ (s. Anm. 12), 34–41.
[59] AAS 40 (1948) 5–7.
[60] DH 1326.
[61] Vgl. Hans-Joachim SCHULZ, Ein Blick in die Zukunft: Was können die Kirchen vom Päpstlichen Orientalischen Institut erwarten für den ökumenischen Fortschritt und für die

Ihren Niederschlag fand diese autoritative Entscheidung von PIUS XII. dann auch in der Apostolischen Konstitution *Pontificalis Romani*, die von Papst PAUL VI. bei der Veröffentlichung der neuen Ordinationsriten am 18. Juni 1968 ausdrücklich wiederholt wurde: „Die Materie der heiligen Diakonen-, Priester- und Bischofsweihe ist allein die Handauflegung: die ebenfalls einzige Form sind die den Vollzug dieser Materie in ihrem Sinn bestimmenden Worte […].“[62]

• Durch philologische, strukturelle, historisch-kritische und theologische Vergleiche können die exakten reformatorischen sowie katholischen Einflüsse auf die Aus- und Weiterbildung der anglikanischen Ordinationsriten herausgestellt werden,[63] was natürlich auch weitreichende dogmatische und ökumenische Auswirkungen hat, z.B. hinsichtlich der Anerkennung der unter Papst LEO XIII. 1896[64] für nichtig erklärten anglikanischen Ordinationen und das daraus resultierende Amtsverständnis.

Lange Zeit wurde in der liturgiewissenschaftlichen Forschung nämlich angenommen, dass die anglikanischen Ordinationsriten im Wesentlichen aus Kürzungen der vorreformatorischen Ordinationsformulare des in England im 16. Jahrhundert vorherrschenden *Sarum-Pontificale*[65] hervorgegangen sind.[66] Durch Heranziehung liturgischer und außer-

theologische Wissenschaft, in: TAFT – DUGAN, Il 75° anniversario del Pontificio Istituto Orientale (s. Anm. 45), 197–212, hier 199f.

62 Zitiert nach Heinrich RENNINGS – Martin KLÖCKENER (Hgg.), Dokumente zur Erneuerung der Liturgie. Bd. 1: Dokumente des Apostolischen Stuhls 1963–1973 [= DEL I], Kevelaer 1983, Nr. 1084; vgl. AAS 40 (1948) 6. – Ein besonderer ökumenischer Hinweis erscheint ebenfalls in dieser Apostolischen Konstitution von 1968: „… Aufgrund der Überlieferung nämlich, die vorzüglich in den liturgischen Riten und im Gebrauch der Kirche des Ostens wie Westens deutlich wird, ist es klar, daß durch die Handauflegung und die Worte der Weihe die Gnade des Heiligen Geistes so übertragen und das heilige Mal so eingeprägt wird …“ (DEL I, Nr. 1081).

63 Vgl. FEULNER, Das „Anglikanische Ordinale“ (s. Anm. 55); DERS., Die anglikanische Ordinationsliturgie der Kirche von England, in: LJ 47 (1997) 23–40; DERS., Zu den eucharistischen „Opfer“- bzw. „Darbringungs“-Aussagen in der Ordinationsliturgie der Kirche von England, in: LJ 50 (2000) 117–126.

64 Hinter dieser Regelung steht die Entscheidung von Papst LEO XIII. aus dem Jahre 1896, als er in seinem Apostolischen Schreiben *Apostolicae Curae* die anglikanischen Ordinationen als „völlig ungültig und gänzlich nichtig“ erklärt hat: „… Itaque omnibus Pontificum Decessorum in hac ipsa causa decretis usquequaque assentientes, eaque plenissime confirmantes ac veluti renovantes auctoritate Nostra, motu proprio certa scientia, pronunciamus et declaramus, ordinationes ritu anglicano actas, irritas prorsus fuisse et esse, omninoque nullas …“ [ASS 29 (1896/97) 193–203, hier 202]. – Siehe auch John J. HUGHES, Absolut Null und Nichtig. Zur Ablehnung der anglikanischen Weihen durch die Bulle Leos XIII. „Apostolicae curae“ vom 13. September 1896 (Studia Anglicana 2), Trier 1970; George TAVARD, A Review of Anglican Orders: The Problem and the Solution, Collegeville 1990; Giuseppe RAMBALDI, Ordinazioni Anglicane e Sacramento dell'Ordine nella Chiesa. Aspetti storici e teologici: A cento anni dalla bolla Apostolicae curae di Leone XIII, Roma 1995; R. William FRANKLIN (ed.), Anglican Orders: Essays on the Centenary of *Apostolicae Curae*, 1896–1996, London 1996; Christopher HILL – Edward YARNOLD (ed.s), Anglican Orders: The Documents in the Debate, Norwich 1997; Margaret O'GARA, *Apostolicae Curae* After a Century: Anglican Orders in Light of Recent Ecumenical Dialogue on Ordained Ministry in the Church, in: Canon Law Society of America Proceedings 60 (1998) 1–18.

65 Vgl. William MASKELL (ed.), Monumenta Ritualia Ecclesiae Anglicanae […], vol. II, Oxford ^{2}1882.

liturgischer Quellen, durch Strukturierung der Liturgieformulare in sinnvolle Einheiten, durch philologische Analysen der teilweise unedierten Texte, durch den strukturellen und inhaltlichen Vergleich der liturgischen Einheiten sowie durch die Herausarbeitung ihres historisch-theologischen Wandels konnte nunmehr gezeigt werden, dass die anglikanischen Ordinationsriten, besonders in ihren Kernelementen, auf den im englischen Exil lebenden elsässischen Reformator Martin BUTZER (1491–1551) zurückgehen[67] und lediglich an *sekundären* Stellen mit Elementen des katholischen *Sarum-Pontificale* ergänzt wurden.

Der ziemlich komplizierte Entwicklungsprozess lässt sich folgendermaßen schematisch darstellen [„Ordinale“ = liturgisches Buch mit den Ordinationsriten]:[68]

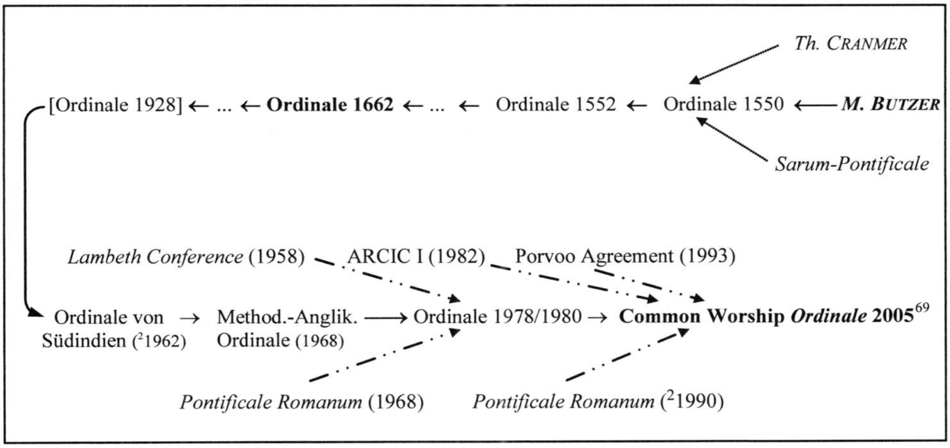

• Der u.a. auch durch eine *liturgievergleichende* Untersuchung darstellbare historische Wandel der Strukturen und der *theologischen* Inhalte der anglikanischen Ordinationen zieht natürlich auch sakramenten-theologische und ekklesiologische Implikationen nach sich. Nach Abschluss einer umfassenden liturgievergleichenden Studie zum *Ordinale* in *allen* anglikanischen Teilkirchen

66 So z.B. Paul F. BRADSHAW, The Anglican Ordinal. Its History and Development from the Reformation to the Present (Alcuin Club Collection 53), London 1971; Marion J. HATCHETT, Commentary on the American Prayer Book, San Francisco 1995, 506–512.

67 Martini BUCERI, Scripta Anglicana fere omnia [...], ed. a Con. HUBERTO, Basel 1577.

68 Überarbeitete Version von FEULNER, Die anglikanische Ordinationsliturgie (s. Anm. 63), 28. – Siehe auch Paul BRADSHAW (ed.), A Companion to Common Worship, vol. 2 (Alcuin Club Collection 81), London 2006, 219–241.

69 Die *Common Worship – Ordination Services* wurden 2005 von der General Synod der *Church of England* approbiert. Als Studienausgabe gedruckt: Common Worship, Services and Prayers for the Church of England: Ordination Services, London 2007 (²2008). – Vgl. auch: Baptism, Eucharist and Ministry (Faith and Order Paper no. 111), Geneva 1982; Together in Mission and Ministry. The Porvoo Common Statement with Essays on Church and Ministry in Northern Europe, London 1993; Paul GIBSON, Anglican Ordination Rites. The Berkeley Statement: “To Equip the Saints.” Findings of the Sixth International Anglican Liturgical Consultation, Berkeley, California, 2001 (Grove Worship Series 168), Cambridge 2002.

kann möglicherweise eine neue Diskussionsbasis in der festgefahrenen theologischen Kontroverse um die Anerkennung der anglikanischen Ordinationen durch die römisch-katholische und auch durch die östlichen Kirchen eröffnet werden, was weitreichende ökumenische Auswirkungen haben kann.[70]

Aus dem Einfluss des nachkonziliaren *Pontificale Romanum* (1968; ^{2}1990) haben sich außerdem bereits einige pastoral-liturgische Impulse für die 2005 approbierte Neugestaltung der anglikanischen Ordinationsformulare der *Church of England* ergeben.[71]

(2) Das zweite Beispiel ist aus dem Bereich der Eucharistie genommen: In den letzten vier Jahrzehnten hat die liturgiewissenschaftliche Erforschung der östlichen Anaphoren eine herausragende Rolle eingenommen. Auch hier haben Vertreter einer *liturgievergleichenden* Methodik wichtige Erkenntnisse zum Verständnis des Eucharistischen Hochgebetes beitragen können. Bereits vor dem II. Vatikanischen Konzil hatten Bernard BOTTE OSB,[72] Alphonse RAES SJ (1896–1983)[73] und nicht zuletzt Josef A. JUNGMANN SJ (1889–1975)[74] in ihren liturgiewissenschaftlichen Studien, die sich bewusst oder unbewusst auch einer *liturgievergleichenden* Methode bedienten, wegweisende Ergebnisse vorgelegt, die die nachkonziliare Reform der Eucharistiefeier der katholischen Kirche we-

[70] Natürlich sind die Frauenordinationen in einigen anglikanischen Teilkirchen ein erhebliches Hindernis im ökumenischen Dialog! Ein anvisiertes Forschungsprojekt beim FWF (= Fonds zur Förderung der wissenschaftlichen Forschung in Österreich) soll die Erforschung der Anglikanischen Ordinationsriten in zwei weiteren Teilbänden vorantreiben (s. auch Anm. 63).

[71] Die Liturgiekommission der *Church of England* hatte bei der Überarbeitung der damals von 1980–2000 (verlängert bis Ende 2005) geltenden Ordinationsriten im *Alternative Service Book* auch einige nicht-anglikanische Mitarbeiter und Gutachter aus verschiedenen Ländern und Kirchen ausgewählt. Deren Aufgabe war es, aufgrund von pastoralliturgischen Erfahrungen ihrer eigenen Kirchen Gestaltungsmöglichkeiten bei der Neuordnung der anglikanischen Ordinationsformulare aufzuzeigen und auch zu liturgie-theologischen Fragen Stellung zu beziehen: Im Einzelnen ging es z.B. um den Ort der Ordinationen, um den liturgischen Dienst der Neugeweihten in der Feier ihrer Ordination, um den möglichen Einbezug von Familienangehörigen, um die angemessene Gestaltung der ausdeutenden Riten, um die bessere Einbindung der sakramentalen Handauflegung, um die inhaltliche Überarbeitung der Ordinationsgebete, um die Wiedereinführung der in der Reformationszeit verloren gegangenen Ordinationssalbungen *etc.* [vgl. Common Worship: Ordination Services (s. Anm. 69)].

[72] Bernard BOTTE, L'anaphore Chaldéenne des Apôtres, in: OCP 15 (1949) 259–276; DERS., Note historique sur la concélébration dans l'Église ancienne, in: Maison-Dieu 35 (1953) 9–24; DERS., Problèmes de l'Anamnèse, in: JEH 5 (1954) 16–24; DERS., Problèmes de l'anaphore syrienne des Apôtres Addai et Mari, in: OrSyr 10 (1965) 89–106 u.a.

[73] Vgl. Alphonse RAES, Les paroles de la consécration dans les anaphores syriennes, in: OCP 3 (1937) 486–504; DERS., Le récit de l'institution eucharistique dans l'anaphore chaldéenne et malabare des Apôtres, in: OCP 10 (1944) 216–226; DERS., Introductio in Liturgiam orientalem, Roma 1947; DERS., Un nouveau document de la Liturgie de S. Basile, in: OCP 26 (1960) 401–411; DERS., ΚΑΤΑ ΠΑΝΤΑ ΚΑΙ ΔΙΑ ΠΑΝΤΑ. En tout et pour tout, in: Oriens Christianus IV/12 (1964) 216–220 etc. – RAES edierte außerdem eine Fülle von west-syrischen Anaphoren in der von ihm begründeten Reihe *Anaphorae Syriacae*.

[74] Vgl. Josef A. JUNGMANN, Die Stellung Christi im liturgischen Gebet (LQF 19/20), Münster ^{2}1962; DERS., Missarum Sollemnia. Eine genetische Erklärung der römischen Messe I-II, Wien ^{5}1962 u.a.

sentlich mitbeeinflussten und die bereits auch ökumenische Auswirkungen zeigen.

• Besonders bedeutsam waren die *liturgievergleichenden* Studien der zahlreichen west-syrischen Anaphoren.[75] Die neuen römisch-katholischen Hochgebete von 1968/70 sind in ihrer klaren Struktur besonders dem antiochenischen Anaphora-Typus nachempfunden, wie die Übersicht erkennen lässt:

antiochenische Anaphoren	röm.-kath. Hochgebete II-IV (1968/1970)[76]
Eröffnungsdialog	Eröffnungsdialog
Oratio ante Sanctus	Präfation
Sanctus–Benedictus	Sanctus–Benedictus
Oratio post Sanctus	Postsanctus
——	[*Konsekrations-*]*Epiklese*
Einsetzungsworte	Einsetzungsworte
Spezielle Anamnese	Spezielle Anamnese
+ Darbringungsaussage	+ Darbringungsaussage
[*Konsekrations-*]*Epiklese*	[*Kommunion-*]*Epiklese*
Interzessionen/Diptychen	Interzessionen
Doxologie	Doxologie

• Auch hinsichtlich der Darbringungs- bzw. Opferaussagen in den eucharistischen Liturgien hat es vermittels einer *vergleichenden* Liturgieforschung Bewegung im ökumenischen Verständnis gegeben.[77]

[75] Vgl. auch Albert GERHARDS, Entstehung und Entwicklung des Eucharistischen Hochgebets im Spiegel der neueren Forschung. Der Beitrag der Liturgiewissenschaft zur liturgischen Erneuerung, in: Gratias agamus. Studien zum eucharistischen Hochgebet. Für Balthasar Fischer, hg. v. Andreas HEINZ – Heinrich RENNINGS, Freiburg u.a. 1992, 75–96.

[76] Vgl. DEL I, Nr. 1032–1043, 2060.

[77] Vgl. beispielsweise Hans-Joachim SCHULZ, Ökumenische Glaubenseinheit aus eucharistischer Überlieferung, Paderborn 1976, 48–53; DERS., Ökumenische Aspekte der Darbringungsaussagen in der erneuerten römischen und in der byzantinischen Liturgie, in: Archiv für Liturgiewissenschaft 19 (1978) 7–28; DERS., Liturgischer Vollzug und sakramentale Wirklichkeit des eucharistischen Opfers, in: OCP 45 (1979) 245–266; 46 (1980) 5–19; DERS., Das frühchristlich-altkirchliche Eucharistiegebet. Überlieferungskontinuität und Glaubenszeugnis, in: Internationale kirchliche Zeitschrift 70 (1980) 139–153; DERS., Patterns of Offering and Sacrifice, in: Studia Liturgica 15 (1982) 34–48; DERS., Hochgebet und eucharistische Darbringung. Das wiedererschlossene Zeugnis der Liturgie in seiner ökumenischen Bedeutsamkeit, in: Erich RENHART – Andreas SCHNIDER, Sursum Corda. Variationen zu einem liturgischen Motiv. Für Philipp Harnoncourt zum 60. Geburtstag, Graz u.a. 1991, 140–146; B. SCHULTZE, Die patristische Eucharistielehre im Gespräch evangelischer und orthodoxer Theologen, in: Ostkirchliche Studien 28 (1979) 97–144; Gabriele WINKLER, Zur Erforschung orientalischer Anaphoren I: Anmerkungen zur Oratio post Sanctus und Anamnese bis Epiklese, in: OCP 63 (1997) 363–420; DIES., Zur Erforschung orientalischer Anaphoren in liturgievergleichender Sicht III: Der Hinweis auf „die Gaben" bzw. „das Opfer" bei der Epiklese, in: Albert GERHARDS – Klemens RICHTER (Hgg.), Das Opfer. Biblischer Anspruch und liturgische Gestalt (Quaestiones Disputatae 186), Freiburg u.a. 2000, 216–233 etc.

• Besonders das *Eucharistische Hochgebet IV* mit seiner *feststehenden* Präfation ist in seiner Gesamtschau der Heilsgeschichte inhaltlich sehr stark von östlichen Anaphoren beeinflusst, besonders von der ägyptischen *Basilius-Anaphora.*[78]

• Für einige Kirchen der Reformation sind das *Eucharistische Hochgebet IV* und auch das aus der so genannten *Traditio Apostolica* entlehnte Hochgebet II zum Vorbild bei der Einführung neuer Eucharistiegebete geworden.[79] So beispielsweise bereits 1971 in der *Evangelischen Kirche der Union* (EKU),[80] in der ökumenischen Kommunität von Taizé,[81] und im Jahre 1975 als „Common Eucharistic Prayer"[82] bei den Methodisten,[83] Lutheranern[84] sowie Presbyterianern[85]

[78] Siehe Annibale BUGNINI, Die Liturgiereform 1948–1975. Zeugnis und Testament, Freiburg 1988, 490–492. – Vgl. Bruno KLEINHEYER, Erneuerung des Hochgebetes, Regensburg 1969, *passim*; Die eucharistischen Hochgebete II–IV. Ein theologischer Kommentar, hg. v. Otto NUSSBAUM (Lebendiger Gottesdienst 16), Münster 1971, 82–107 [Heinzgerd BRAKMANN]; Heinzgerd BRAKMANN, Foedera pluries hominibus. Anmerkungen zur Revision des Eucharistischen Hochgebets IV, in: LJ 50 (2000) 211–234; Norbert LOHFINK, Der Alte Bund im 4. Hochgebet, in: Bibel und Liturgie 73 (2000) 33–46; Georg BRAULIK, Das göttliche Bundesangebot an die Menschheit. Zum 4. Hochgebet, in: Streit am Tisch des Wortes? Zur Deutung und Bedeutung des Alten Testaments und seiner Verwendung in der Liturgie, hg. v. Ansgar FRANZ (Pietas Liturgica 8), St. Ottilien 1997, 841–853; DERS., Gott für Israel preisen. Zur Heilsprärogative Israels und zum vierten Hochgebet, in: Dialog oder Monolog? Zur liturgischen Beziehung zwischen Judentum und Christentum, hg. v. Albert GERHARDS – Hans Hermann HENRIX (Quaestiones Disputatae 208), Freiburg 2004, 223–253; Daniela KRANEMANN, Israelitica dignitas? Studien zur Israeltheologie eucharistischer Hochgebete (Münsteraner Theologische Abhandlungen 66), Altenberge 2001, 139–152; Hans B. MEYER, Eucharistie. Geschichte, Theologie, Pastoral (Gottesdienst der Kirche 4), Regensburg 1989, 350 u.a.

[79] Vgl. Ottfried JORDAHN, Die ökumenische Bedeutung der Hochgebete der erneuerten römischen Liturgie, in: Una Sancta 31 (1976) 245–256; Frank C. SENN (ed.), New Eucharistic Prayers. An Ecumenical Study of their Development and Structure, New York – Mahwah/NJ 1987, 63–163 (H. Boone PORTER), 74–79 (Gail RAMSHAW-SCHMIDT), 80–95 (James F. WHITE), 96-123 (Arlo D. DUBA); Frieder SCHULZ, Das Eucharistiegebet in den Kirchen der Reformation als Frucht ökumenischer Konvergenz. Rezeption und Revision, in: Karl SCHLEMMER (Hg.), Gemeinsame Liturgie in getrennten Kirchen? (Quaestiones Disputatae 132), Freiburg u.a. 1991, 82–118, bes. 103f.: „In den USA bildete sich 1975 eine Arbeitsgruppe aus Gliedern der anglikanischen, methodistischen und presbyterianischen Kirche sowie aus dem Bereich der [...] Consultation on Church Union und der katholischen Kirche mit dem Ziel, ein gemeinsames Eucharistiegebet zu verfassen. Das Arbeitsergebnis wurde als 4. Eucharistiegebet in das neue Book of Common Prayer der Anglikaner in den USA aufgenommen. Aufgrund der gleichen altkirchlichen Grundlage entspricht es weitgehend dem 4. katholischen Hochgebet. [...] Schließlich ist noch festzuhalten, daß das altkirchliche Eucharistiegebet aus der Kirchenordnung des Hippolyt faktisch ein ökumenisches Hochgebet geworden ist, nachdem es von den englischen und amerikanischen Anglikanern, den amerikanischen Lutheranern und Presbyterianern sowie von den französischen Reformierten der Schweiz in ihre Sammlung der Eucharistiegebete aufgenommen worden ist." [vgl. dazu auch MEYER, Eucharistie (s. Anm. 78), 438f.].

[80] Gebete zur Ergänzung von Agende I der Evangelischen Kirche der Union, Düsseldorf 1971.

[81] Eucharistie à Taizé, [ed. par] TAIZÉ-COMMUNAUTÉ, Taizé 1971. – Vgl. MEYER, Eucharistie (s. Anm. 78), 438.

[82] A Common Eucharistic Prayer, [ed. by] THE COMMITTEE OF A COMMON EUCHARISTIC PRAYER, o.O. 1975.

[83] At the Lord's Table/Supplemental Liturgical Resources, Nashville/TN 1981/84. – The Methodist Service Book (1975) in England besitzt allerdings nur ein einziges Eucharistiegebet, bei dem Gemeinde-Akklamation, Anamnese und Epiklese den Einsetzungsworten

in den USA und im Jahre 1979 dann sogar im offiziellen *Book of Common Prayer* der amerikanischen Anglikaner (Rite II).[86] Auch im erneuerten Messbuch der deutschen Alt-Katholiken von 1995 (^{3}2006)[87] befindet sich ein Text, der eine stark verkürzte Fassung des römischen *Hochgebetes IV* darstellt.

• Auch die unter der Bezeichnung *Lima-Liturgie* bekanntgewordene und 1982 in englischer, französischer, spanischer und deutscher Sprache veröffentlichte Ordnung einer ökumenischen Abendmahlsfeier ist unter anderem die Frucht einer umfassenden *liturgievergleichenden* Forschung und hat überraschend breite Beachtung und Aufmerksamkeit gefunden.[88]

• Die Ausweitung der *Konzelebration* im Römischen Ritus nach dem II. Vatikanischen Konzil (*SC* 57–58) hat ebenfalls durch neuere liturgiegeschichtliche Einsichten, besonders aus den östlichen Kirchen, wichtige Impulse erfahren.[89]

(3) Wenden wir uns in einem dritten Beispiel dem Wirken des Heiligen Geistes in den Sakramenten der Kirche zu: Die nachkonziliare Erneuerung der

folgen. Die anglikanische Gottesdienstreform in England bot bereits im Alternative Service Book (London 1980) vier neue, im Wesentlichen gleich strukturierte Eucharistiegebete mit geteilter Epiklese, Gemeinde-Akklamation und Darbringungsgebet.

84 Lutheran Book of Worship. Ministers' Edition. Prepared by the Churches participating in the Inter-Lutheran Commission on Worship, Minneapolis – Philadelphia 1978.

85 The Service for the Lord's Day/Supplemental Liturgical Resources 1, Philadelphia/PA 1984.

86 The Book of Common Prayer and Administration of the Sacraments and Other Rites and Ceremonies of the Church Together with The Psalter or Psalms of David According to the use of The Episcopal Church, New York 1979.

87 Die Feier der Eucharistie im Katholischen Bistum der Alt-Katholiken in Deutschland, Bonn ^{3}2006. – Vgl. auch Sigisbert KRAFT, Die Erneuerung der Liturgie in den alt-katholischen und anglikanischen Kirchen, in: SCHLEMMER, Gemeinsame Liturgie in getrennten Kirchen? (s. Anm. 79), 11–28, hier 15–20.

88 Die Eucharistische Liturgie von Lima, Frankfurt/M. 1983 (Sonderdruck aus: Ökumenische Perspektiven von Taufe, Eucharistie und Amt, hg. v. Max THURIAN, Frankfurt/M. 1983, 213–235); Frieder SCHULZ, Die Lima-Liturgie. Die ökumenische Gottesdienstordnung zu den Lima-Texten. Ein Beitrag zum Verständnis und zur Urteilsbildung, Kassel 1983; DERS., Die Rezeption der Lima-Liturgie, in: JLH 31 (1987/88) 1–37; Hans-Christoph SCHMIDT-LAUBER, Die Bedeutung der „Lima-Liturgie" für die ökumenische Bewegung, in: LJ 35 (1985) 131–147 u.v.m.

89 DEL I, Nr. 57f., 387–392a-t, 945f. [in der zu *SC* 57 (*olim* 44) gehörigen *Declaratio* auf dem II. Vatikanischen Konzil wurde bei der Konzelebration ausdrücklich auf die lange liturgische Tradition der östlichen Kirchen verwiesen: Acta et Documenta Concilio Oecumenico Vaticano II – Apparando. Ser. II, vol. III/2, Vatikan 1969, 33f.; vgl. auch BUGNINI, Liturgiereform (s. Anm. 78), 145–156; MEYER, Eucharistie (s. Anm. 78), 371, 488–491]. – Siehe ebenso: Alphonse RAES, La concélébration eucharistique dans les rites orientaux, in: La Maison-Dieu 35 (1953) 24–47; Archdale A. KING, Concelebration in the Christian Church, London 1966, bes. 13–17, 102–132; André JACOB, La concélébration de l'anaphore à Byzance d'après le témoignage de Léon Toscan, in: OCP 35 (1969) 249–256; William F. MACOMBER, Concelebration in the East Syrian Rite, in: The Malabar Church. Symposium in Honour of Rev. Placid J. Podipara C.M.I. (OCA 186), ed. by Jacob VELLIAN, Roma 1970, 17–22; Heinzgerd BRAKMANN, "Καὶ ἀναγινώσκουσι πάντες οἱ Ἱερεῖς τὴν εὐχαριστήριον Εὐχήν". Zum gemeinschaftlichen Eucharistiegebet byzantinischer Konzelebranten, in: OCP 42 (1976) 319–367; Robert F. TAFT, Ex Oriente Lux? Some Reflections on Eucharistic Concelebration, in: DERS., Beyond East and West (s. Anm. 20), 111–132.

Liturgie hat die *pneumatologische* Dimension der Sakramente deutlicher zum Ausdruck gebracht.[90] Auch hierfür haben *liturgievergleichende* Studien und Vorarbeiten in den vorangegangenen Jahren den Weg gewiesen:

• Die Firmung galt schon immer – trotz der komplizierten Wechselgeschichte – als Sakrament des Heiligen Geistes.[91] In der nachkonziliaren Liturgiereform wurde die Spendeformel der Firmung entsprechend den damaligen liturgievergleichenden Untersuchungen neu gestaltet und der byzantinischen Form aus dem fünften Jahrhundert angeglichen.[92] Sie lautet in der deutschen Fassung: „Sei besiegelt durch die Gabe Gottes, den Heiligen Geist".[93]

• Auch die anderen sakramentalen Spendeformeln sind nun *pneumatologisch* geprägt: z.B. die neugestaltete Absolutionsformel beim Sakrament der Buße,[94] die Formel bei der Krankensalbung[95] und schließlich die Neuformulierung im Bischofsweihegebet.[96]

• Zur komplexen Entwicklungsgeschichte der Epiklese und deren Stellung im Eucharistischen Hochgebet sind mehrere liturgietheologische, liturgiegeschichtliche und *liturgievergleichende* Untersuchungen vorgelegt worden (beispielsweise Bernard BOTTE,[97] Sebastian P. BROCK,[98] Robert F. TAFT[99] und Gabriele

[90] Vgl. Yves CONGAR, Der Heilige Geist, Freiburg 1982, 454–495.

[91] Vgl. CONGAR, Der Heilige Geist (s. Anm. 90), 454–463. Siehe auch: Burkhard NEUNHEUSER, Taufe und Firmung (HDG IV/2), Freiburg ²1983; Georg KRETSCHMAR, Firmung, in: TRE 11, 192–204; Gabriele WINKLER, Confirmation or Chrismation? A Study in Comparative Liturgy, in: Worship 58 (1984) 2–17; Bruno KLEINHEYER, Sakramentliche Feiern I: Die Feiern der Eingliederung in die Kirche (Gottesdienst der Kirche 7/1), Regensburg1989, *passim*; Manfred HAUKE, Die Firmung. Geschichtliche Entfaltung und theologischer Sinn, Paderborn 1999 u.a.

[92] „Σφραγὶς δωρεᾶς πνεύματος ἁγίου." (Schreiben eines Patriarchen von Konstantinopel [GENNADIUS?] an den Metropoliten MARTYRIUS von Antiochia [PG 119, 899f.]). – Vgl. Francois RECKINGER, „Accipe signaculum". Die Firmung in neuer Gestalt, in: Heiliger Dienst 26 (1972) 164–174, 27 (1973) 13–23; H. ROSSI, Siegel und Gabe – Eine Besinnung über die neue Firmformel als Hilfe zu deren Erklärung, in: Schweizerische Kirchenzeitung 141 (1973) 181–184.

[93] Die Feier der Firmung in den katholischen Bistümern des deutschen Sprachgebietes, hg. im Auftrag der Bischofskonferenzen Deutschlands, Österreichs und der Schweiz und der Bischöfe von Bozen-Brixen und von Luxemburg, Freiburg u.a. 1973, 34. – In der dazugehörenden Apostolischen Konstitution *Divinae consortium naturae* vom 15. August 1971 nimmt Papst PAUL VI. bewusst auch Bezug auf die liturgische Praxis der Kirchen des byzantinischen Ritus, deren Formel nahezu wörtlich übernommen wurde (siehe ebd. 16; DEL I, Nr. 2599).

[94] „Gott, der barmherzige Vater hat durch den Tod und die Auferstehung seines Sohnes die Welt mit sich versöhnt und den Heiligen Geist gesandt zur Vergebung der Sünden. Durch den Dienst …" (Die Feier der Buße nach dem neuen Rituale Romanum. Studienausgabe, Freiburg u.a. 1974, 32 Nr. 46).

[95] „Durch diese heilige Salbung helfe der Herr in seinem reichen Erbarmen, er stehe Dir bei in der Kraft des Heiligen Geistes." (Die Feier der Krankensakramente. Die Krankensalbung und die Ordnung der Krankenpastoral […], Freiburg u.a. ²1994, 92 Nr. 28).

[96] „Gieße jetzt aus über deinen Diener, den du erwählt hast, die Kraft, die von dir ausgeht, den Geist der Leitung …" (Pontifikale I: Die Weihe des Bischofs, der Priester und der Diakone [Handausgabe mit pastoralliturgischen Hinweisen], Salzburg u.a. 1994, 42).

[97] Vgl. Bernard BOTTE, L'épiclèse de l'anaphore d'Hippolyte, in: RThAM 14 (1947) 241–251; DERS., L'épiclèse dans les liturgies syriennes orientales, in: Sacris Erudiri 6 (1954) 48–72.

WINKLER[100]). Am wichtigsten ist aber, besonders unter ökumenischen Gesichtspunkten, die Erneuerung der Eucharistie-Epiklese, das heißt die Herabrufung des Heiligen Geistes auf die eucharistischen Gaben von Brot und Wein.[101] Eine solche Konsekrations-Epiklese findet sich in allen *neuen* eucharistischen Hochgebeten im römischen Ritus.[102]

Eine ausdrückliche Geist-Epiklese findet sich in der dem HIPPOLYT zugeschriebenen so genannten *Traditio Apostolica*,[103] und eine konsekratorische Wirkung wird ihr erstmals in den *Mystagogischen Katechesen* des CYRILL VON JERUSALEM zugeschrieben (vgl. *myst. cat.* 5,7).[104] Von der Konsekrations-Epiklese ist die Kommunion-Epiklese zu unterscheiden, welche um einen fruchtbaren geistlichen Empfang der Kommunion bittet. Während die Kommunion-Epiklese in vielen *Postcommunio*-Gebeten der römischen

98 Sebastian P. BROCK, The Epiklesis in the Antiochene Baptismal Ordines, in: Symposium Syriacum 1972. Célébré dans les jours 26–31 octobre 1972 à l'Insitut Pontifical Oriental de Rome. Rapports et communications (OCA 197), Roma 1974, 183–215; DERS., Towards a Typology of the Epicleses in the West Syrian Traditions, in: Hans-Jürgen FEULNER et al. (ed.s), Crossroad of Cultures: Studies in Liturgy and Patristics in Honor of Gabriele Winkler (OCA 260), Roma 2000, 173–192; DERS., Invocations to/for the Holy Spirit in Syriac Liturgical Texts: Some Comparative Approaches, in: Acts of the International Congress (s. Anm. 23), 377–406.

99 Vgl. Robert F. TAFT, From Logos to Spirit: The Early History of the Epiclesis, in: Gratias agamus (s. Anm. 75), 489–502.

100 Vgl. Gabriele WINKLER, Nochmals zu den Anfängen der Epiklese und des Sanctus im Eucharistischen Hochgebet, in: Theologische Quartalschrift 174 (1994) 214–231; DIES., Weitere Beobachtungen zur frühen Epiklese (den Doxologien und dem Sanctus). Über die Bedeutung der Apokryphen für die Erforschung der Entwicklung der Riten, in: Oriens Christianus 80 (1996) 177–200; DIES., Further Observations in Connection with the Early Form of the Epiklesis, in: Le Sacrament de l'Initiation. Origines et Prospective (Patrimoine Syriaque. Actes du Colloque 3), Antélias 1996, 66–80; DIES., Zur Erforschung orientalischer Anaphoren in liturgievergleichender Sicht I: Anmerkungen zur Oratio post Sanctus und Anamnese bis Epiklese, in: OCP 63 (1997) 363–420; DIES., Zur Erforschung orientalischer Anaphoren in liturgievergleichender Sicht III: Der Hinweis auf „die Gaben“ bzw. „das Opfer“ bei der Epiklese, in: Albert GERHARDS – Klemens RICHTER (Hgg.), Das Opfer. Biblischer Anspruch und liturgische Gestalt (Quaestiones Disputatae 186), Freiburg u.a. 2000, 216–233; DIES., The Epiclesis and Institution Narrative of the Anaphora of Basil: Their Evolution and Theological Meaning, in: Orthodox Teaching on the Sacraments of the Church: The Acts of the 5th International Theological Conference of the Russian Orthodox Church (Moscow, 13–16 November 2007) vol. I, Moskau 2009, 382–399 [in Russ.] u.a.

101 Vgl. John H. MCKENNA, Eucharist and Holy Spirit. The Eucharistic Epiclesis in the 20th Century Theology (Alcuin Club Collection 57), Great Wakering 1975; DERS., Eucharistic Prayer: Epiclesis, in: Gratias agamus (s. Anm. 75), 283–291; B. SCHULTZE, Die dreifache Herabkunft des Heiligen Geistes in den östlichen Hochgebeten, in: Ostkirchliche Studien 26 (1977) 105–143; Yves CONGAR, Der Heilige Geist, Freiburg ²1986, 464–488. – Zur Epiklese als Kontext der Konsekration im Hochgebet vgl. Achim BUDDE, Die Darbringung im Gedankengang des Eucharistischen Hochgebetes. Eine entwicklungsgeschichtliche Skizze, in: GERHARDS – RICHTER, Das Opfer (s. Anm. 77), 185–202.

102 Vgl. dazu auch Richard ALBERTINE, The Post-Vatican Consilium's (Coetus X) Treatment of the Epiclesis Question in the New Eucharistic Prayers, in: Ephemerides Liturgicae 100 (1986) 489–507; K.-W. DE JONG, Questions à propos de la double épiclèse. Le Problème de la double épiclèse, en particulier dans les prières eucharistiques II-IV, in: Questions Liturgiques 68 (1987) 256–276; Bruno KLEINHEYER, Artikel 55 der Allgemeinen Einführung in das Römische Meßbuch zu Anamnese und Epiklese des Eucharistiegebetes, in: Gratias agamus (s. Anm. 75), 167–181.

103 Fontes Christiani 1, 226f. (Wilhelm GEERLINGS).

104 Fontes Christiani 7, 150–153 (Georg RÖWEKAMP).

Liturgie immer erhalten blieb, ist die Konsekrations-Epiklese im Römischen Kanon nur rudimentär in dem den Einsetzungsworten vorangehenden Gebet *Quam oblationem* enthalten. Dagegen kommt ihr in den östlichen Liturgien, wo sie *nach* den Einsetzungsworten gesprochen wird, seit dem vierten Jahrhundert eine grundlegende Bedeutung zu.[105]
Die unterschiedliche Entwicklung in Ost und West war schon Gegenstand vieler Kontroversen. Während die westliche Tradition seit AMBROSIUS[106] die Einsetzungsworte als Konsekrationsworte verstand,[107] schreibt die orthodoxe Schultheologie die Konsekration der Epiklese zu, was seit der ersten Hälfte des 14. Jahrhunderts zu einer kontroversen Diskussion über den genauen Zeitpunkt der Konsekration führte.[108] Im Rahmen ökumenischer Gespräche, vor allem mit der östlichen Theologie, aber auch im *liturgievergleichenden* Studium der liturgischen Gegebenheiten und ihrer geschichtlichen Entwicklung, hat sich der Blick mittlerweile geweitet.[109] Im Allgemeinen gehören die kontroversen Epiklese-Diskussionen heute der Vergangenheit an, da das Eucharistische Hochgebet ein Ganzes ist und es als Ganzes epikletisch-konsekratorischen Charakter hat.[110] Umso wichtiger war es, dass bei der nachkonziliaren Liturgiereform in die neuen Eucharistischen Hochgebete wieder eine explizite Epiklese eingefügt wurde. Und auch heute bleiben in der westlichen Tradition Eucharistische Hochgebete mit einer konsekratorischen Epiklese *nach* den Einsetzungsworten in Gebrauch, wo der Heilige Stuhl den altspanischen Ritus erlaubt, und zwar in vielen der variablen *Post-Pridie-Gebeten* des *Missale Hispano-Mozarabicum* von 1991.

Der bekannte orthodoxe Theologe Paul EVDOKIMOV (1901–1970) hat angeführt, dass die Erneuerung der Epiklese in den neuen Eucharistischen Hochge-

[105] Vgl. Johannes BETZ, Die Eucharistie in der Zeit der griechischen Väter I/1, Freiburg 1955, 328–341; Palle DINESEN, Die Epiklese im Rahmen altkirchlicher Liturgien, in: StTh 16 (1962) 42–107 u.a.

[106] AMBROSIUS, De sacramentis IV, 14–23, V, 24 (Fontes Christiani 3, 142–151, 172–175 [Josef SCHMITZ]); De mysteriis, 52 (Fontes Christiani 3, 246f. [DERS.]).

[107] Seit im 14. Jh. die Lateiner im Osten auf die orthodoxe Position über die Rolle der Epiklese gestoßen sind, gab es in der Folge eine ganze Reihe von päpstlichen Erklärungen, wonach die Einsetzungsworte die Form des Sakraments und der Zeitpunkt der Konsekration der Elemente sind: DH 1017, 1083, 2718, 3556 u.a. – Siehe auch das „Armenierdekret" (1439): DH 1321; vgl. DH 1352.

[108] Vgl. Nikolaus KABASILAS, Ἑρμηνεία τῆς θείας Λειτουργίας [Erklärung der Göttlichen Liturgie], Kap. XXIX [Explication de la Divine Liturgie (Sources Chrétiennes 4bis), ed. René BORNERT et al., Paris 1967]. – Vgl. Robert F. TAFT, Ecumenical Scholarship and the Catholic-Orthodox Epiclesis Dispute, in: Ostkirchliche Studien 45 (1996) 201–226; DERS., The Epiclesis Question in the Light of the Orthodox and Catholic Lex orandi Traditions, in: Bradley NASSIF (ed.), New Perspectives on Historical Theology. Essays in Memory of John Meyendorff, Grand Rapids – Cambridge 1996, 210–237.

[109] Vgl. Sigisbert KRAFT, Die eucharistische Epiklese als ökumenisches Problem, in: Una Sancta 40 (1985) 226–231.

[110] Vgl. beispielsweise Johannes BETZ, Eucharistie in der Schrift und Patristik (HDG IV/4a), Freiburg 1979, 42; MEYER, Eucharistie (s. Anm. 78), 99f.; Burkhard NEUNHEUSER, Das Eucharistische Hochgebet als Konsekrationsgebet, in: Gratias agamus (s. Anm. 75), 315–326; Winfried HAUNERLAND, Das eine Herrenmahl und die vielen Eucharistiegebete. Traditionen und Texte als theologische und spirituelle Impulse, in: DERS., (Hg.), Mehr als Brot und Wein. Theologische Kontexte der Eucharistie, Würzburg 2005, 119–144, hier 122f. u.a.

beten der römischen Liturgie für den heutigen ökumenischen Dialog sehr bedeutsam sei.[111] Lukas VISCHER (1926–2008), der frühere Vorsitzende des Ökumenischen Rates der Kirchen, hat die Epiklese einmal Zeichen der Einheit und ein Unterpfand für einen neuen Durchbruch der Ökumene genannt.[112] Die Erneuerung der Eucharistie-Epiklese ist weit mehr als die Änderung eines Ritus, da sie auch etwas Grundsätzliches über das Wesen der Kirche und der Sakramente aussagt.

Auch reformatorische Liturgietraditionen haben solche Epiklesen in ihre wiederentdeckten Eucharistiegebete integriert, teilweise sogar den Einsetzungsworten nachgestellt, so etwa die kalvinistische Kirche Schottlands, die anglikanische *Episcopal Church* in den USA, die amerikanischen Lutheraner und die englischen Methodisten.[113]

Die Sakramente sind nicht einfach die Verlängerung von Person und Wirken Jesu Christi im Raum der Kirche: die Kirche muss vielmehr um den Geist bitten, damit er Jesus Christus und sein Heilswerk vergegenwärtigt. Die Kirche selbst hat eine epikletische Struktur. Sie besitzt nicht den Hl. Geist und verfügt nicht über ihn, sie kann und darf jedoch vollmächtig um sein Kommen bitten, und sie ist der Erhörung dieser Bitte sicher.

(4) Auch die überaus große ökumenische Bedeutung der nachkonziliaren Perikopenordnung (1969; ^{2}1981 für die liturgischen Lesungen sei erwähnt.[114] Die-

[111] Paul EVDOKIMOV, Eucharistie – Mystère de l'Église, in: La Pensée Orthodoxe 2 (1968) 53–69, hier 62 Anm. 33; DERS., L'Ésprit Saint dans la tradition orthodoxe, Paris 1969, 101 Anm. 42.

[112] Lukas VISCHER, Epiklese, Zeichen der Einheit, der Erneuerung und des Aufbruchs, in: Oecumenica. Jahrbuch für ökumenische Forschung 2 (1967) 302–312 [nachgedruckt in: DERS., Ökumenische Skizzen. Zwölf Beiträge, Frankfurt/M. 1972, 46–57].

[113] Vgl. SENN, New Eucharistic Prayers (s. Anm. 79), *passim*; SCHULZ, Eucharistiegebet in den Kirchen der Reformation (s. Anm. 79), 99–102. – Book of Common Order of the Church of Scotland, Edinburgh ^{2}1996; Lutheran Book of Worship (s. Anm. 84); The Methodist Service Book, Letchworth 1975; Book of Common Prayer (s. Anm. 86).

[114] So verweist z.B. die „Pastorale Einführung“, in: Die Feier der Heiligen Messe: Messlektionar. Für die Bistümer des deutschen Sprachgebietes [...] Bd. 1: Die Sonntage und Festtage im Lesejahr A, Einsiedeln u.a. 1986, 11*–40*, darauf, dass bei der Erstellung der Leseordnung nicht nur „die Tradition des Römischen Ritus gewahrt blieb“, sondern auch „alle Formen der Auswahl, der Anordnung und des Gebrauchs von biblischen Lesungen in anderen Liturgiefamilien und einigen Teilkirchen gebührend berücksichtigt“ wurden (Nr. 59). Die „Zuordnung bestimmter Bücher zu bestimmten Zeiten des Kirchenjahrs“ sei „aufgrund sachlicher Zusammenhänge und gemäß der liturgischen Tradition“ erfolgt. Deshalb werde beispielsweise „entsprechend westlicher (ambrosianischer und [alt]spanischer) wie auch östlicher Überlieferung in der Osterzeit die Apostelgeschichte gelesen“ (Nr. 74) [vgl. Georg BRAULIK, Pentateuch-Bahnlesung an den Sonntagen im Jahreskreis. Bemerkungen zur Kritik der „Wiener Perikopenordnung“, in: DERS. – Norbert LOHFINK (Hgg.), Liturgie und Bibel. Gesammelte Aufsätze (Österreichische Biblische Studien 28), Frankfurt/M. 2005, 225–266, hier 228f. m. Anm. 17]. – Siehe auch Ansgar FRANZ, Wortgottesdienst der Messe und Altes Testament. Katholische und ökumenische Lektionarreform nach dem II. Vatikanum im Spiegel von Ordo Lectionum Missae, Revised Common Lectionary und Four Years Lectionary: Positionen, Probleme, Perspektiven (Pietas Liturgica. Studia 14), Tübingen – Basel 2002, bes. 99–130; Elmar NÜBOLD, Entstehung und Bewertung der neuen Perikopenordnung des römischen Ritus für die Messfeier an Sonn- und Festtagen, Paderborn 1986.

se Leseordnung ist nämlich über die Grenzen der katholischen Kirche hinaus weit akzeptiert und adaptiert worden,[115] z.B. ab 1992 in Nordamerika im *Revised Commmon Lectionary*[116] auch für Anglikaner, Baptisten, Lutheraner, Methodisten, Presbyterianer und Unitarier (*Unitarian Universalist Christian Fellowship*).[117]
Unbeschadet dieser im Horizont der Liturgiegeschichte außergewöhnlichen Bedeutung ist das vatikanische Lektionar in den vergangenen Jahren zunehmend in Kritik geraten, besonders bezüglich der Auswahl der alttestamentlichen Perikopen. Einige neuere Vorschläge für eine künftige Reform bedienen sich eines *liturgievergleichenden* Studiums der westlichen und östlichen Lesungsordnungen der Vergangenheit wie der Gegenwart. So orientiert man sich mit gewissem Erfolg an den Tora-Lesungen in den Lektionaren der west- und ostsyrischen Kirchen,[118] wofür Anton BAUMSTARK bereits 1921 eine immer noch maßgebliche Monographie vorlegte.[119]

(5) Nachdem der „Päpstliche Rat zur Förderung der Einheit der Christen“ den mit Rom unierten Chaldäern am 20. Juli 2001 erlaubt hat,[120] unter bestimm-

[115] Ansgar FRANZ bemerkt zu Recht: „Trotz aller immer wieder konstatierter Mängel ist der vatikanische *Ordo Lectionum* (OLM) ein mutiger, bedeutender und kaum zu überschätzender Durchbruch zu einer weiten ‚Öffnung der Schatzkammer der Bibel‘ (SC 51). Das erneuerte Meßlektionar […] dürfte […] das im ökumenischen Bereich am stärksten rezipierte Dokument des II. Vatikanischen Konzils sein.“ [DERS., Die Rolle des Alten Testaments in den Perikopenreformen des 20. Jahrhunderts, in: DERS., Streit am Tisch des Wortes? (s. Anm. 78), 619–648, hier 621].

[116] The Revised Common Lectionary, ed. by CONSULTATION ON COMMON TEXTS, Norwich 1992 (Nachdruck: Minneapolis 2012). – Das RCL ist eine Revision des seit 1983 erprobten *Common Lectionary*.

[117] Vgl. FRANZ, Rolle des Alten Testaments (s. Anm. 115), 638–642; DERS., Wortgottesdienst der Messe (s. Anm. 114), 99–106. – Eine Liste der Kirchen und kirchlichen Gemeinschaften, die das RCL weltweit benutzen (Stand: 1998): http://www.commontexts.org/rcl/usage.html [Abruf: 19.7.2012]. – The Worshipbook: Services and Hymns, Philadelphia 1970; Book of Common Worship, prepared by THE THEOLOGY AND WORSHIP MINISTRY UNIT, Louisville – London 1993; Lutheran Book of Worship (s. Anm. 84); The United Methodist Book of Worship, Nashville/TN 1992 (^{16}2007).

[118] Siehe dazu vor allem Pauly KANNOOKADAN, The East Syrian Lectionary. An Historico-Liturgical Study, Rom 1991 [s. dazu: K.D. JENNER, The Development of Syriac Lectionary Systems: A Discussion of the Opinion of P. Kannookadan, in: The Harp 10 (1997) 9–24]. Vgl. auch Heinzgerd BRAKMANN, Der christlichen Bibel erster Teil in den gottesdienstlichen Traditionen des Ostens und Westens. Liturgiehistorische Anmerkungen zum sog. Stellenwert des Alten/Ersten Testaments im Christentum, in: FRANZ, Streit am Tisch des Wortes? (s. Anm. 78), 565–604, hier 583–586; BRAULIK, Pentateuch-Bahnlesung (s. Anm. 114), 255f.; DERS., Die Tora als Bahnlesung. Zur Hermeneutik einer zukünftigen Auswahl der Sonntagsperikopen, in: DERS. – LOHFINK, Liturgie und Bibel (s. Anm. 114), 125–149, hier 142–149.

[119] Anton BAUMSTARK, Nichtevangelische syrische Perikopenordnungen des ersten Jahrtausends im Sinne vergleichender Liturgiewissenschaft untersucht (LF 3), Münster 1921 [(LWQF 15), Münster 1972].

[120] Vgl. Dokumente wachsender Übereinstimmung [= DwÜ] III, hg. v. Harding MEYER u.a., Paderborn – Freiburg 2003, 599–601. – Textedition der Anaphora in: Anthony GELSTON, The Eucharistic Prayer of Addai and Mari, Oxford 1992, 47–55. Vgl. die deutsche Übertragung in Andreas HEINZ, Licht aus dem Osten. Die Eucharistiefeier der Thomas-Christen, der Assyrer und der Chaldäer mit der Anaphora von Addai und Mari (Sophia 35), Trier 2008, 378–386.

ten Bedingungen die Kommunion in der nicht-unierten „Assyrischen Kirche des Ostens“ zu empfangen, hat man auch die Gültigkeit der in den ältesten Handschriften ohne Einsetzungsworte überlieferten sehr altertümlichen *Anaphora von Addai und Mari* anerkannt. Diese weitreichende Entscheidung war nur durch vorangehende, jahrelange intensive *liturgievergleichende* Studien möglich gewesen.[121]

(6) Aufgrund des in der Theologie allgemein rezipierten Axioms *lex credendi – lex orandi*, also der Anerkennung der Liturgie als *locus theologicus*, können gerade auch *liturgievergleichende* Untersuchungen die in offiziellen gemeinsamen Erklärungen zwischen verschiedenen Kirchen zum Ausdruck gebrachten, fundamentalen Glaubensübereinstimmungen weiter untermauern. Grundlegend hierfür war u.a. die so genannte „Wiener Christologische Formel“ der Ersten Pro-Oriente-Konsultation (7.–11. September 1971).[122] In einer kleineren *liturgievergleichenden* Studie aus dem Jahre 1953 konnte Hieronymus ENGBERDING bereits nachweisen,[123] dass sich im gesamten Bereich der Liturgien der nicht-chalkedonensischen Kirchen eine Schmälerung der Menschheit Christi, eine Minderbewertung seines Heilswirkens und seiner Selbsthingabe, wie sie dem traditionell gewordenen Bild vom „Monophysitismus“ entspricht, als charakteristischer Wesenszug nicht mit Sicherheit erkennen lässt. Inwiefern solche Untersuchungen dann indirekt Eingang gefunden haben in die beachtenswerten gemeinsamen Erklärungen zwischen der Römisch-Katholischen Kirche einerseits und der Koptisch-Orthodoxen (10. Mai 1973),[124] der Syrisch-Orthodoxen (23. Juni 1984)[125] und der Armenisch-Apostolischen (13. Dezember 1996 bzw. 25. Januar 1997),[126] oder der Assyrischen Kirche des Ostens (11.

[121] Vgl. Robert F. TAFT, Mass Without the Consecration? The Historic Agreement on the Eucharist between the Catholic Church and the Assyrian Church of the East Promulgated 26 October 2001, in: Worship 77 (2003) 482–509; MATTHIEU SMYTH, Une avance oecuménique et liturgique. La note romaine concernant l'Anaphore d'Addai et Mari, in: La Maison-Dieu 233 (2003) 137–154; Nicholas V. RUSSO, The Validity of the Anaphora of *Addai and Mari*: Critique of the Critiques, in: Issues in Eucharistic Praying in East and West. Essays in Liturgical and Theological Analysis, ed. by Maxwell E. JOHNSON, Collegeville 2010, 21–62. – Kritisch dagegen Uwe M. LANG (Hg.), Die Anaphora von Addai und Mari. Studien zu Eucharistie und Einsetzungsworten, Bonn 2007.

[122] Vgl. den Text der „Wiener Christologischen Formel“ bei: Dietmar W. WINKLER, Koptische Kirche und Reichskirche. Altes Schisma und neuer Dialog (Innsbrucker Theologische Studien 48), Innsbruck – Wien 1997, 264.

[123] Hieronymus ENGBERDING, Das chalkedonensische Christusbild und die Liturgien der monophysitischen Kirchengemeinschaften, in: Alois GRILLMEIER – Heinrich BACHT (Hgg.), Das Konzil von Chalkedon. Geschichte und Gegenwart II, Würzburg 1953, 697–733.

[124] Vgl. DwÜ I, Paderborn – Freiburg ^{2}1991, 529–531; Peter HOFRICHTER – Johann MARTE (ed.s), Documents on Unity in Faith between the Oriental Orthodox Churches and the Roman Catholic Church (Pro Oriente 36), Innsbruck – Wien 2013, 25–27.

[125] Vgl. DwÜ II, Paderborn – Freiburg 1992, 571–574; HOFRICHTER – MARTE, Documents on Unity in Faith, 35–38.

[126] Vgl. DwÜ III, 582–584, 584–587; HOFRICHTER – MARTE, Documents on Unity in Faith, 53–56, 57–60.

November 1994)[127] andererseits, lässt sich nicht mit Bestimmtheit sagen und bedarf noch der wünschenswerten Erforschung.[128]
Es wird aber noch einmal deutlich, wie zentrale liturgische Texte, die seit Jahrhunderten zum lebendigen Glaubensgut einer Kirche gehören, nicht nur in dogmatischer, sondern auch in ökumenischer Hinsicht von weitreichender Bedeutung sein können. Auch hierfür kann eine *liturgievergleichende Methodik* einen wichtigen Beitrag liefern.

5. ABSCHLIESSENDE BEMERKUNGEN

Die heute mehr denn je notwendig gewordene Pflege des ökumenischen Dialogs und die Bedeutung der Ökumene für das Leben der Kirche mögen zeigen, wie wichtig gegenwärtig auch eine *ökumenisch* ausgerichtete Liturgiewissenschaft innerhalb der Theologie ist. Eine modifizierte *liturgievergleichende* Methodik mit ihrer historisch-kritischen und systematisch-theologischen Arbeitsweise ist *per se* ökumenisch und dürfte hierbei ein wichtiges Arbeitsinstrument sein, um den römischen Ritus im Kreise der *gesamten* christlichen Riten *in Ost und West* zu untersuchen, auf die Gegenwart hin kritisch zu durchleuchten und die liturgische Erneuerung weiterzuführen.[129] In einer so verstandenen *Vergleichenden Liturgiewissenschaft* geht es darum, auch die Theologie der verschiedenen Liturgien zu erforschen und zu verstehen, womit nicht nur die faktische Vielfalt der Liturgien in Ost und West wahrzunehmen, sondern auch die Kontextualität zu beachten ist. Das Verstehen der *anderen* Liturgien, ihrer gegenseitigen Beeinflussungen und der Motivation für ihre Änderungen bringt ein besseres Verstehen der *eigenen* Liturgie mit sich. Eine so verstandene *Vergleichende Liturgiewissenschaft* ist zugleich auch eine wahrhaft *Ökumenische* Liturgiewissenschaft.[130] Bereits das Ökumenismus-Dekret des II. Vatikanischen Konzils empfiehlt in Artikel 9, dass man sich auch eine „bessere Kenntnis ... [des] liturgischen Lebens" der getrennten Kirchen erwerben soll.[131] Die am 22. April 2001

[127] Vgl. DwÜ III, 596–598; HOFRICHTER – MARTE, Documents on Unity in Faith, 103–106.

[128] Vgl. beispielsweise Dietmar W. WINKLER, Ein Passus aus der koptischen Basiliusliturgie und der syrischen Vita Dioscori als Quellen der Wiener Christologischen Formel, in: Stephen EMMEL u.a. (Hgg.), Ägypten und Nubien in spätantiker und christlicher Zeit. Akten des 6. Internationalen Koptologenkongresses, Münster, 20.–26. Juli 1996, Bd. I (Sprachen und Kulturen des Christlichen Orients 6/1), Wiesbaden 1999, 534–545.

[129] Gerard ROUWHORST warnt allerdings angesichts der liturgischen Reformbestrebungen der letzten Jahrhunderte (und auch v.a. Jahrzehnte) zu Recht vor den beiden Versuchungen, nämlich zum einen eine bestimmte liturgiegeschichtliche Periode als „Gründungsepoche" zu idealisieren und zum anderen die historische Kontinuität der als authentisch angesehenen liturgischen Tradition zu überschätzen [DERS., Historical Periods as Normative Sources. The Appeal to the Past in the Research on Liturgical History, in: Religious Identity and the Problem of Historical Foundation. The Foundational Character of Authoritative Sources in the History of Christianity and Judaism (Jewish and Christian Perspectives Series VIII), Leiden 2004, 495–512].

[130] Vgl. FEULNER, Armenische Athanasius-Anaphora (s. Anm. 12), 74; DERS., Liturgiewissenschaft in Wien (s. Anm. 12), 250.

[131] DEL I, Nr. 370a [lat. Text: AAS 57 (1965) 98].

in Straßburg unterzeichnete „Charta Oecumenica“ hebt in Punkt 5 hervor,[132] die Gottesdienste anderer Kirchen kennen und schätzen zu lernen, was natürlich auch eine wissenschaftliche Beschäftigung mit den verschiedenen Liturgien einschließt.

Wir alle sind ermahnt, den ökumenischen Dialog noch weiter zu intensivieren, die erreichten Ergebnisse anzunehmen und noch anstehende Probleme und Hindernisse im geschwisterlichen Geist der Liebe gemeinsam auszuräumen. Dazu kann und soll auch die Liturgiewissenschaft einen wichtigen Beitrag leisten, wobei jedoch noch einmal herausgestellt sei, dass eine *liturgievergleichende* Methode nur eine unter mehreren sein darf, um den Ansprüchen einer „Liturgiewissenschaft“ als theologischer Disziplin gerecht zu werden.

Eine Liturgiewissenschaft, die sich nicht ganz selbstverständlich als eine *ökumenische* versteht, wie bereits oben erwähnt, würde also von vornherein ihr Thema verfehlen. Gerade heute wird durch die zunehmenden internationalen Kontakte der Gesellschaften mit ihren vielfältigen Bekenntnissen auch der interreligiöse Dialog mit anderen Weltreligionen immer bedeutender, was natürlich ganz besonders das Judentum (und ggf. ebenso den Islam) betrifft.[133]

Insofern wäre es sicherlich hilfreich und deshalb wünschenswert, wenn im offiziellen ökumenischen Dialog besonders die östlichen Liturgien, als die *Orthopraxie*, noch viel stärker berücksichtigt sowie die einschlägigen Forschungsergebnisse der (östlichen) Liturgiewissenschaft zur Kenntnis genommen werden würden. Ein intensiverer Blick auf die östlichen Liturgien aller Riten bzw. Ri-

[132] Der Text der *Charta Oecumenica* ist publiziert in: Ökumenische Rundschau 50 (2001) 506–514, hier 510. Im Internet ist er u.a. zu finden bei: http://www.ceceurope.org/file|admin/filer/cec/CEC_Documents/ChartaOecumenicaDE.pdf [Abruf: 20.6.2012].

[133] Die asiatischen, afrikanischen und lateinamerikanischen Religionen bieten eine Fülle von Forschungsaufgaben, deren Ergebnisse für den Dialog und die Möglichkeiten der Inkulturation von Bedeutung sind. Im Zuge des Zusammenwachsens der Kulturen wird die interreligiöse vergleichende Erforschung des Gottesdienstes zunehmen [vgl. Franz KOHLSCHEIN, Liturgiewissenschaft – Selbstverständnis einer „Konzilswissenschaft“, in: Georg KRAUS (Hg.), Theologie in der Universität. Wissenschaft – Kirche – Gesellschaft. FS zum Jubiläum 350 Jahre Theologie in Bamberg (Bamberger Theologische Studien 10), Frankfurt/M. u.a. 1998, 193–207, hier 203]. – Vgl. beispielsweise auch: Hans H. HENRIX (Hg.), Jüdische Liturgie. Geschichte – Struktur – Wesen (Quaestiones Disputatae 86), Freiburg/Br. 1979; Klemens RICHTER, Jüdische Wurzeln christlicher Liturgie im Spiegel der neueren katholischen Liturgiewissenschaft, in: Marcel MARCUS u.a. (Hgg.), Israel und Kirche heute. Beiträge zum christlich-jüdischen Dialog […], Freiburg/Br. 1991, 135–147; Benedikt KRANEMANN, Gottesdienst als ökumenisches Projekt, in: Christian GRETHLEIN – Günter RUDDAT (Hgg.), Liturgisches Kompendium, Göttingen 2003, 77–100, hier 98f.; Albert GERHARDS, Impulse des christlich-jüdischen Dialogs für die Liturgiewissenschaft, in: Methodische Erneuerung der Theologie. Konsequenzen der wiederentdeckten jüdisch-christlichen Gemeinsamkeiten (Quaestiones Disputatae 200), hg. v. Peter HÜNERMANN – Thomas SÖDING, Freiburg/Br. 2003, 183–211; DERS. (Hg.), Identität durch Gebet. Zur gemeinschaftsbildenden Funktion institutionalisierten Betens in Judentum und Christentum (Studien zu Judentum und Christentum), Paderborn u.a. 2003; DERS., Kontinuität und Unterbrechung: Gottesdienst und Gebet in Judentum und Christentum (Studien zu Judentum und Christentum), Paderborn u.a. 2005; DERS. – Clemens LEONHARD (ed.s), Jewish and Christian Liturgy and Worship: New Insights Into Its History and Interaction (Jewish and Christian Perspectives Series 15), Leiden 2007; Johannes SPORER, „Der Lobpreis Gottes“: Mönchsliturgien, Araberstämme und der Koran (unveröffentl. Dissertation der Universität Wien), Wien 2012.

tenfamilien (sowie auf einige liturgische Traditionen der aus der Reformation hervorgegangenen Kirchen und kirchlichen Gemeinschaften[134]) wäre sicherlich eine nicht zu unterschätzende Bereicherung für die liturgische (Aus-/Weiter-) Bildung[135] und die *ars celebrandi* vieler für westliche Liturgiefeiern Verantwortlicher und damit eine lohnenswerte Aufgabe für die Zukunft – nicht zuletzt ganz besonders im Rückblick auf 50 Jahre *Sacrosanctum Concilium*.
In der ersten päpstlichen Enzyklika über den Einsatz für die Ökumene hat Papst JOHANNES PAUL II. den ökumenischen Weg als den Weg der Kirche bezeichnet und ihn im Einheitswillen Christi begründet gesehen: „An Christus glauben heißt, die Einheit wollen; die Einheit wollen heißt, die Kirche wollen; die Kirche wollen heißt, die Gnadengemeinschaft wollen, die dem Plan des Vaters von Ewigkeit her entspricht."[136] Auch Papst BENEDIKT XVI. hat bereits in seiner ersten Botschaft nach seiner Wahl als „vorrangige Verpflichtung" die Aufgabe bezeichnet, „mit allen Kräften an der Wiederherstellung der vollen und sichtbaren Einheit aller Jünger Christi zu arbeiten".[137]

[134] Hier wäre beispielsweise die Anglikanische Liturgie und auch der daraus hervorgegangene „Anglican Use [des Römischen Ritus]" mit seinem liturgischen *Anglican Patrimony* zu nennen (vgl. dazu auch Hans-Jürgen FEULNER, "Anglican Use of the Roman Rite"? The Unity of the Liturgy in the Diversity of Its Rites and Forms, in: Antiphon 17/1 (2013) 31–72 [dt. Version: DERS., „Anglican Use" des Römischen Ritus?, in: Stefan HEID (Hg.), Liturgiereformen (in Vorbereitung)].

[135] Vgl. auch PÄPSTLICHER RAT ZUR FÖRDERUNG DER EINHEIT DER CHRISTEN, Direktorium zur Ausführung der Prinzipien und Normen über den Ökumenismus, 25. März 1993 (VAS 110), Bonn 1993, bes. Nr. 55–91.

[136] JOHANNES PAUL II., Ut unum sint, Nr. 9 [VAS 121, 11]. – Vgl. ebd., Nr. 50: „Anerkannt wurden die große liturgische und spirituelle Tradition der orientalischen Kirchen, die besondere Eigenart ihrer historischen Entwicklung, die eigenen Kirchenordnungen [...] sowie die ihnen eigene Weise, die Lehre zu verkünden. Das alles in der Überzeugung, daß die legitime Verschiedenartigkeit in keiner Weise der Einheit der Kirche entgegensteht, sondern vielmehr ihre Zierde und Schönheit vermehrt und zur Erfüllung ihrer Sendung in nicht geringem Maße beiträgt." [VAS 121, 38]. – Siehe auch der nachdrückliche Aufruf zum Kennenlernen des christlichen Ostens in Liturgie und Spiritualität sowie der Wunsch zum Kennenlernen der Liturgien der Ostkirchen, zur Vertiefung der Kenntnis von den geistlichen Traditionen der Väter und Lehrer des christlichen Orients und auch die Ausbildung von Liturgiewissenschaftlern in Einrichtungen, die auf den christlichen Osten spezialisiert sind, damit sie ihrerseits die Kenntnis von den Kirchen des Ostens verbreiten können [SEKRETARIAT DER DEUTSCHEN BISCHOFSKONFERENZ, Apostolisches Schreiben *Orientale Lumen* von Papst JOHANNES PAUL II. an den Episkopat, den Klerus und die Gläubigen zum hundertsten Jahrestag des Apostolischen Schreibens *Orientalium dignitas* von Papst LEO XIII. (2. Mai 1995)(VAS 121), Bonn 1995, 111f. (Nr. 24)].

[137] BENEDIKT XVI., Messaggio alla Chiesa Universale al termine della Santa Messa con i Cardinali Elletori nella Capella Sistina, in: Insegnamenti di Benedetto XVI vol. I 2005, Città del Vaticano 2006, 1–7; dt. in: Papst BENEDIKT XVI. / Joseph RATZINGER, Predigten und Ansprachen April/Mai 2005 (VAS 168), Bonn 2005, 24f. – Vgl. auch Konstantin NIKOLAKOPOULOS (Hg.), Benedikt XVI. und die Orthodoxe Kirche. Bestandsaufnahmen, Erwartungen, Perspektiven, St. Ottilien 2008; Werner THIEDE (Hg.), Der Papst aus Bayern. Protestantische Wahrnehmungen, Leipzig 2010.

Die byzantinische Bischofsweihe in der melkitischen Kirche*

Hanna Ghoneim

1. Einführung

Ein immer noch unerfülltes Desiderat in der Liturgiewissenschaft ist die Erforschung der Rezension der griechisch-byzantinischen Euchologia in der melkitischen Kirche; die Melkiten[1] bilden nämlich einen byzantinischen Sprengel im heute arabophonen Nahen Osten.
Infolge der christologischen Auseinandersetzungen nach dem Konzil von Chalkedon (451) im syrischen Sprachgebiet haben sich die Melkiten allmählich im Laufe der Geschichte vom angestammten antiochenischen Ritus entfernt und langsam den der Kaiserstadt adoptiert und adaptiert. Im Patriarchat von Antiochien kam dieser Byzantinisierungsprozess zu seinem gewissen definitiven Abschluss Anfang des 13. Jahrhunderts; analog gilt das auch für das Patriarchat Jerusalem. Die Melkiten gebrauchten anfangs das Griechische, später ab dem 9. Jahrhundert wurde das Syrische vor allem im ländlichen Bereich neben dem im städtischen Bereich gebräuchlichen Griechisch als liturgische Sprache verwendet. Später kam zuerst als Glossen und Anmerkungen in den Handschriften das arabische Element dazu. Bis zum 17. Jahrhundert waren Griechisch und Syrisch nebst Arabisch gebräuchlich, bis das letztere, insbesondere im Patriarchat von

* S. dazu nun auch: Hanna Ghoneim, Der byzantinische Bischofsweiheritus in der Melkitischen Kirche. Eine liturgiegeschichtliche vergleichende Untersuchung (unveröffentl. Dissertation der Universität Wien), Wien 2010.

[1] Ursprünglich bezeichnete man als „Melkiten" jene Christen der Patriarchate Antiochien, Alexandrien und Jerusalem, die als Zeichen ihrer Treue zu Konstantinopel, dem Kaisersitz (*Melko* auf Syrisch bedeutet „König/Kaiser") zuerst im Glauben von Chalkedon, später auch der byzantinischen Liturgie gefolgt sind. 1724 ereignete sich eine Spaltung im melkitischen Patriarchat von Antiochien; ein Teil der Gläubigen wollte eine Union, eine Wiederherstellung der Communio mit Rom; der andere nicht, so entstanden ab dieser Zeit zwei melkitische Patriarchate in Antiochien: Das *griechisch-orthodoxe* und *griechisch-katholische* Patriarchat. Die Orthodoxen lehnen die Bezeichnung „Melkiten" mehrheitlich ab, die Katholiken haben ihn fast als Eigenname genommen. Die ersten bezeichnet man im arabischen Sprachraum als *rūm-orṯodoks*, die Katholiken *rūm-kaṯūlīk* (arab. ‚Rum' = Angehörige des Neuen Rom – Konstantinopel). Nach der Trennung erfährt die byzantinische Liturgie bei den Melkiten, aufgrund der nun verschiedenen Einflüsse, leichte Veränderungen, die man als verschiedene Rezensionen bezeichnen kann. In unserer Studie deutet der Begriff „Melkiten" auf beide Patriarchate vor der Trennung und danach hin, da beide nach wie vor in der gleichen Tradition wurzeln. Kennzeichnend für ihre Liturgie ist die Verwendung des Arabischen neben Griechisch und früher Syrisch. Die orthodox gebliebenen nach der Trennung 1724 werden in der Studie *Rum-Orthodox*, die Katholiken *katholische Melkiten* genannt.

Antiochien, die beiden anderen Sprachen verdrängt hat und dann fast die ausschließliche Liturgiesprache geworden ist.
Diese Studie will anhand der arabischen liturgischen Handschriften und Druckausgaben die Rezension der byzantinischen Bischofsweihe im Patriarchat von Antiochien aufzeigen.[2] Sie beabsichtigt skizzenhaft die verschiedenen Weiheformulare aufzuzeigen, die die Melkiten kennen und kannten und sucht nach ihren griechischen Quellen. Wohl bemerkt, nicht alle melkitischen Handschriften, die die Bischofsweiheliturgie beinhalten, konnten hier einbezogenen werden. Eine kurze Darstellung der Bischofsweiheordnung nach den griechischen Euchologia scheint zu unserem Zweck hilfreich zu sein.

2. DIE BYZANTINISCHE BISCHOFSWEIHELITURGIE

Die heutigen griechisch-byzantinischen Euchologion-Drucke kennen drei verschiedene Ordnungen für die Bischofsweihe,[3] alle haben aber folgende Elemente gemeinsam, so dass wir vermuten können, dass diese Elemente den Kernritus bilden:

- Vorstellung des Weihekandidaten
- Erwählungsformel + ἡ θεία χάρις (Die göttliche Gnade)
- Kyrie-Ruf
- Auflegung des Evangeliars
- Dreimalige Bekreuzigung des Hauptes des Weihekandidaten
- Handauflegung
- Das erste Weihegebet
- Litanei/Diakonika
- Das zweite Weihegebet
- Anlegen des Omophorion
- Axios-Akklamation
- Friedenskuss (*aspasmos*)

Das älteste Zeugnis für dieses Schema ist die Bischofsweiheordnung der Hs. *Barberinianus graecus 336* (8. Jh.), heute in der Bibliotheca Apostolica Vatica-

[2] Zu diesem Thema speziell verfügen wir über eine ‚einsame' Studie von Daniel Z. AWIKÉ, L'Ordination épiscopale dans l'Eglise Melkite, Vatikan 1994, die als Lizentiatsarbeit am Ponitificio Istituto Orientale eingereicht wurde. Diese Studie (48 Seiten) basiert auf einer von Joseph Hallit angefertigte Ordnung, die AWIKÉ als allein gültige in der melkitisch-katholischen Kirche hält. Er erwähnt aber vier weitere Ordnungen, zwei bei den orthodoxen Melkiten, MASSARRA und HAWAWEENY (dazu s. unten) und zwei bei den katholischen, i.e. Großes Euchologion von Jerusalem 1865 und SKAF. Es handelt sich in der Studie lediglich um eine Darstellung der Bischofsweiheordnung und lässt die Liturgiegeschichte und Quellenfrage eigentlich unberücksichtigt.

[3] Die folgenden Ausführungen über die byzantinisch-griechische Bischofsweihe stützen sich auf die Abhandlung von Heinzgerd BRAKMANN, Metrophanes von Nyssa und die Ordnungen der byzantinisch-griechischen Bischofsweihe, in: Hairesis [Festschrift für Karl HOHEISEL] (JAC Ergänzungsband 34), Münster 2002, 303–326.

na, der ältesten uns bekannten Euchologion-Handschrift der byzantinischen Liturgie überhaupt; der Kodex stammt aus dem italo-griechischen Raum und hat auch Elemente der Melkiten aus Palästina und Ägypten.[4]
Ein analoges Schema finden wir auch bei den Weihen zum Presbyterat und Diakonat, so dass leicht zu erkennen ist, dass die Weihen des klassischen dreigliedrigen Weiheordo überhaupt ähnlich schlicht strukturiert sind, und so ihren ursprünglichen Kern in den handschriftlichen und später gedruckten Euchologien erstaunlich konstant bewahrt haben.[5]
Die ältesten handschriftlichen liturgischen Quellen zeigen generell nur ganz wenige Rubriken. In der handschriftlichen Tradition zeigen sie, bzw. weisen hin auf die Praxis der Riten für den Auftraggeber bzw. den Bestimmungsort der Handschrift in einem konkreten Kontext mit zeitgeschichtlichen und lokalen Einflüssen; die ‚editio typica' ist ein sehr modernes Konzept. Gerade hier, in den Rubriken also, erfolgen im Laufe der Geschichte die entscheidenden Veränderungen und Anpassungen, auch kommen neue Elemente dazu, wie das Glaubensbekenntnis und die Erwählung des Weihekandidaten. Mit der Erfindung des Buchdruckes wurden, wie alle liturgischen Bücher, auch die Bischofsweiheriten dann stärker vereinheitlicht und lassen sich so auf drei Grundordnungen reduzieren.

a) Taxis I[6]

Zum ersten Mal erscheint die Ordnung der Bischofsweihe im venezianischen Euchologion-Druck von 1571. Die ältesten Zeugnisse für diese Taxis sind in den alten Euchologion-Handschriften zu finden wie Hs. *Paris Coislin 213* (1027), *Grottaferrata Γβ 1* (11./12. Jh.)[7] u. a. Diese Weiheordnung bildet in der Tat die Basis für die späteren Entwicklungen, obwohl sie in eben dieser Form, wie sie auch noch in den ersten Euchologion-Drucken zu finden ist, schon längst nicht mehr praktiziert wird. Ihr ehrwürdiger altertümlicher Charakter ist wohl der Grund, warum sie auch noch in allen Ausgaben der griechischen Euchologion-Drucken seit 1571 zu finden ist.[8] Da wir allgemein vor dem 8. Jahrhundert über keine früheren handschriftlichen Zeugnisse der byzantinischen Tradition verfügen, können wir annehmen, dass diese Taxis die älteste, zugleich

4 Siehe die Edition dieser Handschrift: Stefano PARENTI – Elena VELKOVSKA, L'Eucologio Barberini gr. 336 (BEL.S 80), Rom ²2000, hier 165–167.

5 Vgl. die Texte der Priester- und Diakonenweihe, PARENTI – VELKOVSKA, Eucologio, 167–172.

6 BRAKMANN, Metrophanes (s. Anm. 3), 305–307.

7 Der Bischofsweihetext in beiden Handschriften in: Miguel ARRANZ, L'eucologio constantinopolitano agli inizi del secolo XI. Hagiasmatarion und Archieratikon (Rituale & Pontificale) con l'aggiunta del Leiturgikon (Messale), Rom 1996, 142–146.

8 Der älteste Euchologion-Druck ist 1545 in Venedig erschienen. Ein Exemplar findet sich in der Bayerischen Staatsbibliothek München (Sig. ESlg/4 Liturg. 222); dort finden wir die Priester- und Diakonenweihe, aber keine Spuren der Bischofsweihe. Vgl. BRAKMANN, Metrophanes (s. Anm. 3), 305, Anm. 14.

patriarchale Weihepraxis der oströmischen Reichshauptstadt Konstantinopel repräsentiert.

b) Taxis II[9]

Grundlage dieser Taxis ist die Hs. *Barberinianus graecus 390* (J. 1575),[10] die dann aus dem Besitz des Leo ALLATIUS[11] (1586–1669), später in die Vatikanbibliothek kam. Ursprünglich war die Handschrift im Besitz des Germanos KOUSKONARIS.[12] Der gelehrte Dominikaner Jacques GOAR (1601–1653) hat als erster den Kodex Barb. gr. 390 in seinem monumentalen Werk *Euchologion sive Rituale Graecorum* (Paris ^{1}1647 / Venedig ^{2}1730) publiziert.[13] Aufgrund einer Fehleinschätzung bzw. einer Frühdatierung GOARS erlangte die Handschrift eine posthume Berühmtheit in Urbe durch das Collegio Greco, wo ALLATIUS und nach ihm GOAR sie zur Hand hatten. Die Veröffentlichung von GOAR hat diese Taxis der Bischofsweihe bekannt gemacht und erhielt ihre offizielle Approbation im römischen Euchologion Papst BENEDIKT XIV. (1754) für die Byzantiner in Süditalien und Sizilien und hatte eine spätere Nachwirkung insbesondere bei den Melkiten und den Ruthenen.[14]
Der Text der Bischofsweihe in diesem Kodex repräsentiert in der Tat die Weihepraxis auf Zypern im 16. Jahrhundert, die möglicherweise auf die Zeit der Kreuzzüge im 14. Jahrhundert zurückgeht. Dieser Ritus wurde ins römische Euchologion von 1754 (im Appendix) aufgenommen, das fast einhundert Jahre früher angekündigt worden war.[15] Diese Taxis aber hatte sich bereits seit 1705

9 BRAKMANN, Metrophanes (s. Anm.3), 310–314.

10 Zu dieser Handschrift s. Gregorios A. IOANNIDES, Il manoscrito Barberini greco 390: edizione e commento liturgico (unveröffentl. Dissertation des Pontificale Istituto Orientale), Rom 2000.

11 Leo ALLATIUS (1586–1669), aus griechisch-orthodoxer Familie von Chios, Student am Griechischen Kolleg (Collegio Greco) St. Atanasius zu Rom (1600), später Professor am gleichen Kolleg (zwei Jahre), im Auftrag des Papstes oftmalige Übersetzung von griech. Werken ins Lateinische, Scriptor graecus der Bibliothreca Apostolica Vaticana, sammelte viele griech. Werke aus dem Orient für die Vaticana, Papst ALEXANDER VII. (1655–1667) ernannte ihn zum Kustos der Vatikanischen Bibliothek.

12 Γερμανὸς Κουσκωνάρις, ἐπίσκοπος Γραικὸς Λεφακαράν, ἤτοι Ἀμαθοῦντος ... ἐν τῇ νήσῳ Κύπρου, vgl. IOHANNIDES, Barberini gr. 390, Diss. (s. Anm. 10), 26; Er war Bischof von Amathounta auf Zypern. Am 31. August 1595 wurde er als katholisch-unierter Weihbischof für den byzantinischen Ritus in Italien ernannt († 1610), vgl. BRAKMANN, Metrophanes (s. Anm. 3), 311. bes. Anm. 57.

13 GOAR nennt die Handschrift in seinem Werk ‚Euchologium Allatianum'. In einem Katalog von Antonio POSSEVINUS, Apparatus sacer 3, Venezia 1606, 134 (Appendix) wird die Handschrift bezeichnet: „Pontificale S. De ordinatione, & officio Episcopi, & collationem ordinum", vgl. IOHANNIDES, Barberini gr. 390, Diss. (s. Anm. 10), 42.

14 Für die Melkiten vgl. das Jerusalemer Euchologion von 1865, s.u. S. 8–9; bei den unierten Ruthenen bis in die letzte offizielle Ausgabe der Bischofsweihe, vgl. die ‚editio typica' des kirchenslawischen Archieratikon der ‚recensio ruthena', publiziert durch die Ostkirchenkongregation: Arkhieratikon ili Sluzhebnik Svjatitel'skij, Rom 1973, 254–269. Für diesen und andere wertvolle Hinweise bin ich Dr. Stephan J. KOSTER dankbar.

15 Zur Dokumentation über die Bestrebung Roms zu einem dem ‚katholischen Glauben konformen' griech. Euchologion siehe Michael ABRAS, Tārīḫ 'al-'ifḫoloǧion 'al-kabīr 'al-

in den griech. venezianischen Euchologia der Orthodoxen – vermutlich über Goars Werk – eingebürgert.
Diese zypriotische Bischofsweiheordnung ist eine *Collage* von zwei, wohl ursprünglich nicht miteinander verbundenen Riten:

Ritus A: *Glaubensbekenntnis, Professio Fidei.* Nach der Vorstellung des Weihekandidaten wird dieser in einem Ritenkomplex aufgefordert, seinen Glauben zu erläutern; er verliest drei Symbola, die er mit der Hand geschrieben haben soll. Dieser Ritus findet außerhalb des Bêma (*sanctuarium*) statt, aber bereits innerhalb der Pontifikalliturgie der Weihe.

Ritus B: Die eigentliche Weihe, *Consecratio.* Sie beginnt mit: „Die göttliche Gnade“; es folgt das erste und zweite Weihegebet und zum Schluss die Verleihung des Omophorion. Sie findet innerhalb des Bêma am Altar statt.

Die zypriotische Taxis II unterscheidet sich von der konstantinopolitanischen Taxis I in Folgendem:

- Sie enthält zusätzlich zur Ordinatio (Ritus B) einen präliminaren Ritus (Ritus A), der einen Dialog-Charakter hat; Schwerpunkt ist die Professio Fidei.[16]
- Ritus A erfolgt unmittelbar vor Ritus B und beide erfolgen innerhalb der göttlichen Liturgie nach dem ersten Einzug (πρώτη εἴσοδος) und vor dem Trisagion. Im Gegensatz zu Taxis I, wo die Weihe erst nach dem Trisagion vollzogen wird, das ja der ursprüngliche alte Einzugsgesang Konstantinopels ist.[17]
- Die Erwählungsformel „Er wurde gewählt und bestätigt … Die göttliche Gnade“ wird vom Hauptkonsekrator gesprochen, während das Evangeliar auf dem Haupt und Nacken des Ordinandus liegt; in Taxis I wird das Evangeliar nach der Verlesung der Formel aus der χάρτης, wohl einem Kanzleidokument, auf Haupt und Nacken gelegt.
- Fehlen des Chartophylax, ursprünglich der Archivar, der die Aufgabe hat, diese Urkunde, in der die Erwählungsformel und „Die göttliche Gnade“ steht, dem Hauptkonsekrator zu überreichen. Sie ist quasi die Weiheurkunde.
- Verleihung des Epigonation und des Hirtenstabes durch den Hauptkonsekrator vor der Weihe am Ende des Ritus A; gleich zu Beginn von Ritus B. Diese Zeremonie hat keinerlei Entsprechung in Taxis I[18] und ist ein absolutes Novum.

maṭbūʿ fī l-Quds (= Geschichte des großen Euchologion, das in Jerusalem gedruckt wurde), in: Al-Massra 84 (1998) 534–548; 1094–1107, hier 540–542.

[16] Die lateinische Besetzung Zyperns (1191–1570/71) könnte auf diesen Ritus Einfluss genommen haben; vgl. Olivier RAQUEZ, Les confessions de foi de la Chirotonie épiscopale des églises grecques, in: Giustino FARNEDI (Hg.), Traditio et progressio. Studi liturgici in onore del Prof. A. Nocent OSB (Analecta Liturgica 12 = StAns 95), Rom 1988, 469–485, hier 475.

[17] RAQUEZ, Confessions de foi, 474.

[18] Nach heutiger und der klassischeren Praxis wird der Stab am Ende der göttlichen Liturgie verliehen; das Epigonation, falls der Ordinandus es als Hegoumenos oder Archimandrit

Zusammenfassend könnte bezüglich Taxis II gesagt werden: Es handelt sich um eine zypriotische Rezension der byzantinischen Bischofsweihe, die den Ursprungsritus durch einen Präliminarium-Ritus erweitert hat und zusätzlich zwei sehr späte und periphere Elemente, fast im Sinne einer ‚traditio instrumentorum' zum Beginn der eigentlichen Weihe in den Mittelpunkt stellt: die Verleihung des Epigonation und des Bischofsstabes, den der Weihekandidat so bereits während seiner eigenen Weihe in den Händen hält.[19] Das älteste Zeugnis für diese Taxis ist die Hs. *Barb. gr. 390*.[20]

c) Taxis III: Ordo des METROPHANES VON NYSSA[21]

Zum ersten Mal erscheint diese Taxis im Archieratikon[22] von Venedig 1714, das ebenso den Namen des Redaktors der Taxis trägt, sie lautet dann auch später so im Archieratikon und Euchologion: Τάξις ἐπὶ χειροτονίᾳ ἐπισκόπου κατὰ τὴν ἑρμηνείαν Μητροφάνους Νύσσης. Sie ist ab 1776 in den Euchologion-Drucken eingegangen. Keine handschriftliche Vorlage dafür ist uns bekannt. Es handelt sich in der Tat um eine neue revidierte Version der in Konstantinopel üblichen Weiheordnung der Diataxis des GEMISTOS,[23] die sich parallel zur zypriotischen Weihetradition im 14.–15. Jahrhundert entwickelt hat. Es handelt sich im Grunde genommen um eine erweiterte Redaktion von Taxis I.[24] Die Erweiterungen bestehen in folgenden Elementen:

- Taxis III enthält Ritus A, dieser erfolgt aber getrennt vor dem Beginn der göttlichen Liturgie, geht also der Weihe nicht unmittelbar voraus wie in Taxis II. Die Texte der drei Glaubensbekenntnisse sind der Taxis II entnommen,[25] nur werden sie hier zusammen verlesen ohne weitere Befragung durch die weihenden Bischöfe.

noch nicht hat, bei der Bekleidung mit den bischöflichen Gewändern zum Abschluss der eigentlichen Weihe (Ritus B).

19 Das römischen Arkhieratikon der Ruthenen (s. Anm. 14), 263, vgl. auch das Jerusalemer Euchologion der kath. Melkiten von 1865 (s. Anm. 28).

20 Es gibt ältere Zeugnisse dieser Taxis auf Zypern, die aber verschiedene Textvarianten zeigen, vgl. Jean DARROUZÈS, Textes synodaux chypriotes, in: Revue des études byzantines 37 (1979) 5–122, bes. 14–14. Die Dokumente sind in RAQUEZ, Confessions de foi, 474 und BRAKMANN, Metrophanes, 311–312 nochmals angeführt.

21 Zu Metrophanes von Nyssa s. Anm. 72.

22 Dieses liturgische Buch, eigentlich ein Auszug aus dem Euchologion mit den Riten und Weihen für den Gebrauch eines Bischofs, was seinen Namen erklärt, entspricht dem *Pontifikale* des römischen Ritus.

23 Diese Diataxis erfährt im handschriftlichen Material viele Versionen. Zur Diataxis s. Alexander RENTEL, The 14th Century Patriarchal Liturgical Diataxis of Dimitrios Gemistos. Edition and Commentary [unveröffent. Dissertation des Pontificio Istituto Orientale], Rom 2003.

24 Mit diesem Archieratikon-Druck sinkt laut BRAKMANN die handschriftliche Produktion der griech. Archieratika schlagartig: BRAKMANN, Metrophanes (s. Anm. 3), 315.

25 Ursprünglich gab es in der Diataxis des GEMISTOS nur ein Glaubensbekenntnis, das der Weihekandidat vielleicht selbst formulieren und dann schreiben musste.

- Am Anfang der eigentlichen Weihehandlung (Ritus B) schreitet der Weihekandidat, begleitet von zwei Bischöfen, dreimal um den Altar herum (χορεία).[26]

Nach dieser knappen Darstellung der Weiheformulare in den griechischen Euchologion-Drucken wirft sich die Frage auf: Welche Ordnungen haben die Melkiten übernommen und wie haben sie sie rezipiert?

3. DIE REZENSIONEN DER BYZANTINISCHEN BISCHOFSWEIHE IN DER MELKITISCHEN KIRCHE

Zunächst gilt es die Druckausgaben zu befragen, um die heute geltenden Ordnungen zu erfahren; zweitens versuchen wir durch die uns bisher bekannten handschriftlichen Quellen die älteren Ordnungen kennen zu lernen.
Zu den hier vorgestellten Bischofsweiheformularen der melkitisch-arabischen Rezensionen wird versucht, nach ihren griechischen Vorlagen zu suchen, und zugleich sollen die Besonderheiten der Melkiten hervorgehoben werden.
Nach der gegenwärtigen Quellenlage können wir fünf arabische Rezensionstypen der byzantinischen Bischofsweihe erkennen. Drei finden sich in den gedruckten Büchern und zwei in den handschriftlichen Quellen.

a) Die arab. Bischofsweiheformulare in den Druckausgaben

Hier begegnen uns drei Quellen: Die erste betrifft die Griechisch-Katholischen (Kath. Melkiten), nämlich ihr Großes Euchologion von Jerusalem 1865[27] (Euch. Jer.); die anderen beiden die Griechisch-Orthodoxen (Rum-Orthodoxen), nämlich das Archieratikon von MASSARRA (^{1}1890 / ^{2}1925) (Arch. Mas.) und das Große Euchologion von HAWAWEENY (^{1}1913 / ^{2}1955) (Euch. Haw.).

b) Bischofsweiheritus des Großen Eucholgion Jerusalem 1865 bei den katholischen Melkiten

Die katholischen Melkiten kennen in ihrer Liturgiegeschichte einen einzigen Druck des arabischen Großen Euchologion,[28] das 1865 in Jerusalem durch die

[26] Diese Zeremonie ist in vielen alten griech. liturgischen Dokumenten aus dem 14. Jh. bezeugt, wie z. B. in der *Diataxis des Gemistos*, Protonotarios der 'Großen Kirche', der Haghia Sophia Konstantinopels (um 1380) später Megas Sakellarios (1394), und Symeon von Thessalonikê († 1429).

[27] AWIKÉ (s. Anm. 2) erwähnt dazu noch zwei Quellen bei den kath. Melkiten: Skaf und Hallit; zu den zwei Ordnungen s. am Ende dieser Studie.

[28] Kitāb al-ifẖoloğion al-kabīr isti'māl kahanat ar-rūm al-kāthūlīk. ṭubi'a bi'ūrašalīm fī dair al-ābā al-fransiskān sanat 1865 (Das Buch des Großen Euchologion. Verwendung der

Kustodie der Franziskaner gedruckt wurde.[29] Es enthält zwei Formulare für die Bischofsweihe. Beide haben die gleiche Überschrift „Ordo der Cheirotonia eines Bischofs, sei es Episkopos oder Metropolit“.[30]
Das erste Weiheformular stammt aus dem Euchologion von KARMA;[31] das zweite ist eine Übersetzung der Ordnung aus dem römischen Euchologion von 1754 (Euchologium Benedicti XIV. PP.), es handelt sich also um die uns bereits bekannte Taxis II. Das letztgenannte Formular hat nach der Spaltung im antiochenischen Patriarchat der Melkiten 1724 das erste abgelöst und wurde zur allein gültigen Ordnung für die katholischen Melkiten. Der Karma-Text wurde dennoch als ‚Relikt‘ ins Jerusalemer Euchologion als fertige Übersetzung von Taxis I übernommen, die ja auch im römischen Euchologion von 1754 als erste Ordnung angeführt ist.
Eine Handschrift der Bibliothek der melkitisch-katholischen Erzdiözese Aleppo, Hs. *Alep Arch. Cath. 213* (J. 1768),[32] bezeugt, dass Taxis II aus dem römischen Euchologion von 1754 bereits in den 70er Jahren des 18. Jahrhunderts bekannt war, denn diese Handschrift enthält das gleiche Weiheformular wie in Euch. Jer., allerdings mit vielen Abweichungen in Satzstruktur und Vokabular. Identisch zeigt sich hingegen der Text der Taxis II in Euch. Jer. mit Texten in anderen Handschriften, deren Verfasserschaft, Herkunft und Datierung bisher nicht zu erschließen sind, wie *Alep Arch. Cath. 229* (18.–19. Jh.), *Harissa 91* (18. Jh.),[33] *Hauran 15* (19. Jh.) und *Damas Patr. Cath. 18* (19.–20. Jh.).[34]
Die arabische Übersetzung der Taxis II in Euch. Jer. ist dem griechischen Ursprungstext nicht ganz getreu. Das veranlasst den Leser, den Text der Bischofsweihe als fehlerhaft und korrekturbedürftig anzusehen. Vergleichend mit dem Text des römischen Euchologion von 1754 fallen zwei Punkte im zweiten Bischofsweiheformular des Euch. Jer. auf:

- Die Adlerzeremonie im Ritus A fehlt.
- Beim Anlegen des Epigonation wird eine Begleitformel angeführt, die im römischen Euchologion und auch im Ursprungstext des *Barb. gr. 390* nicht vorhanden ist.

Griechisch-Katholischen Priester. Es wurde gedruckt in Jerusalem, im Kloster der Franziskaner-Patres 1865).

29 Vgl. Cyrille KOROLEVSKIJ, Histoire des Patrairchates Melkites, Bd. 3, Rom 1911, 122–124; Georg GRAF, Geschichte der christlichen arabischen Literatur, Bd. 1 (StT 118), Città del Vaticano 1944, 636. Über die Genese dieses liturgischen Buches s. den Beitrag von Machael ABRAS, Geschichte (s. Anm. 15); die Studie könnte weiter vertieft werden.

30 Euch. Jer., 13.

31 Nur Rubriken mit einigen Abänderungen. Zum Karma-Euchologion s. unten 177-181.

32 Neuer Digitalcode GCAA 00213. Eine Studie dieser interessanten Handschrift ist vorgesehen.

33 Joseph NASRALLAH, Catalogue des manuscrits du Liban. Bd. 1: Bibliothèque des Monastaires de Saint Paul (Harissa), Bibliothèque du Séminaire de l'Annonciation (Ain-Traz), o. O., o. J. [Harissa 1960], 110–111.

34 Der Inhalt der letzten Handschrift ist identisch mit dem des Euch. Jer.

Kurz gesagt: Taxis II findet sich im arabischen Großen Euchologion 1865 und wurde für die katholisch-melkitische Kirche mit einigen Änderungen bestimmend.

c) Bischofsweiheritus bei den Rum Orthodoxen

Nach dem Schisma im antiochenischen Patriarchat im Jahr 1724 wurde der Patriarch der Rum-Orthodoxen – nicht ohne Einfluss des Patriarchen von Konstantinopel – immer aus den griechischsprachigen Mönchen gewählt. Seit dieser Zeit wird folgerichtig die in Konstantinopel gebräuchliche Ordnung des METROPHANES (Taxis III) üblich. Bis 1898 war das Oberhaupt auf dem Patriarchenthron ein Grieche, d. h. bis zu dieser Zeit wurde der griechische Text bei den Orthodoxen verwendet. Später wurde diese Taxis in zwei Formen ins Arabische übersetzt, die eine von MASSARRA und die andere von HAWAWEENY.

Weiheformular des Archieratikon von MASSARRA

Zum ersten Mal in der Neuzeit finden wir 1890 bei den Orthodoxen ein nur auf Arabisch abgefasstes Archieratikon, das von Gerasimos MASSARRA[35] herausgegeben wurde (Arch. Mas.).[36] Die Bischofsweihe in diesem Archieratikon ist keine wörtliche Übersetzung der Taxis des METROPHANES. Sie ist in der Tat eine Kombination zwischen Taxis II und Taxis III.
Der Redaktor hat sich mehrerer griechischer Vorlagen – wohl auch unter Einschluss des arabischen Großen Jerusalemer Euchologion von 1865 – bedient, um seine Weiheordnung anzufertigen. Er selber erwähnt keine Quelle im Vorwort seines Archieratikon, aber aus dem Text der Bischofsweihe lassen sich folgende Vorlagen vermuten:

- Das griechische Archieratikon von Konstantinopel 1820,[37] das nur Taxis III enthält;
- das griechische Große Euchologion von Venedig 1862[38] (oder ein Nachdruck vor 1890), dem Elemente aus Taxis II entnommen wurde;

[35] Gerasimos MASSARRA (Lattakia 1858 – Beirut 1936), Mönch 1873, Theologiestudium in Chalki 1875–1879, Priesterweihe und Archimandrit 1889, hat in Alexandrien gewirkt von 1889 bis 1902, Metropolit von Beirut (1902–1936). Er hat viele liturgische und dogmatische Bücher aus dem Griechischen ins Arabische übersetzt.

[36] Leider war mir kein Exemplar dieses Archieratikon zugänglich. Eine zweite revidierte Ausgabe des Buches finden wir 1925. Diese Ausgabe war die Grundlage für diese Studie.

[37] Vgl. die Ähnlichkeit des Buchtitels des Arch. Mas. zu dem griech.: Ἀρχιερατικὸν, περιέχων τὰς θείας, καὶ ἱερὰς λειτουργίας Ἰωάννου τοῦ Χρυσοστόμου, Βασιλείου τοῦ Μεγάλου καὶ Γρηγορίου Διαλόγου, ἤτοι τῶν Προηγιασμένων, ἔτι δὲ καὶ τὰς τάξεις πασῶν τῶν χειροτονιῶν, τὴν ἀκολουθλίαν τοῦ ἀρραβῶνος καὶ τοῦ στεφανώματος τὴν ἀκολουθίαν τοῦ μικροῦ ἁγιασμοῦ, καὶ μέρος τῆς ἱερὰς μεταλήψεως, καὶ ἄλλας ἀναγκαίας τοῖς ἀρχιερεῦσιν εὐχὰς. Ἐκδοθὲν ἤδη εἰς χρῆσιν τῶν ἀρχιερέων, ἐπιμελείᾳ συντόνῳ τῶν πανιερωτάτων ἐφόρων τῆς Πατριαρχικῆς τυπογραφίας, ἐν Κωνσταντινουπόλει ͵αωκ΄ 1820.

- und die ausführlichen Erklärungen des SYMEON VON THESSALONIKE über die Ordination.[39]

Ritus A (vorbereitender Ritus) wurde der Taxis II entnommen und erweitert, während Ritus B (die Weihe) der Taxis III entstammt. Die Rezitation der Glaubensbekenntnisse geschieht nicht laufend hintereinander, sondern in drei Schritten in einer je eigenen Zeremonie mit der folgenden Struktur:

- Schreiten auf dem Adlerteppich auf den Konsekrator hin
- Vorstellung des Erwählten durch einen Archimandriten
- Frage seitens des weihenden Bischofs
- Rezitation eines Glaubensbekenntnisses
- Ausruf „κέλευσον"
- Segen
- Friedenskuss

Taxis III im griechischen Archieratikon 1820 kennt diesen Komplex nicht. Dort wird die fortlaufende Rezitation der drei Symbola mit dem Ausruf „πρόσχωμεν" eingeleitet und danach kommt „κέλευσον, κελεύσατε", Segen und Friedenskuss. Wir haben überraschenderweise nach MASSARRAS Ordnung mit vier Segnungen und viermaligem Friedenskuss zu tun.
Mit der dritten Segensformel im Anschluss an die Rezitation des dritten Glaubensbekenntnisses läuft die Ordnung wörtlich nach dem griechischen Archieratikon bis zum Schluss. Nach dem Abschluss der Göttlichen Liturgie vollzieht sich eine zusätzliche Zeremonie, die keine Entsprechung in der griechischen Version hat, nämlich die *Übergabe des Hirtenstabes* mit Begleitformel: „Nimm diesen Stab, um damit die dir anvertraute Herde Christi zu weiden. Er soll für dich den Gehorsamen gegenüber ein Stab der Betreuung und des Schutzes sein".[40]
Bei der Kombination der zwei Taxeis aus dem griechischen Euchologion zeigt MASSARRA eine gewisse Rubrikenüberlappung. Wir finden die Rubrik über den kleinen Einzug (εἴσοδος) zwei Mal vor. Ritus A beginnt laut Arch. Mas. einerseits nach dem ersten Einzug der Göttlichen Liturgie, an dem der Weihekandidat teilnimmt, der das Evangeliar mit den drei darin steckenden zu rezitierenden Symbola hält, so wie in Taxis II angegeben wird; andererseits findet Ritus B nach dem Beginn der Göttlichen Liturgie statt, und beim Einzug zieht der Weihekandidat *nicht* mit, sondern er wird nach der Vollendung des Trisagion und der Phêmê[41] von zwei Priestern durch das nördliche Seitenschiff in das Haupt-

[38] Εὐχολόγιον τὸ Μέγα τῆς κατὰ ἀνατολᾶς ὀρθοδόξου καθολικῆς ἐκκλησίας (Ἐν Βενετίᾳ 1862).
[39] PG 155, 396D–425A.
[40] Arch. Mas. 95, Spalte 1. Diese Zeremonie wurde in der zweiten Ausgabe des Archieratikon von MASSARRA 1925 aus dem Großen Euchologion von HAWAWEENY 1913 übernommen, das seinerseits dem russischen Brauch entnommen wurde.
[41] Φήμη (= Stimme, Ruf, Reputation), in einer bischöflichen Liturgie werden Name und Titel des zelebrierenden Patriarchen bzw. Bischofs vor der Apostellesung vom Diakon

schiff geführt, indem diese rufen: κέλευσον, κελεύσατε, bis sie zu den Königlichen[42] (heiligen) Türen gelangen; dann wird der Weihekandidat von zwei Bischöfen empfangen, und diese führen ihn dreimal um den Altartisch, so wie es in Taxis III dargelegt wird.
Was die Übersetzung der Glaubensbekenntnisse, Formeln und Weihegebete betrifft, gibt MASSARRA den griechischen Text wortwörtlich wieder. An einigen Stellen werden veraltete arabische Vokabeln angewandt. Die Übersetzung zeigt aber eine Beheimatung des Übersetzers sowohl in der griechischen Sprache als auch in der arabischen literarischen Sprache. Das Weiheformular des MASSARRA wird bis heute im orthodoxen Patriarchat von Antiochien verwendet.[43]

Weiheformular des Euchologion von HAWAWEENY

Rafael HAWAWEENY[44] übersetzt seinerseits die Taxis III in seinem Großen Euchologion 1913 (Euch. Haw.)[45] fast wörtlich. Die griechische Vorlage seiner Übersetzung ist, wie er selber angibt, das Εὐχολόγιον τὸ Μέγα (Venedig 1885). In der Hinführung auf die Ordnung gibt HAWAWEENY einen Hinweis, dass sie *neu* ist und in den griechischen Kirchen gebraucht wird. Am Schluss deutet er darauf hin, dass die griechische Ordnung (von METROPHANES)[46] die Stabübergabezeremonie nicht kennt. So übernimmt er diese aus dem russisch-slawischen Brauch. Die Texte der Glaubensbekenntnisse, die Formeln und die Gebete stimmen fast wortwörtlich mit denen im Arch. Mas. mit geringfügigen Abweichungen überein.
HAWAWEENY übersetzt zugleich Taxis II aus dem griechischen Euchologion 1885 und führt sie in seinem Euchologion als *„die alte Ordnung bei den Grie-*

mit lauter Stimme in einem Huldigungsruf proklamiert, dies wird gr. φήμη, in slaw. ‚pokhvaly' (= Huldigungs- und Lobruf) genannt; bei den Russen ist der Brauch heute auf die Patriarchalliturgie beschränkt.

42 Die ‚Königlichen Türen' sind jene, durch die der Basileus einzog, eigentlich die Türen zum ‚Naos', die der Ikonostase sind korrekt die ‚heiligen Türen', erst später vermischen sich die Termini, nachdem es keinen Basileus mehr gibt.

43 Eine neue Überarbeitung der Ordnung finden wir im neuerschienenen Archieratikon von Youhanna Yazigi 2006, die Einfluss der katholischen Version aufzeigt.

44 HAWAWEENY (* Beirut 20.11.1860, † Brooklyn/NY 27.2.1915), Theologiestudium auf Chalki (1879–1886) und anschließend in der Geistlichen Akademie in Kiew (1888–1889), Diakonatsweihe auf Chalki (20.12.1885), Priesterweihe in Kiew (16.6.1889), Archimandrit (28.7.1889) in Moskau, Exarch des antiochenischen orth. Patriarchen in Moskau, unterrichtete an der Geistlichen Akademie in Kazan. Bischof von Brooklyn (1904–1915), heilig gesprochen durch die Orthodox Church in America am 29.3.2000. Er hat mehrere liturgische Bücher aus dem Griechischen und Slawischen ins Arabische übersetzt, gerade das Euchologion; vgl. Paul D. GARRETT, The Life and Legacy of Bishop Raphael Hawaweeny, The First One Hundred Years, Englewood/NJ 1995.

45 Zweite unveränderte Auflage 1955.

46 Die Überschrift der Weiheliturgie ist in Euch. Haw.: „Taxis des Offiziums der Cheirotonie des Episkopos, d. h. des Archiereus". Der Name „Metrophanes von Nyssa", nach dem diese Ordnung ursprünglich benannt wird, wird nicht erwähnt, ebensowenig in Arch. Mas.

chen“ an; allerdings nur die Rubriken und nur zur Kenntnisnahme und nicht zum liturgischen Gebrauch. Seine Übersetzung für die Rubriken steht dem Ursprungstext näher als die Übersetzung des katholischen Euchologion 1865.

Revision des Weiheformulars von MASSARRA

Seit der Besteigung des antiochenischen Patriarchenthrones bei den Rum-Orthodoxen durch arabischsprachige einheimische Kandidaten[47] befolgt die Kirche bis heute ausschließlich die Fassung des Arch. Mas. Da diese aber bei manchen liturgischen Vollzügen nicht klar ist, hat neuerdings Yūḥannā YAZIGI[48] eine Revision in seinem Archieratikon vorgelegt[49] und die Rubriken ausführlicher ausgearbeitet; z. B. wenn der Patriarch den Kairos[50] nimmt, geht er in den Altarraum hinein und *grüßt alle Bischöfe* und legt seine Paramente an; oder bei der Vorstellung des Weihekandidaten durch einen Archimandriten wird diesem nach der Vorstellungsformel „der Erwählte und Bestätigte …“ *vom Diakon das Evangeliar gegeben*, in dem die Symbola stecken. Nach der Göttlichen Liturgie finden wir bei YAZIGI zusätzliche Rubriken, die keine Entsprechung in der griechischen Fassung haben.
Der Beginn von Ritus A wird laut YAZIGI wie bei MASSARRA interessanterweise immer noch nach dem kleinen Einzug angesetzt, während Ritus B dem Trisagion folgt. Die heutige Praxis des rum-orthodoxen Patriarchates von Antiochien entspricht jener in Griechenland. Ritus A findet nach dem feierlichen Orthros vor der Liturgie statt. Ritus B hat seinen Platz nach dem Trisagion und der Phêmê in der Liturgie; d.h. vor dem Evangelium.

47 Der erste arabischsprachige orthodoxe Patriarch von Antiochien war MELETIOS II. DUMANI (1899–1906).

48 Geboren in Lattakia 1955, Abschluss an der theologischen Fakultät der orthodoxen Universität von Balamand (1978), Dissertation über das Sakrament der Taufe an der Universität von Thessalonike (1983) zugleich studierte er kirchliche Musik, Diakonatsweihe (1979) Priesterweihe (1983), seit 1981 unterrichtet er Liturgie in Balamand, von 1988–1991 und 2001–2005 war er Rektor der dortigen theologischen Fakultät, 1995 Ernennung zum Bischof von Al-Husn und 2008 zum Metropolit des West- und Zentraleuropa, Autor und Übersetzer viele Bücher in Theologie, Liturgie, Musik, Hymnographie und Pädagogik. 17.12.2012 Wahl zum Patriarchen von Antiochien mit dem Namen Johannes X.

49 Kitāb ḫidmat ru’asā’ al-kahana, yaštamil ‘alā mā yaḫtaṣṣu bi-ḫidmat ru’asā’ al-kahana mina al-quddās al-ilāhi li-lḏ-ḏahabī al-fam wa li-Basīlius al-kabīr wal-Brōǧiāzmīnī, wa ar-risāmāt al-kahnūtia wa ṣalawāt al-ġurūb ws-sahar wa taqdīs al-mā’ wa as-saǧda wa al-maṭālibsi wa afāšīn limunāsabāt muḫtalifa ma‘a aš-šurūḥāt al-wāǧibap 2006 (= Buch des Dienstes der Bischöfe enthält, was zum Dienst der Bischöfe gehört: die göttliche Liturgie des Chrysostomos, des Basilios des Großen, und der Vorgeweihten Gaben, sowie die priesterlichen Weihen, die Abend- und Morgengebete, die Wasserweihe, das Kniebeugegebet, Metalepsis und Gebete für verschiedene Anlässe mit den dazu gehörenden Erklärungen, [Baouar/Libanon] 2006) 293–306. Das neue Archieratikon von YAZIGI stützt sich auf aktuelle Ergebnisse der Liturgiewissenschaft, cf. Robert TAFT, Miguel ARRANZ, Alexander SCHMEMANN u. a.

50 καιρός (= die rechte / „qualitative“ Zeit in Opposition zu χρόνος), hier sind die Vorbereitungsgebete vor den heiligen Türen der Ikonostase zu Beginn der Liturgie gemeint.

d) Zusammenfassung

Wir haben also in den arabischen liturgischen Drucken beider Obödienzen des melkitischen Patriarchates von Antiochien drei verschiedene Textmodelle der byzantinischen Bischofsweihe:

1. Formular des Großen Euchologion Jerusalem 1865 als Übersetzung von Taxis II (kath. Rezension);
2. Formular des Archieratikon von MASSARRA 1890/1925 als Kombination aus Taxis II und III mit Einführung eigener Elemente, die dem Kommentar des SYMEON VON THESSALONIKE entstammen. Diese Rezension wurde von Yuhanna YAZIGI revidiert (1. orth. Rezension);
3. Formular des Euchologion von HAWAWEENY als Übersetzung von Taxis III (2. orthodoxe Rezension).

Eine Frage drängt sich nun auf: Wie haben die Melkiten vor der Trennung 1724 die Bischofsweihe gefeiert? Hierfür ist die handschriftliche Tradition zu befragen.

4. BISCHOFSWEIHEFORMULARE IN DEN HANDSCHRIFTEN[51] MELKITISCHER TRADITION

Hier stoßen wir auf zwei Bischofsweiheformulare: Zum einen die Rezension des Euchologion von KARMA (Euch. Karma), und das zweite ist die bisher älteste greifbare Rezension aus einer Handschrift, die in der *Bibliothèque Orientale* der Jesuitenuniversität Saint Joseph in Beirut aufbewahrt wird unter der Nummer 867 (*Beirut Orientale 867*).

a) Weiheformular des Euchologion von KARMA[52]

Meletius KARMA[53] (* Hama 1572, † Aleppo 1635), Bischof von Aleppo (1612–1634), später Patriarch von Antiochien als EUTHYMIOS II. (1634–1635), bildet eine sehr wichtige Wende in der Liturgiegeschichte der Melkiten, gerade des Patriarchats von Antiochien. Als Bischof von Aleppo hat er die Fülle der liturgischen Texte mit ihren vielen verwirrenden Textvarianten in verschiedenen Sprachen (Griechisch, Syrisch und Arabisch) und das Chaos in den liturgischen Büchern, bisher zumeist Handschriften, bemerkt. Als Mönch des Klosters Mar

[51] Wir beschränken uns selbstverständlich auf die bisher bekannten arabischen Handschriften.

[52] Der übliche Titel des Buches: Kitāb afġolǧion aṣ-ṣalawāt waṭ-ṭalibāt yaḥtāǧu ilaihi al-kāhin fī ǧamī‘ al-awqāt fassarhu min al-luġati al-yunāniyā bikaddin wa ta‘ab al-faqīr Malātios al-muṭrān bimadīnati ḥalab (= Buch des Euchologion der Gebete und der Fürbitten, das ein Priester braucht in allen Zeiten. Wurde übersetzt vom Armseligen Malatios, dem Bischof (Metropoliten) in der Stadt Aleppo).

[53] Zur Person von Meletios KARMA s. Joseph NASRALLAH, Histoire du mouvement littéraire dans l'Église Melchite du Ve au XXe siècle, Bd. 4/1, Paris 1979, 70–87 mit weiterführender Literatur über seine Biographie und Werke.

Saba bei Jerusalem (vor seiner Priesterweihe in seiner Heimatdiözese Hama 1604) hatte er Griechisch gelernt.[54] So wollte er die liturgische Sprache vereinheitlichen. Er begann sein Projekt, die liturgischen Bücher anhand einiger venezianischer griechischer Drucke, die er von Rom erbat,[55] zu revidieren und in Arabisch herauszugeben in der Hoffnung, sie mit Hilfe der Kongregation „Propaganda Fide" drucken zu können.[56] Kurz vor seiner Wahl zum Patriarchen am 10. Mai 1634, hat er ein Euchologion angefertigt und mit einem Horologion zum Druck nach Rom geschickt. Dort wollte man aber den Inhalt des Euchologion verifizieren, so musste das Euchologion zuerst ins Lateinische übersetzt werden. Zur gleichen Zeit fasste die „Propaganda Fide" ins Auge, das griechische Euchologion zu revidieren und eine neue dem katholischen Glauben entsprechende Ausgabe zu erstellen. So wurde der Auftrag berühmten Gelehrten wie Jakob GOAR OP und Leo ALLATIUS anvertraut.[57] Ein Projekt, das erst 1754 im besagten Euchologion Papst BENEDIKTS XIV. seine Erfüllung fand. Bis dahin gab es für das Patriarchat keine andere Lösung, als das Euchologion von Karma handschriftlich immer wieder zu kopieren, so dass aus diesem Euchologion viele Abschriften entstanden sind; die Ab- und Nachschriften sind aber nicht alle gleichmäßig identisch, viele enthalten – typisch für handschriftliche Quellen, je nach Bedarf des Kopisten und/oder des Auftraggebers – nur Auszüge des Textes, dessen Inhalt eigentlich aus 117 Kapitel besteht.[58]

Euch. Karma überliefert uns die melkitische Ordnung zur Bischofsweihe. Es handelt sich um die Übersetzung des Weiheformulars des venezianischen Eu-

[54] NASRALLAH, Histoire Bd. 4/1 (s. Anm. 53), 72.

[55] Es gibt Versuche, seinen Willen zur Katholizität hervorzuheben. Dieses Thema gehört aber nicht zum Rahmen unserer Thematik.

[56] Vgl. Carsten-Michael WALBINER, Und um Jesu Willen, schickt sie nicht ungebunden. Die Bemerkungen des Meletius Karma (1572–1635) um den Druck arabischer Bücher in Rom, in: Rifaat EBIED – Herman TEULE (Hgg.), Studies on the Christian Arabic Heritage: in Honor of Father Prof. Dr. Khalil Samir SJ at the Occasion of his Sixty-Fifth Birthday (Eastern Christian Studies 5), Leuven – Paris – Dudley/MA 2004, 163–175.

[57] Vgl. ABRAS, Geschichte (s. Anm. 15), 539–542.

[58] NASRALLAH führt einige Kodizes an: NASRALLAH, Histoire, Bd. 4/1 (s. Anm. 53), 83–84, 267. Zum vollständigen Inhaltsverzeichnis des Euchologion s. Angelo MAIO, Scriptorum veterum nova collectio e vaticanis codicibus edita, Bd. 4, Rom 1831, n. 618, 561–564; auch Georg GRAF, Katalog christlich-arabischer Handschriften in Jerusalem. Die arabischen Handschriften des melkitischen Seminars Sainte-Anne, in: Oriens Christianus N.S. 4 (1914) 97–101. Zum Vorwort des Euch. Karma s. eine französische Übersetzung in KOROLEVSKIJ, Histoire Bd. 3 (s. Anm. 27), 121–122, wo das Anliegen des Bischofs zur liturgischen Liturgie zum Ausdruck kommt. Eine Kopie des Euchologion existiert in der Vatikanischen Bibliothek Vaticanus arab. 618 (vom Jahr 1643), Vgl. MAIO, Scriptorum veterum; Cyrille KARALEVSKIJ (CHARON), Histoire du rite byzantin dans l'Église melkite, in: Studi e ricerche intorno a S. Giovanni Crisostomo a cura del comitato per il XV centenario della sua morte (ΧΡΥΣΟΣΤΟΜΙΚΑ), Rome 1908, 498–625, hier 615–620. Eine lateinische Übersetzung des Euch. Karma bildet Codex *Vat. lat. 189*, der im Auftrag des Kardinals Stefano Borgia (1731–1804) geschrieben wurde, als er Sekretär der Kongregation *Propaganda Fide* war (1770–1780), vgl. KOROLEVSKIJ, Histoire (s. Anm. 29), 122. Eigentlich soll die Handschrift auf das Jahr 1633 datiert werden, wie im Vorwort des Euchologion steht.

chologion-Druckes 1571. Der folgende Vergleich beider Weihestrukturen zeigt die Abweichungen der arabischen von der griechischen Vorlage:

Euchologion von Karma (1633)	***Euchologion Venedig 1571***
Der [weihende] Bischof *sitzt* vor den Altar	Der [weihende] Bischof *geht* auf die Altarstufe hinauf
Der Weihekandidat kommt mit drei Bischöfen[59] von der rechten Seite	Der Weihekandidat wird von drei Bischöfen vorgeführt von der rechten Seite
Der Chartophylax steht an der linken Seite und gibt dem Konsekrator die Urkunde des *Zeugnisses des Volkes*	Der Chartophylax gibt dem Konsekrator von der linken Seite die Urkunde
Inhalt der Urkunde: „Durch die Wahl/ Überprüfung[60] der Gott liebenden Bischöfe und die Wahl der Priester".	Inhalt der Urkunde: „Durch die Wahl und Überprüfung der von Gott geliebten Episkopoi und gerechten Priestern" † „Die göttliche Gnade …".
Der weihende Bischof nimmt die Urkunde und liest sie laut	Der weihende Bischof nimmt die Urkunde und liest sie laut
Übergabe des Glaubensbekenntnisses an den Weihekandidaten	
Rezitation des Glaubensbekenntnisses	
Dreimal „Kyrie eleison"	
Das Gebet: „Die göttliche Gnade"	Der Konsekrator sagt laut: „Durch die Wahl…die göttliche Gnade"
Dreimal „Kyrie eleison"	Dreimal „Kyrie eleison"
Auflegung des Evangeliars auf Haupt und Nacken des Weihekandidaten	Auflegung des Evangeliars auf Haupt und Nacken des Weihekandidaten
Dreimalige Bekreuzigung des Hauptes	Dreimalige Bekreuzigung des Hauptes
Handauflegung	Handauflegung
Das erste Weihegebet	Das erste Weihegebet

59 Die alten arabischen Euchologien verwenden zwei Begriffe für das Bischofsamt: „Mutrān" (Metropolit) und „Usquf" (Episkopos), die kirchenrechtliche Unterschiede aufweisen. Der Begriff „Raīs kahna" (Erzpriester) ist die wörtliche Übersetzung des griech. Ἀρχιερεύς, er ist ein strikt liturgischer Begriff und bedeutet in diesem Sinne „Bischof". Im dargestellten Schema ist „Bischof" die Wiedergabe des arabischen Begriff „Raīs kahna", während „Metropolit" für „Mutrān" und „Episkopos" für „Usquf" steht.

60 In manchen Handschriften steht اختيار (Wahl), in anderen اختبار (Überprüfung), der Unterschied ist ein Punkt unter dem zweiten Buchstaben, der leicht zu übersehen ist.

Die Diakonika	Die Diakonika
Das zweite Weihegebet	Das zweite Weihgebet
Abnahme des Evangeliars	Abnahme des Evangeliars
Anlegen des Omophorion	Anlegen des Omophorion
Dreimalige Axios-Akklamation	Dreimalige Axios-Akklamation
Friedenskuss	Friedenskuss
	Anokathedra (Sessio)
„Friede sei mit dir/euch“[61] zum Apostolos	εἰρηνεύει
Kommunion	Kommunion
Klerus und Volk empfangen den Segen vom Neugeweihten	

Wir merken an der Ordnung von KARMA folgendes:

1. Der Incipit der Weihe ist wie im griechischen Euchologion: „Nach der Vollendung des Trisagion setzt (sic) sich der Archiereus“.[62]
2. Auffällig ist die Einbettung des Glaubensbekenntnisses in die Weiheordnung. Dieses wird zwischen der Erwählungsformel „Durch die Wahl und Überprüfung ...“ und der als *Gebet* bezeichneten Formel „Die göttliche Gnade“ eingefügt.[63] Das liegt auf der Hand, denn das Glaubensbekenntnis war mittlerweile ein wesentlicher Bestandteil der Weihe geworden.[64] Das Glaubensbekenntnis wird vom Chartophylax[65] dem Weihekandidaten zum Verlesen *übergeben*. Bemerkenswert ist, dass der Weihekandidat das Glaubensbekenntnis auf der Altarstufe verliest daraufhin antworten Klerus und Volk mit einem dreimaligen „Kyrie eleison“ ohne Aufruf zum Gebet oder Ähnliches. Dieser Brauch hat keine Entsprechung im griechischen Euchologion, geschweige denn die Form des Glaubensbekenntnisses.

[61] In einigen Handschriften steht in arabischer Schrift „εἰρήνη πᾶσοι“ (Plural); in anderen „εἰρήνη σοι“ (Singular).

[62] Μετὰ τὴν τοῦ τρισαγίου συμπλήρωσιν ἄνεισιν ὁ ἀρχιερευς.

[63] Die Formel lautet im Karma-Text: „Durch die Wahl/Überprüfung der Gott liebenden Bischöfe und die Wahl/Überprüfung der gerechten Priester“. Diese Formel wird in einer Urkunde dokumentiert, die der Chartophylax dem weihenden Patriarchen bzw. Bischof übergibt. Diese Urkunde wird in Karma-Version interessanterweise „Zeugnis des Volkes“ genannt. Es ist wegen des eingeschobenen Glaubensbekenntnisses nicht klar, ob die Formel „Die göttliche Gnade“ Teil der Urkunde ist.

[64] Eine Handschrift der Bibliothek der melk. Erzdiözese in Aleppo, *Alep Arch. Cath.* 254 (214) [J. 1622], die möglicherweise von KARMA selbst geschrieben wurde, enthält eine arabische Übersetzung der Taxis I aus dem venezianischen Euchologion 1571; in der Ordnung finden wir aber kein Glaubensbekenntnis.

[65] Ein Chatophylax wird im Euchologion definiert als „der größte (älteste/würdigste) unter den Priestern“. Gemeint wird wahrscheinlich der Protopresbyteros; ursprünglich wurde der Notar der bischöflichen bzw. patriarchalen Kanzlei als Chartophylax bezeichnet.

3. Der Ritus der ‚Anokathedra'[66] fehlt in Euch. Karma. Dass der Bischof und die Bischöfe mit den Priestern nach dem Trisagion zum Synthronon ziehen, ist aus den meisten arabischen handschriftlichen zeitgenössischen Quellen bekannt.
4. Der Segen durch den Neugeweihten nach dem Abschluss der Göttlichen Liturgie ist in den griechischen Euchologien nicht bezeugt.

Diese Unterschiede zur griechischen Vorlage lassen vermuten, dass die Ordnung im Euch. Karma keine direkte Übersetzung im strengen Sinne ist. Im Grunde genommen ist das Formular im KARMA zugeschriebenen Euchologion eine spätere Bearbeitung einer defekten und mangelhaften Übersetzung von KARMA selbst mit Rücksicht auf eigene liturgische Gebräuche.[67]
Es bleibt noch ein Wort zu sagen: Diese Ordnung in Euch. Karma war in der Melkitischen Kirche von Antiochien, Jerusalem und vielleicht in Alexandrien gebräuchlich, bevor die ersten arabischen Drucke des Euchologion erschienen sind. Das bezeugen die vielen liturgischen Handschriften aus dem 17. und 18. Jahrhundert.[68] Die gleiche Ordnung wird für die Patriarchenweihe verwendet.
Es interessiert uns noch die Frage nach der Form der Bischofsweihe vor der Rezension von KARMA. Hier geben uns zwei Handschriften Aufschluss. Die eine stammt aus dem 15. Jahrhundert und ist in der *Bibliothèque Orientale* der Universität St. Joseph in Beirut aufbewahrt *Beirut Orientale 867*; die andere in der Bibliothek der griechisch-melkitischen katholischen Erzdiözese Aleppo *Alep Arch. Cath. 264* (olim 224) aus dem Jahr 1544.[69]

b) Das älteste arabische Weiheformular der Bischofsweihe in der Melkitischen Kirche

BRAKMANN erwähnt zu den drei Taxeis in den venezianischen Drucken noch eine vierte Ordnung, die zu der konstantinopolitanischen Tradition zählt; es handelt sich um die Ordnung der *Diataxis des Demetrios Gemistos* (Taxis G).[70] Diese Ordnung ist eine Entwicklung von Taxis I, sie hat aber keinen Eingang in

[66] Hinaufsteigen des/der Bischöfe samt Priestern zum Synthronon, nach dem Trisagion und während des Phemê (Sessio, meistens hinter dem Altar).
[67] Die Handschrift *Alep Arch. Cath. 254* (214) [J. 1622] steht hierfür als greifbare Urquelle im Verdacht. Diese Handschrift kann von KARMA selbst stammen.
[68] Diese Ordnung ist auch im kath. Jerusalemer Großen Euchologion angeführt, allerdings nur die Rubriken in roter Schrift und in abgeänderter Form. Siehe Kapitel 6 im Euchologion, 14.
[69] Zur Beschreibung der Handschriften und Edition der Bischofsweihe in beiden Dokumenten s. Hanna GHONEIM, Ein Bischofsweiheritus in der melkitischen Kirche nach einem Dokument aus dem 15. Jahrhundert, in: Samir KHALIL SAMIR (Hg.), Actes du Colloque Melkites, Jounieh, Janvier 2008 (Parole de l'Orient 34), Jounieh 2009, 361–411. Die Bischofsweiheordnung in beiden Handschriften ist identisch mit zuweilen unterschiedlichen Textvarianten. Beide lassen sich mit den bereits erwähnten Weiheordnungen kaum vergleichen.
[70] BRAKMANN, Metrophanes (s. Anm. 3), 307–310.

die Euchologion-Drucke gefunden.[71] Grund dafür mögen m. E. die vielen Textvarianten dieses Ordo gewesen sein, der den turbulenten Zeiten des byzantinischen Reiches während und nach den Kreuzzügen, insbesondere den Zerstörungen Konstantinopels beim vierten Kreuzzug 1204 und dem daraus resultierenden Zusammenbruch der alten Kathedralliturgie der Hagia Sophia, angepasst werden musste.[72] SYMEON VON THESSALONIKE hat diese Ordnung aus einer uns heute unbekannten Vorlage gekannt, weiter entwickelt und interpretiert,[73] bis sie ihre endgültige Gestalt durch METROPHANES VON NYSSA[74] erhalten hat.[75] BRAKMANN bemerkt zu Recht eine enge Beziehung zwischen Taxis I und Taxis III; die letzte hat zum ersten Mal die verschiedenen Varianten der handschriftlichen Bischofsweihetexte abgelöst.[76]
Der Bischofsweihetext der Hs. *Beirut Orientale 867* bildet eine arabische Wiedergabe einer der Rezensionen der Diataxis von GEMISTOS[77] mit Einflüssen aus Zypern. Die griechische Vorlage bleibt uns unbekannt.

Einige Merkmale lassen Berührungen beider Ordnungen erkennen:

- Die anwesenden Bischöfe tragen weiße Phelonia;
- der Weihekandidat küsst das Knie des weihenden Bischofs;
- der Weihekandidat ist ein Mönchpriester.

Die Gestalt der Weihe in *Beirut Orientale 867* ist sehr vereinfacht dargestellt, denn die Ordnung war nicht für eine Kathedrale wie Hagia Sophia bestimmt, sondern eher für eine Klosterkirche.

71 Ebd., 307.
72 Taxis II ist eine Rezension der Taxis I auf Zypern, auf die die lateinische Hierarchie der Kreuzfahrerzeit Einfluss genommen hat. Vgl. DARROUZÈS, Textes synodaux (s. Anm. 20), 7, 14–22.
73 PG 155, 396D–425A.
74 Geboren auf der Insel Thasos, Mönch in Athos-Kloster Dionysiou; dann Hegumenos des Cotroceni-Kloster in Bukarest, zugleich Beichtvater des Fürsten der Moldau Brâncoveanu; 1707 zum (Titular-)Bischof von Nyssa geweiht; 1716 auf den Bischofsstuhl von Bukarest berufen als Nachfolger des aus Georgien stammenden Metropolit Antim IVIREANUL (1708–1716), vgl. BRAKMANN, Metrophanes (s. Anm. 3): „Wer war Metrophanes?", 318–323, bes. 321–322.
75 Vgl. die Synopse der beiden Weihefonmulare in: Daniel GERGOPOULOU, Ἱερὰ Ἀνθολογία περὶ τῶν σεπτῶν καὶ θείων ἑπτὰ μυστηρίων τῆς Ἐκκλησίας, Venedig 1833, 55–60.
76 Vgl. BRAKMANN, Metrophanes (s. Anm. 3), 310.
77 Eine Abschrift dieser Diataxis ist die Hs. *Jerusalem S. Saba 362* (607) (14. Jh. ?), ediert in: Alexander DMITRIEVSKIJ, Opisanie litugičeskich rukopisej chranjaščichsja u bibliotekach pravoslavnago vostoka, Bd. 2: Εὐχολόγια, Kiev 1901, 298–301; auch in: P. N. TREMPELAS, Μικρὸν Εὐχολόγιον, Ά: Αἱ ἀκολουθίαι καὶ τάξεις Μνήστρων καὶ Γάμου, Εὐχελαίου, Χειροτονιῶν καὶ Βαπτίσματος κατὰ τοὺς ἐν Ἀθήναις ἰδίᾳ κώδικας, Athene 1950, 253–254 (hier wird der Kodex in das 16. Jh. datiert). Der Text zum Vergleich mit dem der *Beirut Orientale 867* wurde der zweiten Edition entnommen. Andere Abschriften der Diataxis s. BRAKMANN, Metrophanes, 308. Das Original der Gemistos Diataxis ist uns nicht bekannt, die Editionen beziehen sich auf spätere Rezensionen, vgl. Alexander RENTEL, The 14th Century (s. Anm. 23), 30.

5. Zusammenfassung und Ergebnis

Die arabisch-melkitischen Rezensionen der byzantinischen Bischofsweihe sind chronologisch in vier Zweige einzuordnen:

- Die Ordnung von der Hs. *Beirut Orientale 867* als Rezension der hoch entwickelten konstantinopolitanischen Taxis I. Repräsentant dieser Ordnung ist die Diataxis des Gemistos (v. J. 1383) und später Symeon von Thessalonike.
- Die Ordnung des Euchologion von Karma ist eine Rezension der Taxis I der griechischen Euchologion-Drucke.

Nach dem Schisma 1724 im melkitischen Patriarchat von Antiochien zwischen Katholiken und Orthodoxen erkennen wir zwei Rezensionen von zwei Ordnungen aus den griechischen Euchologion-Drucken:

- Die Ordnung des Großen Euchologion Jerusalem 1865, als Übersetzung der zypriotischen Taxis II, über das griechische Euchologion Papst Benedikts XIV. (Rom 1754) aus Goar entnommen, die von den unierten Katholiken des byzantinischen Ritus befolgt wird.
- Die Ordnung des Archieratikon von Massarra Beirut 1890/1925, die eine Kombination aus Taxis II und III darstellt. Diese Ordnung hat die bisher gebrauchte griechische Ordnung aus dem Archieratikon von Konstantinopel 1820 abgelöst. Die Orthodoxen haben sich zuerst der griechischen Texte bedient, da der Patriarch und einige Bischöfe bis 1898 aus dem griechischen Sprachraum stammten. Die Ordnung des Großen Euchologion von Hawaweeny ist eine Übersetzung der Taxis III aus dem griechischen venezianischen Großen Euchologion 1885.

Wir können das Ergebnis summarisch folgendermaßen darstellen:

Taxis I (11. Jh.)	=> Rezension von Karma (1633)
Gemistos Diataxis (14. Jh.)	=> Beirut Orientale 867 (15. Jh.)
Taxis II (1575)	=> Euchologion von Jerusalem (1865) (*kath. Melkiten*)
Taxis III (1714)	=> Archieratikon von Massarra (1890) und Euchologion von Hawaweeny (1913) (*Rum-Orthodoxe*)

Damit erfahren wir, dass die Melkiten in ihrer Liturgiegeschichte alle bekannten Hauptordnungen der byzantinischen Bischofsweihe gekannt haben. Sie haben versucht sie ins Arabische zu übersetzen, das Ergebnis war die Entstehung verschiedener Weiheformulare, die nicht unbedingt mit dem Urtext ganz übereinstimmen.

5. DIE HEUTIGE PRAXIS DER BISCHOFSWEIHE BEI DEN MELKITEN

Die Rum Orthodoxen

Wie bereits erwähnt feiern die Orthodoxen des Patriarchats von Antiochien die Bischofsweihe nach der Version von MASSARRA, nur der vorbereitende Ritus A wird vor der Göttlichen Liturgie durchgeführt und nicht nach dem kleinen Einzug, wie in demselben Buch und auch in YAZIGI's Archieratikon (2006) festzustellen ist. Für die Wahl eines Bischofs haben die Orthodoxen einen eigenen Ritus, den MASSARRA in seinem Archieratikon aufführt, von dem er sagt, dass er ihn in einem Dokument im Archiv des Patriarchates gefunden habe. Dieser Ritus ist in einer anderen Form in *Beirut Orientale 867* und *Alep Arch. Cath. 264* bezeugt. Es handelt sich um eine vorausgehende zeremonielle Wahl eines Bischofs. Dieser Ritus hat keine Entsprechung sowohl in den anderen arabischen als auch in den griechischen Drucken.[78]
Die von Yuhanna YAZIJI revidierte Ordnung MASSARRAS hat noch keine allgemeine Befürwortung bei den Orthodoxen von Antiochien gefunden. Die Ordnung aus dem Großen Euchologion von HAWAWEENY wurde zugleich kaum praktiziert. HAWAWEENY führt auch die Übersetzung der Taxis II an mit Anweisung auf die Glaubensbekenntnisse, Formeln und Gebete in der übersetzten Taxis III.

Die katholischen Melkiten

Die Katholiken haben bis Ende der 80er Jahre des vergangenen Jahrhunderts die Version im Jerusalemer Euchologion 1865 (Übersetzung von Taxis II) verwendet. Diese wurde aber immer als korrekturbedürftig angesehen. Niemand wagte – vielleicht mangels fachlicher Kompetenzen – den Versuch, eine neue korrigierte Fassung für die Bischofsweihe vorzulegen. Die Revision des erwähnten Euchologion steht immer noch als Desiderat an. Eine neue Fassung benötigt Rückgriff auf die Quellen, oder gar auf die Ordnungen anderer byzantinischer Traditionen. Da die Fülle der Textvarianten im Umlauf so groß ist, legt sich die Versuchung nahe, dass es frei stehe, aus den verschiedenen Rituselementen eine jeweils neue Weiheordnung zu komponieren. Hierher zählt auch die Vorlage von Euthymios SKAF BS[79] (1914–2005). Er hat 1983 dem heiligen Synod eine

[78] MASSARRA vermerkt, dass dieser Erwählungsritus ein alter Brauch im Patriarchat Antiochien sei. SYMEON VON THESSALONIKE kennt diesen Ritus, vgl. PG 155, 401–407 (Kap. 191–197). – Auch die slavischen Arkhieratiká kennen diesen Ritus der Erwählung in einfacherer Form, s. das ruthenische Arkhieratikon (s. Anm. 14), 251–253, der russische Chinovnik, Moskau 1983, Tom. 2, 5–9. Hinweis von Dr. Stephan J. KOSTER.

[79] Aftīmōs SKAF († 2005), kath. melk. Basilianer Salvatorianer, nach Theologie- und Philosophiestudium am Angelicum in Rom 1939 zum Priester geweiht, sein Lehrer für Liturgie war Placide DE MEESTER, mit Ausbruch des zweiten Weltkrieges Rückkehr 1940 ins Mutterhaus seines Ordens in Ǧūn (nahe von Sidon), im Priesterseminar der Kongregation

Ordnung vorgeschlagen, deren Grundlage eine Beschreibung des Ritus von Placide De Meester OSB bildet.[80] Die von De Meester dargestellte Weiheform ist kein Weiheformular zum liturgischen Gebrauch, sondern eine wissenschaftliche Darlegung der byzantinischen Weiheelemente. Basis dieser Darstellung ist das römische Euchologion von 1754 und die Ausführungen des Symeon von Thessalonike. Skaf fügt in seinem vorgeschlagenen Weiheformular zu den Rubriken seinerseits eigene Überschriften hinzu, um die liturgischen Vollzüge auszudeuten Skaf liefert auch eine *eigene* Kurzfassung für das zweite und dritte Glaubensbekenntnis. Die ausführliche Rezitation geschieht nämlich in seinem Vorschlag am Vorabend der Weihe. Wir können die Ordnung von Skaf als Bearbeitung der Darstellung von De Meester mit eigenen Einfügungen betrachten, die wir sonst in keinem Dokument in der byzantinischen Tradition finden.

Die vorgeschlagene Ordnung Skafs wurde nochmals von Joseph Hallit MSP[81] in sein liturgisches Werk „Anthologion"[82] eingeführt als – wie Awike in seiner Studie angibt – „die gültige Weiheordnung des griechisch-melkitischen katholischen Patriarchats von Antiochien und dem ganzen Orient, von Alexandrien und Jerusalem".[83] Es sei bemerkt, dass die Veröffentlichung dieses Anthologion nicht die Zustimmung der liturgischen Kommission und der Synode der melkitisch-katholischen Kirche gefunden hat, also einer Approbation durch die Hierarchie der Kirche entbehrt.

Die Bestrebung nach einer einheitlichen, verbindlichen Ordnung der Bischofsweihe für die (katholischen) Melkiten bleibt immer noch ein Desiderat. Diese Studie will hierzu einen kleinen Beitrag leisten. Es gilt weiterhin die Ergebnisse weiterer Forschungen der Liturgiewissenschaft im Auge zu behalten. Eine Mystagogie über die Bischofsweihe auf biblischer und patristischer Basis wäre wünschenswert zum Verständnis des Ritus und der Bedeutung des Dienstes des Bischofsamtes in der Kirche. Nicht zuletzt müsste die Bischofssynode des melkitisch-katholischen Patriarchates irgendwann eine verbindliche Ordnung der Bischofsweihe verabschieden. Denn Liturgie ist eigentlich ein Werk der Kirchengemeinschaft als Antwort auf die Gnade Gottes und keineswegs ein literarisches Werk von einzelnen Personen.

Professor für Dogmatik, Philosophie und Patristik, trotz pastoralem Einsatz Unterricht an der „Université de Saint Esprit–Kaslik" und am „Institut St. Paul–Harissa" im Libanon und kurz Liturgie am „Pontificio Istituto Orientale" in Rom, lange Jahre Mitglied der liturgischen Kommission der kath.-melk. Kirche.

80 Placide De Meester, Studi sui sacramenti secondo il rito bizantino, Rom 1947, 262–274.

81 ‚Missionaire de Saint Paul' von Harissa und Begründer des „Auferstehungsordens" in der katholischen melkitischen Kirche.

82 Joseph Hallit, Al-Anṯolōǧion ṣalawāt muḫtārat (= Das Anthologion, ausgewählte Gebete), Faraya 1988; das Buch ist eine Kompilation aus Horologion und Euchologion.

83 Awiké, Ordination épiskopale (s. Anm. 2), 3.

"JUST LIKE IN THE EARLY CHURCH": HERMENEUTICS OF THE USE OF EARLY LITURGICAL PRACTICE FOR MODERN LITURGICAL REFORM

BASILIUS J. GROEN

Those of us that ever dealt with the psychological Rorschach test know how much one's own thoughts, emotions, expectations, fears, and other experiences influence our perception.[1] In the inkblots some discern threatening dragons; others see aroused sexual organs, yet others shining suns, stars, and so on. Phenomenology teaches us that our own frame-of-mind, the way our senses function, and our emotions profoundly affect our observations. From the history of fine arts we know that many painters depict buildings, garments, or utensils which were used in the periods in which the artists themselves lived, on paintings of events from earlier times. Thus, in many Medieval or Renaissance paintings of the Annunciation or the Crucifixion, for instance, we observe that these salvific events occur in Italian, Dutch or other environments. Another interesting example concerns the parish church of St Prisca on the Aventine hill in Rome. On the altar painting by Domenico Cresti (1560-1636) we see St Peter baptizing Prisca: Peter sprinkles water from a tray upon Prisca's head whilst a boy dressed like a sixteenth- or seventeenth-century altar boy holds a service book in his hands from which Peter reads the prayers.[2] It is highly unlikely that Peter performed baptism in this way.

Numerous other examples could be given. What does all of this mean for the science of historiography? Does it mean that it is impossible to reconstruct the history of worship as it really was and that studies on liturgical history are more or less the result of our own imagination and prejudices? Can we really perceive liturgy as the Orthodox faithful of the Eastern Roman Empire saw it: "Through their own eyes"?[3] The renowned Greek author, Nikos Kazantzakis, in his key work "Asceticism, Salvatores Dei" (partly written during the author's stay in Vienna in 1922) said that our hearts should encompass the "onward march of mankind" through as many centuries as possible.[4] However, is this not a 'mis-

[1] I wish to thank Steven Hawkes-Teeples, S.J. (St. Louis) who carefully revised this text.

[2] Andrea LEMMA – Antonio LOMBARDI, La Chiesa di Santa Prisca e il suo Mitreo, Rome 2000, 15; cf. 20.

[3] Robert F. TAFT, Through Their Own Eyes: Liturgy as the Byzantines Saw It, Berkeley 2006.

[4] Nikos KAZANTZAKÊS, Askêtikê. Salvatores Dei, Athens [2]1962, 44; Nikos KAZANTZAKIS, The Saviors of God. Spiritual Exercises. Translated, with an Introduction, by Kimon FRIAR, New York 1960, 78. Kazantzakis died fifty years before the conference where this paper was given, viz. on 26 October 1957.

sion impossible', because our hearts are so affected by passions and prejudices that we cannot perceive historical events in a more or less 'objective' way?

Here hermeneutics play an indispensable role in the encounter between us and events or persons from the remote past. The art of hermeneutics interprets and tries to understand those persons and events.[5] Using hermeneutics we realize that all of us have preconceptions, a *Vorverständnis*, prejudices, socio-cultural traditions and that all of us live in certain socio-economic conditions, in given historical, geographical, religious and ecclesiastical contexts. We also realize that we are not abstract genderless human persons, but men or women with our own specific observations.[6] Only if we become aware of these preconceptions, this *Vorverständnis* may we be able to do 'justice' to history.

The historical-critical component and method of liturgical studies with respect to the early church has made great progress during the last centuries. One needs only think of the historical-genetical method, the *liturgie comparée* and studies examining the social-cultural factors and mental attitudes.[7] Not only have the official liturgical books and the hierarchy's role been investigated, but current research projects are also examining the social, cultural, economic, and political contexts, as well as other sources, such as the architecture of churches, garments, the people's role, and devotional practices (religious popular culture, or so-called 'para-liturgy'), in order to get a more or less realistic picture of actual ritual practice and the meaning people gave it. For this, texts, buildings, artefacts like chalices and paintings, and skeletal remains including relics must suffice.[8] Yet this requires realizing our own *Vorverständnis*, our own specific con-

5 Axel BÜHLER, Hermeneutik, in: Hans Jörg SANDKÜHLER (Ed.), Enzyklopädie Philosophie. Bd. 1, Hamburg 1999, 547–551; Lutz GELDSETZER, Hermeneutik, in: Wulff D. REHFUS (Ed.), Handwörterbuch Philosophie (UTB 1830), Göttingen 2003, 382–387; Michael INWOOD, Hermeneutics, in: Edward CRAIG (Ed.), The Shorter Routledge Encyclopaedia of Philosophy, London – New York 2005, 367–368; Gaetano CHIURAZZI – Gianni VATTIMO, Ermeneutica, in: Enciclopedia Filosofica 4 ²(2006) 3547–3557; Taylor CARMAN, Phenomenology as Rigorous Science, in: Brian LEITER – Michael ROSEN (Eds.), The Oxford Handbook of Continental Philosophy, Oxford 2007, 9–29; Michael N. FORSTER, Hermeneutics, in: LEITER – ROSEN, The Oxford Handbook of Continental Philosophy, 30–74; Claus VON BORMANN, Hermeneutik. 1. Philosophisch–theologisch, in: TRE 15 (1986) 108–137; Henning SCHRÖER, Hermeneutik. 4. Praktisch–theologisch, in: Theologische Realenzyklopädie 15 (1986) 150–156; Georg WIELAND, Hermeneutik. 1. Begriff und Geschichte, in: LThK 5 (special edition 2006) 1–3. Cf. Hans–Georg GADAMER, Hermeneutik, in: Joachim RITTER (Ed.), Historisches Wörterbuch der Philosophie 3 (1974) 1061–1074.

6 Anne JENSEN, Hermeneutik. 5. Feministisch–theologisch, in: LThK 5 (special edition 2006) 8–9; Teresa BERGER, Gender Differences and the Making of Liturgical History. Lifting a Veil on Liturgy's Past, Farnham 2011.

7 For a short survey, see Albert GERHARDS – Benedikt KRANEMANN, Einführung in die Liturgiewissenschaft (Einführung Theologie), Darmstadt 2006, 35–41, 45–48.

8 Cf. Robert TAFT, Anton Baumstark's Comparative Liturgy Revisited, in: Robert TAFT – Gabriele WINKLER (Eds.), Acts of the International Congress "Comparative Liturgy Fifty Years After Anton Baumstark (1872–1948)", Rome, 25–29 September 1998 (OCA 265), Rome 2001, 191–232, here 196, fn 11.

text as well as making a careful and empathic contrast and comparison between our own world and that of early Christianity, including the difficult attempt at understanding the early Christian *Verstehenshorizont*. Hermeneutics are an essential part of the historical-critical and systematic-theological investigations done within the international school of the *liturgie comparée*[9], because they aim at understanding: they contribute to making us understand the historical developments and changes that led to current practice and help us to understand that current practice is relative, not absolute.[10]

An important objective of many a liturgical reform during the twentieth century has been to return to the worship practice of the early church. Also for the liturgical renewal inaugurated by the Second Vatican Council (1962-1965), the exploration of sources and textual resources of early Christian liturgy was (and is) a foremost goal. Thus the council also wished to contribute to inter-Christian unity. The principle of return to the sources (French: *ressourcement*) was reinforced by seminal research on liturgy, scripture, patrology and further theological history which was done during the nineteenth and twentieth centuries.[11]
What, however, do we mean by the notion 'early church'? It is broad and covers three or more centuries. Moreover, there were significant regional and other contextual differences in the early church. Some denominations, especially 'high churches' that appeal to the early church properly speaking, mean the fourth and fifth centuries: the 'golden' age of the prolific church fathers, a period of expansion and blossoming of ecclesiastical culture. Yet other faith communities, in particular Protestant 'free churches', appeal directly to the first century only to biblical evidence and reject later developments.
Furthermore, when we speak about 'return' it must be remarked that a large-scale 'return' to the period of two thousand years ago is impossible, because social and cultural contexts were quite different. In addition, there is only a small quantity of texts, objects, and buildings that has 'survived' and come

[9] See, for instance, Gabriele WINKLER – Reinhard MEßNER, Überlegungen zu den methodischen und wissenschaftstheoretischen Grundlagen der Liturgiewissenschaft, in: Theologische Quartalschrift 178 (1998) 229–243.

[10] According to Robert TAFT, Über die Liturgiewissenschaft heute, in: Theologische Quartalschrift 177 (1997) 243–255, the aim of the study of the history of worship is to understand the present situation, to develop a sense for its being relative, not absolute (247), as the past is instructive, not normative (248). Similar statements can be found in his article 'Anton Baumstark's Comparative Liturgy Revisited', 227–232. See also his study Through Their Own Eyes, 1–27: we always *interpret* historical facts.

[11] See, *e.g.*, Martin KLÖCKENER, Die Zukunft der Liturgiereform – im Widerstreit von Konzilsauftrag, notwendiger Fortschreibung und „Reform der Reform", in: Andreas REDTENBACHER (Ed.), Die Zukunft der Liturgie. Gottesdienst 40 Jahre nach dem Konzil, Innsbruck – Vienna 2004, 70–118, here 72–88; Martin KLÖCKENER, Die Vision einer lebendigen Liturgie, in: IDEM – Eduard NAGEL – Hans-Gerd WIRTZ (Eds.), Gottes Volk feiert … Anspruch und Wirklichkeit gegenwärtiger Liturgie, Trier 2002, 9–36, here 10–18; Herman WEGMAN, Liturgie in der Geschichte des Christentums, Regensburg 1994, 352–356.

down to us and we hardly know whether these witnesses, that are not uniform but often quite diverse, are truly representative of certain areas and periods. Indeed, the period of the early church is constitutive for the Christian religion, but differentiation is most necessary when speaking of this period.[12]
As Robert Taft says, the past cannot be normative, but it may be instructive.[13] At the same time, elements that are fundamental for Christian faith, such as scripture, the creed, baptism, eucharist, and ministry, as well as diakonia and justice, remain normative. Yet these elements are historical, their forms continuously change, and churches have different opinions about the significance of these historical forms.
In particular, ministry is the object of many inter-ecclesiastical differences of opinion. Both 'high' and 'low' churches base their ministry forms on the so-called 'early church'. Orthodox and Roman Catholic canon law, for instance, prescribes the maleness of episcopacy, priesthood and diaconate, presupposing that this regulation originates from the New Testament and early church. However, feminist and other critical theologians – also within the Orthodox and Roman Catholic churches – assert that the authorities of their faith communities overlook sources from the apostolic age of women presiding in liturgical assemblies.[14] For their part, the 'free churches', that have various other forms of ministry, claim that these are biblical and, therefore, genuine. Another example concerns the reinstatement of the permanent deaconate during the Second Vatican Council (*Lumen Gentium*, No. 29). Thereby, the council, too, appealed to the 'early church'. However, the council's permission for deacons to preside at certain sacramental celebrations, such as baptism and matrimony, is not the result of historical investigations but of present-day pastoral need.[15]

[12] Reinhard MEßNER, Über einige Aufgaben bei der Erforschung der Liturgiegeschichte der frühen Kirche, in: Martin KLÖCKENER – Benedikt KRANEMANN – Angelus A. HÄUßLING (Eds.), Liturgie verstehen. Ansatz, Ziele und Aufgaben der Liturgiewissenschaft (ALW 50 (2008)), Fribourg 2008, 207–230; Martin WALLRAFF, Spätantike Liturgien und ihr normativer Wert in den Liturgiereformen des 20. Jahrhunderts, in: Benedikt KRANEMANN – Helmut Jan SOBECZKO (Eds.), Liturgie in kulturellen Kontexten. Messbuchreform als Thema der Liturgiewissenschaft. Liturgia w kontekstach kulturowych – reforma mszału w Kościołach krajów europejskich XX w. (Colloquia Theologica 11), Opole – Trier 2010, 39–60.

[13] See fn. 10.

[14] See, e.g., Ute E. EISEN, Amtsträgerinnen im frühen Christentum. Epigraphische und literarische Studien (Forschungen zur Kirchen- und Dogmengeschichte 61), Göttingen 1996; Kevin MADIGAN – Carolyn OSIEK, Ordained Women in the Early Church. A Documentary History, Baltimore 2005; Gary MACY, The Hidden History of Women's Ordination. Female Clergy in the Medieval West, Oxford 2008.

[15] Josephus ALBERIGO et al., Conciliorum Oecumenicorum Decreta, Bologna ^{3}1973, 874. Cf. Peter NISSEN, Het Tweede Vaticaans Concilie en het herstel van het permanente diaconaat, in: Gian ACKERMANS – Adelbert DAVIDS – Peter NISSEN (Eds.), Kerk in beraad. Opstellen aangeboden aan prof. dr. J.C.P.A. van Laarhoven bij gelegenheid van zijn afscheid als hoogleraar aan de Katholieke Universiteit Nijmegen, Nijmegen 1991, 301–319; Stephan STEGER, Der Ständige Diakon und die Liturgie. Anspruch und Lebenswirklichkeit eines wiedererrichteten Dienstes (Studien zur Pastoralliturgie 19), Regensburg 2006, 65–165; Christian WESSELY, Gekommen, um zu dienen. Der Diakonat aus funda-

Here I shall briefly examine two cases. Firstly, I discuss the anointing of the sick, limiting myself to the Western liturgical tradition. Secondly, I investigate iconography, concentrating on the Eastern liturgical tradition. I realize that the anointing of the sick is also celebrated in Eastern Christianity and that also Western Christian churches have sacred art, but for reasons of limitation I will not make further explorations in these fields. Finally, I shall make some reflections on the relationship between liturgical research and ecumenism.

ANOINTING OF THE SICK

As is well known, during the Second Vatican Council, the decision was taken to reform the theory and practice of the anointing of the sick. The name 'anointing of the sick' (*unctio infirmorum*) was chosen instead of 'extreme unction', 'last anointing' (*extrema unctio*) and it was decided that this was not only for the dying, but could also be given to the sick and elderly who were in peril of death. The order penance – viaticum – anointing was also reinstated in the original form, namely penance – anointing – viaticum. This again made it clear that, as in the Orthodox Church, not the unction, but 'last communion' is the real sacrament for the dying. In addition, the council laid down that the number of unctions had to be adapted and the prayers revised.[16]

In 1972, the new Roman rite for the anointing of the sick appeared.[17] According to the *Ordo*, unction is for those weakened by severe illness and age. The basic form consists of the following elements: greeting, confession, scripture reading, intercessions, laying-on of hands, prayer of blessing or thanksgiving over the oil, anointing, a prayer for healing or for the situation in question, Our Father, and the final blessing. The formula for the anointing contains assistance, forgiveness of sins, salvation and alleviation. Foreheads and hands are anointed. Only a priest may perform the ceremony of anointing. Unction of the sick can also take place during the eucharist, between the 'service of the word' and the eucharistic liturgy itself. Further, in the case of imminent death, the *ritus continuus*, that is confession, anointing and viaticum applies.

mentaltheologisch–ekklesiologischer Sicht, Regensburg 2004, 20–46; Margret MORCHE, Zur Erneuerung des Ständigen Diakonats. Ein Beitrag zur Geschichte unter besonderer Berücksichtigung der Arbeit des Internationalen Diakonatszentrums in seiner Verbindung zum Deutschen Caritasverband, Freiburg i.B. 1996; Klemens ARMBRUSTER – Matthias MÜHL (Eds.), Bereit wozu? Geweiht für was? Zur Diskussion um den ständigen Diakonat (Quaestiones Disputatae 232), Freiburg i.B. 2009.

16 Sacrosanctum Concilium 73–75. See ALBERIGO, Conciliorum Oecumenicorum Decreta, 834.

17 Ordo unctionis infirmorum eorumque pastoralis curae, Vatican City 1972. A second, slightly adapted edition appeared in 1975.

A year before (1971), the new formula for the blessing of the oils during the Chrism Mass in the cathedral on Maundy Thursday had appeared.[18] In that mass, not only the oil for the catechumens and the oil for the sick are blessed and the chrism is consecrated, but the priests of the diocese must also renew their vows of allegiance to the bishop. During the blessing of the oil for the sick, the presence of the Holy Spirit is invoked on the oil, so that God protect body, soul and spirit, banishing pain and illness.

Did Roman Catholic 'decision makers' (mainly the pope, cardinals and bishops as well as several theologians) take the results of historical-critical studies into account? Which elements did they adopt, which ones not? What was their *Vorverständnis*? Let us have a look at the practice of anointing the sick in the early church. We shall also examine whether the conciliar reform has been 'successful' so far.

An important function of oil – usually olive oil – in Mediterranean regions was alleviating pain and healing wounds.[19] For instance, the Good Samaritan poured oil and wine on the victim's wounds (Luke 10:34) and the Gospel of Mark reports that the twelve apostles anointed the sick with oil and healed them (Mark 6:13). When anointing is done together with a prayer to the Lord, as, for instance, in the Letter of James (James 5:14-16a), we already have the first phase of the historical development of the anointing of the sick. This rite, that is anointing with oil with a prayer, was, in early Christianity, aimed in the first place at curing the illness and secondarily – and then only in combination with the illness – at the forgiveness of sin and the curing of the soul. However, these aspects may not be played off against one another, because in the early church, there is a close link between: a) sickness, sin and possession; b) forgiveness, healing, and liberation from demons; and c) anointing, penance, and exorcism. These sicknesses were both minor and serious ones, including handicaps such as blindness and possession by evil spirits. Dying persons could be anointed, too, maybe penitents as well. The Syrian author, Pseudo-Dionysius Areopagite (ca. 500), also describes the unction of deceased persons.
Anybody could anoint the sufferer: lay persons, monks, nuns, deacons, deaconesses, or priests. It was also possible for the sick person to anoint him- or herself

[18] Ordo benedicendi oleum catechumenorum et infirmorum et conficiendi chrisma, Vatican City 1971. Other liturgical books, namely the Lectionary, the Missal and the Ceremonial, contain more regulations on the blessing of oils on this day. See Ordo lectionum missae, Vatican City 1969, 25; Lectionarium 1. De tempore. Ab Adventu ad Pentecostem, Vatican City 1970, 652–654; Missale Romanum ex decreto sacrosancti oecumenici concilii vaticani II instauratum auctoritate Pauli pp. VI promulgatum, editio typica tertia, Vatican City ^{3}2002, 291–296; Caeremoniale Episcoporum, Vatican City 1984, 83–86 (Chrism Mass), 155–158 (collective anointing of the sick).

[19] A good overview of the history of the anointing of the sick, as well as discussion of some formularies in current use can be found in Reiner KACZYNSKI, Feier der Krankensalbung, in: Sakramentliche Feiern 1/2 (GDK 7, 2), Regensburg 1992, 249–338.

or to drink or sip the oil. The liturgical accent was not on the unction or the drinking of the oil, but on its blessing. This was done by the bishop, sometimes by a priest or a monk. In several cases the oil came from a lamp that burnt in the church. In particular from the third, fourth, and fifth centuries we have a number of prayers of blessing of the oil, in which God is asked to bless the oil for the comfort and health of those who use the oil. Important sources of this are the Apostolic Tradition, the Canons of Hippolytus, the Apostolic Constitutions, the Testament of Our Lord Jesus Christ, and the Euchologion of Serapion of Thmuis. According to Pope Innocent I, the anointing with the holy ointment oil (*sancto oleo chrismatis*) that is 'made' (and blessed) by the bishop (*quod ab episcopo confectum*) may be performed by all Christians (*non solum sacerdotibus sed et omnibus uti christianis licet, in sua aut in suorum necessitate unguendum*).[20] However, the pope forbids that penitents be anointed with this oil, since it belongs to the category of sacraments (*quia genus est sacramenti*). Usually, the faithful brought the oil to the church and after its blessing they took it back home.

After the Carolingian reforms, there were changes in the Western church, of which I mention only a few. First, lay persons could no longer do the anointing; this was limited to a priest. Second, the anointing was linked with penance and the last communion, viaticum. Since penance was hard, many in the early church postponed it until the end of their lives. By linking the anointing to penance, this too was often postponed. Third, because of the high death rate, priests were ordered to anoint the dying and the very sick first. Later this order read: *Those not critically ill or dying should not be anointed.* Fourth, the text of the holy anointing with oil was included in the same service book for penance and the rituals for the dying, thus strengthening the connection of unction with the death-bed. Fifth, the spiritual effects of the anointing of the sick, in particular the forgiveness of sins, were given increasing prominence, and the bodily effects, the healing, less and less. Sixth, at the end of the Middle Ages, the order of the sacraments for the dying was changed from penance – anointing – viaticum to penance – viaticum – anointing, thus making the unction of the sick the very last ritual for the dying. Seventh, during the Middle Ages, priests were forbidden to consecrate the olive oil themselves.

Whether modern Roman Catholic liturgical renewal is consistent with the liturgical practice in the early church is a very difficult question. As I said before, socio-cultural conditions almost two millennia ago were very different. One

[20] Roger CABIÉ, La Lettre du pape Innocent Ier à Décentius de Gubbio (19 mars 416). Texte critique, traduction et commentaire (Bibliothèque de la Revue Ecclésiastique 58), Leuven 1973, 30–33, 56–61; Antoine CHAVASSE, Étude sur l'onction des infirmes dans l'Église latine du IIIe au XIe siècle. Tome 1: Du IIIe siècle à la réforme carolingienne, Lyon 1942, 89–99.

should think only of the tendency to perceive demonic activity everywhere. The most learned Greek church father, Gregory of Nazianzus, for example, was convinced that Christians including himself were attacked and tricked by demons almost all the time and that, therefore, a continuous warfare was required.[21] His namesake, the Roman pope, Gregory the Great, usually advised people to make the sign of a cross over lettuce before eating it, lest a demon sitting on one of the leaves would cause damage.[22]

The conciliar reform certainly widened the theology of extreme unction, maybe the most neglected sacrament. However, the regulation that those who are anointed must be *very seriously* sick (*pericolose aegrotans*)[23] is actually a compromise between early Christian and medieval Western practice. Would it not be more fitting if anointing could be provided for all who find themselves sick, bodily or mentally, in a crisis, in other words, all afflicted people in the broadest sense, and not only weakened elderly or very sick people? Do not authentic 'prayer of faith', the laying-on of hands and anointing with olive oil strongly appeal to the senses of many infirm and can they not promote wholeness? Is not the anointing a ritual for the healing of the whole person; a celebration for the meeting between God and Man and between people in a crisis situation, in which being broken and the contingency of human existence are felt in one's own body; a celebration, in which God's 'friendliness to humankind' (*Philanthropia*) can be passed on to us all; or a sacrament that can make any sick person receptive to God's mystery and, at the same time, give strength?[24] These questions need further investigation, also in an ecumenical setting.

One also has to be aware of diachronicity and the co-existence of incongruent phenomena: a) Medieval Scholastic theology and canons of the Council of Trent; b) twentieth-century theological approaches (Louis-Marie Chauvet, Karl Rahner, and Edward Schillebeeckx, for instance); c) the renewed rites after the Second Vatican Council and their attempt at a *ressourcement* to early Christianity; d) various ritual and devotional practices. These opinions and practices,

[21] Dayna S. KALLERES, Demons and Divine Illumination. A Consideration of Eight Prayers by Gregory of Nazianzus, in: Vigiliae Christianae 61 (2007) 157–188.

[22] William DALRYMPLE, From the Holy Mountain. A Journey in the Shadow of Byzantium, London 1997, 55.

[23] Ordo unctionis infirmorum eorumque pastoralis curae, 14 (no. 5), 15 (no. 8).

[24] See, for instance, Josef LAMBERTS, Geborgen in Zijn liefde. Het sacrament van de ziekenzalving (Woord en Beleving 14), Tielt 1987; Cor TRAETS, The Sick and Suffering Person. A Liturgical/Sacramental Approach, in: Questions Liturgiques 71 (1990) 30–49; Bert GROEN, Ziekenzalving in een algemeen ziekenhuis. Perspectieven, in: Ad BLIJLEVENS et al. (Eds.), Liturgie met zieken. Vol. 1, Baarn 1993, 152–174, here 154–155, 160, 162–163; Karin E. LEITER, Wenn Gott uns streichelt. Krankensalbung erleben, Innsbruck 1997. Cf. Adolf KNAUBER, Salbung und Gebet des Glaubens. Das apostolische Sakrament der Kranken. Liturgie, Pastoral, Spiritualität, Doktrin der Krankensalbung (pastoral–katechetische Hefte 60), Leipzig 1978, 50–51, 69, 71–72.

which date from very different periods, actually co-exist nowadays, and this inevitable phenomenon may cause confusion and tension.[25]

Another thorny issue concerns the celebrant. The discussion of the *minister proprius* in the Roman Catholic Church is not only related to the present problems of ministry and ordination, but is also fed by the fact that there have been many different moments as the principal focus of the celebration in the course of history. As I mentioned before, according to several third-, fourth-, and fifth-century sources, the sacerdotal liturgical moment was the blessing of the oil, not the anointing itself. One could envisage the 'up-grading' of the bishop's blessing of the oil during the Chrism Mass. In order to clarify the bishop's blessing of the oil and parish practice, it is essential to festively present the blessed oils in the parish church, for instance during the Last Supper Mass on Maundy Thursday and that prayers are said for those to be anointed with it in the coming year.[26]

For the subject of this article it is also relevant to point at the different ways how the words 'elders of the church' (*presbyterous tês ekklêsias*) from the Letter of James (5:14) often have been translated. Some authors, especially Roman Catholics and Orthodox, used to render this passage with 'priests of the church', whilst others, Protestants in particular, preferred 'elders of the congregation', not to mention middle courses and other variations. Their interpretation was probably also influenced by the denominations to which they belonged. Although nowadays many exegetes work with historical-critical methods, differences in ecclesial backgrounds may still play a significant role in the interpretation of several scriptural passages. One need only think of Matthew 16:18 and discussions on ministry and primacy.

More ecclesiological and ecumenical research is necessary on the issue of the presider of the celebration of anointing, especially on the question whether all those who, in the name of the church, are working in pastoral care and liturgy for the sick, can be authorized to anoint. Comparison with distribution of holy communion by lay persons comes to mind. Amongst most Western European Catholic liturgical scholars, there is consensus that performing anointing should not be limited to priests. Nevertheless, on 11 February 2005, the Vatican Congregation for the Doctrine of the Faith repeated the regulation of present canon law (*omnis et solus sacerdos*, Canon 1003, Art. 1)[27] laying down that only a priest may administer the anointing of the sick and that 'this doctrine has to be kept for ever' (*definitive tenenda*).[28]

[25] Patrick PRÉTOT, Sacrements et guérison. Un essai de typologie des relations entre deux dimensions de salut, in: MD 245 (2006/1) 7–46, here 40–42.

[26] See the relevant practical suggestions in Iris BLECKER, Zur Heilung und Stärkung. Die Heiligen Öle und ihr Empfang in der Gemeinde, in: praxis gottesdienst 2004, no. 4, 1.

[27] Codex Iuris Canonici, Vatican City 1983, 177.

[28] Osservatore Romano, 21 October 2005; www.vatican.va (accessed throughout 2007 and 2008). Cf. Czesław KRAKOWIAK, Czy diakoni i wierni świeccy mogą udzielać sakramentu namaszczenia chorych? in: Roczniki Teologiczne 54 (2007) 8, 119–139; Bruno Fabio

One could also investigate whether the participants, as in the early church, could anoint one another. This is also done in the Orthodox Church in which, after the celebration of the sacrament of the anointing of the sick, many participants fill little bottles with the consecrated oil and take it home for use when they need it. The sacraments of the Orthodox Church are fully recognized by the Roman Catholic Church, including that of the anointing of the sick and its form of celebration. For centuries, the Western church has adopted many liturgical elements from the Eastern church. Here too the Western church could follow Eastern practice, if it chose to do so.

The burden of the past, namely the anointing of the sick as extreme unction, with the priest as herald of death, will have to be borne a little longer in the *Romana*. This becomes clear if we look at present-day practice. In Western Europe, to which I now limit myself, clearly not all the goals of reform have been fulfilled. The practice of only anointing the dying is still prominent in most Roman Catholic parishes, in hospitals, and nursing homes, in continuity with the medieval past. Only the name is often adapted: 'Sacrament for the sick' or 'anointing of the sick' instead of 'extreme unction'. In many cases, the administration of the last sacraments is a hasty affair, sometimes in the middle of the night, while the dying person has already lost consciousness. The next of kin are often present. However, only a minority of dying Roman Catholic patients are anointed. Most of them die without the last rites. Sometimes, as a sign of comfort and farewell for the family, a recently dead person is anointed. But also renewal occurs: sometimes anointing is practiced in the case of serious illness for giving strength and relief – in accordance with liturgical reform initiated by the Second Vatican Council. Incidentally, the practice of extreme unction must not only be seen negatively – as a sign that liturgical renewal is rejected – since it was, and still is, an important transition ritual for the dying.[29]

PIGHIN, Diritto sacramentale (Istituto di Diritto Canonico San Pio X. Manuali 1), Venice 2006, 308–310. See also Ilona RIEDEL–SPANGENBERGER, Das Gewohnheitsrecht in der katholischen Kirche. Zur Spendung der Krankensalbung durch Diakone und Laien, in: Trierer Theologische Zeitschrift 103 (1994) 188–201; Pierre–Marie GY, La question du ministre de l'onction des malades, in: MD 205 (1996/1) 15–24; Andreas HEINZ, Die Krankensalbung im spätantiken Gallien. Das Zeugnis der Martinsschriften des Sulpicius Severus (um 400), in: Trierer Theologische Zeitschrift 106 (1997) 271–287; Franz–Josef NOCKE, Sakramententheologie. Ein Handbuch, Düsseldorf 1997, 233; Peter HÜNERMANN, Das Apostolat für die Kranken und das Sakrament der Krankensalbung. Dogmatische Überlegungen anlässlich der römischen Instruktion vom 13. 11. 1997, in: Theologische Quartalschrift 178 (1998) 29–38; Philippe ROUILLARD, The Anointing of the Sick in the West, in: Anscar J. CHUPUNGCO (Ed.), Handbook for Liturgical Studies. 4: Sacraments and Sacramentals, Collegeville 2000, 171–190, here 186–187.

29 See also the discussion and suggestions in: Andrea GRILLO – Eugenio SAPORI (Eds.), Celebrare il sacramento dell'unzione degli infermi (BEL.S 130), Rome 2005; Genevieve GLEN (Ed.), Recovering the Riches of Anointing. A Study of the Sacrament of the Sick. An International Symposium. The National Association of Catholic Chaplains, Collegeville 2002; Lizette LARSON–MILLER, The Sacrament of Anointing of the Sick (Lex Orandi Series), Collegeville 2005; Bert GROEN, Die Krankensalbung und ihr Platz in der heutigen Krankenhausseelsorge, in: Heiliger Dienst 59 (2005) 100–118.

Furthermore, in many parishes it is increasingly developing into a celebration 'for encouragement and strengthening' of older people. It is then – for instance, during the annual 'Sunday of the Sick' – celebrated as a collective anointing of the sick, sometimes during a normal Sunday service, sometimes during a special celebration of the eucharist. A corporate unction better demonstrates the parish's solidarity and its warmth can be better felt. Besides, in this case the sick can experience it more as a sacrament for recovery, rather than for resignation. Usually, far more women than men participate.

The actual celebrant of the anointing ritual is no longer always a priest. This is the case in many Western European large hospitals, where the pastoral teams mostly consist of both Catholics and Protestants, both ordained and non-ordained. The men and women in these teams often collaborate closely, also in liturgical matters; the various wards are often divided between the team-members. It does not matter to many patients whether they receive pastoral care from a priest or a (female) pastoral worker or a Protestant minister, including the liturgical celebration. They are only interested in the care and trust, not the denomination. It therefore often happens that anointing is provided by a pastoral worker. In countries with a population of mixed denominations, such as Germany and the Netherlands, it sometimes happens that Protestant pastors who have just rediscovered the unction of the sick, provide this for Roman Catholics.[30] Yet in several other large hospitals, for example in the academic hospital of Vienna, a different policy is pursued, viz. the continuous availability of a priest for the entire hospital, for the administration of the anointing of the sick.[31]

Let us now concentrate on other Western churches. The sixteenth-century Reformation held that the anointing of the sick did not originate from Jesus Christ himself – this being the criterion for ecclesiastical administration of sacraments – and that the practice of extreme unction was in sharp contrast to the anointing of the sick in the time of the New Testament (in particular James 5:14-15) and the early church. Some Reformers also thought that the gift of grace, the charisma of healing had ceased after the initial period of Christianity and that for this reason a religious 'ritual of healing' was superfluous. Because of these arguments, the anointing of the sick as a sacrament was stopped and it disappeared from Protestant liturgy for some four centuries.

After centuries-long negation, more interest in the anointing of the sick was shown within the Reformed churches during the second half of the twentieth century, both for research and for practical pastoral care. (Here, I limit myself to

[30] Cf. Corja MENKEN–BEKIUS, Rituelen in het individuele pastoraat. Een praktisch–theologisch onderzoek, Kampen ^{2}2000, 71–72; cf. 220; EADEM, Werken met rituelen in het pastoraat, Kampen 2001, 61, 85–89.

[31] For several formularies used in the Vienna academic hospital, see Jeannette REHM – Gerhard GARY (Eds.), Dein Bleiben war nur geliehen. Abschiedsriten und Liturgien mit Sterbenden im Krankenhaus, Innsbruck 2007.

the Anglican Communion and the Lutheran and Reformed churches. Anointing of the sick, the dipping of cloths in oil in order to brush the sick with them, and so on, have existed much longer in several Pentecostal and a few other Protestant denominations.) This rebirth of anointing must be seen in the context of the general rediscovery of liturgical elements by Protestant pastors and theologians. For a long time, the spoken and heard word (in particular, scripture reading and sermon) was considered much more important than non-verbal signs. 'Life rituals' performed by ministers, such as baptism, marriage, and burial, were thought to be less important than the sermon service. However, at the end of the twentieth century, these ceremonies underwent a revival and were ever more regarded as 'blessing places'. Furthermore, ecumenical contacts and research into the traditions of other churches encouraged the Protestant liturgical movement. The great interest in the body, its health, well-being, 'wellness', and human self-development in the Western world of today probably also contributed to the interest in anointing.[32]

The anointing of the sick has been rediscovered in the Anglican community, and both the Church of England and other denominations within the Anglican Communion, such as the Episcopal Church in the United States of America, have adopted the anointing of the sick in their service books. Also the British Methodists, the Church of Sweden, the Protestant Church in the Netherlands, the United Evangelical-Lutheran Church of Germany (VELKD), the American Lutherans, the American Baptist Church, the United Church of Christ, and other denominations have included unction of the sick in their new service books.

In addition, in several Western European cities, there is great interest in 'anointing services' (*Salbungsgottesdienste*) and the Thomas Masses – liturgical services for those on the border or outside the church – during which laying-on of hands and anointing may take place for those who ask for a personal blessing.[33]

Besides enthusiasm on the part of many Protestant Christians, other members of the Reformed churches are uneasy and fearful. There is, on the one hand, fear of so-called 'Roman Catholic ritualism' and magic and, on the other, fear of the sensational healing services of the American Pentecostal movement, which aim, not only at spiritual re-awakening, but also very much at bodily healing. Good explanations and clarifications within the *Reformata* are therefore very im-

[32] Michael MEYER–BLANCK, Zeichen und Worte im Ernstfall. Das gottesdienstliche Handeln im Krankenhaus und die gegenwärtige Kasualdebatte, in: Wege zum Menschen 50 (1998) 408–421, here 414, 417–420.

[33] See, *inter alia*, Thomas DEGENHARDT – Henner FLÜGGER, Die Thomas–Messe im Bremer St. Petri–Dom. Ein Praxisbericht, in: Jahrbuch für Liturgik und Hymnologie 37 (1998) 80–86, here 85; Heikki KOTILA, Die Thomasmesse. Eine finnische Volksbewegung zur Erneuerung des gottesdienstlichen Lebens, in: JLH 38 (1999) 65–87, here 74, 77, 80; Tillman HABERER, Die Thomasmesse. Ein Gottesdienst für Ungläubige, Zweifler und andere gute Christen, Munich 2000, 89–93, 149–161; Waldemar PISARSKI, Gott tut gut. Salbungsgottesdienste – Grundlagen und Modelle, Munich 2000.

portant, say the protagonists of the anointing ritual. One also points to the reality that only few become healthy again and that everyone dies in the end.
Many Protestant theologians and pastors call the anointing of the sick a 'ritual' or a 'symbolic act' and avoid the term 'sacrament'.[34] Some Anglican theologians call it 'sacramental'[35], but other Anglicans say 'quasi-sacramental'.[36] Here also more discussion with other Western and Eastern churches and theologies is desirable.
The Protestant lack of experience with the anointing of the sick creates openness for new ways and directions. In some churches, for instance in the German Lutheran church, the question of who does the anointing, is answered in a rather 'liberal' way, i.e. not only ordained ministers, but also any well-prepared visitor of the sick can undertake the anointing. However, in the Church of England, any authorised lay-person can perform the imposition of hands, but anointing must be performed by a priest. Also the question of who the recipients are is generally answered in a 'liberal' way, namely the sick in general. Some theologians even advocate that all those present be anointed, since those who allegedly are not infirm also experience the limits of life and since by way of unction empathy with the ailing person is strengthened. Sometimes there is a request for all those present to anoint each other.[37]

ICONOGRAPHY

As a reaction against the opaque iconostasis and an attempt to return to 'the' early Christian liturgical tradition, in several new Orthodox church buildings, for instance in the diocese of Neapolis in Thessalonica, the iconostasis is low (knee- or waist-height) and the people in the nave can easily discern the altar and the liturgical action taking place there. This is also meant to reinforce the active participation of the people in the services. The icons of Jesus Christ, the Mother of God and saints, such as John the Baptist and the church's patron, are

34 Thus, *e.g.*, Frieder SCHULZ, Die Salbung als neu entdeckte Zeichenhandlung. Information über den Gesprächsstand in den evangelischen Kirchen, in: Liturgisches Jahrbuch 48 (1998) 183–189; MENKEN–BEKIUS, Werken met rituelen 61, 85.

35 For instance, several older studies, such as Charles GUSMER, The Ministry of Healing in the Church of England. An Ecumenical–Liturgical Study (Alcuin Club Collections 56), Great Wakering Essex 1974, 117–128; Norman AUTTON, Watch with the Sick, London 1976, 12–13, 32–36.

36 For instance, Colin BUCHANAN, Services for Wholeness and Healing. The Common Worship Orders (Grove Worship Series 161), Cambridge 2000, 16. He argues that an explicit institution of the anointing of the sick by the Lord, required for a sacrament, is missing.

37 Ute MEYER ZU LENZINGHAUSEN, Krankensalbung in der evangelischen Klinikseelsorge. Ein Ritual wird neu entdeckt (Schriftenreihe der Evangelischen Fachhochschule Freiburg 7), Münster 1999, 59–62. MENKEN–BEKIUS, Werken met rituelen, 88 points out that the other participants can show their sympathy by a kiss, a caress, a handshake or their participation in the laying–on of hands.

placed upon small columns or upon a low gate.[38] Such a lowering of the iconostasis provokes contrasting reactions. Proponents are convinced that Eastern Orthodoxy also needs liturgical renewal. Opponents claim that Eastern liturgical worship is the authentic continuation of early Christian liturgy – "*Ostkirche ist Urkiche*" – and that therefore liturgical reform is neither necessary nor appropriate. Yet Thomas Pott, from the Benedictine monastery of Chevetogne, has shown that liturgical reform is an essential part of the history of the Byzantine rite[39] and Marcel Mojzeš has described the process of liturgical reform in Russia and Greece at the beginning of the twentieth century.[40] During the first international congress of the Society of Oriental Liturgy in Eichstätt in July 2006, the Orthodox liturgist, Pavlos Koumarianos, read a paper on the spread of the liturgical movement in Greece.[41] In the same country, important congresses on liturgical reform have been held for several years.

An essential question is which *Vorverständnis* proponents and opponents of the lower iconostasis and of liturgical renewal have. Let me first sketch some historical developments.

'Gradually' and 'slowly' are two key words when we discuss the question of when icons acquired a steady place in the liturgy. The emergence of sacred images of Jesus Christ, Mary, angels, and saints in early Christianity was a long process. The veneration of these images developed only gradually. Discussions of the meaning of these images lasted for centuries and were sometimes very intense and even violent. In the same way the holy images made according to the traditions of the Eastern churches only acquired a central and irrevocable place many centuries after the emergence of the Christian religion.[42]

The first followers of Jesus of Nazareth were Jews who were convinced that in Him the Messiah had come. In the earliest phases of Christian liturgy, pictorial images probably played no role, because the liturgy consisted primarily of prayer, lessons, words of explanation and catechesis, singing, eucharist with bread and wine, baptism with water, signs, such as imposition of hands and anointing with oil, etc. The written and heard word of scripture was accentuated. There

38 Peter GALADZA, The Role of Icons in Byzantine Worship, in: StLi 21 (1991) 113–135, here 134–135.

39 Thomas POTT, La réforme liturgique byzantine. Étude du phénomène de l'évolution non–spontanée de la liturgie byzantine (BEL.S 104), Rome 2000. English translation, authorized by the author: IDEM, Byzantine Liturgical Reform. A Study of Liturgical Change in the Byzantine Tradition, transl. Paul MEYENDORFF, preface Robert TAFT (The Orthodox Liturgy Series 2), Crestwood/New York 2010.

40 Marcel MOJZEŠ, Il movimento liturgico nelle chiese bizantine. Analisi di alcune tendenze di riforma nel XX secolo (BEL.S 132), Rome 2005.

41 Pavlos KOUMARIANOS, Liturgical 'Rebirth' in the Modern Church of Greece. An Ambiguous Effort for a Liturgical Reform, in: Bolletino della Badia Greca di Grottaferrata III series 4 (2007) 119–144.

42 Helmut FISCHER, Die Ikone. Ursprung, Sinn, Gestalt, Hannover 2001, 21–70; Nikolaus THON, Ikone und Liturgie (Sophia 19), Trier 1979, 29–75; Boris ROTHEMUND, Handbuch der Ikonenkunst, Bd. 1, Munich ^{3}1985, 18–68, 252–264.

was no place for sacred visual art, also because the decalogue prohibited making and venerating divine images. The transcendent God is beyond all images made by human hands and venerating such images is even mocked (*e.g.*, Isaiah 44: 9-20). In addition, early Christian theologians rejected the cult of images in other religions, syncretism, and the obligation to sacrifice to the representation of the Roman emperor. (Nevertheless, especially during persecution periods, many Christians made the compulsory sacrifice to the imperial image.) According to St Paul and other proclaimers and theologians of the 'good news', the believers themselves are the temple of God, if they live according to His will, and idols are false (cf. 1 Corinthians 6:16).

Yet in the course of the second century, Christians began to make images of persons and objects that were important for their faith: not only floral, faunal and pastoral designs, and the *orans* figure, but also signs like the Christ monogram and the fish (*ichthus*), a (eucharistic) meal, Old Testament and New Testament scenes. We also see figurative images of Christ Himself.

Making images of holy persons and events in liturgical spaces was strongly promoted during the fourth century when Christianity became an allowed, then privileged and finally the official state religion in the Roman Empire. The cult of images was also promoted by the need of ordinary, 'simple' Christians to have something tangible and visible. Theological debates, 'bare' monastic spirituality did not move their hearts. Concrete depictions of the protagonists of their religion, relics, and souvenirs filled their religious needs much better. Moreover, they wanted powerful protectors in difficult and risky everyday life. They were looking for comforters who made them feel safe, mediators to whom they could entrust their worries. Christ as *pantokratôr* and Mary as the 'mistress' and the caring 'lady' (*despoina*) fulfilled this need.

Furthermore, the liturgy more and more resembled a series of solemn rites in which the mysteries of salvation were ritually represented and the Son of God was worshipped and glorified. The imperial court in Constantinople and its participation in the liturgy resulted in the adoption of many imperial court rituals in the Christian liturgy, making it even more magnificent.

In the growing veneration of icons, intellectual theology was not a leader, but theology reacted to popular 'material spirituality'.[43] Prominent theologians, such as Tertullian and Origen, had a negative attitude toward the images. During the fourth century, however – now that sacred depictions were widespread – many church fathers, for instance, Basil the Great, Gregory of Nazianzus, and John Chrysostom, were fairly positive, that is to say: they pointed out the positive aspects of the scenes that depicted biblical persons and events. It is doubtful if in this way they also approved the *veneration* of sacred images. Asking this

[43] Anton J. VAN DER AALST, De betekenis van de ikonen, in: IDEM – Anton JACOBS – Cees KRIJNSEN (Eds.), Gebed in beelden. Feestikonen in de oosterse kerken, Baarn 1991, 11–29, here 12.

question is somewhat anachronistic, because the veneration of such images was still 'in its infancy'. Incidentally, there were also some theologians and bishops who were not in favour of sacred images at all.[44] Epiphanius of Salamis, for instance, strongly disapproved of them. Eusebius of Caesarea was (at least) indifferent, probably opposed to them. It is, however, not certain whether his letter to the sister of the Emperor Constantine, in which he rebukes her for her request to him to send her a representation of Christ, is authentic.[45] It is interesting to note that some present proponents of the veneration of icons tend to neglect such critical patristic voices and wish to believe – without scholarly investigations – that, for example, the correspondence of Eusebius regarding his rejection of sacred images definitely is a falsification. Are we not tempted to see what we want to see, and to overlook or reject that what we do not wish to see?

By now the old Judaeo-Christian 'prohibition of images' and the former refusal to venerate the portrait of the pagan emperor had retreated into the background. The emperor himself was now a Christian and the relationship with Judaism had become most problematic. Dominant Christianity liked to consider itself the true Israel and thought that many prescriptions from the *Tanakh* had been necessary before the coming of Christ, but were no longer valid now that Grace was abundant.

During the sixth and seventh centuries, in a multitude of churches all over the Eastern Roman Empire, the veneration of holy images was usual. Some sources mention kissing and burning incense and lights.[46] In addition, icons were ritually washed, incensed, anointed and carried around in processions.

In many fourth- and fifth-century church buildings, there was a barrier between the sanctuary and the nave (*cancelli*), initially a kind of low gate of about one meter high. Important reasons of this partition were the wish to maintain order in the full churches, the growing opinion that only liturgical officiants – especially clergymen – ought to enter the 'Holy of Holies', and that 'the people' have their own place in the nave.[47] Soon little columns with an architrave were added. Between the columns there were curtains that could be closed at certain moments of the service. After eighth- and ninth-century iconoclasm, holy imag-

[44] Short surveys can be found in THON, Ikone und Liturgie, 34–46; Jean-Michel SPIESER, Alle origini dell'iconografia cristiana, in: Sabino CHIALÀ – Lisa CREMASCHI (Eds.), Giovanni di Damasco, un padre al sorgere dell'Islam: Atti del XIII Convegno ecumenico internazionale di spiritualità ortodossa, sezione bizantina, Bose, 11–13 settembre 2005, Magnano 2006, 277–313, here 279–283.

[45] Jean-Baptiste PITRA (Ed.), Spicilegium Solesmense. Vol. 1, Paris 1852, 383–386; Hans-Jürgen GEISCHER (Ed.), Der byzantinische Bilderstreit (Texte zur Kirchen- und Theologiegeschichte 9), Gütersloh 1968, 15–17. On the issue of authenticity, see SPIESER, Alle origini dell'iconografia cristiana, 279–283 (with pertinent literature); Stephen GERO, The True Image of Christ. Eusebius' Letter to Constantia Reconsidered, in: JThS New Series 32 (1981) 460–470.

[46] GALADZA, Role of Icons in Byzantine Worship, 116–119.

[47] WEGMAN, Liturgie in der Geschichte des Christentums, 26, 30, 163; GALADZA, Role of Icons in Byzantine Worship, 127–134.

es were hung from the columns or put upon the architrave. Throughout the centuries, the barrier rose higher and higher, images were also placed *between* the columns. At the end of the fourteenth century, the full iconostasis was a reality. In particular in Russia, a further development of the iconostasis took place, separating sanctuary and nave even more. The iconostasis became almost fully opaque and often reached the ceiling.[48]

It is obvious that proponents of the low iconostasis cannot base their reform on very early Christian practice, but have to suffice with ca. the fourth century. As for the proponents of the high iconostasis, it is clear that they find support in the second millennium, not in the first.

Common to both views is their conviction that the energy of the depicted sacred persons and events is present in the images and that, therefore, these must be venerated. So icons have an almost 'sacramental' meaning: a visible image serves as a carrier of divine reality and is a symbol of transcendence, a 'window to eternity'.[49] In other words, icons reveal God's love and glory. In that way they exhort people to prayer. At the same time, they visibly express human prayer, because they are a theology in painting and colours.[50]

A main stream of Byzantine liturgical theology considers the sanctuary a symbol of heaven/paradise and the nave as a symbol of the earth. From this perspective, the iconostasis is not only the partition between these two spaces, but also their connection. The iconostasis not only veils, but also reveals. Proponents of reform do not deny this, but they point to the lack of active participation by the 'people' and wish to strengthen the role of the laity in the celebration. In the assembly (*ekklêsia*, *synaxis*) the people must be more involved than is now the case. Various critical theologians also point out that, for many centuries, women have been marginalized, and they advocate the official recognition of the essential role women play in the liturgical assembly, for instance, the reinstatement of the ministry of deaconesses.[51]

[48] Here I cannot examine other geographical and chronological differentiations. See, *e.g.*, Markiyan FILEVYCH, The Iconography of the Byzantine Sanctuary Screen in the Context of the Liturgy and the Church's Interior (Master Thesis, University of Graz), Graz 2004.

[49] Marcel QUENOT, L'Icône. Fenêtre sur l'Absolu (Collection « Bref » 3), Paris 1987; Gennadios LIMOURIS (Ed.), Icons. Windows on Eternity – Theology and Spirituality in Colour (Faith and Order Paper 147), Geneva 1990; Anton JACOBS, Iconen uit het christelijk Oosten, in: Herman TEULE – Anton WESSELS (Eds.), Oosterse christenen binnen de wereld van de islam, Heerlen – Kampen 1997, 144–150; John BAGGLEY, Festival Icons for the Christian Year, Crestwood/New York 2000.

[50] Edmond VOORDECKERS, Ikonen. Theofanie en gebed (Schrift en liturgie 5), Bonheiden ^{2}1988; Leonid OUSPENSKY, The Meaning and Language of Icons, in: IDEM – Vladimir LOSSKY, The Meaning of Icons, Crestwood/New York 1982, rev.ed., 23–49.

[51] See, for example, Kyriaki Karidoyanes FITZGERALD, Women Deacons in the Orthodox Church. Called to Holiness and Ministry, Brookline 1998; Marcel METZGER, Le diaconat féminin dans l'histoire, in: Kanon XVI, 144–166; Euaggelos (Evangelos) THEODÔROU, Hoi diakonisses stên historia tês Ekklêsias, in: Pantelês KALAÏTZIDÊS – Nikos NTONTOS, (Eds.), Fylo kai thrêskeia. Hê thesê tês gynaikas stên Ekklêsia (Cheimerino programma 2002–2003). Hiera Mêtropolis Dêmêtriados, Akadêmia Theologikôn Spoudôn, Athens

In Byzantine-rite services, looking is extremely important, whereas in Protestant and many modern Roman Catholic services hearing comes in first place. Yet seeing and hearing complement one another. On the one hand, language can interpret realities, objects and feelings that otherwise would remain unclear. Water, for instance, can both purify and destroy, but the spoken word – during baptism, a blessing, etc. – interprets and indicates the meaning of the water. On the other hand, in the world-wide ecumenical movement where Protestantism, Anglicanism, Orthodoxy, Catholicism, and so on, meet and dialogue, despite all kind of tensions, Western churches have learnt from their Eastern brothers and sisters to esteem icons. It is relevant that nowadays in many Western churches one can find icons and in ecumenical services holy scripture and icons are simultaneously used.

Solid investigations of the origins and the historical development and changes of both the anointing of the sick and icons are irreplaceable if we wish to understand their present meaning. It is important not merely to examine current liturgical practice in just one particular church, but in several ecclesiastical communities, comparing the different practices with one another and defining similarities and differences in various Christian traditions from the inside, thus providing an interesting ecumenical picture. Indeed, by its very nature, liturgiological research is ecumenical, not only because it presupposes cooperation between scholars from different churches (Orthodox, Oriental Orthodox, Catholics, Anglicans, Lutherans, Reformed, Pentecostals, etc.), but also because of its content, procedure, and method. Its aim is to understand hermeneutically the plurality of Christian liturgies – not only their continuities, but also their discontinuities and ruptures – and the plurality of the men and women celebrating these liturgies. Liturgiological research investigates not merely service books, but the actual celebration itself and the context in which it takes place.[52] Besides 'prescribed faith', 'lived faith' has to be on the research agenda.[53] The study of

2004, 185–208; John WIJNGAARDS, No Women in Holy Orders? The Women Deacons of the Early Church, Norwich 2002; Dietmar W. WINKLER (Ed.), Diakonat der Frau. Befunde aus biblischer, patristischer, ostkirchlicher, liturgischer und systematisch–theologischer Perspektive (orientalia – patristica – oecumenica 2), Münster – Berlin – Vienna 2010. Cf. Élisabeth BEHR–SIGEL – Mgr. Kallistos WARE, L'ordination de femmes dans l'Église orthodoxe, Paris 1998, 12–13, 50, 60–65. See also fn. 14.

52 Cf. Kevin IRWIN, Context and Text. Method in Liturgical Theology, Collegeville/Minnesota 1994. Also Teresa BERGER, Die Sprache der Liturgie, in: Hans-Christoph SCHMIDT-LAUBER – Michael MEYER-BLANCK – Karl-Heinrich BIERITZ (Eds.), Handbuch der Liturgik. Liturgiewissenschaft in Theologie und Praxis der Kirche, Göttingen ³2003, 798–806, here 802 (cf. 805), states: "Die liturgische Rede ist im Kern … vor allem Vollzug, Handlung, Redegeschehen. Bei einem Blick auf liturgische Texte nähert man sich deshalb nur einem kleinen Teil der Wirklichkeit der Sprache der Liturgie." The same view in other words in: Teresa BERGER, Breaking Bread in a Broken World. Liturgy and Cartographies of the Real, in: StLi 36 (2006) 74–85, especially 75–78.

53 A good example of accounting for the social, political and cultural contexts of the history of liturgy is: WEGMAN, Liturgie in der Geschichte des Christentums. A recent survey can be found in: Louis VAN TONGEREN, Een gemeenschappelijke oriëntatie. Over de Ritual

worship also aims at discerning the presence and energy of the Holy Spirit in the celebrations.[54] An important additional objective of comparative research – be it on the history of worship or on its current practice – is that the diverse ecclesiastical communities can learn from one another. Actually, liturgical celebrations may not only bring faithful together, but they also reveal their separation. Our churches are still divided and we live in a broken world. Our faith communities and liturgical assemblies also need healing.[55] *Omnes ecclesiae semper reformandae sunt. Nonne etiam hodierna forma ecclesiae catholicae romanae defectus habet?!* (All churches are in constant need of reform. Does not also the current shape of the Roman Catholic Church have deficiencies?!)[56] Fortunately, in the Faith and Order Commission of the World Council of Churches, for instance, a great deal of fruitful thought on liturgy and worship has taken place, *inter alia* on the celebration and meaning of the sacraments, proclamation of the Word of God, ecclesiastical year, veneration of saints, epiclesis, anamnesis, and doxology. Very significant is the Lima Report on Baptism, Eucharist and Ministry (1982). Nearly all Orthodox, Oriental Orthodox, Anglican, Old Catholic, Lutheran, and Reformed churches are members of the World Council. Although as yet the Roman Catholic Church formally does not belong to the Council, it fully participates in the Faith and Order Commission.[57] Also the official liturgical reforms initiated by the Second Vatican Council, or the agreements in various bilateral dialogues would have been unthinkable without the previous results of comparative liturgical inquiries.[58] At first sight, contrasting experiences may alienate, but at second, closer sight, they are an important contribution to a better understanding of one's own tradition and to the pursuit of unity.

Studies en ontwikkelingen binnen het liturgiehistorisch onderzoek, in: Jaarboek voor liturgie–onderzoek 22 (2006) 135–151; IDEM, Eine gemeinsame Zielrichtung. Die *ritual studies* und die Entwicklungen in der Liturgiegeschichtsforschung, in: Benedikt KRANEMANN – Paul POST (Eds.), Die modernen Ritual Studies als Herausforderung für die Liturgiewissenschaft – Modern Ritual Studies as a Challenge for Liturgical Studies (Liturgia Condenda 20), Leuven 2009, 111–132. In the field of Byzantine studies and hagiography, for instance, many researchers take the above-mentioned contexts into account.

54 Cf. Friedrich LURZ, Für eine ökumenische Liturgiewissenschaft, in: Trierer Theologische Zeitschrift 108 (1999) 273–290, here, 280, 289–290.

55 BERGER, Breaking Bread in a Broken World, 78–80.

56 According to the declaration by the Vatican Congregation for the Doctrine of the Faith, issued on 29 June 2007, "Responsa ad quaestiones de aliquibus sententiis ad doctrinam de Ecclesia pertinentibus", the fullness of Catholicity and the Church of Christ can only be found in the Catholic Church. See Acta Apostolicae Sedis 99 (2007) 604–608. This statement was hotly debated both in other churches and among Catholic ecumenists.

57 On the structure and members of the World Council of Churches, see Huibert VAN BEEK (Ed.), A Handbook of Churches and Councils. Profiles of Ecumenical Relationships, Geneva 2006.

58 Cf. Gabriele WINKLER – Robert TAFT, Introduction, in: WINKLER – TAFT, Acts of the International Congress "Comparative Liturgy Fifty Years After Anton Baumstark", 9–29, here 14–28.

Theological research into early Christian liturgy and its ecumenical relevance should not only deal with the forms and contents of the *liturgical* assembly. The word of God celebrated in worship is inseparably connected with the word of scripture heard in catechesis and God's word lived in diakonia and caritas. If they are separated, the liturgy risks becoming only navel-gazing, "a noisy gong or a clanging cymbal" (cf. 1 Corinthians 13:1).[59] As the Romanian Orthodox theologian, Ion Bria, states, there also is the 'liturgy after the liturgy',[60] or – I might add – the 'liturgy before the liturgy'.[61] Yet since liturgy is such an important *locus theologicus* and worship assemblies reach much more people than academic theology, the study of liturgy is extremely important.

This kind of research is also important for Jewish-Christian dialogue. After centuries of anti-Judaism in Christian liturgy[62] and the *Shoa*, nowadays, in research, dialogue and liturgical practice, many Christians – particularly Western Christians – are attempting to re-establish the central liturgical place of Israel and Judaism. The revelation to Israel was not revoked at Christ's manifestation, but extended throughout the world. The God of Israel, who appeared to His people and all nations, appears to the world in Jesus and still manifests Himself today. God acts in Jesus Christ without 'eliminating' Jewish tradition. The Son of God Himself, Mary, and the apostles had 'Semitic faces'.[63]

Here, our current preconceptions are definitely different from those of many bishops and theologians who lived in, for instance, the third and fourth centuries and acutely polemicized against Judaism,[64] not only on account of the 'substitution theology' but also for reasons of competition and 'market' rivalry. Such polemics, which we currently feel as most deplorable, had devastating effects, a terrible *Wirkungsgeschichte* for living Jews. Yet it is anachronistic to say that

[59] Louis–Marie CHAUVET, Du symbolique au symbole. Essai sur les sacrements (rites et symboles 9), Paris 1979, 81–122.

[60] Ion BRIA, The Liturgy after the Liturgy. Mission and Witness from an Orthodox Perspective, Geneva 1996.

[61] Basilius J. GROEN, Liturgie und Armut. Der Gottesdienst vor und nach dem Gottesdienst, in: Leopold NEUHOLD – Livia NEUREITER (Eds.), Muss arm sein? Armut als Ärgernis und Herausforderung (Theologie im kulturellen Dialog 15), Innsbruck – Vienna 2008, 104–156.

[62] See, *e.g.*, Bert GROEN, Antijudaismus in der christlichen Liturgie und Versuche seiner Überwindung, in: Joachim KÜGLER (Ed.), Prekäre Zeitgenossenschaft. Mit dem Alten Testament in Konflikten der Zeit – Internationales Bibel-Symposium Graz 2004 (Bayreuther Forum Transit. Kulturwissenschaftliche Religionsstudien), Münster 2006, 247–278; Bert GROEN, Anti-Judaism in the Present-Day Byzantine Liturgy, in: The Journal of Eastern Christian Studies 60 (2008) 369–387.

[63] Dieu est vivant. Catéchisme pour des familles par une équipe de chrétiens orthodoxes, Paris 1979, 164–171.

[64] Heinz SCHRECKENBERG, Die christlichen Adversus Judaeos–Texte und ihr literarisches und historisches Umfeld (1.–11. Jh.) (Europäische Hochschulschriften XXIII), Frankfurt [4]1998; Adelbert DAVIDS, Anti-judaïsme en antisemitisme in de eerste eeuwen van het christendom, in: TEULE – WESSELS, Oosterse christenen binnen de wereld van de islam, 47–56.

those church fathers should have been aware of the excesses of later anti-Judaism and anti-Semitism.
Currently in the work of several liturgical scholars a change of paradigm can be observed. The Jewish roots of Christian worship are being accentuated. But the issue at stake is not only to lay emphasis on the similarities between both religions, instead of ignoring the Jewish tradition. The alleged dependency of Christian liturgy upon Jewish worship along the lines of a model of a mother (Judaism) and daughter (Christianity) is rightly being questioned, because there are still many uncertainties and gaps regarding the historical development of Jewish and early Christian liturgy and their mutual relations.[65] For that reason, much historical research and interdisciplinary cooperation, especially in Old and New Testament exegesis, Jewish studies and religious studies, will be required. Since in this new paradigm we try to understand not just the similarities, but also the differences between Jewish and Christian worship,[66] comparative Jewish-Christian liturgical studies are imperative.

Research on the history of worship and applying its results in modern liturgical reform certainly are different from making a Rorschach test. Yet realizing what are one's preconceptions, what is one's *Vorverständnis*, in a hermeneutical way is essential for good scholarly work.

[65] See the article by Paul BRADSHAW in this book, pp. 47–59.

[66] See, for instance, Albert GERHARDS, Jüdische und christliche Liturgie. Gemeinsamkeiten, Differenzen, Herausforderungen, in: Heiliger Dienst 58 (2004) 20–31; IDEM, Jüdische Liturgie und christliche Liturgiewissenschaft. Zum Stand der Forschung, in: IDEM – Hans H. HENRIX (Eds.), Dialog oder Monolog? Zur liturgischen Beziehung zwischen Judentum und Christentum (Quaestiones Disputatae 208), Freiburg i. B. 2004, 34–49; Albert GERHARDS – Andrea DOEKER – Peter EBENBAUER, Identität zwischen Tradition und Neuschöpfung. Liturgisches Beten in Judentum und Christentum als Quelle eines unabschließbaren Prozesses religiöser Selbstbestimmung, in: EIDEM (Eds.), Identität durch Gebet. Zur gemeinschaftsbildenden Funktion institutionalisierten Betens in Judentum und Christentum (Studien zu Judentum und Christentum), Paderborn 2003, 13–19; Daniela KRANEMANN, "Unsere Väter, die Söhne Israels…„. Zeitgenossenschaft von Israel und Kirche in der christlichen Liturgie – Chancen und Desiderate, in: Heiliger Dienst 58 (2004) 45–58; Peter EBENBAUER, Mehr als ein Gespräch. Zur Dialogik von Gebet und Offenbarung in jüdischer und christlicher Liturgie (Studien zu Judentum und Christentum), Paderborn 2010.

Le tropaire Ὁ Μονογενής dans les liturgies orientales et sa signification œcuménique

Sebastià Janeras

Le tropaire Ὁ Μονογενής est une hymne bien connue, qui est chantée au début de la Divine Liturgie dans le rite byzantin.[1] En voici le texte:[2]

1. Ὁ Μονογενὴς Υἱὸς καὶ Λόγος τοῦ Θεοῦ,
2. ἀθάνατος ὑπάρχων,
3. καὶ καταδεξάμενος διὰ τὴν ἡμετέραν σωτηρίαν
4. σαρκωθῆναι
5. ἐκ τῆς ἁγίας Θεοτόκου καὶ ἀειπαρθένου Μαρίας
6. ἀτρέπτως ἐναθρωπήσας,
7. σταυρωθείς τε,
8. Χριστέ, ὁ Θεός,
9. Θανάτῳ θάνατον πατήσας,
10. εἷς ὢν τῆς ἁγίας Τριάδος,
11. συνδοξαζόμενος τῷ Πατρί, καὶ τῷ ἁγίῳ Πνεύματι.
12. Σῶσον ἡμᾶς.

Ce tropaire se trouve parmi les éléments par lesquels s'ouvre la Divine Liturgie de rite byzantin. Plus en concret, il est chanté avec le *Gloria Patri* du deuxième antiphone de l'Ἔναρξις. Celle-ci se compose de trois antiphones, c'est-à-dire

[1] Sur ce tropaire, cf. Julien Puyade, Le tropaire ὁ Μονογενής, dans: Revue de l'Orient Chrétien 7 (1912) 253–267; Venance Grumel, L'auteur et la date de composition du tropaire ὁ Μονογενής, dans: EOr 22 (1923) 398–418; Egon Wellesz, A History of Byzantine Music and Hymnography, Oxford 1961², 178–179; Ilona Borsai, Le tropaire byzantin «O Monogenés» dans la pratique du chant copte, dans: Studia Musicologica 14 (1972) 329–354; Jan H. Barkhuizen, Justinian's Hymn ὁ Μονογενὴς Υἱὸς καὶ Λόγος τοῦ Θεοῦ, dans: Byzantinische Zeitschrift 77 (1984) 3–5; Jean Breck, The Power of the Word: In the Worshipping Church, Crestwood 1986, chap. VI. Confessing the Monogenes: The Only–Begotten Son (traduction française: La puissance de la Parole. Une introduction à l'herméneutique orthodoxe, Paris 1996); Gernot Bühring – Siegbert Uhlig, Antiochenisches und Justinianisches im Hymnus "Eingeborener Sohn", dans: Ostkirchliche Studien 37 (1988) 297–307; Robert Taft, Monogenes, Ho, dans: Oxford Dictionary of Byzantium, 2, New York – Oxford 1991, 1397; Sebastià Janeras, Valor ecuménico del tropario ὁ Μονογενής, dans: Diálogo ecuménico 34 (1999) 299–315 (il faut regretter que les textes y ont été mal placés); S. I. Nikitine, Jedinorodnyj Syne, dans: Pravoslavnaja Enciklopedija 18 (Moscou 2008) 51–54. Pour toute l'histoire qui entoure le tropaire, cf. Karl-Heinz Uthemann, Kaiser Justinian als Kirchenpolitiker und Theologe, dans: Aug. 39 (1999) 5–83.

[2] Je le divise en incises, numérotés, pour mieux le comparer avec la version syro–antiochienne que je donne plus bas.

trois psaumes, accompagnés de litanies et de prières. Les psaumes habituels chez les grecs ce sont les psaumes 91, 92 et 94, tandis que chez les slaves on chante régulièrement les Τυπικά, c'est-à-dire, les psaumes 102, 103 et les Béatitudes. Ici aussi le Tropaire ὁ Μονογενής est chanté avec le *Gloria Patri* du deuxième psaume.

Au début, comme chant d'entrée de la Liturgie, on ne chantait qu'un psaume, alterné avec un verset ou un tropaire.[3] Parmi ces chants d'entrée on trouve le Trisagion, mais aussi le tropaire ὁ Μονογενής, comme le témoigne un Diaconal sinaïtique du IXe siècle, le ms. Saint-Pétersbourg 44.[4] Le psaume que présentent les anciens livres liturgiques est le psaume 94 (95), lequel constitue aujourd'hui le troisième antiphone.

L'office des trois antiphones dérive de la liturgie stationnale de Sainte-Sophie de Constantinople. Plus tard on ajouta les trois antiphones à toutes les célébrations de la Divine Liturgie, même sans stations. Avec l'introduction de nouveaux tropaires, le tropaire ὁ Μονογενής fut transposé à sa place actuelle, après le deuxième antiphone. Et sur le modèle de ces trois antiphones de la Liturgie on chantait à Sainte-Sophie, d'après son *Typikon*, trois psaumes, le dernier avec le tropaire ὁ Μονογενής, dans le petit office de la Τριτοέκτη.[5] Mais le tropaire ὁ Μονογενής pouvait être un chant processionel même sans antiphones, comme il apparaît dans le *Typicon* de la Grande Église le mercredi après la Pentecôte.[6] Ce tropaire apparaît encore à l'office cathédrale des vêpres constantinopolitaines, avec le groupe des trois petits antiphones (Ps. 114, 115, 116), concrètement avec le deuxième.[7] Cela est témoigné par le Codex Barberini 336 (VIIIe siècle).[8]

À la place des antiphones de la Liturgie, on peut chanter, comme j'ai dit plus haut, les Τυπικά, qui sont d'origine palestinienne et qui faisaient partie d'un

[3] Sur les questions qui suivent, voir surtout Juan MATEOS, La célébration de la parole dans la liturgie byzantine (OCA 191), Roma 1971, chapitres I–III.

[4] Publié par Jean Baptiste THIBAUT, Monuments de la notation ekphonétique et hagiopolite de l'Église Grecque, Saint-Pétersbourg 1913, 3e partie, 7.

[5] Cf. Juan MATEOS, Le Typicon de la Grande Église. Ms. Sainte-Croix nº 40, Xe siècle, II (OCA 166), Rome 1963, 4; Sur la τριτοέκτη, cf. Ioannis FOUNTOULIS, Τριθέκτη (Κείμενα Λειτουργικῆς 1), Thessalonique 1969, 5–44; Miguel ARRANZ, Les prières presbytérales de la Tritoekti de l'ancien Euchologe byzantin, dans: OCP 43 (1977) 70–93. Sur la tritoekti le Vendredi–Saint, cf. Sebastià JANERAS, Le Vendredi–Saint dans la tradition liturgique byzantine. Structure et histoire de ses offices (StAns 99 – Analecta Liturgica 13), Rome 1988, 307–311. D'après Syméon de Thessalonique, au XVe siècle, les psaumes de la τριτοέκτη étaient: 24, 26 et 100, mais sans ὁ Μονογενής, puisque pour le troisième antiphone on chantait Alléluia. Cf. De sacra precatione (PG 155, 649 et 652).

[6] La procession allait de la Grande Église à l'église des saints Anges au Nouveau Palais au chant du tropaire ὁ Μονογενής. Cf. MATEOS, Le Typicon (cf. n. 3), 2, 142.

[7] Cf. Miguel ARRANZ, L'office de l'Asmatikos Hesperinos («vêpres chantées») de l'ancien Euchologe byzantin, 2, dans: OCP 44 (1978) 391–419; Alexander LINGAS, Cathedral Vespers in Late Byzantium, dans: OCP 63 (1997) 421–448.

[8] Cf. Stefano PARENTI – Elena VELKOVSKA, L'Eucologio Barberini gr. 336 (BEL.S 80), Rome 1995, 54.

office de communion après la neuvième heure.[9] Dans cet office étaient chantées seulement les Béatitudes, sans psaumes. Mais lorsque plus tard, à Constantinople, l'office des Τυπικά fut uni à la Liturgie, au lieu des antiphones (psaumes 91, 92, 94) on introduisit les psaumes 102 et 145, celui-ci suivi du tropaire ὁ Μονογενής, le tout précédant le chant des Béatitudes. Cet ensemble est passé, d'après l'*Horologion* grec, à l'office des *Typika* en dehors de la Liturgie (et sans communion), donc avec le ὁ Μονογενής. Dans le *Služebnik* slavon par contre cet office des Τυπικά ne possède ni les psaumes ni le tropaire.
Mais il n'y a pas que le rite byzantin qui possède le tropaire ὁ Μονογενής. D'autres liturgies orientales l'emploient aussi. En tout premier lieu la liturgie syro-antiochienne, dans laquelle le tropaire occupe une place semblable, pendant une petite procession du prêtre, avec l'évangéliaire, autour de l'autel avant les lectures. Ce tropaire (en syriaque *ma'nitho*), attribué au patriarche d'Antioche Sevère, commence, dans les livres: *Eram^{e}rmokh Mor Malko Iḥidoyo,* etc. Nous avons ici à faire avec l'incipit du psaume 144: «Je t'exalte, Seigneur Roi» (*Eram^{e}rmokh Mor Malko*) suivi du *ma'nitho,* c'est à dire: *Iḥidoyo Bro...* Souvent les traducteurs ne l'ont pas remarqué et ont traduit le tout comme une seule pièce. Ainsi, par exemple, Guy Le Fèvre de la Boderie (Fabricius Boderianus) dans sa version latine, en 1572: «Exaltabo te, Domine mi rex, cuius Unigenitus...».[10] Union donc du verset psalmique (adressé à Dieu) avec le tropaire par le moyen de *cuius* (suivi de la troisième personne). Même interprétation chez Brightman: « I will magnify thee, o God my King, whose only-begotten Son who was immortal in his nature... »[11] Même Mgr. Gabriel Khouri-Sarkis, syro-antiochien lui-même et bon connaisseur de sa liturgie, traduisit en français, dans un petit livre par ailleurs remarcable et très utile: « Je vous exalte, ô mon Seigneur-Roi, Fils unique et Verbe du Père céleste qui, par sa nature, est immortel... »,[12] traduction qui s'est maintenue dans la brochure plus récente en usage dans la paroisse syrienne catholique de Paris. Dans cette traduction on passe du vocatif du verset à la trosième personne du tropaire. Dans la traduction allemande de Johannes Madey tout le texte, verset et tropaire, est adressé au Christ, au vocatif et à la deuxième personne: «Ich will dich hochverherrlichen, mein Herr und mein König, eingeborener Sohn…»[13] Même le P. Puyade, lequel, dans son étude sur ce tropaire, présente en parallèle le texte grec et le texte syriaque, fait commencer celui-ci par le verset comme faisant un

9 Juan MATEOS, Un Horologion inédit de Saint-Sabas. Le Codex synaïtique grec 863 (IXe siècle), dans: Mélanges Eugène Tisserant 3 (StT 233), Cité du Vatican 1964, 64–66.
10 Fabricius BODERIANUS, D. Severi Alexandrini quondam patriarcha de ritibus baptismi et sacrae synaxi apud syros christianos receptis liber, Anvers 1572, 119. À noter que, d'après cet auteur, Sévère est patriarche d'Alexandrie (!).
11 Frank Edward BRIGHTMAN, Liturgies Eastern and Western, Oxford 1896, 77.
12 Gabriel KHOURI–SARKIS, La Liturgie syrienne. Anaphore des Douze Apôtres, Paris 1950, 32–33.
13 Johannes MADEY – Georg VAVANIKUNNEL, Qurbana oder die Eucharistiefeier der Thomaschristen Indiens, Paderborn 1968, 143.

tout.[14] Il est néanmoins de toute évidence qu'il s'agit d'un chant composé d'un verset de psaume et d'une *ma'nitho.*

Les maronites ne possèdent pas cette *ma'nitho.* On la trouve cependant dans un Missel du début du XVIe siècle (ms. Bkerké 115), mais, d'après Pierre Gemayel, il s'agit d'un missel « jacobitisé ».[15] Chez les arméniens le tropaire ὁ Μονογενής constitue le chant d'entrée des dimanches ordinaires.[16]

Pour ce qui est de la tradition alexandrine et copte, on trouve ce tropaire (toujours en grec) comme chant d'entrée dans la Liturgie de Marc.[17] Il apparaît encore dans la cérémonie d'intronisation du patriarche d'Alexandrie et dans la consécration épiscopale, toujours après les lectures de l'Ancien Testament et des Actes des Apôtres, là où trouve aussi sa place le Trisagion.[18] Le tropaire ὁ Μονογενής apparaît encore le Vendredi Saint, dans la synaxe de la sixième heure, consacrée à la mémoire de la crucifixion et de la mort du Christ. Après la lecture de l'Ancien Testament et de l'Apôtre, on chante ce tropaire, suivi du Trisagion, la lecture de l'Évangile et le rite caractéristique de la tradition copte appelé Μνήσθητι (en copte ⲁⲣⲓⲡⲁⲙⲉⲩⲓ).[19]

Sous l'influence du rite byzantin sur la liturgie de Jerusalem le tropaire ὁ Μονογενής y fut aussi accepté. D'après le lectionnaire géorgien, ce tropaire (en géorgien *ohit'aj*) se trouve comme chant d'entrée le jour de Pâques.[20] Le lectionnaire ne donne ici que l'incipit: *Mẖolodšobili,* mais on trouve le texte entier dans le *Iadgari.*[21] Dans le Diaconal sinaïtique mentionné ci-dessus, de la liturgie de Jérusalem, le tropaire ὁ Μονογενής est un chant d'entrée des dimanches ordinaires. Et ici il apparaît clairement que le tropaire est chanté sous forme responsoriale, puisqu'on trouve indiquée une fois, après le *Gloria Patri*, la répétition de la dernière partie du tropaire: εἷς ὢν τῆς ἁγίας Τριάδος...[22] Encore, pour ce qui est de la liturgie de Jérusalem, il faut signaler que la Liturgie de Saint Jacques signale ce tropaire comme chant d'entrée.[23]

14 PUYADE, Le tropaire (cf. n. 1), 252. Dans le commentaire qui suit, il en donne une traduction française (255): «Je te loue, Seigneur Roi, unique Fils du Père céleste, qui est immortel...», et il ajoute en note: «Suivant le génie du syriaque, on passe de la seconde personne à la troisième.».

15 Pierre GEMAYEL, L'avant–messe maronite. Histoire et structure (OCA 174), Rome 1965, 58.

16 BRIGHTMAN, Liturgies (cf. n. 11), 421.

17 BRIGHTMAN, Liturgies (cf. n.11), 116–117.

18 Henricus DENZINGER, Ritus orientalium coptorum, syrorum et armenorum in administrandis sacramentis. 2, Würzburg 1864, 19 et 41.

19 Cf. Anton BAUMSTARK, Drei griechische Passionsgesänge ägyptischer Liturgie, dans: OrChr 3e série 3–4 (1928–1929) 75–78; Oswald H. E. BURMESTER, The greek Kirugmata, Versicles and Responses and Hymns in the Coptic Liturgy, dans: OCP 2 (1936) 388; JANERAS, Le Vendredi Saint (cf. n. 4), 175.

20 Michel TARCHNISCHVILI, Le grand lectionnaire de l'Église de Jérusalem (V^e^–VIIIe siècle), t. 1, n° 745 (CSCO 188), Louvain 1959.

21 Elene METREVELI – Caca ČANKIEVI – Lili XEVSURIANI, Udzvelesi Iadgari, Tbilisi 1980, 216.

22 THIBAUT, Monuments (cf. n. 4), 7.

23 BRIGHTMAN, Liturgies (cf. n. 11), 83.

Il est intéressant finalement de signaler la présence du tropaire ὁ Μονογενής dans la Liturgie d'origine italo-grecque dite de Saint Pierre. Celle-ci est une messe latine en grec dans une structure byzantine. Eh bien, dans cette Liturgie le tropaire ὁ Μονογενής apparaît comme faisant fonction d'Introïtus, accompagné du psaume 94.[24]

En conclusion, le tropaire ὁ Μονογενής est, de par son origine, un chant d'entrée de la Liturgie, qui s'est répandu bientôt jusqu'à devenir un patrimoine de plusieurs liturgies orientales.

LE TEXTE

Le texte originel du tropaire ὁ Μονογενής fut rédigé en grec. Même si Sévère d'Antioche en aurait été l'auteur, on ne peut pas oublier qu'il écrivait en grec. Le tropaire fut bientôt traduit en syriaque, une traduction d'ailleurs amplifiée. Il en existe cependant une traduction syriaque littérale, que l'on peut voir dans un *Horologion* melkite (c'est-à-dire, de rite byzantin mais en syriaque) du neuvième siècle.[25] Les autres traditions du même rite byzantin on traduit petit à petit le tropaire dans les diverses langues : géorgien, slave, roumain, etc. Dans tous ces cas il s'agit d'une traduction littérale de l'original grec. La traduction arménienne est somme toute littérale, bien qu'elle omette un pair de mots. Et chez les coptes, puisque, comme j'ai déjà dit, le tropaire a été chanté toujours en grec, le texte n'a pas subi de transformations. Par contre, la version propre à l'Église syro-antiochienne se présente amplifiée, ce qui d'ailleurs n'est pas étonnant dans les textes de langue syriaque. Voici une traduction de cette version, divisée d'accord avec le texte grec donné au début:[26]

1. Le Fils unique et Verbe du *Père céleste*
2. qui, par sa nature, est immortel,
3. a accepté *et il est venu, dans sa bonté* pour *la vie et* la rédemption du genre humain,
4. et il a pris chair
5. de la sainte *et glorieuse* Vierge *pure*, Mère de Dieu, Marie,
6. sans changement il s'est fait home
7. et il a été crucifié pour nous,
8. le Christ Dieu,
9. et par sa mort il a écrasé *et tué notre* mort,

[24] Humphrey William CODRINGTON, The Liturgy of Saint Peter (LWQF 30), Münster 1930, 138.
[25] Mathew BLACK, A Christian Palestinian Syriac Horologion (Berlin, ms. Or. Oct. 1019), Cambridge 1954, 234–235 (fols. 53b–54a du ms. Berlin Or. Oct. 1019).
[26] Je signale en italiques les leçons variantes et les amplifications.

10. et il est Un de la sainte Trinité,
11. *adoré et* glorifié ensemble avec *son* Père et *son* Esprit Saint.
12. Aie pitié de nous.

On devrait dire un mot sur la construction grammaticale du tropaire. Si l'on ne tient pas compte du vocatif Χριστὲ ὁ Θεός et de la supplique finale Σῶσον ἡμᾶς, il ne reste que des participes, sans un seul verbe à la forme indicative. Les premiers mots: ὁ μονογενὴς Υἱὸς καὶ Λόγος peuvent être considérés comme des nominatifs ou comme des vocatifs. Si on les prend pour des nominatifs, le tropaire est une exposition, une sorte de confession de foi. Si on les considère comme des vocatifs, le tropaire devient une prière. Dans le premier cas, on doit comprendre et traduire le texte à la troisième personne; dans le deuxième cas, par contre, à la deuxième personne. En général les versions ont rendu le texte du tropaire au vocatif, avec le verbe à la deuxième personne. Ainsi la version slavonne : *Jedirodnyj Sine i Slove...* ; aussi la version syrienne melkite : *Bro Iḥidoyo wmelto d'Aloho dlo moyutho…*, ou la version roumaine : « Unulenăscut Fiule și Cuvinte al lui Dumnezeu, cela ce ești fără de moarte… » La version géorgienne présente les substantifs au nominatif et donc les verbes à la troisième personne : « Le Monogène, Fils et Verbe de Dieu, Être immortel, prit tout sur lui…»[27] La traduction de l'Église syro-antiochienne (non la version syriaque melkite) est aussi rédigée à la troisième personne : « Le Fils unique et Verbe du Père céleste, lequel par nature est immortel... »[28] Seulement à la fin vient, comme toujours, la supplique à la deuxième personne : *ḥus al kulan* (« Aie pitié de nous tous »). La traduction latine de la Liturgie de saint Jean Chrysostome faite par Léon Toscan (XIIe siècle), et celle de la Liturgie de saint Basile faite par Nicolas d'Otrante (XIIIe siècle) conservent au début la forme ambigüe du grec : *Unigenitus Filius* (et non *Unigenite Fili) et Verbum Dei...,* mais elles continuent à la deuxième personne : *cum sis immortalis...*[29]

L'AUTEUR

D'après la tradition byzantine le tropaire ὁ Μονογενὴς aurait été composé par l'empereur Justinien. Par contre, la tradition syro-antiochienne l'a toujours attribué au patriarche Sévère d'Antioche. Sur cette question avaient écrit jadis le

[27] Udzvelesi Iadgari (cf. n. 21), 216.
[28] Il s'agit évidemment du *ma'nitho* sans le verset qui le précède.
[29] André JACOB, La traduction de la Liturgie de saint Jean Chrysostome par Léon Toscan, dans: OCP 32 (1966) 143; ID., La traduction de la Liturgie de saint Basile par Nicolas d'Otrante, dans: Bulletin de l'Institut Historique Belge de Rome 38 (1967) 63. Le même phénomène se produit avec le Trisagion. Cf. Sebastià JANERAS, Le Trisagion: une formule brève en liturgie comparée, dans: Robert F. TAFT – Gabriele WINKLER, Comparative Liturgy fifty Years after Anton Baumstark (1872–1948) (OCA 265), Rome 2001, 528–533.

bénédictin Julien Puyade en 1912 et le byzantinologue Venance Grumel en 1923.[30] Puyade plaidait pour la paternité sévérienne du tropaire, tandis que Grumel, qui mène son étude avec plus de rigueur et avec un sens plus critique, penche pour Justinien, bien qu'il conclue à propos de cette paternité : « C'est possible, c'est plus que probable, ce n'est pas sûr ». Nous y reviendrons.
Il y a encore un troisième auteur auquel a été attribuée la paternité du tropaire : Cyrille d'Alexandrie. Cette attribution se trouve seulement, à ma connaissance, chez Syméon de Thessalonique (XVe siècle),[31] mais elle ne doit pas être retenue. Toutefois, une relation lointaine avec Cyrille, du point de vue doctrinal, faut-il la reconnaître.[32]
Pour Germain de Constantinople ce furent Joseph d'Arimathée et Nicodème les auteurs du tropaire. Lorsqu'ils ensevelirent le corps du Christ furent initiés par le corps du Seigneur et par sa divinité inséparable. Toutefois, Germain connait l'attribution à Justinien: « ἔνιοι δὲ λέγουσιν, ὅτι τὸ αὐτὸ τροπάριον ἐκπεφώνηται παρὰ τοῦ τῆς θείας λήξεως βασιλέως Ἰουστινιανοῦ ».[33] Mais l'attribution à Joseph et Nicodème ne manque pas d'intérêt. La même attribution à Joseph et Nicodème est faite d'une forme constante à propos du Trisagion dans toute la tradition syro-antiochienne, d'après laquelle Joseph et Nicodème, lorsqu'ils ensevelirent le corps du Christ entendirent les anges chanter : « Saint Dieu, Saint Fort, Saint Immortel », et ils ajoutèrent : « Toi, qui as été crucifié pour nous, aie pitié de nous ».[34]
Évidemment, dans ce dernier cas il n'est pas question du tropaire ὁ Μονογενής mais du Trisagion. Mais il y a vraiment une étroite relation entre les deux textes. On peut le voir déjà de par leur place dans la Liturgie. Dans la tradition syrienne, aussi bien que dans des anciens documents byzantins, le Trisagion suit immédiatement le tropaire. Et Nicolas d'Andida, au XIIe siècle, lequel attribue le tropaire à Justinien, après avoir commenté – ou plutôt paraphrasé – ce chant, dit : « Nos pères lui adaptèrent le Trisagion, afin que celui qui est loué dans le tropaire soit proclamé Un de la Trinité ».[35]

Qui est vraiment l'auteur du tropaire ὁ Μονογενής? D'après l'historien Théophane (IXe siècle),[36] Justinien établit que le tropaire ὁ Μονογενής devait être chanté dans les églises, sans toutefois dire un mot sur sa paternitè. Ce fait est placé par Théophane dans l'année 6028 de l'ère byzantine, ce qui correspond à

[30] Voir la bibliographie de la note 1.
[31] Τοῦτο δὲ παρὰ τοῦ θείου Κυρίλλου ἐκτέθεται: De sacra precatione, 348 (PG 155, 633).
[32] On a pu dire que le tropaire ὁ Μονογενής a canonisé la doctrine de Cyrille d'Alexandrie et sa formule Μία φύσις τοῦ Θεοῦ Λόγου σεσαρκωμένη.
[33] GERMAIN DE CONSTANTINOPLE, Ecclesiastica hierarchia (PG 98, 404). Ce texte est le premier document qui parle du tropaire ὁ Μονογενής à ce moment de la Liturgie.
[34] JANERAS, Le Trisagion (cf. n. 29), 551–552.
[35] NICOLAS D'ANDIDA, Protheoria, 12–13 (PG 140, 433). La paraphrase de Nicolas reprend celle de Germain.
[36] THÉOPHANE, Chronographia (PG 108, 477).

l'année 535–536 du calendrier julien. Dom Puyade ne croyait correcte cette datation et voulait rapporter le tropaire plus tôt, vers la fin du Ve siècle ou au début du VIe. Grumel de son côté a montré la précision du chroniste Théophanes. Je suis en partie son exposition, en y ajoutant des nouveaux éléments, tout particulièrement en relation avec le Trisagion.

LE MILIEU DANS LEQUEL APPARAIT LE TROPAIRE ὁ Μονογενής

C'est justement par le Trisagion que je vais commencer, parce que je crois qu'il y a une vraie liaison entre les deux textes. Dans son origine le Trisagion était christologique, même si les byzantins lui ont donné dès le début un sens trinitaire. Les Églises orthodoxes orientales par contre ont toutes maintenu toujours le sens christologique.[37]

Il est bien connu qu'à la fin de la première session du concile de Chalcédoine (451) les métropolites et les évêques orientaux (c'est à dire, antiochiens) chantèrent le Trisagion parmi des acclamations:

> Longues années au sénat!
>
> Ἅγιος ὁ Θεός, Ἅγιος ἰσχυρός, Ἅγιος ἀθάνατος, ἐλέησον ἡμᾶς.
>
> Longues années aux empereurs! (...)[38]

Mais avant ce texte, rapporté d'habitude comme étant le premier témoignage du Trisagion, Nestorius, dans son *Livre d'Héraclide*, en parle déjà, en disant que cette hymne reconnait le Christ comme Dieu, Saint et Immortel, contre ceux qui voient le Christ soumis à la souffrance et mortel. À ce Trisagion, comme il est bien connu, le patriarche monophysite d'Antioche Pierre le Foulon, pour mieux exprimer son sens christologique, lui ajouta : « Toi qui as été crucifié pour nous » (ὁ σταυρωθεὶς δι'ἡμᾶς).

En 512, sous l'empereur Anastase et le patriarche Timothée, tous les deux de tendance monophysite, il y eut des graves tumultes à Constantinople à cause du Trisagion. Le 4 novembre les monophysites chantèrent du haut de l'ambon de l'église de Saint Théodore le Trisagion avec l'addition ὁ σταυρωθεὶς δι' ἡμᾶς, à quoi les chalcédoniens opposèrent le Trisagion sans l'addition. La même chose se répéta deux jours après au Forum de Constantin, où l'émeute finit avec des incendies et des morts.[39] Sévère d'Antioche, qui cette même année était devenu patriarche d'Antioche, avait visité peu avant la ville impériale.

Toutefois la victoire des non-chalcédoniens ne dura pas longtemps. En 518, sous l'empereur Justin et le patriarche Jean, pendant la célébration de la Litur-

[37] Je renvoie une fois de plus à mon article déjà cité sur le Trisagion.
[38] Eduard SCHWARTZ, Acta Conciliorum Oecumenicorum, t. 2, vol. 1, Berolini – Lipsiae 1933, 195.
[39] Cf. MARCELLINUS COMES, Chronicon (PL 51, 937.938).

gie, le dimanche 15 juillet, le peuple demanda, avec des cris sans cesse qui arrêtèrent même la célébration, la proclamation pour le lendemain de la commémoraison du concile de Chalcédoine et l'anathème de Sévère, Timothée et d'autres. La scène se répéta le lendemain, pendant la célébration de cette commémoraison.[40] Le peuple obtint enfin l'anathème contre Sévère et Timothée. Tous ces faits furent inclus dans les actes du concile de Constantinople de 536.

Dans la célébration liturgique du 16 juillet la chronique mentionne, parmi les chants d'entrée, le cantique de Syméon, le « Benedictus », sous forme antiphonale, suivi du Trisagion.[41] Le tropaire ὁ Μονογενής n'y apparaît pas; ces faits se passaient en 518.

Cette même année Sévère était envoyé en exil. Et vers cette même époque un autre évêque syrien et théologien monophysite, Philoxène de Mabboug, qui avait écrit *De uno e sancta Trinitate incarnato et passo*,[42] connaissait aussi l'exil. Dans un autre endroit il avait écrit : « Les antiochiens (c'est-à-dire, les nestoriens) refusent de confesser la Vierge comme Mère de Dieu, aussi que le Christ comme un de la Trinité, crucifié pour nous ».

Au même temps, en 519, retentissait dans la capitale de l'empire le cri des moines scythes : *Unus de Trinitate crucifixus est.* Avec cette formule ils prétendaient interpréter d'une manière orthodoxe le concile de Chalcédoine, contre certains chalcédoniens qui penchaient pour le nestorianisme.[43] Cette formule, à propos de l'incarnation du Christ, apparaît déjà dans Proclus de Constantinople (431-446) dans sa lettre aux Arméniens : « Nous confessons que Dieu le Logos, Un de la Trinité, s'est incarné »,[44] et aussi dans une lettre à Jean d'Antioche : « Nous confessons que Un de la Trinité fut crucifié dans la chair ».[45] Cela apparaît tout particulièrement dans le douzième anathematisme de Cyrille d'Alexandrie : « Quiconque ne confesse que le Verbe de Dieu a souffert dans la chair, a été crucifié dans la chair et a goûté la mort dans la chair (...) soit anathème ! »[46]

[40] Sur tous ces faits, cf. Sebastià JANERAS, Una celebrazione liturgica tutta particolare a Costantinopoli nel secolo sesto, dans: Bert GROEN – Steven HAWKES–TEEPLES – Stefanos ALEXOPOULOS (eds.), Inquiries into Eastern Christian Worship: Selected Papers of the Second International Congress of the Society of Oriental Liturgy, Rome, 17 – 21 September 2008 (Eastern Christian Studies 12), Louvain – Paris – Walpole/MA 2012, 173–187.

[41] Sur cela, voir l'article cité dans la note précédente.

[42] Édité en partie par Marcel BRIERE dans: PO 15/4 (1920) et Marcel BRIERE – François GRAFFIN dans: PO 18/3 (1977). Sur Philoxène, voir surtout André DE HALLEUX, Philoxène de Mabbog. Sa vie, ses écrits, sa théologie, Louvain 1963.

[43] Sur les moines scythes, cf. Emile AMMAN, Scythes (moines), dans: Dictionnaire de Théologie catholique 14, 1746–1753; et surtout Charles MOELLER, Le chalcédonisme et le néochalcédonisme en Orient de 451 à la fin du VIe siècle, dans: Aloys GRILLMEIER – Henri BACHT (eds.), Das Konzil von Chalkedon. 1, Würzburg 1951, 637–720.

[44] Tomus ad armenios (PG 65, 865).

[45] Ad Ioannem Antiochenum (PG 65, 877).

[46] Eduard SCHWARTZ, Acta Conciliorum Oecumenicorum, t. 1, vol. 1, partie 1, Berolini – Lipsiae 1927, 42.

Justinien, avant de devenir empereur, mais associé au trône de Justin, et agissant déjà en théologien[47], ne voyait de bon œil, au début, l'activité des moines scythes, qui voulaient répandre la formule *Unus de Trinitate crucifixus est,* et dans ce sens il écrivit au pape Hormisdas. Mais il changea bientôt sa pensée et devint même un avocat convaincu de la formule scythe, dans laquelle il voyait une possibilité de réconcilier monophysites et chalcédoniens et obtenir ainsi l'unité de l'empire. Ses lettres de 520 et 521 au pape, dans lesquelles il employait l'expression *unus de* (ou *in* ou *ex*) *Trinitate,* n'obtinrent aucune réponse :

> « Nobis videtur quoniam Filius Dei vivi Dominus noster Iesus Christus ex Virgine Maria natus, quem praedicat summus apostolorum carne passum, recte dicitur unus in Trinitate cum Patre Spirituque Sancto regnare ; sicut enim ambiguum dicere simpliciter unum de Trinitate, non praemisso nomine Domini nostri Iesu Christi, sic eius personam in Trinitate cum Patris Spiritusque Sancti personis non dubitamus esse. »[48]

> « Nobis videtur quoniam Filius Dei vivi Dominus noster Iesus Christus ex Maria Virgine natus, quem praedicat summus apostolorum carne passum, recte dicitur unus ex Trinitate cum Patre Spirituque Sancto regnare, maiestatisque eius personam in Trinitate et ex Trinitate non infideliter credimus. »[49]

Entretemps Justinien devenait empereur, en 527, et depuis lors, sous l'influence de sa femme l'impératrice Théodora, il penchait de plus en plus pour les monophysites. Le mois de mars 533 il publia un édit contre une interprétation nestorienne de la définition de Chalcédoine.[50] Dans son deuxième article il anathématise tous ceux qui ne confessent pas que « Jésus Christ, le Fils de Dieu et notre Dieu, lequel se fit homme et fut crucifié, est un de la Trinité » (voir dans le tableau: Justinien *b*).

Justinien envoya cet édit au pape Jean II avec une profession de foi personnelle, toujours avec le but de soutenir l'expression *Unus de Trinitate*. Par deux fois pouvons-nous lire dans cette lettre non seulement les mêmes idées, mais aussi le même texte (voir dans le tableau: Justinien *c* et *d*).[51]

En novembre de cette même année Justinien écrivit encore une *Confessio rectae fidei adversus Tria Capitula,* toujours dans le même sens. On peut rapprocher ce texte du tropaire ὁ Μονογενής, aussi que du symbole de foi de Nicée-Constantinople, avec lesquels le parallélisme est évident (voir dans le tableau: Justinien *a*).[52]

Le pape Jean II approuva la doctrine de Justinien, même la formule *Unus de Trinitate*, ce qu'il confirme clairement dans une lettre aux sénateurs:

47 Sur Justinien théologien, voir Mario AMELOTTI – Livia MIGLIARDI ZINGALE, Scritti teologici ed ecclesiastici di Giustiniano, Milano 1977; UTHEMANN, Kaiser Justinian (cf. n. 1).
48 Lettre de 520 (PL 63, 496).
49 Lettre de 521 (PL 63, 508).
50 Cet édit est rapporté par le Chronicon Paschale (PG 92, 893).
51 PL 66, 15 et 16.
52 PG 86, 995.

> « Justinianus [...] de his tribus quaestionibus orta certamine fuisse signavit, utrum unus ex Trinitate Christus et Deus noster dici possit [...]. An Deus Christus carne pertulerit impassibili deitate. An proprie et veraciter Mater Domini Dei nostri Christi Maria sempre Virgo debeat appellari. Probavimus in his catholicam imperatoris fidem. »[53]

Le mois de novembre de cette même année 533 Constantinople connut un nouveau tremblement de terre, qui nous est rapporté par le *Chronicon Paschale.*[54] Ce tremblement se produisit le soir. Le peuple se ramassa au Forum, et pendant toute la nuit on ne cessait de prier et de crier: « Saint Dieu, Saint Fort, Saint Immortel, toi qui as été crucifié pour nous, aie pitié de nous ». Le matin arrivé, lorsque tout était déjà calme, ils crièrent encore: « Le sort des chrétiens a vaincu. Toi, qui as été crucifié pour nous, sauve nous et notre ville ».
Depuis l'automne 534 jusqu'en février 536 Sévère d'Antioche était de nouveau présent dans la ville impériale, accueilli par l'impératrice Théodora. Depuis 535 siégeait dans le trône patriarcal Anthime, lui aussi monophysite. C'est dans cette période, probablement en 535 et certainement avant le mois de février 536 que le tropaire ὁ Μονογενής fut composé et introduit dans la liturgie.
En effet, en février 536 le nouveau pape Agapet se rendit à Constantinople, où il s'opposa à l'empereur, déposa le patriarche Anthime et à sa place fut intronisé le patriarche Menna. Un concile fut convoqué, dans lequel furent lus les récits des faits qui eurent lieu en 518, à propos de la fête du concile de Chalcédoine, et inclus dans les Actes conciliaires.[55] Le mois d'août Justinien publiait une Constitution contre Sévère, Anthime, Pierre et Zoaras.[56] Sévère connut l'exil définitif, où il devait mourir deux ans après.
Le tropaire ὁ Μονογενής fut composé avant tous événements; certainement avant le bannissement de Sévère et sûrement avant la déposition du patriarche Anthime le mois de février. Cela explique que byzantins et non byzantins eussent pu accepter et introduire dans la liturgie le tropaire ὁ Μονογενής. Après 536 cela aurait été impossible.
Revenons maintenant à la question de l'auteur du tropaire: Justinien ou Sévère? Les quelques textes apportés par Puyade manifestent certes la même pensée et contiennent des expressions pareilles à celles du tropaire, par exemple:

> « Un donc de cette essence sublime, un de la Trinité, le Verbe de Dieu, Dieu de Dieu est descendu du ciel (...) et pour notre salut il est entré et il a habité dans le sein de la chair, dans la Vierge Marie (...). Il s'est fait homme, lui qui est Dieu ; il est devenu ce qu'il n'était pas, sans aucun changement de ce qu'il était. »[57]

[53] PL 66, 20.
[54] PG 92, 889.
[55] Cf. SCHWARTZ, Acta Conciliorum Oecumenicorum (cf. n. 38), 3, 71–76.
[56] Voir le texte de la Constitution en PG 86, 1095–1104, ou dans Mansi 8, Paris 1901, 1149–1156.
[57] Cité d'après Joseph LEBON, Le monophysisme sévérien, Louvain 1909, 180–181.

On pourrait citer encore d'autres textes, tels que certains hymnes de Sévère, où il est toujours question des expressions « Un de la Trinité » et « sans changement ».[58]

Mais les textes de Justinien mis dans le tableau ci-joint présentent des parallélismes littéraux très étroits et plaident avec force pour la paternité de l'empereur. Cependant on ne doit pas oublier l'histoire que je viens d'esquisser : Sévère se trouvait à Constantinople lorsque le tropaire est né. Justinien pouvait avoir été influencé par Sévère, lequel aurait pu même collaborer dans la rédaction. D'autre part, Sévère pourrait être l'auteur de ce texte, à la diffusion duquel Justinien aurait contribué avec son autorité impériale. En tout cas, la formule scythe *Unus de Trinitate crucifixus est* s'accorde bien avec l'addition foulonienne du Trisagion, et les expressions principales du tropaire peuvent se trouver chez Justinien aussi bien que chez Sèvère. Si Justinien donc en est l'auteur, l'attribution syrienne à Sévère ne manque pas quand même de sens.

On peut donc dire que le tropaire ὁ Μονογενής est un fruit du néo-chalcédonisme. Chalcédoniens et non chalcédoniens s'y retrouvent. Et on peut remarquer encore la présence dans le tropaire d'un adverbe accepté par tous: ἀτρέπτως (« sans changement » ; en syriaque : *dlo šuḥlofo*) et qui se trouve aussi justement dans la définition du concile de Chalcédoine.

On a comparé encore le texte du tropaire ὁ Μονογενής avec l'hymne christologique de Philippiens 2, 6-11, ce qui est important pour bien saisir tout le contenu doctrinal du tropaire. Jean Breck le fait brillamment dans son livre *La puissance de la Parole*. Il résume en schéma les rapports entre les deux hymnes: « Chacune commence par une proclamation de la condition éternelle et divine du Christ ; chacune continue par Son humiliation volontaire, Sa descente, Son incarnation et Sa crucifixion pour notre salut : Sa victoire sur la mort et Son exaltation consécutive; enfin Sa glorification comme Dieu. »[59] Il faut noter que ce rapprochement était déjà fait par Justinien dans sa *Confessio rectae fidei*.[60]

SIGNIFICATION ŒCUMÉNIQUE

Après tout ce que nous venons de dire, la signification œcuménique du tropaire ὁ Μονογενής est indéniable. On ne peut plus dire, comme certains auteurs l'on fait jusqu'aujourd'hui, que le tropaire ὁ Μονογενής est antinestorien et antimo-

[58] Cf. Ernest Walter BROOKS, James of Edessa. The Hymns of Severus of Antioch and others, dans: PO 6/1 (1909), passim. Puyade se réfère, en plus de Sévère, à la tradition monophysite en général.

[59] BRECK, La puissance de la Parole (cf. n. 1), 198. Dans son examen, plus bref, du contenu stylistique et doctrinal du tropaire, BARKHUIZEN, Justinian's Hymn (cf. n. 1), se rèfère aussi à l'hymne de l'épître aux Philippiens.

[60] PG 86, 997.

nophysite. On pourrait accepter un but antinestorien à cause de la formule *Unus de Trinitate crucifixus est*, bien que dans le tropaire les membres « crucifié » et « Un de la Trinité » se trouvent séparés sans former une seule phrase. Mais surtout le tropaire n'est pas antimonophysite, parce que, comme il apparaît clair, il reflète la christologie néochalcédonienne et sévérienne. Après tant de discussions et de luttes à propos de l'expression *Unus de Trinitate crucifixus est,* chalcédoniens et non-chalcédoniens, byzantins, syro-antiochiens, arméniens et coptes confessent et proclament dans la Liturgie: le Christ est le Verbe de Dieu, Un de la sainte Trinité, fait homme sans changement et crucifié, et il est glorifié ensemble avec le Père et le Saint-Esprit.

À cause de la relation entre le tropaire ὁ Μονογενής et le Trisagion, je voudrais apporter un petit exemple d'une attitude non œcuménique, voire même ignorante, de Rome vis-à-vis des Églises orientales catholiques. En 1635 la Congrégation *De Propaganda Fide* défendit aux arméniens catholiques d'introduire l'addition au Trisagion, *secundum theopaschitarum haeresim.*[61] Et, ce qui est pire, les syriens catholiques, dans le Synode de Charfet (Liban) de 1888, ont refusé – eux-mêmes ! – l'addition comme une *blasphemia et impietas*:

> « Appendix quam Petrus Cnaphaeus unus ex coryphaeis monophysitarum [...] Trisagio, id est seraphico hymno qui est : « Sanctus Deus, Sanctus Fortis, Sanctus Immortalis, miserere nostri » addidit, quae est : « Qui crucifixus es pro nobis » ante « miserere », quamque Iacobitae ab ipso acceperunt et usque ad hunc diem in usu habent, haec, inquimus, appendix est impietas et blasphemia, cum in ea crucifixio Sanctissimae Trinitati tribuatur. Propterea illam condemnamus et anathematizamus, prohibemusque illius additionem ad Trisagium quocumque sensu et quocumque pretextu, quemadmodum condemnamus et reicimus interpolationem quem Iacobitae in suis libris liturgicis introduxerunt ad Trisagium, illud referendo ad Filium, cum Ecclesia illud semper usurpet directum ad Sanctissimam Trinitatem. »[62]

Mais on peut voir encore aujourd'hui des liturgistes, des théologiens, des historiens parler du Trisagion « théopasquite ». Alors la liturgie latine est aussi théopasquite, puisqu'elle chante le Trisagion le Vendredi Saint pendant l'adoration de la Croix! On devrait parler tout simplement du Trisagion, avec ou sans addition, ou encore du Trisagion trinitaire (byzantins) et du Trisagion christologique (non-byzantins, occidentaux, sens originel). Un malentendu à ce propos avait coûté autrefois beaucoup d'encre et même de sang.

De même pour le tropaire ὁ Μονογενής. Cette perle de la liturgie n'est pas un texte « anti » ou « contre », qui appartienne seulement à une partie, mais plutôt un texte, pourrions-nous dire, de réconciliation de la chrétienté, pour employer les paroles de Klum-Böhmer à propos du Trisagion.[63] Ce texte est une confession de foi, à côté du symbole de Nicée, comme dit Jean Breck, lequel intitule le

[61] Cf. Johannes Michael HANSSENS, Institutiones liturgicae de ritibus orientalibus, t. 3, Rome 1953, 139.
[62] Synodus Sciarfensis Syrorum in Monte Libano celebrata anno MDCCCLXXXVIII, Rome 1896, 22.
[63] Edith KLUM-BÖHMER, Das Trishagion als Versöhnungsformel der Christenheit. Kontroverstheologie im V. und VI. Jahrhundert, München–Wien 1979.

chapitre 6 de son livre: « Le tropaire ὁ Μονογενής, symbole de foie orthodoxe ». En prenant le mot « orthodoxe » dans son sens plénier, j'aimerais mieux dire: une confession de foi œcuménique que tous les chrétiens, d'Orient et d'Occident, tout comme le symbole de Nicée-Constantinople, peuvent proclamer.

CREDO	TROPAIRE	JUSTINIEN (a)	JUSTINIEN (b)	JUSTINIEN (c)	JUSTINIEN (d)
Πιστεύω [...]		ὁμολογοῦμεν δὲ αὐτὸν	μὴ ὁμολογοῦντας	denegantes	praedicantes
εἰς ἕνα Κύριον Ἰησοῦν Χριστὸν		τὸν Δεσπότην ἡμῶν Ἰησοῦν Χριστὸν		Dominum nostrum Jesum Christum	Dominum nostrum Jesum Christum
τὸν Υἱὸν τοῦ Θεοῦ τὸν μονογενῆ,	ὁ μονογενὴς Υἱὸς	τὸν μονογενῆ Υἱὸν τοῦ Θεοῦ	τὸν Υἱὸν τοῦ Θεοῦ	Unigenitum Filium Dei	
	καὶ Λόγος τοῦ Θεοῦ	Θεὸν Λόγον	καὶ Θεὸν ἡμῶν	et Dominum nostrum	et Verbum Dei
		τὸν πρὸ αἰώνων καὶ ἀχρόνως			et ante saecula et sine tempore
τὸν ἐκ τοῦ Πατρὸς γεννηθέντα		ἐκ τοῦ Πατρὸς γεννηθέντα,			
πρὸ πάντων τῶν αἰώνων.					
Φῶς ἐκ φωτός,					
Θεὸν ἀληθινὸν ἐκ Θεοῦ ἀληθινοῦ,					
γεννηθέντα,					
οὐ ποιηθέντα,		οὐ ποιηθέντα,			
ὁμοούσιον τῷ Πατρί,					
δι'οὗ τὰ πάντα ἐγένετο.					
		ἐπ'ἐσχάτων τῶν ἡμερῶν			in ultimis diebus
	ἀθάνατος ὑπάρχων,				
	καὶ καταδεξάμενος				
Τὸν δι'ἡμᾶς τοὺς ἀνθρώπους,		δι'ἡμᾶς			
καὶ διὰ τὴν ἡμετέραν σωτηρίαν	διὰ τὴν ἡμετέραν σωτηρίαν	καὶ διὰ τὴν ἡμετέραν σωτηρίαν			
κατελθόντα ἐκ τῶν οὐρανῶν,		κατελθόντα ἐκ τῶν οὐρανῶν,			descendisse de caelis
καὶ σαρκωθέντα	σαρκωθῆναι	καὶ σαρκωθέντα	τὸν σαρκωθέντα	Incarnatum	et incarnatum
ἐκ Πνεύματος Ἁγίου		ἐκ Πνεύματος ἁγίου		de Sancto Spiritu	de Spiritu Sancto
	ἐκ τῆς ἁγίας	καὶ τῆς ἁγίας ἐνδόξου		et ex sancta atque gloriosissima	et ex sancta atque gloriosa
καὶ Μαρίας τῆς παρθένου,	Θεοτόκου καὶ ἀειπαρθένου Μαρίας	Θεοτόκου καὶ ἀειπαρθένου Μαρίας		semper Virgine Deigenitrice Maria	Virgine Deigenitrice Maria
ἐνανθρωπήσαντα,	ἀτρέπτως ἐνανθρωπήσας,	καί γεννηθέντα ἐξ αὐτῆς,	καὶ ἐνανθρωπήσαντα	hominem factum	natum et hominem factum
σταυρωθέντα τε ὑπὲρ ὑμῶν	σταυρωθείς τε,		καὶ σταυρωθέντα	atque crucifixum	et crucifixum,
ἐπὶ Ποντίου Πιλάτου					
	Χριστὲ ὁ Θεός,				
καί παθόντα, καί ταφέντα					
	θανάτῳ θάνατον πατήσας,				
		ὅς ἐστι Κύριος Ἰησοῦς Χριστός,			
	εἷς ὢν τῆς ἁγίας Τριάδος,	εἷς τῆς ἁγίας Τριάδος	ἕνα εἶναι τῆς ἁγίας καὶ	unum esse sanctae et	unum esse sanctae et
			ὁμοουσίου Τριάδος	consubstantialis Trinitatis	consubstantialis Trinitatis
			[…] συμπροσκυνούμενος	et coadorandum	et coadorandum
	συνδοξαζόμενος		καὶ συνδοξαζόμενος	et conglorificandum	et conglorificandum
	τῷ Πατρὶ		τῷ Πατρὶ	Patri	Patri
	καὶ τῷ ἁγίῳ Πνεύματι.		καὶ τῷ ἁγίῳ Πνεύματι	et Spiritui Sancto	et Sancto Spiritui
	Σῶσον ἡμᾶς.				

ZUR ENTSTEHUNGSGESCHICHTE DES "KÖNIGLICHEN" ANFANGS DES BYZANTINISCHEN MORGENGOTTESDIENSTES

VASSA LARIN

A. EINLEITUNG

Der „königliche" Dienst [KD], mit dem der tägliche byzantinische Orthros beginnt, besteht aus: Den Psalmen 19 und 20, einer Inzensierung der ganzen Kirche, den Kreuztroparia, einer kurzen Litanei und der Ausrufung „Δόξα τῇ ἁγίᾳ καὶ ὁμοουσίῳ ...". Viele Typika schreiben während dieses „königlichen" Anfangs vor, dass die Gläubigen „ohne Metanoia" (ἄνευ μετάνοιῶν) beten sollen. Die byzantinische Liturgiewissenschaft schenkte diesem kurzen Ritus bisher sehr wenig Aufmerksamkeit. Jene Liturgiker, die sich bis jetzt mit dem Orthros befassten, behandelten die Entstehungsgeschichte des KD entweder gar nicht,[1] oder begnügten sich mit einigen wenigen Anmerkungen.[2] Sie führten vor allem an, dass der KD ursprünglich nur in „kaiserlichen" Klöstern zelebriert wurde. So schrieb J. Matéos im Jahre 1961: „... il était célebré, semble-t-il, dans les monastères de fondation impériale".[3] Auch R. Taft wiederholte 1986 fast wortwörtlich das Gleiche: „... there is the so-called Royal Office, a brief service for the sovereign celebrated, apparently, in imperial monastic foundations".[4] Darüber hinaus wird vermutet, der KD sei "extraneous to the structure of matins", und würde von Mönchen willkürlich an den Anfang des täglichen Morgengottesdienstes hinzugefügt: „Because monks are fond of adding but only rarely subtract material from their offices".[5] Ziel dieser Arbeit ist es, diese Hypothesen auf Basis der byzantinischen monastischen Typika der 10.-14. Jahrhunderte zu überprüfen. Zuerst werfen wir einen Blick auf den „Kathedral"-Anfang des täglichen Orthros in der Hagia Sophia, um die *strukturellen* Möglichkeiten für einen KD an dieser Stelle des Stundengebets zu veranschaulichen. Schließlich soll festgestellt werden, wer für diese Interpolation verantwortlich war bzw. ob sie tatsächlich auf eine monastische Initiative zurückgeht.

[1] Cf. Mikhail SKABALLANOVIČ, Tolkovyj Tipikon 1, Kiew 1910; Nikolaj D. USPENSKY, Vsenoščnoe bdenie, Moskau 2004.
[2] Ioannis FOUNTOULIS, Monachikos orthros, Thessaloniki 1978, 7.
[3] Juan MATEOS, Quelques problèmes de l'orthros byzantin, in: Proche–Orient Chretien 11 (1961) 201.
[4] Robert TAFT, The Liturgy of the Hours in East and West, Collegeville 1986, 277.
[5] TAFT, Liturgy of the Hours (s. Anm. 4), 277.

B. DER ORTHROS DER HAGIA SOPHIA: EIN STRUKTURELLER PRÄZEDENZFALL?

Die ᾀσματικὴ ἀκολουθία der Hagia Sophia in Konstantinopel ist in diesem Zusammenhang von großer Bedeutung, weil die studitisch geprägten „Reform-Klöster" des 11.-12. Jahrhunderts, die als erste den „königlichen" Dienst anführten, unter dem Einfluss dieses Ritus ihrer Herkunftsstadt standen.
Wegen der bruchstückhaften Quellen- und Forschungslage[6] basiert diese Untersuchung des Orthros der Hagia Sophia größtenteils auf dem Bericht des hl. Symeon von Thessaloniki († 1429), den er uns in seinem „De Sacra Precatione" hinterließ.[7] Über den täglichen Orthros berichtet der hl. Symeon, dass der Gottesdienst im Narthex der Kirche mit der Ausrufung „Εὐλογημένη ἡ βασιλεία..." beginnt. Darauf folgt eine Große Ektenie (τὰ εἰρηνικά) und Psalmen schließen an. Während des 118. Psalms wird zuerst der Narthex vom Priester inzensiert, dann tritt er durch die Seitentüren in die Kirche ein, beweihräuchert die Kirche und zuletzt den Altarraum. Dort legt er das Weihrauchgefäß ab, nimmt das Kreuz und geht in den Narthex zurück (wieder durch die Seitentüren). Zunächst stellt er das Kreuz vor die Haupttüren, die sich zwischen Narthex und Kirche befinden. Während des 170. Verses (Ἐγγισάτω ἡ δέησίς μου ἐνώπιόν σου, Κύριε...) beginnt der feierliche Einzug in die Kirche: Der Priester öffnet die Türen, singt „τὸ εἰσοδικόν" (Einzugsvers) mit dem „Alleluia", wobei er das Kreuz hält, an dem drei brennende Kerzen befestigt sind (wohl die Anfänge der heutigen österlichen Riten).[8] Der Priester segnet den Einzug mit den Worten, „Εὐλογημένη ἡ εἴσοδος τῶν ἁγίων σου, Κύριε" und tritt durch die Haupttüren in die Kirche ein. Ihm folgt der Bischof, (der hier sonst keine Funktion innehat) und geht zu seinem Stasidion. Das Volk tritt durch die Seitentüren in die Kirche ein. Hierauf geht der Priester zum Altarraum und stellt das Kreuz vor dessen Türen. Psalm 118 wird bis zum Ende gesungen, worauf das „Εὐλογεῖτε" (das Lied der drei Jünger) folgt.
Hier soll Symeons Bericht unterbrochen werden, ohne den letzten Teil des Orthros zu berücksichtigen, denn der Fokus der Arbeit liegt auf dem Anfang des Ritus. Der Orthros beginnt außerhalb des Altarraums, ja sogar außerhalb der

[6] Die noch unveröffentlichte Dissertation von Gregor M. HANKE, Vesper und Orthros des Kathedralritus der Hagia Sophia zu Konstantinopel. Eine strukturanalytische und entwicklungsgeschichtliche Untersuchung unter besonderer Berücksichtigung der Psalmodie und der Formulare in den Euchologien, Philosophisch–Theologische Hochschule Sankt–Georgen, Frankfurt am Main 2002, blieb der Verfasserin unzugänglich. Übersichten bzw. Annäherungen an die Struktur des Orthros im Kathedralritus geben Juan Mateos und Ilarion Alfeev: Juan MATÉOS (Hg.), Le Typicon de la Grande Église 1 (OCA 165), Rom 1962, XXII–XXIII; Ilarion ALFEEV, Prepodobnyj Simeon Novyj Bogoslov i Pravoslavnoe Predanie, Moskau 1998, 116. Beide Autoren bleiben jedoch die Fundierung aus den Quellen schuldig, weswegen sie hier nicht weiter berücksichtigt werden.

[7] PG 155, 247C–249A.

[8] SKABALLANOVIČ, Tolkovyj Tipikon (s. Anm. 1), 383.

Kirche im Narthex. Dass dieser Teil des Berichts von Symeon tatsächlich den Ritus der Hagia Sophia wiedergibt, lässt sich nicht bezweifeln, denn auch ein russischer Pilger, Erzbischof Antonij von Novgorod, berichtet am Ende des 12. Jahrhunderts über den Gottesdienst in Konstantinopel: Der Orthros in der Hagia Sophia „wird zuerst im Narthex vor den königlichen Türen gesungen, dann geht man herein und singt in der Kirche“.[9]

So lässt sich eine strukturelle Parallele zum „königlichen“ Anfang feststellen: Etwas „weniger Feierliches“ am Anfang des Orthros der Hagia Sophia, währenddessen die Kirche inzensiert wurde, wie später dies während des „königlichen“ Dienstes gemacht werden soll. Erst nach dieser *Vorbereitung* beginnt der feierliche Teil des Orthros mit dem Einzug und einem Einzugsvers, dem im „königlichen“ Dienst die feierliche Ausrufung „Δόξα τῇ ἁγίᾳ καὶ ὁμοουσίῳ“ folgt. Interessanterweise begann auch der Kathedralritus der Jerusalemer Anastasis-Kirche des vierten Jahrhunderts mit einem „weniger feierlichen“ Teil (vor dem Einzug des Bischofs), wie uns Egeria in ihrem Pilgerbericht überliefert.[10] Deshalb sind die strukturellen Entfaltungsmöglichkeiten für einen „königlichen“ Dienst gerade am Anfang des Orthros nicht zu übersehen.

C. DIE FRÜHEN ZEUGNISSE DES „KÖNIGLICHEN“ DIENSTES

C. I. Geschichtliches

Die ersten hier behandelten, klösterlichen Typika spiegeln eine konstantinopolitanische Tradition wider, die im 11. Jahrhundert eine „Studitische Synthese“ aus den hagiopolitischen und Hagia Sophia-Riten darstellte.[11]

Der geschichtliche Hintergrund der zu untersuchenden Typika ist ganz von der monastischen Reformbewegung des 11.–12. Jahrhunderts geprägt. Zu den ideo-

[9] Paul SAVVAITOV, Putešestvie Novgorodskago episkopa Antonia v Tsar'grad, St. Petersburg 1872, 93. Zitat in: SKABALLANOVIČ, Tolkovyj Tipikon (s. Anm. 1), 382.

[10] Nach Egeria wurde der Anfang dieses täglichen Gottesdienstes (vor der Morgendämmerung) von Presbytern und Diakonen – ohne den Bischof – zelebriert, unter Anwesenheit von: Mönchen und Jungfrauen (monazontes et parthenae) und den eifrigeren Laien (et laici praeterea – viri aut mulieres). Zu diesem Teil des Orthros wurden „Hymnen, Psalmen und Antiphone“ responsorisch gesungen (dicuntur ymni et psalmi responduntur, similiter et antiphonae). Bei Morgendämmerung beginnt man die „morgendlichen Hymnen“ (matutinos ymnos). Erst zu diesem Moment erscheint der Bischof mit dem Klerus und tritt sofort in das Heilige Grab (intro spelunca) ein (Itinerarium 24, 1–4). Otto PRINZ (Hg.), Itinerarium Egeriae (Peregrinatio Aetheriae), Heidelberg 1960, 31.

[11] Robert TAFT, Vizantijskij Tserkovnyj Obrjad, St. Petersburg 2000, 74. Das gleiche schrieb Skaballanovič ein Jahrhundert früher: „...заимствуя въ храмѣ Воскресенія и у Палестинскихъ монастырей чинъ суточнаго богослуженія, пр. Феодоръ долженъ былъ произвесть въ немъ нѣкоторые измѣненія... И понятно, въ какую сторону могли клониться эти измѣненія. Палестинскій чинъ богослуженія въ К–полѣ естественно было приспособить къ уставу св. Софіи и соборныхъ церквей“: SKABALLANOVIČ, Tolkovyj Tipikon (s. Anm. 1), 396.

logischen Zügen dieser Bewegung zählen die Vorliebe für das koinobitische Leben und die Betonung des Vorrangs des Gebets vor der körperlichen Arbeit.[12] Außerdem strebten die „Reformatoren" die Selbständigkeit der Klöster gegenüber dem berüchtigten Charistikariersystem an. Laut diesem System, das sich wohl seit dem mönchsfeindlichen Kopronymos (741–775) einbürgerte,[13] konnte ein Kloster einer Privatperson (χαριστικάριος) als eine Art Geschenk (διὰ χαριστικῆς) übergeben werden. Diese Gepflogenheit, die seit dem 10. Jahrhundert besonders große Verbreitung fand, diente im Idealfall zur wirtschaftlichen Stärkung der Klöster, weshalb sie von mehreren angesehenen Bischöfen verteidigt wurde.[14] Es führte jedoch zu Missbräuchen, da der „Charistikarios" das Kloster für seinen eigenen Profit ausnutzte. Manchmal verkaufte er sogar das Kloster an jemanden Dritten, oder zog selbst mit der Familie in das Kloster ein.[15] Charistikarier konnten sowohl Geistliche als auch Laien sein, ja sogar Frauen, wobei manchmal Frauenklöster an Männer und Männerklöster an Frauen verliehen wurden.[16] Wiederholt versuchten Kirchensynoden (1027, 1028) diese Missbräuche abzustellen, was allerdings nicht gelang, da die Beschlüsse der Synoden ignoriert wurden. Daher versuchte eine neue Bewegung innerhalb des Mönchtums, die man monastische „Reformbewegung" nennt, andere Schutzherren für die Klöster zu finden.

Das 11. Jahrhundert war von der heftigen Kontroverse über die Säkularisierung des Kirchenguts geprägt. So konfiszierte 1057–1058 Isaak Komnenos (1057–1059) Klostergut, was u. a. kurz darauf zur Absetzung des Patriarchen Michael Kerullarios führte.[17] Die Situation spitzte sich erneut zu, als Alexios I. Komnenos (1081–1118) im Jahre 1082 Kirchengeräte verpfänden ließ, um den Krieg mit Robert Guiscard zu finanzieren, worauf der Kaiser auf eine starke Opposition in Kirchenkreisen stieß.[18] Nichtsdestoweniger wandten sich die Reform-Mönche dem Kaiser als Schützer ihres Eigentums zu.

In verschiedenen Ktitor-Typika des 11.–12. Jahrhunderts finden wir eine nachdrückliche Erklärung, dass das Kloster selbständig (αὐτοδέσποτα), selbstverwaltend (αὐτεξούσια) und frei (ἐλεύθερα) sei.[19] Eine solche Erklärung war bei weitem noch keine Garantie für die zukünftige Selbständigkeit des Klosters. Um den Status „selbständig" zu bestätigen, erwirkten einige der „Reform"

[12] John THOMAS – Angela C. HERO (Hgg.), Byzantine Monastic Foundation Documents 2 (Dumbarton Oaks Studies 35) [BMFD], Washington/D.C. 2000, 447.
[13] Nikolai Af. SKABALANOVIČ, Vizantijskoe Gosudarstvo i Tserkov' v XI veke I, St. Petersburg 2004, 395–403.
[14] Georg OSTROGORSKY, Geschichte des Byzantinischen Staates, hrsg. von Walter OTTO (Byzantinisches Handbuch T. 1, Bd. 2), München 1940, 263.
[15] SKABALANOVIČ, Vizantijskoe Gosudarstvo 1 (s. Anm. 13), 395–403.
[16] Ibid., 400.
[17] Nikolaj Af. SKABALANOVIČ, Vizantijskoe Gosudarstvo i Tserkov' v XI veke II, St. Petersburg 2004, 102–103.
[18] THOMAS – HERO, BMFD 2 (s. Anm. 12), 450. Cf. auch OSTROGORSKY, Geschichte (s. Anm. 14), 263.
[19] THOMAS – HERO, BMFD 1 (s. Anm. 12), 167.

Klöster einen Chrysobullos vom Kaiser, der die Selbständigkeit garantierte. Die Gewährung eines solchen Chrysobullos war nicht automatisch mit einer Machtbefugnis des Kaisers über das Kloster verbunden. Beispielsweise wissen wir, dass Alexios Komnenos verschiedenen Klöstern (z. B. Eleousa, Pakourianos) Chrysobullen gewährte, ohne sich diese Klöster anzueignen oder Einfluss auf das klösterliche Leben auszuüben. Vermutlich beteten die Mönche als Gegenleistung für die Gewährung des Chrysobullos für den Kaiser. Zumindest fühlte sich der Mönch Christodoulos († 1093), der für sein Kloster auf Patmos einen Chrysobullos von Alexios bekam, in seinem „Testament“ verpflichtet, für den Kaiser zu beten; dazu fordert er auch seinen Nachfolger auf: „für unseren mächtigsten und heiligen Kaiser zu singen und zu beten.“[20] Auf die Person Alexios I. Komnenos wird etwas näher eingegangen, denn die Ursprünge des „königlichen“ Dienstes scheinen mit seinem Namen eng verbunden zu sein.

Das zweideutige Verhältnis zwischen Alexios und dem klösterlichen Eigentum ist ein anschauliches Beispiel einer Tragik des orthodoxen Kaisers in Spätbyzanz. Einerseits unterstützten die Kaiser verschiedene Klöster, oder begründeten sogar eigene, „kaiserliche“ Klöster, wo viele von ihnen begraben wurden oder auch die letzte Jahre ihres Lebens (manchmal als Mönche) verbrachten. Die labile politische Lage in Spätbyzanz, als jeder Kaiser mit der Möglichkeit rechnen mußte, sein Leben im Kloster zu beenden, rief eine besondere Beziehung zwischen dem Kaiser und dem Mönchsleben hervor.[21] Die kaiserlichen Ktitoren bauten in ihren Klöstern Familiengrüfte und erhofften sich so von den Mönchen Gebete für die eigene Familie und für das gesamte Reich. Einige kaiserliche Ktitoren gewährten ihren Klöstern liturgische Typika, die u.a. das Gebet für die Ktitoren vor und nach ihrem Tod genau regelten. Der Rechtsstatus eines „kaiserlichen“ Klosters war für die Mönche vorteilhaft, da ein „kaiserliches“ Kloster vom Beitrag der Diözesenverwaltung befreit war. Zusätzlich war es auch in administrativen Angelegenheiten gegenüber dieser Verwaltung selbständig. Der Bischof hatte hier keine Rechte, auch nicht τὴν ἀναφοράν (der Erwähnung seines Namens im kirchlichen Gebet).[22] Die kirchenrechtliche Problematik ist in diesem Fall offensichtlich, fällt aber nicht in den Rahmen dieser Arbeit. Es sei nur angemerkt, dass bestimmte „bischofsfeindliche“ Züge der klösterlichen Typika dieser Zeit, wobei der Kaiser mitunter als Schützer des Klosters vor dem eigenen Bischof fungierte, mit der Rolle mancher Bischöfe als Charistikarier verbunden sind. D. h. eine „bischofsfeindliche“ Einstellung einiger Klöster lag nicht in der Natur der Sache (in der bischöflichen Macht), sondern in den vorübergehenden Umständen des Charistikariersystems.

[20] Testament [B5]: THOMAS – HERO, BMFD 2 (s. Anm. 12), 595. Leider enthält das Typikon nur sehr generelle liturgische Hinweise, so dass ein „königlicher“ Dienst am Anfang nicht festzustellen – aber auch nicht auszuschließen ist.

[21] SKABALANOVIČ, Vizantijskoe Gosudarstvo 2 (s. Anm. 17), 146–149.

[22] Ibid., 152.

Andererseits gab es noch eine weitere Seite der Beziehung zwischen Kaiser und Kloster bzw. Kirchengut. Wie immer man diese Beziehung auch beurteilen will, der Kaiser war in seiner Rolle als Schützer der Grenzen des Reiches nicht immer auch Schützer der Kirche. Die politischen Verhältnisse in der spätbyzantinischen Zeit zwangen den Kaiser immer wieder zu Handlungen, denen die Kirche nicht zustimmen konnte, – sei es Konfiskationen sakraler Kirchengeräte, sei es Verhandlungen mit Rom in Zeiten der Not (1091,[23] 1274, 1439 u. a.). Diese Umstände blieben nicht ohne Konsequenzen für die Einstellung der Kirche zum Kaiser, was im kirchlichen Gebet für den Kaiser Ausdruck fand: Der Kaiser bedarf des Gebets der Kirche, während die Kirche lediglich des Schutzes Gottes bedarf. In diesem Sinne schreibt H. G. Beck über die spätbyzantinische Kirche: Die Kirche „rückt auf bedeutsame Weise vom Kaiser als ihrem Garanten ab, weil diesen die politischen Verhältnisse zwingen, eine Linie zu verfolgen, welche in den Augen der Orthodoxie nur als unzuverlässig erscheinen konnte.“[24] Genau auf diesem Hintergrund entsteht das Gebet für den König am Anfang des Orthros.

C. II. Die Quellen-Typika

Wie bereits erwähnt, gehen heutige Liturgiker im Hinblick auf den „königlichen“ Dienst von der Vermutung aus, dass dieser Ritus ursprünglich nur in „kaiserlichen“ Klöstern gefeiert wurde. Daher ist es erforderlich, im nächsten Teil dieser Arbeit zu prüfen, ob eine nähere Erforschung der monastischen Typika von *Eleousa*, *Evergetis*, *Kecharitomene*, *Pantokrator* u. a. diese Hypothese bestätigen kann. Die Frage lautet daher: Hing ursprünglich der „königliche“ Dienst nur mit dem „kaiserlichen“ Status der Klöster, die ihn einführten, zusammen, oder nicht? Außerdem ließe sich durch die genaue Untersuchung der verschiedenen Redaktionen „königlichen“ Dienstes in den Typika möglicherweise ein besseres Verständnis der Struktur und des Inhaltes des gesamten Ritus gewinnen.

C. II. 1. Eleousa

Das Kloster der Gottesmutter *Eleousa* wurde 1080 von Bischof Manuel von Stroumitza (heute Stroumica im Südosten Makedoniens) gegründet.[25] Manuel war ursprünglich Mönch des hl. Auxentios-Klosters bei Chalkedon, wurde danach Bischof von Stroumitza und kaufte mit eigenem Geld ein Grundstück, auf dem er sein Kloster erbaute. Obwohl Manuel nur eingeschränkt als Vertreter der

[23] S. den Brief des Kaisers Alexios Komnenos an die Kaiser Westeuropas von 1091. Zitiert in: Feodor I. USPENSKY, Istoria Vizantijskoj Imperii IV, Moskau 2002, 112–113.
[24] Hans-Georg BECK, Das Byzantinische Jahrtausend, München 1978, 108.
[25] THOMAS – HERO, BMFD 1 (s. Anm. 12), 167.

Reformbewegung bezeichnet werden kann,[26] strebte er die Selbständigkeit seines Klosters an, um es von allen staatlichen und kirchlichen Steuern zu befreien. Außerdem legte er Wert darauf, dass das Kloster nach seinem Tod nicht vom nächsten Bischof von Stroumitza übernommen würde. Aus diesem Grund bemühte sich Manuel im Juli 1085 um einen Chrysobullos des Kaisers Alexios I. Komnenos. Nach der Gewährung des Chrysobullos bekam das Eleousa-Kloster den Status „αὐτοδέσποτος“, „αὐτεξούσια“ und „ἐλεύθερα“.[27] Ein „selbständiges“ Kloster zu sein hieß, dass es (wie ein „kaiserliches“ Kloster) vom Beitrag der Diözesenverwaltung befreit war. Im Unterschied zu einem „kaiserlichen“ Kloster hatte der örtliche Bischof in einem „selbständigen“ Kloster das Recht auf die Erwähnung seines Namens im Gebet (τὴν ἀναφοράν), auf die Einsetzung (τὴν σφραγίδα) und auf die Disziplin (τὴν διόρθωσιν τῶν σφαλμάτων.[28] In seinem Typikon begrenzte Manuel allerdings das Recht des Bischofs „τὴν σφραγίδα” dadurch, dass die Mönche nur einen bereits gewählten Abt dem Bischof zur Amtseinsegnung (σφραγίς) vorstellen sollten [Typikon §16].[29]

Kaiser Alexios besuchte das Kloster in Stroumitza während eines Feldzugs gegen die Serben.[30] Anna Komnene berichtet (was von Forschern des *Eleousa*-Typikons übersehen wird), dass Alexios bei diesem Feldzug von seiner Ehefrau Eirene Doukaina überall hin begleitet wurde.[31] Man kann davon ausgehen, dass Eirene das Kloster mit ihrem Ehemann besuchte. Nach dem Feldzug gewährte Alexios dem Kloster noch einen weiteren Chrysobullos, laut dem das Kloster zwölf „paroikoi“ (Bauern) erhielt. In der Zeit zwischen den zwei Chrysobullen wurde das *Eleousa*-Typikon von Manuel verfaßt, d. h. zwischen 1085 und 1107.[32] Wir sollten also in Betracht ziehen, dass der Besuch des kaiserlichen Ehepaars zum *Eleousa*-Kloster und die Verfassungszeit seines Typikons zeitlich relativ nahe zusammenfallen. Auf diesen Punkt werden wir später noch zurückkommen.

Manuel bemerkt in seinem Typikon, dass Alexios seinen (ersten) Chrysobullos erließ, damit für den Kaiser im Kloster gebetet werde. Uns ist leider nur die Englische Übersetzung des Textes aus der Dumbarton Oaks Ausgabe zugänglich:

> For, in fact, according to the chrysobull that has been issued to me and is attached to this [typikon] by our most excellent and holy emperor, Lord Alexios, for the sake of a supplicatory prayer on behalf of the permanence of his divine sovereignty, no one of the tax collec-

[26] „Manuel was at best a reluctant follower of the monastic reform movement“. Ebd.
[27] Ebd.
[28] SKABALANOVIČ, Vizantijskoe Gosudarstvo 2 (s. Anm. 17), 152.
[29] THOMAS – HERO, BMFD 1 (s. Anm. 12), 185.
[30] Ebd., 167.
[31] „Er zwang sogar die Augusta, mit ihm zusammen ins Feld zu ziehen“. Anna KOMNENE, Alexias XII, 2, übersetzt von Diether R. REINSCH, Köln 1996, 407.
[32] THOMAS – HERO, BMFD 1 (s. Anm. 12), 167.

tors in the region [...] will be permitted [...] to innovate and to injure or to abuse at all this monastery of the Mother of God. [Typikon §18][33]

Der besagte „supplicatory prayer on behalf of his divine sovereignty", um den Alexios nach den Worten Manuels das Kloster bat (oder um das die Kaiserin Eirene das Kloster bat?), finden wir am Anfang des Orthros. Diesen Anfang des täglichen Gebets legt Manuel in dem sechsten Absatz seines Typikons dar:

- Mesonyktikon im Narthex
- Trisagion[34] (vermutlich in der Kirche)
- Gebet für den König (Text unbekannt)
- „Kommt, lasst uns niederfallen"
- Psalm 19
- Trisagion
- Troparia: Σῶσον, Κύριε
- Δόξα: Ὁ ὑψωθεὶς
- Καὶ νῦν: Ταχὺ προκατάλαβε
- 24 Kyrie eleison
- Hexapsalm

Der heutige „königliche" Dienst unterscheidet sich von der Version aus *Eleousa* durch das Fehlen der Vorschrift „ἄνευ μετάνοιῶν" (ohne Metanoia) und durch das besondere Gebet für den König; ferner fehlt der 20. Psalm und die kurze Ektenie am Ende, die hier durch das 24-malige Kyrie eleison ersetzt wird. Es gibt auch keine feierliche Ausrufung (Δόξα τῇ ἁγίᾳ...) vor dem Hexapsalm, die den „königlichen" Dienst vom weiteren Teil des Orthros abgrenzen würde. Ob der Weihräucherungsritus fehlt lässt sich nicht feststellen, weil Manuel generell keine Hinweise auf die Handlungen des Priesters gibt.

Zusammenfassend kann festgestellt werden, dass die Einführung des „königlichen" Dienstes im Fall Eleousa nicht mit dem Status eines „königlichen" Klosters zusammenhing, sondern mit einer anderen Art Verhältnis zwischen Kaiser und Kloster; Alexios Komnenos eignete sich dieses Kloster zweifellos nicht an. Vielmehr ist die Bedingung des Kaisers, ausgesprochen in seinem Chrysobullos, dass für ihn gebetet wird, entscheidend: der Kaiser bietet dem Kloster Unterstützung und Privilegien an. Damit gewinnt er nicht ein eigenes Kloster, sondern das tägliche Gebet der Mönche. In der Hypothese, der „königliche" Dienst hinge mit dem „kaiserlichen" Status des Klosters zusammen, lässt sich eine Korrektur anbringen: die Grundlage für den „königlichen" Dienst ist nicht die juristische Macht des Kaisers, sondern sein Bedürfnis nach Gebet.

[33] Ebd., 187.

[34] Mit dem Begriff *Trisagion* meinen wir hier und auch weiterhin die Reihe von Gebeten: Heiliger Gott...(dreimal), Ehre und jetzt, Allerheilige Dreieinigkeit..., Kyrie eleison (dreimal), Ehre und jetzt, Vaterunser.

C. II. 2. Evergetis

Das Kloster *Evergetis* wurde 1048 in der Nähe von Konstantinopel von einem gewissen Paulus († 1054), dem ersten Abt des Klosters, gegründet.[35] Der Nachfolger des Paulus, Timotheos († nach 1067), baute das Kloster weiter aus und gilt als Verfasser des liturgischen Typikons. Die Handschrift dieses Typikons (*Cod. Atheniensis 788*), die uns heute in der Ausgabe Dmitrievskys zur Verfügung steht, stammt allerdings erst aus dem 12. Jahrhundert.[36] Laut seinem Typikon erhielt Timotheos Chrysobullen von unbenannten „Kaisern“ für sein Kloster, die dem Kloster den Status „ἐλεύθερος“ und „αὐτοδέσποτος“ verliehen.[37] Obwohl wir die Namen der „Kaiser“ nicht kennen, lässt sich eine Verbindung zwischen dem Kloster und der Komnenen-Dynastie herstellen. Johannes Doukas, Schwager des Kaisers Alexios I. Komnenos, trat in dieses Kloster als Mönch Antonios irgendwann nach 1097 ein.[38]

Das Evergetis-Typikon gilt als das einflussreichste Typikon der monastischen Reformbewegung des 12. Jahrhunderts, weil es vielen anderen „Reform“-Typika (Kosmoteira, Phoberos, Kecharitomene, Pantokrator) als Vorbild diente.[39] Für uns ist der „Prologos“ dieses Typikons besonders wichtig, da wir hier eine detaillierte Darlegung des „königlichen“ Dienstes finden, der dem heutigen Ritus fast genau entspricht. Es wird vermutet, dass der „Prologos“ aus den ersten Jahrzehnten des 12. Jahrhunderts stammt,[40] d.h., in einer Zeit der engen Verbindung des Klosters mit der kaiserlichen Familie. Der Status dieses Klosers lässt sich aber nicht als „kaiserlich“ bezeichnen.

Der Anfang des Orthros wird im Typikon des Klosters Evergetis ausführlich beschrieben: nach einem Mesonyktikon, das jeder Mönch in der eigenen „Zelle“ liest, werden alle Mönche zu dem „ἑωθινὴν δοξολογίαν“ (Doxologie der Morgendämmerung, Orthros) durch den großen Semantron berufen. Nach dem Segen des Priesters, der im Altarraum und in der Kirche inzensiert, singen die Mönche den folgenden „königlichen“ Dienst:

- Trisagion
- Psalm 19 [Weihräuchern]
- Psalm 20
- „Gewöhnliche Troparia“
- Kyrie eleison
- Ausrufung
- Hexapsalm

[35] Alexij DMITRIEVSKY (Hg), Opisanie Liturgičeskich Rukopisej 1, Kiew 1895, XXXVI.
[36] Ebd., XL.
[37] Ebd., 630.
[38] THOMAS – HERO, BMFD 2 (s. Anm. 12), 467.
[39] THOMAS – HERO, BMFD 1 (s. Anm. 12), 211.
[40] THOMAS – HERO, BMFD 2 (s. Anm. 12), 455–6.

Wir haben also fast den heutigen Ritus vor uns, auch mit zwei Psalmen. Der Verfasser scheint einen schon allgemein bekannten Ritus zugrunde zu legen, denn er hält es nicht für nötig, die „gewöhnlichen“ Troparia oder die Anzahl der „Kyrie eleison“ zu nennen. Er führt demnach nichts Neues ein, so dass wir feststellen können, dass es sich beim Verfasser des Typikons *Evergetis* nicht um den Erfinder des „königlichen“ Dienstes handelt. Während sich die Troparia bereits eingebürgert haben (mit Abweichungen nur beim Theotokion), müssen die Psalmen genau benannt werden, denn sie haben zu diesem Zeitpunkt in unterschiedlichen Klöstern verschiedene Gestalt. Im Typikon *Eleousa* gab es nur einen Psalm, in anderen Typika werden wir noch weitere Variationen vorfinden. Das bestätigte auch Mateos, als er zum Schluss kam: „Dans cet office, les psaumes sont plus récents que les tropaires“.[41]
Ein Vergleich der *Eleousa* und *Evergetis* Strukturen vom Anfang des Stundengebets weist auf einen Einfluss des Hagia Sophia-Orthros hin, der im Narthex begann:

Eleousa	Evergetis
• *Mesonyktikon im Narthex*	• (Mesonyktikon „in den Zellen“)
• Trisagion (vermutlich in der Kirche)	• Trisagion
• Gebet für die Kaiser	• Psalm 19
• Δεῦτε, προσκυνήσωμεν	• Psalm 20
• Psalm 19	[Weihräuchern]
• Troparia	• Troparia
• 24 Kyrie eleison	• Kyrie eleison
	• *Ekphonesis*
• Hexapsalmos	• Hexapsalmos

Im Unterschied zur *Eleousa* haben wir im *Evergetis*-Ritus nur ein paraliturgisches Mesonyktikon „in den Zellen“ und zugleich eine feierliche Ausrufung vor dem Hexapsalm, die in der *Eleousa* fehlte, und die hier den „königlichen“ Dienst vom weiteren Teil des Orthros *abgrenzt*. Dies lässt sich wohl auf den Einfluss des Orthros der Hagia Sophia zurückführen:[42] In der Hagia Sophia gab es den „weniger feierlichen“ Teil des Orthros, der im Narthex zelebriert wurde. Danach trat man in die Kirche ein, mit einem „Einzugsvers“ als Übergang in den weiteren Teil des Orthros. Um diesen Ablauf (weniger feierlicher Anfang und weiterer Teil) beizubehalten braucht der struktursensitive Byzantiner unbedingt einen „weniger feierlichen Anfang“ des Orthros, *abgegrenzt* vom „weiteren Teil“ des Gottesdienstes. Im Fall *Eleousa* hatte man ein Mesonyktikon im

[41] MATEOS, Quelques problèmes (s. Anm. 32), 201.
[42] Der Verfasser des Typikons Evergetis führt selbst an, dass er auf dem Ritus der Großen Kirche basiert: „τῶ τῶ τύπῳ τῆς μεγάλης ἐκκλησίας ἀκολουθοῦντες...“ DMITRIEVSKY, Opisanie 1 (s. Anm. 35), 442.

Narthex, das als „Anfang“ fungierte. Dort hatten wir daher keine Ausrufung vor dem Hexapsalm: Der „königliche“ Dienst brauchte nicht vom weiteren Teil des Orthros abgegrenzt zu werden, denn er befand sich schon (wegen des Mesonyktikons) im „weiteren Teil“. Im *Evergetis*-Typikon haben wir dagegen kein kirchliches Mesonyktikon, also muß der „königliche“ Dienst als „weniger feierlicher Anfang“ fungieren, der dann naturgemäß vom „weiteren Teil“ (dem Hexapsalm) durch die Ausrufung abgegrenzt wird. In der späteren Entwicklung wird diese Struktur des Gottesdienstes der Hagia-Sophia zwar nicht immer beibehalten (z. B. ein Mesonyktikon im Narthex *und* die Ausrufung kommen gleichzeitig vor), sie bleibt aber wichtig für das Verständnis der heutigen Platzierung des „königlichen“ Anfangs innerhalb des Orthros.

C. II. 3. Kecharitomene und Pantokrator

Die Geschichte des Frauenklosters der Gottesmutter *Kecharitomene* haben wir bereits kurz angesprochen. Das Kloster wurde in den ersten Jahren des 12. Jahrhunderts von der Kaiserin Eirene Doukaina, der Frau von Alexios I. Komnenos gegründet. Kaiserin Eirene wohnte hier nach dem Tod ihres Ehemannes mit ihrer berühmten Tochter, Anna Komnene. Das neue Kloster wurde neben dem alten, ehemaligen Männerkloster *Philanthropos* in der nordwestlichen Ecke Konstantinopels errichtet und dem alten Kloster angeschlossen.[43] Das Ktitor-Typikon dieses zweifellos „kaiserlichen“ Klosters reicht in die Jahre 1110–1116 zurück und wurde vermutlich von der Kaiserin selbst verfasst.[44] Dieses Typikon gilt als ein anschauliches Beispiel des Siegs der Reformbewegung am Anfang des 12. Jahrhunderts, weil es von dieser Bewegung stark geprägt ist.[45] Das Typikon der Kaiserin Eirene spiegelt generell die evergetische Reform-Tradition wider, der „königliche“ Dienst der Kecharitomene ist jedoch in vielen Einzelheiten einzigartig.
Bei der Analyse des *Kecharitomene*-Ritus bedienen wir uns der englischen Übersetzung der Dumbarton Oaks Ausgabe.[46] Im Unterschied zur *Evergetis* wird das Mesonyktikon dieses Klosters im Narthex der Kirche gesungen. Anschließend beginnt der Orthros (ein Weihräucherungsritus ist nur kurz angesprochen) mit dem Trisagion, den Psalmen 19 und 20, „gewöhnlichen“ Troparia und Kyrie eleison (Anzahl nicht erwähnt). Danach führt die Kaiserin eine außergewöhnliche Vorschrift ein, nach der andere Psalmen und andere, todesgedenkende Troparia gesungen werden sollten, wenn ihr Ehemann eines Tages stirbt. Die Kaiserin schreibt also zwei Riten vor:

[43] THOMAS – HERO, BMFD 2 (s. Anm. 12), 649.
[44] Einige Forscher stellen die Verfasserschaft in Frage. Ebd., 651.
[45] Ebd., 650.
[46] Ebd., 664–724.

(1) Zu Lebzeiten des Kaisers:

- Mesonyktikon im Narthex
- Trisagion
- Psalm 19 [Weihräuchern]
- Psalm 20
- „Gewöhnliche" Troparia
- Kyrie eleison
- Hexapsalm

(2) Nach dem Tod des Kaisers:

- Mesonyktikon im Narthex
- Trisagion
- Psalm 22 [Weihräuchern]
- Psalm 64
- Todesgedenkende Troparia
- Trisagion
- Hexapsalm

Bei den zwei Versionen fällt in erster Linie die unterschiedliche Psalmenauswahl ins Auge. Die Psalmen 19 und 20 passen zum Gebet für den König, vor allem weil sie den Begriff „βασιλεύς" thematisieren (Ps 19, 10; Ps 20, 1 und 8). Für die zweite, todesgedenkende Version ihres „königlichen" Dienstes schreibt die Kaiserin die Psalmen 22 und 64 vor, die den Begriff „König" nicht verwenden, vielmehr thematisieren sie den Tod (Ps 22, 4; Ps 64, 5). Außerdem steht Psalm 64 am Anfang des neunten „Kathisma", welches heute zum samstäglichen (d. h. am „todesgedenkenden" Wochentag) Mesonyktikon gelesen wird. Der „königliche" Dienst konnte also auch ein *todesgedenkender* Dienst sein, der ihn an die traditionelle Thematik des Mesonyktikons anschließt. Wir nehmen an, dass sich gerade aus diesem Grund die zweite Version des „königlichen" Dienstes der Kaiserin Eirene in der Tradition nicht durchsetzte: Ein todesgedenkender Dienst passt liturgisch-theologisch zu dem täglichen Mesonyktikon,[47] nicht aber zu dem täglichen Anfang des Orthros, der traditionell mit einer feierlichen Auferstehungsthematik verbunden ist.[48] Wir vermuten außerdem, dass der todesgedenkende Dienst, den wir heute am Ende des Mesonyktikons finden, in Verbindung mit dem von Kaiserin Eirene eingeführten Ritus steht. Wir sind also angehalten darauf hinzuweisen, dass außer dem „königlichen" Dienst das Ende des Mesonyktikons den einzigen *zwei*psalmigen Dienst des Stundengebets darstellt und folgendermaßen aussieht:

Das Ende des Mesonyktikons

- Δεῦτε, προσκυνήσωμεν
- Psalm 120
- Psalm 133
- Trisagion
- Todesgedenkende Troparia
- Kyrie eleison 12 Mal
- *Gebet „Μνήσθητι, Κύριε"*

[47] Afanasiy SACHAROV, O pominovenii usopšich po ustavu Pravoslavnoj Tserkvi, St. Petersburg 1999, 23.

[48] „Всякая вообще утреня разсматривалась древними, о чемъ свидѣтельствуютъ другіе памятники... какъ служба въ честь воскресенія Христова". SKABALLANOVIČ, Tolkovyj Tipikon 1 (s. Anm. 1), 48.

- Ektenie

Im Grunde fehlt uns in der Version (2) der Kaiserin Eirene nur das Gebet „Μνήσθητι, Κύριε", um dies für eine Kopie ihrer Struktur zu halten. Allerdings taucht genau dieses Gebet am Anfang des Orthros im Ktetor-Typikon des „kaiserlichen" *Pantokrator* Klosters auf.[49] Kaiser Johannes II. Komnenos (1118–1143), Sohn der Kaiserin Eirene Doukaina, gründete dieses Kloster. Wie seine Mutter Eirene hinterlässt Johannes seinem Kloster zwei verschiedene Riten des „königlichen" Dienstes: Einen Ritus für seine Lebenszeit und einen anderen für die Zeit nach seinem Tod. In der zweiten, *todesgedenkenden* Version des Ritus führt der Verfasser den vollen Text des „Gebets für den verstorbenen Kaiser" (Μνήσθητι, Κύριε) an.
Wir können also gemeinsame Züge der zwei Riten, das Ende des Mesonyktikons und der „königliche Anfang", feststellen:

Das Ende des Mesonyktikons	Der „königliche" Dienst
• Δεῦτε, προσκυνήσωμεν	• Δεῦτε, προσκυνήσωμεν
• Psalm 120	• Psalm 19
• Psalm 133	• Psalm 20
• Trisagion	• Trisagion
• Todesgedenkende Troparia	• Kreuztroparia
• Kyrie eleison 12 Mal	
• Gebet „Μνήσθητι, Κύριε"	
• Ektenie	• Ektenie

Angesichts der Gemeinsamkeiten dieser *zwei*psalmigen Riten stellt sich die Frage, in welche Richtung sich die beiden Riten beeinflussten. Der letzte Teil des Mesonyktikons entstand vermutlich in der gleichen Periode wie die angeführten Zeugnisse des „königlichen" Dienstes, die eine zweipsalmige Struktur aufweisen.[50] Beide Riten scheinen also gegenseitig ihre Stellung innerhalb des Stundengebets beeinflusst zu haben: Der KD gab alle todesgedenkenden Elemente auf, die am Anfang des Orthros thematisch deplatziert waren, während der unmittelbar vorhergehende Ritus, das Ende des Mesonyktikons, diese Elemente übernahm.
Wurden die beiden Riten nach dem Muster irgendeiner zweipsalmigen todesgedenkenden Litia aufgebaut? In dem studitischen Typikon des Patriarchen Alexios (vor 1043) finden wir zwar todesgedenkende Troparia im Mesonyktikon (въ

[49] DMITRIEVSKY, Opisanie 1 (s. Anm. 35), 656–702. Der „königliche" Dienst: 658–659.
[50] SKABALLANOVIČ, Tolkovyj Tipikon 1 (s. Anm. 1), 431–2.

полунощие), allerdings fehlen die Psalmen.[51] In dem besagten Typikon finden wir aber eine Litia für den verstorbenen Ktitor, die dem „königlichen" Dienst gewissermaßen ähnlich ist:

- Kommt, lasst uns niederfallen
- Psalmen 19, 22 und 24
- Trisagion
- Todesgedenkende Troparia
- Kyrie eleison 40 Mal

Gemeinsame Züge sind unverkennbar, dieser vorliegende Ritus ist jedoch *drei*-psalmig, wie viele Dienste des Stundengebets. Eine Verbindung zwischen dieser Litia und dem „königlichen" Dienst, die wir nicht näher bestimmen können, lässt sich nicht ausschließen.

C. II. 4. Weitere Beispiele: Phoberos und Hilandar

Über die Geschichte des Klosters des hl. Johannes des Vorläufers, *Phoberos,* wissen wir wenig, zumeist nur das, was das Typikon (Ὑποτυπώσεις) des Klosters[52] berichtet. Das Typikon *Phoberos* wurde nach 1113 von Abt Johannes verfasst und gilt als ungefähre Kopie des Typikons *Evergetis.*[53] Johannes lässt uns wissen, dass sein Kloster den Status „ἐλευθέραν", „αὐτοδέσποτον" und „ἰδιοδέσποτον" besitzt, der ihm durch ein Schreiben (ὑπόμνημα) des Patriarchen Nikolaos III. Grammatikos (1084–1111) gewährt wurde (Typikon §33). Es gibt keine Belege, dass *Phoberos* ein kaiserliches Kloster war. Zwischen dem Kloster und den hochgestellten Familien der Botaneiates und Komnenen gab es jedoch eine enge Verbindung: die Nichte des Kaisers Alexios I. Komnenos, Eudokia Komnene Botaneiates, Ehefrau eines Nikephoras Botaneiates (nicht des Kaisers), galt als Patronatsträgerin des Klosters. Eudokia wird im Typikon sogar als „zweite Stifterin" des Klosters (δευτέρα ἡμῖν κτητόρισσα) geehrt [§50].[54] Das von Johannes verfasste Typikon wurde zu Lebzeiten der Eudokia Komnene, ca. 1144, überarbeitet.[55] Die Überarbeitung scheint hastig gewesen zu sein, womit auch die Wiederholungen des Textes (z. B., §8A und §8B, §53A und §53B) zu erklären sind.

Die etwas verwirrende Darstellung des „königlichen" Dienstes in diesem Typikon lässt sich anscheinend auf die hastige Überarbeitung von 1144 zurückführen. Im Folgenden wird nur der Anfang des Ritus zitiert, denn der übrige Teil entspricht fast wortwörtlich dem KD von *Evergetis*. Nach *Phoberos* beginnt das

[51] Aleksij PENTKOVSKY, Tipikon Patriarcha Aleksija Studita v Vizantii i na Rusi, Moskau 2001, 413.

[52] Athanasios I. PAPADOPOULOS–KERAMEUS (Hg.), Noctes Petropolitanae, St. Petersburg 1913, 1–88.

[53] THOMAS – HERO, BMFD 3 (s. Anm. 12), 872.

[54] PAPADOPOULOS–KERAMEUS, Noctes (s. Anm. 52), 62.

[55] THOMAS – HERO, BMFD 3 (s. Anm. 12), 872.

tägliche Stundengebet mit einem Mesonyktikon „in den Zellen“, für das drei Kathismata vorgeschrieben sind (9, 16 und 18, die in *Evergetis* nicht vorkommen)[56], währenddessen ein Bruder die Lampen in der Kirche anzündet. Nach dem Mesonyktikon versammeln sich die Brüder im Narthex, wo der „Amomos“ (Ps 118) gelesen wird (ein zweites Mesonyktikon?). Danach [wir unterstreichen die für unsere Überlegungen relevanten Teile]:

> ...εἰσερχομένων ἡμῶν ἔσωθεν τοῦ ναοῦ, ψάλλειν τρισάγιον εὐθέως μετὰ καὶ τῶν συνήθων τροπαρίων, τὸ «Ἐπακοῦσαί σου Κύριος» [die ersten Worte des 19. Psalms] καὶ τὸ «Κύριε ἐλέησον», προσέχοντας ἐξισοῦν ἐφ' ὅσον τε εἰκός, τούτων ψαλλομένων, αὐτόν τε τὸν ἱερέα περιϊέναι τὸν θεῖον ναοὸν ἅπαντα καὶ πάντας θυμιᾶν...[57]

Das Weihräuchern schließt mit der gewöhnlichen Ausrufung. Die seltsame Reihenfolge der verschiedenen Bestandteile des „königlichen“ Dienstes weist wohl auf die mangelhafte Überarbeitung von ca. 1144 hin:

- Trisagion
- „Gewöhnliche“ Troparia
- Psalm 19 [Weihräuchern]
- Kyrie eleison
- Ausrufung

Der Überarbeiter des Typikons war anscheinend nicht um Genauigkeit bemüht, so dass diese Reihenfolge möglicherweise nicht der Praxis entsprach. Immerhin liegt auch hier ein „königlicher“ Dienst in einem „nicht-kaiserlichen“ Kloster vor.

Als ein letztes Beispiel des „königlichen“ Dienstes im 12. Jahrhundert betrachten wir noch das Typikon des hl. Sabbas von Serbien. Dieses slawische Typikon wurde im Jahre 1199 vom hl. Sabbas auf Basis des *Evergetis*-Typikons für das auf dem Athos gelegene Kloster *Hilandar* verfaßt. Dieses alte Kloster baute der hl. Sabbas mit der Erlaubnis des Kaisers Alexios III. Angelos (1195–1203) und mit Hilfe seines Vaters, des Königs Stefan Nemanja (1166–1196) wieder auf.[58] Deshalb ist das Kloster „Hilandar“ als ein serbisches „kaiserliches“ Kloster anzusehen. Ich zitiere die Beschreibung des „königlichen“ Dienstes des Klosters *Hilandar* nach der Ausgabe des Originaltextes von Vladimir Ćorović:[59] nach dem Segen des Priesters,

> вы же „аминь“ чающе трьсветое пѣти, абие по ѲІ и К-номъ ѱлмѣ и по ѡбычаиныхь тропарихь и по „ги поміли“ сьблоудающе по тькьмо, ѣко подобно сихь пѣти...[60] (ihr sagt „Amen“, wenn ihr das Trisagion singen sollt, und gleich danach, beim 19. und 20. Psalm, bei den gewöhnlichen Troparia und beim „Kyrie eleison“ sollt ihr diese so singen, wie es sich gehört...[Die gewöhnliche Ermahnung, zusammen zu singen.]

[56] Heute werden alle drei Kathismata jeden Samstag gelesen: die 18. Kathisma am Freitagabend in der Vesper, die 9. Kathisma im Mesonyktikon, und die 16. Kathisma im Orthros.
[57] PAPADOPOULOS–KERAMEUS, Noctes (s. Anm. 53), 24.
[58] THOMAS – HERO, BMFD 4 (s. Anm. 12), 1331.
[59] Vladimir ĆOROVIĆ (Hg.), Spisi Sv. Save, Belgrad – Sr. Karlovtsi 1928.
[60] ĆOROVIĆ, Spisi (s. Anm. 60), 43–44.

Dieses Beispiel ist deshalb wichtig, weil der hl. Sabbas diesen Ritus als erster auf dem Athos einführte, und dies nicht aufgrund einer kanonischen Verpflichtung gegenüber dem byzantinischen Kaiser.

D. DIE VORSCHRIFT „OHNE METANOIA"

Die Ursprünge der Vorschrift „ohne Metanoia" (ohne Verbeugungen), die in späteren Redaktionen des „königlichen" Dienstes auftaucht, stellen ein Rätsel dar, denn keine der frühesten Versionen des „königlichen" Dienstes verbietet Metanoia am Anfang des Orthros. Tatsächlich scheint die Vorschrift ursprünglich nicht mit dem „königlichen" Dienst verbunden zu sein; sie erschien am Anfang des Orthros unabhängig von diesem Ritus.
Das Typikon *Evergetis* schreibt am Vorabend der Großen Fastenzeit (am Abend des Sonntags der Butterentsagung) sowohl keine „Pannichida" als auch „Metanoia" während des Apodeipnons vor, weil man zum letzten Mal ein nicht fastengerechtes Abendessen zu sich nahm, welches die „Metanoia" erschweren könnte. Das Essen am Vorabend der Fastenzeit heißt „Paraklesis" (Trost): Παννυχίδα δὲ ἀφ' ἑσπέρας οὐ ψάλλομεν διὰ τὴν παράκλησιν, ἀλλ' οὐδὲ εἰς τὸ ἀπόδειπνον ποιοῦμεν μετανοίας...[61] Darüber hinaus sollen die Mönche am ersten Tag zwei Stunden später als an den anderen Tagen der Fastenzeit aufstehen, ebenfalls „διὰ τὴν παράκλησιν".[62] Diese Vorschrift hat das russische Typikon beibehalten, indem es zum ersten Tag der Großen Fastenzeit bemerkt: „Am Montag der ersten Woche soll der Paraekklesiarch später läuten, des abendlichen Trostes wegen".[63] Die gleiche Vorschrift finden wir auch in Jerusalemer Typika der 12.–16. Jahrhunderte. Der erste Beleg dafür findet sich im Jerusalemer Typikon Nr. 1094 des 12.–13. Jahrhunderts, das zum Beginn des Orthros anführt:

> ...ψάλλεται τὸ Τρισάγιον ·μετάνοιαν οὐ ποιοῦμεν. Κύριε ἐλέησον ιβ καὶ εὐθὺς το Δόξα ἐν ὑψίστοις Θεῷ ἄνευ μετάνοιῶν (d. h., Anfang des Hexapsalms ohne Metanoia).[64]

Eine sinaitische Redaktion des Jerusalemer Typikons Nr. 1097 von 1214, schreibt ebenfalls am Anfang des Orthros vor: ἀρχόμεθα Τρισαγίου καὶ οὐ ποιοῦμεν μετάνοιαν.[65] Die gleiche Vorschrift steht in einem späteren Jerusalemer-Konstantinopler Typikon der Patriarchenbibliothek in Jerusalem, Nr. 311 des 16. Jahrhunderts: ἀπὸ τοῦ Τρισαγίου ἄνευ μετανοίας.[66] Außerdem wurde die Vorschrift aus dem gedruckten Typikon von 1603 übernommen, das eben-

[61] DMITRIEVSKY, Opisanie 1 (s. Anm. 35), 512.
[62] Ebd.
[63] Tipikon siest' ustav §49, Graz 1964, 343.
[64] Aleksij DMITRIEVSKY, Opisanie Liturgičeskich Rukopisej 3, Petrograd 1917, 8.
[65] Ebd., 395.
[66] Ebd., 350.

falls keinen KD kennt. Nur für den Anfang des Orthros, an Wochentagen der Großen Fastenzeit, schreibt dieses Typikon vor: Τρισάγιον χωρὶς μετανοιῶν und ὁ ἑξάψαλμος χωρὶς μετανοιῶν.[67]
Daraus schließen wir, dass sich die Vorschrift „ohne Metanoia“ unabhängig vom KD entwickelte und nicht mit seiner Thematik zu erklären ist. Weil die alten Jerusalemer Typika, die diese Vorschrift enthielten, gar keinen „königlichen“ Dienst kannten, können wir mit Sicherheit sagen, dass die Vorschrift mit irgendeinem *anderen* Aspekt des Orthros zusammenhängt. Gleich wie der Jerusalemer Orthros des vierten Jahrhunderts immer in der Anastasis-Kirche stattfand und beim Heraustreten des Bischofs aus dem hl. Grab besonders von der Auferstehungsthematik geprägt war, könnte man bei der ursprünglichen Jerusalemer Vorschrift „ἄνευ μετάνοιῶν“ diese Thematik des Orthros einbringen. Auf die Auferstehungsthematik weisen auch ähnliche frühere Vorschriften hin, beispielsweise der 20. Kanon des ersten Ökumenischen Konzils, der alle Verbeugungen an Sonntagen und in der ganzen Pfingstperiode untersagt.[68]
Die Untersagung der „Metanoia“ am Anfang des monastischen Tages, der mit ziemlich großen körperlichen Anstrengungen verbunden ist, lässt sich außerdem auf die asketische Maßhaltung der alten Typika zurückführen. Die Typika versuchten, jede Übertreibung bei körperlichen Anstrengungen während des Gebets zu vermeiden.

E. ZUSAMMENFASSUNG

Abschließend fassen wir unsere Forschungsergebnisse in drei Thesen zusammen:
(1) Die Platzierung des „königlichen“ Dienstes am Anfang des Orthros hängt mit der Struktur des Orthros der Hagia Sophia zusammen. Beim Orthros der Hagia Sophia fand ein „weniger feierlicher“ Anfang immer im Narthex statt, während die Kirche vom Priester inzensiert wurde. Im Jerusalemer Orthros des vierten Jahrhunderts, beschrieben von Egeria, haben wir ebenfalls einen „weniger feierlichen“ Anfang festgestellt, der möglicherweise auch einen Einfluss auf die Platzierung des „königlichen“ Dienstes ausübte. Aus diesem Grund können wir der folgenden Aussage von Robert Taft nicht zustimmen:

> [The Royal Office] is really a separate service, extraneous to the structure of matins. Because monks are fond of adding but only rarely subtract material from their offices, it has become permanently prefixed to Byzantine matins.[69]

[67] To paron Typikon 1603, Bayerische Staatsbibliothek, 2 Liturg. II. Paginierung fehlt.
[68] Joseph WOHLMUTH (Hg.), Dekrete der Ökumenischen Konzilien, Paderborn–München 1973, 16.
[69] TAFT, Liturgy of the Hours (s. Anm. 4), 277.

Wir haben gesehen, dass sich die „vorbereitende" Funktion des „königlichen" Dienstes ursprünglich mit der Funktion des Mesonyktikons überschnitt, später aber verselbständigten sich beide Riten. Der KD wurde in die Thematik und Struktur des Orthros integriert, während das Mesonyktikon die „todesgedenkenden" Elemente des „königlichen" Dienstes übernahm.

(2) Der KD in den nicht-„kaiserlichen" Typika von *Eleousa*, *Evergetis*, *Phoberos* und *Hilandar* bringt neue Fragestellungen in die Forschung über diesen Teil des Orthros ein. Die Entstehung des „königlichen" Dienstes lässt sich nicht mehr ausschließlich vom „kaiserlichen" Status eines Klosters ableiten, vielmehr entspringt dieses Gebet für den „König / Kaiser" den persönlichen, finanziellen (im Sinne von Unterstützung vom Kaiser) und geistlichen Beziehungen eines Klosters mit dem Kaiser und seiner Familie. Was auch immer die Beweggründe für diese Beziehungen sein mochten, sie brachten das Kloster dazu, dem Bedürfnis des Kaisers nach Gebet entgegenzukommen. Dieses Bedürfnis, und nicht eine kanonische Pflicht, schafft die Grundlagen für den KD. Insofern dürfen wir die Entstehung dieses Ritus nicht aufgrund einer Macht des Kaisers betrachten, sondern vom Gesichtspunkt der Schwäche und Bedürftigkeit, die allen Menschen gemeinsam ist.

(3) Die Ursprünge des „königlichen" Dienstes sind mit dem kaiserlichen Ehepaar Alexios und Eirene Komnenos verbunden. Ob Bischof Manuel, vom Kloster *Eleousa*, irgendeinen Fingerzeig von Alexios oder Eirene bezüglich des „königlichen" Dienstes erhielt, können wir nicht nachweisen. Immerhin ist ein „supplicatory prayer on behalf of the permanence of his divine sovereignty" im Chrysobullos von Alexios 1107 überliefert. Die gewagte Hypothese, dass die Kaiserin Eirene hinter der Einführung des „königlichen" Dienstes in *Eleousa* stehen könnte, ist nicht auszuschließen, denn wir wissen, dass sie gemeinsam mit ihrem Mann ca. 1106 dieses Kloster besuchte. Ferner berichtet Anna Komnene, dass ihre Mutter in engem Kontakt mit dem Mönchtum war, mit besonderem Interesse für den monastischen Gottesdienst[70].

Offensichtlich fehlen uns die Informationen, um mehr als eine Hypothese aufzustellen. Trotz ihrer kleinen Unterschiede, gibt es keinen Zweifel daran, dass die verschiedenen „königlichen" Dienste einer gemeinsamen Quelle entspringen.

[70] Alexias XII, hrsg. und übersetzt von Diether R. REINSCH, Köln 1996, 407.

"EVEN AT THE GRAVE, WE MAKE OUR SONG:" THE DIVERGENCE OF ECUMENICAL REMEMBERINGS OF THE DEAD

LIZETTE LARSON-MILLER

1. INTRODUCTION

I would like to begin by expressing my gratitude to the *Institut für Liturgiewissenschaft an der Universität Wien*, all those who have worked to put together this symposium, and above all to Professor Hans-Jürgen Feulner, for his kind invitation to be part of this very interesting conference.

Robert Taft has written, "history is a science not of past happenings, but of present understanding,"[1] a phrase which takes on a particular meaning with regard to what we are about during this conference. Exploring the impact of research in early church liturgy on liturgical development throughout later centuries and especially on the major liturgical developments of the twentieth century is a timely task in both broadening our knowledge of liturgical history and in understanding some of the tensions within contemporary liturgical discussions. It appears that liturgical 'growing pains' are shared in many parts of the church today, from calls to simplify and translate the complex liturgies of the Christian East, especially among younger generations in the diaspora churches, to the tensions in the Roman Catholic Church balancing different interpretations of reform, especially between post-Vatican II and pre-Vatican II views of liturgy, to the tensions throughout the Anglican Communion over the balance between scripture and liturgy, as well as Protestant and Catholic emphases, to the tensions in many Protestant churches just discovering and implementing weekly worship based on liturgical tradition, both regionally and congregationally.

All of these very present realities raise questions about how important the inheritance of early liturgy is, how comprehensive or integral the adoption of early practices have been, how radically different cultural, geographical, political and temporal realities between 'then' and 'now' make direct comparisons difficult or impossible, and how to assess the ecumenical relevance of early church liturgical developments while acknowledging that one cannot ignore the intervening 1200-1500 years. The biases of the liturgical movement of the nineteenth and twentieth centuries in Western Christianity were often quite transparent in the preference for seeing the first five to eight centuries of Christianity as the font of all liturgical theology and practice, and the subsequent centuries, allowing for

[1] Robert TAFT, Beyond East and West: Problems in Liturgical Understanding, Washington/D.C. 1984, 153.

varying denominational and confessional stances, as a slow disintegration of sacramental theology and/or a corruption of 'pure' liturgical practice.[2]

In a small book that I have used as a text when I taught non-specialist university students in the sacraments, Kenneth Stevenson summarized these biases by writing of three primary reasons why we should look to the early church for our inspiration.

1. "First of all, how early Christians worshiped *is accessible*," but these accessible texts were "sadly lost for many subsequent centuries." Because of this, the early church influence was very minimal on worship in the Middle Ages and at the Reformation. "This latter point is crucial to any discussion of liturgy, because the Reformers sought to purge the medieval worship that they had inherited of supposedly Catholic accretions. Had they had access to some of the texts…we may well ask whether their liturgical work might have been more balanced, less wordy, and more deeply traditional."[3]
2. The second argument is against those who feel the early church is *irrelevant.* "How those early Christians, direct heirs to the New Testament, carried out their central cultic acts must be relevant to us because they grew out of the formative era of our religion. To study origins is a necessary and sobering exercise. And it changes and alters as a process as time goes on, because we return to them with fresh concerns."[4]
3. "Thirdly, to study the era of origins has to provide us with some basic *norms* in the sense that they challenge the way we worship today." While acknowledging the differences in world views between contemporary Christians and early Christians, Stevenson still holds the early church patterns as normative; "We don't have to *imitate* the early centuries – but there can be little doubt that they propose to us certain significant norms that ought to challenge our own discipleship and the quality and depth of our worship."[5]

Bishop Stevenson's introduction is intended to be itself accessible and popular, but his stress on accessibility, relevance and normativity as key reasons to prejudice the early church liturgical pattern is echoed in official and scholarly works as well. While more recent scholarship would challenge just how accessible our understanding and knowledge of these early practices actually is,[6] contemporary commentaries and ritual texts have favored Stevenson's conviction that not all centuries of liturgical development are created equal.

[2] See the discussion in John F. BALDOVIN, Reforming the Liturgy: A Response to the Critics, Collegeville 2008, 159, in which he addresses the critique by some that liturgical history is considered "an exercise in antiquarianism".

[3] Kenneth STEVENSON, The First Rites. Worship in the Early Church, Collegeville 1989, 10. Emphasis is Stevenson's.

[4] STEVENSON, The First Rites, 11.

[5] STEVENSON, The First Rites, 10–11.

[6] See Paul F. BRADSHAW, The Search for the Origins of Christian Worship. Sources and Method for the Study of Early Liturgy, Oxford [2]2002, especially chapter 1.

Much of this approach to early church liturgy, especially the understanding that what is closest to the origin – Jesus Christ – is the most normative, centers on the great sacraments of initiation and eucharist. Thus, in *Sacrosanctum Concilium*, Chapter II on "The Most Sacred Mystery of the Eucharist" we read:

> The rite of the mass is to be revised in such a way that the intrinsic nature and purpose of its several parts, as well as the connection between them, may be more clearly manifested, and that devout and active participation by the faithful may be more easily achieved. For this purpose the rites are to be simplified, due care being taken to preserve their substance. Parts which with the passage of time came to be duplicated, or were added with little advantage, are to be omitted. Other parts which suffered loss through accidents of history are to be restored to the vigor they had in the days of the holy Fathers, as may seem useful or necessary.[7]

Above all, the restructuring of the rites of initiation, particularly inclusive of the catechumenate, reflects this return to the early church pattern as both relevant to the contemporary situation of the church and theologically normative in the focus on adults able to speak for themselves. The *praenotanda* of the revised RCIA states:

> This rite includes not simply the celebration of the sacraments of baptism, confirmation, and eucharist, but also all the rites belonging to the catechumenate. Endorsed by the ancient practice of the church, a catechumenate that would be suited to contemporary missionary activity in all regions was so widely requested that the Second Vatican Council decreed its restoration, revision, and adaptation to local traditions.[8]

But are other rites of the church as transparently dependent on the earliest centuries of Christianity? Certainly we can see preferences for early church texts and ritual patterns in initiation and eucharist, as well as in ordination rites, in anointing of the sick, and elsewhere, at the same time as we see a juxtaposition of second millennium practices with early church liturgical inheritance.

I would like to look at the rites for the dead, the funeral rites, as one example of how complex it can be to base contemporary theology and ritual practice on ancient liturgical patterns. I propose to show first that several contemporary churches very deliberately intended to echo, follow, and even imitate in part the patterns of the early church in their funeral rites. Second, drawing from our incomplete knowledge of early church funeral practices, I will emphasize just two elements: ritual patterns and liturgical texts from which to base a comparison of the rites. Lastly, I will return to the contemporary rites to assess whether the similarities outweigh the differences, and what those similarities and differences can tell us regarding belief in the theological efficacy of the rites, what is happening, for whom is it being celebrated, and what does it do.

7 The Constitution on the Sacred Liturgy, 50. in: Austin FLANNERY (Ed.), Vatican Council 2: The Conciliar and Post Conciliar Documents, Collegeville 1980, 17.

8 The Rites of the Catholic Church as revised by the Second Vatican Ecumenical council, Vol. 1. Collegeville 1990, 35.

2. THE EARLY CHURCH AS SOURCE FOR CONTEMPORARY FUNERAL RITES

Roman Catholicism

The *Order of Christian Funerals 1989* represents the most recent (vernacular typical edition) English language version of the 1969 *Ordo Exsequiarum, (Rite of Funerals)* of the post-Vatican II reform decrees. It is a rich collection of rites and texts, grouped around a threefold ritual movement: vigil, funeral liturgy, rite of committal. Does it intentionally and self-consciously draw on early church patterns and theology? The *Constitution on the Sacred Liturgy* sets the hopes and guidelines for the post-conciliar reforms that were to come. When speaking of funeral rites, the document says that "Funeral rites should express more clearly the paschal character of Christian death, and should correspond more closely to the circumstances and traditions found in various regions."[9] One has to look elsewhere to find the confirmation that the return to a focus on the paschal mystery (in funerals and throughout many of the rites) was understood to be a return to the roots of early church theology.[10] While the entire *Constitution on the Sacred Liturgy* is permeated with language of the paschal mystery, its direct link to early church liturgical theology is best seen throughout the theological introduction to the revised RCIA, using the instructions around the celebration of confirmation as an example:

> In accord with the ancient practice followed in the Roman liturgy, adults are not to be baptized without receiving confirmation immediately afterward, unless some serious reason stands in the way. The conjunction of the two celebrations signifies the unity of the paschal mystery, the close link between the mission of the Son and the outpouring of the Holy Spirit, and the connection between the two sacraments through which the Son and the Holy Spirit come with the Father to those who are baptized.[11]

The link to baptism and full initiation is an important factor in the revised funeral rites, as baptismal elements frame the funeral liturgy itself making a ritual statement of contextualizing the funeral in the theology of the paschal mystery, understood throughout the liturgical documents as both the passion, death and resurrection of Christ *and* the participation of Christians "into the mystery of Christ: they die with him, are buried with him, and rise with him."[12] This same

[9] Sacrosanctum concilium, 81.
[10] The link of 'paschal mystery' theology to the early church is also a source of critique by opponents. See the claim that stressing the paschal mystery is unfaithful to 'classic Roman Catholic Theology', Society of St. Pius X, The Problem of Liturgy Reform, Kansas City 2001.
[11] Introduction, Christian Initiation of Adults, 215.
[12] Sacrosanctum concilium, 6.

mystery continues as from the time of Pentecost "...the church has never failed to come together to celebrate the paschal mystery."[13]

The normativity of early church liturgical patterns is seen in the introduction to *The Order of Christian Funerals*, for example with regard to processions.

Processions continue to have special significance in funeral celebrations, as in Christian Rome where funeral rites consisted of three "stages" or "stations" joined by two processions...The funeral liturgy mirrored the journey of human life, the Christian pilgrimage to the heavenly Jerusalem.[14]

Other elements of the liturgy itself, as well as the theological explanation in the introduction point again and again to a stress toward baptism, paschal mystery and Easter as well as commendation, clear shifts away from the foci of the rite found in the *Rituale Romanum* of 1614, where the absolution rite had substituted for earlier commendation practices, and the prayer texts revealed a tug of war between the 'confident hope' language of early prayers and the 'fear of judgment' prayers which abound in the second millennium of Christianity.[15]

Are these rites adapted and created with their theological and ritual roots in the early church? They are certainly a shift away from the emphases of the pre-Vatican II Requiem Mass toward both a theological framework based on a renewed understanding of the paschal mystery, and a ritual re-working that owes a debt in many cases to elements in the first eight centuries of Western Christian funeral practice. "They offer us a vastly restored proclamation of faith and constitute the current stage in a process..."[16] The restoration of the proclamation of faith seems very much founded on the relevance and normativity that Stevenson argued for in his popular treatment of early church liturgical relevance.

Anglicanism

Unlike the Roman Catholic *Order of Christian Funerals* link to the more universal Latin Urtext of the *Ordo Exsequiarum,* Anglican rites have a family resemblance one to another based more on good will and common purpose, than on legislative mandate. For that reason, it is best to choose one, and I will use the Episcopal Rite of the United States as found in the *1979 Book of Common Prayer* as well as the very recent expansion for adult burial, referred to, thus far, as *Enriching Our Worship III.*[17]

The *praenotanda* of the Burial Rites in the 1979 *Book of Common Prayer* are particularly weak, far more a listing of suggested rubrics than a theological ex-

[13] Sacrosanctum concilium, 6.

[14] General Introduction, The Order of Christian Funerals, 42.

[15] Frederick S. PAXTON, Christianizing Death: The Creation of a Ritual Process in Early Medieval Europe, Ithaca 1990, 206.

[16] Richard RUTHERFORD, The Death of a Christian. The Order of Christian Funerals, Collegeville 1990, 109.

[17] Burial Rites for Adults (Enriching Our Worship 3), New York 2007, iv.

planation of the rites. This is the unfortunate result of both the hurried writing of the burial rites, as well as a general approach to the 1979 prayer book that resisted the theological introductions found in subsequent prayer books throughout the Anglican communion. In an article on the composition of the burial rites in the prayer book, Gregory Howe admits that a looming publishing deadline kept the rite from its possible fullness, "we made it through "The Burial of the Dead: Rite One," and the clock stopped us about halfway through Rite Two."[18] Only at the conclusion of the rite, in the notes added literally at the end, is there a theological statement. "The liturgy for the dead is an Easter liturgy. It finds all its meaning in the resurrection. Because Jesus was raised from the dead, we, too, shall be raised."[19] The end notes go on to describe that the liturgy is, "therefore, characterized by joy, in the certainty that…nothing will separate us from the love of God," as well as acknowledging human grief at the loss of a loved one. "So, while we rejoice that one we love has entered into the nearer presence of our Lord, we sorrow in sympathy with those who mourn."[20]

There is nothing in the notes that overtly suggests the model is to be found in the early church, but there is an obvious reliance on the Roman Rite, notably the first typical edition of the post-conciliar rites, *The Rite of Funerals* of 1969. This is especially evident in the nascent vigil service, the funeral liturgy proper beginning at the door and concluding with the commendation, and the committal service, the same three-step movement with similar prayers at several points throughout the liturgy. This is different from its predecessor, the 1928 prayer book, in which the funeral was, at least on paper, seen as a two step process, funeral liturgy and committal. The 1979 prayer book also added prayers stressing an Easter, and by extension, early church emphasis, most noticeably in the first (and therefore normative) collect for the burial of an adult, which is the collect for Tuesday of Easter Week:

> O God, who by the glorious resurrection of your Son Jesus Christ destroyed death, and brought life and immortality to light: grant that your servant *N.*, being raised with him, may know the strength of his presence, and rejoice in his eternal glory; who with you and the Holy Spirit lives and reigns, one God, for ever and ever, Amen.[21]

The shift towards theology and ritual anchored in the liturgical movement's adoption of early church practices is far more apparent in the new BCP supplement, *Enriching Our Worship III.* There a *praenotanda* begins with "we are Easter people…" and moves on to explain this scripturally, traditionally and ritually. There is also an explanation, for the first time, of the addition of East-

[18] Gregory M. HOWE, Death. Appearance and Reality. A Consideration of the Burial Rites of the 1979 BCP, in: Ruth MEYERS (Ed.), A Prayer Book for the 21st Century, New York 1996, 130–143.
[19] 1979 Book of Common Prayer, New York 1990, 507.
[20] Ibid.
[21] The Burial of the Dead, Rite 2, 493.

ern Christian elements by means of the journey language of the funeral rites so dominant in the early church:

> Through both the burial rite and the pastoral rituals surrounding death and burial, we acknowledge that the living are on the same journey toward the heart of the holy and undivided Trinity. As the ancient Eastern Orthodox memorial service proclaims, *Give rest, O Christ, to your servants with your saints, where sorrow and pain are no more, neither sighing, but life everlasting. All of us go down to the dust; yet even at the grave we make our song: Alleluia, alleluia, alleluia.*[22]

As with a number of different liturgies in most recent Anglican books, drawing from Eastern Orthodox liturgical texts has been a way to deepen the connection to earlier traditions while broadening the theological scope beyond the 'worship wars' of much of Anglican history.

The Christian Church (Disciples of Christ)

While the Roman Catholic and Anglican examples above come from churches rooted in historical liturgical tradition, the funeral presented in *Chalice Worship,* represents a very different community, a Protestant group for whom much of the historical liturgical tradition has not been central to their experience or concern. The Disciples of Christ is a fairly unique Protestant denomination in the United States in that they were from the beginning committed to a weekly celebration of the Lord's Supper. The contemporary denomination called *Disciples of Christ* grew, ironically, from an early nineteenth-century hope for a Christianity that could end divisions between denominations by returning believers to the New Testament, in principles and practices. Alexander Campbell (1788-1866) is often considered the 'founder', but he was one of several who became known leaders in what was called the "Restoration Movement." The 1997 worship book, *Chalice Worship,* has its roots in the *Disciples of Christ* but is intentionally ecumenical and has in practice become one of the most widely used worship resources for American Protestants interested in "liturgy," which for many groups is a very new concept.

There are noticeable differences in the construction of the worship book and in the specific rites for the deceased on which we are focusing. First, where official liturgical texts from liturgical churches generally have no "author" but are composite works of anonymous (or semi-anonymous) committees, *Chalice Worship* is the work of two authors, who compiled and edited a variety of materials. The introductory material is clearer in direction and scope than many liturgical church *praenotandae* because it is not bound by the variety of opinions of multiple committee members nor beholden to maintaining continuity with centuries of tradition. In describing the Sunday service models in the book, the authors say that it "is inappropriate to summarize Disciples worship as a service

22 Burial Rites for Adults (see fn 17), iv.

of word and sacrament. To do so would be to ignore the complexity of celebrative activities through which the gathered faithful meet the risen Lord."[23] In spite of that, the models suggested are generally informed by studies of how the church in the first four centuries struggled to deal with the new aspects of worship that varied from Hebrew heritage. They reflect what appears to be a growing convergence of understanding among Christians around the world as to the shape of worship. The order generally follows the pattern set forth by Justin Martyr: readings from the gospels, sermon by the president, prayers by all the people, bread, wine, and water are brought, extempore prayer of thanksgiving, people's response: amen, distribution and reception of elements.[24]

The ritual patterning of the Lord's Supper is clearly modeled on early church patterns. Turning to the funeral liturgy, which is entitled "A Service of Memory and Hope" two contradictory perspectives are immediately obvious. First, the variety of texts reveals a use of several early church funeral texts, pointing again to the use of early liturgy as a source. However, the introduction to the funeral rites states that the funeral is to be fit to the circumstances of the individual deceased, inclusive of "those for whom death is the end of personal existence; and others for whom death is the gateway to eternal life with God."[25] It is probably safe to say that this is a long ways from early church theological assumptions! Expanding this to several other service books, it becomes apparent that this is increasingly common among the "ecumenical" Protestant service books, which represent a great deal of mutual sharing, common assumptions, and links to the "emergent church" pattern in the United States.
Setting aside this brief look at contemporary church claims of early church liturgical roots, let us turn to a few aspects of rites for the dead from the early centuries of Christian liturgical development.

3. FUNERAL RITES IN THE EARLY CHURCH

Early Christian rites for the dead were both consistent with cultural religious patterns shared and transformed through interactions around the Mediterranean as well as interpretively transformed by organic Christian beliefs in life after death, judgment, the relationship between the body and the soul, the ongoing relationship between the living and the dead, and the articulation of the connection between the death of Christ and the death of each Christian. In reconstructing ritual patterns in the first five to six centuries of Christian practice, we rec-

[23] O. I. Cricket HARRISON, The Lord's Day Service Among Disciples Congregations, Chalice Worship, St. Louis 1997, 3.
[24] Ibid., 4.
[25] Ibid., 58.

ognize that the various sources, liturgical texts, archeology, hagiography, apologetics, and poetry give us an incomplete picture while recognizing local variety, occasionally idiosyncratic perspectives, and the constant temptation to "fill in the blanks" ourselves to complete the picture. With that caveat, what can we say about the two elements, ritual patterns and consistency in liturgical texts in light of the theological efficacy of the rites, on which we are basing the analysis of contemporary use of ancient practices?

Ritual patterns

We know that Christian burial practices are born of three primary sources: first, the need to bury bodies quickly before decomposition became overwhelming; second, the continuation of cultural and religious practices from Judaism and elsewhere of washing and wrapping the body as both honorific and practical; and thirdly, the overwhelming preference of Christians for burial in imitation of Jesus' burial.[26] In addition to the burial preference, a much-observed Christian distinction was their willingness to touch the corpses themselves, rather than relegate that care to others.[27] Thus, the first step of a Christian ritual pattern is the care of the body, generally in the home, by those closest to the deceased. Between the third and fourth centuries there are witnesses that this first step was accompanied by prayers, psalms and hymns, although references to specific psalms reveal that no set pattern of choices was in place. Depending on the time of day that death occurred, there may have been a period of waiting between the preparation of the body and the actual burial, so the practice of keeping watch with the body, whether from fear of revenge from the dead inherited from pagan practices or in imitation of the vigiling surrounding Jesus' own body, seems to have been accompanied by extended psalm singing, scripture reading and prayers.

The next step of the ritual pattern is the necessity of moving the body to the place of burial from the home or other place of preparation. This procession was another important step in death rituals throughout the Mediterranean that was broadly seen as not simply a necessity but imbued with symbolism of journey and movement. The earliest Christian description is from Aristides (mid-second century), who wrote that the Christians "rejoice and give thanks and accompany

[26] See Lizette LARSON-MILLER, To Imitate Their Perfection. A comparison of the Relationship of Christology and Martyrial Liturgy in Sixth century Gaul and Syria. PhD Dissertation, Graduate Theological Union Berkeley 1992, 13–19.

[27] "These gestures of closing the eyes, washing the body, and clothing it in burial clothes were usually done in the home, by the family and/or close friends. Here there was a variance from the Jewish practice of maintaining a distinct group of burial workers who performed most of the actions dealing with the dead body, relieving the family from some facts of ritual impurity." Ibid., 14–15. See also Apostolic Constitutions vi.30 for a later codification of this practice.

the corpse, for he has emigrated from one place to another."[28] For centuries to come, the Christian procession to burial was described as a journey and accompanied by singing of psalms and hymns, a deliberate counterpart to the expansive expressions of grief against which some Christian leaders railed.

In the most commonly referenced ritual patterns surrounding death, the next step was the burial itself. At the grave, which was sometimes in a covered cemetery that would in later centuries be considered as a church building,[29] the earliest references we have report that "rites and prayers" were performed.[30] Here a brief excursus must be added to say that the ritual pattern of two stations, home and grave, with a procession between, is thus augmented by an additional station, the church building, in some places. In other words, the burial site for some was a church, for others it was not. But in some geographical areas by the late third century, there is evidence of a station at the church for a service separate from burial, and this pattern will continue and grow in the Western church in the subsequent centuries. So, we have evidence of a three-station pattern, home-church-grave, with two processions linking the three places.

Returning to the rites done, there is evidence that in some geographical churches those rites included a celebration of the Eucharist. In the Latin-speaking church, probably the most famous example is that of Augustine of Hippo, comparing the different traditions of Rome (Ostia) and his own North Africa in reference to the burial of his mother. Describing her burial in Ostia, Augustine writes:

> When her body was carried away, we went out, and we returned without tears. Not even in those prayers we poured forth to you when the sacrifice of our redemption was offered up in her behalf, with the corpse already placed beside the grave before being lowered into it, as is the custom of that place, not even during those prayers did I shed tears.[31]

He describes here a celebration of the eucharist at the grave in the presence of the body, after which the body was placed in the grave. This is apparently in contrast to what is recorded by the Council of Hippo in 393 which prohibited the celebration of eucharist in the presence of the corpse.[32]

[28] ARISTIDES, Apology 15 (Joseph Armitage ROBINSON (Ed.), The Apology of Aristides, Nendeln ^{2}1967, 49–50).

[29] The difference between the burial site (grave) and church is ambiguous in the earliest evidence. Eventually there is a clear second step before the grave, which results in a pattern of home, procession to the church, service in the church, procession to the grave, committal.

[30] EUSEBIUS, De vita Constantini iv.66, 71 (Friedhelm WINKELMANN (Ed.), Berlin 1975, 147–149).

[31] AUGUSTINE, Confessiones ix.12 (CChr.SL 27, 151).

[32] It was the continuing practice of giving communion to the dead that was the primary concern of the canon: "certain osent célébrer les sacrifices corps présent et communier le cadaver sans vie avec une parcelle du sait corps. A notre avis, cette coutume est à prohiber." Conc. Hippon. 393, canon 4. Cited in Victor SAXER, Morts, martyrs, reliques, Paris 1980, 152.

Lastly in the ritual process, there is early and widespread evidence of commemorative celebrations, most notably on the third day following death. In Jewish mourning there were three 'days of weeping',[33] as well as counterparts in other religious groups.[34]
The initial three-day period of mourning had its roots in a popular Near Eastern belief that the soul lingered near the corpse for three days after death, hoping to reenter the body. Only when the soul observed the face of the corpse begin to change in the process of decay did it give up hope and go on its way.[35]
The Christianizing of this pattern found the resurrection of Christ as the most obvious link and continued to observe the third day with a meal at the grave as did many non-Christians, the *refrigerium* recounted in writings and in art.[36] The belief in the three day sojourn of the soul (as well as of Christ) is most commonly depicted in the priority given to the Jonah cycle in early Christian grave decorations. In the pre-Constantinian collation of visual themes, the re-worked Jonah cycle is overwhelmingly the most common find, as evidenced in Graydon Snyder's work, *Ante Pacem*, where the Jonah cycle appears 108 times out of a total of 181 pictoral scenes.[37]
Other days of commemoration (such as the seventh, the thirtieth, the fortieth, the fiftieth, and above all, the annual anniversary of death) were also observed, but the earliest evidence and most common observance is that of the third day.

Liturgical Texts

Of the prayers and other texts used in early funeral liturgies, including scripture, adapted scripture, and original compositions, there are few in the first six centuries which cross geographical, linguistic, and cultural lines. The continuity often rests in repeated images used in liturgical texts, and similarly-themed scriptural passages, rather than in uniformity. A liturgical prayer from the mid-fourth cen-

33 Geoffrey ROWELL, The Liturgy of Christian Burial, London 1977, 5.
34 For evidence of the Greek tradition of honoring the dead on the third day with the funeral feast, see Franz CUMONT, After Life in Roman Paganism, New York 1959, 50–53.
35 Frederick PAXTON, Christianizing Death, Ithaca 1990, 21.
36 Again AUGUSTINE's remembering of his mother's activities in North Africa which were forbidden in Milan. Describing her usual practice at the *refrigerium,* he says: "When she had brought her basket with the accustomed festival-food, to be but tasted by herself, and then given away, [she] never joined therewith more than one small cup of wine, diluted according to her own abstemious habits, which for courtesy she would taste. And if there were many churches of the departed saints, that were to be honoured in that manner, she still carried round that same one cup, to be used everywhere…" Confessions, vi.
37 Graydon SNYDER, Ante Pacem. Archeological Evidence of Church Life Before Constantine, Macon 1982, 43. "In the first scene Jonah stands in a boat as an Orant, about to be cast into the sea. Sometimes he has already been cast out, or perhaps has dived out, but still frequently maintains an awkward Orant gesture. Occasional the *ketos,* the sea animal, receives the cast-out Jonah…but normally the *ketos* is spewing Jonah out and once more Jonah normally maintains the Orant gesture…in the third scene Jonah lies nude under a tree or vine with obvious pastoral décor in the background." Ibid., 46.

tury, used at the home before the body was processed to the grave, captures many of the images that recur again and again:

> God, who has the power of life and death, God of the spirits and Master of all flesh, God who brings death and gives life, who leads down to the gates of hades and brings back again, who creates the spirit of people and who receives the souls of the saints and gives them rest. You who change and convert and transform your creatures as is right and expedient; you yourself alone are immortal and unchanging and eternal. We pray to you for the repose and rest of this man, your servant [or, this woman your servant]. Let his soul and his spirit rest in green places and in secret places of rest with Abraham and Isaac and Jacob and all your saints and raise up his body on the day which you have appointed according to your trustworthy promises in order that also you may bestow, with respect to him, the inheritances in your holy pastures. Do not remember his trespasses and sins, make his departure peaceful and blessed. Heal the griefs of his relatives by the Spirit of comfort and give to us all a good end, through your only-begotten Jesus Christ through whom be to you the glory and the power in the holy Spirit both now and to all the ages of ages, amen.[38]

The contrast between the omnipotence and immutability of God and the changing mortality of humanity, the rest in green places with all the saints (especially Abraham), the resurrection of the body on the last day, and the plea to not remember sins will reappear again and again in prayers, as well as the use of scripture (here Wisdom 26:13; Numbers 26:22; I Samuel 2:6, Psalm 23:2; Titus 1:2) incorporated into the composition of liturgical prayer.[39] The image of death as rest or sleep until the final day of resurrection is also present in funereal art and graphic inscriptions in Greek and Latin speaking Christianity in particular.
The psalms sung during the procession to the grave are mentioned by John Chrysostom as Psalms 22, 23, and 116. Psalm 116 in particular is also mentioned in the sixth book of the *Apostolic Constitutions*[40] and appears a bit later in the Armenian, Coptic and Gallican prayers. The psalms would be used as the voice of the deceased in medieval Western tradition, especially verses 8-9, and verse 15 of Psalm 116:

> For you have delivered my soul from death, my eyes from tears, my feet from stumbling. I walk before the Lord in the land of the living. I kept my faith, even when I said, "I am greatly afflicted." Precious in the sight of the Lord is the death of his faithful ones.

If scholarly consensus following on the work of Damien Sicard's proposal for fifth century origins for the old Roman *ordo defunctorum* can be followed,[41] then the framework of funeral rites given in *Ordo XLIX* gives us a few more texts with which to work. In Frederick Paxton's synthesis of variants from Sicard's chart, the ordo reveals that first, at the moment of death, Psalms 114 (When Israel went out from Egypt) and 115 (Not to us, O Lord, not to us, but to

[38] The Sacramentary of Sarapion of Thmuis, 18 (R.J.S. BARRETT-LENNARD (ed.), Nottingham 1993, 50–51).
[39] Most notably in the Apostolic Constitution, where several prayers bear a close resemblance to that of Sarapion's Book VIII, section 41.
[40] VI, 30, 3.
[41] See the defense and argument for fourth/fifth-century origins in PAXTON, Christianizing Death, 37–44.

your name give glory) were used, along with two liturgical texts which will reappear in Latin language rites, the response *Subvenite sancti dei* and the verse *Suscipiat te Christus.* Based on the Lukan story of Lazarus and the rich man (Luke 16:19-31), the person of Lazarus becomes the model for the just-deceased Christian:

> Aid him, saints of God: run to meet him, angels of the Lord – you who receive his soul, you who offer him to the sight of the most high. May Christ, who created you, receive you and may the angels lead you to the bosom of Abraham. May a chorus of angels receive you and may you have eternal rest with Lazarus the poor man.[42]

At the home, after the washing and preparation of the body, Psalm 93 (The Lord is king, he is robed in majesty) is used, along with the antiphon "My redeemer, you formed me from the earth and dressed me in flesh: Lord resuscitate me on the last day."[43] As the procession to the grave begins, Psalms 23 (The Lord is my shepherd) and 33 (Rejoice in the Lord, O you righteous), are used, both of which speak of God as "helper and protector."[44] While awaiting burial, Psalm 42 (As a deer longs for flowing streams) is sung, followed by Psalm 115 again, along with other unnamed psalms and chants and a reading from the book of Job in a "vigil", otherwise unknown. Because two of the antiphons are taken from Job, one might speculate that the reading reiterates "My redeemer, you formed me from the earth…" (drawn from Job 19:25-27).
Finally, "as the body is placed in the tomb" the antiphon "Open to me the gates of justice and let me enter, for I will confess to the Lord. The Lord's just ones will enter by this gate," is sung with the remainder of Psalm 118. Sicard sees a great unity in the texts used, reiterating the themes

> God is the giver of life, the recreator, the resurrector. He is attended by angels who carry the souls of the dead to join the community of souls already in repose. The dying person identifies with Christ through the reading of the Passion and, fortified for the final judgment with the body and blood of Christ, dies in the assurance of entry into the community of saints. The church organized the rite as a passage. It conducted its dead member symbolically from earth to heaven, praying in the name of the deceased, using the first person of the psalms. The funeral cortege was an *adventus*, a triumphal procession into perpetual light.[45]

While this represents a small sampling, it is perhaps enough in this limited space to return to the contemporary rites and see the similarities, differences and implications of the same for theological meaning.

[42] Ibid., 39–41.
[43] Ibid., 40. "De terra formasti me et carnem induisti me redemptor meus domine, resuscita me in novissimo die."
[44] Ibid., 41.
[45] PAXTON's summary, 42.

4. THE INHERITANCE OF EARLY LITURGICAL DEVELOPMENT

In the Roman Catholic rite described above, the pattern has clear affinities with historical patterns of Christian funerals. Although listed out of order, there are prayers after death and presumably at the place of death. There is a vigil, a transfer of the body to the church or place of committal, the station at the church (with eucharist as normative) a procession to the place of committal, and the committal itself.

In the prayer language of the first station, one of the central prayers uses the imagery of the early church prayers:

> Holy Lord, almighty and eternal God, hear our prayers for your servant N., whom you have summoned out of this world. Forgive his/her sins and failings and grant him/her a place of refreshment, light, and peace. Let him/her pass unharmed through the gates of death to dwell with the blessed in light, as you promised to Abraham and his children for ever. Accept N. into your safekeeping and on the great day of judgment raise him/her up with all the saints to inherit your eternal kingdom…[46]

The same imagery of forgiveness of sins, a place of refreshment, light and peace, passage of the soul, and safekeeping until the day of judgment are very consistent with Sarapion of Thmuis and subsequent prayers. Only the order, listing forgiveness first, is a noticeable change. The prayers for gathering in the presence of the body also contain verses from Psalms 115 and 116, again reminiscent of the early patterns. In the procession to the church or committal, the primary psalm suggested is Psalm 122 (I rejoiced when I heard them say: Let us go to God's house), which is not prominent in the first six centuries of Christian history, but does come in by the eighth and ninth centuries in the West.

The second station in the church begins with overtly baptismal elements, the placing of a white pall on the coffin (the baptismal garment) and the sprinkling with holy water. Neither is known from the earliest centuries of liturgy, but they are consistent with the resurrection focus that was evident there.

The Old Testament scripture readings noted in the earliest liturgies are all offered as options in the Liturgy of the Word, the psalms are varied but Psalms 33, 114, and 115 are not listed as options at all. The only gospel reference we have from the earliest centuries is the Lukan story of Lazarus and the rich man, but, oddly enough, of all the gospels presented as options, that passage is not included. The commendation rite at the end of the church station includes the response and verse from the old Roman *ordo defunctorum*, as well as the versicle and response, "eternal rest grant unto her, O Lord, and let perpetual light shine upon her" which comes not from the earliest centuries but from the traditions of the eighth century.

At the final station, the committal, the ritual pattern retains the ancient structure but the liturgical texts have changed. The earliest stratum revealed a dependence

[46] Concluding Prayers in: Prayers After Death (Order of Christian Funerals), 107.

on psalmody, especially Psalm 118, while the contemporary Roman Catholic committal uses short scripture passages from the gospels, prayers for the mourners, and texts which have been consistently used from the eighth century on.

The Episcopal church in the United States also has developed a ritual pattern very consistent with the earliest centuries, especially in the augmentation of EOW III. There, the prayers at death and for a vigil in the home have suggestions that psalms be used, but again missing Ppsalms 33, 114, and 115. The litanic prayers contain the images of the early church prayers:

> That it may please you mercifully to pardon all his sins, *We beseech you to hear us, good Lord.* That it may please you to grant him a place of refreshment and everlasting blessedness, *We beseech you to hear us, good Lord.* That it may please you to give him joy and gladness in your kingdom, with your saints in light, *We beseech you to hear us, good Lord.*[47]

As with the Roman vigil and prayers, the primary prayers are the *commendatio animae* and the *profisicere*, prayers which come from the eighth or ninth century and carry through the intervening centuries.[48] Interspersed with the imagery of the early church are prayers which pray for deliverance from evil, which clearly date from a later Christian period, as well as prayers which speak of joy in the presence of God ("Let his heart and soul now ring out in joy to you, O Lord, the living God, and the God of those who live.").

Turning to the funeral liturgy proper, there is the same series of overt baptismal rituals (the white pall and the sprinkling rite), and a collect which mentions for the first time "the last day" and the "fullness of your promises" as something that will come later. The suggested readings include the option of Psalm 118, seen in the *ordo defuntorum*, but neither the reading from Job nor from Luke that are directly or indirectly referenced in the early rites. As in the Roman Rite, this centers on the celebration of the Eucharist. The commendation rite ends with the Eastern Orthodox Kontakion which echoes much of the prayer for the dead of Sarapion of Thmuis, but the closing prayers are drawn from later centuries, including the prayer:

> Blessed Jesus, Son of the living God, we pray you to set your passion, cross, and death between your judgment and our souls, now and in the hour of our death. Give mercy and grace to the living, pardon and peace to the dead; to your holy church peace and concord, and to us sinners everlasting life and glory; for with the Father and the Holy Spirit you live and reign, one God, now and for ever. Amen.[49]

This prayer combines elements from the late Middle Ages and an original prayer of Lancelot Andrewes from the early seventeenth century. It is situated next to eighth-century prayers and the Easter troparion borrowed from the Eastern

47 Book of Common Prayer, "Ministration at the Time of Death", 463.

48 See John S. LAMPARD, Go Forth, Christian Soul: The Biography of a Prayer, Peterborough 2005, for a treatment of the *profisicere* prayer.

49 Enriching our Worship 3 (see fn 17), 40.

Orthodox tradition. The committal itself, like the Roman Rite, is composed mostly of prayers focused on Christ and drawn from gospel images and late medieval litanies from the Sarum rite, rather than the psalms of the early church.

Finally, turning to the multi-denominational Protestant texts in *Chalice Worship,* there is a discernable gap between the ritual pattern of the early church and what is suggested here. While there is an option of doing the committal first and then the funeral liturgy in earlier Anglican rites, it is not presented as such in the ritual order, and is soundly denounced in the subsequent EOW III. In *Chalice Worship,* the committal comes first and is followed by the "Service of Grateful Memory." The primary prayer in the committal service is:

> God of heaven and earth, in your Son Jesus Christ you have given us a true faith and a sure hope. Strengthen this faith and hope in us all our days, that we may live as those who believe in the communion of the saints, the forgiveness of sins, and the resurrection to eternal life; through your Son Jesus Christ our Lord. Amen.[50]

The prayer is not focused on the deceased at all, but on those who are gathered for the liturgy. The prayer is preceded by a purpose statement, which functions not as a prayer but as a moment of catechesis. It is interesting that the dual focus presented there is to give thanks to God for the gift of the deceased "to us" and to "commit their earthly body with confidence."[51] No specific scripture passages are commended, and no hints of prayer texts from the first millennium of Christianity are to be found.

The primary funeral service (judging from length) contains none of the early church prayer language, but includes in the several scripture passages that might be used Psalm 23 and Psalm 42, both dating back to the early church texts. The only baptismal reference is in a prayer following the preaching:

> Remind us of our baptism in which we were baptized into Christ's death that we might rise to newness of life. United with him in a death like his, we will certainly be united with him in a resurrection like his.[52]

The service continues with the possibility of the Lord's Supper ("If the Lord's Supper is observed, an emphasis may be made upon communion with the host of Christians believers of all times and places. The invitation should make clear the Lord's Supper's meaning and that participation is open to all Christ's followers.") The conclusion is simply a dismissal with blessing; no commendation rite is offered as an option.

[50] Chalice Worship, committal service, 59.
[51] Ibid.
[52] Chalice Worship, 68.

5. CONCLUSION

The contemporary funeral rites logically draw from centuries of Christian practice rather than just from the first five or six centuries of Christian liturgy. In all three traditions presented as examples here, however, there is a claim of returning, of reclaiming, or of rooting themselves in the traditions and theology of the early church. In the Roman and Anglican rites, there is an order of funeral rites which is patterned on the ritual practices of the early church. In both of those traditions, there are also still prayers based on the imagery found in the few early church prayers that are discernible. The ecumenical collection of ritual texts and patterns found in *Chalice Worship* seems to have very little in common with the limited evidence that we have from the early church.

All three have commonalities not observed above, however. The first is the emphasis on the mourners in prayers, rituals and scriptural choices. In the early liturgical texts described above, only the prayer of Sarapion mentions the mourners at all: "Heal the griefs of his relatives by the Spirit of comfort…". In all the contemporary rites, the prayers for the mourners make up more than half of the options presented in the full rites.

The second observation is that the prayers accessible to us from earliest liturgical rites almost uniformly stress the distance between death and final judgment. The bodies and souls wait for the final judgment in a place of light, peace and refreshment. Contemporary rites, having crossed over the bridge from *refrigerium interim* to purgatory and back to *refrigerium interim* in some cases, seem far less clear about the divide. The contemporary prayers mix and match the current fullness of rest in God with future fullness, reluctant to name the unknown timing and placement of where Christians are after death.

The third observation, most obvious in the liturgical texts of the third set of churches, the protestant group centered around the Disciples of Christ, is the distaste for naming or in anyway praying for the dead. This is an obvious inheritance of reformed Christians who have emerged from the teachings of Calvin, Knox, Zwingli and others, but in the ecumenical soup of the twenty-first century, and in light of the claims of drawing on the early church, it is surprising that the structure of the rites, (a committal and then a return to the church building), still echo the protest against prayers for the dead or even prayers in the proximity of the dead. But the contemporary option that substitutes for praying for the dead is praying for the living. This is not so much in the tradition of the reformation which prayed that the living might take the confrontation with death so apparent at a funeral and convert their own lives, but prayers that pray for the living in their own confident hope of resurrection. These are hinted at even in the Roman and Anglican rites, but are quite obvious in the Disciples of Christ prayers.

The fourth observation is the question at the heart of the funeral rites – what is it that they do? The contemporary Roman rites state a threefold purpose: to worship God, to console the mourners, and to commend the dead to God. Two of the three are certainly prominent in the early church liturgies also. The Anglican rites would probably add the reverent disposal of the body with a stress on the incarnation and the importance of the body, but otherwise agree with the threefold Roman emphasis. The Disciples of Christ introduction does not describe the purpose of the rite at all, but perhaps the stress on "grateful memory" of the deceased could be interpreted as a primary reason for doing the rite.

But written texts are only part of the lived experience of funeral rites, and increasingly the cultural stress on "celebration of life" in North America is influencing even those rites which have a clear idea of why they are celebrated. A funeral whose primary purpose is to celebrate the life of the deceased looks backwards to the former life, rather than forward to eternal life. The emphasis is very different, and it is either death-denying or life-denying, in the sense of eternal life. This is an emphasis that seems far removed from the practice and belief of the early church, with the language of journey, of confident hope, of Easter joy, of triumph in the resurrection, of rest in a place of peace, light and refreshment, of confidence in the forgiveness of sins, and delight in the communion of saints.

At the beginning of this essay I described Kenneth Stevenson's three criteria for the importance of understanding and practicing the liturgy of the early church. The third point he made was the normativity of early church liturgy: "We don't have to imitate the early centuries but there can be little doubt that they propose to us certain significant norms that ought to challenge our own discipleship and the quality and depth of our worship."[53] There is much ecumenical rhetoric about returning to the liturgical development of the early church, from the mid-twentieth century to current discussions. The evidence suggests that there may be more rhetoric than reality in some of the rites which we practice. Perhaps revisiting the "quality and depth of our worship" in light of the funeral rites would result in a greater depth and authenticity between belief and practice.

[53] The First Rites, 12.

North African Liturgical Readings: The Augustinian Legacy and Some Western Parallels

Michael Margoni-Kögler*

The literary works of St. Augustine, above all his approximately 750 sermons recorded up to now, which were held during eucharistic and other liturgical assemblies, constitute the main source for our knowledge of the North African Christian worship in Late Antiquity. Most of these sermons contain direct or indirect references to one or more of their immediately preceding biblical lessons. In view of only poorly preserved primary liturgical sources originating in the late patristic era (e.g. "lectionaries" or *Typika*, such as the so called "Armenian Lectionary of Jerusalem" contemporary to the late Augustine, or simple listings of scriptural readings) liturgico-historical research depends almost exclusively on the evaluation of such homiletic testimonials – a task which for the vast amount of the Augustinian homiletic *œuvre* had already been accomplished in parts in the twentieth century.[1] Although a thorough analysis of this entire *corpus*, based on a more consciously reflected methodology as well as on augmented source material (cf. the "*sermones* Dolbeau" and the recently discovered "*sermones* Erfurt"[2]), surely enlarges and corrects the spectrum of these scriptural readings as it has been drawn up by previous scholarship, it does not enable us to reconstruct and arrange them as comprehensively as later reading lists or lectionaries do. In many cases either the detection of the pericopes themselves or their attribution to certain feasts or periods of the liturgical year remains rather hypothetic. Based on the results of our doctoral thesis, our investigation now shifts to the question whether comparative liturgy may help to draw any conclusions where the Augustinian sources lack or obscure evidence:

* The following article represents the slightly enlarged version of my lecture delivered at the Symposium liturgicum Vindobonense in November 2007. The same topic is discussed at some length in the closing chapter of my study Die Perikopen im Gottesdienst bei Augustinus. Ein Beitrag zur Erforschung der liturgischen Schriftlesung in der frühen Kirche (Sitzungsberichte der Österreichischen Akademie der Wissenschaften. Philosophisch–historische Klasse 810 = Veröffentlichungen der Kommission für die Herausgabe des Corpus der Lateinischen Kirchenväter 29), Wien 2010, 602–620, which settles the basic questions concerning identifiability and assignment of biblical lessons detected in the Augustinian sources.

1 Especially by Geoffrey G. Willis' reconstruction of St Augustine's Lectionary (Alcuin Club Collection 44), London 1962, the inevitable limitations of which I outlined in my Perikopen im Gottesdienst bei Augustinus, 38–40. For a review of further investigations in this area cf. ibid. 19–25.

2 Editio princeps in two parts by Isabella Schiller – Dorothea Weber – Clemens Weidmann, Sechs neue Augustinuspredigten, in: Wiener Studien 121 (2008) 227–284; 122 (2009) 171–213.

Which, if any, parallels or at least similarities to biblical lessons attested by different eastern and especially western authors contemporary with or slightly later than Augustine and also by the earliest extant *capitularia* (lists of pericopes) of Late Antiquity and the early Middle Ages, testifying traces of well established reading practice passed on through the centuries, may corroborate hypothetic identifications of biblical lessons individually chosen or traditionally followed by Augustine, or may even supply hints for their proper heortological attribution, or may simply display parallels between St. Augustine's North African liturgy and other liturgical families? A few selected crucial points drawn from my analysis of the Augustinian festal homilies, leaving apart the *Sanctorale*, shall shed some light on the hitherto rather obscure relation of the North African liturgy to other liturgical families.

1. THE NATIVITY CYCLE

St. Augustine's rootage in the *western* heortological framework is not very astonishing if we remember North Africa together with North Italy as among the first Churches that took over the December 25 Nativity feast from Rome.[3] Thus, even if the separate celebration of Christ's birth on December 25 was already established by the mid-380s (at the latest) in Cappadocia and in the Antioch of John Chrysostom[4], but not yet in Jerusalem as its absence in the Armenian Lectionary reveals, the shifting of festal themes in accordance with the balance with Epiphany becomes obvious especially from St. Augustine's Christmas homilies and places him in close vicinity to the Christmas sermons of Leo the Great (*tract.* 21-30), preached only a few decades after his death: Whereas e.g. Gregory of Nyssa deals at length not only with Christ's birth itself, but also with the adoration of the Magi and Herod's slaughter of the Innocents – for Epiphany will be centred around the baptism of Christ –, we encounter Augustine focussing mainly on the mystery of the *verbum caro factum* humiliating itself by accepting his birth from a virgin-mother and taking

[3] Thus, also the oldest extant Christmas sermon goes back to a Numidian bishop, Optatus of Milevis (c. 360); cf. André WILMART, Un sermon de saint Optat pour la fête de Noël, in: Revue des sciences religieuses 2 (1922) 271–302.

[4] Cf. GREGORY OF NYSSA, diem nat. (Gregorii Nysseni Opera 10/2, 235–296); GREGORY OF NAZIANZUS, or. 38 (PG 36, 311–334); JOHN CHRYSOSTOM, nativ. (PG 49, 351–362; § 1: "οὔπω δεκατόν ἐστιν ἔτος"). Cf. especially Jochen REXER, Die Festtheologie Gregors von Nyssa. Ein Beispiel der reichskirchlichen Heortologie (Patrologia 8), Frankfurt/M. 2002, 5f., 36–40, 88–97; Jill Burnett COMINGS, Aspects of the Liturgical Year in Cappadocia (325–430) (Patristic Studies 7), New York 2005, 61–69; Reiner KACZYNSKI, Das Wort Gottes in Liturgie und Alltag der Gemeinden des Johannes Chrysostomus (Freiburger Theologische Studien 94), Freiburg i. Br. 1974, 158f.; Hans FÖRSTER, Die Feier der Geburt Christi in der Alten Kirche. Beiträge zur Erforschung der Anfänge des Epiphanie- und des Weihnachtsfestes (Studien und Texte zu Antike und Christentum 4), Tübingen 2000, 60–85.

on the form of a servant (cf. Philippians 2:6-8). It is exactly this theology of Christmas that Augustine's choice of the biblical lessons reflects, comprising primarily Luke 2 and – in all likelihood – Philippians 2*, both attested by explicit indications[5], and alternatively possibly also a reading of John's Prologue, unambiguous indications for which, however, are missing. Unfortunately St. Leo's sermons on the Nativity, displaying the same heortological accentuation as Augustine's, lack any such indications referring to the gospel or epistle that has been heard/read out just before, but from the predominance of quotations from these very biblical chapters (Philippians 2; Luke 2; John 1) we can guess with the utmost probability that also the festal readings were taken from them. We do not know for sure whether at Leo's time the *missa in nocte* in the Liberian Basilica was already celebrated in addition to the *missa in die* at St. Peter's. If it was, Luke 2 would have been the gospel during the night and John 1 in the morning; but the Augustinian records do not reveal any hints for a mass at midnight.[6] The festal pericopes would vary from year to year in St. Augustine's community at Hippo.[7]

On Epiphany – in St. Augustine's North Africa an already firmly established, but still rather young feast (since Optatus included the Magi still in his Christmas sermon) – the bishop of Hippo consequently dealt primarily with the adoration of the Magi, but – as several of his sermons reveal and one of them states explicitly – also the slaughter of the Innocents was or at least could be chosen as part of the feastday's gospel.[8] The closest parallels can again be drawn to the Epiphany sermons of Leo the Great (*tract.* 31-38), whereas the great North Italian bishops at the same time or slightly later focus upon those themes which finally lead to the commemoration of the *tria miracula*; thus, for Maximus of Turin the two dominating heortological contents are Christ's baptism in the Jordan and the miracle at Cana, which presumably also dominate at St. Chromatius's Aquileia, as far as we can guess from his fragmentary *sermo* 34, whereas the homilies of Peter Chrysologus of Ravenna already reveal the full *trias* by combining these motifs with the adoration of the Magi.[9] To be

[5] Cf. sermo (= s.) 189,4; 190,4; 193,1; 196,2; 196A (= ÉTAIX 2), to be paralleled with LEO'S tract. 21–30, passim.

[6] *Pace* Edmund HILL, Sermons (184–229Z) on the Liturgical Seasons (The Works of Saint Augustine 3/6), New Rochelle/NY 1993, 52[8]. Cf. also Germain HUDON, Le mystère de Noël dans le temps de l'Église d'après saint Augustin, in: MD 59 (1959) 60–84, 64.

[7] For further references concerning the Christmas pericopes in early Western liturgies cf. the instructive overview in Franco SOTTOCORNOLA, L'anno liturgico nei sermoni di Pietro Crisologo: Ricerca storico–critica sulla liturgia di Ravenna antica (Studia Ravennatensia 1), Cesena 1973, 356–358.

[8] Cf. s. 373,2: "Multa igitur consideranda sunt, fratres, in hac quam audivimus euangelica lectione." The 10 Augustinian sermons on Epiphany recorded up to now are s. 199–204; Étaix 4 (= 204A); 373; Dolbeau 23 (= 374augm.); 375. For a detailed analysis cf. my Perikopen im Gottesdienst bei Augustinus, 70–77.

[9] Cf. MAXIMUS, especially s. 64,1; 65,1 (cf. Andreas MERKT, Maximus I. von Turin. Die Verkündigung eines Bischofs der frühen Reichskirche im zeitgeschichtlichen, gesellschaftlichen und liturgischen Kontext [Supplements to Vigiliae Christianae 40],

sure, Augustine also mentions the wine-miracle in one of his sermons on Epiphany[10], but based on this single remark we cannot deduce an integration of John 2:1-12 into the spectrum of the Augustinian pericopes for Epiphany, even if the early Gaulish sources together with the North Italian homilies just mentioned point in this direction, e.g. the Lectionary of Luxeuil – the least Romanized of all old Gallican lectionaries – giving a gospel-harmonic cento (a specific feature of the Visigothic and old Gallican liturgy) consisting of Matthew 3:13-17; Luke 3:23 (baptism) and John 2:1-11 (Cana) for the feastday, whereas Matt. 2 has formed the gospel already on December 28 "*in natale Infantum ad missam*".[11]

A hypothetic reconstruction of a reading from Isaiah 60 – the pilgrimage of the peoples to Zion – derived from some allusions in *s.* Dolbeau 23,15.20[12], could possibly be supported with evidence from the same Lectionary (Isaiah 60:1-16) and the Lectionary of Schlettstadt (Isaiah 60:1-6) as well as from the oldest extant Roman list of Epistles, the *Capitula lectionum* of the "*Comes* Würzburg" (Isaiah 60:1-6)[13], being well aware that the compilation of these documents took place not earlier than almost three centuries after Augustine, of course preserving traditional liturgical reading practice. An interesting feature to conclude with is the Epistle reading from Ephesians 2 on the peace Christ's apparition made between Christians and Jews which, as far as my research led, is not attested by any western author or lectionary nor included in the vast amount of biblical lessons the so called Armenian Lectionary provides for Epiphany[14] nor in the somehow strange earliest East Syriac lectionary system, the so called "Burkitt Manuscript" (last quarter of the fifth century).[15]

Leiden 1997, 152–155, 181–193); PETER CHRYSOLOGUS, s. 156; 157; 160 (cf. SOTTOCORNOLA, L'anno liturgico [see fn 7], 240–250). Further Adolf SMITMANS, Das Weinwunder von Kana. Die Auslegung von Jo 2, 1–11 bei den Vätern und heute (Beiträge zur Geschichte der biblischen Exegese 6), Tübingen 1966, esp. 165–186. – Unfortunately, the writings of St. Ambrose give no hints concerning the biblical lessons that were read during the Christmas and Epiphany services at Milan in the fourth century.

10 S. Dolbeau 23,11: "Convertit aquam in vinum Christus, magnum miraculum: quis alius facit hoc in vite omni anno?"

11 Cf. Pierre SALMON, Le Lectionnaire de Luxeuil (Paris, ms. lat. 9427). 1: Édition et étude comparative (Collectanea biblica latina 7), Roma 1944, LXXI, CVI, 57–60.

12 Put forward by Martin KLÖCKENER, Die Bedeutung der neu entdeckten Augustinus–Predigten (Sermones Dolbeau) für die liturgiegeschichtliche Forschung, in: Goulven MADEC (ed.), Augustin prédicateur (395–411). Actes du Colloque International de Chantilly (5–7 septembre 1996) (Collection des Études Augustiniennes. Série Antiquité 159), Paris 1998, 129–170, 166.

13 Cf. SALMON, Lectionnaire de Luxeuil (see fn 11), CVI–CVII; Germain MORIN, Le plus ancien *Comes* ou Lectionnaire de l'Église romaine, in: Revue bénédictine 27 (1910) 41–74, 48.

14 Cf. Athanase RENOUX (ed.), Le codex arménien de Jérusalem 121. II. Édition comparée du texte et de deux autres manuscrits (PO 36/2), Turnhout 1971, 211–217.

15 B.M. Add. 14528, fol. 152r–191v; cf. Francis C. BURKITT, The Early Syriac Lectionary System, in: Proceedings of the British Academy 10 (1921–1923) 301–338, 306.

2. THE PASCHAL CYCLE

2.1 Quadragesima

Turning to the paschal cycle, the Augustinian indications for the detection of his quadragesimal pericopes are more numerous and the spectrum of the readings, compared with the data listed by Willis, has therefore been enlarged.[16] Thus, we have to pick out some specific features. A difficulty that arises (not only concerning the Lenten sermons, but in their case particularly noticeable) and unfortunately cannot be solved in most instances is the identification of the proper type of liturgical service in which a sermon was delivered. In the case where we are informed about a gospel preceding the sermon, this ensures that Augustine preached during a Eucharist; if no gospel reading becomes evident, we cannot state with certainty whether the sermon arose from a eucharistic or non-eucharistic service, e.g. an additional Liturgy of the Word in the morning on high feasts, or perhaps a Liturgy of the Hours for his monastic community, or simply a catechetical instruction addressed mainly (but maybe not exclusively) to the catechumens, especially in Lent. As most of the quadragesimal sermons listed within the Old Testament- and Epistle-squares of the table at the end of our article reappear within the Gospel-square, the detected pericopes were mainly read during eucharistic services. Among them, primarily the Old Testament lectures are worth noting.

In three of the six extant sermons Augustine preached as a kind of Quadragesima-Opening he abundantly quotes from Isaiah 58:3-7 on the true, spiritual fasting, i.e. good deeds based on solidarity (*caritas*).[17] Even if he does not refer to this pericope by means of an explicit reference, we can – based on the appropriate liturgical coherence and the proper biblical context of the passage – guess that it has been read in the very Eucharist in which each of these sermons was held. Now we find Isaiah 58 as a lesson at the beginning of Lent for example also in the "Burkitt Manuscript" as the tenth of the twelve Old Testament readings[18] as well as during the sixth Lenten week in some other ancient systems preserved by the Greek Church[19], but not testified (as a pericope) by the North Italians (Gaudentius, Chromatius, Peter Chrysologus, Maximus of Turin, Ambrose) nor by the Old Spanish *Liber Commicus* of Silos (Toledo) nor by the later South Gaul Caesarius of Arles, whereas it is listed e.g.

[16] Compare WILLIS, St Augustine's Lectionary (see fn 1), 23–24, with my investigation in Perikopen im Gottesdienst bei Augustinus, 81–95.

[17] These are s. 205,3; 206,3; 207,1.

[18] Cf. BURKITT, Lectionary System (see fn 15), 306.

[19] Cf. Alfred RAHLFS, Die alttestamentlichen Lektionen der griechischen Kirche, in: Nachrichten von der Königlichen Gesellschaft der Wissenschaften zu Göttingen. Philologisch–historische Klasse aus dem Jahre 1915 (Mitteilungen des Septuaginta–Unternehmens 1,5), Berlin 1916, 28–136, 38.

in the Luxeuil Lectionary "*in inicium quadragensimae*" and equally in the Schlettstadt Lectionary.[20] Also the Roman liturgy testifies to Is. 58:1-9, since the *Capitula lectionum* of the "*Comes* Würzburg" appoint it to Friday before the first Lenten Sunday.[21] If *s.* 5 was preached within the Quadragesima, as traditionally assumed due to the allocution of the *competentes*[22], explicit indications reveal Genesis 32-33 as the underlying Old Testament reading (Jacob's fight with the angel *and* his reconciliation with Esau) and additionally Psalm 42. This could lend probability to the hypothesis that also in St. Augustine's Church certain chapters of Genesis were traditionally read during the Quadragesima following more or less a limited *lectio continua* (i.e. *Bahnlesung*), thus agreeing not only with eastern practice[23], but also with some of his western bishop-colleagues, e.g. St. Ambrose stating in the opening chapters of *de mysteriis* and *de Ioseph* that during Lent the stories of the patriarchs are read as biblical lessons, and the later Caesarius testifying to a *Bahnlesung* of Genesis 12-42.[24] This hypothesis could further be supported by the interpretation of a slightly cryptic question Augustine poses in the exordium of his *s.* 5: "*Istae lectiones quae vobis leguntur, numquid modo primum vobis leguntur, et non eaedem cotidie repetuntur?*" Not every day, of course, the same lessons were repeated, but perhaps he alludes with "istae lectiones" to the specific Lenten readings which are repeated every year daily. The two further Old Testament lessons, both taken from the Books of Kings – Elijah raising the son of the widow of Sareptah (1 Kings 17:8-16/24), Elisha rising the son of the Shunemite woman from the dead (2 Kings 4:8-37)[25] –, similarly testify to regionally standard Lenten readings if we again take a look at Caesarius who deals with them as the homily immediately preceding readings in the last week

[20] Cf. SALMON, Lectionnaire de Luxeuil (see fn 11), CVIII, 75–77 (Isaiah 58:1-14).

[21] Cf. MORIN, Comes (see fn 13), 49.

[22] This assumption was questioned by Drobner who would prefer the Quinquagesima (baptism at Whit Sunday); cf. Hubertus R. DROBNER, Augustinus von Hippo, Predigten zum Buch Genesis (Sermones 1–5). Einleitung, Text, Übersetzung und Anmerkungen (Patrologia 7), Frankfurt/Main 2000, 168.

[23] Cf. JOHN CHRYSOSTOM'S hom. in Gen., the Armenian Lectionary of Jerusalem assigning long pericopes from Gen. to Monday till Thursday of the Great Week, and the later tradition of the Greek Church (as *lectio continua* from Monday to Friday of the first till the fourth Lenten week, as *Bahnlesung* in the two following weeks; cf. RAHLFS, Lektionen [see fn 19], 34–38, 64).

[24] Cf. AMBR., myst. 1: "De moralibus cottidianum sermonem habuimus, cum vel patriarcharum gesta vel Proverbiorum legerentur praecepta, …"; CAES., s. 81–93, with explicit references to the foregoing lesson from Gen. ("cum divina lectio legeretur, audivimus" or similar; for a listing see Karl BERG, Cäsarius von Arles. Ein Bischof des sechsten Jahrhunderts erschließt das liturgische Leben seiner Zeit [Frühes Christentum. Forschungen und Perspektiven 1], Thaur 1994, 84f.).

[25] Cf. AUG., s. Lambot 10 (= 136B),4: "Animadvertistis quid dixerit sancto Heliae: «Vade in Sarepta Sydoniae, ibi mandavi mulieri viduae ut pascat te» (1 Kings 17:9). … Audistis quid dixerit: «Tantum habeo quod sola cum filiis meis consumam, et moriar» (ibid. v. 12). …"; s. 136,5f. (recapitulation of 2 Kings 4:29-35).

before the Holy Week.[26] Besides, the list of Epistles in the "*Comes* Würzburg" also appoints these two readings to Tuesday of the second, Friday of the fourth, and Tuesday of the third Lenten week respectively.[27] In this instance comparative liturgical analysis indeed helps to corroborate our hypothetic identification of Augustine's biblical lessons and to confirm their proper heortological attribution.

Concerning the Epistle readings which become obvious from four Augustinian Lenten homilies, parallels can be drawn in two instances: The *Liber Commicus* of Silos, an admittedly late source reflecting the Visigothic reading practice at Toledo, appoints verses 7-10 of 1 John 2 to the Saturday before Palm Sunday and verses 8-12 of the same chapter to the morning service of the third Sunday in Lent as parts of a quadragesimal *Bahnlesung* of the Catholic Epistles.[28] Whether the North African liturgy of St. Augustine's time was familiar with a similar reading practice or not, must of course remain undecided due to the lack of further Augustinian testimonies. The second Lenten lesson that allows a comparison becomes evident from Augustine's only fragmentarily preserved *s.* 162B (= 392,1), i.e. *s.* frg. Verbraken 11, reflecting – in all likelihood – a reading from 2 Corinthians 5 (the recommended reconciliation with God), which would also have included the very beginning of chapter 6, the καιρὸς of the ἡμέρα σωτηρίας. As a matter of fact, 2 Corinthians 6:1-10 is attested by several liturgical primary sources for the first Sunday in Lent, viz. by various *Libri commici* of the Old Spanish liturgy, by the Missale of Bobbio reflecting the Old Gallican liturgy, and by the list of Epistles in the Roman "*Comes* Würzburg" and later sources, thereby continuing a tradition that can be traced back to Leo's *tract.* 40 and 42 "*de ieiunio Quadragesimae*".[29]

[26] CAES., s. 124 and 128 (cf. Corpus Christianorum. Series Latina 103, 514–518 and 526–530). Also CHROMATIUS in his s. 25 deals with the pericope 1 Kings 17:1-16 just read out; cf. its Incipit: "De sancto Helia nobis lectio insinuata est. Et congrue tempore ieiunii de sancto Helia lectum est, …" (text: ibid. 9A, 113ff.).

[27] Cf. MORIN, Comes (see fn 13), 51–53. Likewise, Leo the Great alludes to 1 Kings 17:9-16 in his tract. 42, 2 (text: CChr.SL 138A, 242).

[28] Cf. Fray Justo PEREZ DE URBEL – Atilano GONZALEZ Y RUIZ–ZORRILLA (eds.), Liber Commicus. Tomo 1 (Monumenta Hispaniae sacra. Serie litúrgica 2), Madrid 1950, 311 and 204. AUGUSTINE's sermo 211,2 reads: "Si advertistis <*lacuna*> quid advertistis? Beati Iohannis, cum eius epistola legeretur, debuit vos terrere sententia. Ait enim: «Tenebrae transierunt, lux vero iam lucet» (1 John 2:8c). Deinde secutus adiunxit: «Qui se dicit in lumine esse et fratrem suum odit, in tenebris est usque adhuc» (ibid. v.9). …". The biblical context supports the conclusion that the pericope comprised at least verses 7-11 or rather verses 7-17 of 1 John 2.

[29] Cf. Liber Commicus 1 (see fn 28), 81; SALMON, Lectionnaire de Luxeuil (see fn 11), CVIII (synopsis), 77; MORIN, Comes (see fn 13), 49. LEO THE GREAT, tract. 40,2: "Unde oportune auribus nostris lectio apostolicae praedicationis insonuit dicens: «Ecce nunc tempus acceptum, ecce nunc dies salutis» (2 Corinthians 6:2)"; 42,1: "… verbis Apostoli, in quo Christus loquebatur, incipiam dicamque quod lectum est: «…» (ibid.)." From tract. 42,2f.6 it becomes clear that the pericope ended with 2 Corinthians 6:16.

Among the various gospel passages that an analysis of the Augustinian Lenten homilies reveals[30], a short treatment of those taken from John (chapters 5; 6; 9), lying at the base of his sermons 125, 132, and 136 respectively, shall shed some light on their predominance. The *Capitulare evangeliorum* of the "*Comes* Würzburg" testifies to a kind of "interrupted *Bahnlesung*" (i.e. not always following strictly the narrative order of the biblical chapters and sometimes interspersed even with other biblical lessons) of John 2; 4-12 in Lent; quite similar, and without any interruptions by other gospel-pericopes, is the arrangement that several Visigothic *Libri Commici* display.[31] Besides, Augustine's contemporaries Ambrose of Milan and Chromatius of Aquileia also bear witness to a reading of John 9 (the healing of the man born blind) during Lent.[32] Whether Augustine had already followed a continuous reading of selected chapters of John or not, we cannot argue convincingly on the base of these testimonies, always bearing in mind the restrictions caused by textual transmission[33]; but at least we are allowed a glimpse into the development of supra-regional liturgical reading conventions including the North African liturgy as attested by its most famous exponent.

2.2 Easter Vigil

Concerning the programme of biblical lessons during St. Augustine's Easter Vigil[34] we encounter very traditional readings that are attested by various

[30] For a quick overview see the table at the end of this article, the presuppositions of which are discussed in my Perikopen im Gottesdienst bei Augustinus, 83–90.

[31] Cf. Henri LECLERCQ, Liber comicus, in: Dictionnaire d'archéologie chrétienne et de liturgie 9/1 (1930) 220–243, 225–230. Unfortunately the Luxeuil Lectionary cannot provide us with information in this instance, as almost the whole Quadragesima is lacking in it due to a textual loss.

[32] Cf. AMBROSE, ep. 67 (Maur. 80),1: "Audisti, fili, lectionem evangelii, in qua decursum est quod «praeteriens dominus Iesus vidit a generatione caecum» (John 9:1) …" (cf. also §§ 3–9 [text: CSEL 82/2, 165ff.]); de sacramentis 3,11: "Hoc est mysterium, quod legisti in evangelio, si tamen legisti – certe audisti –: Caecus obtulit se salvatori, ut curaretur … in libro evangelii, qui scribitur secundum Iohannem" (CSEL 73, 43); CHROMATIUS, s. 27 (topically referring to John 11, but retrospectively to John 9): "… Superius caecum a nativitate lumine oculorum illuminavit visibili opere …; in praesenti vero lectione Lazaro mortuo vitam donavit" (text: CChr.SL 9A, 124). For further Lenten lessons taken from John according to Chromatius's homilies cf. SOTTOCORNOLA, L'anno liturgico (see fn 7), 390.

[33] For example, the extant Augustinian sources do not reveal any traces of Augustine's preaching on the transfiguration (as e.g. Leo I. did in his tract. 51) or on the temptation of Christ (common to almost all liturgical families at the beginning of Lent) which of course must not be excluded on the base of an *argumentum e silentio*.

[34] For the hypotheses concerning the structure of St. Augustine's Easter Vigil cf. Anton ZWINGGI, Die Osternacht bei Augustinus, in: LJ 20 (1970) 4–10. More recently, cf. Drobner's comprehensive introduction into his German translation of the Augustinian Easter sermons, dealing with liturgical structure, rhetoric style, and of course the Easter theology itself: Hubertus R. DROBNER, Augustinus von Hippo, Predigten zum österlichen Triduum (Sermones 218–229/D). Einleitung, Text, Übersetzung und Anmerkungen (Patrologia 16), Frankfurt/M. 2006, 43–112, esp. 52–84 and 90–100.

liturgical families in East and West which Baumstark has treated in his *Nocturna Laus*.[35] Again we are confronted with the limitations caused by the transmission process, for it is hard to believe that in the Easter Vigil of Hippo merely four Old Testament lessons – apart from the Psalm – were read, viz. Genesis 1, the canticles Exodus 15 and Daniel 3, and Isaiah 2 (verses 1-5 at least). We miss core elements of the Paschal Vigil such as Genesis 22 and Jonah to which most of the liturgical families testify. On the other hand, given the Augustinian evidence, we notice a very strong parallel to the short *tractatus* his younger contemporary Zeno delivered in the Veronese Easter Vigil commenting on almost exactly the same biblical lessons[36], viz. Genesis 1, Exodus 12, and Exodus 14-15 (from which we could guess that the Exodus-story itself would equally have been part of the Augustinian Easter Vigil, not only the canticle chapter 15), Daniel 3, and – the only difference – not Isaiah 2, but Isaiah chapters 1 and 5 (which again could lend probability to the hypothesis that Isaiah 2 was in Hippo perhaps embedded within a broader framework). Otherwise it is only the Luxeuil Lectionary that is the first to testify to a reading of the first five chapters of Isaiah.[37]

2.3 Ascension

The Augustinian pericopes for the feast of the Ascension – quite young a feast at his time, nevertheless already “toto orbe terrarium” celebrated (cf. *s.* 262,3) – display some affinity to the Old Gallican and Spanish habit of reading parts of Acts and Revelation as a *Bahnlesung* at least during the Easter Octave (LectLux), or even till Pentecost (LibComm), but often apart from the biblical course of the chapters: on Ascension itself both provide the New Testament lesson from Acts 1; the *Liber Commicus* appoints Revelation 4:2-4.10f. for the Sunday after Ascension, the Luxeuil Lectionary provides Revelation 5:1-13 for Wednesday in the Easter Octave[38], while Augustine’s *s.* Guelf. 21 bears witness to Revelation 5:1-14 as an eligible lesson on Ascension Day. The closest parallel can be found in the Old Gallican *Missale of Bobbio*, according to which Revelation 7:9-12 is read “*in Ascensione Domini*”[39] – a passage that represents a

[35] See Anton BAUMSTARK, Nocturna Laus. Typen frühchristlicher Vigilienfeiern und ihr Fortleben vor allem im römischen und monastischen Ritus (LWQF 32), Münster 1957 [^{2}1967], 46–61, especially the tables on pp. 46–48.

[36] Cf. Gordon P. JEANES, The Day Has Come! Easter and Baptism in Zeno of Verona (Alcuin Club Collection 73), Collegeville/Minn. 1995; Miguel S. GROS, La vigile pascale à Vérone dans les années 360–380, in: Ecclesia Orans 18 (2001) 11–23; Aimé SOLIGNAC, Les lectures de la vigile et du jour de Pâques à Vérone au temps de Zénon, in: Revue des études augustiniennes 45 (1999) 261–275.

[37] Cf. SALMON, Lectionnaire de Luxeuil (see fn 11), CXII and 106f.

[38] Cf. ibid. CXII and 119–132; Liber Commicus 2 (see fn 28), 388–438.

[39] Cf. The Bobbio Missal: A Gallican Mass–Book (Ms. Paris. Lat. 13246). Text ed. by Elias A. LOWE. Notes and Studies by André WILMART, Elias A. LOWE and Harold A. WILSON (HBS 58 & 61), Woodbridge 1991, 90. As Gospel pericope Luke 24:36–53 follows, as it

kind of summary of the pericope chosen by Augustine focussing upon the adoration of the lamb and the enthroned God. For the two Epistle readings I proposed with a certain degree of probability (Colossians 3:1f.[-?] and 1 Corinthians 15*), I did not find any parallels except the fact that the Luxeuil Lectionary has singled out four parts of 1 Corinthians 15 which were recited during the Octave of Easter. Finally, a further Augustinian specification is the gospel pericope John 14:(?-)25-28(-?): though widely attested for the Day of Pentecost, it is not – as Augustine obviously could choose – attached to the Ascension Day.[40]

2.4 Day of Pentecost

The Old Testament reading for Pentecost, Tob. 2* (mentioning the Jewish feastname of the *dies pentecostes*) remains similarly unparalleled. However, this explicit reference in *s.* Dolbeau 31,2 could rather point back to a non-eucharistic morning service, as Augustine underlines by "*audistis mane*". Whereas a reading from Acts 2 quite naturally constitutes the New Testament lesson on Whit Sunday, with Matthew 9:(14?-)17 – the new wine that must not be put in old wineskins – we encounter a singular gospel pericope referring to the apostles who are ebrious not from wine, but from the Holy Ghost. As far as my research led, I did not notice any parallel in other liturgical families. The very exegetical link, however, that for Augustine clearly arises from the association with Acts 2:13, can be encountered in a theologically similar matter in two homilies Maximus of Turin held (but not on Whit Sunday), identifying the new wine with the grace of the Holy Spirit and the new wineskins with the newly baptised ("*neophyte*"), cleansed by the *puritas lavacri*.[41]

does in the Libri Commici of Silos and San Millán (cf. LECLERCQ, Liber comicus [see fn 31], 234), in the Syriac "Burkitt–Lectionary" (cf. BURKITT, Lectionary System [see fn 15], 312) and in the Armenian Lectionary of Jerusalem (preceded by Ps. 23). Also Augustine could choose this very common Gospel reading for Ascension day (cf. s. Morin 17,1).

40 Cf. AUGUSTINE, s. Liverani 8 (= 265A),1: "Ascensionis domini nostri Iesu Christi sanctus et sollemnis dies hodie illuxit: «Exultemus et iocundemur in eo» (Ps. 117:24a). ... Non de alio aliquo loquimur vobis, nisi de illo qui modo ex evangelio loquebatur omnibus nobis, et ascensurus ad patrem dicebat discipulis suis: «Haec locutus sum vobis, cum adessem vobiscum. Paraclitus autem spiritus veritatis, quem mittet pater in nomine meo, ille vos docebit omnia, et commonebit vos omnia quaecumque dixi. Non turbetur cor vestrum neque formidet. Audistis quia dixi vobis: 'Vado ad patrem meum', quia pater maior me est» (John 14:25–26.27c.28aα.bβ.c)."

41 Cf. MAXIMUS, s. 28,3 ("... Legimus vinam in ecclesia specialiter abundare, sicut in evangelio dictum est vinum novum in utres novos esse condendum [cf. Matthew 9:17], hoc est in novos homines neofytos spiritus sancti gratiam conferendam. ...") and s. 65,1 ("... ipse dominus manifestius declaravit dicens in utres novos vinum novum esse condendum [cf. ibid.]. In novitate enim utrium lavacri puritas, spiritus sancti gratia significatur in vino"; texts: CChr.SL 23, 109 and 273). Cf. further PETER CHRYSOLOGUS, s. 31 ad Matt. 9:14-17 (CChr.SL 24, 178–181).

3. CONCLUSION

The diversity of the converging and diverging elements that became obvious in the course of our comparative liturgical analysis of the Augustinian biblical lessons, as far as they can be detected from his festal sermons, does not allow a definite answer to the question on the relationship(s) of the North African liturgy to other liturgical families contemporary with or slightly later than Augustine. None of the points of contact we observed seems to be close enough to fix a striking relationship with exactly this or that liturgy. In any case, the comparative analysis allowed the validation of some liturgical readings that we could establish only with a certain degree of probability or as merely hypothetic. On the one hand we find Augustine embedded in supra-regionally spreading lessons, on the other hand we encounter some peculiar features concerning their choice, his liturgico-theological *proprium* so to speak. Thus, we can agree with Willis "that the African scheme has its own characteristics and its own affinities" and that "it is clearly not Roman." Nevertheless, his final conclusion that "its closest relations are with the non-Roman Western use, for example the Gallican, and above all the Mozarabic"[42], deserves correction or at least modification, as we found parallels and similarities to early Roman reading practice, attested e.g. by Leo the Great and the lists of pericopes in the "*Comes* Würzburg", that are by no means less noticeable than those to contemporary North Italian and slightly later Gaulish or, as far as preserved by later tradition, Visigothic-Spanish sources. The lively interchange of different liturgical traditions and reading practices at St. Augustine's time is still in progress; we cannot make out one distinctive influence upon, or the aftermath of, the North African biblical lessons revealed by St. Augustine's homilies.

[42] WILLIS, St Augustine's Lectionary (see fn 1), 102. Of course one must beware of identifying the liturgical readings Augustine's sermons display with any fixed form of a North African lectionary ("the African scheme").

TABLE

Christmas Augustine closest parallels

O.T.	Isaiah 7* (v. 14 > Matt. 1:23)	*s.* 370,3	
Epistle	Phil. 2* (vv. 6-8) [maybe Rom. 5:1-5; Rom. 13:12-13]	*s.* Étaix 2 (= 196A) [*s.* 185,3; *s.* 190,1]	cf. Leo I., *tr.* 21-25; 27-30
Psalm	Ps. 84 (ℜ v. 12) probably Ps. 95 (ℜ v. 1-2); Ps. 18 (ℜ v. 6)	*s.* Frang. 4 (= 189),2 e.g. *s.* 190,4; 195,3	cf. id., *tr.* 24,3
Gospel	Luke 2* (vv. 1-14/20 *vel* 1-32/35 *vel* 1-38/40) Matt. 1:18-25 probably John 1:1-18	*s.* 189,4; 193,1; 190,4; 196,2 *s.* 370,3 e.g. *s.* 186,2	cf. id., *tr.* 21-27; 29-30 (esp. Luke 2 / John 1) id., *tr.* 23,1; 29,2 cf. (e.g.) id., *tr.* 27,1

Epiphany Augustine closest parallels

O.T.	- - [Isaiah 60:1-6/16 ?]	[*s.* Dolbeau 23,15.20]	LectLuxeuil; LectSchlettstadt; *Comes* Würzburg
Epistle	Eph. 2:11-22	*paene passim* (implicitly)	
Psalm	Ps. 18 (ℜ v. 2)	*paene passim* (implicitly)	cf. Leo I., *tr.* 32,1
Gospel	Matt. 2* (vv. 1-18/23 *vel* 1-12)	*s.* 373,2-3; etc. (cf. 'Innocentes' in *s.* 200,2; 202,2; 373,3; 375)	e.g. Leo I., *tr.* 31-38, esp. 33,1; 34,3.5; 35,1; 36,1f.; 38,1

Quadragesima Augustine closest parallels

O.T.	probably Is. 58:1-10f./14 (vv. 3-7) presumably Gen. 32-33 1 Kgs. 17:8-16(-24?) probably 2 Kgs. 4:8-37	e.g. *s.* 205,3; 206,3; 207,1 *s.* 5,5-6 *s.* Lambot 10 (= 136B),4 *s.* 136,5-6	Burkitt; LectLux; *Comes* Würzburg e.g. Ambr.; Caes., *s.* 88; East Caes., *s.* 124; *Comes* Würzb. cf. Caes., *s.* 128; *Comes* Würzburg
Epistle	1 John 2* (vv. 8-9) 1 Cor. 13:1-8a (v. 8a) Gal. 4:8-20 (v. 16) presumably 2 Cor. 5* (v. 20) [–6*?]	*s.* 211,2 *s.* 352,4 *s.* 392^{2-6},4 *s.* frg. Verbr. 11 (= 392^{1} = 162B)	Libri Commici *Comes* Würzburg *paene passim* (2 Cor. 6*!)
Psalm	probably Ps. 26 probably Ps. 35 presumably Ps. 42 (ℜ v. 1) Ps. 50 (ℜ v. 11)	*s.* 216,1.5.8 e.g. *s.* 213 = Guelf. 1,1 *s.* 5,3 *s.* 352,1	
Gospel	probably Luke 6* (vv. 37-38) Matt. 6:5/7-15 (*traditio orationis dominicae*) presumably Matt. 18:23-35 presumably John 5:1-18	e.g. *s.* 205,3; 206,2; 208,2; 210,12 *s.* 58,1; 59,1 *s.* 5,2 *s.* 125,1	 very common *Comes* Würzb.;

	John 6* (vv. 55f.)	*s.* 132,1	LibCom
	John 9	*s.* 136,1 (*s.* Mai 130; Lambot 10;11)	ibd.
	presumably Luke 13:10-17	*s.* frg. Verbr. 11 (= 392^{1} = 162B)	ibd.; Ambrose; Chroma-tius

Easter Vigil

		Augustine	closest parallels
O.T.	Gen. 1	*s.* Denis 2 (= 223A),1	ArmLect; Zeno; LectLux(?); LibCom
	Exod. 15	*s.* Wilmart 5 (= 223E),1-2	ArmLect; cf. Zeno; LectLux; LibCom
	Dan. 3	*c. litt. Pet.* 2,211	ArmLect; Zeno; LectLux; LibCom
	Is. 2* (vv. 1-5[-?])	*ep. Io. tr.* 1,13	LectLux
Psalm	Ps. 41	*en. Ps.* 41,1; cf. *s.* Denis 2,4	e.g. *Comes* Murbach
	maybe Ps. 17 (℞ v. 29)	*s.* 221 = Guelf. 5,1-2	
Epistle	?		
Gospel	Matt. 28* (vv. 1-10[-?])	*s.* 235,1	very common

Ascension

		Augustine	closest parallels
N.T.	Acts 1:1-11[-?]	*s.* 265,1	*paene passim* (*Comes* Würzburg; Lect Lux; LibCom)
	Rev. 5:1-14 (v. 5)	*s.* 263 = Guelf. 21,2	cf. Bobbio Missal; LectLux (Easter Octave!)
	probably Col. 3:1-2(-?)	*s.* Mai 98,1; 395,1	
	maybe 1 Cor. 15* (v.50-53)	*s.* 264,6	cf. LectLux (Easter Octave!)
Psalm	Ps. 96 (℞ v. 9)	*s.* Lambot 16 (= 265E),2	
	Ps. 56 ([℞:] v. 6a = 12a)	*s.* 262,4	
	[maybe Ps. 23]	[*s.* 377 (authentic?)]	cf. ArmLect; Burkitt-Ms; Gregory Nyss.
Gospel	Matt. 28:(16-)20	*s.* 263 = Guelf. 21,3	
	Luke 24:36(?)-53	*s.* Morin 17 (= 265D),1	very common (e.g. LectLux; LibCom)
	John 14:(?-)25-28(-?)	*s.* Liverani 8 (= 265A),1	cf. e.g. ArmLect, LectLux (on the 50th Day)
	John 20:?-17-?	*s.* Lambot 25 (= 265F),1f	

Day of Pentecost

		Augustine	closest parallels
O.T.	"*mane*": Tob. 2:1-2(-?)	*s.* Dolbeau 31 (= Mai 158augm.),2	
N.T.	Acts 2:1-15(-?)	*s.* 267,2; 378	*paene passim*
Psalm	? [Vigil: Ps. 140; 117]	[*s.* 266,1.8; 29,1.3; Dolb. 8,1]	
Gospel	Matt. 9:(14?-)17	*s.* 267,2	[cf. Maximus Taur., *s.* 28,3; 65,1]

L'ECOUTE VAUT PLUS QUE LE SACRIFICE (1 SAMUEL 15,22)

MARCEL METZGER

1. L'IMMIXTIO, COMME ICONE DE LA RESURRECTION DU CHRIST

Dans ses *Homélies catéchétiques,* l'évêque Théodore de Mopsueste (350-428) expliquait ainsi le sens de l'*immixtio*, qui suit la fraction du pain, avant la communion:

> «C'est une règle de jeter peu à peu dans le calice le pain vivifiant», pour montrer que le corps et le sang sont inséparables, qu'ils sont un en vertu, et que c'est une seule et même grâce qu'ils donnent à ceux qui les reçoivent[1].

Selon Théodore de Mopsueste, l'association du pain et du vin sanctifiés représente la réunion du corps et du sang de Jésus, qui avaient été dissociés par la mise à mort. Or, corps et sang sont les deux composantes de l'être humain, dans la pensée biblique. La réunion des oblats eucharistiques devient, de ce fait, une icône du retour à la vie, et donc du Sauveur ressuscité. Cette interprétation de l'*immixtio* a été reçue également dans les Églises d'Occident, parmi d'autres explications[2].

Une telle façon de présenter l'*immixtio* concorde pleinement avec cette compréhension de l'eucharistie, comme réalisation du Mystère pascal, qu'exprime l'acclamation de l'anamnèse dans les prières eucharistiques:

> Ta mort, Seigneur, nous la proclamons, et nous confessons ta sainte résurrection et ton ascension[3].

Cette acclamation est à présent bien connue, du fait de son insertion dans le Missel du pape Paul VI. L'ancien *Missale romanum* l'ignorait.

De renouveler la proclamation de la résurrection du Christ juste au moment de la communion, cela conforte et affermit la foi des participants en cet instant où ils s'approchent pour recevoir son corps et son sang. En outre, une telle proclamation donne sens également au rite de la communion *sub utraque* par intinction : le pain sanctifié trempé dans la coupe est signe de résurrection et de vie recréée, par la réunion des deux composantes, c'est une représentation du Vivant, du Ressuscité, et une nourriture de résurrection.

[1] THÉODORE DE MOPSUESTE, Homélies catéchétiques 16,17 (Les homélies catéchétiques de Théodore de Mopsueste (StT 145), édition Raymond TONNEAU – Robert DEVREESSE, Rome 1949, ristampa anastatica Dini Modena 1981, 559); traduction: Hans-Joachim SCHULZ, Die byzantinische Liturgie, Glaubenszeugnis und Symbolgestalt, Trier [3]2000, 73.

[2] Hans Bernhard MEYER, Handbuch der Liturgiewissenschaft, 4, 207, § 532 C c.

[3] Achim BUDDE, Die ägyptische Basilios-Anaphora. Text, Kommentar, Geschichte, Münster 2004, 159.

Le rituel et les signes qu'il comporte manifestent ainsi que la liturgie, de façon générale, et l'eucharistie en particulier, sont pour les croyants la source de la Vie, une «Vie en Christ», selon l'admirable expression de Nicolas Cabasilas, et une participation actuelle à la résurrection du Christ, dans la célébration elle-même.

Dans ce contexte se pose une question pastorale incontournable: les fidèles, enfants et adultes, sont-ils assez sensibles à cette admirable signification de l'eucharistie? En sont-ils instruits par les commentaires liturgiques, la catéchèse et la prédication? Or, dans les publications parues en France, car je ne parlerai pas des Églises d'autres pays, théologiens et catéchètes s'en tiennent à des présentations devenues classiques seulement depuis le catéchisme du concile de Trente (1566), même quand elles sont formulées dans un langage plus moderne. Cet enseignement se limite à expliquer des notions théologiques, voire apologétiques, appliquées à la messe : sacrement, sacrifice, et présence réelle. Cinquante ans après le concile Vatican II, on continue actuellement à publier de telles initiations à l'eucharistie, qui négligent à ce point les enseignements donnés par la liturgie elle-même, qu'elles ne citent même pas les prières eucharistiques[4].

Les exposés sur la notion de sacrifice sont du même genre. L'enseignement commun dans l'Église catholique romaine part d'une définition du sacrifice empruntée à l'histoire des religions[5]. À cet égard, l'article «Opfer» du *LThK* est représentatif de l'argumentation généralement mise en œuvre; en effet, l'exposé liturgique y est placé en dernier, après des exposés de théologie systématique et de théologie éthique:

> Pour l'Église en prière, l'offrande qu'a faite le Christ de sa personne sur la croix et sa réception dans la résurrection est un sacrifice particulier, qui inclut toutes les entreprises sacrificielles ... En raison de la valeur expiatoire du sacrifice de la croix, les participants comprennent leur propre offrande non seulement comme un sacrifice de louange, mais aussi comme un sacrifice de supplication[6].

Le constat est flagrant: dans ces définitions, on ne trouve aucune référence aux enseignements des anciens catéchètes, tel Théodore de Mopsueste. La résurrection est à peine mentionnée; rien n'est dit de ses effets pour les participants, alors que l'eucharistie est puissance de l'Esprit Saint pour la vie nouvelle des fidèles, en tant que par le baptême ils sont ressuscités avec le Christ et sont

[4] Réflexions exposées dans notre article: «La liturgie, source de la catéchèse», in Job GETCHA – Michel STAVROU (dir.), Le Feu sur la terre. Mélanges offerts au Père Boris Bobrinskoy (Analecta Sergiana 3), Paris 2005, 69–80.

[5] Par contre, dans le Catéchisme de l'Église catholique (1992), l'exposé sur l'eucharistie n'est pas contaminé par cette définition (§ 136–1372).

[6] LThK 7, 1070: Für die betende Kirche ist die Hingabetat Christi am Kreuz und seine Annahme in der Auferweckung das einzigartige Opfer, das alle menschliche Opferversuche in sich einschließt... Wegen der Sühnekraft des Kreuzes-Opfer verstehen die Feiernden ihre Oblation nicht nur als Opfer des Lobes, sondern auch als Bittopfer.

nourris de dimanche en dimanche (jour de la résurrection) par le pain de Vie et la coupe du salut.
Pour le dire en d'autres termes: dans ses explications de l'eucharistie, la doctrine catholique romaine habituelle ne procède pas d'un regard sur les actions liturgiques, comme c'était l'usage dans les catéchèses du christianisme antique, elle se complaît dans une déduction de la notion de sacrifice. De ce fait, elle ne prend en considération que l'offrande que le Christ fit de lui-même, et non pas le Repas du Seigneur, avec nourriture et boisson[7], tel que le Christ l'a institué et qui est offert aux participants comme *pharmakon athanasias* (remède d'immortalité). Et si l'exposé fait mention de la communion des fidèles, c'est à la façon de M. Olier, comme participation à l'offrande du Christ, sans référence à la résurrection:

> Comme une union à l'Hostie pour la dilater, pour faire un plus grand sacrifice et pour faire de tous les offrants et adorateurs autant de victimes à Dieu[8].

Dans cette perspective, on ne perçoit dans l'offrande du Christ que la forme suprême du sacrifice. Qu'on est loin de la théologie du Mystère pascal et de l'école de Dom Odo Casel!
C'était le premier point de mon exposé: la présentation de ma problématique. Je traiterai à présent les points suivants:
2. Pour l'Église catholique romaine, le concile Vatican II a reconnu à nouveau la liturgie comme sommet et source de tous les actes de l'Église. Mais dans la réalité, il reste encore tant à faire, parce que les réformes du concile se heurtent sans cesse aux mentalités et aux pratiques héritées d'un passé récent.
3. L'offrande du Christ dans l'eucharistie est le fondement de la liturgie de la Parole: les lectures bibliques initient les participants à la pensée du Christ et les conduisent à communier à ses dispositions, ou son intention (Philippiens 2,5).
4. La liturgie de la Parole doit être reconnue comme le sommet de la communication actuelle de Dieu avec ses communautés, et comme la source de toutes les autres formes d'enseignement dans les Églises.
5. La pratique des médias modernes est un stimulant pour une pratique liturgique adaptée à notre temps, dans une perspective œcuménique.

[7] Cette omission dans le discours peut s'expliquer par le fait que la communion des fidèles avait été détachée de la messe; la réforme liturgique conciliaire a mis fin à cette dérive, mais a-t-on assez vérifié quelles conséquences subsistent encore dans les usages et les mentalités?

[8] MONSIEUR OLIER (Saint Sulpice, Paris, 1608 – 1657), Explication des cérémonies de la grand'messe de paroisse, l. 8, chap. 3, cité in: Liturgia, encyclopédie populaire des connaissances liturgiques, Paris 1930, 22.

2. LA LITURGIE COMME SOMMET ET SOURCE

Après une longue glaciation, qui s'est étendue sur près d'un millénaire, le concile Vatican II a reconnu à nouveau la liturgie comme sommet et source pour l'ensemble de la vie et des actions de l'Église. Pourtant, pour passer vraiment dans les pratiques, une telle reconnaissance semble demander encore beaucoup de temps. On a même le sentiment que certains éléments de la réforme liturgique, parfois des éléments essentiels, sont actuellement contestés, voire niés. Après la ferveur des premières mises en œuvres de ces réformes conciliaires, au temps du pape Paul VI, on assiste à présent à un retour manifeste à certaines habitudes précédentes, dont la plus évidente est la remise en service de l'ancien *Missale romanum* du pape Pie V.

Cela n'étonne qu'à moitié. En effet, dans le passé, la réception des conciles s'est régulièrement heurtée à des difficultés d'application. Ce fut le cas en particulier après le concile de Nicée II (787). À l'époque, les pères conciliaires étaient encore majoritairement imprégnés par la doctrine iconoclaste, au point que survint bien vite un second conflit iconoclaste. De même, les réformes du concile de Trente (1545–1563) ne furent appliquées, pour certaines, qu'avec beaucoup de lenteur, parfois et en certains pays deux siècles après leur promulgation.

Quant à la reconnaissance de la place centrale de la liturgie dans l'Église catholique romaine en notre temps, la plus grande difficulté vient de ce que, pendant des siècles, évêques et théologiens prenaient d'autres réalités pour le sommet et la source de leur action pastorale ou de leur réflexion doctrinale. La mise en œuvre des réformes du concile de Trente, dont le motif principal était la réaction contre les thèses de la Réformation protestante et ses applications, a donné la priorité à la défense de la doctrine, celle-ci étant considérée comme un ensemble de vérités à croire. De ce fait, la foi a été davantage perçue comme l'adhésion à un dogme, que dans le sens d'une *sequela Christi,* chemin de vie à la suite du Christ. C'est l'affirmation objective des «vérités» qui passait de fait pour le sommet et la source des institutions ecclésiales et de leur fonctionnement.

L'organisation interne de la Curie romaine reflète cette façon de considérer les institutions ecclésiales. En effet, la priorité étant toujours reconnue à la formulation doctrinale, la Congrégation pour la doctrine de la foi a pris le contrôle sur les décisions des autres congrégations, par exemple sur la Congrégation pour l'enseignement catholique. Les dicastères ont été établis principalement pour contrôler les Églises locales et les théologiens. Dans le domaine liturgique, ces contrôles ont à nouveau été renforcés depuis quelques années. On peut regretter leur investissement excessif pour des détails, comme l'énorme mobilisation à propos de la traduction des mots *pro multis* dans le récit de la dernière Cène.

La preuve la plus évidente que dans les déclarations des instances romaines c'est la doctrine, et non la liturgie, qui est considérée comme le sommet et la source, on la perçoit dans le renversement de la célèbre formule *Lex orandi, lex credendi.* Dans le texte originel, le propos est plus développé: *ut legem credendi lex statuat supplicandi,* ce qui signifie: «que la règle de la prière détermine la règle de la foi[9]». Mais la pratique du Magistère romain tend à adapter les textes liturgiques à l'évolution de ses propres formulations doctrinales.

La reconnaissance de la liturgie comme sommet et source de la vie en Église rend donc nécessaire un renversement de tendance dans la gouvernance de l'Église catholique. Cette mutation n'est pas encore acquise.

3. L'OFFRANDE DU CHRIST DANS L'EUCHARISTIE COMME FONDEMENT DE LA LITURGIE DE LA PAROLE

La récente affaire du *Missale romanum* tridentin a de nouveau attiré l'attention sur la compréhension sacrificielle de l'eucharistie. Pourtant, comme je l'ai expliqué dans mon introduction, on ne peut pas déduire de la notion générale de sacrifice, définie par l'histoire des religions, une compréhension adéquate de l'eucharistie chrétienne. En effet, en entrant en personne dans notre humanité, par son Fils, Dieu a transformé radicalement et renouvelé toutes les représentations et institutions humaines en place. Cela vaut tout particulièrement pour les institutions religieuses et cultuelles.

Les Pères de l'Église en témoignent de façon éloquente, par le fait même que leurs démonstrations théologiques découlaient de leur contemplation des saints mystères[10]: les Pères ont rendu compte de ce qui se réalisait dans les célébrations de la liturgie. C'est de leur tradition qu'il faut s'inspirer, pour expliquer l'action spécifique qui s'opère dans l'eucharistie, puisque celle-ci est un *unicum* dans l'histoire des religions[11].

Plus précisément, quelques réflexions me paraissent nécessaires ici sur la compréhension sacrificielle de l'eucharistie. Il faut d'abord prendre en compte les premières expressions des Pères de l'Église sur le sujet. De Justin de Rome, le philosophe et martyr, nous sont parvenus des propos éclairants sur la transformation de la notion de sacrifice. Dans son *Dialogue avec Tryphon*, son interlocuteur juif, il exprime leur commun accord à ce sujet: tous les deux convenaient que les sacrifices agréés par Dieu ne pouvaient plus être les immolations sanglantes du Temple de Jérusalem:

> En revanche, les prières émanant des hommes de cette race qui se trouvaient alors dans la dispersion, il (Dieu) aurait dit les agréer, appelant ces prières *sacrifices.* Or que les prières comme les actions de grâce, si elles sont présentées par ceux qui en sont dignes, soient les seuls *sacrifices* parfaits et agréables à Dieu, je l'affirme moi aussi. Car c'est cela seul que

[9] PROSPER D'AQUITAINE (vers 435); Paul DE CLERCK, L'intelligence de la liturgie, Paris 1995, 66.

[10] C'est la «Théoria» des Pères grecs; René BORNERT, Les commentaires byzantins de la divine liturgie du VIIe au XVe siècle, Paris 1966, 65, 92, etc.

[11] Michel Yves PERRIN, «Pratiques et discours eucharistiques dans les premiers siècles», in: Maurice BROUARD (dir.), Eucharistia. Encyclopédie de l'Eucharistie, Paris 2002, 120.

> les chrétiens *ont reçu prescription* de faire, et en particulier dans le *mémorial* de leur repas, – aliments et liquides – , à l'occasion duquel ils commémorent aussi la Passion que pour eux souffrit le Fils de Dieu[12].

La notion de sacrifice se trouve ainsi radicalement modifiée dans le langage des chrétiens, en accord avec certains milieux juifs: la dénomination de sacrifice doit s'appliquer aux prières et aux actions de grâce, et non plus à des immolations[13].

L'offrande du Christ, dans le mystère pascal de sa mort et de sa résurrection, telle qu'elle est célébrée dans l'eucharistie, se distingue radicalement des anciens sacrifices du Temple de Jérusalem, et cela, à bien des égards, en particulier parce qu'elle est devenue une source de vie pour les croyants. En effet, au Temple, les victimes animales étaient détruites par le feu. Il n'en devait rien subsister, ces immolations étaient des holocaustes, et non pas des sacrifices de communion. Certes, Jésus a donné sa vie sur la croix et fut déposé mort dans le tombeau ; mais Dieu, son Père, l'a relevé, si bien que la vie de Jésus n'a pas été anéantie, contrairement à celle des victimes des sacrifices. Sur la croix, Jésus a remis son Esprit entre les mains de son Père céleste, il lui a été rendu par la résurrection, et il l'a insufflé à ses disciples, afin qu'à leur tour ils le communiquent aux croyants par le baptême et l'eucharistie.

Les catéchèses mystagogiques des Pères évoquent à peine l'offrande du Christ, l'eucharistie y est présentée bien plutôt comme don de Dieu, et précisément dans ce sens: Jésus Christ nourrit son Église par le pain et la coupe de son corps et de son sang, un aliment de résurrection et de vie éternelle, comme l'explique Théodore de Mopsueste à propos de l'*immixtio*.

Par leur participation à la célébration eucharistique, les fidèles sont entraînés par le Seigneur dans une communion totale avec lui; ils ne font plus qu'un avec lui, il leur communique son Esprit par tout ce que comporte son repas de communion: Parole, action de grâce, pain et coupe. La communauté des croyants accomplit dans le mémorial du Seigneur ce qu'il lui a lui-même confié; en agissant ainsi, les croyants communient aux sentiments du Christ Jésus et se les approprient, selon la recommandation de l'apôtre: «Ayez en vous les mêmes sentiments qui sont dans le Christ Jésus» (Philippiens 2,5).

Suivre le Christ (Jean 1,43, etc.) dans l'eucharistie conduit aussi les fidèles à s'approprier, comme leur Maître, les paroles du Psaume 39,7-9 (H 40): «Tu n'exigeais ni holocauste ni victime, tu m'as ouvert l'oreille, alors j'ai dit: Voici, je viens, pour accomplir tes volontés.» La parole sur l'oreille, ou l'ouïe, s'accomplit pour les participants par l'écoute des Écritures proclamées pendant

[12] JUSTIN, Dialogue avec Tryphon 117, 2–3 (JUSTIN MARTYR, Dialogue avec Tryphon, édition critique, Philippe BOBICHON, 496–499).

[13] Dans le même sens, EUSEBE DE CESAREE, Historia Ecclesiastica X, 4,68, (SC 55, 103): «les sacrifices non sanglants et immatériels qui sont offerts par les prières». Matthias KLINGHARDT, Gemeinschaftsmahl und Mahlgemeinschaft, Soziologie und Liturgie frühchristlicher Mahlfeiern, Tübingen–Basel 1996, 403–404: «θυσία heisst häufig einfach das Gebet…», avec nombreuses références.

l'eucharistie, et cette proclamation réalise la parole du prophète Jérémie, citée deux fois dans l'Épître aux Hébreux: «Je mettrai mes lois dans leur pensée, je les graverai dans leur cœur» (Jérémie 31,33 ; Hébreux 8,10 ; 10,16). Or les plus anciennes descriptions des assemblées chrétiennes, en particulier dans les écrits de Tertullien[14], témoignent explicitement du zèle des Églises à se laisser instruire par les saintes Écritures.

Avant d'entrer dans sa Passion, Jésus avait révélé le sens de son Mystère pascal au cours de la dernière Cène, et l'apôtre Paul a rendu compte de la tradition ainsi reçue du Seigneur (1 Corinthiens 11,23-26): l'eucharistie est un repas de communion au Christ, dans lequel la Parole de Dieu introduit les participants dans la pensée du Christ, pour les rendre capables d'accomplir son commandement: «Faites ceci en mémoire de moi». La participation à l'offrande du Christ dans l'eucharistie exige donc une disposition à l'écoute de la Parole de Dieu et de l'Évangile. Voilà pourquoi la liturgie de la Parole fait une partie intégrante de la célébration eucharistique.

4. LA LITURGIE DE LA PAROLE COMME SOMMET ET SOURCE DE LA COMMUNICATION ACTUELLE DE DIEU AVEC SES COMMUNAUTES

Dans l'Église catholique romaine, qui pendant des siècles a considéré les proclamations dogmatiques de son Magistère comme le sommet et la source de son fonctionnement, il reste bien du chemin à faire pour reconnaître la liturgie de la Parole comme sommet de la communication actuelle de Dieu avec ses communautés et comme source et modèle de toutes les autres formes d'enseignement ecclésial.

Pour exposer cette thèse, je procéderai à la façon des Pères de l'Église, c'est-à-dire: je commencerai par observer et exposer ce qui se passe dans la liturgie de la Parole. En effet, dans la liturgie, Dieu entre en communication avec son Peuple, représenté par les fidèles de chaque communauté locale, qui à leur tour lui répondent. La liturgie de la Parole n'est pas un exposé sur Dieu, mais un entretien et un dialogue avec lui, comme le manifestent les acclamations de l'évangile. Celles-ci sont en effet une forme d'entretien personnel avec le Seigneur: «Gloire à toi, Seigneur», ou «Louange à toi, ô Christ». Dans la liturgie de la Parole s'accomplit le début de l'*Épître aux Hébreux*: «Après avoir, à maintes reprises et sous maintes formes, parlé jadis aux Pères par les prophètes, en ces jours (c'est-à-dire maintenant dans la célébration eucharistique) il nous parle par son Fils» (Hébreux 1,12).

[14] Apologeticum 39 (CSEL, 19).

Nulle part ailleurs dans l'Église la proclamation de la Parole de Dieu n'est aussi directe et immédiate. La liturgie de la Parole est le sommet de la communication de Dieu avec son Peuple. Il ne s'agit pas seulement d'un enseignement sur Dieu, dans lequel on parle de lui, mais d'une conversation, d'un échange, dans lequel il nous parle et nous lui répondons. Ce qui est proclamé dans la liturgie de la Parole n'est pas la parole de l'Église, comme dans les nombreuses déclarations du Magistère[15], mais la Parole de Dieu, qui est confiée à son Église, dans les communautés locales, afin qu'elles l'écoutent, en fassent leur nourriture, en vivent et ensuite la proclament. À cet égard, depuis la réforme des lectionnaires, la proclamation dominicale des trois lectures bibliques assure à l'annonce de la Parole de Dieu une audience élargie ; elle est reçue par les fidèles même en dehors des assemblées, puisqu'elle est largement diffusée et relayée par la presse et les émissions catholiques de la radio et de la télévision.
Pendant plusieurs siècles, et jusqu'à une époque récente, ce qui était considéré dans l'Église catholique romaine comme la source pour l'annonce de la foi et pour l'enseignement religieux, ce n'était pas la proclamation de la Parole de Dieu dans la liturgie, mais un manuel, reproduisant une synthèse résumée des traités dogmatiques classiques, à savoir le catéchisme[16].
Dans ce genre de document, la source de l'annonce de la foi, ce n'est pas la liturgie, mais un petit traité scolastique. Ce traité est l'aboutissement d'un processus de théorisation. Lointainement formé à partir des catéchèses antiques et des exposés sur les quatre documents essentiels de la foi chrétienne, c'est-à-dire le Symbole de foi, les Béatitudes (Matthieu 5,3-12), les Dix Commandements et le *Notre Père,* augmentés d'un élément plus récent, la doctrine post-tridentine des sept sacrements, le catéchisme catholique classique est un produit scolaire, pour un enseignement notionnel et déductif.
Est-il pensable que l'enseignement de la foi par les instances du Magistère ne soit pas influencé par la proclamation conciliaire sur la liturgie, comme sommet et source? Certes, il y eut quelques légers progrès en ce domaine, voilà trente ans. L'épiscopat français avait alors publié une brève présentation de la foi chrétienne en lui donnant un titre emprunté à la liturgie: «Il est grand le Mystère de la foi»; c'est, dans le missel français, l'acclamation de l'anamnèse après le récit de la Cène. Ce livret exposait l'ensemble du mystère chrétien en commentant la prière eucharistique 4. Hélas, cette heureuse initiative n'eut de loin pas le même succès que le *Catéchisme de l'Église catholique* de 1992.

15 Synode des évêques 2008, extrait du document préparatoire, n 18: «Ainsi que cela a déjà été mentionné, les livres des Saintes Écritures libèrent une force d'appel direct et concret que n'ont pas d'autres interventions ou textes ecclésiaux.»

16 Cependant, je m'empresse de signaler un élément très appréciable du Catéchisme de l'Église catholique de 1992: pour la première fois dans l'histoire de ces manuels, un catéchisme catholique propose une initiation à la liturgie; elle occupe les § 1066–1112 et introduit le chapitre (très classique, lui) sur les sacrements.

Il faudrait pourtant reconnaître que les prières eucharistiques et toutes les autres bénédictions de la liturgie sont les professions de foi les plus explicites dont disposent nos Églises. Cela vaut tout particulièrement pour la prière eucharistique 4: elle est bien plus complète, dans l'annonce de la Bonne Nouvelle que les symboles de foi usuels (*Credo*). Elle donne l'occasion de présenter l'ensemble de l'économie (histoire du salut), les missions de l'Esprit Saint, la réalisation du salut dans le temps présent, et jusqu'au sort des défunts. Or, cela vaut pour tous les textes de la liturgie: ils sont le langage commun de la foi, ils contiennent d'innombrables emprunts aux Saintes Écritures, leurs paroles sont entendues et prononcées par l'ensemble des fidèles, dont ils nourrissent la mémoire. Pour que la liturgie soit effectivement sommet et source, cela exige que la catéchèse et l'enseignement officiel lui donnent la préférence, dans l'exposé de la foi.

5. LES MEDIAS MODERNES COMME DEFI POUR UNE LITURGIE VIVANTE

Pendant ces dernières décennies, la culture générale des populations de nos pays a évolué rapidement, et en profondeur. Elle s'est éloignée d'une manière significative des façons de penser et des représentations des civilisations biblique, antique et médiévale. Dans le même temps, les mass médias modernes se sont développés d'une façon prodigieuse, tant et si bien, qu'avec la publicité, ils sont devenus les maîtres de la communication.

La culture actuelle évolue sous différentes influences, en particulier dans le domaine religieux. La communication dans les Églises, et en particulier dans la liturgie, doit en tenir compte et se mettre à la recherche de nouvelles voies. Qu'on songe tout simplement à la règle de base de la communication moderne, qui accorde autant d'attention à chacune de ces trois composantes: l'émetteur, le message et le récepteur. Mais le Magistère catholique ne semble pas s'en être aperçu, bien qu'utilisant les techniques modernes. Comme il y a quatre ou cinq siècles, il continue à s'intéresser bien plus à l'émetteur et au message qu'au récepteur.

Au concile Vatican II il en fut autrement. Ainsi, entre autres, la réforme liturgique fut décidée et menée dans l'intérêt des «récepteurs» de la communication, les fidèles, en l'occurrence. Cette intention a été clairement annoncée, par exemple dans le principe de base pour la réforme des lectionnaires: «Pour apprêter plus richement pour les fidèles la table de la Parole de Dieu, on ouvrira plus largement les trésors de la Bible[17]».

[17] Constitution sur la sainte Liturgie, n 51 (Les conciles œcuméniques, t. 2, Giuseppe ALBERIGO (dir.), Paris 1994, 1691).

Or, des Églises non catholiques ont également adopté les nouveaux lectionnaires romains. Cet intérêt a conduit à la création de commissions réunissant plusieurs Églises chrétiennes d'un même pays, en particulier en Amérique du Nord. Au congrès de la *Societas liturgica* à Palerme, en août 2007, on a cependant regretté que les instances romaines fassent obstacle, depuis quelques années, à cette collaboration entre Églises, en prenant diverses dispositions réductrices, par exemple par de nouveaux règlements sur les traductions liturgiques[18]. Pourtant, dans la pastorale liturgique, la prise en compte des mentalités actuelles et des nouveaux intérêts culturels de nos contemporains est une mission commune à toutes les communautés chrétiennes. Aussi, les Églises devraient-elles unir leurs forces et s'entraider dans la recherche de nouvelles formes de communication du message chrétien. Un tel investissement est à leur portée, puisque déjà dans le domaine des études bibliques elles collaborent avec bonheur et grand profit.

Deux pensées pour conclure

1. Dans l'immense trésor des traditions ecclésiales on a redécouvert, grâce à une connaissance renouvelée des Pères de l'Église, la façon particulière qu'avaient mise en œuvre les Églises de l'Antiquité pour expliquer les célébrations liturgiques, à savoir la mystagogie, comme contemplation des dons que Dieu accorde à son peuple *hic et nunc,* dans le temps présent des assemblées. Cet art s'est perdu au fil du temps. La mystagogie a été supplantée par la pratique scolastique, qui n'avait pas d'objectif pastoral. Mais le temps est venu de s'intéresser à nouveau à la mystagogie, en théologie pratique (ou pastorale), et pour la mettre en œuvre dans les célébrations et la catéchèse, mais aussi pour poursuivre la réforme conciliaire.
2. Avant le concile et ses réformes, la liturgie était considérée comme un devoir à rendre à Dieu, si bien que dans les manuels de théologie, jusqu'au début du XXe siècle, elle était rangée dans les chapitres de la théologie morale. Dans la compréhension catholique courante, le sacrifice était considéré comme un don de l'homme, ou comme une restitution; certes, il s'agit de l'offrande suprême, celle du Seigneur Jésus Christ. Mais les enseignements de la Bible et des Pères renversent radicalement de telles représentations. La liturgie doit être comprise avant tout comme un don de Dieu à ses fidèles : don de la vie divine dans le Repas du Seigneur, dans la Parole, le pain, le vin, l'eau et l'huile. Voilà pourquoi la liturgie se déploie fondamentalement dans l'action de grâce, qui en grec se dit «eucharistie».

[18] David HOLETON, «Le partenariat œcuménique en liturgie. Des débuts mouvementés», in: MD 253 (2008/1) 93–112.

Towards a Baptismal Ecclesiology

Paul Meyendorff

It would be no exaggeration to say that, from both theological and pastoral perspectives, the twentieth century was the age of eucharistic ecclesiology. Building upon developments in biblical and patristic theology that began already in the nineteenth century, twentieth-century theologians rediscovered the centrality of the eucharist in the life of the Church. Basing themselves on key scriptural passages, as well as the writings of Ignatius of Antioch, Maximus the Confessor, Nicholas Cabasilas, and others, leading modern Orthodox theologians – Nicholas Afanassiev, Alexander Schmemann, John Meyendorff, John Zizioulas, and their followers – focused on the eucharist as the visible expression and manifestation of the Church.[1]

Nor was this eucharistic focus unique to the Orthodox. Leading western, Roman Catholic scholars, including Jean Daniélou, Louis Bouyer, and Yves Congar, similarly rediscovered eucharistic ecclesiology through their reading of the Greek fathers. These scholars laid the groundwork for the liturgical reforms of Vatican II, with their similar emphasis on the centrality of the eucharist. Thus, this council's decree on the liturgy, "Sacrosanctum Concilium," states categorically that "the liturgy… most of all in the divine sacrifice of the eucharist, is the outstanding means whereby the faithful may express in their lives and manifest to others the mystery of Christ and the real nature of the true Church."[2] Subsequent to Vatican II, many Protestant churches similarly underwent eucharistic revivals, and the language of "koinonia," with its strong eucharistic overtones, entered the ecumenical vocabulary.

This eucharistic revival was not limited to the theological level alone, but had immediate pastoral effects as well. In ever-increasing parts of the Orthodox world, ordinary lay persons now receive communion much more regularly and frequently. In fact, in those churches most directly touched by this revival, a majority of the faithful receive communion every Sunday. Nor was the revival limited to the more frequent reception of communion. In many cases, the revival also included significant changes in the way the liturgy was celebrated, includ-

[1] It would be an exaggeration to say that the eucharistic revival in the Orthodox Church arose out of nothing in the twentieth century. Already in the nineteenth century, the Kollyvades in Greece, as well as St John of Kronstadt in Russia, placed a strong emphasis on more frequent communion. Even earlier in the fourteenth-fifteenth centuries, the hesychast movement placed great stress on the eucharist and on its reception – see especially the writings of Nicholas Cabasilas, The Life in Christ and the Commentary on the Liturgy.

[2] Constitution on the Sacred Liturgy, Par. 2.

ing the use of the vernacular language, the recitation of the so-called "silent prayers" aloud, a renewed emphasis on preaching, changes in the practice of confession,[3] etc.

Few today would deny the positive aspects of this eucharistic revival, which has now entered into the mainstream of Orthodox theological reflection. Eucharistic ecclesiology provides a coherent, holistic understanding of the Church, both as it has been and continues to be realized in time and place, as well as in the world to come. Here and now, in the eucharist, we can experience a foretaste of the heavenly banquet, the image of the Kingdom. Here and now, in the eucharist, we can experience that true unity with God and with one another for which humanity, and indeed the whole cosmos, was created.

I would suggest, however, that there is something lacking in this vision, both theologically and pastorally. If, indeed, the eucharist is the primary ecclesiological criterion, then the vast majority of Orthodox Christians, who receive communion only rarely, are not really members of the Church most of the times that the liturgy is celebrated. By refusing communion, they reject the invitation to "draw near" offered by Christ himself. The purpose of the liturgy, after all, is not simply to transform the bread and wine into the Body and Blood of Christ, but to transform us, to make us truly sharers of his Body, to grant us the communion of the Holy Spirit – in other words, to affirm our own membership in the Church and to realize the Church in the here and now. Where is the Church, then, when only the priest and a tiny number of the faithful share in communion? And are those who refuse the invitation really members of Christ's Body, the Church?

A further problem arises in the case of Orthodox relations with others who call themselves Christian, but with whom we are not "in communion." On this issue, the Orthodox have in recent decades been entirely consistent in rejecting any possibility of "intercommunion." For communion requires total unity in faith and in ecclesial structures. It is an all or nothing proposition – we are either in communion, or we are not, and there is no possibility to be in "partial communion." Yet such an approach flies in the face of reality. Do we not share much that is essential with other Christians, particularly those who share the same creeds with us, who celebrate many of the same sacraments, whose ecclesial structures closely resemble ours, and who manifest many of the same signs of holiness in the lives of their faithful? Few Orthodox, for example, would deny the real holiness of Mother Theresa of Calcutta. Yet we cannot meet together at

[3] Chiefly in the Slavic churches, confession has for several centuries been required before each time a person receives communion. Obviously, this poses a serious obstacle to frequent communion. One response to this was the introduction of general confession, proposed by Fr Schmemann and approved by the Synod of Bishops of the Orthodox Church in America (cf Alexander SCHMEMANN, Confession and Communion: Report to the Holy Synod of Bishops of the Orthodox Church in America [Orthodox Church in America, 1972]).

the Lord's Table, because to do so would be dishonest, as St Paul reminds the Corinthians: because of the divisions in the community, "It is not the Lord's Supper that you eat,"[4] even if the rite is properly performed. Yet those other Christians with whom we are unable to eat are Christians, at times even better Christians than we!

Here we come to the limitations of an ecclesiology that is based almost exclusively on the eucharist. Something is clearly missing.

In reviewing the writings of the chief proponents of eucharistic ecclesiology, I am struck by the virtual absence of references to baptism, and the relative paucity of references to the Holy Spirit. It is clear that baptism, so central in the life of the early Church, has largely been lost from the Church's memory. Yet much of the early patristic literature, particularly the mystagogical catecheses of the fourth century, was focused precisely on baptism – at a time when converts were flocking to the Church, and when adult baptism was common. It is not surprising that baptism would have such a prominent role at that particular time, nor that the importance of baptism began to fade once the empire became Christian and infant baptism replaced adult baptism almost completely. One of the consequences of this shift was the virtual disappearance of the catechumenate as well – it survived only vestigially in Byzantine practice in the litany of the catechumens at the liturgy.[5] In subsequent centuries, for a variety of reasons, the frequency of communion declined as well, leading to a greatly reduced focus on the eucharist and its theological and ecclesiological implications. If, in the twentieth century, the centrality of the eucharist has been rediscovered, it is now time to rediscover baptism, without which the eucharist, and all that flows from it, is impossible.

It is in baptism and chrismation that we "put on Christ," that we become members of the "Body of Christ," that we "receive the gift of the Holy Spirit," that our fallen humanity is restored, that we are adopted into sonship, and that we can dare to call God "Abba."[6] At Pentecost, after the Holy Spirit descends upon the apostles, Peter preaches his first sermon in which he demonstrates that Jesus is both Lord and Savior.[7] After hearing these words, his listeners then ask, "Brethren, what shall we do?" Peter responds: "Repent and be baptized every one of you in the name of Jesus Christ for the forgiveness of your sins; and you shall receive the gift of the Holy Spirit."[8] The remainder of the Book of Acts

4 1 Corinthians 11:20.

5 Today, even this litany has largely dropped out of use except in the Slavic churches. And catechumens have not actually been dismissed since at least the seventh century.

6 All translations of this word, including the Greek, miss its intimate character. It takes incredible boldness to go from not even being able to pronounce the name of God, to call him "Abba" – "Daddy" – the most intimate form of address. This boldness (*parrhesia*) is expressed in the introduction to the Lord's Prayer in the liturgy.

7 Cf Acts 2: 14–36. This sermon is often referred to as the "Protoevangelion," the first proclamation of the good news.

8 Acts 2: 37–8.

then describes in detail the spread of the Church through the proclamation of the gospel, the baptism of countless converts, first from Judaism and then from among the Gentiles, and the bestowal of the Spirit through the laying on of hands.[9]

Not surprisingly, all the early church orders, the *Didache*, the *Apostolic Tradition* of Hippolytus, the *Didascalia Apostolorum*, as well as the subsequent documents that drew from them, largely concern themselves with the stages of initiation: first catechesis, then the baptismal rites in increasingly elaborate form, all being fulfilled in the procession to the church, where the gathered assembly of baptized Christians await the neophytes, greet them with the kiss of peace, and then celebrate the (paschal) eucharist. In this way, typically on Pascha night, they would greet the newly-baptized who had just shared, through the waters of baptism, in Christ's own death and resurrection. The eucharist here stands not on its own, but as the climax of a long journey in which candidates for baptism put off the "old man," and "put on Christ," received the Holy Spirit, and were thus fully integrated into the Church, the Body of Christ. Again in the words of the Acts of the Apostles, "...they devoted themselves to the apostles' teaching and fellowship, to the breaking of bread and the prayers."[10] Precisely through their continued participation in the life of the Church, particularly the eucharist, that baptismal reality they experienced once in the waters was nourished and maintained. In other words, a eucharistic ecclesiology makes sense only through the prism of a baptismal ecclesiology.

The Church's other rites and sacraments are also closely related to baptism. Confession, for example, was considered to be a "second baptism," a return to baptismal grace available to those who fell away and cut themselves off from the life of the Church (and therefore from the eucharist). The anointing of the sick, closely related to the sacrament of penance, contains rich baptismal imagery (in the Byzantine baptismal rite itself, the prayer of consecrating the "oil of gladness" is actually a prayer for the blessing of healing oil). The consecration of a church includes the washing and chrismation of the altar table and walls of the building. The funeral rites are the completion of our baptism, with elements similarly borrowed from the baptismal rite, such as, at various times, anointing or the final kiss.[11] All this should not surprise us, and it points to the absolute centrality of baptism in the life of the Church.

The main point, then, is that the Church, as the Body of Christ, is comprised of those who hear the gospel, repent, are baptized into Christ, and receive the Holy Spirit in baptism. The baptized alone then are able to gather each week to par-

[9] The importance of the laying on of hands is typical of the Lukan corpus. Later, particularly in Syrian practice, this is replaced by anointing with chrism.

[10] Acts 2:42.

[11] In ancient times, the newly-baptized were greeted with the kiss of peace when they entered the church for the paschal eucharist immediately following their baptism. Now, as they depart this world, the same kiss is offered in farewell.

ticipate in the eucharist. In doing so, they affirm the continued reality of their baptism, by which they were grafted into Christ's Body. The Church has known and understood this from the very beginning, but it has come to take it for granted. I would therefore argue that, after almost a century of eucharistic revival, it is now time for a baptismal revival.

Symptoms of baptismal neglect are all around us. Theologians have recently paid little attention to baptism, and therefore it does not inform their thought. On the liturgical level, a rite that once comprised the essence of the paschal liturgy is now often performed as a private ceremony, with only close family and friends in attendance, and with no connection to Pascha on either the practical or cognitive level. The contemporary rite has reduced to some 45 minutes what once took three years or more. In some parts of the Orthodox world, baptism is not even performed in a church building, but in private homes or apartments. Baptism's connection to the eucharist remains in vestigial form only, with the newly-baptized either receiving communion from the presanctified gifts, or at the liturgy the following Sunday. As a result, baptism has been privatized, and it is no longer experienced as an ecclesial event. For many of the faithful, it typically takes second place to the elaborate party that follows, with everyone commenting on the cute baby and the beautiful white dress, but with little if any understanding of the radical significance of the event that has just occurred.

Our challenge for this century, therefore, is to strive for the restoration of the centrality of baptism, just as the twentieth century saw a return to proper eucharistic understanding and practice. Just as with the eucharistic revival, this must take place on multiple fronts, both theological and pastoral. The Church today faces very much the same kinds of challenges it faced in the fourth century. We now face a world that is religiously fragmented, and where Christianity is no longer the dominant force. The Orthodox can no longer depend on a Christian empire for support, and even the traditionally Orthodox countries are becoming increasingly secularized. Western Europe, despite its Christian foundations, is largely rejecting its Christian roots, as is evident from the rejection of any mention of Christianity in the proposed European constitution. Our post-modern world largely rejects Christian values, while at the same time facing the threat of a resurgent, often fundamentalist, Islam. At times, particularly in North America, the response is a type of fundamentalist Christianity that has lost its bearings, using ostensibly Christian values to support economic and military hegemony. Thus, authentic, Orthodox Christianity now faces the formidable task of preaching the Gospel in an increasingly hostile world – a world not too different from that of the third-fourth centuries.

This was a world in which both individuals and society needed to be converted. The gospel had to be proclaimed, individuals needed to hear it, to repent of their sins, and to move from a world of darkness and shadow into one where light and truth ruled. And it was precisely the whole baptismal process, including catechesis, moral and ethical as well as theological, that prepared the way for baptism, chrismation, and full sharing in the eucharistic, corporate life of the

Church. Today, we face the same challenge; and, in order to respond properly, we need to revitalize our baptismal theology and practice, restore it to the prominence it once enjoyed.

How is this to be accomplished? First, I would suggest, we need to restore the ecclesial experience of baptism. Baptism will never be central to the Church's life if it is hidden under a bushel. Private celebrations of baptism must be replaced by fully ecclesial ones, with the attendance and participation of the local parish. Already in 1974, in his seminal work, *Of Water and the Spirit*,[12] Fr Alexander Schmemann argued for the celebration of baptism at the regular Sunday liturgy. His suggestion was taken up in many parishes and is now frequently followed in the United States and Western Europe.[13] For the majority who were themselves baptized as infants, this marked the first time that they had witnessed a baptism. This approach is particularly effective when, as Schmemann also proposed, the key prayers, in particular the blessing of water, are read aloud in a language the people can understand. These prayers express the chief elements of the Christian understanding of baptism. Thus, when people hear these prayers again and again, they are reminded of the significance and implications of their own baptism. They begin to understand that baptism not only transforms individuals, but also incorporates them into the communion of the Church. In an age of almost absolute individualism, this rediscovery of "being as communion," in the words of Metropolitan John (Zizioulas) is essential – and begins precisely with baptism! In this way, baptismal practice can also revitalize the parish – a critical need in many parts of the Orthodox world today.

Such a revival of corporate baptismal practice will naturally vary from place to place, as local circumstances differ. It is much easier to do this in smaller, more closely-knit parishes, than in much larger urban or suburban churches, where people do not know each other well. It will also generate objections that the

[12] (Crestwood/NY: St Vladimir's Seminary Press 1974). More recently (2005) the Moscow Patriarchate, with the patriarch's blessing, published a service book containing the text and rubrics for a baptismal liturgy.

[13] The following structure is typical:

- Rites of the catechumenate, exorcisms, renunciation of Satan, adhesion done in advance – on the eve or before the beginning of the liturgy
- "Blessed is the Kingdom…"
- Great Synapte, with special petitions from the rite of baptism
- Blessing of baptismal water, read aloud from "Great are You, O Lord…"
- Blessing of oil of catechumens and pre-baptismal anointing
- Baptism
- Chrismation
- Procession around the font, with "As many as have been baptized" replacing the Trisagion
- Baptismal Prokeimenon, Epistle, Alleluia, Gospel (Sunday readings may be done as well)
- Litanies and prayers of the faithful
- Cherubikon, followed by the eucharistic liturgy as usual, through the Prayer Behind the Ambo and Dismissal
- Rites of ablution and tonsure following the dismissal

service is too long, but that need not be the case. For example, the preliminary rites, including the exorcisms, can be done on the eve, or before the normal starting time for the liturgy. The three antiphons of the liturgy can be omitted, as they are not historically an integral part of the liturgy.[14] The concluding rites of ablution and tonsure can be done after the dismissal of the liturgy.

A common objection to such a communal practice is the potential cost to the family of the baptized, who feel obliged to host an elaborate reception or banquet. This is indeed a challenge, but it is symptomatic of the problem. For the real reception, the real baptismal banquet is not the elaborate party at the home, but the eucharistic banquet, which naturally involves the entire local church and is itself the foretaste of the Banquet of the Kingdom.

In whatever way baptism and eucharist are integrated, the main purpose is to involve the entire community in the event. For it is the local eucharistic community which comprises the Church, the Body of Christ, in that time and place. This is the community into which the candidate is now being united, and thus both they and the individual are directly affected. Through baptism, the community accepts new members and assumes responsibility for them, as the newly-baptized do for the community.

It is not only the baptismal rite itself that needs to be restored, but also the entire catechetical process. This restoration will naturally take different forms in different parts of the Orthodox world. In Orthodox countries such as Greece, infant baptism will remain the norm, and so catechesis will have to follow baptism. In Orthodox cultures of the past, the elaborate liturgical structures of the daily, weekly, and annual cycles fulfilled that function, but that is no longer the case. Elsewhere, whether in former Communist lands, where the majority are unchurched, or in the West, where Orthodoxy is experiencing a surge of new, adult converts, the Church needs to develop more adequate forms of pre-baptismal catechesis, both moral and theological. Simply handing the potential convert a book to read – the typical practice – is not sufficient. Here again, the past can be instructive. Group instruction for enquirers and catechumens (with the faithful invited as well) can be held at various times during the year in preparation for baptism/chrismation on the Church's traditional baptismal days: Theophany, Pascha,[15] and Pentecost. I have personally witnessed cases in which six or more persons are incorporated into the Church at the liturgy of Holy Saturday, with the entire parish in attendance.

A renewed baptismal focus will help Orthodoxy to face these contemporary challenges, which are both internal and external. But it will help in other areas as well.

[14] They are omitted, for example, when the eucharistic liturgy is celebrated with vespers, as on the eves of Christmas, Theophany, and Pascha.

[15] The original paschal, baptismal liturgy is now celebrated on Holy Saturday.

A solid baptismal theology will help the Church to rediscover the priesthood of the laity.[16] For, by being incorporated into Christ through baptism, Christians also attain a share in Christ's priesthood. They must be the presence of Christ in the world and are called to offer themselves on behalf of the world. They too must proclaim the good news of God's love and forgiveness to a world that lives in the shadow of sin and darkness. This priestly function of all Christians is strongly affirmed in Scripture, which applies the notion of priesthood only to Christ, who is the high priest, or to all the baptized, the "royal priesthood."[17] This does not, of course, eliminate the need for ordained clergy – bishops in particular, but also presbyters, and deacons – who are essential for maintaining order in the Church and for visibly expressing its unity. Within the Church, they are charged also with preaching and teaching. But the goal of that preaching and teaching must be to empower the faithful to exercise their priestly ministry in the world in which they live.

Historical developments in recent centuries have led to increased clericalism within Orthodoxy. The gradual monasticization of the episcopate helped to foster a divide between bishops and their flocks. As a result of Turkokratia, clergy attained increased civil powers in addition to the pastoral and spiritual authority they had always wielded. Bishops became civil rulers, and both religious and civil powers were centralized in the episcopal office in a way that confused pastoral and legal authority and absolutized its power. Since the seventeenth century, the development of seminaries as professional schools for training clergy, while certainly desirable, has had the unintended consequence of fostering a clergy-laity divide: the clergy are perceived as the real Christians, while the laity is only there to pay, pray, and obey. The result is a passive laity, which lacks the knowledge, conviction, or courage to assume its proper responsibilities. A renewed emphasis on the implications of baptism for all the baptized would help to overcome these negative developments.

I would propose as well that further reflection on baptismal ecclesiology may help the Orthodox Church in its relations with other Christians. Almost alone among Christian churches, Orthodoxy has rejected the possibility of "intercommunion," arguing that eucharistic communion is possible only after full agreement has been reached and structural unity restored. This is a position I fully support and have forcefully argued in my representation of the Orthodox Church at the World Council of Churches.[18] But relying solely on eucharistic ecclesiology is not sufficient, as it leaves no middle ground between "full com-

16 On this issue, see my article, The Priesthood of the Laity, in: Ann Mitsakos BEZZERIDES, Christ at Work. Orthodox Christian Perspectives on Vocation, Brookline 2006, 209–227.

17 1 Peter 2:9.

18 I was a member of the Worship Committee for the 1998 Assembly of the WCC, which decided that no eucharistic service was to appear on the official program of the assembly. Subsequently, I participated in the drafting of the "Guidelines for Common Worship" produced for the WCC Special Commission, in which this principle and the reasons for it were clearly spelled out.

munion" and "no communion." This has led to confusion and wide differences among the Orthodox about the ecclesial status of other Christians. And it has also led to confusion and differences about the way in which individuals or groups from other Christian bodies are received into Orthodoxy – whether by [re]baptism, chrismation, or just confession and communion.

Orthodox practice regarding the reception of converts has been generally consistent since the fourth century. Canonical guidelines make it clear that persons who underwent Trinitarian baptism were generally not [re]baptized, but were received either through chrismation or confession/communion. These canonical precedents, of course, addressed only the situation at the time, before the East-West schism and the Reformation. Thus, in order to address the confused situation of his own time and basing himself on the ancient canonical models, Metropolitan Peter Moghila of Kiev developed guidelines to deal with Non-Chalcedonians, Roman Catholics, Uniates, and Protestants.[19] Confirmed Roman Catholics and Uniates, for example, were to be received by confession (of sin) and communion; Protestants through confession of faith, chrismation, and communion. His approach has largely been adopted by the Slavic churches.

How are we to explain this approach? Is it, as some would have it, an exercise in *oikonomia*, whereby the baptism performed outside the canonical limits of the Orthodox Church is of no value, but it is given value by the authority of the bishop? Or is it rather an exercise of *discernment*, by which the bishop recognizes that which is true and authentic – the work of the Holy Spirit – outside the Church? Though there is clearly no consensus on this question within Orthodoxy today, I would argue for the authenticity of the second position. If this latter view is correct, it is based precisely on a baptismal ecclesiology, which sees the Church as being based on the baptism of its members – an ecclesiology based on a correct catechesis about the faith, a correct creed (liturgically, creeds are baptismal statements of faith, hence the formula "I believe…"), a proper baptism in the name of the Trinity, followed by ongoing sacramental, eucharistic life. To the extent that these can be discerned outside the visible limits of the Orthodox Church, they are marks of ecclesial reality.[20] In this way, Christian bodies which are not Orthodox nevertheless share an ecclesial reality, to a greater or lesser extent, with the "one, holy, catholic, and apostolic" Orthodox Church. However, because something is lacking in them, full, eucharistic communion is not yet possible.

19 See my article, The Liturgical Reforms of Peter Moghila. A New Look, in: SVTQ 29 (1985) 101–114.

20 This is taken to its furthest point with Roman Catholics, even whose ordinations are generally recognized as valid, so that Roman Catholic priests received into Orthodoxy are typically received in their rank and only vested, but not re-ordained. For further reflection on the question of mutual recognition of baptism, see Thomas F. BEST (ed.), Baptism Today: Understanding, Practice, Ecumenical Implications (Faith and Order Paper 207), Collegeville/MN 2008, and particularly my article in Part 2: "Toward Mutual Recognition of Baptism," 195–206.

I mention the above examples only by way of demonstrating the potential benefits of a renewed emphasis on baptism and its ecclesiological implications. I am fully aware of the controversial nature of some of the issues I have raised, but I am convinced that such an emphasis on baptism by our theologians and our pastors will be helpful to the Orthodox Church as it confronts the internal and external challenges it faces in the twenty-first century.

East Meets West in Liturgy: Mutual Influence Through the Centuries

Mark M. Morozowich

1. Introduction

The identity of Eastern Christians, so firmly rooted in their liturgical expression, provides a window revealing theological truths as well as long held myths. Western Christians share this same attachment, especially as witnessed in the Roman Catholic liturgical discussions of the past decades, the turmoil around translations, and the debate about which version of the Roman Catholic liturgy should be, could be, or might be celebrated. This attachment to song, prayer, movement, gesture, and symbol has been fodder for modern ritual studies revealing shared cross-cultural realities that describe an almost hard-wiring of the human person. However, limited horizons and scopes of interest have long obscured cogent arguments for a more effective and life giving liturgical practice. All too often the argumentation focuses on what makes one group different or actually better than another group with little attention given to the vicissitudes, complexities, and depth of tradition. This study provides a short review of tradition in the liturgical sense in order to focus our attention on its specific usage, then a few examples will illustrate the mutual influence of East and West.

2. Tradition

The more than a century-long modern liturgical movement, nourished by painstaking historical-liturgical research, provides a comprehensive, compelling, synthetic view of the two millennial span of Christian tradition. Yet this very concept of tradition continues to perplex and vex the ordinary person, the student, and even the theologian. A clarification of terms helps to focus this discussion. Robert Taft provides an eloquent and measured definition:

> Of course all true history is not just chronicle but an interpretation of the past resulting from patterns perceived or imposed by the mind of the historian. For the historian of Christian tradition, however, that pattern is not so much a quest for tradition as its test. Tradition is not history, nor is it the past. Tradition is the church's self-consciousness now of that which has been handed on to it not as an inert treasure, but as a dynamic principle of life. It is the

> church's contemporary reality understood genetically, in continuity with that which produced it.[1]

Tradition bespeaks a broader understanding that conveys the living reality of life in Christ today with an awareness of the various stages that have brought us to today. This important definition of tradition provides a background to facilitate discussion regarding what is liturgical-historical research and how that research directly impacts the lived worship experience today. Many speak about liturgical history in a normative and determinative manner, however, as Taft clearly evaluates tradition, "(Tradition) is the church's contemporary reality understood genetically, in continuity with that which produced it."[2] So this understanding of tradition demands a deeper appreciation of how we normally utilize this term tradition as most people limit their thinking to their own experience or to their immediate relative's experience. In many instances, the appeal to what was handed down to me by my parents becomes the measuring stick for all future change and the de facto definition of tradition. In contrast, the importance of historical study lies in its ability to yield principles defining tradition: these principles function as guides, not as a litmus test.

The liturgical historian does not solve the immediate issues of pastoral life. Taft describes the work of the scholar: "In liturgical renewal the work of the historian is to remove obstacles to understanding produced by a misreading of the past. Historical scholarship cannot tell the church what it must do. It can only help the church to see what it could do if those in the pastoral ministry deem it feasible."[3] This caveat might seem to negate the influence and impact of the liturgical historian; on the contrary, the role of historical liturgical scholarship has influenced and impacted many modern ecumenical discussions.

Tradition entails identity. The popular tendency to totally separate various distinct liturgical traditions as if they were and are totally separate, isolated, unrelated entities is wrong-headed. Many think that early ritual churches lived in a vacuum untouched by other ritual churches until the so-called evils of the last several hundred years with various unions of Eastern Churches to the Latin Rite Catholic Church. Liturgical historians have demonstrated the contrary. Many liturgical families exerted influence upon one another throughout history. Some examples are: the Christmas and Epiphany dyad,[4] the impact of Jerusalem upon Rome and Constantinople,[5] the entrance of the sanctus into all anaphorae,[6]

[1] Robert F. TAFT, Response to the Berakah Award, in: ID. Beyond East and West, 2nd Ed. Edizioni Orientalia Christiana, Rome 1997, 290.

[2] IBID., 290.

[3] IBID., 289.

[4] For an exhaustive treatment see: Susan K. ROLL, Toward the Origins of Christmas, Kampen 1995.

[5] Miguel ARRANZ, "Les grandes étapes de la liturgie byzantine. Palestine – Byzance – Russie. Essai d'aperçu historique, in: Liturgie de l'Église particulière et liturgie de l'Église universelle (BEL.S 7), Rome 1976, 43–72; Anton BAUMSTARK, Ausstrahlungen des vor-byzantinischen Heiligenkalendars von Jerusalem, in: OCP 2 (1936) 129–144; Anton BAUMSTARK, Denkmäler der Enstehungsgeschichte des byzantinischen Ritus, in:

and the influence of Constantinople and Rome upon the Armenian Liturgy tradition in the tenth to thirteenth centuries.[7] These historical facts debunk myths that viewed liturgical families as distinct entities untainted by one another and fanciful concepts of ritual purity. The comparative study of liturgy, founded by Anton Baumstark, provides the major methodological practice that undergirds these studies.[8] One could even look at the developing study of icons that demonstrates their existence as a common phenomenon of the Roman Empire, both Eastern and Western. Certainly, distinctive qualities for each liturgical family exist and must be encouraged. However, one must always realize that these traditions did not develop in a vacuum nor did they exist in isolation; rather, they existed side by side and influenced one another through the centuries.

3. EAST-WEST ISSUES – *LATINIZATION*

The impact of the modern, almost universal, presence of the Latin liturgical tradition throughout the world provokes fear and anxiety among many Eastern Christians. This fear is not unfounded when one looks at some of the historical liturgical effects of union with the Latin Church in the lived reality of the Eastern Catholic Churches. Primarily this effect is pejoratively described as uniatism and the people of these churches were often labeled pejoratively as uniates.[9]

This long and tortuous history remains beyond the scope of this paper; however, I intend to provide several modern examples of scholarly developments that illustrate positive ecumenical results. These selected examples treat issues that directly impact ecumenical discussion regarding the Catholic and Orthodox communions.

The basic criticism heaped upon the Eastern Catholics, the so-called uniates, remains latinization, which is a technical term applied to the deviances from the

OrChr 3rd Series 2 (1927) 1–32; Robert F. TAFT, The Byzantine Rite: A Short History (American Essays in Liturgy), Collegeville 1992.

6 For good studies on the Sanctus see: Bryan D. SPINKS, The Sanctus in the Eucharistic Prayer, Cambridge 1991; Gabriele WINKLER, Das Sanctus: Über den Ursprung und die Anfänge des Sanctus und sein Fortwirken (OCA 267), Rome 2002.

7 For a good overview see: Claudio GUGGEROTTI, La Liturgia Armena delle Ordinazione e l'epoca Ciliciana. Esiti rituali di una teologia di comunione tra Chiese (OCA 264), Rome 2001, 221–387.

8 Anton BAUMSTARK, Comparative Liturgy, third edition revised by Bernard BOTTE, trans. Frank Leslie CROSS. Westminster/Maryland 1958. For an update comprehensive study see: Robert. F. TAFT, Anton Baumstark's Comparative Liturgy Revisited, in: Robert F. TAFT – Gabriele WINKLER (Eds.), Comparative Liturgy Fifty Years After Anton Baumstark (1872-1948) Rome, 25-29 September 1998 (OCA 265), Rome 2001, 191–232.

9 For an overview of the issues and a developed bibliography see: Robert F. TAFT, Reflections on *Uniatism* in the Light of Some Recent Books, in: OCP 65 (1999) 153–184.

Byzantine liturgical tradition based upon Latin influence. Taft describes this hybridization phenomenon by comparing the liturgical symbological system to a language.[10] He observes that one cannot simply make up the rules as one goes along; rather, grammar and the inherent linguistic system of a language dictate its proper use. The analogy then stresses that the same must be said for liturgy. The understanding of any particular liturgical tradition depends on its coherent symbological and theological system. The symbol system of a tradition must be followed in order to make sense. The only way to make sense of it is to study it in depth. This negative example of liturgical influence often jades any discussion on the issues. Robert Taft provides a good overview:

> Some Eastern Catholic clergy see their history as a progress from schism and spiritual stagnation to a life of discipline, renewal, and restored religious practice in the Catholic communion. For this group, the adoption of certain Latin — they would say "Catholic" — devotions and liturgical uses is a sign of this new identity. Such attitudes reflect an interior erosion of the Eastern Christian consciousness, a "latinization of the heart" resulting from a formation insensitive to the true nature of the variety of traditions within the Catholic Church.[11]

This unfortunate state reflects the oft lived reality resulting from years of diminishing liturgical identity of the Eastern Catholic Churches, a bad effect of mutual influence. So many prelates, clergy, and laity lacked the proper intellectual and spiritual formation to understand and live the Eastern liturgy. We see this issue clearly addressed at the Second Vatican Council in *Orientalium Ecclesiarum 6*:

> All members of the Eastern Rite should know and be convinced that they can and should always preserve their legitimate liturgical rite and their established way of life, and that these may not be altered except to obtain for themselves an organic improvement. All these, then, must be observed by the members of the Eastern rites themselves. Besides, they should attain to an ever greater knowledge and a more exact use of them, and, if in their regard they have fallen short owing to contingencies of times and persons, they should take steps to return to their ancestral traditions.[12]

Although this council ended in 1965, we find that even today this mandate still has not taken a deep hold in some Eastern Catholic Churches.[13] The formative events of history could not be undone with a simple decree. For many years, the Roman curia viewed the Eastern liturgical traditions as an aberration from the Roman liturgical norms: the Eastern Catholics were placed under the Congregation for the Propagation of the Faith.[14] The attitudes of suspicion

[10] Robert F. TAFT, The Liturgy in the Life of the Church, given at the "Encounter of Eastern Catholic Bishops of America and Oceania," Boston, November 8–12, 1999, ECJ 7 (2000) 74.

[11] IBID., 78–79.

[12] http://www.vatican.va/archive/hist_councils/ii_vatican_council/documents/vat-ii_decree_19641121_orientalium-ecclesiarum_en.html (Accessed October 2, 2008).

[13] For an example see Part II of Peter GALADZA, The Theology and Liturgical Work of Andrei Sheptytsky (1865–1944) (OCA 272), Rome 2004.

[14] C. CAPROS, Origine e sviluppo della S. C. Orientale, in: La Sacra Congregazione per le Chiese Orientali nel cinquantesimo della fonazione 1917-1967, Rome 1969, 27–64.

regarding union have existed for centuries. An early sixteenth century report by John Łaski, Archbishop of Gniezno, Poland to the Fifth Lateran Council at its eleventh session exemplifies the sentiment of that period.[15] His long and detailed report contains a section entitled: "De sacramentis, sint eorum sacramenta vera et ab eis administrabilia." Among the problems enumerated is idolatry during the Great Entrance,[16] the use of teplota/zeon,[17] and the administration of Chrismation by priests.[18] There is no record, however, that this report was read at the council; rather, it provides an important historical testament to a mentality that did not approve of divergences from the Latin liturgical tradition. Around the same period, at the end of the sixteenth century, the Union of Brest, uniting the churches of the Kyivan Metropolia with Rome and its assurances that the ritual practices of the Ruthenians would be preserved produced a tumultuous result.[19] Just a few short years later, the 1720 Synod of Zamosc' clearly stepped away from the original intentions of the Brest Union and eliminated infant communion and the use of teplota/zeon.[20] This situation even continued into the nineteenth century when Pius IX (1792–1878) issued his Encyclical, *Omnem Sollicitudinem* on May 13, 1874, concerning the need to purify certain Eastern liturgical customs as had been done in the past.[21] The encyclical even states that the Synod of Zamosc' is a model of liturgical legislation.

The long standing approach of latinization began to change at the end of the nineteenth century when Pope Leo XIII (1810–1903) began to highlight the importance of the Eastern churches and their own liturgical and theological traditions:[22] he manifested the serious intent of instituting a change of direction

[15] Jan KRAJCAR, A Report on the Ruthenians and their Errors, in: OCP 29 (1963) 75–94.

[16] IBID., 88.

[17] IBID., 89.

[18] IBID., 90.

[19] For a complete history of this Union see: Bernard DUPUY, Recherches sur l'Union de Brest, in: Istina 35 (1990) 17–42; Borys A. GUDZIAK, Crisis and Reform: the Kyivan Metropolitanate, the Patriarchate of Constantinople, and the Genesis of the Union of Brest, Cambridge 2001; Sophia SENYK, Vicissitudes de l'Union de Brest au XVIIe siècle, in: Irénikon 65 (1992) 462–87; ID., The Background of the Union of Brest, in: Analecta Ordinis Sancti Basilii Magni 21 (1996) 103–144; Silverio SAULLE, L'Unione de Brest. Genesi e sviluppi storici, in: Studie sull'Oriente cristiano 2/1 (1998) 137–164, 2/2 (1998) 137–167. See also: Ambroise JOBERT, De Luther à Mohila. La Pologne dans la crise de la Chrétienté, 1517–1648, (Collection historique de l'Institut d'études slaves), Paris 1974. For the articles of the Union see: M. DELMOTTE (trans.), Les Articles de Brest, in: Istina 35 (1990) 43–49.

[20] Laurence Daniel HUCULAK, The Divine Liturgy of St. John Chrysostom in the Kievan Metropolitan Province during the Period of Union with Rome (1596–1839) (Analecta Ordinis Sancti Basilii Magni, Series 2, Section 1, vol. 47), Rome 1990, 333–335; Meletius Michael SOLOVEY, The Byzantine Divine Liturgy: History and Commentary, Washington 1970, 318.

[21] Pius IX, Acta. Pars Prima. Vol. 6. Acta exhibens quae ad ecclesiam universam spectant, Rome n.d., 316–323. See also the online reference: Pius IX, Omnem Sollicitudinem, http://www.papalencyclicals.net/Pius09/p9omnems.htm.

[22] For an overview see: Claude SOETENS, Le Congrès Eucharistique international de Jérusalem (1893) dans le cadre de la politique orientale du Pape Léon XIII (Recueil de

in his encyclical *Orientalium Dignitas*, from November 30, 1894.[23] It was Pope Benedict XV (1854–1922) who created the Oriental Congregation[24] and the Pontifical Oriental Institute[25] in 1917 in order to raise the status of the Eastern Catholic Churches to their proper dignity. These important institutions have provided an invaluable service to the Eastern churches, both Catholic and Orthodox, not only from a juridical and administrative point of view, but perhaps more crucially on the academic level with the specialized study of their liturgical traditions, thus leaving speculation and emotion aside in order to focus on facts and verifiable truths. In fact, the Oriental Institute has been an important bastion of ecumenical scholarship since its foundation.

4. EASTERN CHURCHES: SOCIAL AND POLITICAL SITUATION

A quick appraisal of the situation of various Catholic and Orthodox Eastern churches reveals that they faced difficult socio-economic situations with various wars and political upheavals which restrained the development of academic studies. This effected both the Eastern Catholic and the Orthodox Churches.
The often-overlooked period of liturgical-historical scholarship in the Russian Orthodox Church of the nineteenth and the beginning of the twentieth century provides an important backdrop when considering liturgical issues.[26] Russian Liturgical scholarship during this period developed under the direction of such

travaux d'histoire et de philologie – Université de Louvain, série 6, fasc. 12), Louvain 1977; Rosario F. ESPOSITO, Leone XIII e l'Oriente cristiano: Studio storico-sistematico, Rome 1960, 367–384; Joseph HAJJAR, Les chrétiens uniates du Proche-Orient, Paris 1962, 309–311; for further bibliography on Leo's policies regarding the East consult Giuseppe M. CROCE, La Badia Greca di Grottaferrata e la rivista "Roma e l'Oriente." Cattolicesimo e ortodossia fra unionismo e ecumenismo (1799–1923), 2 vols., Vatican City 1990, vol. 1, 126 n. 48; Robert F. TAFT, Eastern Catholic Theology – Is There Any Such Thing? Reflections of a Practitioner, in: Logos: A Journal of Eastern Christian Studies 39 (1998) 13–58.

23 http://www.papalencyclicals.net/Leo13/l13orient.htm (accessed October 3, 2008).

24 For the history of the Congregation see: La Sacra Congregazione per le Chiese Orientali nel cinquantesimo della fonazione 1917–1967, Rome 1969.

25 For the history of the Pontifical Oriental Institute see: Edward G. FARRUGIA (ed.), The Pontifical Oriental Institute the First Seventy Five Years 1917–1992, Rome 1993.

26 This subject has been widely studied and the following are recommended: James W CUNNINGHAM, A Vanquished Hope. The Movement for Church Renewal in Russia, 1905–1906, Crestwood 1981; Igor SMOLITSCH, Geschichte der Russischen Kirche 1700–1917, vol. 1 (Studien zur Geschichte Osteuropas 9), Leiden 1964; id. Vol. 2 (Forschungen zur osteuropäischen Geschichte 45), Leiden 1991; C. SIMON, L'Église orthodoxe russe à la fin du XIXe et au début du XXe siècles: isolement et intégration, in: Histoire du Christianisme 11 (1995) 733–792; Nicolas M. ZERNOV, The Russian Religious Renaissance of the Twentieth Century, London 1963. For an earlier view see Nikolaj D USPENSKY, The Collision of Two Theologies in the Revision of the Russian Liturgical Books in the Seventeenth Century, in: ID, Evening Worship in the Orthodox Church, trans. Paul LAZOR, Crestwood/NY 1985, 191–240.

notable figures as Dmitrievsky, Skaballanovich, Karabinov, and Sokolov.[27] Various councils addressing church reform were held:[28] in particular, the liturgical reforms at the Council of 1917–1918 in Moscow provide a startling look into proposals that seem to have only been taken seriously many years later in the West. This council has been the subject of several new studies.[29] These studies provide detailed presentations of the tremendous liturgical movement that preceded the council as well as demonstrate an intense interest in aggiornamento. Among the issues of the 1917–1918 Council, they addressed the lack of participation in the liturgy, the possibility of liturgical reform especially in the case of the typikon, liturgical language, music, the iconostasis, and the restoration of the ancient ambo. This astounding list of liturgical issues confounds many outside observers long afflicted with a notion that the Orthodox Church never discusses liturgical change or even had any interest in it.

The Bolshevik Revolution forced the untimely closure of the 1917–1918 Moscow Council and severely disrupted the intellectual life of the Russian Orthodox Church by incarcerating scholars or by deporting them. This scholarship continued in centers of learning in various Western centers. Perhaps one of the best known liturgists of this time is Alexander Schmemann. His seminal work *Introduction to Liturgical Theology*,[30] published originally in 1960 in Paris, influenced not only Eastern, but also Western Liturgists.[31] This important period and the series of contributions witness to the need for the great role that the East has to play in the church at large.

27 For a general overview of many of these authors see: Peter GALADZA, Liturgy and Life: The Appropriation of the Personalization of Cult in East-Slavic Orthodox Liturgiology, 1869–1996, in: StLi 28 (1998) 213–220.

28 Aleksandr Aleksandrovich BOGOLEPOV, Church Reforms in Russia 1905–1918: In Commemoration of the 50th Anniversary of ht All-Russian Church Council of 1917–1918, Bridgeport: Publications Committee of the Metropolitan Council of the Russian Orthodox Church of America, 1966.

29 Н. БАЛАШОВ, На пути к литургическому возрождению: Дискуссии Православной Российской Церкви начала XX века. Поместный Собор 1917–1918 гг. и предсоборный период (Серия: Церковные реформы), Moscow 2000; А.Г. КРАВЕЦКИЙ, Священный Собор Православной Российской Церкви. Из материалов Отдела о богослужении, проповедничестве и храме, in: Богословские труды 34 (1998) 200–388; Marcel MOJZEŠ, Il movimento liturgico nelle chiese bizantine: Analisi di alcune tendenze di riforma nel XX° secolo (BEL.S 132), Rome 2005.

30 Alexander SCHMEMANN, Introduction to Liturgical Theology, Crestwood/NY 1986.

31 See Kevin W. IRWIN, Context and Text: Method in Liturgical Theology, Collegeville/MN 1994; David W. FAGERBERG, What is Liturgical Theology? A Study in Methodology, Collegeville/MN 1992.

5. SACRAMENTS OF INITIATION: A CASE STUDY[32]

Numerous liturgical studies demonstrate the effect of scholarly research on various churches.[33] Schmemann's 1974 seminal study, *Of Water and the Spirit* on the Sacraments of Initiation, impacted both Eastern Orthodox and Eastern Catholic Churches.[34] Schmemann profited from the intellectual world of Paris and read various studies regarding the Sacraments of Initiation.[35] He examined the liturgies of initiation as celebrated in the Byzantine tradition and urges reflection on deepening the pastoral unity of the liturgical celebrations with the celebrating community. This important theological development comes from the years of liturgical historical study of the early sources and looks at tradition from the perspective illustrated by Taft: Miguel Arranz's work is seminal for understanding this history of the Mysteries of Initiation.[36] Schmemann's work, almost contemporaneous with the reform of the Rites of Initiation in the Latin Church, provides an important contextualization for understanding these issues.[37]

Lest one think that this liturgical historical research did not yield results, I direct your attention to one of its most important fruits as seen in a Russian Orthodox Church publication of a revised Order of Initiation – *Posledovanie Kreščal'noj Liturgii* from 2000,[38] as well as the Ukrainian Catholic Eparchy of St. Josaphat in Parma, Ohio, who published *The Mysteries of Christian Initiation* in 2002.[39] This Ukrainian Catholic text resulted from a lengthy study of the issue of Christian Initiation in the late eighties and by 1991 a provisional text was in circulation. Both of these liturgical texts incorporate Baptism and Chrismation into a normal Eucharistic liturgy and are virtually identical. Little has been published regarding the development of the Moscow text. Schmemann's study as well as Miguel Arranz's work on the Constantinopolitan Euchologia demonstrated the original location of initiation at the Easter Vigil thus providing the impetus for the eventual reunification of the Initiation Sacraments within the

32 See my complete study of this issue: Mark MOROZOWICH, Liturgical Changes in Russia and The Christian East? A Case Study: The Mysteries (Sacraments) of Initiation with the Eucharistic Liturgy," in: Worship 83 (2009) 30–47.

33 For an example and good overview see: Robert F. TAFT, Eastern Presuppositions and Western Liturgical Renewal, in: Antiphon 5:1 (2000) 10–22.

34 Alexander SCHMEMANN, Of Water and the Spirit: A Liturgical Study of Baptism, Crestwood/New York 1986.

35 See Schmemann's cursory bibliography in ibid., 155–158.

36 Miguel ARRANZ, Les Sacrements de l'ancien Euchologe constantinopolitain (1-10), in: OCP 48 (1982) 284–335; OCP 49 (1983) 42–90, 284–302; OCP 50 (1984) 372–397; OCP 51 (1985) 60–86; OCP 52 (1986) 145–178; OCP 53 (1987) 59–106; OCP 55 (1989) 33–62, 317–338.

37 See also Maxwell JOHNSON, The Rites of Christian Initiation: Their Evolution and Interpretation, Collegeville/MN 1999, 291–325.

38 Posledovanie Kreščal'noj Liturgii, Moskovskij Patriarxat, Moscow 2000.

39 The Mysteries of Christian Initiation: Baptism, Chrismation, and Eucharist, Parma/OH 2002.

Eucharistic celebration of the community, one of the major themes of *Sacrosanctum Concilium*.[40] It also represents the renewal of the practice of infant communion among Eastern Catholic Churches.[41]
This intriguing similarity provides for an interesting reflection. As the acknowledgement indicates, this Parma text resulted from over twelve years of work.[42] So obviously the work that was being done in Parma was almost completely identical to the work accomplished in Moscow, although there was no collaboration on the project. This clearly indicates the role of liturgical-historical scholarship helping to bring unity in liturgical practice. This eliminates latinization for the Eastern Catholics, and introduces a common celebration in the Orthodox Church. At the same time, it has to be noted that the changes instituted by the Second Vatican Council regarding the Rites of Initiation provided an impetus for both of these churches to reflect on how they are most effectively living their Christian tradition in this regard. So we see not only an influence from the scholarly in the person of Schmemann, but also the lived pastoral situation.

6. THE WORDS OF INSTITUTION – ADDAI AND MARI

Another example of the fruits of liturgical-historical study is found in one of the most explicit latinizations which occurred when various churches of the Antiochean tradition came into union with Rome and were forced to add the words of institution to the Addai and Mari Anaphora in order to prove that it was a valid anaphora. The copious studies on the history of the anaphorae conducted in mostly Western scholarly circles, clearly demonstrated that this was not an omission, but rather reflects the antiquity of this prayer.[43] The varied implications have important ecumenical effects. The Catholic Church recognized the validity of the Anaphora of Addai and Mari at the onset of the twenty-first century – in 2001 after beginning this study in May 1998.[44] Here are the salient points of the decree:

> The Anaphora of Addai and Mari is notable because, from time immemorial, it has been used without a recitation of the Institution Narrative. As the Catholic Church considers the

[40] For a more comprehensive study, see: Mark MOROZOWICH, Liturgical Changes in Russia and The Christian East? A Case Study: The Mysteries (Sacraments) of Initiation with the Eucharistic Liturgy (fn. 32).
[41] See Mark MOROZOWICH, Eastern Catholic Infant Communion: Has Catholic Dogmatic Teaching Prohibited It?, in: Logos: A Journal of Eastern Christian Studies 49 (2008) 71–90.
[42] The Mysteries of Christian Initiation: Baptism, Chrismation, and Eucharist, Parma/OH 2002, 224.
[43] For a comprehensive summary of this scholarship see: Robert TAFT, Mass Without the Consecration?, in: Worship 77 (2003) 489–494.
[44] See Robert TAFT, Mass Without the Consecration?, in: Worship 77 (2003) 484.

> words of the Eucharistic Institution a constitutive and therefore indispensable part of the Anaphora or Eucharistic Prayer, a long and careful study was undertaken of the Anaphora of Addai and Mari, from a historical, liturgical and theological perspective, at the end of which the Congregation for the Doctrine of Faith on January 17th, 2001, concluded that this Anaphora can be considered valid. H.H. Pope John Paul II has approved this decision. This conclusion rests on three major arguments.
>
> In the first place, the Anaphora of Addai and Mari is one of the most ancient Anaphoras, dating back to the time of the very early Church; it was composed and used with the clear intention of celebrating the Eucharist in full continuity with the Last Supper and according to the intention of the Church; its validity was never officially contested, neither in the Christian East nor in the Christian West.
>
> Secondly, the Catholic Church recognizes the Assyrian Church of the East as a true particular Church, built upon orthodox faith and apostolic succession. The Assyrian Church of the East has also preserved full Eucharistic faith in the presence of our Lord under the species of bread and wine and in the sacrificial character of the Eucharist. In the Assyrian Church of the East, though not in full communion with the Catholic Church, are thus to be found "*true sacraments, and above all, by apostolic succession, the priesthood and the Eucharist*" (U.R., n. 15).
>
> Finally, the words of Eucharistic Institution are indeed present in the Anaphora of Addai and Mari, not in a coherent narrative way and *ad litteram*, but rather in a dispersed euchological way, that is, integrated in successive prayers of thanksgiving, praise and intercession.[45]

Predominantly, scholarship that took place in the West provided an opportunity for the Assyrian and the Chaldean Churches to broach an important theological crisis. So the reality of liturgical scholarship aimed at understanding the development of the liturgy yielded a very important result bringing two separated Eastern Churches closer together with one another while at the same time bridging the theological gap with the Latin Church and moving a step closer to full unity between the Assyrian and the Catholic Churches.

7. CONCLUSIONS

These two contemporary examples illustrate the wide ranging impact of historical-liturgical study. The importance of uniting tradition and history remain very important. All too often people simply want to choose a particular period in history to validate a liturgical practice. Liturgical reform is a vast undertaking. Taft's comments on the nature of reform guide this discussion:

> No true reform can be based on the "pick-a-century" game. The past is always instructive but never normative. What its study, like all study, should provide is understanding, an understanding that challenges myths and frees us from the tyranny not just of any one frozen slice of the past, but also from the tyranny of the latest cliché, so that we can move

[45] http://www.vatican.va/roman_curia/pontifical_councils/chrstuni/documents/rc_pc_chrstuni_doc_20011025_chiesa-caldea-assira_en.html (Accessed 9 November 2007).

> ahead to solutions suitable for today in faithful freedom, faithful to living tradition that is always indebted to but free of the past.[46]

So one should not fear historical research or be bound to a particular mode of liturgical form that has been experienced. Rather, it is the ability to understand the deeper theological and pastoral issues that must be addressed in current worship or, more accurately, the current expression of the tradition. In the example of the Mysteries of Initiation, it is intriguing to see that two different churches of the same liturgical tradition but different ecclesial communions have yielded identical results without mutual collaboration.

These brief examples point to a bright future for the liturgy of the church. They demonstrate the ability to use tradition and liturgical scholarship to provide concrete answers to today's problems. The varied experiences point to the role of scholarship as the very engine of the aggiornamento in progress today. This intellectual development will hopefully help to bridge the gap between the various churches and be a true ecumenical tool.

[46] TAFT, Beyond East and West (fn. 1), 291.

The Baptisteries of Late Antique Asia Minor (Western Turkey): What Do They Tell Us About Christian Initiation?

H. Richard Rutherford

Abstract

This parallel session returns to the recurring question of the role of monumental baptisteries at sites clearly independent of episcopal sees and churches. A brief overview of several familiar examples, such as baptisteries at the basilica of St. John (Ephesus) and the putative "monastery" at Alahan (Isauria), will introduce a more in-depth examination of the baptistery and ecclesial complex at the lesser-known site of the Monastery of St. Symeon the Younger (Mons Admirabilis near Antioch on the Orontes). The session will offer a summary of current thinking on the topic and open a discussion of, among others, questions about why such baptisteries exist in these places; what rites of Christian Initiation celebrated there might look like; what relationship, if any, would these centers have had with bishops under whose jurisdiction they fell.

The guiding notes to set the stage for this brief article are the following:

- "Today's designs" include form and function: shape, size, location, water source, patterns of movement, etc.
- "Ancient fonts" are but a sampling from fifth and sixth century Asia Minor (today's Western Turkey and the Mediterranean Islands) – one of the most extensive treasuries of extant baptisteries with fonts.
- "What can we learn?" While there is much more to be said, these three points stand out. There are still many more questions than answers, and even some of the questions await refinement.

"Baptisteries are everywhere!"

Baptisteries appear, as one expects, in the basilicas of episcopal sees, but also in churches at shrines to well known martyrs and other patron saints, at monasteries, and even in churches at cemeteries (likely once linked also to memorial shrines or martyria). Furthermore, within ecclesial complexes, baptisteries are both outside the basilica, as free standing structures, and inside, occupying a space clearly designated and designed for its purpose. Whether outside or inside the church, baptisteries stand in the east end, as at Xanthus, and in the west, as at Ephesus, as well as in the north, (e.g. Elaiussa Sebaste) or south (Anemurium).

The location of the baptistery in relation to the church, or of the font within the baptistery, appears to have no explicit theological meaning. In certain regions, of course, the location may have local significance, for example as in relation to a tomb of a martyr. Another factor determining placement may have been the availability of water, as may be the case at Alahan, Isauria (see Fig. 1, 2, and 3).

Fig. 1. Alahan, Isauria

Fig. 2. Alahan, Isauria

Fig. 3. Alahan, Isauria

What do we learn from this for today's designs? Theological symbolism, such as passing the baptismal font in the entry way or narthex as a reminder of entering the Church through one's own baptism, or contemporary pastoral concerns, such as visibility by the congregation during baptisms, may be meaningful to us. Such things do not appear to concern the communities whose extant ruins we observe from afar. Indeed, those baptisteries might caution us not necessarily to expect theological symbolism from the location of their fonts.

"FONTS RESIDE IN BAPTISTERIES!"

After personally visiting more than 75 archaeological sites with baptisteries and extant fonts I cannot insist enough on this seeming truism. In other words, except for a hand full of examples removed from their original locations, fonts are always in liturgy-specific spaces apart from the principal room for Eucharistic worship.

Furthermore, when it comes to size and location, baptisteries and their fonts appear to reflect local liturgical emphases and practice. Larger monumental, often free-standing baptisteries tend to house large fonts, and reveal clear patterns of liturgical movement within the larger church complex.

Large fonts, centrally placed or located along a lateral wall, with passages in and out, suggest elaborate processional celebrations, as we see in the episcopal basilica at Xanthus (see Fig. 4 and 5),

Fig. 4. Xanthus

Fig. 5. Xanthus

or in the shrine churches of Alahan (see Fig. 6 and 7),

Fig. 6. Alahan, Isauria

Fig. 7. Alahan, Isauria

and of St. John at Ephesus (see Fig. 8 and 9).

Fig. 8. St. John, Ephesus

Fig. 9. St. John, Ephesus

In smaller baptisteries, sometimes little more than a small room within the larger church or ecclesial complex, fonts tend to be smaller, often nestled alone against an apse or side wall. These seem to reflect simpler rites. Examples include the episcopal basilicas at Anemurium (see. Fig. 10 and 11), where the baptistery is located south of the apse,

Fig. 10. Anemurium

Fig. 11. Anemurium

and Elaiussa Sebaste, where the baptistery is located directly north of the apse (see Fig. 12 and 13),

Fig. 12. Elaiussa Sebaste

Fig. 13. Elaiussa Sebaste

as well as the cupola church at the nearby Shrine of St. Thecla in Seleucia, with a baptistery north-east of the apse (see Fig. 14 and 15).

Fig. 14. Shrine of St. Thecla

Fig. 15. Shrine of St. Thecla

Fig. 16. Shrine of St. Thecla. Font viewed in 1999

Fig. 17. Shrine of St. Thecla. Font viewed in 2007.

Documenting the treasury of extant baptismal fonts before further loss due to the herding of large animals, vandalism, tourism, etc., is essential to preserving the archaeological record.

Some fonts are large enough and deep enough to accommodate baptism by full immersion or submersion (see Fig. 18 and 19).

Fig. 18. St. John, Ephesus

Fig. 19. St. John, Ephesus

Others, though deep enough, scarcely fit one person inside, as seen in the font at Alahan (see Fig. 20 and 21).

Fig. 20. Alahan, Isauria

Fig. 21. Alahan, Isauria

Still others, while relatively large, are shallow, suggesting baptism by infusion (see Fig. 16).

Despite all the variations, however, one thing we learn for today is that the space in which a baptismal font is located and the size of the font are related and that both location and size play a role in shaping the celebration of Christian Initiation.

"FONTS COME IN ALL SHAPES AND SIZES!"

Most readers of these pages are familiar with octagonal and cruciform designs, and perhaps the oval or womb-like plans, each reflecting a specific symbolic reference to theologies of baptism. Some will also recognize the so-called tri-lobed fonts with their Trinitarian emphasis. Beyond these familiar shapes, one finds also quatri-lobed, square, round, U-shaped, as well as coffin-like fonts (see Fig. 22 and 23). Some of these fonts have steps on two, three, or four sides, apparently to lead into and out of a central piscina; some fonts have steps on one side only; others have no steps at all (see Fig. 24 and 25).

Fig. 22. Vizari, Crete. Round with steps into coffin-like font area.

Fig. 23. Panormos, Crete. U-shaped with steps.

Fig. 24. St. George, Peyia, Cyprus. Circle (?) with steps from the west only.

Fig. 25. Istanbul Archaeological Museum, Istanbul, Turkey. Cruciform exterior with oval interior.

What do we learn from this wide variety of ancient font designs? Authentic artistic creativity, rather than any attempt to emulate certain "ideal" forms with explicit symbolism, should be our guide to today's designs. Indeed, with such historical diversity, it is hard to imagine any modern design for a functional baptismal font that does not have its precedent in antiquity anyway.

WHAT IS THE BIGGEST LESSON I'VE LEARNED FROM THIS RESEARCH?

The faith of the Church gathered to celebrate the liturgies of Christian Initiation and the unfolding of the rites themselves are what gives symbolism to the font. Just as the sacraments embrace many layers of meaning simultaneously, so too authentic spiritual creativity will design contemporary baptisteries and fonts to capture those many layers of symbolism for today. Furthermore, it is not out of the question that purely practical concerns, such as terrain, materials at hand, accessibility to water, models familiar from secular use, and the like will contribute to our designs just as they had done in late antique Christianity.

APPENDIX: BRIEF DESCRIPTION OF SITES

Sites in Turkey

Alahan

In his archaeological survey of the Göksu River Valley, Dr. Hugh Elton, former Director of the British Archaeological Institute in Ankara, describes the ecclesial complex at Alahan as "one of the most spectacular sites in Turkey." Situated on a ledge in the Taurus Mountains and once identified as a monastery, the site includes an original cave "church," two basilicas, a baptistery, living quarters, and a small cemetery. Scholars today believe it to be more a pilgrimage center than a monastery.

Anemurium

An ancient site, situated on the southernmost tip of Turkey's eastern coastline and about 40 miles north of Cyprus, Anemurium has been inhabited from at least the fourth century B.C. From the fourth to seventh centuries A.D. the city prospered and was home to an active Christian population. Three basilicas from the sixth century survive, including one in the city's extensive necropolis.

Elaiussa Sebaste

Elaiussa Sebaste is located on the Mersin-Silifke highway within the boundaries of the village Kumkuyu. The city was founded in the Late Hellenistic Age (second–first century B.C.) and enjoyed natural fortifications. It was inhabited until the late ninth century A.D. Excavations have revealed a theater, an agora, a vast thermal bath complex, a necropolis and a Byzantine basilica (fifth–sixth centuries A.D.).

Ephesus

Situated in Southwest Turkey, Ephesus was one of the leading cities of the region throughout Antiquity. As the effective capital of the Roman province of Asia, it boasted a population of between 50,000 and a half million inhabitants by the year A.D. 300 and from New Testament times a major Christian center as well. In A.D. 431 Ephesus, by then a metropolitan see, was the site of the third ecumenical council held in the basilica of St. Mary. Nearby on Ayasuluk Hill is the shrine marking the traditional burial place of St. John, the Beloved Disciple. The magnificent ruins on the site today reflect the glory of the work of Emperor

Justinian who replaced a simpler wooden basilica built there in the fourth century.

Hagia Thecla (Meryemlik)

A walled pilgrimage center with cells for both monks and nuns, Meryemlik is believed to have been the home of St. Thecla, the purported companion of St. Paul. Located near modern Silifke on the Gösku River just north of the eastern Mediterranean coast, the site attracted Christian pilgrims en route to and from Jerusalem, among them Egeria and the Pilgrim of Bordeaux. Although the site of several churches and monasteries from the fourth to seventh centuries, little remains today beyond the excavated cave where Thecla is said to have spent the final years of her life.

Xanthus

After a long and glorious history as the principal city of ancient Lycia, mentioned already by Homer and extending to early Byzantine times, Xanthus was reduced to a mere village after the seventh century. The ruins of its large and magnificent basilica, with delicate mosaic floors rivaled by none, reveal the opulence of this episcopal see just before its nadir. It was restored to use again, albeit on simpler scale, in the tenth century.

Sites in Crete & Cyprus

Panormos

An important port on the north coast of Crete from the ninth century B.C. well into Byzantine times, Panormos (Axos in Roman times) was also an episcopal see. North of the village a large basilica (fifth–sixth century) with a wooden roof, dedicated to Holy Wisdom has been excavated. It is believed to be the largest early Christian church on Crete. The basilica has three aisles; each aisle was separated from the other by four columns.

Vizari

Renowned for its villas in Roman and early Byzantine eras, this once affluent village nestled in the lush Amari Valley is home to one of the largest basilicas (seventh–eighth century) on the Island of Crete outside metropolitan centers. Situated close to the north central coast of the island, Vizari suffered multiple invasions throughout history but survives today as a landmark to Cretan resistance well into modern times.

Peyia

A Roman and early Christian settlement at Cape Drepnon on the westernmost point of Cyprus, St. George near Peyia was a well known pilgrimage center like its counterpart on the eastern point of the island, St. Andrew the Apostle. Situated about half way between Alexandria and Rhodes, it is believed to have been a port of call for the ships carrying grain from Egypt to the capital at Constantinople and well endowed by Emperor Justinian in the sixth century.

SELECT BIBLIOGRAPHY

BRADSHAW, Paul F., Baptismal Practices in the Alexandrian Tradition, Eastern or Western?, in: Paul F. BRADSHAW (ed.), Essays in Early Initiation (Alcuin/GLS 8), Nottingham 1988.

BRADSHAW, Paul F., The search for the origins of Christian worship: sources and methods for the study of early liturgy, 2nd revised edition, New York 2002.

CASTELFRANCHI, Marina Falla, Battisteri e Pellegrinaggi, in: Ernst DASSMANN – Josef ENGEMANN (Hgg.), Akten des XII. Internationalen Kongresses für Christliche Archäologie. Bonn, 22.-28. September 1991, Münster 1995, 234–248.

DJOBADZE, Wachtang, Vorläufiger Bericht über Grabungen und Untersuchungen in der Gegend von Antiochia am Orontes, in: Istanbuler Mitteilungen 15 (1965) 218–242.

DJOBADZE, Wachtang, Archeological Investigations in the Region West of Antioch on-the-Orontes. Stuttgart 1986.

DOWNEY, Glanville, A History of Antioch in Syria: from Seleucus to the Arab Conquest, Princeton 1961.

DUFAŸ, Bruno, Les baptistères paléochrétienes ruraux de Syrie du Nord, in: Géograpie historique du Monde Méditerraneén (Byzantina Sorbonensia 7), Paris 1988, 67 ff.

DUFAŸ, Bruno, A propos du baptême: L'évêque, la ville et la champagne, in: Actes du XIe Congrès International d'Archéologie Chrétienne 1, Roma 1989, 637–650.

EQUINI SCHNEIDER, Eugenia (ed.), Elaiussa Sebaste. 2. Un porto tra Oriente e Occidente, Roma 2003 [Floorplan: figure 162, p. 223].

ELTON, Hugh W., Alahan and Zeno, in: Anatolian Studies 52 (2002) 153–157.

GOUGH, Michael (ed.), Alahan: An Early Christian Monastery in Southern Turkey (Texts and Studies 73), Toronto 1985.

HARVEY, Susan Ashbrook, The Stylite's Liturgy: Ritual and Religious Identity in Late Antiquity, in: Journal of Early Christian Studies 6 (1998) 523–539.

HILL, Stephen, The early Byzantine churches of Cilicia and Isauria, Brookfield/VT 1996.

JENSEN, Robin M., Baptism ad Sanctos, Paper presented at the annual meeting of the North American Academy of Liturgy, Louisville/KY, January 6–9, 2005.

JENSEN, Robin M., Living Water: Images, Symbols, and Settings of Early Christian Baptism, Leiden 2011.

LASSUS, Jean, Sanctuaires chrtiens de Syrie, essai sur la genèse, la forme et l'usage liturgique des édifices du culte chrétien, en Syrie, du IIIe siècle a la conquête musulmane. Paris 1947.

MITCHELL, Stephen, Anatolia: Land, Men and Gods in Asia Minor. Vol. 2: The Rise of the Church, Oxford 1993.

RISTOW, Sebastian, Frühchristliche Baptisterien, Münster 1998.

RUSSELL, James, Christianity at Anemurium (Cilicia): Recent Discoveries, in: Studi di antichita cristiana 41 (1991) 1621–1637.

RUTHERFORD, H. Richard, What Can We Learn from Ancient Baptismal Fonts for Today's Designs? in: EnVisionChurch, March 4, 2008. http://www1.georgetown.edu/ centers/liturgy/envisionchurch/44007.html (accessed October 31, 2008).

VAN DEN VEN, Paul, La Vie Ancienne de S. Syméon Stylite le Jeune (521–592). Tome Ier Introduction et texte grec., Bruxelles 1962.

VERZONE, Paolo, Il Santuario di S Simeone il Giovane sul Monte delle Meraviglie, in: Corsi di Cultura sull'Arte Ravennate e Bizantina 21 (1974) 273–286.

Die liturgische Verehrung der Heiligen des Alten Testaments in der lateinischen Kirche. Ein vergessenes Desiderat der Konzilsgeneration*

Nikodemus C. Schnabel

1. Nostra aetate

„Der Prozeß, in dem die Konzilserklärung *Nostra aetate* entstand, war ein leidenschaftlicher und höchst dramatischer *Streit*, der die überwiegende Mehrheit der Konzilsväter und der im Umfeld des Konzils arbeitenden Theologen in einen … erstaunlichen Lernprozeß hineingerissen hat.“[1] Dieser Lernprozess, in dem die „Kirche mutig begonnen“ hat, „Schutt und Schmutz aus der Geschichte ihres Verhaltens gegenüber dem Judentum abzutragen und neue Wege der geforderten Solidarität mit dem jüdischen Volk zu bahnen“[2] hat in den Jahrzehnten nach dem Zweiten Vatikanischen Konzil eine so breite Dynamik entfaltet, dass eine diskursfähig bleiben wollende Theologie von ihm nicht mehr absehen kann. Dies trifft auch auf die Liturgiewissenschaft zu, deren Vertreter sich in jüngster Zeit in zahlreichen Publikationen mit dezidiert jüdisch-christlichen Fragestellungen auseinandersetzen.[3] Signifikant hierfür ist das deutschsprachige Handbuch der Liturgiewissenschaft *Gottesdienst der Kirche*, das dieser Thematik in seinem aktuellsten Teilband aus dem 2008 einen großen Platz einräumt.[4]

* Siehe dazu: Nikodemus C. Schnabel, Die liturgische Verehrung der Heiligen des Alten Testaments in der lateinischen Kirche. Versuch einer historischen und ökumenischen Spurenlese (unveröffentl. Dissertation), Wien 2013.

1 Erich Zenger, Nostra aetate. Der notwendige Streit um die Anerkennung des Judentums in der katholischen Kirche, in: Günther Bernd Ginzel – Günter Fessler (Hgg.), Die Kirchen und die Juden. Versuch einer Bilanz, Gerlingen 1997, 49–81, hier 53 [Hervorhebungen im Original]. – Diesen Beitrag möchte ich den Mönchen der Benediktinerabtei Unserer Lieben Frau zu den Schotten in Wien in Dankbarkeit für die gewährte Gastfreundschaft in den vergangenen Jahren widmen.

2 Ebd., 51.

3 Es sei exemplarisch nur auf folgende Sammelbände verwiesen: Albert Gerhards – Clemens Leonhard (Hgg.), Jewish and Christian Liturgy and Worship. New Insights into its History and Interaction (Jewish and Christian Perspective Series 15), Leiden – Boston 2007; Albert Gerhards – Stephan Wahle (Hgg.), Kontinuität und Unterbrechung. Gottesdienst in Judentum und Christentum (Studien zu Judentum und Christentum o.B.), Paderborn 2005; Albert Gerhards – Hans Hermann Henrix (Hgg.), Dialog oder Monolog? Zur liturgischen Beziehung zwischen Judentum und Christentum (Quaestiones Disputatae 208), Freiburg – Basel – Wien 2004; Albert Gerhards – Andrea Doeker – Peter Ebenbauer (Hgg.), Identität durch Gebet. Zur gemeinschaftsbildenden Funktion institutionalisierten Betens in Judentum und Christentum (Studien zu Judentum und Christentum o.B.), Paderborn 2003.

4 Vgl. Gerard Rouwhorst, Christlicher Gottesdienst und der Gottesdienst Israels. Forschungsgeschichte, historische Interaktionen, Theologie, in: Martin Klöckener – Ange-

Auffällig ist jedoch, dass bei dem zur Zeit erwachten Interesse der liturgiewissenschaftlichen Forschung an den liturgischen Beziehungen zwischen Judentum und Christentum ein Aspekt fast völlig außen vor bleibt, der bei den Theologen im Vor- und Umfeld des Zweiten Vatikanischen Konzils noch auf ein gesteigertes Interesse gestoßen ist[5] und der beinahe Eingang als eigener Gegenstand in die ursprünglich geplante Fassung der „Judenerklärung" des Konzils gefunden hätte, die dann nach einem hart errungenen Prozess mit einigen Kompromissen[6] letztlich zu Artikel 4 der umfassenderen „Erklärung über das Verhältnis der Kirche zu den nichtchristlichen Religionen" *Nostra aetate* wurde.[7] Die Rede ist von der liturgischen Verehrung der großen Gestalten des Alten Testaments als Heilige in der lateinischen Kirche.[8]

lus A. HÄUßLING – Reinhard MESSNER (Hgg.), Theologie des Gottesdienstes. Band 2: Gottesdienst im Leben der Christen. Christliche und jüdische Liturgie (Gottesdienst der Kirche. Handbuch der Liturgiewissenschaft 2,2), Regensburg 2008, 491–572.

5 Vgl. Bernard BOTTE, Le culte de Saints de l'Ancien Testament dans l'Église chrétienne, in: Cahiers Sioniens 4 (1950) 38–47; DERS., Une fête du prophète Élie en Gaule au VIe siècle, in: Cahiers Sioniens 4 (1950) 170–177; DERS., Abraham dans la liturgie, in: Cahiers Sioniens 5 (1951) 180–187; DERS., Le culte du prophète Élie dans l'Église chrétienne, in: Études Carmélitaines 35 (1956) 208–218; DERS., Les Saints de l'Ancien Testament, in: MD 52 (1957) 109–120; Jean BLANC, La fête de Moïse dans le rite byzantin, in: Cahiers Sioniens 8 (1954) 464–466; Henri Irénée MARROU, Les Saints de l'Ancien Testament au Martyrologe Romain, in: Mémorial Joseph Chaine « 1888–1948 » (Bibliothèque de la Faculté Catholique de Théologie de Lyon 5), Lyon 1950, 281–290; Marcel SIMON, Les Saints d'Israël dans la dévotion de l'Église Ancienne, in: Revue d'Histoire et de Philosophie Religieuses 4 (1954) 98–127; John HENNIG, Abel's Place in the Liturgy, in: Theological Studies 7 (1946) 126–141; DERS., The Literary Tradition of Moses in Ireland, in: Traditio 7 (1949–1951) 233–261; DERS., Zur Stellung Abrahams in der Liturgie, in: Archiv für Liturgiewissenschaft 9,2 (1966) 349–366; DERS., Zur Stellung Davids in der Liturgie, in: Archiv für Liturgiewissenschaft 10,1 (1967) 157–164; DERS., Zur liturgischen Tradition der Jünglinge im Feuerofen, in: Heiliger Dienst 22 (1968) 151–156. – Es ist darauf hinzuweisen, dass auch der wegweisende Aufsatz von Yves CONGAR, Ecclesia ab Abel, in: Marcel REDING (Hg.), Abhandlungen über Theologie und Kirche. Festschrift für Karl Adam, Düsseldorf 1952, 79–108 im selben zeitlichen Kontext entstanden ist.

6 Immer noch am ausführlichsten skizziert bei Johannes OESTERREICHER, Kommentierende Einleitung der Erklärung über das Verhältnis der Kirche zu den nichtchristlichen Religionen, in: Lexikon für Theologie und Kirche. Ergänzungsband 2 (1967) 405–478.

7 Nostra aetate 4 ist mit seiner heilsgeschichtlich orientierten Ekklesiologie keineswegs ein isolierter Text innerhalb der Konzilsdokumente, sondern diese Theologie ist auch im 2. und 6. Artikel der Dogmatischen Konstitution über die Kirche Lumen gentium, im 5. Artikel der Liturgiekonstitution Sacrosanctum Concilium und im 11., 14. und 15. Artikel der Dogmatischen Konstitution über die göttliche Offenbarung Dei verbum fest verankert.

8 Dass dieses Thema in jüngster Zeit nicht völlig in Vergessenheit geraten ist, ist namentlich Georg Braulik, dem emeritierten Ordinarius für Altes Testament an der Katholisch-Theologischen Fakultät der Universität Wien, zu verdanken, der in einem Vortrag anlässlich seiner Ehrenpromotion durch die Philosophisch-Theologische Hochschule Sankt Georgen in Frankfurt am Main am 21. Juni 2006 dieses Thema in pointierter Weise aufgegriffen hat: Vgl. Georg BRAULIK, Verweigert die Westkirche den Heiligen des Alten Testaments die liturgische Verehrung?, in: Theologie und Philosophie 82 (2007) 1–20. Der verstorbene Wiener Ordinarius für Liturgiewissenschaft, Hansjörg Auf der Maur, muss in diesem Zusammenhang ebenfalls erwähnt werden, der im Faszikel über die Heiligenverehrung im aktuellen Handbuch der Liturgiewissenschaft diese Thematik immer wieder aufgreift: Vgl. Hansjörg AUF DER MAUR, Feiern im Rhythmus der Zeit. Feste und Gedenktage der Heiligen (GDK 6,1), Regensburg 1994, 65–358, hier besonders 117–122

2. DIE GRUNDSATZSTUDIE VON 1961

Anfang Februar 1961 wurde der Benediktinerabt der Jerusalemer Dormitio-Abtei, Leo von Rudloff, zum Vorsitzenden der „Unterkommission für den Jüdischen Problemkreis" berufen, die am Päpstlichen Einheitssekretariat unter der Leitung von Augustin Kardinal Bea angesiedelt war.[9] Bea verkündete auf dem ersten Gesamttreffen aller Mitglieder und Konsultoren des Einheitssekretariats am 14. und 15. November 1960, dass seinem Sekretariat der Auftrag von Papst Johannes XXIII. zugeteilt worden sei, sich der *Quaestiones de Iudaeis* anzunehmen, woraus durch die Initiative durch Gregory Baum OSA die erwähnte Unterkommission eingerichtet wurde. Neben Baum und von Rudloff bildete Johannes Oesterreicher[10] als Konsultor den Kern dieser Unterkommission, die von Fall zu Fall durch verschiedene Mitarbeiter erweitert wurde.

Sie bekam den Auftrag, für die dritte Generalversammlung des Einheitssekretariats vom 6. bis zum 21. April 1961 in Ariccia in den Albanerbergen eine Grundsatzstudie vorzulegen. Am 20. April verlas Gregory Baum diese Grundsatzstudie auf Englisch, die aber auch in französischer und lateinischer Übersetzung verteilt wurde. Nach ihrer Verlesung kam es zu einer überraschenden Ak-

(„Feste biblischer Gestalten"), aber auch 83–88 („Alttestamentlich-jüdische ‚Verehrung' von Märtyrern und Gerechten"). Ausdrücklich zu dieser Thematik geäußert haben sich auch Bert GROEN, Old Testament saints and anti-Judaism in the current Byzantine liturgy, in: Marcel BARNARD – Paul POST – Els ROSE (Hgg.), A cloud of witness. The cult of saints in past and present (Liturgia condenda 18), Leuven – Paris – Dudley/MA 2005, 145–159, wobei die Situation in der lateinischen Kirche in seinem Beitrag nicht zur Sprache kommt; und Gerard ROUWHORST, The Cult of the Seven Maccabean Brothers and Their Mother in Christian Tradition, in: Joshua SCHWARTZ – Marcel POORTHUIS (Hgg.), Saints and role models in Judaism and Christianity (Jewish and Christian perspectives series 7), Leiden – Boston 2004, 183–204, der aber eine grundsätzliche Behandlung des Themas vermeidet und sich allein auf die historische Genese der Verehrung der Makkabäischen Märtyrerbrüder als Heilige im Christentum beschränkt – umso bedauerlicher ist es, dass derselbe Autor dieses Thema in seinem von ihm verantworteten Faszikel im Handbuch der Liturgiewissenschaft völlig ausspart (s. Anm. 4). Als populärwissenschaftliche Publikation ist zu nennen Bertrand DE MARGERIE, Les Saints Prohètes du Christ Prophète, Paris 2002. – Schon etwas älter ist der Beitrag von Georg KRETSCHMAR, Die Heiligen Israels im Gottesdienst der Kirche, in: Gerhard Ludwig MÜLLER (Hg.), Heiligenverehrung – ihr Sitz im Leben des Glaubens und ihre Aktualität im ökumenischen Gespräch (Schriftenreihe der Katholischen Akademie der Erzdiözese Freiburg o.B.), München – Zürich 1986, 31–63, dessen Ausführungen aber bezüglich ihrer substitutionstheologischen Implikationen kritisch anzufragen sind, besonders 49–57 („Die Heiligen Israels und unsere Theologie heute"). Positiv zu erwähnen ist abschließend noch die Lizentiatsarbeit von Daniela KRANEMANN, Israelitica dignitas? Studien zur Israeltheologie Eucharistischer Hochgebete (Münsteraner Theologische Abhandlungen 66), Altenberge 2001, welche die Nicht-Verehrung der Heiligen des Alten Testaments im aktuellen liturgischen Festkalender der lateinischen Kirche im Gesamtzusammenhang einer christlichen Israeltheologie ausdrücklich problematisiert, besonders 39–41.

[9] Im folgenden stütze ich mich weitgehend auf die Dokumentation von Johannes OESTERREICHER, Kommentierende Einleitung (s. Anm. 6), 414–426.

[10] Zur Würdigung Oesterreichers und Kardinal Beas vgl. Dorothee RECKER, Die Wegbereiter der Judenerklärung des Zweiten Vatikanischen Konzils. Johannes XXIII., Kardinal Bea und Prälat Oesterreicher – eine Darstellung ihrer theologischen Entwicklung, Paderborn 2007.

klamation der anwesenden Bischöfe.[11] Die endgültige Fassung der Grundsatzstudie konnte nach Berücksichtigung der Diskussionsbeiträge schließlich auf der vierten Generalversammlung im August 1961 in Bühl, in Deutschland vorgelegt werden.[12]
Die Grundsatzstudie[13] ist in drei Teile gegliedert, und zwar erstens „Dogmatische Prinzipien", zweitens „Moralische und liturgische Erwägungen" und drittens „Praktische Anregungen". Am Ende der Studie sind sieben Voten angeschlossen, die sich direkt an die Konzilsväter richten.
Von großem Interesse ist der zweite Teil der Grundsatzstudie, der mit „Moralische und liturgische Erwägungen" überschrieben ist. Während der erste Abschnitt dieses Teils jedwede Form von Rassenhass und Antisemitismus unmissverständlich verurteilt, widmet sich der zweite Abschnitt Fragen der Liturgie.[14] Einleitend an das alte Axiom *Legem credendi lex statuat supplicandi* – das hier aber im weitesten Sinne verstanden wird – erinnernd, sei die Weise zu Beten nicht nur Ausdruck der Glaubensüberzeugung, sondern forme auch das Glaubensleben. Für die Mehrheit der Gläubigen sei die Liturgie immer noch die eigentliche Erzieherin zum geistlichen Leben. Aus diesem Grund sei es sehr bedauerlich, dass mit den Makkabäischen Märtyrerbrüdern nur eine einzige Kommemoration alttestamentlicher Gestalten im Liturgischen Kalender (1. August) verankert sei. „Die spirituelle Bedeutung der Makkabäer sei jedoch weitaus geringer als die vieler anderer Männer *und Frauen* Israels. Würde es nicht zum

[11] „Es sei aber schon hier vorweggenommen, daß die erste Verlesung in Ariccia – entgegen allen Gepflogenheiten des Sekretariats – mit Applaus aufgenommen wurde... [W]enn meine Erinnerung mich nicht täuscht, war das spontane Händeklatschen, mit dem die Studie am 20. 4. 1961 begrüßt wurde, die einzige solche Bekundung für ein vorbereitendes Dokument. Es scheint ein Beweis dafür zu sein, daß hier ein Anliegen deutlich ausgesprochen wurde, das die meisten bis dahin nur vage gefühlt hatten. Was bisher vielfach nur im Unterbewußtsein geschlummert hatte, wurde nun ins helle Licht des Tages gehoben. Die applaudierenden Bischöfe erwiesen sich hier als wahre Vertreter des Volkes Gottes: Die Studie leistete für sie denselben Dienst, den später die promulgierte Erklärung der gesamten Kirche erwies und noch erweisen wird." OESTERREICHER, Kommentierende Einleitung (s. Anm. 6), 417.

[12] Dass diese Grundsatzstudie bislang kaum von der Forschung rezepiert wurde, hat ihren entscheidende Grund sicher darin, dass sie nicht in allgemein zugänglicher Form vorliegt. So fehlt sie etwa in der wichtigen Dokumentensammlung von Rolf RENDTDORFF – Hans Hermann HENRIX, Die Kirchen und das Judentum. Dokumente von 1945 bis 1985 (Gemeinsame Veröffentlichung der Studienkommission Kirche und Judentum der Evangelischen Kirche in Deutschland und der Arbeitsgruppe für Fragen des Judentums der Ökumene-Kommission der Deutschen Bischofskonferenz o.B.), Paderborn – München 1988. – Der neuste deutschsprachige Standard-Kommentar zum Zweiten Vatikanischen Konzil verweist bezüglich der Grundsatzstudie lediglich auf die Dokumentation bei OESTERREICHER, Kommentierende Einleitung (s. Anm. 6), 417–426: Vgl. Roman A. SIEBENROCK, Theologischer Kommentar zur Erklärung über die Haltung der Kirche zu den nichtchristlichen Religionen *Nostra aetate*, in: Peter HÜNERMANN – Bernd Jochen HILBERATH (Hgg.), Herders Theologischer Kommentar zum Zweiten Vatikanischen Konzil. Band 3, Freiburg – Basel – Wien 2005, 591–693, hier 636f.

[13] Wie SIEBENROCK, Theologischer Kommentar (s. Anm. 12) bin ich hier auf die Dokumentation bei OESTERREICHER, Kommentierende Einleitung (s. Anm. 6), 417–426 angewiesen.

[14] Vgl. OESTERREICHER, Kommentierende Einleitung (s. Anm. 6), 419f.

Nutzen vieler Gläubigen sein, wenn jene Feste der Gerechten des Alten Bundes, die das lateinische Patriarchat von Jerusalem feiert, irgendwie auf die ganze Kirche ausgedehnt würden? Dies könnte z.B. in der Form eines neuen Festes der Patriarchen und Propheten geschehen.“[15] Um aber das Heiligenjahr gegenüber dem Herrenjahr zurücktreten zu lassen, gemäß dem Wunsch der „Kirche von heute“[16], „schlugen die Unterzeichner der vorbereitenden Studie vor, die Feste des Jerusalemer Patriarchats dem Römischen Missale nach Möglichkeit als Votivmessen einzuverleiben.“[17]

Zwar kämen die Gestalten des Alten Testaments in den liturgischen Gebeten immer wieder vor, aber besondere „Messen zu Ehren der verschiedenen Patriarchen und Propheten würden das Wissen um die Einheit der Heilsgeschichte im Verstand und Herzen vieler noch tiefer verankern. Ihre Einfügung in das Römische Messbuch würde – selbst wenn diese Meßfeiern nur selten stattfänden – ...zu einer fruchtbaren Atmosphäre jüdisch-christlicher Beziehung beitragen.“[18] Der Abschnitt schließt mit einem Gebetsbeispiel aus dem Proprium des lateinischen Patriarchats von Jerusalem.[19]

Resultat dieser Überlegungen ist schließlich das fünfte der sieben Voten,[20] die am Ende der Grundsatzstudie stehen: „Es möchte dafür Sorge getragen werden, daß die Feste der Gerechten des Alten Bundes, wie sie zur Zeit im lateinischen Patriarchat von Jerusalem gefeiert werden, auf die Gesamtkirche ausgedehnt würden, sei es als Votivmessen oder als ein Fest der Patriarchen und Propheten.“[21]

3. DIE DEBATTEN

Sowohl auf der dritten Generalversammlung des Einheitssekretariats im April 1961 wie auf der vierten im August 1961 kam es zu Diskussionen über die Grundsatzstudie und ihre Voten.[22] Auf beiden Versammlungen, besonders aber der im August tagenden stieß das fünfte Votum überraschend auf Widerstände.[23] Im April wurde geklärt, dass das fünfte Votum ursprünglich an die Adresse der Ritenkongregation gerichtet sei, worauf der „Unterkommision für den Jüdischen Problemkreis“ von den anwesenden Bischöfen zu Verstehen gegeben wurde, dass die Ritenkongregation zusätzliche Feste nicht wolle und dass es ja bereits

15 Ebd., 420 [Hervorhebung durch N.C.S.].
16 Ebd.
17 Ebd.
18 Ebd.
19 Vgl. ebd.
20 Siehe oben.
21 Ebd., 421.
22 Dokumentiert ebd., 422–426.
23 „Merkwürdigerweise löste das fünfte Votum eine sehr lebhafte Debatte aus.“ Ebd., 423.

eine Anrufung der Patriarchen und Propheten gebe und dass Abraham bereits einen prominenten Platz im Kanon der Messe innehabe.[24]
In der Versammlung im August wurde auf die Eigenfeier des Propheten Elija bei den Karmeliten hingewiesen und darauf, dass das Offizium des Advents dem Gedächtnis der Patriarchen und Propheten gewidmet sei. Auch wurde auf die Sterbegebete verwiesen, in denen die Kirche Gott den Sterbenden anempfehle und ihn an sein Erbarmen erinnere, dass er bereits den Gerechten des Alten Bundes erwiesen habe. „Eine andere Wortmeldung galt den heiligen Frauen, die in unserem Votum nicht übersehen werden sollten."[25]
Als dezidierte Argumente gegen das fünfte Votum wurden von einem Bischof ins Feld geführt, dass „die Feste unseres Herrn, der allerseligsten Jungfrau und der Apostel insgesamt ‚jüdische' Feste" seien[26] und damit eine Einführung von Festen zu Ehren der alttestamentlichen Gerechten schlichtweg unnötig. Ein anderes Argument verwies auf den lokal begrenzten Charakter der Feste des lateinischen Patriarchats und dass es der kirchlichen Gewohnheit widerspräche ortsgebundene Feste auf die Gesamtkirche auszudehnen. Ein drittes Gegenargument verwies auf den ungünstigen Zeitpunkt: Die gegenwärtige liturgische Erneuerung sei nicht gerade geeignet für die Einführung neuer Feste.[27]
Hält man sich die Grundsatzstudie bezüglich der liturgischen Erwägungen und die Argumente gegen sie in den Debatten vor Augen, muss man feststellen, dass sich nicht nur die Ausgangslage gewandelt hat, sondern auch die meisten Gegenargumente nicht mehr verfangen:
War bis zum neuen Generalkalender von 1969 wenigstens die Commemoratio der Makkabäischen Märtyrerbrüder am 1. August noch im Kalender verankert, gibt es heute nicht ein einziges Fest alttestamentlicher Heiliger im Generalkalender mehr. Der Römische Kanon, das Erste Eucharistische Hochgebet mit der Anrufung Abels, Abrahams und Melchisedeks, ist nur noch eines von verschiedenen möglichen Hochgebeten, das ob seiner Länge sich in der pastoralen Praxis eher seltener Verwendung erfreut. Die summarische Anrufung der heiligen Patriarchen und Propheten in der Allerheiligenlitanei für die Osternachtsvigil ist gestrichen worden und die erwähnten Sterbegebete sind heute nicht mehr gebräuchlich.
Gleichwohl aber wurden und werden immer wieder neue Heiligengedenktage in den Generalkalender aufgenommen, über deren „wahrhaft universale Bedeutung"[28] man zu einem differenzierten Urteil gelangen kann. Auch wurden durch

[24] Vgl. ebd., 422.
[25] Ebd., 423
[26] Ebd.
[27] Vgl. ebd., 423f.
[28] Auf das Kriterium des *„momentum universale revera prae se ferentes"* wird in wörtlicher Zitation von *Sacrosanctum Concilium* 111 wiederholt und ausdrücklich bei der Kalenderreform verwiesen: Vgl. Calendarium Romanum ex decreto Sacrosancti Oecumenici Concilii Vaticani II instauratum auctoritate Pauli PP. VI promulgatum. Editio typica, Vatikanstadt 1969, hier 9; 68 und 70.

die Kalenderreform 1969 bis dato nur lokal oder regional verwurzelte Feste auf die Gesamtkirche ausgedehnt.
Fakt ist aber, dass das fünfte Votum der Grundsatzstudie nicht mehr weiter verfolgt wurde und auch nicht Eingang gefunden hat in den Erstentwurf des *Decretum de Iudaeis* vom Dezember 1961.[29]

4. DER EINWAND VON BERNARD BOTTE

Ein Hauptargument gegen die Einführung liturgischer Feste alttestamentlicher Heiliger in den Generalkalenders der Römischen Kirche, das auch in der Debatte vom August 1961 durchschimmert, ist – neben der immer wieder zurecht beklagten Hypertrophie des gesamtkirchlichen Sanktorales – der Vorwurf des „künstlichen Charakters“[30] solcher Feste, die einer historisch gewachsenen Tradition im Westen entbehrten. Die Situation in den Ostkirchen sei demgegenüber eine völlig andere und so sei es auch nachvollziehbar, dass die Verehrung der Heiligen des Alten Testaments dort bis heute lebendig sei. Rein theologisch gesehen, spräche nichts dagegen, die großen Gestalten des Alten Testaments als Heilige zu verehren, aber für die Westkirche sei dies als gekünsteltes Konstrukt abzulehnen.
In Kürze lässt sich so der Aufsatz „Les Saints de l’Ancien Testament“ in *La Maison-Dieu* des Benediktinergelehrten Bernard Botte aus dem Jahr 1957 zusammenfassen, der mit dem programmatischen Satz beginnt: „Parmi les différences qui distinguent la piété orientale de celle de l’Occident, l’attitude envers les saints de l’Ancien Testament est caractéristique.“[31] Während im Osten durch das Pilgern zu den Stätten der alttestamentlichen Heilsgeschichte und den Gräbern der Gerechten des Alten Bundes schon früh deren Verehrung einen Sitz im Leben der Gläubigen einnehmen konnte, muss deren Verehrung im Westen doch immer abstrakt bleiben:
„Il faut savoir comprendre et apprécier les différentes traditions, mais pas nécessairement imiter. Certaines formes de piété parfaitement légitimes en Occident, parce qu’elles ont répondu ou répondent encore à une exigence historique, seraient déplacées dans les rites orientaux. Il en est de même de certaines formes de la piété orientale pour les Occidentaux. Il faut se garder des constructions artificielles faites à coups de raisonnements. Il y a une différence entre la logique abstraite et la logique de la vie.“[32]

[29] Vgl. Vgl. OESTERREICHER, Kommentierende Einleitung (s. Anm. 6), 426, dort auch Wiedergabe des Wortlautes des Entwurfs.
[30] „Caractère artificiel“: Vgl. BOTTE, Les Saints de l’Ancien Testament (s. Anm. 5).
[31] Vgl. ebd., 109.
[32] Ebd., 120. – Eine Sonderrolle nimmt aber im Westen für Botte Irland ein, wie er in seinem Aufsatz betont, wo schon früh, unabhängig vom Osten, eine lebendige Verehrung der Heiligen des Alten Testaments aufgeblüht sei: Vgl. ebd., 115–117.

Dieser Einwand Bottes ist in der jüngeren Literatur von der Sache her immer wieder anzutreffen, wenn es um die liturgische Verehrung der Heiligen des Alten Testaments geht. So schreibt Gerard Rouwhorst im Jahr 2004 über das Phänomen der Verehrung „vor-christlicher Heiliger“[33] im Christentum: „From the fourth-century Armenian Lectionary which provides a detailed and reliable picture of the liturgical traditions of Christians living in Jerusalem at the end of the fourth and during the fifth century, it becomes clear that this category of ‚saints‘ [sic] was very popular in that city and in the Holy Land then. In addition, traces of their veneration are also found in most Eastern liturgical rites as well in *some ancient western* liturgical traditions, in particular those of Gaul and Irish Christianity.“[34]
Auch wenn Rouwhorst eine Verehrung mancher alttestamentlicher Heiliger (speziell der Makkabäischen Märtyrerbrüder) in einigen westlichen Traditionen zur Kenntnis nimmt, geht auch er von einem klaren Ost-West-Gefälle aus. Letztlich bedauert er auch nicht die Streichung der Makkabäischen Brüder aus dem Generalkalender der Römischen Kirche, sondern hält sie für die folgerichtige Konsequenz aus einem im Mittelalter beginnenden Marginalisierungsprozess ihrer Verehrung.[35]
Es soll an dieser Stelle anhand eines bewusst nicht aus dem keltischen oder gallischen Liturgiebereichs gewählten Beispiels geprüft werden, ob sich das Bild der marginalen liturgischen Verehrung alttestamentlicher Gestalten im Westen erhärten lässt, und zwar für den heutigen deutschsprachigen Raum.[36]

5. BAMBERG ALS BEISPIEL

Für das Hochstift Bamberg, das bislang noch in keiner Literatur im Zusammenhang mit der liturgischen Verehrung der Heiligen des Alten Testaments Erwähnung gefunden hat, sind im Mittelalter folgende Feste nachweisbar (in alphabetischer Reihenfolge):[37]

33 „pre-Christian“: Vgl. ROUWHORST, The Cult of the Seven Maccabean Brothers (s. Anm. 8).
34 Ebd., 183 [Hinweis und Hervorhebungen durch N.C.S.].
35 Vgl. ebd., 202–205.
36 Eine erste Auseinandersetzung mit Bottes Aufsatz von 1957 findet sich bei BRAULIK, Verweigert die Westkirche den Heiligen des Alten Testaments die Verehrung? (s. Anm. 8), 14–18: Er argumentiert mit einem Beispiel aus der irischen Tradition.
37 Die folgenden Ausführungen stützen sich auf das Quellenmaterial, das Adolf Lagemann in seiner 1952 in Würzburg eingereichten historischen Dissertation ediert hat: Vgl. DERS., Der Festkalender des Bistums Bamberg im Mittelalter. Entwicklung und Anwendung (Sonderausgabe aus dem 103. Bericht des Historischen Vereins Bamberg), Bamberg 1967. Die berücksichtigten Quellen umfassen den Zeitraum von der Gründung des Bistums Bamberg im Jahre 1007 bis zum Jahr 1500, als sich das Festwesen zu festigen und vereinheitlichen begann: Vgl. ebd., 27. – Es sei hierbei ausdrücklich betont, dass es sich bei den untersuchten Handschriften um Liturgische Kalendarien handelt, die wirklich ein Hinweis auf ein liturgisches Gedächtnis geben und nicht um bloße Martyrologien: Vgl.

Heilige(r)[38]	Gedenk-/Festtag	Handschriftliche Zeugen[39]
Aaroni pph[40]	1. Juli	Ls[41] (15. Jh.)
Abacuc pph (in Palaestina)	15. Januar	D4[42] (11. Jh.); Ls (15. Jh.)
Abrahae patriarchae	9. Oktober	M[43] (12. Jh.)
Abraham, Isaac et Jacob patr.	6. Oktober	*C1*, *C2* (14. Jh.); *C3*, C5, C6[44], *C7*, C8, Ls (15. Jh)[45]
Amos pph	31. März	Ls (15. Jh.)
Assumptio Moysi	4. September	D8[46] (13. Jh.); Ls (15. Jh.)
Danielis pph	21. Juli	D4 (11. Jh.); M (12. Jh.); Ls (15. Jh.)
David reg (et pph)	30. Dezember	C6, Ls, U3[47] (15. Jh.)

ebd.,20–26. Dies ist umso wichtiger zu betonen, da Lagemanns Arbeit genau in dieser Hinsicht pauschalisierender Kritik ausgesetzt war, insbesondere durch Adalbert KURZEJAS Rezension im ALW 13 (1971), 307f. So ist etwa bei Lagemann durchaus ersichtlich, welcher Kalendareintrag einem liturgischen Fest – Kennzeichnung durch Kursivsetzung in diesem Beitrag – und welcher lediglich einer *Memoria* entspricht. Im Gegenzug bleibt an Kurzeja die kritische Rückfrage zu stellen, was er genau unter „martyrolog[ischem] Füllmaterial" versteht, da er hierfür weder ein Beispiel benennt noch diesen Vorwurf argumentativ in irgendeiner Form stützt. Dass es sich bei den von Lagemann untersuchten und ausgewerteten Quellen um Kalendarien, und nicht um Martyrologien, handelt, besteht kein Zweifel. – Hierfür ist als Unterscheidungskriteriologie immer noch hilfreich John HENNIG, Kalendar und Martyrologium als Literaturformen, in: ALW 7,1 (1961) 1–44.

38 Die Heiligen werden nach den in den Handschriften bezeugten Festbezeichnungen aufgeführt, wobei vereinzelt abweichende Lesarten in Klammern gesetzt sind: Vgl. ebd., 51.

39 Die Sigel der Kalender-Handschriften sind von Lagemann übernommen und werden im folgenden durch eine Anmerkung bei Erstnennung aufgelöst. Für eine detaillierte Beschreibung der jeweiligen Handschrift sei auf Lagemanns Arbeit verwiesen.

40 Die Abkürzung „pph" steht hier wie andernorts für „prophetae".

41 Ls: Nürnberg, Losungsstube: Kalender der Nürnberger Losungsstube, Staatsarchiv Nürnberg Rep. 52a, Nr. 425. Pergamenthandschrift, 19 Bl., 15. Jh. Vgl. ebd., 47.

42 D4: Bamberg, Dom: Sacramentarium (Gregorianum) et Graduale Bambergense, Staatsbibliothek Bamberg Msc. Lit. 4 (Ed. IV. 3). Pergamenthandschrift, 235 Bl., ausgehendes 11. Jh. Vgl. Adolf LAGEMANN, Der Festkalender des Bistums Bamberg, 29.

43 M: Bamberg, Michelsberg (Benediktiner): Sammelhandschrift, Badische Landesbibliothek Karlsruhe Msc. 504. Pergamenthandschrift, 191 Bl., Kalendarium ab dem 12. Jh. Vgl. ebd., 40f.

44 C6: Bamberg, Carmelitenkloster: Diurnale Carmelitarum, Staatsbibliothek Bamberg Msc. lit. 96 (Ed. VII. 49). Papierhandschrift, 347 Bl., 15. Jh. Vgl. ebd., 38.

45 Alle C-Sigel sind Handschriften des Bamberger Carmelitenkloster. Von den acht dort erhaltenen Handschriften weisen sieben das für den Karmelitenorden früh bezeugte Eigenfest der drei alttestamentlichen Patriarchen Abraham, Isaak und Jakob am 6. Oktober auf; bei den kursiv gesetzten Handschriften ist dieser Tag besonders als hoher Festtag herausgehoben. Da außer C6 die anderen Handschriften keine besonderen Auffälligkeiten bezüglich Gedenktagen von anderen alttestamentlichen Heiligen aufweisen, sei bezüglich der Beschreibung dieser Handschriften auf die Seiten 36–39 in Lagemanns Arbeit verwiesen. – Für die interessante Entwicklung der Eigenfeiern des Karmelitenordens vgl. James BOYCE, Praising God in Carmel. Studies in Carmelite Liturgy, Washington/D.C. 1999.

46 D8: Bamberg, Dom: Psalterium dispositum per hebdomadem cum ordinario de tempore, Staatsbibliothek Bamberg Msc. Lit. 63 (Ed. III. 16). Pergamenthandschrift, 332 Bl., 13. Jh. Vgl. ebd., 30f.

(Depos) (Hi)ezechielis pph	10. April	D1[48], D2[49] (11. Jh.); D5[50], M, D6[51] (12. Jh.); D8, D9[52], A[53] (13. Jh.); D10[54], D12[55], D13[56], D14[57], D15[58], D16[59] (14. Jh.); D17[60], *D18*[61], D22[62], D23[63], J[64], Ls (15. Jh.)
Helisei pph	19. Juli	*C6* (15. Jh.)[65]
Jesajas pph	6. Juli	M (12. Jh.); Ls (15. Jh.)
Job servi dei	10. April	M (12. Jh.)

[47] U3: Unbekannte Provenienz: Lateinischer Kalender, Staatsarchiv Nürnberg Rep. 52a, Nr. 426. Papierhandschrift, 51 Bl., 15. Jh. (vor 1431). Vgl. ebd., 48.

[48] D1: Bamberg, Dom und Bamberg, Michelsberg (Benediktiner): Sacramentarium Gregorianum, Staatsbibliothek Bamberg Msc. lit. 1 (A. II. 52). Pergamenthandschrift, 255 Bl., 11. Jh.; geschrieben in Fulda für Kloster Michelsberg, kam wohl bald nach der Mitte des 11. Jhs. in den Dom. Vgl. ebd., 27f.; 40.

[49] D2: Bamberg, Dom: Sacramentarium Gregorianum, Staatsbibliothek Bamberg Msc. lit. 3 (Ed. V. 4). Pergamenthandschrift, 187 Bl., Anfang 11. Jh.; Lüttich. Vgl. ebd., 28.

[50] D5: Bamberg, Dom: Sammelhandschrift, Staatsbibliothek Bamberg Msc. lit. 161 (Ed. II. 14). Pergamenthandschrift, 81 Bl., 12. Jh. Vgl. ebd., 29f.

[51] D6: Bamberg, Dom: Graduale et Missale Bambergense, Staatsbibliothek Bamberg Msc. lit. 11 (Ed. III. 6). Pergamenthandschrift, 342 Bl., Ende 12. Jh. Vgl. ebd., 30.

[52] D9: Bamberg, Dom: Eberhardi Directorium vetus pro Choro Bambergensi, Staatsarchiv Bamberg Rep. B 86/11, Nr. 64. Pergamenthandschrift, 135 Bl., Mitte 13. Jh. bzw. spätes 14. Jh. Vgl. ebd., 31.

[53] A: (Wahrscheinlich) Augustiner-Eremiten: Psalterium feriatum, Staatsbibliothek Bamberg Msc. lit. 62 (A. I. 32). Pergamenthandschrift, 172 Bl., 13. Jh. Vgl. ebd. 36.

[54] D10: Bamberg, Dom: Calendarium Bambergense, Staatsarchiv Bamberg Rep. B 86/11, Nr. 61. Pergamenthandschrift, 38 Bl., Anfang 14. Jh. Vgl. ebd., 31f.

[55] D12: Bamberg, Dom: Capitula et Collecta in ecclesia per annum lege solita, Staatsbibliothek Bamberg Msc. Lit. 111 (Ed. IV. 14) Pergamenthandschrift, 124 Bl., 14. Jh. Vgl. ebd., 32.

[56] D13: Bamberg, Dom: Calendarium fratrum Cathedralis Bambergensis, Staatsbibliothek Bamberg Msc. lit. 163 (Ed. II. 21). Pergamenthandschrift, 46 Bl., 14. Jh. Vgl. ebd., 32f.

[57] D14: Bamberg, Dom: Calendarium ecclesiae cathedralis Bambergensis, Staatsbibliothek Bamberg Msc. lit. 162 (Ed. II. 20). Pergamenthandschrift, 30 Bl., 14. Jh. Vgl. ebd., 33.

[58] D15: Bamberg, Dom: Missale Bambergense, Staatsbibliothek Bamberg R. B. Msc. 173. Pergamenthandschrift, 265 Bl., 14. Jh. Vgl. ebd., 33.

[59] D16: Bamberg, Dom: Calendarium Bamberg. Ecclesiae, Staatsbibliothek Bamberg R. B. Msc. 46. Papierhandschrift, 46 Bl., 14. Jh. Vgl. ebd., 33f.

[60] D17: Bamberg, Dom: Anniversarium, Staatsarchiv Bamberg Rep. B 86/11, Nr. 79. Pergamenthandschrift, 185 Bl., 15. Jh. Vgl. ebd., 34

[61] D18: Bamberg, Dom: Liber statuorum et documentorum fraternitas ecclesiae cathedralis Bambergae, Staatsarchiv Bamberg Rep. B 86/11, Nr. 67. Pergamenthandschrift, 47 Bl., 15. Jh. Vgl. ebd., 34. – Der Gedenktag des Propheten Ezechiel ist in dieser Handschrift durch eine rote Unterstreichung als Festtag besonders gekennzeichnet: Vgl. ebd., 96f..

[62] D22: Bamberg, Dom: Copialbuch mit Kalendarium, Staatsarchiv Bamberg Rep. B 86/11, Nr. 67. Papierhandschrift, 235 Bl., 15. Jh. Vgl. ebd., 35.

[63] D23: Bamberg, Dom: Liber Anniversariorum, Staatsarchiv Bamberg Rep. B 86/11, Nr. 59. Pergamenthandschrift, 110 Bl., 15. Jh. Vgl. ebd., 35.

[64] J: Bamberg, St. Jakob (Kollegiatstift): Zins- und Anniversarienbuch, Staatsarchiv Bamberg A 221/9, Nr. 3951. Abschrift auf Papier, Original angelegt ab 1505. Vgl. ebd., 40.

[65] Der Gedenktag des Propheten Elischa ist in dieser Handschrift eindeutig als ein hoher Festtag besonders herausgehoben: Vgl. ebd., 146f.

Jocae (?)[66] et Eliae pph	14. Juli	Ls (15. Jh.)
Johelis pph	6. Juli	M (12. Jh.)
Joppe pph[67]	11. April	Ls (15. Jh.)
Loth pph	10. Oktober	Ls (15. Jh.)
VII Machabeorum (fratrum)	1. August	D1, D2, D3, D4 (11. Jh.); *D5*, *M*, D6 (12. Jh.); D7, *D9*, A (13. Jh.); D10, D11, S[68], L1, P1, D13 (14. Jh.); K1, P3 (14./15. Jh.); D19, D20, D24, D25, CL2, C3, L2, L3, L4, L5, L6, L7, K2, K3, K4, K5, P4, E, U2 (15. Jh.)[69]
Samuelis pph	20. August	D6 (12. Jh.); A (13. Jh.); S (14. Jh.); J, Ls (15. Jh.)
Sydrach, Midrach[70]	24. April	Ls (15. Jh.)

Es ist hier nicht der Ort auf manch interessantes Detailphänomen näher einzugehen, doch die bezeugte heortologische liturgische Verehrung[71] von 19 Gedenk- bzw. sogar Festtagen von alttestamentlichen Heiligen im Hochstift Bamberg im Hoch- und Spätmittelalter lassen das Bild eines Westens, der die Verehrung alttestamentlichen Heiligen nur in Ausnahmefällen kennt, fraglich werden, zumal die Situation sich für den gesamten deutschsprachigen Raum –

66 Bei diesem von Lagemann mit einem Fragezeichen versehenen Heiligen wird es sich meiner Meinung nach wohl am wahrscheinlichsten um den Propheten Josua handeln.

67 Bei Job servi dei und Joppe pph handelt es sich offensichtlich beide Mal um denselben Heiligen, nämlich den Propheten Ijob. Anscheinend handelt es sich hier um zwei getrennte Verehrungstraditionen, worauf die unterschiedlichen Namens- und Attributsbezeichnungen und das ungleiche Datum hinweisen. Auffällig ist jedoch die sehr große Terminnähe, die für einen gemeinsamen Festursprung sprechen könnte.

68 S: Bamberg, St. Stephan (Kollegiatsstift): Liber variarum orationum et benedictionum aliarumque rerum cum calendario eccl. s. Stephani, Staatsarchiv Bamberg Rep. B 115, Nr. 46. Pergamenthandschrift, 69 Bl., 14. Jh. Vgl. ebd., 42.

69 37 Bamberger Kalendarien verzeichnen den Gedenktag der Sieben Makkabäischen Märtyrerbrüder (drei von ihnen – D5, M und D9 – sogar als herausgehobenen Festtag): Dies ist die Mehrzahl der erhaltenen Handschriften. Viele verzeichnen aber neben den Makkabäischen Brüdern keine weiteren Gedenktage alttestamentlicher Heiliger, daher sei für die Beschreibung dieser Handschriften auf die Seiten 27–50 in Lagemanns Arbeit verwiesen.

70 Es handelt sich hier offensichtlich um die drei Jünglinge im Feuerofen, Schadrach, Meschach und Abed-Nego aus Dan 3, wobei das Fehlen des Namens des dritten Jünglings auffällig ist.

71 Auch wenn die Kalendare allein natürlich noch keinen Aufschluss über die konkret gefeierte Liturgie geben – dies ist Gegenstand eines größeren Forschungsvorhabens des Autors (s. Anm. 79) – sind sie jedoch als gewachsene und nicht gemachte liturgie-präskriptive Quellen von einem nicht zu unterschätzenden Wert: Vgl. HENNIG, Kalendar und Martyrologium (s. Anm. 36), 25–34, hier besonders 32.

trotz immer wieder zu beobachtender spezieller territorialer Akzentsetzungen – ähnlich darstellt.
Interessant wäre in diesem Zusammenhang auch eine flächendeckende Untersuchung sowohl der zahlreichen alttestamentlichen Kirchen-, Altar-, Glocken-, Bruderschafts- und Schutzpatrozinien im Mittelalter und in der Neuzeit als auch der vielerorts verehrten Reliquien von alttestamentlichen Personen[72] oder von heilsgeschichtlich relevanten Orten des Alten Testaments. So befinden sich etwa allein im Reliquienschatz des Münsteraner Doms drei Reliquien vom Stab Aarons und in derselben Diözese zusätzliche noch in der Stiftskirche von Freckenhorst und in der ehemaligen Benediktinerabtei Liesborn.[73] In Höxter im Bistum Paderborn wurde 1336 eine Tobias-Bruderschaft zum Wohle von ansteckenden Krankheiten und zur Besorgung eines christlichen Begräbnisses für Fremde und Pilger bestätigt.[74] In der Erzdiözese Köln gibt es in der Pfarrei Weiden im Dekanat Eschweiler eine St. Jobs-Kapelle;[75] und der Prophet Daniel ist im Spätmittelalter und in der frühen Neuzeit der bedeutendste Schutzpatron der Bergleute in der Alpenregion, bevor er schrittweise durch die Hl. Barbara verdrängt wurde.[76] Die Beispiele ließen sich mühelos fortsetzen. Dabei ist zu bedenken, dass es bei den gewählten Beispielen bewusst um bislang wenig untersuchte Phänomene für eher abseits gelegene Regionen handelt, die natürlich nicht mit einer Stadt wie Venedig konkurrieren können, in der allein sieben (!) Kirchen alttestamentlichen Heiligen geweiht waren,[77] wovon in fünf heute noch regelmäßig Liturgie gefeiert wird.[78]

[72] Die Fragestellung nach der „Echtheit" dieser Reliquien ist in diesem Fall natürlich müßig.
[73] Vgl. Peter ILISCH – Christoph KÖSTERS, Die Patrozinien Westfalens von den Anfängen bis zum Ende des Alten Reiches. Herausgegeben vom Institut für Religiöse Volkskunde Münster (Westfalia Sacra 11), Münster 1992, 1.
[74] Vgl. ebd., 677.
[75] Vgl. Leonhard KORTH, Die Patrocinien der Kirchen und Kapellen im Erzbistum Köln. Ein Beitrag zur Geschichte des religiösen Lebens und der kirchlichen Organisation in den Rheinlanden, Düsseldorf 1904, 93.
[76] Vgl. Wilhelm DEUER, Die Bergbauheiligen Kärntens und ihre künstlerische Darstellung, in: Grubenhunt & Ofensau. Vom Reichtum der Erde. Landesausstellung Hüttenberg – Kärnten, 1995. Klagenfurt 1995, 559–565.
[77] Vgl. Antonio NIERO, Culto dei santi dell'antico testamento, in: Silvio TRAMONTIN [u.a.] (Hrsg.), Culto dei Santi a Venezia (Biblioteca Agiografica Venezia 2), Venedig 1965, 155–180.
[78] Und zwar S. Giobbe, S. Geremia, S. Moisé, S. Samuele und S. Raffaele Arcangel. Vgl. hierzu Nina GOCKERELL, Kirchen mit alttestamentarischen Patrozinien in Venedig. Materialien zu Geschichte und Ikonographie der Kirchen S. Giobbe, S. Geremia, S. Moisé, S. Samuele, S. Simeone und S. Zaccaria (Centro Tedesco di Studi Veneziani 11), Venedig 1978. – Gockerell bezieht in ihre Untersuchung auch die neutestamentlichen Propheten geweihten Kirchen S. Simeone und S. Zaccaria mit ein, übersieht jedoch die im Westen des Sestiere Dorsoduro gelegene Kirche S. Raffaele Arcangel: vgl. unter anderem Herbert ROSENDORFER, Kirchenführer Venedig, Leipzig 2008, 110f.

6. AUSBLICK

Es scheint nicht nur theologisch gut begründbar zu sein, die großen Gestalten des Alten Bundes, als Heilige prominenter im Westen liturgisch zu verehren, sondern es scheint hierfür auch eine historisch gewachsene Tradition von der frühen Kirche[79] durch das Mittelalter hindurch bis zur Neuzeit zu geben. Auch wenn die liturgische Verehrung der Heiligen des Alten Testaments nie so in Blüte wie im Osten stand, ist das Bild einer generellen westlichen Nichtverehrung dieser Heiligen kritisch anzufragen.

Es scheint an der Zeit, sich wieder auf das fünfte Votum der Grundsatzstudie von 1961 zu besinnen, wobei auch die großen Frauengestalten des Alten Bundes nicht unberücksichtigt bleiben sollten, auch wenn für sie in der Tat der liturgiehistorische Befund sowohl im Westen als auch im Osten eher bescheiden ausfällt.[80]

[79] Vgl. etwa 1. Clemensbief 9,1–12,8; 17,1–19,3 und 45,6–8.

[80] Das in diesem Beitrag lediglich anfanghaft benannte Thema der liturgischen Verehrung der Heiligen des Alten Testaments in der lateinischen Kirche ist Forschungsgegenstand der liturgiewissenschaftlichen Dissertation des Autors dieses Beitrags, die voraussichtlich im Frühjahr 2014 publiziert werden wird. – Ich danke Georg BRAULIK OSB für die kritische Lektüre des Manuskripts.

DOKUMENTATION

DES SYMPOSIUMS

GRUSSWORT

Hochwürdigster Herr Weihbischof DDr. KRÄTZL, verehrte Kolleginnen und Kollegen aus nah und fern, liebe Studierende, meine Damen und Herren!

Es ist für mich eine große Freude und Ehre, Sie heute Abend im Namen des *Instituts für Liturgiewissenschaft* der Universität Wien und der Stiftung *Pro Oriente* zur Eröffnung des internationalen *Symposium Vindobonense* im Don Bosco-Haus begrüßen zu dürfen.
Vor etwa drei Jahren überlegten wir uns am Institut erstmals, ob, wann und unter welchem Thema wir ein solches Liturgie-Symposium hier in Wien organisieren könnten. Nach umfänglichen Planungen, unzähligen Gesuchen um finanzielle Unterstützung, terminlichen Verschiebungen und vielen Vorarbeiten ist es uns nun gelungen, dieses kleine, aber wohl feine Symposium in der österreichischen Hauptstadt zu organisieren.

Die Liturgiekonstitution „Sacrosanctum Concilium“ (vom 4. Dezember 1963) des II. Vatikanischen Konzils billigt dem Gottesdienst in Artikel 10 einen hohen Stellenwert zu – was auch über den römisch-katholischen Bereich hinaus Gültigkeit besitzt –, wenn es dort gleich eingangs heißt:

> „[D]ie Liturgie [ist] der Höhepunkt, dem das Tun der Kirche zustrebt, und zugleich die Quelle, aus der all ihre Kraft strömt …“

Die Feier der Liturgie ist also zentral für das Glaubensleben (*lex credendi – lex orandi*) und auch für das Selbstverständnis der verschiedenen Kirchen in Ost und West. Im Bereich der Liturgie sowie der Liturgiewissenschaft hat sich seit dem II. Vatikanischen Konzil – nicht zuletzt auch aufgrund wegweisender liturgiehistorischer Untersuchungen der letzten Jahrzehnte – eine erstaunliche Annäherung der christlichen Konfessionen vollzogen, bis in die liturgische Feierpraxis hinein.
Schon jede Form menschlichen Tuns ist ein äußerst komplexes Gebilde, zu dessen Erklärung oft verschiedene Wissenschaften herangezogen werden müssen. Noch mehr gilt das für das liturgische Tun der Kirche. Hier müssen auch die verschiedensten theologischen Disziplinen herangezogen werden, um die je verschiedenen Seiten des liturgischen Geschehens zu erfassen.
Die Versuche, die Komplexität des liturgischen Geschehens durch die eine oder andere der klassischen theologischen Disziplinen *allein* in den Griff zu bekommen, müssen als gescheitert angesehen werden. Nur das Zusammenspiel aller theologischen Disziplinen und die Anwendung der verschiedenen Methoden kann es ermöglichen, zu einer gewissen Gesamtschau zu gelangen.
Vielenorts ist in diesem Zusammenhang oft der Vorwurf zu vernehmen, dass eine *historische* Beschäftigung mit der Liturgie und deren geschichtlicher Ent-

wicklung für die heutige Feierpraxis irrelevant sei oder zumindest kaum Nutzen brächte. Dass dies nicht unbedingt so sein muss, lässt sich bei genauerer Betrachtung durchaus erschließen, zumal die Liturgie in den verschiedenen Kirchen im Laufe der Jahrhunderte mehr oder weniger organisch gewachsen ist. Mit Hilfe einer historischen Methode gelang auch der Aufbau einer eigenen *Liturgiegeschichte*, die Unterscheidung der wichtigsten Epochen und der in ihnen wirkenden Kräfte. Nur so wird es möglich, die *heutige* Liturgie in ihrem geschichtlichen Werden zu erkennen, den Bedeutungsgehalt der einzelnen Akte auszumachen und das Wichtige vom Unwichtigen zu unterscheiden (SC 21). Natürlich genügt es dabei nicht, *allein* auf die Geschichte der liturgischen Handlungen zu sehen. Es muss das gesamte christliche Leben der verschiedenen Jahrhunderte im Hinblick auf seinen Einfluss auf die Liturgie untersucht werden. Auch die Liturgiereform, die durch das II. Vatikanum eingeleitet wurde, ist ohne die liturgie-geschichtliche Forschung nicht denkbar. Die historische Forschung hat die Grundstrukturen der Liturgie erarbeitet, an denen die liturgietheologischen Überlegungen der Reform dann anknüpfen konnten.
Die Liturgiegeschichte lehrt außerdem, den rechten Zusammenhang zur Tradition des kirchlichen Lebens zu wahren, die Erfahrung über den Erfolg oder auch Misserfolg bestimmter liturgischer Maßnahmen auszuwerten. Damit kann auch die Richtung erkannt werden, in die das liturgische Leben der Kirche treibt. Die Liturgiegeschichte kann also positive Impulse geben für eine ständig sich erneuernde Liturgie. Sie ebnet die Wege, wieder aufzuzeigen oder wieder stärker zu betonen, was einmal bewährter Bestandteil der Liturgie in den verschiedenen Riten war, später dann leider in den Hintergrund trat oder sogar vergessen und aufgegeben wurde. Eine historisch-philologische Methode darf aber natürlich nicht dazu verleiten, nur wohlgeordnete Archive anzulegen, sondern sie muss zugleich die Möglichkeit schaffen, diese Ergebnisse für die lebendige Liturgie der Gegenwart fruchtbar zu machen, und zwar im ökumenischen Kontext.
Deshalb haben wir uns entschlossen, das Symposium unter das Leitthema: *Liturgies in East and West: Ecumenical Relevance of Early Liturgical Development* zu stellen.
Der ökumenische Beitrag und die jüdischen Wurzeln der christlichen Liturgie sollen in diesem Symposium durch international anerkannte WissenschaftlerInnen aus verschiedenen christlichen Konfessionen aufgezeigt und auf die Praxis hin fruchtbar gemacht werden.

Unser Dank gilt den verschiedenen Sponsoren, die durch ihre finanzielle Unterstützung die Durchführung erst ermöglicht haben: neben der Stiftung *Pro Oriente* sind dies die *Erzdiözese Wien*, vertreten durch Weihbischof Helmut KRÄTZL, das *Bundesministerium für Wissenschaft und Forschung*, die *Universität Wien* mit ihrem Rektor Univ.-Prof. Dr. Georg WINCKLER, die *Superiorenkonferenz der männlichen Ordensgemeinschaften Österreichs* und auch die *Stadt Wien*.

Herzlichen Dank an alle Vortragenden von nah und fern. Ich freue mich, dass doch so viele Kollegen der kurzfristigen Einladung nach Wien Folge leisten konnten. Wir alle freuen uns schon sehr auf die interessanten Vorträge, die Diskussionen und die sicherlich vielen Gespräche und Gedankenaustausche. Danke auch natürlich an alle Gäste, Interessierte, Studierende und Kollegen, die nicht die Mühe gescheut haben, am Symposium teilzunehmen. Möge auch Ihnen die Teilnahme in vielfältiger Weise Frucht und Anregung bringen.
Und schließlich: Ein ganz herzlicher Dank gilt den Mitarbeiterinnen unseres Instituts, die ich ganz besonders erwähnen möchte! Ohne die Mithilfe aller Mitarbeiterinnen wäre das Symposium nicht zustande gekommen: Frau Renate KOS, Frau Mag. Monika SCALA, Frau Mag. Manuela ULRICH, Frau Mag. Petra SCHILLER und Frau Ing. Justyna OKOLOWICZ. Dank auch an Herrn Florian MAYR von der Studentenvertretung unserer Fakultät, der die Homepagegestaltung mitübernommen hat.

Ich wünsche Ihnen allen eine erfolgreiche und fruchtbringende Teilnahme und bedanke mich für Ihr Kommen.

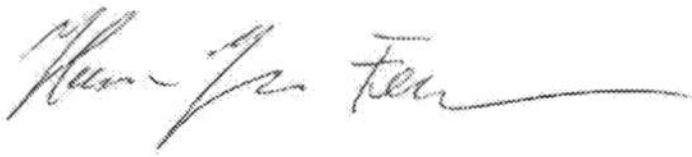

Univ.-Prof. Dr. Hans-Jürgen Feulner
Institut für Liturgiewissenschaft
Universität Wien

Your Excellency, Bishop KRÄTZL, distinguished colleagues from near and far, dear students, ladies and gentlemen!

It is an honor and a great pleasure to welcome you on behalf of our Department of Liturgical Studies and the Foundation *Pro Oriente* to the opening of this international *Symposium Vindobonense* here at the Don Bosco-Haus.
Three years ago, we first considered when, where, and how to best organize such a liturgy symposium here in Vienna. After an extensive period of planning, writing various grant applications, managing time conflicts and immersing ourselves in preparatory work, we succeeded in organizing this small but constructive Symposium here in the capital city of Austria.

Article 10 of the Constitution on Sacred Liturgy, "Sacrosanctum Concilium" (December 4, 1963), of the Second Vatican Council awards the liturgy a high significance – even beyond the Roman-Catholic sphere – when one reads at the very beginning:

> "[T]he liturgy is the summit toward which the activity of the Church is directed; at the same time it is the font from which all her power flows …"

Celebrating liturgy is the central element of a living faith (*lex credendi – lex orandi*) and the mission of different churches in the East and West. Ever since Vatican II and due to seminal work in the field of historico-liturgical studies, various Christian denominations have been striving to approach each other, reaching out to each other also in terms of how to celebrate the liturgy.
Any aspect of human action is an extremely complex structure and can often only be explained by applying various methodologies. This applies even more to the liturgical activity of the Church. One has to employ various theological disciplines in order to understand the manifold aspects of the liturgical events.
It has been shown that all attempts to explain the complexity of liturgical actions by relying upon one or another theological discipline alone have failed. Only the cooperation of all theological disciplines and the application of the various methods can help to achieve a certain kind of overall view.
In this respect, in many places one can hear complaints that it is irrelevant or at least of no use for the current way of celebrating the liturgy to look at liturgy from a historical point of view as well as observing its historical development. However, this does not necessarily need to be the case as one can see when taking a closer look at things and particularly when accepting the fact that the liturgy has, more or less, been growing organically over the last centuries. It was possible to establish a *Liturgical History* with the aid of a historical method. Liturgical History in this sense means a differentiation of the most important eras and their most influencing powers. With that in hands, this is the only way possible to recognize our current liturgy in its historical development, to understand the significant content of single passages and articles, and to distinguish between important and unimportant aspects (*Sacrosanctum Concilium* 21). Of

course, it is not enough to *only* focus on the history of liturgical acts. In order to fully understand the liturgical developments, it is necessary to research Christian life as a whole, looking at various centuries and examining how far Christian life as such has influenced the celebration of the liturgy. The liturgical reform, initiated by Vatican II, cannot be imagined without liturgico-historical research. It is the seminal work of historical research that developed a basic structure for liturgy, and which was then followed by liturgico-theological thoughts and research.
This is why we decided and chose "*Liturgies in East and West: Ecumenical Relevance of Early Liturgical Development*" as a guiding theme for our Symposium. In their talks and presentations, different internationally renowned scholars belonging to various Christian denominations will try to indicate the ecumenical aspect and the Jewish roots of Christian liturgy. Hereby our aim is to gain fruitful aspects for the practical experience of the different liturgies.

Let me express my thanks to our various sponsors. Their generous financial support enabled us to organize and realize this Symposium. Along with the *Pro Oriente* Foundation, we would like to thank the *Archdiocese of Vienna*, represented by Bishop Helmut KRÄTZL, the *Federal Ministry of Science and Research*, the *University of Vienna* and its rector Univ.-Prof. Dr. Georg WINCKLER, and also the *Conference of the Major Superiors of Austria*, as well as the *City of Vienna*.
Many thanks to all the speakers from near and far. I am pleased that so many colleagues could make it to Vienna despite the short notice. We are all looking forward to the upcoming talks, lectures, presentations, as well as discussions, conversations, and the exchange of ideas. Thanks also to all our guests, the interested public, students, and colleagues, who spared no efforts to participate in our Symposium. May your participation challenge you and trigger new thoughts and ideas.
Last but not least, I would particularly like to thank my entire staff at our Department. Without their help, this Symposium would not have taken place: Renate KOS, Monika SCALA, Manuela ULRICH, Petra SCHILLER, and Justyna OKOLOWICZ. Thanks also to Florian MAYR, one of the faculty's student representatives, for helping design our webpage.

I wish you all a successful, inspiring, and fruitful participation in our *Symposium Vindobonense* and thank you all for coming!

Univ.-Prof. Dr. Hans-Jürgen Feulner
Institut für Liturgiewissenschaft
Universität Wien

SYMPOSIUM
VINDOBONENSE
LITURGIES IN EAST AND WEST
ECUMENICAL RELEVANCE OF EARLY LITURGICAL DEVELOPMENT

http://www.univie.ac.at/liturgiewissenschaft

universität wien INSTITUT FÜR LITURGIEWISSENSCHAFT

PRO ORIENTE

SYMPOSIUM VINDOBONENSE 2007

LITURGIES IN EAST AND WEST

ECUMENICAL RELEVANCE OF EARLY
LITURGICAL DEVELOPMENT

17. - 20. November 2007

Don Bosco-Haus Wien

INFORMATION
http://www.univie.ac.at/liturgy-symposium

BM.W_F[a] universität wien StaDt Wien Wien ist anders. Superiorenkonferenz

INSTITUT FÜR LITURGIEWISSENSCHAFT | SCHENKENSTRASSE 8-10 | 1010 WIEN | TEL. +43 1 4277 31301 | LITURGY_SYMPOSIUM@UNIVIE.AC.AT

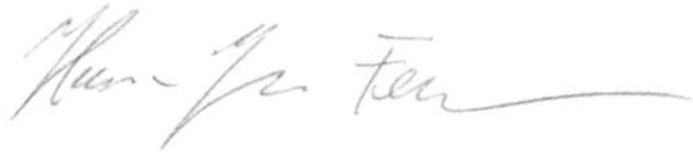

ABSCHLUSSBERICHT Symposium Vindobonense 2007

SYMPOSIUM VINDOBONENSE
LITURGIES IN EAST AND WEST
ECUMENICAL RELEVANCE OF
EARLY LITURGICAL DEVELOPMENT

Liturgies in East and West: Ecumenical Relevance of Early Liturgical Development

Vom **17.–20. November 2007** fand im Don Bosco-Haus ein liturgiewissenschaftliches Symposium zum Thema „*Liturgies in East and West. Ecumenical Relevance of Early Liturgical Development.*" statt, das vom *Institut für Liturgiewissenschaft der Universität Wien* (Leitung: Univ.-Prof. Dr. Hans-Jürgen FEULNER) in Kooperation mit der *Stiftung Pro Oriente* veranstaltet wurde. Der Einladung waren namhafte WissenschaftlerInnen aus Europa, Asien und den USA, Studierende österreichischer theologischer Fakultäten und Interessierte aus unterschiedlichen Bereichen gefolgt.

Vesper und Eröffnung am Samstag, 17. November 2007, Don Bosco-Haus

Eröffnet wurde das Symposium am Samstag, 17. Nov. 2007 in der Kapelle des Don Bosco-Hauses mit der feierlichen Vesper, der Weihbischof DDr. Helmut KRÄTZL vorstand. In seiner Homilie beleuchtete KRÄTZL die Liturgie als Lobpreis und ging dabei auch auf die Bedeutung der unterschiedlichen christlichen Traditionen ein: „*Liturgie ist im Tiefsten Lobpreis. Lobpreis mit allen Sinnen, allen Künsten, allen Ausdrucksmöglichkeiten, die der Mensch hat. Ein Lobpreis mit lautem Jubel, oder im schweigenden Staunen. Es ist gut, dass die verschiedenen christlichen Traditionen, auch von Ost und West, sich dabei gegenseitig bereichern, ja sogar herausfordern, jene ‚Instrumente' und Zeichen zu finden, die Altehrwürdiges weitergeben, aber auch in der Stimme, Sprache und Symbolik der jeweiligen Zeit.*"

Die anschließende *Eröffnung des Symposiums* nahm Hans-Jürgen FEULNER, Vorstand des Instituts für Liturgiewissenschaft an der Universität Wien, vor. In seiner Eröffnungsrede hob FEULNER die Bedeutung der historischen Liturgieforschung gerade für die Feierpraxis hervor: „*Vielenorts ist in diesem Zusammenhang oft der Vorwurf zu vernehmen, dass eine historische Beschäftigung mit der Liturgie und deren geschichtlicher Entwicklung für die heutige Feierpraxis irrelevant sei, oder zumindest kaum Nutzen brächte. Dass dies nicht unbedingt so sein muss, lässt sich bei*

genauerer Betrachtung durchaus erschließen, zumal die Liturgie in den verschiedenen Kirchen im Laufe der Jahrhunderte mehr oder weniger organisch gewachsen ist. Mit Hilfe einer historischen Methode gelang auch der Aufbau einer eigenen Liturgiegeschichte, die Unterscheidung der wichtigsten Epochen und der in ihnen wirkenden Kräfte. Nur so wird es möglich, die heutige Liturgie in ihrem geschichtlichen Werden zu erkennen, den Bedeutungsgehalt der einzelnen Akte auszumachen und das Wichtige vom Unwichtigen zu unterscheiden (SC 21). *Natürlich genügt es dabei nicht, allein auf die Geschichte der liturgischen Handlungen zu sehen. Es muss das gesamte christliche Leben der verschiedenen Jahrhunderte im Hinblick auf seinen Einfluss auf die Liturgie untersucht werden.*"

Beim Abendessen im Don Bosco-Haus ergaben sich bereits die ersten Gespräche zwischen ReferentInnen und StudentInnen

Erster Sitzungstag am Sonntag, 18. November 2007, Katholisch-Theologische Fakultät

Die Vorträge des ersten Tages fanden an der Katholisch-Theologischen Fakultät statt. Lizette LARSON-MILLER (Church Divinity School of the Pacific an der Graduate Theological Union der University of California–Berkeley), eröffnete am Sonntagnachmittag mit ihrem Vortrag zum Thema „*Even At The Grave, We Make Our*

Song': The Divergence Of Ecumenical Rememberings of The Dead", in dem sie der Frage nach der Relevanz der frühen liturgischen Entwicklung für die Kranken- und Sterberiten unterschiedlicher christlicher Traditionen nachging. Dabei ging sie sowohl auf entscheidende Reformen der 60er und 70er Jahre des 20. Jh. als auch auf aktuelle Entwicklungen ein, wobei sie ihren Fokus auf die westlichen Traditionen legte.
Der weitere Nachmittag widmete sich im Rahmen mehrerer paralleler Kurzvorträge einzelnen Spezialaspekten liturgischer Entwicklungen in den christlichen Traditionen des Ostens und Westens. So beleuchtete etwa Stefanos ALEXOPOULOS (damals CYA International Center for Hellenic and Mediterranean Studies/Athen) die Diskrepanz von Theorie und Praxis in Bezug auf die Akzeptanz von Konvertiten in der orthodoxen Kirche, Anthony F. CARR (Pontificio Ateneo Sant'Anselmo/Rom) sprach über die Diakonissenordination in der syrischen Tradition, und Mark MOROZOWICH (Catholic University of America in Washington/DC) behandelte den gegenseitigen Einfluss von östlicher und westlicher Liturgie im Laufe der Geschichte. Parallel beschäftigte sich Reinhard MESSNER (Universität Innsbruck) mit der äthiopischen Version der Markusliturgie, Richard RUTHERFORD (University of Portland/OR) stellte seine Arbeit am Aufbau einer internationalen Datenbank zu frühchristlichen Baptisterien vor, und Monika SCALA (Wien – Klosterneuburg) sprach über die Passio Perpetuae.

Öffentlicher Vortrag von Paul Bradshaw im Schottensaal des Schottenstifts

Den Abschluss dieses Tages bildete der öffentliche Vortrag von Paul BRADSHAW (University of Notre Dame, South Bend/IN), der im Schottensaal des Schottenstifts stattfand. Der Einladung waren neben den Teilnehmern und Teilnehmerinnen des Symposiums auch zahlreiche interessierte ZuhörerInnen gefolgt. BRADSHAW sprach in seinem Vortrag über den jüdischen Einfluss auf die frühe christliche Liturgie und ging in diesem Rahmen auch auf das Verhältnis von Juden und Christen in der frühchristlichen Zeit ein. Dabei sprach er sich für die Notwendigkeit einer differenzierten Betrachtung dieser Entwicklung aus und räumte mit vorschnellen Pauschalaussagen – positive wie negative – auf.

Zweiter Sitzungstag am Montag, 19. November 2007, Don Bosco-Haus

Der zweite Tag wurde am Vormittag von Basilius GROEN (Karl-Franzens-Universität in Graz), zum Thema „*'Just Like In The Early Church': Hermeneutics of The Use of Early Christian Liturgy for Modern Liturgical Reform*" eröffnet. Anhand der westlichen Praxis der Krankensalbung und der Diskussion um die Ikonostase in orthodoxen Kirchen behandelte GROEN die Frage nach den Bedingungen für einen Rückgriff auf die frühchristliche Praxis bei liturgischen Reformen und Entwicklungen und ging auf aktuelle Fragen im ökumenischen Kontext ein. Dabei machte er deutlich, dass bei derartigen Diskussionen immer nach dem jeweiligen Vorverständnis zu fragen ist, das Reformen zugrunde gelegt wird bzw. wurde.

Die folgenden Kurzvorträge gaben den TeilnehmerInnen wieder die Möglichkeit, sich nach Interesse mit weiteren Spezialaspekten auseinander zu setzen. Paul MEYENDORFF (St. Vladimir's Orthodox Theological Seminary, Crestwood/NY) sprach über die Taufekklesiologie, die Gebets- und Fastenpraxis in der orientalisch-orthodoxen Tradition wurde von Biji CHIRATHILATTU (Malankara-Syrisch-Orthodoxe Kirche in Wien) diskutiert; parallel bot Harald BUCHINGER (Universität Wien bzw. Universität Regensburg) einen Überblick über Ursprung und Frühgeschichte der Quadragesima und Michael MARGONI-KÖGLER (Wien) präsentierte die liturgischen Schriftlesungen in Nordafrika, ausgehend von Augustinus im Vergleich mit weiteren westlichen Quellen. Im letzten Vortrag stellte Sebastià JANERAS (Theologische Fakultät Kataloniens in Barcelona/Spanien) den Text des Troparions Ὁ μονογενής in den verschiedenen Ostliturgien und seine ökumenische Bedeutung vor.

Der Nachmittag stand den TeilnehmerInnen für die „Erkundung Wiens" zur Verfügung. Einige nahmen an einer Stadtführung durch die Innenstadt teil, andere besuchten gemeinsam die aktuelle Ausstellung in der Albertina „*Picasso bis Monet*". Beliebter Schlusspunkt war das Hotel Sacher bzw. das Café Mozart.

Öffentlicher Vortrag von Marcel Metzger im Don Bosco-Haus

Prof. METZGER (im Vordergrund) bei der Vorbereitung seines Vortrags

Am Abend versammelten sich die TeilnehmerInnen und weitere ZuhörerInnen zum öffentlichen Vortrag von Marcel METZGER (emer. Professor an der Université Marc Bloch in Strasbourg), in dem er über Liturgie als Verkündigung sprach und dabei die Bedeutung der Verkündigung von Gottes Wort hervorhob.

Dritter Sitzungstag am Dienstag, 20. November 2007, Don Bosco-Haus

Der Vormittag des letzten Tages bot noch einmal die Möglichkeit, sich mit Spezialfragen auseinander zu setzen. Dabei standen an diesem Tag verschiedene Dissertations- und Forschungsprojekte im Vordergrund. Diliana ATANASSOVA (Universität Salzburg) stellte das FWF-Projekt der Katholisch-Theologischen Fakultät Salzburg zu den Typika des Schenute-Klosters vor, Manuela ULRICH (Wien) ihr damaliges Dissertationskonzept zu den Verkündigungsorten in der stadtrömischen Liturgie. Nikodemus SCHNABEL (Wien und Jerusalem) sprach bezugnehmend auf seine Dissertation zur liturgischen Verehrung der Heiligen des Alten Testaments, und Hanna GHONEIM (Damaskus und Wien) besprach die Quellen seiner Arbeit zur Feier der byzantinischen Bischofsweihe in der Melkitischen Kirche.

Den Abschlussvortrag des Symposiums hielt Hans-Jürgen FEULNER zur ökumenischen Relevanz einer vergleichenden Liturgiewissenschaft. Er stellte dabei – ausgehend von der Methode der vergleichenden Liturgiewissenschaft nach Anton Baumstark – eine modifizierte liturgievergleichende Methodik vor, die verstärkt auch die westlichen Traditionen mit einbezieht. An den Vortrag schloss sich eine rege Diskussion an, die auch gleichzeitig wichtige Positionen und Themen der letzten Tage aufgriff und damit den offiziellen Schlusspunkt der Veranstaltung bildete.

Prof. FEULNER bei seinen Ausführungen zur Vergleichenden Liturgiewissenschaft

Gruppenbild der Vortragenden
(mit unserem Ehrengast, Metropolit Dr. Kuriakose Mor THEOPHILOSE/Kerala)

Autorenverzeichnis

Rev. Dr. Stefanos ALEXOPOULOS, Catholic University of America, Washington/DC, Assistant Professor of Liturgical Studies and Sacramental Theology

Dr. Diliana ATANASSOVA, Universität Salzburg, FWF-Projekt (Patristik und Kirchengeschichte): „Die Typika des Schenute-Klosters“

Rev. Dr. Paul F. BRADSHAW, University of Notre Dame, South Bend/IN, Emeritus Professor of Liturgical Studies

Priv.-Doz. Dr. Heinzgerd BRAKMANN, Universität Bonn, Privatdozent für Liturgiewissenschaft und Ostkirchenkunde, katholisch-theologische Fakultät

Univ.-Prof. Dr. Harald BUCHINGER, Universität Regensburg, Professor für Liturgiewissenschaft

Rev. Dr. Anthony (Ephrem) F. CARR, O.S.B., Pontifical Liturgical Institute, Rome, Emeritus Professor of Liturgical Studies

Rev. Dr. Biji Markose CHIRATHILATTU, Pfarrer der Malankara-Syrisch-Orthodoxen Gemeinde, Wien

Univ.-Prof. Dr. Hans-Jürgen FEULNER, Universität Wien, Professor für Liturgiewissenschaft und Sakramententheologie

Rev. Dr. Hanna GHONEIM, Seelsorger der melkitisch-katholischen Gemeinde in Wien und früherer Direktor des katechetischen Zentrums in Damaskus/Syrien

Univ.-Prof. Dr. Basilius J. GROEN, Karl-Franzens-Universität, Graz, Professor für Liturgiewissenschaft und Sakramententheologie sowie UNESCO Chair of Intercultural and Interreligious Dialogue in Southeastern Europe

Dr. Sebastià JANERAS, Facultat de Teologia de Catalunya, Barcelona, Emeritus Professor

Sr. Dr. Vassa LARIN, Universität Wien, FWF-Projekt (Liturgiewissenschaft): „The Enarxis of the Byzantine Divine Liturgy"

Rev. Dr. Lizette LARSON-MILLER, Church Divinity School of the Pacific, Berkeley/CA, Nancy and Michael Kaehr Professor of Liturgical Leadership

Dr. Michael MARGONI-KÖGLER, Co-Autor des Augustinus-Lexikons, freier Mitarbeiter beim CSEL in Wien

Rev. Dr. Marcel METZGER, Faculté de Théologie Catholique de Strasbourg, Université de Strasbourg, Professeur émérite

Dr. Paul MEYENDORFF, St. Vladimir's Orthodox Theological Seminary, Crestwood/NY, The Alexander Schmemann Professor of Liturgical Theology

Rev. Dr. Mark M. MOROZOWICH, Catholic University of America, Washington/DC, Associate Professor of Liturgical Studies and Sacramental Theology and Dean of the School of Theology and Religious Studies

Rev. Dr. H. Richard RUTHERFORD, C.S.C., University of Portland/OR, Emeritus Professor of Pastoral Liturgical Studies

Rev. Nikodemus C. SCHNABEL, O.S.B., Dormitio Abtei auf dem Berg Zion, Jerusalem, Leiter des Jerusalemer Instituts der Görres-Gesellschaft

Liborius Olaf Lumma

Qui manducat carnem meam et bibit sanguinem meum

Theologische Implikationen der Gregorianischen Communio-Antiphonen de evangelio im Messproprium des Temporale

30 Communiones (Kommuniongesänge in der römischen Eucharistiefeier) aus dem Repertoire des Gregorianischen Chorals bilden das Thema der vorliegenden Studie. Im Mittelpunkt steht die Frage, welche inhaltlichen Zusammenhänge zwischen dem Gesang der Communio und der Handlung der eucharistischen Kommunion bestehen.

In der Tradition der Gregorianischen Semiologie legt der Autor Interpretationsvorschläge vor, in deren Licht Communio und Eucharistie zum wechselseitigen hermeneutischen Schlüssel werden, und zieht Schlussfolgerungen für die biblische Theologie und die liturgische Praxis heute.

Bd. 5, 2009, 312 S., 39,90 €, gb., ISBN 978-3-643-50023-6

LIT Verlag Berlin – Münster – Wien – Zürich – London

Auslieferung Deutschland / Österreich / Schweiz: siehe Impressumsseite

Vergessene Theologen

Peter Browe

Die Eucharistie im Mittelalter

Liturgiehistorische Forschungen
in kulturwissenschaftlicher Absicht

Mit einer Einführung
herausgegeben von Hubertus Lutterbach
und Thomas Flammer

6. Auflage 2011

Vergessene Theologen Bd. 1

LIT

Peter Browe
Die Eucharistie im Mittelalter
Liturgiehistorische Forschungen in kulturwissenschaftlicher Absicht. Mit einer Einführung herausgegeben von Hubertus Lutterbach und Thomas Flammer

Wie kein anderer vor ihm hat sich der Jesuit Peter Browe († 1949) in den 1920er bis 1940er Jahren um die Erforschung der Eucharistie im Mittelalter verdient gemacht. Diese quellengesättigten und interdisziplinären, ehedem „verstreut" publizierten Studien werden hier „auf einen Blick" neu zugänglich gemacht: Forschungen u. a. zur Verehrung und zum Empfang der Eucharistie, zum „magischen" Einsatz und zur Aufbewahrung der heiligen Materie, zur Handhabung der Eucharistie an heiligen Orten und zur Austeilung der Kommunion während heiliger Zeiten. Die Untersuchungen des zu Unrecht vergessenen Theologen Browe eröffnen einen liturgiehistorischen Zugang zum Mittelalter. Für eine interdisziplinär-kulturgeschichtliche Mediävistik sind sie unverzichtbar.

Prof. Dr. Hubertus Lutterbach lehrt Katholische Theologie an der Universität Essen.

Bd. 1, 6. Aufl. 2011, 576 S., 29,90 €, br., ISBN 978-3-8258-6233-6

LIT Verlag Berlin – Münster – Wien – Zürich – London

Auslieferung Deutschland / Österreich / Schweiz: siehe Impressumsseite